The Regions of Normandie Cotentin

Western Normandy – *see the map opposite.*

For Eastern Normandy,
(Normandie Vallée de la Seine), see the inside back cover.

THE**GREEN**GUIDE
Normandy

Half-timbered house, Pont l'Évêque © Loïc Durand/Calvados Attractivité

 MICHELIN

THE GREEN GUIDE **NORMANDY**

Editorial Director	Cynthia Clayton Ochterbeck
Editor	Sophie Friedman
Principal Writer	Terry Marsh
Production Manager	Natasha George
Cartography	Peter Wrenn
Picture Editor	Yoshimi Kanazawa
Interior Design	Chris Bell
Layout	Natasha George
Cover Design	Chris Bell, Christelle Le Déan

Contact Us

Michelin Travel and Lifestyle North America
One Parkway South
Greenville, SC 29615
USA
travel.lifestyle@us.michelin.com

Michelin Travel Partner
Hannay House
39 Clarendon Road
Watford, Herts WD17 1JA
UK
☎01923 205240
travelpubsales@uk.michelin.com
www.viamichelin.co.uk

Special Sales

For information regarding bulk sales, customized editions and premium sales, please contact us at:
travel.lifestyle@us.michelin.com

Note to the reader Addresses, phone numbers, opening hours and prices published in this guide are accurate at the time of press. We welcome corrections and suggestions that may assist us in preparing the next edition. While every effort is made to ensure that all information printed in this guide is correct and up-to-date, Michelin Travel Partner accepts no liability for any direct, indirect or consequential losses howsoever caused so far as such can be excluded by law.

HOW TO USE THIS GUIDE

PLANNING YOUR TRIP

The blue-tabbed PLANNING YOUR TRIP section at the front of the guide gives you **ideas for your trip** and **practical information** to help you organise it. You'll find tours, practical information, a host of outdoor activities, a calendar of events, information on shopping, sightseeing, kids' activities and more.

INTRODUCTION

The orange-tabbed INTRODUCTION section explores Normandy's **Nature** and geology. The **History** section spans Roman times through William the Conqueror to the modern day. The **Art and Culture** section covers architecture, art, literature and music, while **Normandy Today** delves into modern Normandy.

DISCOVERING

The green-tabbed DISCOVERING section features Principal Sights by region, featuring the most interesting local **Sights**, **Walking Tours**, nearby **Excursions**, and detailed **Driving Tours**. Admission prices shown are normally for a single adult.

ADDRESSES

We've selected from the best hotels, restaurants, cafés shops, nightlife and entertainment to fit all budgets. See the Legend on the cover flap for an explanation of the price categories. See the back of the guide for an index of where to find hotels and restaurants.

Sidebars

Throughout the guide you will find blue, orange and green-coloured text boxes with lively anecdotes, detailed history and background information.

😊 A Bit of Advice 😊

Green advice boxes found in this guide contain practical tips and handy information relevant to your visit or to a sight in the Discovering section.

STAR RATINGS★★★

Michelin has given star ratings for more than 100 years. If you're pressed for time, we recommend you visit the ★★★, or ★★ sights first:

★★★	**Worth a special journey**
★★	**Worth a detour**
★	**Interesting**

MAPS

- 🐶 Principal Sights map.
- 🐶 Region maps.
- 🐶 Maps for major cities and villages.
- 🐶 Local tour maps.

All maps in this guide are oriented north, unless otherwise indicated by a directional arrow. The term "Local Map" refers to a map within the chapter or Tourism Region. A complete list of the maps found in the guide appears at the back of this book.

© Hervé Hughes/hemis.fr

PLANNING YOUR TRIP

INTRODUCTION TO NORMANDY

DISCOVERING NORMANDY

CONTENTS

Welcome to Normandy

This former dukedom today incorporates all or part of seven French *départements*, with Rouen as the capital. The Norman coast offers elegant resorts, while cows, orchards and hedgerows provide rural charm. Castles and abbeys such as Mont St-Michel evoke a long history of power struggles, not least the 1944 Normandy Landings. The cuisine, favouring cream, is justly celebrated.

Trouville-sur-Mer, Côte Fleurie and Pays d'Auge

© Guy Thouvenin/age fotostock

VEXIN NORMAND AND PAYS DE BRAY (pp160–180)

Richard the Lion Heart and Philippe Auguste clashed in the Vexin Normand for ownership of these lands; today a region of history but also one of art, being the very cradle of Impressionism with the gardens of Giverny. Yet the Pays de Bray offers renewal to nature lovers longing for dense forests and wild landscapes.

CÔTE FLEURIE AND PAYS D'AUGE (pp181–213)

Elegant summer holidays are to be had on the fine sand beaches and in the restaurants of the Côte Fleurie, running from the Pays d'Auge to east of Calvados. Gourmets on the lookout for Norman authenticity will be drawn to the Pays d'Auge for its lush greenery and its cream, butter, milk and cheeses.

PLAIN DE L'EURE AND PAYS D'OUCHE (pp214–236)

This is where you can glimpse the authentic Normandy. Time is suspended here in a countryside of small farms, enclosed and protected by hedgerows, with little villages nestling around their country church and the occasional horse rider out for a canter in the sun.

PERCHE (pp237–252)

The Perche is a region of deep forests, hedgerows, gentle hills and valleys, dotted with manor houses like small stone fortresses. The region's name is also that given to the horse that evolved centuries ago in this countryside: the gentle, powerful Percheron. People like to eat and

ROUEN AND THE BOUCLES DE LA SEINE (pp82-123)

Rouen, the capital of Normandy, rose from the ashes of World War II to become the dynamic, historic city it is today. The Seine meanders here, bringing trade to towns and villages, nourishing gentle, rich landscapes and inspiring Impressionist painters.

COTE D'ALBÂTRE AND PAYS DE CAUX (pp124–159)

The Pays de Caux, lying between Rouen and Le Havre, is charming and intimate. The appealing landscape invites exploration on foot, by bicycle or on horseback; it contrasts sharply with countryside made for walkers, one of sea spray, cliffs, wheeling gulls and endless sky known as the Alabaster Coast.

drink here, and cider is a long Perche tradition, now proudly returning to its place of prominence.

CAEN AND THE LANDING BEACHES *(pp253–297)*

With the conquest of England by Duke William, Caen was bound to its powerful neighbour. The region was to become the stage for the greatest battle of the Second World War; Caen was almost completely razed, yet rose from its ashes to become a modern and vibrant town.

The nearby beaches and villages carry the memory of the great sacrifices made in 1944 with the Normandy Landings, and today have become a place for contemplation and for peace.

LE BOCAGE AND PAYS D'ARGENTAN *(pp298–318)*

The gentle hills and dales of the Bocage stand in sharp contrast with the little mountains sculpted by the rushing rivers of the Suisse Normande. While this part of Normandy suffered as well in the Allied bombings of June 1944, it has been rebuilt and today is a delight for holiday-makers out to enjoy the lush countryside in which the River Orne meanders.

ALENÇON AND THE PARC NORMANDIE-MAINE *(pp319–341)*

The Parc Régional Normandie-Maine was created in 1975 with a total area of 234 000 hectares. It contains a vast variety of natural riches; its landscapes range from heath to limestone hills and its wildlife includes many rare species. Alençon, meanwhile, awaits with its history and tradition of lace making, and its architectural treasures.

THE NORTH OF THE MAYENNE *(pp342–357)*

The portion of the Mayenne *département* that extends into Normandy includes the cities of Laval, with its medieval centre and terraced Perrine Gardens, and Mayenne, with its 8C castle. Ruins of the Roman town of Jublains recall Julius Caesar's Gaul, while the countryside offers forests, castles, and fields where horses graze. Along the River Mayenne, visitors can bathe and rent watercraft.

GRANVILLE AND THE BAY OF MONT ST-MICHEL *(pp358–381)*

Granville, on the Cotentin peninsula at the mouth of the Bosq and Pointe du Roc, closes the Bay of Mont St-Michel. Its old town preserves the history of its military and religious past. The Bay of Mont St-Michel awaits holiday-makers, nature lovers and amateur biologists and botanists alike with the wealth of flora and fauna waiting to be discovered here.

LA PRESQU'ÎLE DU COTENTIN *(pp382–420)*

Shaped like a snail's head, this rocky peninsula extends into the English Channel with the port of Cherbourg-Octeville at its tip. Lighthouses, bays and splendid views line the coast. A national park offers excellent bird watching.

CHANNEL ISLANDS *(pp421–453)*

Off the west coast of Normandy, much closer to France than to Britain, the Channel Islands (*Îles Anglo-Normandes* or *Îles de la Manche*) offer English charm, extensive tourist amenities, bathing beaches, and delightful rambles along country lanes. The principal islands are Alderney, Guernsey and Jersey, as well as little Sark, where cars are banned.

The islands are considered as the remnants of the Duchy of Normandy, and are not part of the United Kingdom, although they are British Crown Dependencies.

PLANNING YOUR TRIP

Port-Racine, St-Germain-des-Vaux, Pointe de la Hague, La Presqu'Île du Cotentin
© Hervé Lenain/hemis.fr

When and Where to Go

☺ Plan Your Itinerary ☺

The website http://en.normandie-tourisme.fr, produced by the Normandy Regional Tourist Board, offers downloadable guidebooks and brochures so you can plan a personalised itinerary. One booklet covers parks and gardens; another describes historical sites and monuments, yet another lists how to enjoy golf holidays in Normandy. There are also guidebooks devoted to D-Day and the Battle of Normandy, and to Activities for the Family.

SEASONS

The most pleasant time of year here is July to September, although the mildness of the coastal climate makes it possible to visit Normandy at any time of the year. In spring, the blossoming of the apple trees transforms the Normandy countryside. Apples flower last, after the Gaillon cherries and the Domfront pears. Apple blossom time is really without equal, and this is the ideal time to explore the countryside by driving through the Pays d'Auge and along the Seine valley.

In summer, the hot weather comes earlier inland than on the coast.

Cows under apple trees in spring, Essay

© Leroy Arthur/age fotostock

The beach season does not begin before June, when the last storms have died away. From Le Tréport to Mont St-Michel, the coast is taken over by people in search of sea air, relaxation and amusement. The sky remains hazy, and the sunshine has a special quality, filtered through the light clouds. Inland, the fine weather inspires long rambles through the picturesque countryside, and the many recreational areas along the winding rivers provide opportunities to cool off in bucolic surroundings. The autumn months are the wettest of the year but as soon as November approaches there are many magnificent days. It is the time of year to enjoy the wonderful changing colours of the forest trees. The light is incomparably soft, making the stone buildings appear all the more substantial. It is never very cold.

THEMED TOURS
HERITAGE TRAILS

To help tourists discover France's national heritage in its historical context, municipalities, recently aided by the **Fédération nationale des Routes Historiques**, have set up a number of routes focussing on a given theme. Each itinerary is clearly signposted by panels laid out along the roads and is described in leaflets available from the tourist offices for each *département* or locality. In Calvados, for example, you could choose the Route of the Old Mills, through Fontaine-Henry and Creully; in Orne you could explore the land of Sir Lancelot, around Domfront, Lassay and La Ferté-Macé, or perhaps the Forest Route, taking in the countryside between Essay and Domfront.

THEMATIC ITINERARIES

Driving tours are given throughout this guide. Others, on more specific themes, have been mapped out for you by French specialists.

Visiting Mont St-Michel Bay

The bay surrounding Mont St-Michel, which features on UNESCO's list of World Nature and Culture Heritage Sites, is also an exceptional place on account of its tidal range – the greatest in continental Europe. During spring tides, the sea level can rise up to 15m between low and high tide. The water recedes 15km/9mi from the coast, then rushes back, accelerating in pace towards the end.

Throughout the year, the **Maison de la Baie** at Le-Vivier-sur-Mer (on the Brittany side) and the **Eco-Musée de la Baie** in Vains-St Léonard, welcome tourists, organise tours of the bay, provide information and stage exhibits aimed at promoting the heritage of the bay. From July to August they are open every day of the week; weekdays only the rest of the year.

Maison de la Baie (visits to oyster beds by tractor, visits on foot to the bay to explore its landscapes and enjoy its flora and fauna, such as the seals), Port Est Le Vivier, Le Vivier-sur-Mer. ℘02 99 48 84 38. www.maison-baie.com.

Eco-musée de la Baie (demonstration of salt-making, excursions to discover the bay's flora and fauna), Route du Grouin du Sud, 50300 Vains-St Léonard. ℘02 33 89 06 06. www.manche.fr/patrimoine.

Crossing the Bay to Mont St-Michel – Visitors should know that it is dangerous to cross the Bay alone, even if there are no barriers. Rivers, sand bars and areas of mud and quicksand change constantly with the currents and winds, and the sea level can rise with the incoming tide at a speed sometimes said to be as fast as a galloping horse. Therefore, for your safety, cross to Mont St-Michel only with one of the licensed Bay guides. Indeed, in the past the first guides were the Bay's fishermen and hunters; they passed their knowledge down to the next generation from which many of today's guides come, making the crossings safer and quite unforgettable.

⊡ To obtain further information, or to make reservations (essential), apply to the Office de Tourisme Intercommunal de Sartilly Porte de la Baie at either 4 place des Halles, 50 530 Genêts ℘08 99 36 22 24 (€3 + service provider's charge) or ℘118 612 (€2.99 + €2.99/min + service provider's charge). www.annuaire-mairie.fr/office-tourisme-intercommunal-sartilly-porte-la-baie.html.

Two **private guide companies** organise crossings to Mont St-Michel:

♦ Chemins de la Baie du Mont Saint-Michel, 34 rue de l'Ortillon, 50530 Genêts. ℘02 33 89 80 88. www.cheminsdelabaie.com.

♦ Découverte de la Baie du Mont Saint-Michel, La Maison du Guide, 1 rue Montroise, 50530 Genêts. ℘02 33 70 83 49. www.decouvertebaie.com.

There are also several private guides conducting interesting specialised tours (nature, history, as a pilgrimage, etc.). Consult www.ot-montsaintmichel.com.

Mont St-Michel bay at low tide

© Francis Leroy/hemis.fr

Anniversaries of the D-Day landings

During the summer of 2014, the world's attention was drawn to the events of June 1944, with the D-Day landing beaches and the sites of the Battle of Normandy took centre stage. The 70th anniversary of the Allied Invasion was commemorated by Allied Heads of State and hundreds of thousands of visitors.

Five years later, in June 2019, the 75th anniversarsy was celebrated across Normandy in a rich and unprecedented programme of events devised to bring to life the memory of this tragic period. In particular, The skies over the UK and Normandy were filled with Douglas DC-3/C-47 Dakotas and hundreds of Paratroopers (DAKS over Normandy. www.daksovernormandy.com). Other events included a Normandy WWII International Film Festival; the Opening of the new 360° immersive room at Caen Memorial, and a Giant picnic at Omaha Beach.

Following in William the Conqueror's Footsteps
A suggested itinerary, with supporting information and links, follows the career of the Conqueror from Fécamp through 20 towns and sites. www.la-normandie.info/normandie-decouverte/routes-historiques.

Route des Colombiers Cauchois
Visit Normandy's famous dovecotes nestling along the valleys of the Durdent, Valmont or Gonzeville. www.normandie-echappees-plaisirs.fr.

Route de la Pomme et du Cidre
The countryside stretching from the Pays de Caux and the Pays de Bray is dotted with *cour-masures* planted with venerable apple trees. Leaflets about apples and cider making are available from local tourist offices or www.larouteducidre.com.

There is also a museum that relates information about Poiré, a sparkling drink made from pears: Musée du Poiré, 50720 Baranton. ✆02 33 59 56 22. www.parc-naturel-normandie-maine.fr.

Route Historique des Abbayes Normandes
This route takes you to 33 abbeys and priories (of 60 surviving in Normandy) as well as 24 châteaux and museums along the valley of the Seine, around Caen and in Basse-Normandie.

Contact Route historique, 28, rue Raymond Aron, BP 52, 76824 Mont-Saint-Aignan. ✆02 35 12 41 60. www.abbayes-normandes.com.

Route Historique du Patrimoine Cultural Québécois
Three circuits have been developed especially for French Canadians seeking to learn about the land of their ancestors.
Comité Chomedey de Maisonneuve, Centre Culturel Maisonneuve, Place Paul Chomedey de Maisonneuve, 10190 Neuville-sur-Vanne, Aube. http://comite.maisonneuve.free.fr. ✆03 25 40 68 33.

MUSEUMS OF NORMANDY
The extraordinary cultural heritage of Normandy is reflected in museums of all types: art, traditional industry and crafts, natural history, etc., many tucked into out-of-the-way villages you might easily miss. The website www.normandie-tourisme.fr lists museums (including those devoted to Impressionist art).

GARDENS OF NORMANDY
The mild climate has long inspired Normans to cultivate lovely gardens which are the perfect setting for a leisurely stroll.
The **Comité Régional de Tourisme de Normandie** (www.normandie-tourisme.fr) offers a downloadable listing some 65 gardens open to the public. The **Comité des Parcs and Jardins de France** has

regional associations in Normandy. The excellent website, www. parcsetjardins.fr (in French only), lets you locate gardens by type, region, name or on interactive maps. Local garden organisations, under the umbrella of the national Comité, are:

♦ **Union des Parcs et Jardins de Basse-Normandie**
106 Route de Bretagne, 14760 Bretteville-sur-Odon.
℘02 31 15 57 35.

♦ **Union des Parcs et Jardins de Haute-Normandie**
114 ter, avenue des Martyrs de la Résistance, 76100 Rouen.
℘02 32 18 76 18.

A selection of gardens and parks:
♦ Jardin des Plantes in Avranches.
♦ Gardens of the Château de Brécy.
♦ Park and gardens of Thury-Harcourt.
♦ Botanical gardens in Vauville.
♦ Parc Emmanuel-Liais and its greenhouses in Cherbourg.
♦ Jardin des Plantes Quesnel-Morinière in Coutances.
♦ Jardin Christian-Dior in Granville.
♦ Park of the Château de Nacqueville.
♦ Floral park of the Bois des Moustiers at Varengeville-sur-Mer.
♦ Jardin des Plantes at Rouen.
♦ Park of the Château de Miromesnil.
♦ Gardens and terraces of the Château de Sassy.
♦ Park of the Château d'Acquigny.
♦ Park of the Château de Beaumesnil.
♦ Parc zoologique Jean-Delacour at Clères.
♦ Claude Monet's garden at Giverny.
♦ Park of the Château de Launay.

BATTLE OF NORMANDY ITINERARIES

Eight themed itineraries, under the general title The Historical Area of the Battle of Normandy (signposted in French along the routes as Normandie: Terre-Liberté) take in the sites, museums and memorials relating to the events of June 1944 in the Manche, Calvados and Orne

---

 D-Day Tours

Normandy Sightseeing Tours *(5474 blvd. Winston Churchill - 14400 St Vigor Le Grand. ℘02 31 51 70 52. www.normandy-sightseeing-tours. com)* offer D-Day Tours departing from Bayeux. You can take a half- or full-day tour, taking in such historic sites as Omaha Beach, Ste-Mère-Église, Dead Man's Corner Museum, Canadian Cemetery and Ardenne Abbey.

---

départements. The symbol to follow along the roads is a seagull.
For detailed maps and descriptions of the sights, contact the Maison du Département, 98 route de Candol, 50000 St-Lô. ℘02 33 05 98 70. www. manchetourisme.com.

♦ **Overlord-L'Assaut** *(70km/43.5mi)* from Pegasus Bridge to Bayeux via Sword, Juno and Gold beaches.
♦ **D-Day-Le Choc** *(130km/81mi)* from Bayeux to Carentan taking in Omaha Beach and St-Lô.
♦ **Objectif-Un Port** *(95km/59mi)* from Carentan to Cherbourg via Ste-Mère-Église and Valognes.
♦ **L'Affrontement** *(207km/128.6mi)* Overlord-L'Assault, from Bénouville to Vire coming back by Caen.
♦ **Cobra-La Percée** *(155km/96mi)* from Cherbourg to Avranches via Coutances.
♦ **La Contre-Attaque** *(162km/100mi)* from Avranches to Alençon via Mortain.
♦ **L'Encerclement** *(145km/90mi)* from Alençon to L'Aigle via Chambois and Montormel.
♦ **Le Dénouement** *(122km/76mi)* from Caen to L'Aigle via Montormel and Vimoutiers.

Normandy Campaign
For a day-by-day account of the Normandy Campaign, from the landings on 6 June 1944 to the liberation of Paris on 25 August, with detailed maps, go to the website of the American Battle Monuments Commission, at www.abmc.gov.

What to See and Do

OUTDOOR FUN

CANOEING/KAYAKING

The fast-flowing rivers in the Suisse Normande are particularly good for canoes and kayaks.

Notable sites in Normandy are Pont-d'Ouilly, Clécy, Sillé-le-Guillaume and St-Léonard-des-Bois. The rivers **Eure** (around Dreux-Louviers) and **Risle** (around L'Aigle-Seine estuary) have excellent sites; contact clubs in **Rouen** or **Belbeuf**.

You can also practice sea-kayaking out of major nautical centres such as Le Havre and Fécamp.

- **Canoë-Kayak Calvados**. Calvados Attractivité, 8 rue Renoir, 14054 Caen. ℘02 31 27 90 30. www.calvados-tourisme.com/autour-de-leau.
- **Fédération Française de Canoë-Kayak**
  Base Olympique et Paralympique 2024, Route de Torcy, 77360 Vaires sur Marne. ℘01 45 11 08 50. www.ffcanoe.asso.fr.

The Fédération publishes a book, *Le guide du canoë en France*, a guide to all good canoeing and kayaking watercourses. It can be obtained from the English-speaking bookshop Le Canotier, 206 rue du Moulin à Vent, 76760 Yerville. ℘02 35 96 61 31. www.canotier.com.

- **Comité régional Normandie de Canoë-Kayak** –
  1 rue Masson 76350 Oissel. ℘09 63 64 23 97. https://canoekayaknormandie.org.

CRUISES ON THE RIVER SEINE

A number of boats able to accommodate between 80 and 350 passengers visit the main harbours (Le Havre, Honfleur, Rouen).

Trips can take half a day or a whole day, including meals on board, or you can opt for luxury cruises between Paris and Honfleur lasting up to a week, with stops along the way.

The following list features the most popular boats offering this type of excursion.

- **CroisiEurope** – ℘0826 101 234. www.croisieurope.com. Cruises between Paris and Honfleur.
- **Le Guillaume-le-Conquérant** – Contact Rives de Seine Croisières, rue du Bac, 27740 Poses. ℘02 35 78 31 70. www.bateau-guillaume-le-conquerant.com. Shorter cruises between Poses and Muids, about 4h with a meal.

Kayaking along the Grande-Grève beach in front of the Éléphant rock, Îles Chausey

© Christophe Boisvieux/hemis.fr

CLIMBING

Climbers are attracted to the steep rocky slopes of the Alpes Mancelles and Suisse Normande, particularly the vertical walls of the Rochers des Parcs near Clécy or the Fosse-Arthour northwest of Domfront. For information apply to Tourist Information Centres or to:

♦ **Club Alpin Français de Caen**
   92 rue de Geôle, 14000 Caen.
   ℘02 31 86 29 55.
   www.clubalpin-caen.fr.

♦ **Fédération française de la montagne et de l'escalade**
   www.ffme.fr.

CYCLING

Good cycling country is found in the Brotonne forest, Lyons forest, Eure valley, Seine valley and along the Caux coast; there are steeper gradients in the Alpes Mancelles, the Suisse Normande and the Cotentin peninsula. Voies vertes (ecolo-paths for all-terrain bikes) are being developed throughout the region. Consult tourist offices. You can take the train for part of your circuit; your bike travels for free. Certain train stations even rent bikes, which you can turn in at another station. For up-to-date information, consult:

♦ **Fédération Française de Cyclotourisme**
   12 rue Louis-Bertrand,
   94207 Ivry-sur-Seine.
   ℘01 56 20 88 88.
   https://ffvelo.fr.
   The Fédération supplies itineraries covering most of France, giving mileage, difficult routes and sights to see.

♦ **Fédération Francaise de Cyclisme**
   1 rue Laurent Fignon, CS 40 100,
   78180 Montigny le Bretonneux .
   ℘08 11 04 05 55. www.ffc.fr.
   This group produces information on more than 46 000km/ 28 750 mi of marked trails for all-terrain bicycling.

♦ **Comité Départemental de Cyclotourisme de l'Eure**
   Le Clos Tiger, 27170 Beaumonte.
   ℘02 32 45 35 06.
   www.codep-eure.fr.

♦ **Comité départemental de Cyclotourisme de Seine-Maritime**
   ℘02 35 24 50 21/℘06 47 69 35 00.
   http://codep76.e-monsite.com.

♦ **Comité Départemental de Cyclotourisme de la Manche**,
   3 Boulevard de la Dollée
   50000 Saint-Lo. ℘02 33 56 84 62.
   http://www.cyclisme50.com.

FISHING

For those interested in freshwater fishing, it is necessary to know the dates of the *saison de la pêche*: all over France, the second Saturday in March heralds the start of the fishing season for rivers belonging to the first category *(première catégorie)*, ending on the third Sunday in September. In the case of second-category rivers *(deuxième catégorie)*, fishing is permitted all year round, except for pike, which can usually be caught between July and January, depending on the area.

Normandy is dotted with a great many lakes, rivers and ponds of astounding variety. This particular type of topography makes it one of France's most treasured regions for fishing. The fast-flowing rivers abound in fario trout, a local variety, and rainbow trout, brought over from America, whereas the various lakes and ponds are the favourite haunt of carnivorous species such as pike, pikeperch and salmon. The most popular rivers among anglers are the **Risle** (brown trout, carnivores), the **Iton** (pike, rainbow trout), the **Charentonne** (trout), the **Huisne** (grayling, brown trout), the **Touques** (brown trout), the **Yères** (brown trout), the **Bresle** (sea trout), the **Arques** (salmon and sea trout) and the **Durdent** (brown trout, sea trout).

Anglers are expected to comply with legislation on fishing, in particular concerning the size of their catch. They are expected to throw back certain fish into rivers if their length does not meet the required standards (40cm in the case of pike; 23cm in the case of trout).

It is possible to take up sea fishing, both along the coast and on board one of the boats leaving from Trouville, Honfleur, Fécamp, Dieppe, Le Tréport or St-Valery-en-Caux. The waters near Dieppe are said to be teeming with fish and anglers who settle near the piers, often to see their patience rewarded by landing mackerel, pollock, sole or bass. Details are available from regional tourist offices.

Wherever you choose to go fishing, make sure you obey the laws on angling and apply for details from the relevant federations and associations. Any person wanting to fish in France must first get a permit (carte de pêche) from the local AAPPMA (Associations Agrées de Pêche et de Protection du Milieu Aquatique) affiliated fishing association, and obtain permission from the landowner if you wish to fish on private land. See also www.cartedepeche.fr.

- ♦ **Fédération de Calvados pour la pêche**
  3 rue de Bruxelles, 14120 Mondeville.
  ℘02 31 44 63 00.
  www.federation-peche14.fr.
- ♦ **Fédération de la Manche pour la pêche**
  71 Zone Artisanale, 50750 Canisy.
  ℘02 33 46 96 50.
  www.peche-manche.com.
- ♦ **Fédération de l'Orne pour la pêche**,
  4 rue des Artisans, 61003 Alençon.
  ℘02 33 26 10 66.
  www.peche-orne.fr.
- ♦ **Fédération de l'Eure pour la pêche et la protection du milieu aquatique**
  avenue de l'Europe, 27500 Pont-Audemer. ℘02 32 57 10 73.
  www.eure-peche.com.
- ♦ **Fédération de Seine-Maritime pour la pêche,**
  11 cours Clemenceau,
  76100 Rouen. ℘02 35 62 01 55.
  www.federationpeche.fr/76.

GOLF

Normandy has more than 40 golf courses; all the major resorts have clubs, many very beautiful. ℘See http://en.normandie-tourisme.fr. For information about golf in Calvados, la Manche or Orne *départements*, contact:

- ♦ **Ligue de Golf de Basse-Normandie**
  2 av. du Grand-Hôtel, 143 Le Home Varaville. ℘02 31 28 31 00.
  www.lgolfbn.fr.

For information about courses in the Sarthe and La Mayenne départements, contact:

- ♦ **Ligue de Golf des Pays de la Loire**
  9 rue du Couédic 44000 Nantes.
  ℘02 40 08 05 06.
  www.ligue-golf-paysdelaloire.asso.fr.

For the Eure and Seine-Maritime contact:

- ♦ **Ligue Golf de Haute-Normandie**
  11 Pl. Félix Faure, 76170 Lillebonne.
  ℘ 02 32 65 26 39. https://liguegolfnormandie.fr.
- ♦ **Fédération Française de Golf**
  68 rue Anatole-France,
  92309 Levallois-Perret.
  ℘01 41 49 77 00.
  www.ffgolf.org.

WALKING

Walking is one of the best ways of discovering the Normandy countryside – the superb beech forests and the occasional manor houses on well-kept farms. Throughout the region there are long-distance footpaths (*sentiers de grande randonnée*, or *GR* – one- or two-day walks) marked with red-and-white lined posts and shorter, local paths (*petite randonnée* or PR) marked on posts with a single yellow line. Detailed topographical guides are available showing the routes and giving good advice to walkers. The Topo-guides are published by the **Fédération Française de la Randonnée Pédestre** (Comité

Horse-riding on Omaha Beach, Plage de Vierville-sur-Mer

National des Sentiers de Grande Randonnée) and are on sale at https://boutique.ffrandonnee.fr/topoguides.

Several of these well-marked footpaths cross Normandy.

♦ The **GR 2** follows the north bank of the Seine and crosses the Londe and Roumare forests.

♦ The **GR 21** runs up the Lézarde valley to meet the coast at Étretat.

♦ The **GR 22** from Paris to Mont St-Michel crosses the southwest of Normandy up to Mamers.

♦ The **GR 23** follows the left bank of the Seine and crosses the Forest of Brotonne.

♦ The **GR 221** crosses parts of the Suisse Normande and the Cotentin peninsula.

♦ The **GR 223** (444km/276mi) runs along the north coast and the Cotentin peninsula, often following old customs agents' trails with superb views, notably at Cap de la Hague.

♦ The **GR Sur les traces du chasse-marée** (on the trail of the fishmongers) follows the ancient medieval cart-track that, until the arrival of the railway in 1848, brought fish from Dieppe to Rouen and Paris. Information is available from the Dieppe tourism office ℘02 32 14 40 60 and the tourist office of the *département* of Seine-Maritime (*www.seine-maritime-tourisme.com*).

♦ The **Chemins de Saint-Michel** follow routes taken by pilgrims in the years when Mont St-Michel drew penitents from all over France. These trails, long forgotten, have been progressively traced and marked with bright blue posts. Two 200km/124mi trails in the North Cotentin are collectively named the *Chemins aux Anglais*, while the *Chemin de l'Intérieur* leaves from Barfleur and crosses Ste-Mère-l'Église, Carentan, St-Lô, Coutances, La Haye-Pesnel, to arrive in Genêts. The *Chemin Côtier* links Cherbourg with Genêts following the sea coast. Other trails lead to St-Michel from Caen, Rouen, Chartres and Paris.
For information, contact:
Les Chemins du Mont St-Michel, r. de Picardie, 14500 Vire. ℘02 31 66 10 02. www.lescheminsdumontsaint michel.com.

♦ **Voies vertes, sentiers de découverte and sorties natures** are shorter, less ambitious trails organised locally or in regional parks. Contact tourist offices for information.

HORSE-RIDING

In such a well-known horse-breeding region many riding clubs and centres organise rides on the many miles of bridle paths through the woodlands or exhilarating canters along the shore as well as pony-trekking holidays. There are many local gymkhanas and equestrian events and racegoers are spoiled for choice for a day at the races. From September to Easter, experienced riders can hunt in the forests of Écouves or Andaines to the sound of the horn. Some *gîtes* will even put up both you and your horse!

◆ **Fédération Française d'Equitation**
This governing body for horsemanship in France, delivers licences, conducts training, is responsible for the regulatory framework and oversees competitions.
☏02 54 94 46 00.
www.ffe.com.

◆ **Comité Départemental de Tourisme Équestre du Calvados**
4, chemin de la grande Bruyère 14190 St Germain Le Vasson.
☏02 31 90 52 01.

◆ **Comité Départemental de Tourisme Équestre de la Manche**
Le Presbytère,50160 Brectouville.
☏06 30 18 30 09. https://tourisme-equestre-cdte-manche.ffe.com.

◆ **Comité Départemental d'Equitation de l'Orne**
25, rue des Iris, 61250 Damigny.
☏02 33 29 19 92.
www.acor-orne.fr.

Horse-drawn caravans
In the Orne and Calvados *départements* you can hire a horse-drawn caravan *(roulotte)*. Enquire at local tourist information centres.

HUNTING

For all enquiries apply to the various *Fédérations départementales de Chasse*:

◆ **Calvados**
r. des Compagnons, 14000 Caen.
☏02 31 44 24 87.
www.fdc14.fr.

◆ **Manche**
31 r. des Aumônes, La Malherbière, 50750 Bourgvallées.
☏02 33 72 63 63.
www.fdc50.com.

◆ **Orne**
La Briqueterie, RD113, CS 70015 61310 Gouffern en Auge.
☏02 33 67 99 39.
www.fdc61.com.

◆ **Eure**:
r. de Melleville,
27930 Angerville-la-Campagne.
☏02 32 23 03 15.
www.fdc27.com.

◆ **Seine-Maritime**
Maison de la Chasse et de la Nature, rte. de l'Étang,
76890 Belleville-en-Caux.
☏02 35 60 35 97.
www.fdc76.com.

◆ **Fédération Nationale des Chasseurs**
13 rue du Général Leclerc 92136 Issy les Moulineaux .
☏01 41 09 65 10.
www.chasseurdefrance.com.

LAND SAILING

The great stretches of sandy beach on the Calvados and Cotentin coasts are ideal for land sailing *(char-à-voile)*, an exhilarating sport performed on a three-wheeled cart equipped with a sail; speeds can reach 100kph/62mph. **Speed sailing**, a form of windsurfing on wheels is also available. Further information may be obtained from:

◆ **Fédération Française de Char à Voile**
Bâtiment Igesa, 2 chemin d'exploitation, 91220 Le Plessis Pâté. ☏01 60 84 17 71.
www.ffcv.org.
The federation offers a list of clubs, guidebooks and calendars.

REGIONAL NATURE PARKS

Normandy's four regional nature parks are a popular destination for walkers and nature lovers alike since they provide countless opportunities for a wide range of open-air activities. In these highly protected areas, extensive facilities have been set up to introduce visitors to local flora and fauna and to increase their awareness of environmental concerns.
There are a great many sports in which to indulge, depending on the time of year. **Boucles de la Seine Normande** *(see Forêt de Brotonne, p112)* **Perche** *(see Mortagne-au-Perche, p246),* **Normandie-Maine** *(see Château*

de Carrouges, p330) and **Marais du Cotentin et du Bessin** (🕮*see Presqu'île du Cotentin, p384).*

SAILING

The Channel coast is a favourite venue for boaters and sailors. Many sailing clubs offer lessons at all levels of skill, and in the bigger coastal towns, annual regattas are a glorious sight. The main moorings and marinas for visiting yachtspeople are indicated on the **Places to Stay map** (🕮*pp38–39).* They usually provide fuelling facilities, convenient water stands for drinking water and electricity points, WCs, showers and sometimes laundry facilities, handling equipment and repair facilities and a 24-hour guard.
France Stations Nautiques is an association of coastal villages, tourist sites and marinas offering first-rate facilities for nautical sports.

♦ **France Stations Nautiques**
   17 r. Henri-Bocquillon, 75015 Paris.
   ☎01 44 05 96 55.
   www.station-nautique.com.

For further information on sailing, contact:

♦ **Fédération Française de Voile**
   17 r. Henri-Bocquillon, 75015 Paris.
   ☎01 40 60 37 00.
   www.ffvoile.net.

☺ *Visitors who own or want to rent a boat (with an engine of more than 6hp) in France must take a compulsory test in sailing skills* (Carte Mer).

SKIN DIVING

The right conditions for deep-sea diving are to be found between Dieppe and Le Havre and between Barfleur and Avranches on the Cotentin coast.

♦ **Fédération Française d'Étude et de Sports sous-marins**
   24 quai de Rive-Neuve,
   13284 Marseille.
   ☎04 91 33 99 31. www.ffessm.fr.

SPAS

Normandy has several centres for **thalassotherapy and water cures**. In addition to the bracing climate

and vivifying sea air, they rely on the curative virtues of the local waters, mud and algae:

Bagnoles-de-l'Orne

The Grande Source, **a hot spring** with slightly radioactive mineralised water, is said to provide relief for circulatory problems, especially in the legs, and for arthritis and rheumatism as well as problems of the endocrine glands.

♦ **Thermes de Bagnoles-de-l'Orne**
   rue du Prof.-Louvel,
   61140 Bagnoles-de-l'Orne.
   ☎08 11 90 22 33.
   www.bo-resort.com.

♦ **Centre d'Animation et de Congrès de Bagnoles-de-l'Orne**
   8 rue du Prof.-Louvel, 61140,
   Bagnoles-de-l'Orne.
   ☎02 33 30 72 70.
   www.ornetourisme.com.

Deauville

♦ **Thalsasso-Deauville**
   3 rue Sem, 14800 Deauville.
   ☎02 31 87 72 00.
   www.thalasso-deauville.com.

Granville
Le Normandy:

♦ **Centre de Rééducation et de Réadaptation en Milieu Marin**
   1 rue J.-Michelet, 50406 Granvile.
   ☎02 33 90 33 33.
   www.lenormandy.com.

♦ **Granville Thalasso Previthal**
   Rue de l'Ermitage
   50350 Donville-les-Bains.
   ☎02 33 90 31 10.
   www.previthal.com.

Luc-sur-Mer

♦ **Thalasso des 3 Mondes**
   rue Guynemer, 14530 Luc-sur-Mer.
   ☎02 31 97 32 22.
   www.thalassodes3mondes.com.

Ouistreham

♦ **Thalazur Ouistreham**
   avenue du Cmdt-Keiffer,
   14150 Ouistreham.
   ☎02 31 96 40 40.
   www.thalazur.fr/ouistreham.

Laval on a market day

© Pascal_BELTRAMI/Mayenne Tourisme

SWIMMING

The Normandy beaches are of two types: **sandy** along the Côte Fleurie (Cabourg, Houlgate, Deauville, Trouville, Honfleur, etc.) and **shingle** (stony) along the Alabaster Coast (Étretat, Yport, Fécamp, St-Valéry-en-Caux, Varengeville, Dieppe, etc.). Guarded beaches have a system of flags to warn bathers of possible risks: **green** – safe bathing; **orange** – dangerous, be careful; **red** – bathing prohibited; **violet** – polluted water. If you want to know the water quality of any beach, check on: www. theswimguide.org/beaches/france.

WINDSURFING

This sport, which is permitted on lakes and in sports and leisure centres, is subject to certain rules. Apply to local sailing clubs. Boards may be hired on all major beaches. www.ffvoile.net.

ACTIVITIES FOR KIDS 👫👤

In this guide, sights of particular interest to children are indicated with a KIDS symbol (👫👤). Some attractions may offer discount fees for children.

SHOPPING

In France, the big stores and larger shops are open Mondays to Saturdays from 9am to 6.30 or 7.30pm. Smaller, individual shops may close during the lunch hour, almost universally so in smaller towns. Food shops – grocers, wine merchants and bakeries – are generally open from 7am to 6.30 or 7.30pm; some open on Sunday mornings. Many food shops close between noon and 2pm and on Mondays. Hypermarkets usually remain open non-stop until 9pm or later.

Channel Islands

In Jersey, shops are open from 9am to 5pm, 5.30pm or 6pm, and are closed on Sunday and Thursday afternoon. On Guernsey, shops are open Monday to Saturday from 9am until 5.30pm.

TRADITIONAL MARKETS

All cities and nearly all towns have weekly markets, usually held in the morning. The following are only examples – there are literally thousands across France – 🕐 see www.jours-de-marche.fr.

Calvados

Bayeux (r. St-Jean Wed, pl. St-Patrice Sat); **Honfleur** (Sat; organic produce Wed; antiques 2nd Sun of month; flowers Sat); **St-Pierre-sur-Dives** (Mon); **Trouville** (Wed and Sun).

Eure

Les Andelys (Sat); **Bernay** (Wed,Sat); **Évreux** (town centre Wed and Sat, la Madeleine Sun); **Lyons-la-Forêt** (Thu and weekends); **Le Neubourg** (Wed); **Pont-Audemer** (Mon and Fri); **Verneuil-sur-Avre** (Sat/Sun).

Manche
Coutances (Thu); **St-Hilaire-du-Harcoët** (Wed); **St-Vaast-la-Hogue** (Sat); **Valognes** (Fri).

Orne
L'Aigle (animal market at 7.30am Tue, followed by traditional market); **Bagnoles-sur-l'Orne** (Tue, Wed, Fri and Sat).

Seine-Maritime
Caudebec-en-Caux (Sat); **Dieppe** (Sat); **Étretat** (Thu); **Eu** (Fri); **Fécamp** (Thur and Sat); **Forges-les-Eaux** (Thu and Sat); **Harfleur** (Sun); **Le Havre** (Les Halles centrales Mon–Sat except holidays; antiques, cours de la République, Fri); **Vieux Rouen** place St-Marc (Sun); **Yvetot** (Wed).

SIGHTSEEING
GUIDED TOURS
Many sights, châteaux in particular, can be visited only by guided tour. The departure time of the last tour of the morning or afternoon may be up to 1h before the actual closing time. Most tours are conducted by French-speaking guides; some of the larger and more popular sights may offer guided tours (or audioguides) in several languages.

CHURCHES
Churches are usually closed from noon to 2pm. Visitors should refrain from walking about during services. Visitors to chapels are often accompanied by the person who keeps the keys. A donation is welcome.

BOOKS
BATTLE OF NORMANDY
A Traveller's Guide to D-Day
    Carl Shilleto, Mike Tolhurst (Weidenfeld & Nicolson, 2000)
British Armour in the Normandy Campaign 1944
    John Buckley (Routledge, 2004)
The D-Day Landings
    Philip Warner (Pen & Sword, 2004)
The Americans at Normandy, and

The Americans at D-Day
    Two books by John C McManus (Forge, 2005)
D-Day: the First 24 Hours
    Will Fowler (Spellmount, 2006)
The Germans in Normandy
    Richard Hargreaves, Pen & Sword, 2006)
Overlord-D-Day and the Battle of Normandy, 1944
    Max Hastings (Pan, reissued, 2010)
Normandy '44: D-Day and the Battle for France
    James Holland (Bantam Press, 2019)
The Longest Day: D-Day 75th Anniversary Edition
    Cornelius Ryan (Andre Deutsch Ltd., 2019)
D-Day: the Air Campaign: June 1944 and the role of Anglo-American air power in the Normandy landings
    Ken Delve (Independent, 2019)

CLAUDE MONET
Claude Monet
    Christoph Heinrich (Taschen, revised 2000)
Monet in Normandy
    Richard Brettell (Rizzoli, 2006)

CUISINE
Cuisine Grandmere: From Brittany, Normandy, Picardy and Flanders
    Jenny Baker (Faber and Faber, 1995)
The Cuisine of Normandy
    Princess Marie-Blanche de Broglie (Houghton-Mifflin 1984)
A Flavour of Normandy
    Carole Clements (Headline Book Publishing, 1996)

GARDENS
Gardens in Normandy
    Marie-Françoise Valéry (Flammarion, 2000)
The Magic of Monet's Garden
    Derek Fell (Firefly Books Ltd., 2007)

MONT ST-MICHEL
Mont Saint-Michel from A to Z
    Henry Decaens, Adrien Goetz, Gerard Guiller (Flammarion, 1997)

Tides of Mont St-Michel
Roger Vercel (1938, reissued by Kessinger Publishing, 2005)

NORMAN CONQUEST

The Norman Conquest: A New Introduction
Richard Huscroft (Pearson, 2009)
1066: The Hidden History in the Bayeux Tapestry
Andrew Bridgeford (Walker, 2005)
The Norman Conquest
Marc Morris (Windmill Books, 2013).

FILMS

Jules and Jim (1961)
François Truffaut's tale of two young men and a woman, filmed in Rouen.
The Umbrellas of Cherbourg (1964)
With Catherine Deneuve: Jacques Demy's charming musical about love and loss in Normandy.
A Man and a Woman (1966)
Cult Claude Lelouch film about falling in love again, in Deauville.
Tess (1979)
Scenes from Roman Polanski's version of Thomas Hardy's novel were shot in the lush Norman countryside.
Saving Private Ryan (1998)
Steven Spielberg drama about the Battle of Normandy.

La Vie en Rose (2007)
Based on the life of Edith Piaf; the scenes of squalor during her childhood are set in Normandy.
Le Havre (2011)
A shoeshiner tries to save an immigrant child in the French port.
Angel & Tony (2010)
Drama film telling the story of a widow in a desperate situation who wins the respect of her employery and his community and regains her estranged son.
The Fairy (La Fée) (2011)
A hotel clerk searches Le Havre for the fairy who made two of his three wishes come true.
Comment c'est loin (2015)
Quasi-autobiographical comedy written by French rapper Orelsan and directed by Orelsan and Christophe Offenstein.
Dunkirk (2017)
War film written, directed, and produced by Christopher Nolan that depicts the Dunkirk evacuation of World War II.

Calendar of Events

Especially during summer months, towns and villages throughout Normandy hold fairs, festivals, commemorations of all sorts.
You can plan an itinerary to take in these events, whose dates tend to shift from year to year. Consult *www.normandie-tourisme.fr* for exact dates, and ask at local tourist offices.
For *Gastronomic Fairs* 🕭p28.
For *Channel Islands* 🕭p29.

JANUARY
Argentan – *Foire Saint-Vincent*. Major funfair held in the town centre.
Rouen – *Les Puces Rouennaises*. Antiques Fair. www.pucesrouennaises.com.

APRIL
Caen – Carnival. Europe's largest student carnival. www.caenlamer-tourisme.fr.
Caen – *La Fête de l'Excellence Normande* (FENO: Normandy Excellency Festival). https://evenements.normandie.fr/feno.
Granville – *Carnival*. www.carnaval-de-granville.fr.

Honfleur – *Salon du Vin*. Big wine fair held within the walls of the Greniers à Sel. www.calvados-tourisme.com.

Rouen – *24 Heures Motonautiques*. Offshore powerboat race on the river Seine. www.24heures rouen.com.

MAY

Le Marais Vernier – *Etampage* (Branding of cows). The tradition dates back the 18C. 📞02 32 57 61 62. www.visit-normandy-marais-vernier.com.

Coutances – *Jazz sous les Pommiers* (Jazz under the apple trees) 8-day festival showcasing jazz talent from around the world. 📞02 33 76 78 50. www.jazzsouslespommiers.com.

Deauville – *Festival de Paques* (Easter Festival). Major classical music festival. 📞02 31 14 40 00. https://musiqueadeauville.com.

Mont de Cerisy – *La Fête des Rhodos* (Rhododendron Fair). 📞02 33 65 06 75. www.beauxjardinsetpotagers.fr.

Ste-Adresse – Dixie Days Jazz Festival. www.lehavretourisme.com.

La Perrière – Contemporary art market. 📞02 33 73 35 49.

Saint-Laurent-de-Cuves – *Papillons de Nuit Festival*. International artists of genres ranging from rock to indie to electronic come together for a three-day festival. 📞02 33 69 20 40. https://papillonsdenuit.com.

JUNE

Bayeux – *D-Day Festival*. Each year since 2007, D-Day Festival Normandy has been offering a program of festive events for the anniversary of the Allied Landings of 6th June 1944. https://bayeux-bessin-tourisme.com/en/event/d-day-festival-normandy.

Ste-Mère-Église – Commemoration of the D-Day Landings. 📞02 33 41 41 35.

Utah Beach – Commemoration of the landings of 6 June 1944. 📞02 33 71 58 00.

Cabourg – *Festival du Film de Cabourg* (Cabourg Film Festival). 📞02 31 93 74 30 (ticket office), 📞01 58 62 56 09 (Paris HQ). www.festival-cabourg.com.

Cherbourg – Festival les Art'zimutes. Music festival including street concerts, events, sports. 📞06 38 33 08 63. https://lesartzimutes.com.

Deauville – International Horse Jumping Competitions. 📞02 31 14 40 00.

Deauville – International Sailing Week. www.sail-world.com

Évreux – *Rock Music Festival*. Combines alternative rock with electronic music performances in the town's Hippodrome. www.rockinevreux.org.

Cabourg – *Mon Amour*. On the beach, 3 days of indie and electronic music. https://cabourgmonamour.fr.

JUNE–JULY

Blainville-Crevon – *Archéo-Jazz*, festival of jazz and contemporary music. www.archeojazz.com.

Caen – International Organ Festival. 📞02 31 30 46 86.

Mortagne-au-Perche – *Les Musicales de Mortagne*. Festival of chamber music. 📞02 33 81 60 00.

Rouen – Joan of Arc Festival, performances in medieval dress. www.experienceloire.com/joan.htm.

JULY

Barneville-Carteret – Carteret Sea Race. 📞02 33 04 90 58.

Bayeux – Medieval Festival. https://bayeux-bessin-tourisme.com/en/event/bayeux-medieval-festival.

Granville – *Sorties de Bain* (Festival des Arts de la Rue: Street theatre). A festive and cultural event to be enjoyed by the whole family, and completely free! Dancing, theatre, comedy, story-telling, and singing. www.sortiesdebain.com.

Hérouville-Saint-Clair – *Beauregard Festival*. Huge outdoor graden party attracting big-name artists. www.festivalbeauregard.com.

Le Bourg-Dun– Festival of Linens and Needlework. www.lebourgdun.com.

Dives-sur-Mer – *Festival de la Marionnette* (Puppet Festival). ✆02 31 28 12 73. https://le-sablier.org/festival.

Le Haye-de-Routot – *Feu St Clair* (St-Clair bonfire night). A pagan-origin bonfire. www.ancient-yew.org.

Saint-Aubin-sur-Mer – *Pete the Monkey Fetival*. Vibrant arts, music and food festival. http://petethemonkeyfestival.com/en.

Le Tréport – Festival of the Sea. www.seine-maritime-tourisme.com.

Étretat – *Hello Birds*. indie music and the outdoors combine in this Seapop Fetival. https://hellobirdsfestival.fr.

JULY–AUGUST

Cherbourg – *Les Estivales.* Free guided tours of the historic district, Ravalet chateau, botanical gardens, Voeu abbey. ✆02 33 93 52 02. www.cherbourgtourisme.com.

Dreux – *L'été sous les charmes*, world music festival, free concerts. ✆02 37 38 84 12. www.dreux.com.

La Mayenne region – *Les Nuits de la Mayenne*: entertainment organised around the region. ✆02 43 67 60 90. www.nuitsdelamayenne.com.

Mont St-Michel Bay – *Jazz en Baie Festival*. Jazz and soul music permeates the atmosphere during this 12-day event ✆02 33 51 69 36 or ✆02 33 49 90 76. www.jazzenbaie.com.

AUGUST

Crèvecoeur-en-Auges – *Les Mediévales* (Medieval Festival). ✆02 31 63 02 45. www.chateau-de-crevecoeur.com.

Jobourg – *Foire aux moutons* (Sheep Fair). www.mairie-jobourg.fr.

St-Lô – Normandy Horse Show. ✆02 33 06 09 72. https://polehippiquestlo.fr.

Barfleur – *Le Village des Antiquaires* (Antiques Fair). The biggest fair in the Cotentin peninsula. www.barfleur.fr

Blangy-sur-Bresle – Glass Festival. ✆02 35 93 57 01. www.verredartdelabresle.fr.

Les Mediévales, Crèvecoeur-en-Auges

Biennial international kite festival, Dieppe

© Guy Thouvenin/age fotostock

Deauville – Grand Prix: Horse racing www.france-galop.com.

Deauville – *A Musical August*, a week of classical music. ℘01 56 54 14 80. https://musiqueadeauville.com.

Houlgate – Festijazz. ℘02 31 28 14 00. www.jazzcaen.com/festijazz.htm.

Île de Tatihou – *Les Traversées de Tatihou - Musiques du lage*: Music festival on the island, near St Vaast-la-Hougue (2nd or 3rd week of August, depending on tides). www.manche.fr/culture/ traversees-tatihou.aspx.

Granville – *Festival des Voiles de Travail*. The town celebrates its history with boat excursions, exhibitions, concerts, and sea food sampling. www. festivaldesvoilesdetravail.com.

SEPTEMBER

Heritage Days – *On 21 and 22 September, across Normandy (and the whole of France for that matter), the Heritage Days (Journées Européennes du Patrimoine are an opportunity to visit buildings, monuments and sites, many of which are not normally open to the public. https:// journeesdupatrimoine.culture.gouv. fr. Ask for details at local tourist information offices.*

Alençon, Argentan, Bagnoles del'Orne, Mortagne, Flers, Sées – *Septembre musicale de l'Orne*. Weekend classical music concerts throughout the month. ℘02 33 26 99 99. www. septembre-musical.com.

Deauville – *Festival du cinéma américain* (American Film Festival). Premiere screenings of the latest US film releases and big stars on the red carpet. ℘02 31 14 40 00 (tourist office). www.festival-deauville.com.

Dieppe – Biennial international kite festival (next in 2020). ℘02 32 90 04 95. www.dieppe-cerf-volant.org.

Merville-Franceville-Plage – *Festival 'Cidre et Dragon'*. Joins the worlds of fantasy and imagination. www.cidreetdragon.eu.

Lessay – *Foire de Lessay*: The largest and oldest horse and cattle fair in Normandy. ℘02 33 76 58 80. http://foire-de-lessay.dans-la-manche.fr.

OCTOBER

Bellême – International Mushroom Festival. www.mycologiades.com.

Deauville – Equi'Days. Festival of Calvados horses and races.

Deauville – Paris–Deauville Rally, with classic cars.

Haras national du Pin – Horse racing events; prestigious cross-country race and procession of carriages and stallions. ℰ02 33 36 68 68. www.haras-national-du-pin.com.

Mont St-Michel – *Feast of the Archangel Michael*: mass in the abbey church in the presence of the bishops of Bayeux and Coutances. ℰ02 33 60 14 05.

Le Havre – *Ouest Park Festival*. Music festival held in the Tourneville Fort. www.ouestpark.com.

OCTOBER–NOVEMBER

Caen – *Puces Caennaises* (Fleamarket) ℰ02 31 29 99 99. www.caen-evenements.com.

Calvados – Equi' Days: Horse-riding events throughout the region. ℰ02 31 27 90 30.

Neufchâtel-en-Bray – International/National Agricultural Show. Juried competitions, together with Feast of St Martin Fair. ℰ02 35 93 22 96.

Seine-Maritime and Eure départements – Several cities participate in autumn festivities in Normandy; music, theatre and dance. ℰ02 32 33 79 00.

DECEMBER

Sées – Turkey Fair. An event over a hundred years old. Breeders, juried events, sale of foie gras. ℰ02 33 28 74 79.

Dreux – *Les Flambarts* Carnival over three days. Parades, sailing of tiny lighted boats, Christmas fair, skating rink. Festivities celebrating light. ℰ02 37 42 02 99. www.dreux.com/flambarts.

Caen – Christmas fair. Skating rink, market, parades, storytelling, Christmas lighting.

GASTRONOMIC FAIRS IN NORMANDY

Every year a number of fairs and events are held throughout Normandy offering local specialities and special events. The following is a sample:

MARCH

Mortagne-au-Perche – International Black Blood Sausage Festival Sweet. Savoury blood sausage festival, with over 600 international competitors. ℰ06 73 04 75 35. www.mortagne-evenements.com.

MAY AND JUNE

Cambremer – Festival of AOC and AOP regional products of Normandy. ℰ02 31 63 08 87.

Le Tréport – Mussels Fair. www.seine-maritime-tourisme.com.

Vernon – *Foire aux Cerises*. Cherry Fair. Three days in which to celebrate the cherry. ℰ02 32 51 32 56. www.vernon27.fr/events/foire-aux-cerises.

AUGUST

Livarot – Cheese Fair and many regional products, too.

Créances – Carrot Festival with competitions, regional products.

SEPTEMBER

Neufchâtel-en-Bray Cheese festival with tastings, food markets, street parades and competitions. www.seine-maritime-tourisme.com.

Granville – *Toute la Mer sur un Plateau* Seafood festival around the port. ℰ02 33 91 30 03. www.tourisme-granville-terre-mer.com.

OCTOBER–NOVEMBER

Beuvron-en-Auge – Cider festival in open-air market featuring apple and other products; cider press, tastings. ℰ02 31 63 08 87.

Honfleur – Prawn Festival with concerts, workshops, kids' event, prawn-shelling competition. **Le Neubourg** – Foie gras market. www.eure-tourisme.fr.

Rouen – Festival of gastronomy with cooking demonstrations, regional products. https://en.rouentourisme.com/the-festival-of-gastronomy-of-the-stomach.

Vimoutiers – Apple Fair with apple tart competition, tastings etc.
Dieppe – Herring Fairs, scallops too. **Fécamp**, **Le Tréport**, **Etretat** and **St-Valery-en-Caux**.

THE CHANNEL ISLANDS

🅸 Tourist information offices:
Jersey: Liberation Station, St Helier. 𝄐01534 85 90 00. www.jersey.com.
Guernsey: North Esplanade, St Peter Port. 𝄐01481 723 552. www.visitguernsey.com.
Herm: 𝄐01481 75 00 00. www.herm-island.com.
Sark: The Avenue. 𝄐01481 83 23 45. www.sark.co.uk.
Alderney: 𝄐01481 82 23 33. www.visitalderney.com.

APRIL

Guernsey – Spring Floral Guernsey Festival Week.
Herm – Tuesday garden tours through end August.
Sark – Wildflower Fortnight. Guided tours.

MAY–JUNE

Guernsey & Jersey – Liberation Day (9 May) commemorating WWII liberation of the islands.
Guernsey - Healthspan Spring Walking Week; Photography Festival; Literary Festival (readings, talks, book fair).
Jersey – Spring Walking Week.

JUNE–JULY

Guernsey & Jersey – *Le Tour des Ports de la Manche* yacht race.
Guernsey – La Fete de Musique de Ville at St Peter Port (live music); Le Viaer Marché (food, entertainment, traditional Guernsey evening).
Jersey – Jersey in Bloom Festival (talks, open gardens, floral festival); *Bonne Nuit* Harbour Festival (water and beach events).
Sark – Folk festival (major music event); sheep-racing weekend.

AUGUST

Alderney – Carnival week.
Guernsey – North Show and Battle of Flowers.
Jersey – Samarès Manor Autumn Fair; Battle of Flowers.
Sark – Grand Autumn Show. Preserves, baked goods, produce.

SEPTEMBER

Guernsey & Jersey – Autumn Walking Week (guided walks); Channel Islands Festival of Arts and Crafts.
Guernsey (morning) & Jersey (afternoon) - International Air Display including Battle of Britain memorial flight; one of Europe's major free air displays.
Guernsey – International Food Festival. 𝄐01481 723552. www.visitguernsey.com/food-festival.

OCTOBER

Alderney – Food Festival, includes a varied programme of events and themed food nights. 𝄐01481 822 333. www.visitalderney.com/event.
Guernsey – Floral Guernsey Autumn Festival.
Jersey – Standard Chartered Jersey Marathon (a run through St Helier and across the island); Autumn Cattle, Fruit, Flower and Vegetable Show.

OCTOBER–NOVEMBER

Guernsey & Jersey – Tennerfest, gastronomic festival with meals at reduced prices.

DECEMBER

Alderney – Anniversary of Homecoming Day, which commemorates the return of the first islanders after WW2. www.visitalderney.com.
Jersey – *La Fête de Noué* fair: moonlight walks, light displays, markets, parades, street theatre.

Know Before You Go

USEFUL WEBSITES

http://uk.france.fr
The French Government Tourist Office site is packed with practical information and tips for those travelling to France. The homepage has a number of links to more specific guidance.

www.ViaMichelin.com
This site has maps, tourist information, travel features, suggestions on hotels and restaurants, and a route planner for numerous locations in Europe. In addition, you can look up weather forecasts, traffic reports and service station location, particularly useful if you will be driving in France.

www.france.fr
The French Government Tourist Office site is packed with practical information and tips for those travelling to France. Links to more specific guidance for American or Canadian travellers, and to the FGTO's London pages. Choose your country of origin and then click the French region you're interested in.

You'll find links to individual sites for the Gard, Vaucluse and Bouches-du-Rhône plus contact details for local tourist boards and offices.

www.ambafrance-uk.org and www.ambafrance-us.org
The French Embassies in the USA and the UK have a website providing basic information (geography, demographics, history), a news digest and business-related information. It offers special pages for children and pages devoted to culture, language study and travel, as well as links to other selected French sites (regions, cities, ministries).

TOURIST OFFICES
For information, brochures, maps and assistance in planning a trip to France, travellers should apply to the official French Tourist Office in their own country:

TOURIST OFFICES ABROAD

Australia
French Tourist Bureau, 25 Bligh Street, Sydney, NSW 2000, Australia
℘(0)292 31 62 77;
https://au.france.fr.

Canada
Maison de la France, 1800 av. McGill College, Bureau 1010, Montreal, Quebec H3A 3J6, Canada
℘(514) 288 20 26;
https://ca.france.fr.

South Africa
Block C, Morningside Close,
222 Rivonia Road, Morningside 2196 – JOHANNESBURG
℘00 27 (0)10 205 0201.

UK and Ireland
Lincoln House, 300 High Holborn, London WC1V 7JH. ℘0207 061 66 00;
https://uk.france.fr.

USA
825 Third Avenue, New York, NY 10022, USA. ℘(212) 838 78 00;
https://us.france.fr.

REGIONAL TOURIST OFFICES
A wide range of maps, brochures and other information can be downloaded directly from the website for the Comité Régional de Tourisme de Normandie, the overseeing office of Normandy's individual departmental tourist offices, which can be contacted for more precise local information. All offices respond rapidly during opening hours if you address them by filling out the form found on their websites.

♦ **Comité Régional de Tourisme de Normandie**
14 r. Charles-Corbeau,
27000 Evreux. ℘02 32 33 79 00.
www.normandie-tourisme.fr.

Departmental Tourist Offices

- **Calvados**
  8 r. Renoir, 14054 Caen.
  ✆ 02 31 27 90 30.
  www.calvados-tourisme.com.
- **Eure**
  3 bis rue de Verdun, 27000 Evreux.
  ✆ 02 32 62 04 27.
  www.eure-tourisme.fr.
- **Manche**
  Maison du Département
  98 rte de Candol, 50008 St-Lô.
  ✆ 02 33 05 98 70.
  www.manchetourisme.com.
- **Mayenne**
  84 av. Robert Buron, 53003 Laval.
  ✆ 02 43 53 18 18.
  www.tourisme-mayenne.com.
- **Orne**
  Hôtel du Département
  27, boulevard de Strasbourg,
  61017 Alençon.
  ✆ 02 33 28 88 71.
  www.ornetourisme.com.
- **Seine-Maritime**
  28, rue Raymond Aron, 76824
  Mont-Saint-Aignan.
  ✆ 02 35 12 10 10.
  www.seine-maritime-
  tourisme.com.

TOURIST INFORMATION CENTRES

Contact details for the local tourist
office of each Principal Sight can be
found in the green-coloured Orient
Panels of the *Discovering Normandy*
section of this guide.

INTERNATIONAL VISITORS
DOCUMENTS
Passport

Nationals of countries within the
European Union entering France need
only a national identity card or, in the
case of the British, a valid passport or
ID for the whole length of your stay in
France. Nationals of other countries
must be in possession of a valid
national passport.
☺ In case of loss or theft, report to
your embassy or consulate and the
local police.

☺ *You must carry your documents with
you at all times; they can be checked
anywhere.*

Visa

No entry visa is required for Australian,
Canadian, New Zealand and US
citizens travelling as tourists and
staying less than 90 days, except for
students planning to study in France.
If in doubt, apply to your local French
Consulate.

US citizens – General passport
information is available by phone
toll-free from the Federal Information
Center (item 5 on the automated
menu), ✆ 800-688-9889. US passport
forms can be downloaded from
http://travel.state.gov.

CUSTOMS

The UK Customs website (www.hmrc.
gov.uk) contains information on
allowances, travel safety tips, and to
consult and download documents
and guides.
There are no limits on the amount
of duty and/or tax paid **alcohol and
tobacco** that you can bring back into
the UK as long as they are for your
own use or gifts and are transported
by you. If you are bringing in alcohol
or tobacco goods and UK Customs
have reason to suspect they may
be for a commercial purpose, an
officer may ask you questions and
make checks.
There are no customs formalities when
bringing caravans, pleasure-boats and
outboard motors into France for a stay
of less than six months, but a boat's
registration certificate should be kept
on board.

HEALTH

It is advisable to take out comprehensive travel insurance cover, as tourists
receiving medical treatment in French
hospitals or clinics have to pay for it
themselves.
Nationals of non-EU countries
should check with their insurance

EMBASSIES AND CONSULATES IN FRANCE		
Australia	Embassy	4 rue Jean-Rey, 75015 Paris. ℘01 40 59 33 00. www.france.embassy.gov.au.
Canada	Embassy	37 avenue Montaigne, 75008 Paris. ℘01 44 43 29 00. www.international.gc.ca.
Eire	Embassy	12 ave Foch, 75116 Paris. ℘01 44 17 67 00. www.dfa.ie/irish-embassy/france.
New Zealand	Embassy	103, rue de Grenelle, 75007 Paris. ℘01-45 01 43 43. www.mfat.govt.nz.
South Africa	Embassy	59 quai d'Orsay, 75343 Paris ℘01 53 59 23 23. www.afriquesud.net.
UK	Embassy	35 rue du Faubourg St-Honoré, 75008 Paris. ℘01 44 51 31 88. www.gov.uk/world/france.
	Consulate	16 bis rue d'Anjou, 75008 Paris. ℘01 44 51 31 00. www.gov.uk/world/france.
USA	Embassy	2 avenue Gabriel, 75008 Paris. ℘01 43 12 22 22. http://fr.usembassy.gov.
	Consulate	2 rue St-Florentin, 75001 Paris. ℘01 43 12 22 22. http://fr.usembassy.gov.

companies about policy limitations. Keep all receipts.

British and Irish citizens, if they are not already in possession of an **EHIC** (European Health Insurance Card), should apply for one before travelling. The card entitles UK residents to reduced-cost medical treatment. Apply online at www.ehic.org.uk. The card is not an alternative to travel insurance. It will not cover any private medical healthcare or costs, such as mountain rescue in ski resorts, being flown back to the UK, or lost or stolen property.

Details of the healthcare available in France and how to claim reimbursement are published in the leaflet *Health Advice for Travellers*, available from post offices.

All prescription drugs taken into France should be clearly labelled; it is recommended to carry a copy of prescriptions.

ACCESSIBILITY

Sights with good accessibility are indicated in this guide with a ♿. On French TGV and Corail trains there are wheelchair spaces in 1st-class carriages available to holders of 2nd-class tickets. On Eurostar and Thalys, special rates are available for accompanying adults. All airports offer good accessibility. Disabled drivers may use their EU blue card for parking entitlements.

Information about accessibility is available from **Association des Paralysés de France** (17 bd Auguste Blanqui, 75013 Paris. ℘01 40 78 69 00; www.apf.asso.fr), which also has a nationwide network of branches.

The **Michelin Guide France** and the **Michelin Camping Caravaning France**: Revised every year, these guides indicate where to find facilities accessible to the disabled.

The French railway (Oui.SNCF) gives information on travel at https:// en.oui.sncf, as does Air France at www. airfrance.fr.

PETS

Recent regulations make it much easier to travel with pets between the UK and mainland Europe. All animals must be microchipped, vaccinated against rabies (at least 21 days prior to travel) and have the EU Pet Passport.

Full details are available from the website of the **Department for Environment, Food and Rural Affairs** (www.gov.uk/take-pet-abroad).

THE CHANNEL ISLANDS
ENTRY REGULATIONS
Passports are not required for British subjects. The same requirements apply for other tourists as in France.

TRAVEL
By Air
There are flights to **Jersey**, **Guernsey** and **Alderney**:

Jersey, **Guernsey** and **Alderney** airports are served by British Airways (www.britishairways.com), Flybe (www.flybe.com), Bravofly (www.bravofly.com), Jet2 (www.jet2.com), as well as easyJet (www.easyjet.com).

Aurigny Air Services offers flights between Guernsey, Jersey and Alderney and several British airports as well as Dinard in France. www.aurigny.com.

By Sea
Fast catamaran ferries run to the Channel Islands from England (Poole, Weymouth and Portsmouth) and France (Granville, Diélette, Carteret, St-Malo). Contact www.condorferries.co.uk; www.manche-iles.com. Scheduled ferries run among the islands. Note that, for all ferry services, where they land and at what time depends on tides.

Getting There and Getting Around

BY AIR
The principal cities of Normandy are served out of St-Exupéry airport in Lyons.

Hop (Air France) has flights to and from Caen, Rouen and Le Havre daily. Information and reservations: ☎0820 820 820. www.airfrance.com or www.hop.com.

The regional airports are:
Aéroport de Caen-Carpiquet – ☎02 31 71 20 10. www.caen.aeroport.fr.
Aéroport de Cherbourg-Maupertus – ☎02 33 88 57 60. www.cherbourg.aeroport.fr.
Aéroport Le Havre-Octeville – ☎02 35 54 65 00. www.lehavre.aeroport.fr.
Aéroport Rouen Vallée de Seine – ☎02 35 79 41 00. www.rouen.aeroport.fr.

BY SEA
There are numerous **cross-Channel services** from the United Kingdom and Ireland. To choose the most suitable route between your port of arrival and your destination use the **Michelin Tourist and Motoring Atlas France**, **Michelin map 726** (which gives travel times and mileages) or **Michelin Local maps** from the 1:200 000 series.

* Brittany Ferries ☎0330 159 7000 (UK); 0825 828 828 (France); www.brittanyferries.com. Services from Portsmouth (to Caen, St Malo, Cherbourg and Le Havre), Poole (to Cherbourg) and Plymouth (to Roscoff).
* Condor Ferries ☎01202 207 216 and ☎0845 609 1024 (reservations); www.condorferries.co.uk. Services from Poole and Portsmouth.
* DFDS Seaways operate routes between Dover, Dunkirk and Calais. ☎(UK) 0871 574 7235 and 0800 917 1201; www.dfdsseaways.co.uk.

◆ P&O Ferries ☎0800 130 0030 (UK), or 0825 120 156 (France); www.poferries.com. Service between Dover and Calais.

BY RAIL

Eurostar runs from London (St Pancras) to Paris (Gare du Nord) in 2h15 (up to 20 times daily) ☎03432 186 186 (from UK); ☎+44 (0)1233 617 575 (from outside UK). www.eurostar.com.

Oui.sncf (formerly Voyages-SNCF is the official European distribution channel of the French railways for online sales of high-speed and conventional rail travel throughout France and Europe (https://en.oui.sncf).

The **Corail Intercités** network connects Paris with Normandy cities: Rouen, Le Havre, Dieppe, Trouville, Dreux, L'Aigle, Beauvais and Le Tréport. Trains run several times daily.

Trains express régionaux (TER) form an efficient local network, which also makes use of buses.

France Rail Pass and **Eurail Pass** are travel passes that may be purchased by residents of countries outside the European Union.
Contact: https://en.oui.sncf.

☺ *Tickets for rail travel in France must be validated (composter) by using the (usually) automatic date-stamping machines at the platform entrance (failure to do so may result in a fine).*

The French railway company **OUI-SNCF** operates a telephone information, reservation and prepayment service in English from 7am to 10pm (French time). To buy train tickets in France call ☎3635. More useful advice on rail travel in France is available at www.seat61.com.

BY BUS

Each *département* in Normandy operates local and intercity bus services with inexpensive fares. Information is available, in French, from the website of each *département*.

Calvados: www.calvados.fr
Eure: www.eure-en-ligne.fr
Manche: http://manche.fr
Orne: www.orne.fr
Seine-Maritime: www.seine-maritime-tourisme.com
You can also consult local tourist offices once you arrive in Normandy.

DRIVING IN FRANCE

PLANNING YOUR ROUTE

Michelin **Local** maps give a close, detailed look at two or three *départements*, with maps of major towns. For Normandy, you will need **Local 310** (covering the *départements* of Mayenne, Orne, Sarthe), **303** (Calvados, Manche) and **304** (Eure, Seine-Maritime), and may also want the **Regional 513** (Normandy, including maps of Caen and Rouen) and **517** (Pays-de-la-Loire) maps, which list towns, show secondary roads and offer information for tourists.

The map of France 721 offers a view of all Normandy, with major arteries leading from your point of arrival. The latest Michelin route-planning service is available on the internet, **www.ViaMichelin.com**. Travellers can calculate a precise route using such options as shortest route, route avoiding toll roads, GPS navigation, Michelin-recommended route and gain access to tourist information (hotels, restaurants, attractions).

The roads are very busy during the holiday period (particularly weekends in July and August), and you should consider recommended secondary routes (signposted as *Bison Futé – itinéraires bis*). For information on traffic conditions, call ☎0892 681 077 or visit **www.autoroutes.fr**.

You can get a copy of the **French Highway Code** (in English) from www.frenchhighwaycode.com.

DOCUMENTS

Driving Licence

Travellers from other European Union countries and North America can drive in France with a valid national driving

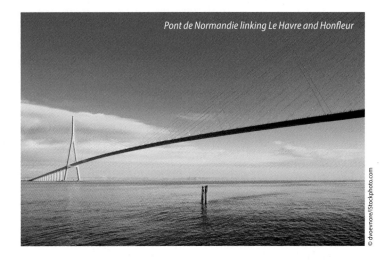

Pont de Normandie linking Le Havre and Honfleur

© dvoevnore/iStockphoto.com

licence. An international driving licence is useful but not obligatory.

😊 *It is not yet clear what the situation will be for UK drivers following exit from the EU.*

Registration papers

For the vehicle, it is necessary to have the registration papers (logbook) and an approved nationality plate.

INSURANCE

Many motoring organisations offer accident insurance and breakdown service schemes for members. Check with your insurance company with regard to coverage while abroad. Because French autoroutes are privately owned, European Breakdown Cover service does not extend to breakdowns on the autoroute or its service areas – you must use the emergency telephones, or drive off the autoroute before calling your breakdown service.

ROAD REGULATIONS

The minimum driving age is 18. Traffic drives on the right. All passengers must wear **seat belts**. Children under the age of 10 must ride in the back seat. Headlights must be switched on in poor visibility and at night; dipped headlights should be used at all times outside built-up areas. Use sidelights only when the vehicle is stationary.

In the case of a **breakdown**, a red warning triangle or hazard warning lights are obligatory, as are reflective safety jackets, one for each passenger, and carried within the car. it is now compulsory to carry an in-car breathalyser kit, too; you can be fined if you do not. UK right-hand drive cars must use headlight adaptors.

In the absence of stop signs at intersections, cars must **give way to the right**. Traffic on main roads outside built-up areas (priority indicated by a yellow diamond sign) and on roundabouts has right of way. Vehicles must stop when the lights turn red at road junctions and may filter to the right only when indicated by an amber arrow.

The regulations on **drinking and driving** (limited to 0.5g/l) and **speeding** are strictly enforced – usually by an on-the-spot fine and/or confiscation of the vehicle.

Speed Limits

Although liable to modification, these are as follows:

◆ **Toll motorways** (*autoroutes*) 130kph/80mph (110kph/68mph when raining);

RENTAL CARS COMPANIES OPERATING IN FRANCE	
Avis	www.avis.fr; www.avis.co.uk
Europcar	www.europcar.fr; www.europcar.co.uk
Budget	www.budget.fr; www.budget.co.uk
Hertz	www.hertz.fr; www.hertz.co.uk
SIXT	www.sixt.fr; www.sixt.co.uk
Enterprise	www.enterprise.fr; www.enterprise.co.uk

- **Dual carriageways** and **motor ways** without tolls 110kph/68mph (100kph/62mph when raining);
- **Secondary roads** that do not have a central separator 80kph/50mph, and in towns 50kph/31mph;
- **Outside lane** on motorways during daylight, on level ground and with good visibility – minimum speed limit of 80kph/50mph.

Parking

In urban areas there are zones where parking is either restricted or subject to a fee; tickets should be obtained from the ticket machines (*horodateurs* – small change necessary) and displayed inside the windscreen on the driver's side; failure to display may result in a fine or towing. Other parking areas in town may require you to take a ticket when passing through a barrier. To exit, you must pay the parking fee (usually there is a machine located by the exit – *sortie*) and insert the paid-up card in another machine which will lift the exit gate.

Tolls

In France, most motorway sections are subject to a toll *(péage)*. You can pay in cash, or with a credit card (Visa, MasterCard), which are being increasingly used at toll stations – so, always have yours handy.

PETROL/GASOLINE

French service stations dispense:
- *sans plomb 98* (super unleaded 98)
- *sans plomb 95* (super unleaded 95)
- *diesel/gazole* (diesel)
- *Premium V-power diesel/gazole* (diesel)
- *GPL* (LPG).

CAR RENTAL

There are car rental agencies at airports, railway stations and in all large towns throughout France. European cars have manual transmission; automatic cars are available only if an advance reservation is made. Drivers must be over 21; between ages 21 and 25, drivers are required to pay an extra daily fee; some companies allow drivers under 23 only if the reservation has been made through a travel agent. It is relatively expensive to hire a car in France.

Car hire and holders of UK driving licences

In 2015, changes to the UK Driving License came into force which mean that because details of fines, penalty points and restrictions are now only held electronically you are going to have to enable a car hire company to access your online driving record by means of a DVLA-issued pass code. Full details are available at www.gov.uk/view-driving-licence.

Where to Stay and Eat

The *Michelin Green Guide* is pleased to offer a selection of accommodations and restaurants for Normandy. Turn to the **Addresses** sections within the individual Sights for descriptions and prices of typical places to stay **(Stay)** and to eat **(Eat)**. The Legend on the cover flap explains the symbols and abbreviations used in these sections.

☺ *Please note: Coin ranges for the Channel Islands are derived from approximate conversions of the euro coin ranges in the same Legend into Pound Sterling (£).*

WHERE TO STAY

FINDING A HOTEL

Turn to the **Addresses** within individual sight listings for descriptions and prices of typical places to stay **(Stay)** with local flair. Use the **Places to Stay** map in the following pages to identify recommended places for overnight stops. It can be used in conjunction with the **Michelin Guide France** – with its well-known star-rating system – which lists an even greater selection of hotels and restaurants.

For further assistance, **La Fédération Loisirs Accueil** is a booking service that has offices in most French *départements*: 280 bd St-Germain, 75007 Paris. ✆01 44 11 10 44. http://www.loisirsaccueilfrance.com.

Relais et Châteaux provides information on booking in luxury hotels with character: 15 r. Galvani, 75017 Paris. ✆01 45 72 90 00. www.relaischateaux.com.

ECONOMY CHAIN HOTELS

If you need a place to stop en route, these can be useful, as they are inexpensive and generally located near the main road.

While breakfast is available, there may not be a restaurant; rooms are small and simple, with a television and bathroom.

Rather than sort through hotels yourself, you can go to websites that cover several chains, from modest to luxurious. These sites allow you to select your hotel based on geographical location, price and level of comfort, and to book online. **www.viamichelin.com** covers hotels in France, including famous selections from the Michelin Guide as well as lower-priced chains.

- **Akena:** www.hotels-akena.com
- **B&B:** www.hotel-bb.com
- **Best Hôtel:** www.besthotel.fr
- **Campanile**, UK ✆0207 519 50 45; France ✆0892 23 48 12; www.campanile.com
- **Kyriad:** UK ✆**0207 519 50 45; France** ✆**0892 23 48 13; www.kyriad.com**
- **Première Classe**: UK ✆**0207 519 5045; France** ✆**0892 23 48 14; www.premiereclasse.com**
- **International Hotels Group:** ✆0800 40 40 40; www.ihg.com
- **Best Western Hotels:** www.bestwestern.fr.
- **Ibis** and **Accor Hotels:** UK ✆0871 663 0628; France ✆0825 88 22 22; **https://ibis.accorhotels.com**

Hotel booking websites

There is a growing number of hotel booking agencies and user-review companies operating online these days, all of them offering hotel rooms at discounted and competitive prices from high-end hotels to budget and economy establishments. It is always worth checking websites such as these to find good value discounts.

☺ *However, the general ease of booking hotel rooms online sometimes makes it worthwhile dealing with the hotels direct, since these can often offer the best rates available at the time of booking.*

RURAL ACCOMMODATION

The **Maison des Gîtes de France et du Tourisme Vert** is an information service on self-catering accommodation in the regions of

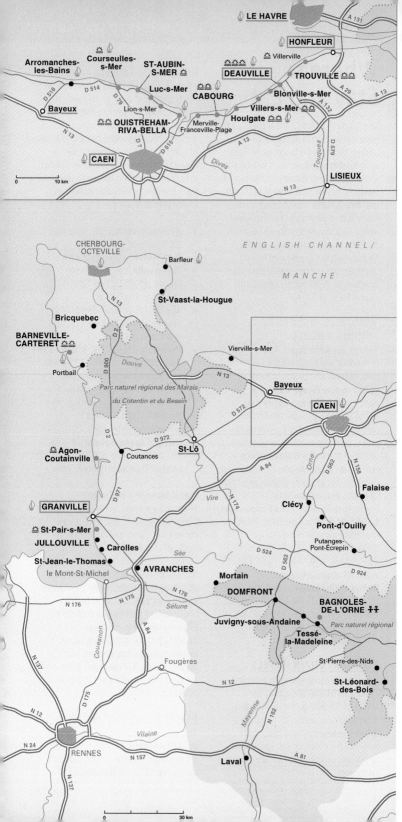

Places to stay

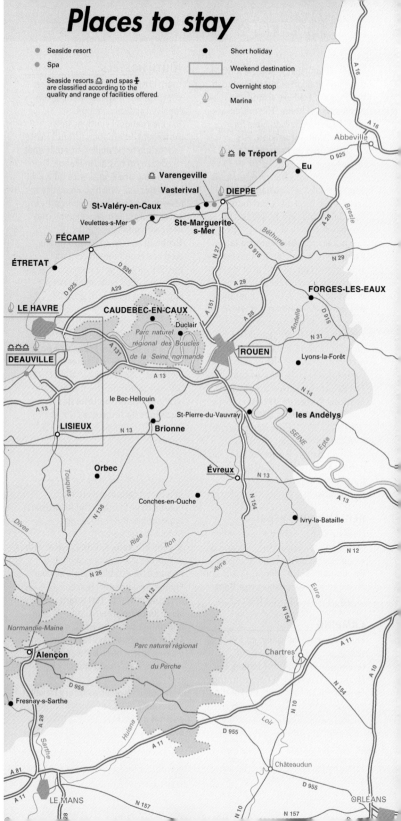

- ● Seaside resort
- ● Spa

Seaside resorts ⚓ and spas ⚕
are classified according to the
quality and range of facilities offered.

- ● Short holiday
- ☐ Weekend destination
- — Overnight stop
- ⛵ Marina

Abbeville

⚓ ⛵ le Tréport

Eu

⚓ Varengeville
Vasterival

⛵ St-Valéry-en-Caux

⛵ DIEPPE

Veulettes-s-Mer
Ste-Marguerite-
s-Mer

⛵ FÉCAMP

ÉTRÉTAT

FORGES-LES-EAUX

⛵ LE HAVRE

CAUDEBEC-EN-CAUX
Duclair

Parc naturel
régional des Boucles
de la Seine normande

ROUEN

Lyons-la-Forêt

⚓⚓⚓

DEAUVILLE

le Bec-Hellouin

St-Pierre-du-Vauvray

les Andelys

LISIEUX

Brionne

Orbec

Évreux

Conches-en-Ouche

Ivry-la-Bataille

Normandie-Maine

Parc naturel régional

Alençon

du Perche

Chartres

Fresnay-s-Sarthe

Châteaudun

LE MANS

ORLÉANS

France. *Gîtes* usually take the form of a cottage or apartment decorated in the local style where visitors can make themselves at home. The organisation also covers specialised gîtes for fishing, camping, walking, etc. Contact **Gîtes de France:** 59 r. St-Lazare, 75439 Paris. 🖉01 49 70 75 75. www.gites-de-france-normandie. com. In total, the association lists some 2 300 rural gîtes and more than 1 500 bed-and-breakfasts in Normandy.

The publication **Bienvenue à la Ferme** lists some 300 Norman farmers who offer accommodation of varying degrees of comfort on their farms, including meals. You can order the free book or download it at www. bienvenue-a-la-ferme.com.

For walkers, climbers, kayakers, bicyclists and others seeking rustic accommodation off the beaten track, consult www.gites-refuges.com. The **Fédération Française des Stations Vertes de Vacances** *(6 rue Ranfer-de-Bretenières, 21000 Dijon. 🖉03 80 54 10 50, www.stationsvertes. com)* lists family-orientated accommodation, leisure facilities and natural attractions in rural locations throughout France, including Normandy.

BED-AND-BREAKFAST

Gîtes de France publishes a selection of bed and breakfast addresses on its website, which lists establishments throughout France offering a room and breakfast at a reasonable price. Book online at www.gites-de-france.com.

CAMPING

There are many officially graded sites with varying standards of facilities throughout the region; the **Michelin Camping & Caravanning France** guide lists a selection of the best campsites, visited regularly by our inspectors. Tourist offices and their websites also provide lists of campsites.

YOUTH HOSTELS

Youth hostels *(auberges de jeunesse)* offer simple, inexpensive and often convivial accommodation.

The international youth hostels movement, International Youth Hostel Federation or Hostelling International, has dozens of hostels in France. There is an online booking service on www. hihostels.com, which you may use to reserve rooms as far as six months in advance. To stay in hostels, you may need a membership card.

To obtain an IYHF or HI card (there is no age requirement) contact the IYHF or HI in your own country for information and membership applications (in the UK 🖉01707 324170).

There are two main youth hostel associations (auberges de jeunesse) in France, the **Ligue Française pour les Auberges de la Jeunesse** *(67 r. Vergniaud, 75013 Paris. 🖉01 44 16 78 78; www.auberges-de-jeunesse.com)* and the **Fédération Unie des Auberges de Jeunesse** *(27 r. Pajol, 75018 Paris. 🖉01 44 89 87 27; www. fuaj.org).*

WHERE TO EAT

A selection of places to eat in the different locations covered in this guide can be found in the **Addresses** appearing in the *Discovering Normandy* section.

Use the **Michelin Guide France**, with its famous star-rating system and hundreds of establishments all over France, for a greater choice.

In the countryside, restaurants usually serve lunch between noon and 2pm and dinner between 7.30pm and 10pm. It is not always easy to find an establishment open between lunch and dinner, as "round-the-clock" restaurants are still scarce in the provinces. However, a hungry traveller can usually get a sandwich in a café, and hot dishes may be available in a brasserie.

Useful Words and Phrases

Commonly Useful Words

	Translation
Goodbye	Au revoir
Hello/Good Morning	Bonjour
Excuse Me	Excusez-moi, Pardon
Thank You	Merci
Yes/no	Oui/non
Please	S'il vous plaît

Sights

	Translation
Abbey	Abbaye
Belfry	Beffroi
Chapel	Chapelle
Cemetery	Cimetière
Cloisters	Cloître
Courtyard	Cour
Convent	Couvent
Lock (Canal)	Écluse
Church	Église
Gothic	Gothique
Covered market	Halle
Garden	Jardin
Town Hall	Mairie
House	Maison
Market	Marché
Monastery	Monastère
Windmill	Moulin
Museum	Musée
Square	Place
Bridge	Pont
Port/harbour	Port
Quay	Quai
Ramparts	Remparts
Roman	Romain
Romanesque	Roman
Tower	Tour

Natural Sites

	Translation
Dam	Barrage
Viewpoint	Belvédère
Waterfall	Cascade
Ledge	Corniche
Coast, hillside	Côte
Pond	Étang
Cliff	Falaise
Forest	Forêt
Cave	Grotte
Lake	Lac
Marsh	Marais
Beach	Plage
River	Rivière
Stream	Ruisseau
Beacon	Signal
Spring	Source
Valley	Vallée

On the Road

	Translation
Car Park	Parking
Diesel	Diesel/Gazole
Driving Licence	Permis de conduire
East	Est
Garage (for repairs)	Garage
Left	Gauche
Motorway/highway	Autoroute
North	Nord
Parking Meter	Horodateur
Petrol/Gas	Essence
Right	Droite
Roundabout	Rond-point
South	Sud
Toll	Péage
Traffic lights	Feu tricolore
Tyre	Pneu
Unleaded	Sans plomb
West	Ouest

Time

	Translation
Today	Aujourd'hui
Tomorrow	Demain
Yesterday	Hier
Week	Semaine
Monday	Lundi
Tuesday	Mardi
Wednesday	Mercredi
Thursday	Jeudi
Friday	Vendredi
Saturday	Samedi
Sunday	Dimanche

Numbers

	Translation
0	Zéro
1	Un
2	Deux
3	Trois
4	Quatre
5	Cinq
6	Six
7	Sept
8	Huit
9	Neuf
10	Dix
11	Onze
20	Vingt
50	Cinquante
60	Soixante
100	Cent
1 000	Mille

Shopping

	Translation
Bakery	Boulangerie
Bank	Banque
Butcher Shop	Boucherie
Chemist's/drugstore	Pharmacie
Closed	Fermé
Cough mixture	Sirop pour la toux
Entrance	Entrée
Exit	Sortie
Fishmonger's	Poissonnerie
Grand	Big
Grocer's	Épicerie
Newsagent/bookshop	Librairie
Open	Ouvert
Painkiller	Analgésique
Plaster (Band-Aid)	Sparadrap
Post office	Bureau de poste
Pound (Half Kilo)	Livre
Pull	Tirer
Push	Pousser
Shop	Magasin
Stamps	Timbres

Food and Drink

	Translation
Beef	Bœuf
Beer	Bière
Butter	Beurre
Bread	Pain
Breakfast	Petit-déjeuner
Cheese	Fromage
Chicken	Poulet
Dessert	Dessert
Dinner	Dîner
Duck	Canard
Fish	Poisson
Fork	Fourchette
Fruit	Fruits
Glass	Verre
Ham	Jambon
Ice cream	Glace
Jug of water	Carafe d'eau
Knife	Couteau
Lamb	Agneau
Lunch	Déjeuner
Meat	Viande
Mineral water	Eau minérale
Mixed salad	Salade composée
Mussels	Moules
Orange juice	Jus d'orange
Oysters	Huîtres
Plate	Assiette
Pork	Porc
Red wine	Vin rouge
Salt	Sel
Sparkling water	Eau gazeuse
Spoon	Cuillère
Sugar	Sucre
Vegetables	Légumes
White Wine	Vin blanc

Personal Documents and Travel

	Translation
Airport	Aéroport
Credit card	Carte de crédit
Customs	Douane
Passport	Passeport
Platform	Voie
Railway station	Gare
Suitcase	Valise
Train/plane ticket	Billet de train/ d'avion
Wallet	Portefeuille

Clothing

	Translation
Coat	Manteau
Dress	Robe
Jumper	Pull
Raincoat	Imperméable
Shirt/blouse	Chemise
Shoes	Chaussures
Trousers	Pantalon

USEFUL PHRASES

Do you speak English?
Parlez-vous anglais?

I don't understand Je ne comprends pas

Speak more slowly, please Parlez plus lentement, s'il-vous plaît

Where is...? Où est...?

When does the ... leave?
A quelle heure part...?

When does the ... arrive?
A quelle heure arrive...?

When does the museum open?
A quelle heure ouvre le musée?

How much does it cost?
Ça coûte combien?

Where is the nearest petrol/ gas station? Où se trouve la station d'essence la plus proche?

Where can I change traveller's cheques? Où puis-je changer un chèque de voyage?

Where are the toilets?
Où se trouve les toilettes?

Do you accept credit cards?
Acceptez-vous les cartes de crédit?

I have an allergy to nuts/dairy products J'ai une allergie aux fruits à coque et à larachide/aux produits laitières

Basic Information

BUSINESS HOURS

Offices and other businesses are open Mon–Fri, 9am–noon, 2–6pm. Many also open Saturday mornings. Town and village shops are generally open Tue–Fri; there are local variations. Midday breaks may be much longer in the south. However, in cities, tourist centres or resorts, businesses may keep longer hours or stay open all day, seven days a week, especially if they primarily serve the tourist market.

ELECTRICITY

The electric current is 220 volts. Circular two-pin plugs are the rule. Adapters should be bought before you leave home; they are on sale in most airports.

EMERGENCIES

International emergency number ✆ **112**
Police (Gendarme): ✆ **17**
Fire (Pompiers): ✆ **18**
Ambulance (SAMU): ✆ **15**
First aid, medical advice and chemists' night-service rotas are available from chemists/drugstores (*pharmacie*, identified by a green cross sign).

MAIL/POST/INTERNET

Look for the bright yellow *La Poste* signs. Main post offices are generally open Mon–Fri 9am–7pm, Sat 9am–noon. Smaller branches generally open 9am–noon, 2–4pm weekdays. There are often automatic tellers (*guichets automatiques*) inside which allow you to weigh packages and buy postage. You may also find that you can change money, make copies, send faxes and make phone calls in a post office.
To mail a letter from the street look for the bright yellow postboxes. Stamps are also sold in newsagents and cafés that sell cigarettes (*tabac*). www.laposte.fr.

WiFi is widely available in cities such as Rouen; check with your hotel if it has Wifi access (there may be a charge, although many now provide this free of charge).

MONEY

CURRENCY

There are no restrictions on the amount of currency visitors can take into France. Visitors wishing to export currency in foreign banknotes in excess of the given allocation from France should complete a currency declaration form on arrival.
Coins and notes – The unit of currency is the **euro** (€). One euro is divided into 100 cents or *centimes d'euro.*
In the Channel Islands, legal tender is the **Pound Sterling** (£). The local currency issued by the banks of Jersey and Guernsey is not legal tender outside the islands. All British clearing banks have branches in the Channel Islands.

BANKS AND CURRENCY EXCHANGE

Banks are generally open Mon–Fri 9am–5.30pm. Some branches are open for limited transactions on Saturday. Banks limit opening hours on the day before a bank holiday. A passport or other ID may be necessary when cashing cheques (traveller's or ordinary) in banks. Commission charges vary and hotels usually charge considerably more than banks for cashing cheques, especially for non-residents.
By far the most convenient way of obtaining French currency is the **24-hr cash dispenser** or ATM (*distributeur automatique de billets* in French), found outside many banks and post offices and easily recognisable by the CB (Carte Bleue) logo. Most accept international credit cards (don't forget your PIN) and almost all also give instructions in English. Note that American Express cards can be used only in dispensers operated by the Crédit Lyonnais bank or by American

Express. Foreign currency can also be exchanged in major banks, post offices, hotels or private exchange offices found in main cities and near popular tourist attractions.

CREDIT CARDS

Major credit and debit cards (Visa, MasterCard, Eurocard, Maestro) are widely accepted in shops, hotels, restaurants and petrol stations. Pay-at-the-pump automatic petrol stations accept most cards (including Maestro debit cards). 😊 *If your card is lost or stolen* call the appropriate 24-hr hotlines listed on www.totallymoney. com/credit-cards/lost-stolen-credit-card. Better still: always carry with you the correct number to call for your particular credit cards.

You must report any loss or theft of credit cards or traveller's cheques to the local police who will issue you with a certificate (useful proof to show the issuing company).

PUBLIC HOLIDAYS

There are 11 public holidays in France. In addition, there are other religious and national festivals days, and a number of local saints' days, etc. On all these days, museums and other

PUBLIC HOLIDAYS	
1 January	New Year's Day *(Jour de l'An)*
Mon after Easter Sun	Easter Monday *(Pâques)*
1 May	Labour Day
8 May	VE Day
Thu 40 days after Easter	Ascension Day *(Ascension catholique)*
7th Sun after Easter	Whit Monday *(Pentecôte)*
14 July	Fête National France's National Day (or Bastille Day)
15 August	Assumption *(Assomption)*
1 November	All Saints' Day *(Toussaint)*
11 November	Armistice Day
25 December	Christmas Day *(Noël)*

monuments may be closed or may vary their hours of admission.

SCHOOL HOLIDAYS

French schools close for holidays five times a year. In these periods, all tourist sites and attractions, hotels, restaurants and roads are busier than usual. These school holidays are one week at the end of October, two weeks at Christmas, two weeks in February, two weeks in spring, and the whole of July and August.

SMOKING REGULATIONS

France has banned smoking in public places such as offices, universities and railway stations. The law also applies to restaurants, cafés, bars, nightclubs and casinos.

TELEPHONES

The telephone system in France is still operated largely by the former state monopoly France Télécom. They offer an English-language enquiries service on ☏0800 364 775 (within France) or ☏00 33 1 55 78 60 56 (outside France). The French **ringing tone** is a series of long tones.

To use a **public phone** you need to buy a prepaid phone card *(télécarte)*. Some telephone booths accept credit cards (Visa, MasterCard/Eurocard). *Télécartes* (50 or 120 units) can be bought in post offices, cafés that sell cigarettes *(tabac)* and newsagents, and can be used to make calls in France and abroad. Calls can be received at phone boxes where the blue bell sign is shown.

MOBILE/CELL PHONES

While in France, all visitors from other European countries and the UK should be able to use their mobile phone as normal. Visitors from other countries need to ensure before departure that their phone and service contract are compatible with the European system (GSM).

The EU abolished roaming charges in June 2017, as a result EU citizens won't be charged extra for calls. But for the foreseeable future the application of this decision in practice remains unclear. If necessary, consult your own provider.

NATIONAL CALLS

French telephone numbers have ten digits. Numbers begin with 01 in Paris and the Paris region; 02 in northwest France; 03 in northeast France; 04 in southeast France and Corsica; 05 in southwest France. However, all ten numbers must be dialled even in the local region.

INTERNATIONAL CALLS

To call France from abroad, dial the country code 33, omit the initial zero of the French number, and dial the remaining nine-digit number. When calling abroad from France dial 00, followed by the country code, followed by the local area code (usually without any initial zero), and the number of your correspondent. **Toll-free numbers** in France begin with 0800.

INTERNATIONAL DIALLING CODES	
Australia	(00+) **61**
Eire	(00+) **353**
United Kingdom	(00+) **44**
Canada	(00+) **1**
New Zealand	(00+) **64**
United States	(00+) **1**

TIME

France is 1hr ahead of Greenwich Mean Time (GMT). In France the 24hour clock is widely applied.

WHEN IT IS **NOON IN FRANCE**, IT IS	
3am	in Los Angeles
6am	in New York
11am	in Dublin
11am	in London
7pm	in Perth
9pm	in Sydney
11pm	in Auckland

TIPPING

Under French law, any service charge is included in the prices displayed for meals and accommodation. Any additional tipping in restaurants and hotels is at the visitor's discretion. However, in bars and cafés it is not unusual to leave any small change that remains after paying the bill, but this generally should not be more than 5 percent.

Taxi drivers do not have to be tipped, but it's usual to give a small amount, not more than 10 percent. Attendants at public toilets should be given a few cents. Tour guides and drivers should be tipped according to the amount of service given: from 2 to 5 euros.

VALUE ADDED TAX

In France a sales tax (*TVA* or VAT) is added to all purchases. For non-EU residents on holiday this tax can be refunded as long as you have bought more than €175 worth of goods at the same time and in the same shop, and have completed the appropriate *Bordereau* form at the shop. Ask for your receipts and the form when at the sales desk, and take these and your purchases to the local customs office at the airport before you check in for your flight.

The amount permitted may vary, so it is advisable to check first with the VAT-refund counter (*Service de détaxe*). Customs Information Centre: ☎08 20 02 44 44 or www.douane.gouv.fr.

Channel Islands

There is no VAT on the Channel Islands, which accounts for the profusion of very busy shops. The most popular purchases are alcohol, tobacco, perfume, and the famous Jersey and Guernsey wool.

Église St-Maclou and half-timbered house, Rouen
© René Mattes/hemis.fr

Normandy Today

21ST CENTURY

Normandy today takes pride in its agricultural and fishing traditions as one of the most rural regions of France, while adapting to the wider European economy as a major centre for maritime trade; technology-based industries are also coming to the fore.

Today, Basse-Normandie (Lower Normandy) markets its milk, cider and Camembert cheese around the world. Haute-Normandie (Upper Normandy) has continued development as a centre for modern industry, although parts remain quite rural.

POPULATION

Although Lower Normandy remains rural in terms of economy, about two thirds of the population lives in and around the urban centres of Alençon, Caen and Cherbourg; in the countryside, demographic decline is a worry, as young people leave. Seaside resorts, on the other hand, have attracted new inhabitants. Upper Normandy, with its industrial and service employment and proximity to Paris, has a more evenly distributed population. Normandy has a fairly young population, with about 25 percent under the age of 20. Life expectancy for men is 77 years, and for women 84 years.

LIFESTYLE

Normandy immediately conjures images of a leisured life along broad beaches, or among verdant pastures and dew-drenched orchards. Curiously, the fact that most inhabitants live in urban areas has left the countryside bucolic.

In addition, quite a few of those pretty half-timbered houses and quaint seaside villas, as well as the many flats in buildings along the coast, belong to Parisians who drive up only on holidays, so roads are rarely crowded during the week. Despite this holiday atmosphere, the locals are famously hard working.

RELIGION

Normandy's rich heritage of churches and abbeys dates, with very few exceptions, to older times. Today, religion plays a far smaller part in daily life. Some 75 percent of Normandy residents profess Roman Catholicism, with a light dusting (1–2 percent) of Protestants and Muslims (1–3 percent), the latter living in urban areas of Upper Normandy. A quarter of inhabitants profess no religion, about the French average. Churches fill up for traditional festivals, but not for Sunday mass. Yet the buildings, which belong to the French state, are carefully maintained. Catholic tradition remains strong.

FOOD

Local Specialities

According to Norman tradition one should eat duck in Rouen, tripe in Caen and La Ferté-Macé, leg of lamb from the salt meadows of Mont-St-Michel Bay and an omelette in Mont-St-Michel; one should also taste Dieppe sole, Duclair duckling, Auge valley chicken garnished with tiny onions, Vire chitterlings (andouillette), black pudding from Mortagne-au-Perche and white pudding from Avranches. Among the tasty meat dishes, try the côtes de veau vallée d'Auge, which are veal cutlets fried in butter and flambéed in Calvados then braised in cider and fresh cream.

As for seafood, there are shrimps and cockles from Honfleur, mussels from Villerville and Isigny, lobsters from La Hague and Barfleur, and oysters, Atlantic crabs, spider crabs, winkles and whelks from Courseulles and St-Vaast. Seafood may be accompanied by rye bread, salted butter and a glass of dry cider.

Fish – sole, turbot and mackerel to mention only a few – is often served with a delicious sauce.

Local pastries, all made with butter, include apple turnovers (chaussons aux pommes), flat cakes baked in the oven (falues or fouaces), biscuits (galettes), shortbread (sablés) and buns (brioches). Douillons are pears hollowed out and filled with butter, wrapped in pastry and baked.

Cream and Normandy Sauce

Cream, the mainstay of the Normandy kitchen, is at its best in the so-called Normandy sauce *(sauce normande)*, which elsewhere is just a plain white sauce, but here both looks and tastes quite different.

Cheese

If cream is the queen of Normandy cooking, cheese is the king of all fare. **Pont-l'Évêque** has reigned since the 13C; **Livarot** is quoted in texts of the same period; the world-renowned **Camembert** probably dates to the 17C, at least.

The Normandy cheeseboard also includes fresh cheese from the Pays de Bray – the **bondons**, *demi-sel* or double cream. Before sweeping France, the **petit-suisse** was a much appreciated farmhouse cheese. **Neufchâtel** cheese can be eaten within 12 days of being made, although a mature Neufchâtel takes up to three months.

CIDER

Apple cider has been made locally since the Middle Ages, and it is still possible to find a farmhouse brew distilled in the traditional way.

The apples are gathered in huge baskets then stored for a short while before being emptied into a circular granite trough, where they are crushed by a round wooden millstone pulled by a horse. The crushed apples *(marc)* are transferred to the press, where they are laid between layers of rye straw and then pressed. The rye straw is then extracted and the apple pulp is put to soak in a vat before being pressed a second time to produce a weaker brew which is kept for use on the farm.

Whether it is *brut* (dry, strongly flavoured with apple with an alcohol content of 4–5 percent), *demi-sec* or *doux* (made artificially sweet by stalling the fermentation process when the alcohol content reaches 2.5–3 percent), cider is the perfect accompaniment for pancakes or apple desserts. It should always be served chilled.

Calvados

Calvados, or *calva* as it is better known, is a cider brandy made from a mash of apples fermented with yeast; it is distilled twice and matured in oak for six to ten years. The tradition of the *trou normand* (Norman hole) is still observed; during a heavy meal a small glass of Calvados is swallowed at one go to help the digestion. Restaurants often serve an apple and Calvados sorbet instead. Calvados is usually drunk after coffee; for just a taste, eat a sugar lump dipped in Calvados. A great many distilleries and storehouses are open to the public.

Perry

Perry *(poiré)* is similar to cider but is made from pears and usually comes from the areas around Mortain and Domfront.

Pommeau

This alcoholic beverage is made by mixing two-thirds of apple juice with one-third of Calvados and features an alcohol content of 16–18 percent. The ageing process is carried out in oak casks for a period of 18 months. It can be drunk chilled as an apéritif, or at room temperature to accompany oysters, foie gras, melon or apple pie. It is also popular for cooking with.

ECONOMY

Normandy's two regions present very different economic profiles. Upper Normandy, which stretches along the Seine river estuary, has a large industrial sector, with Renault car manufacturing plants at Elbeuf and Le Havre, oil refineries, petrochemical plants, a big construction industry and many light industries. The principal import is crude oil; principal exports are refined petroleum and petrochemical products, and cars and car parts. The ports of Le Havre and Rouen are among France's biggest.

In Lower Normandy, three-quarters of the land is agricultural, by far the highest proportion in all France, much of it devoted to dairy cows. Industry occupies only 20 percent of the workforce, and milk processing is the biggest industry. Many people are employed in small businesses and tourism. Norman farms produce grain (wheat, maize, barley), oils (linseed, rape), several sorts of fruit, animal feed, sugar beet and potatoes.

Calvados and Manche produce 12 percent of the French fish catch, much of it shellfish, and nearly all of it sold dockside to wholesellers.

Lower Normandy's agricultural sector sheltered its economy during the 2008–2009 recession. Upper Normandy was hit hardest, although the combination of low fuel prices and good grain harvests kept ports humming, while French holidaymakers choosing to stay at home supported the Norman tourist industry.

GOVERNMENT

The area covered by this book corresponds to the former province of Normandy, divided in 1789 into five *départements*, with remaining bits absorbed by the départements of Eure-et-Loire and Mayenne. Eure and Seine-Maritime make up the region of Upper Normandy, while Calvados, Manche and Orne make up Lower Normandy.

There are 27 **regions** in France (22 within French borders, reduced to 13 on 1 January 2016, and five overseas), governed by elected councils. The regions are composed of **départements** (100 in all of France), each of which is divided into **communes**, governed by municipal councils and mayors. **Cantons** exist only to elect members to the departmental council.

A large *commune*, such as Le Havre, will include several *cantons*. In a rural area, there may be several *communes* in a *canton*. In recent years, the regions have gained more authority over the *départements*. You can tell where people are from by reading the licence plates on their cars: each *département* has its own number.

History

TIMELINE
ROMAN PERIOD

58-51BCE	Roman conquest. New towns appear: Rotomagus (Rouen), Caracotinum (Harfleur), Noviomagus (Lisieux), Juliobona (Lillebonne), Mediolanum (Évreux).
56BCE	The Unelli crushed by Sabinius in the Mont Castre area.
1C	Growth of main settlements (Coutances, Rouen, Évreux, etc.).
2C	Nordic (Saxon and Germanic) invasions of the Bessin region. Conversion to Christianity.
260	Bishopric of Rouen founded by St-Nicaise.
284 and 364	Nordic invasions.

FRANKISH DOMINATION

497	Rouen and Évreux occupied by Clovis.
511	Neustria or the Western Kingdom inherited by Clothaire, Clovis's son.
6C	The first monasteries founded.
7C	Monasteries flourish: St-Wandrille, Jumièges.
709	Mont Tombe consecrated to the cult of St Michael by Aubert, Bishop of Avranches.

VIKING INVASIONS

	The Vikings or Norsemen who sailed from Scandinavia harassed western Europe, parts of Africa and even headed into the Mediterranean.
800	Channel coast invaded by Vikings.
820	Seine valley laid waste by Vikings.
836	Christians persecuted in the Cotentin region.

858	Bayeux devastated by Vikings.
875	Further persecution in the west.
885	Paris besieged by Vikings.
911	Treaty of St-Clair-sur-Epte: Rollo becomes the first Duke of Normandy.

THE INDEPENDENT DUKEDOM

	Under William Longsword the dukedom takes on its final form with the unification of the Avranchin and the Cotentin.
10-11C	Consolidation of ducal powers. Restoration of the abbeys.
1027	Birth of William, the future conqueror of England, at Falaise.
1066	Invasion of England by William. King of France threatened by his vassal, the Duke of Normandy, now also King of England.
1087	Death of William the Conqueror in Rouen.
1087-1135	William's heirs in dispute; ducal authority restored by Henry Beauclerk who becomes King of England as Henry I (1100–35) after his brother William Rufus.
1120	The wreck of the White Ship off Barfleur Point with the loss of Henry I's heir, William Atheling, and 300 members of the Anglo-Norman nobility.
1152	Marriage of Henry II Plantagenet, to Eleanor of Aquitaine, whose dowry included all of southwest France.
1154-89	Henry II of England.
1195	Château-Gaillard built by Richard Lionheart.
1202	Loss of Norman possessions by John Lackland, King of England.
1204	Normandy united to the French crown.

FRENCH DUKEDOM TO THE PROVINCE OF NORMANDY

1315	Granting of the Norman Charter, symbol of provincial status, which remained in being until the French Revolution.
1346	Normandy invaded by Edward III of England.
1364-84	The Battle of Cocherel marks the start of Du Guesclin's campaigns.
1417	Normandy invaded by Henry V of England.
1424	English repulsed by Louis d'Estouteville, defender of Mont-St-Michel.
1431	Trial and burning of Joan of Arc at Rouen.
1437	Founding of Caen university.
1450	Normandy recovered by the French crown after the victory at Formigny and the recapture of Cherbourg.
1469	Charles of France, last Duke of Normandy, is dispossessed of his dukedom.
1514	The Rouen Exchequer becomes the Parliament of Normandy.
1517	Founding of Le Havre.
1542	Rouen created as a self-governing city for treasury purposes.
1589	Henri of Navarre victorious at Arques and the following year at Ivry-la-Bataille.
1625	Alençon also created as a treasury district.
1639-40	Revolt of the Barefoot Peasants provoked by the introduction of the salt tax (gabelle).
1692	Naval battle of La Hougue.
1771-75	Suppression of the Parliament at Rouen.

LATE 18C TO TODAY

1789	The Caen Revolt.
1793	The Girondins' attempted uprising; siege of Granville.
1795-1800	Insurrection of Norman royalists, the Chouans.

1843	Inauguration of the Paris-Caen railway.
1870-71	Franco-Prussian War; occupation of Haute-Normandie and Le Mans.
June 1940	Bresle Front breached.
August 1942	Dieppe Commando raid by Canadian and British troops.
June 1944	Allied landing on the Calvados coast. Battle of Normandy.
1954	René Coty, born in Le Havre, is elected President of the Republic.
1959	Inauguration of the Tancarville Bridge.
1967	Commissioning of the Atomic Centre at La Hague.
1971	Launch of the *Redoutable*, the first French nuclear submarine, at Cherbourg.
1974	Creation of the Brotonne Regional Nature Park.
1975	Creation of the Normandie-Maine Regional Nature Park.
1977	Completion of the Normandy motorway (A13).
1983-84	Start-up of Paluel Nuclear Power Station. Start-up of Flamanville Nuclear Power Station.
1987	Commemoration of the 900th anniversary of William the Conqueror's death.
1991	Inauguration of France's 27th regional nature park in the Cotentin and Bessin area.
6 June 1994	50th anniversary of the Battle of Normandy.
January 1995	Inauguration of the Pont de Normandie.
1997	A violent controversy breaks out between Greenpeace environmentalists and COGEMA over nuclear waste dumped near La Hague.
1999	Tall Ships Armada of the Century on the Seine, from Rouen to Le Havre.
1999	Violent windstorms in December uproot innumerable trees and damage buildings.
2000	Wreck of the *Evoli Sun*, an Italian ship loaded with chemicals, off Cap de la Hague.
2004	60th anniversary of the Normandy landings attended, for the first time, by leaders of Germany and Russia.
2005	The centre of Le Havre is named a UNESCO World Heritage Site.
2006	Port 2000 at Le Havre opened.
2009	The French president approves study to build the a Normandy high-speed train line between Paris and Le Havre, and between Paris, Caen and Cherbourg.
2011	Celebration of Normandy's 11th century.
2014	70th anniversary of the D-Day Landings.
2016	The number of metropolitan regions in France is reduced to 13; combining Basse and Haute Normandie.
2017	Emmanuel Macron is elected President of France, representing his "La République En Marche!" centrist political party.
2019	75th anniversary of the D-Day Landings.

NORMANS THROUGHOUT HISTORY

The story of the Norsemen, or Vikings, who settled in the Frankish kingdom and from there set out on expeditions of conquest to southern Italy and Sicily as well as to England, Wales, Scotland and Ireland, has inspired many tall tales and cinematic extravaganzas.

In the 8C, pagan barbarians from Denmark, Norway and Iceland began their plunder of coastal settlements in Europe and by the 9C they had

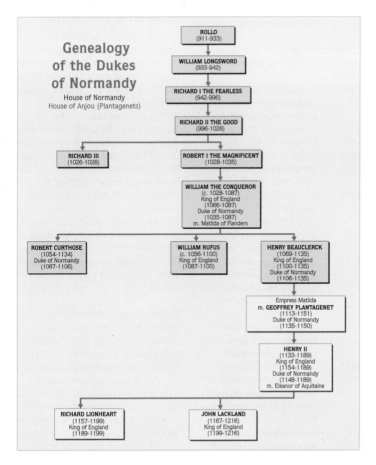

Genealogy
of the Dukes
of Normandy

House of Normandy
House of Anjou (Plantagenets)

ROLLO
(911-933)

WILLIAM LONGSWORD
(933-942)

RICHARD I THE FEARLESS
(942-996)

RICHARD II THE GOOD
(996-1026)

RICHARD III
(1026-1028)

ROBERT I THE MAGNIFICENT
(1028-1035)

WILLIAM THE CONQUEROR
(c. 1028-1087)
King of England
(1066-1087)
Duke of Normandy
(1035-1087)
m. Matilda of Flanders

ROBERT CURTHOSE
(1054-1134)
Duke of Normandy
(1087-1106)

WILLIAM RUFUS
(c. 1056-1100)
King of England
(1087-1100)

HENRY BEAUCLERCK
(1069-1135)
King of England
(1100-1135)
Duke of Normandy
(1106-1135)

Empress Matilda
m. GEOFFREY PLANTAGENET
(1113-1151)
Duke of Normandy
(1135-1150)

HENRY II
(1133-1189)
King of England
(1154-1189)
Duke of Normandy
(1148-1189)
m. Eleanor of Aquitaine

RICHARD LIONHEART
(1157-1199)
King of England
(1189-1199)

JOHN LACKLAND
(1167-1216)
King of England
(1199-1216)

established a permanent foothold in the region that is now Normandy.

In the year 911, **Charles III (The Simple)** signed the treaty of **St-Clair-sur-Epte** with the Viking chief **Rollo**. According to Dudon de St-Quentin, the first historian of Normandy, the Viking simply placed his hands between those of the French king to ratify the agreement creating the dukedom of Normandy: no written treaty was ever drafted.

The Norsemen continued to expand their holdings until well into the 11C, ruling through a succession of ruthless dukes and counts.

Eventually, the Norse converted to Christianity and adopted the French language, but retained a reputation for recklessness, love of combat, cunning and outrageous treachery. At the same time, wherever they went, they showed a remarkable capacity for adapting to local customs. William, Duke of Normandy, became King of England in a coup known as the **Norman Conquest** (1066), while the Norman kingdom of Sicily was founded by the descendants of Tancrède de Hauteville. Norman rulers were among the most powerful and successful of their time, and established enduring political institutions.

In Normandy, the Normans quickly adopted the precepts of feudalism, became masters of cavalry warfare and fostered the cult of knighthood. Eventually, their reputation for fierceness and brutality was softened by religion, marked by pilgrimages to Rome and the Holy Land. In England, their rule made the kingdom safer from foreign invasion and brought discipline to church organisations.

Later still, explorers continued to embark from Normandy in search of new lands:

1402 Jean de Béthencourt, of the Caux region, becomes King of the Canary Islands, but cedes his realm to the King of Castile.

1503 Paulmier de Gonneville, gentleman of Honfleur, reaches Brazil in the Espoir.

1506 Jean Denis, a sailor from Honfleur, explores the mouth of the St Lawrence, preparing the way for Jacques Cartier.

1524 Leaving Dieppe in the caravel *La Dauphine*, Giovanni da Verrazano, a native of Florence and navigator to François I, discovers the site of New York City, which he names Land of Angoulême.

1555 Admiral Nicolas Durand de Villegaignon sets up a colony of Huguenots from Le Havre on an island in the bay of Rio de Janeiro, but they are driven away by the Portuguese.

1563 Led by René de la Laudonnière, colonies of Protestants from Le Havre and Dieppe found Fort Caroline in Florida but are massacred by the Spaniards.

1608 Samuel de Champlain, Dieppe shipbuilder, leaves Honfleur to found Quebec.

1635 Pierre Belain of Esnambuc claims Martinique in the name of the King of France; the colonisation of Guadeloupe follows soon after.

1682 Cavalier de La Salle of Rouen, after reconnoitring the site of Chicago, sails down the Mississippi river and takes possession of Louisiana.

WILLIAM THE CONQUEROR

William was the son of Robert the Magnificent and his concubine Herleva (The Beautiful Arlette), from the town of Falaise. A descendant of the great Viking chief Rollo, he was first known as William the Bastard.

In 1035, when his father died on his way back from the Holy Land, William, then eight years old, became the seventh Duke of Normandy. His tutors instructed him in the rudiments of Latin and the fine points of military strategy, and also instilled in him a deep religious faith.

Later, three of his guardians and his tutor were assassinated by parties who objected to the Bastard's succession. In 1046, barely 20 years old, he confounded yet another plot to undo him, and wisely sought out the support of the King of France, Henri I.

For the Love of Matilda

William built castles (Falaise – his birthplace – and Cherbourg) and towns (Saint-James), expanded Saint-Lô and Carentan, created the city of Caen, and negotiated peace with his enemies.

Between 1054 and 1060, William held fast against the allied forces of the King of France, Guillaume d'Arques and the Geoffrey Martell of Anjou. He consolidated his power by marrying Matilda, daughter of Baldwin V, Count of Flanders. Mindful of all he had suffered as an illegitimate son, William was a faithful and trusting husband. When called away from Normandy, he left the realm in his wife's able hands.

The Conquest

Edward the Confessor, King of England, had recognised William as his heir, but in January 1066 news arrived that **Harold** had claimed the English throne. The duke appealed to the Pope and Harold was excommunicated.

Within seven months, William was master of England. On 12 September 1066, about 12 000 knights and soldiers embarked upon 696 ships followed by smaller boats and skiffs bringing the total number of vessels to 3 000. On 28 September, at low tide, the Normans landed at Pevensey, Sussex. William, the last to disembark, stumbled and fell full length. The superstitious Normans were alarmed, but William laughed and, according to the records, retorted: "My Lords, by the glory of God have I seized this land with my own two hands. As long as it exists it is ours alone."

The Normans occupied Hastings. Harold, who had been busy fighting other attackers, rushed to the scene and pitched camp on a hill. On 14 October, William launched an assault, and after a terrible struggle the Normans were victorious; Harold died in combat.

While remaining Duke of Normandy, William was crowned King of England on Christmas Day, 1066, at Westminster Abbey, London. He suppressed revolts, brought to heel the corrupt aristocracy, encouraged noble Norman families to settle in England, and overcame the Pope's opposition to his control over church affairs. Norman art flourished in England, as the cathedrals at Canterbury, Winchester and Durham show.

Ruling 52 years in Normandy and 21 years in England, William maintained a large measure of peace and justice in his realm. He died on 9 September 1087 near Rouen and was buried at St-Étienne church in Caen, as he had requested.

MONASTICISM IN NORMANDY

Normandy, like Champagne and Burgundy, was a centre of monasticism during the religious revival that swept the 11C, as the many abbeys attest.

Under **Benedictine Rule**, which gradually supplanted other religious rules, nuns and monks made vows of obedience, poverty and chastity. They practised fasting, silence and abstinence. The monks' working day was taken up by prayers scheduled throughout the day, holy reading and, to a greater extent, manual labour, such as baking bread, weaving cloth for the monastic habits, carrying firewood, sweeping, serving meals, preparing the sacristy, growing vegetables, etc. Throughout the Middle Ages monasticism played a vital role in society, securing the propagation of Christianity, promoting the authority of the Pope and contributing to the conservation and transmission of learning.

MEDIEVAL MONASTERIES

The monastic buildings surrounded the cloisters as detailed below.

Cloisters – Generally, four galleries corresponding to the compass points surrounded a central courtyard, often laid out as a medicinal herb garden.

Abbey church – The abbey church was characterised by an extremely long nave; the monks spent long hours in church for mass and other religious offices. In Cistercian churches, a rood screen placed near the high altar separated the monks' choir from that of the lay brothers.

Sacristy – The room in which ecclesiastical garments and altar vessels were stored and in which the priest would don his robes before leading the service.

Chapter House – Used for daily monastic activities, including prayers before the day's work and the reading of a chapter taken from the monastic rule.

Calefactory – The only heated room in the monastery, accessible to all the monks under certain conditions.

Scriptorium – A room reserved for the copying out of manuscripts.

Refectory – A large bare room, endowed with surprisingly good acoustics. During meals, the reader in the elevated pulpit would recite passages from the Bible.

Dormitories – There were generally two: one for the monks above the chapter house and one for the lay brothers above the cellars. In the Cistercian order seven hours were allowed for rest. The monks slept fully dressed in a communal dormitory.

Outbuildings – These included the barns and the porter's lodge, often a grand building with a huge gateway to allow the passage of both carriages and people on foot. The porter's lodge had living quarters on the first floor, where alms were distributed and justice was dispensed to the population.

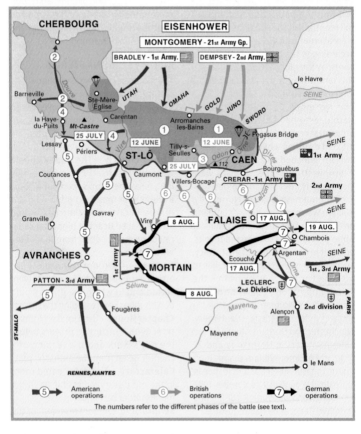

The numbers refer to the different phases of the battle (see text).

The Battle of Normandy

On 6 June 1944, the coast of Normandy was the setting for yet another crucial invasion which would, in its own turn, change the course of history.

From the autumn of 1941, the British authorities had envisaged a landing on the continent of Europe, but it was only after the entry of the United States that offensive action on such a scale could be seriously considered. The COSSAC plan, approved at the Churchill-Roosevelt meetings in Washington and Quebec in May and August 1943, foresaw the landing of invasion troops along the Calvados coast, which was defended by the German 7th Army. This sector was preferred to the Pas-de-Calais (15th German Army) because it meant that the

Germans' lines of communication would be more vulnerable: Lower Normandy would be isolated if the bridges over the Seine and Loire were destroyed. It was also known that the enemy was preoccupied by the defence of the Pas-de-Calais.

Preparation

The building of artificial ports – a lesson learned as a result of the costly Dieppe commando raid of 1942 – and the construction of landing craft was carried out with other training in the winter of 1943–44. On 24 December 1943, General Eisenhower was named Chief of the Allied Expeditionary Force and General Montgomery made responsible for tactical coordination of all land forces (21st Army Group) for **Operation Overlord**.

Air raids to paralyse the French railway system began on 6 March 1944. During the spring of 1944 Field Marshal Rommel had the beaches and their approaches covered with obstacles. It became urgent to find a means of destroying these obstacles by using tanks as bulldozers or sending frogmen to dispose of them.

First Week of the Landing
Circled numbers refer to the map.
① Originally D-Day had been planned for 5 June but it was postponed for 24 hours owing to bad weather.
At dawn on D-Day, 6 June 1944, British and Commonwealth ground forces established beachheads at **Sword**, **Juno** and **Gold** and rapidly linked up with the airborne troops dropped to their east. The Americans, landing on **Omaha Beach**, joined up with their airborne flank only after the capture of Carentan on 12 June.

Layout of the Bridgehead
Advances were substantial but of unequal depth: the Americans threatened Caumont on 13 June; the British and Canadians were held up by very fierce fighting 6km/3.7mi north of Caen in the Tilly-sur-Seulles sector on 7 June and broke through only on the 20th – the village changed hands some 20 times. The Caen sector, as Montgomery had foreseen, became the principal hinge of the whole front.

Isolation of the Cotentin peninsula and the Capture of Cherbourg
② The Americans attacked across the Cotentin peninsula on 13 June and secured it, capturing Barneville on 18 June. Turning north they attacked Cherbourg, which fell on 26 June – a victory in the battle to ensure supply lines.

Battle of the Odon and Capture of Caen
③ On 26 June, a hard battle, which was to last a month, began with a crossing over the Odon upstream from Caen and the taking of Hill 112. Montgomery decided to outflank Caen to the southwest. The city of Caen on the left bank was attacked in force from the west and northeast and fell on 9 July.

Breakthrough Preparation
In early July, General Montgomery laid out his breakthrough strategy:
"Keep the greatest possible number of the enemy divisions on our eastern flank, between Caen and Villers-Bocage, and pivot the western flank of the Army Group towards the southeast in a vast sweeping movement in order to threaten the line of retreat of the German division."

War of the Hedgerows
For the American soldiers of 1944, the Cotentin campaign – the advance to Cherbourg and the Battle of St-Lô – was simply "the war of the hedgerows". Leafy hedges and sunken lanes such as those that divide the Normandy countryside came as an unpleasant surprise for the attackers, but for defensive warfare or guerrilla tactics the terrain offered unending opportunities. Modern arms were not much help: four-inch shells scarcely shook the tree-covered embankments, which constituted natural anti-tank barriers; only the foot soldier could fight successfully in this hell of hedges. The effort of fighting against an invisible enemy was exhausting; every field and orchard crossed was a victory in itself; progress was slow and was often estimated by the number of hedges passed. So that the tanks could operate with a maximum of efficiency, an American sergeant devised a system whereby a sharp steel device, not unlike a ploughshare, was attached to the front of each tank.

The Battle for St-Lô
④ On 3 July, the American 8th Corps launched its offensive, in the face of fierce German resistance, towards the road centre of St-Lô, thus assuring more favourable positions for the large-scale operations to come. Fighting was fierce

for La Haye-du-Puits and Mount Castre. St-Lô fell on 19 July and the Americans entrenched their position behind the Lessay–Périers–St-Lô stretch of road. Progress at this time was slow in the Caen sector. A breakthrough was attempted towards the southwest of the town but was halted in the Bourguébus sector on 19 July.

For one interminable week, from 19 to 25 July, bad weather suspended operations on all fronts.

The Breakthrough (Operation Cobra)

⑤ At midday on 25 July, following intense aerial bombardment, the 7th corps attacked west of St-Lô, the 8th between Périers and Lessay.

By 28 July, Allied armour was driving down the main roads, carrying out vast encircling movements. Coutances fell on 28 July, Granville and Avranches on 31 July. On 1 August, General Patton, taking command of the 3rd Army, hurled it into the lightning war. The 8th Corps burst west into Brittany (Rennes fell on 4 August and Nantes on 12 August), while the 15th Corps and the French 2nd Armoured Division under General Leclerc moved east towards Laval and Le Mans (9 August).

The Thrust South of Caen

⑥ Backing up these operations, Montgomery, with the 1st Canadian Army (General Crerar), moved up to the Caen-Falaise road at the eastern end of the front; the British divisions, pushing southeast from Caumont and Villers-Bocage (5 August), overwhelmed the last defences on the west bank of the Orne.

Battle of the Falaise-Mortain Pocket

⑦ When the German 7th Army was threatened by the American 15th Corps to their rear and the British to the north, Hitler organised a counter-offensive to cut off the 3rd Army from its supply bases by taking control of the Avranches bottleneck. The German 7th Army began its westerly counter attack on 6–7 August in the Mortain region. The Allied air forces crushed the move at daybreak. After a week of bitter fighting the Germans retreated east (12 August). During this time the French 2nd Division moved northwards from Le Mans, took Alençon on 12 August and on 13 August breached the Paris-Granville road at Écouché. The Canadians, halted between the 9 and 14 August at the River Laison, entered Falaise on 17 August, thus forming the northern arm of the pincer movement. Meeting with the Americans at Chambois (19 August), they cornered the German 7th Army and forced its surrender at Tournai-sur-Dives. By the night of 21 August the Battle of Normandy was over – it had cost the Germans 640 000 men, killed, wounded or taken prisoner.

Reconstruction
The Scale of Devastation

Normandy, like Britain and unlike many other French and European territories, is not on any European invasion route and so had remained unscathed since the Wars of Religion; towns had scarcely altered since the 16C. The German invasion of 1940 and the air raids and army operations of 1944 caused widespread devastation and nearly all the great towns suffered – Rouen, Le Havre, Caen, Lisieux. Of the 3 400 Norman *communes*, 586 have been rebuilt to modern standards.

Town Planning and Reconstruction

Modern town planning has altered what were narrow winding main streets into wide straight thoroughfares to accommodate increased traffic, while providing for public gardens, parks and car parks. Houses, flats and offices have been built and an effort has been made to restore individual character to towns and villages; limestone is used for buildings on the Norman sedimentary plain and plateaux, while sandstone, granite and brick are used in the woodland regions. Many historic monuments were damaged but most have been restored and are enhanced by improved settings.

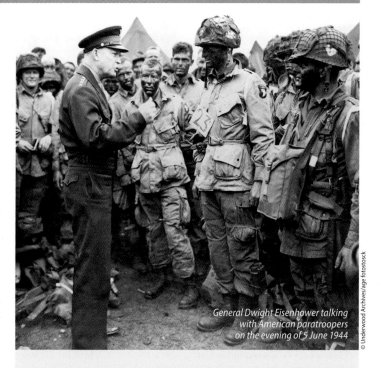

General Dwight Eisenhower talking
with American paratroopers
on the evening of 5 June 1944

© Underwood Archives/age fotostock

Commanders in the Battle of Normandy

General Dwight Eisenhower (1890–1969) was the Supreme Allied Commander for Overlord. He was present when the German capitulation was signed in Berlin on 8 May 1945. Eisenhower was then to become US president from 1953 to 1961.

General George Patton (1885–1945) commanded the 3rd American Army. After the Avranches breakthrough his units swept across Brittany, the Paris basin, participated in the defence of Bastogne in the Battle of the Bulge, then went as far as Bohemia.

General Omar Bradley (1893–1981) commanded the American assault forces during the landing operation. He then led his troops from Brittany across Europe in the Advance to the Elbe.

General Bernard Montgomery (1887–1976) commanded the land forces for the Allied landing operation. Montgomery then led the northern wing of the 21st Army Group through the Netherlands and Denmark in the Drive to the Baltic.

General Philippe de Hauteclocque (1902–47), known as **Leclerc**, commanded the 2nd Armoured Division of Free French Forces. He landed at Utah Beach on 1 August and took the 2nd Armoured Division from Cotentin to Colmar, liberating Paris on the way.

Field Marshal Erwin Rommel (1891–1944) was overall commander of German forces along the North Sea and Atlantic coasts and chief of the armies of the B group. Wounded on 17 June, suspected of having taken part in a plot against Hitler, he committed suicide on 14 October 1944.

Art and Culture

The Norse, a people long considered barbaric, were in fact masters of wood-carving and metalworking, as their sophisticated domestic implements and fine jewellery testify. Over the centuries, their descendants produced the great Norman and Gothic religious architecture of the 11C to 13C, and later proved great innovators in the decorative arts, music (Saint-Saëns, Honegger, Satie), literature (Corneille, de Toqueville, de Maupassant, Flaubert, Maurois), painting (the 19C Impressionists) and, most recently, the cinema.

ARCHITECTURE

NORMAN BUILDING MATERIALS

Rouen and the towns of the Seine are built with chalky limestone from the valley sides. A similar affinity exists between the local materials and the buildings in the Caux region, where pebbles are set in flowing mortar. Clay, in cheap and plentiful local supply, was used for the cob of the timber-framed thatched cottages and for making bricks, which were often ingeniously set to make decorative patterns.

ROMANESQUE (11C–EARLY 12C)

The Benedictines and Romanesque Design

In the 11C, immediately after the period of Viking invasions, the Benedictines returned to their task of clearing the land and constructing churches and other monastic buildings. These architect monks retained the robust building methods employed by the Carolingians and then embellished their constructions with the Oriental dome or the barrel vault used by the Romans for bridges and commemorative arches. This new architectural style, created by the Benedictines, was named Romanesque by Arcisse de Caumont, an archaeologist from Normandy, who in 1840 outlined the theory of regional schools of architecture. Despite its apparent simplicity Romanesque architecture is wonderfully diverse. In England the style is known as Norman.

The Norman School and Its Abbey Churches

The Benedictines, supported by the dukes of Normandy, played an immensely important part in the whole life of the province; only their work as architects and creators of the Norman School is described below.

The first religious buildings of importance in Normandy were the churches of the rich abbeys. Early monastic buildings may have disappeared or been altered, particularly after the Reform of St Maur, but examples of the Benedictine flowering have survived – the ruins of Jumièges Abbey and the churches on Mont-St-Michel, in Cerisy-la-Forêt, St-Martin-de-Boscherville as well as Église St-Étienne and Église de la Trinité in Caen.

The **Norman School** is characterised by pure lines, bold proportions, sober decoration and beautiful ashlared stonework. The style spread to England after the Norman Conquest. Durham Cathedral provides the first official example of quadripartite vaulting, erected at the beginning of the 12C. The Norman style is to be seen in Westminster Abbey, which was rebuilt by Edward the Confessor, in the two west towers and the square crossing tower of Canterbury Cathedral and in the cathedrals of Southwell, Winchester and Ely in England.

Norman architecture also appeared in Sicily in the 11C in the wake of noble Norman adventurers; in France it paved the way for the Gothic style.

The abbey churches are characterised by two towers on either side of the west front, giving the west face an H-like appearance, and a square lantern tower above the transept crossing, which also served to increase the light inside.

The towers, bare or decorated only with blind arcades below, get lighter with multiple pierced bays the higher they rise (in the 13C many were crowned by spires quartered by pinnacles).

ABC of Architecture

Religious Architecture

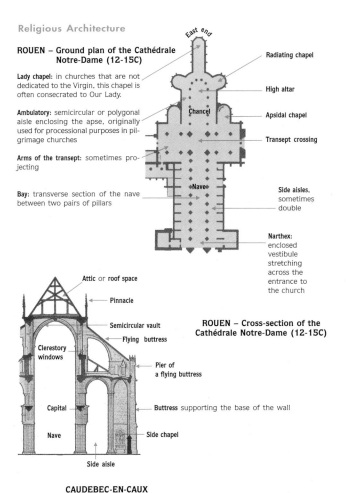

ROUEN – Ground plan of the Cathédrale Notre-Dame (12-15C)

East end

Lady chapel: in churches that are not dedicated to the Virgin, this chapel is often consecrated to Our Lady.

Ambulatory: semicircular or polygonal aisle enclosing the apse, originally used for processional purposes in pilgrimage churches

Arms of the transept: sometimes projecting

Bay: transverse section of the nave between two pairs of pillars

Radiating chapel

High altar

Apsidal chapel

Chancel

Transept crossing

Nave

Side aisles, sometimes double

Narthex: enclosed vestibule stretching across the entrance to the church

Attic or roof space

Pinnacle

Semicircular vault

Flying buttress

Clerestory windows

Pier of a flying buttress

Buttress supporting the base of the wall

Capital

Side chapel

Nave

Side aisle

ROUEN – Cross-section of the Cathédrale Notre-Dame (12-15C)

**CAUDEBEC-EN-CAUX
Vaulting in the Lady Chapel of the
Église Notre-Dame (14C)**

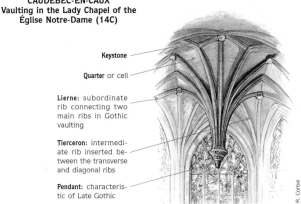

Keystone

Quarter or cell

Lierne: subordinate rib connecting two main ribs in Gothic vaulting

Tierceron: intermediate rib inserted between the transverse and diagonal ribs

Pendant: characteristic of Late Gothic

R. Corbel

61

CAUDEBEC-en-CAUX – Église Notre-Dame (14C)

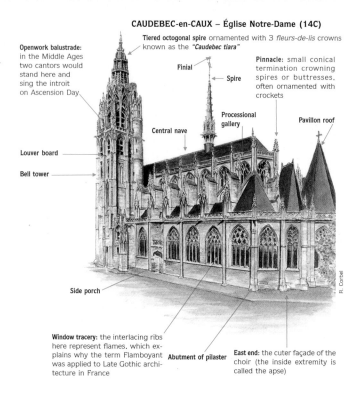

Openwork balustrade: in the Middle Ages two cantors would stand here and sing the introit on Ascension Day

Tiered octagonal spire ornamented with 3 *fleurs-de-lis* crowns known as the *"Caudebec tiara"*

Finial

Spire

Pinnacle: small conical termination crowning spires or buttresses, often ornamented with crockets

Central nave

Processional gallery

Pavillon roof

Louver board

Bell tower

Side porch

R. Corbel

Window tracery: the interlacing ribs here represent flames, which explains why the term Flamboyant was applied to Late Gothic architecture in France

Abutment of pilaster

East end: the cuter façade of the choir (the inside extremity is called the apse)

ROUEN – Portail des Librairies, Cathédrale Notre-Dame (1482)

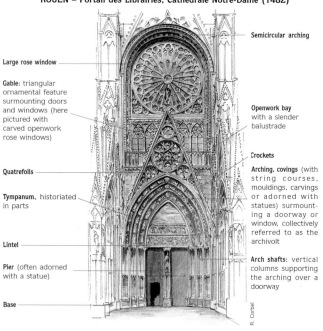

Semicircular arching

Large rose window

Gable: triangular ornamental feature surmounting doors and windows (here pictured with carved openwork rose windows)

Openwork bay with a slender balustrade

Crockets

Arching, covings (with string courses, mouldings, carvings or adorned with statues) surmounting a doorway or window, collectively referred to as the archivolt

Quatrefoils

Tympanum, historiated in parts

Arch shafts: vertical columns supporting the arching over a doorway

Lintel

Pier (often adorned with a statue)

Base

R. Corbel

ROUEN – Chancel and Transept Crossing in the Abbatiale St-Ouen (14C)

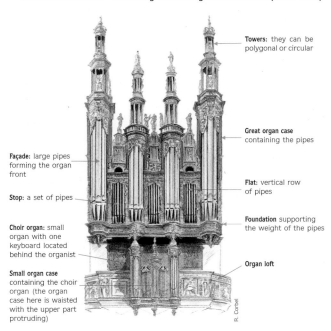

Main arcade

Clerestory windows

Arcature with mouldings

Tracery: ornamental stone ribwork in the upper part of a window

Sculpted spandrel: triangular area comprised between an arch and its framing

Equilateral arch

Mullion: vertical shaft dividing a window into two or several lights

Triforium

Diagonal rib

Compound pier

CAUDEBEC-EN-CAUX – Grand Organ in the Église Notre-Dame (1541-1542)

Towers: they can be polygonal or circular

Great organ case containing the pipes

Façade: large pipes forming the organ front

Flat: vertical row of pipes

Stop: a set of pipes

Foundation supporting the weight of the pipes

Choir organ: small organ with one keyboard located behind the organist

Small organ case containing the choir organ (the organ case here is waisted with the upper part protruding)

Organ loft

R. Corbel

ÉVREUX – Stained glass (early 14C) in the Cathédrale Notre-Dame

The main function of stained glass is to provide a translucent framing for church windows and to regulate the intensity of the light inside the building. "The stained-glass windows in the chancel of Évreux Cathedral are the finest examples of 14C work. They are pure in the extreme, artfully combining light yellows and limpid blues with transparent reds and silvery whites... They are in perfect harmony with the radiant chancel, suffused with dazzling day light", remarked Emile Mâle

Glass edging surrounding the finished panes

French T-bar armature: iron band used between panels to fix them onto the saddle-bar

Ferramenta: iron framework that provides a fixing for the panels within the window

Internal lead: strip of lead used to fit together the pieces of glass in the panel

Silver stain: pigment made of silver nitrate mixed with ochre that produces a lovely yellow after firing in the kiln

Grisaille: pigment made with iron oxide producing a variety of greys and blacks after firing in the kiln

Saddle-bars: iron shafts embedded in the masonry of windows to support the panels

R. Corbel

ÉCOUIS – Stalls in the chancel of the Collégiale Notre-Dame (14C)

High back

Elbow rest

Cheek: narrow upright face forming the end of a row of stalls

Separation between two stalls

Misericord: ledge projecting from the underside of a hinged seat which, when the seat is raised, provides support to worshippers or choir singers out of mercy (per misericordiam). 15C and 16C stalls were often sculpted with amusing grotesques or bizarre creatures called "drolleries"

R. Corbel/MICHELIN

Rural Architecture

Thatched Cottage at LYONS-LA-FORÊT

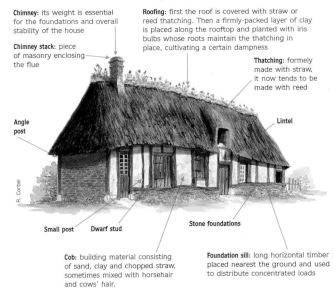

Chimney: its weight is essential for the foundations and overall stability of the house

Chimney stack: piece of masonry enclosing the flue

Roofing: first the roof is covered with straw or reed thatching. Then a firmly-packed layer of clay is placed along the rooftop and planted with iris bulbs whose roots maintain the thatching in place, cultivating a certain dampness

Thatching: formely made with straw, it now tends to be made with reed

Angle post

Lintel

R. Corbel

Small post   **Dwarf stud**

Stone foundations

Cob: building material consisting of sand, clay and chopped straw, sometimes mixed with horsehair and cows' hair.

Foundation sill: long horizontal timber placed nearest the ground and used to distribute concentrated loads

Military Architecture

Château d'HARCOURT (13C)

Although it has suffered from the ravages of time and history, the **Château d'Harcourt** remains a perfect example of medieval defensive architecture.

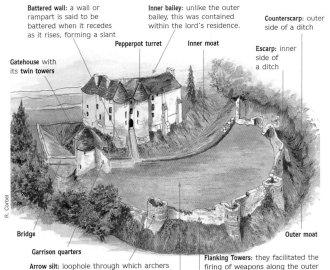

Battered wall: a wall or rampart is said to be battered when it recedes as it rises, forming a slant

Inner bailey: unlike the outer bailey, this was contained within the lord's residence.

Counterscarp: outer side of a ditch

Pepperpot turret

Inner moat

Escarp: inner side of a ditch

Gatehouse with its **twin towers**

R. Corbel

Bridge

Outer moat

Garrison quarters

Arrow silt: loophole through which archers shot their arrows, converted here to receive artillery cannons in the 14C

Flanking Towers: they facilitated the firing of weapons along the outer face of the walls

Curtain wall: enclosing rampart connecting two bastions or towers

Outer bailey: courtyard lying outside the castle perimeter but protected by its ramparts; it was used to accommodate the quartermasters' lodgings and to receive the population in the event of a siege

Seaside Architecture

DEAUVILLE – Villa Strassburger (early 20C)

This villa is a pastiche of the half-timbered mansions typical of the area. Its genuine Norman characteristics are combined with those from Alsace and some other French regions, complemented by a few eccentric touches prompted by the imagination of architect **G. Pichereau**: asymmetrical rooftops, profusion of skylights and dormer windows, projecting eaves.

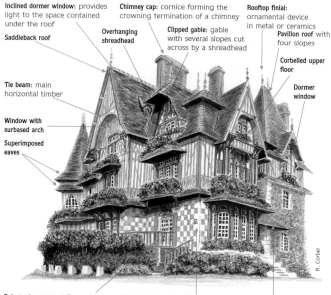

Inclined dormer window: provides light to the space contained under the roof

Saddleback roof

Overhanging shreadhead

Chimney cap: cornice forming the crowning termination of a chimney

Clipped gable: gable with several slopes cut across by a shreadhead

Rooftop finial: ornamental device in metal or ceramics

Pavillon roof with four slopes

Corbelled upper floor

Dormer window

Tie beam: main horizontal timber

Window with surbased arch

Superimposed eaves

Balustrade: parapet formed by a row of balusters

Stacked bond: a bond in masonry in which the bricks form a chequered pattern

Wind-brace

R. Corbel

Civil Engineering

The Pont de NORMANDIE (1988-1994)

Radio relay aerial

Tower head

Staying cables, each consisting of fifty sheathed steel strands

Anti-vibration rods

Pylon struts

Upper brace

Lower brace

Aerodynamic vehicle deck

Piers

Badplates

Entrance providing access inside the pylon

R. Corbel

Charming country churches are often surmounted by Romanesque belfries, which are crowned with a saddleback roof or a four-sided squat wood or stone pyramid, the forerunner of the Gothic spire.

The interior light and size of Norman abbeys is very striking. The naves are wide with an elevation consisting of two series of openings above great semicircular arches – an amazingly bold concept for a Romanesque construction. The Norman monks eschewed the heavy barrel vault in favour of a beamed roof spanning the nave and galleries, reserving groined stone vaulting (the crossing of two semicircular arches) for the aisles. The vast galleries on the first level open onto the wide bays of the nave and repeat the design of the aisles. At clerestory level a gallery or passage in the thickness of the wall circles the church. A dome over the transept crossing supports a magnificent lantern tower which lets in the daylight through tall windows.

Norman Decoration

The abbey churches, like all others of Romanesque design, were illuminated on a considerable scale with gilding and bright colours as were the manuscripts of the time. The main themes were those of Byzantine iconography.

Norman sculptural decoration is essentially geometric; different motifs stand out, of which the most common is the key or fret pattern (straight lines meeting at right angles to form crenellated or rectangular designs). The decorative motifs are sometimes accompanied by mouldings, human heads or animal masks emphasising recessed arches, archivolts, cornices and mouldings. Sometimes the monks executed in low-relief motifs copied from cloth, ivories or metalwork brought back from the Orient; this is the origin of the cornerstones in the great arcade in Bayeux.

Capitals are rare and, where they exist, they are carved with gadroons or stylised foliage.

GOTHIC (12C–15C)

The style, conceived in Île-de-France, apart from quadripartite or rib vaulting, which originated in Norman England, was known as French work or French style until the 16C when the Italians of the Renaissance, who were resistant to the Parisian trend, scornfully dubbed it Gothic. The name survived. The French copied the H-shaped façades and great galleries of the Norman abbeys (the west front of Notre-Dame in Paris is based on that of the Église de la Trinité in Caen and its galleries on those of the Église St-Étienne).

The Cathedrals

Gothic is an ideal artistic style for cathedrals, as it symbolises the religious fervour of the people and the growing prosperity of the towns. In an all-embracing enthusiasm, a whole city would participate in the construction of the house of God. Under the enlightened guidance of bishops and master builders, all the guilds contributed to the cathedral's embellishment: stained-glass makers, painters, wood and stone carvers went to work. The doors became the illustrated pages of history.

Gothic Architecture in Normandy

Gradually the national Gothic style percolated into Normandy before the province was seized by Philippe Auguste in 1204.

In the 13C, the Gothic and traditional Norman styles merged. The best example of this fusion is Coutances Cathedral, where the pure proportions and the lofty austerity of the Norman style combine with Gothic sophistication as in the lantern tower. This was also the period of the superb belfries of the Caen and Bessin plains, typified by their tall stone spires, often pierced to offer less resistance to the wind, and quartered with pinnacles.

The magnificent Merveille buildings of Mont-St-Michel give an idea of total Norman Gothic ornamentation. Sobriety provides the foundation over which foliated sculpture reigns supreme;

plants of every variety decorate the round capitals, cover the cornerstones and garland the friezes. The three- and four-leafed clover in relief or hollowed out is a frequent motif but statuary is rare. Lisieux Cathedral and the Tour St-Romain of Rouen Cathedral show the degree of French Gothic influence in Normandy by the end of the 12C.

The Flamboyant Style

By the 14C, the period of great cathedral building had come to an end. The Hundred Years War (1337–1453) killed architectural inspiration; bits were added, buildings were touched up, but little was created. When the war was over a taste for virtuosity alone remained – and the Flamboyant style was born. Rouen is the true capital of the Flamboyant, which was particularly widespread in Haute-Normandie.

In this new style, the tracery of bays and rose windows resembles wavering flames – the derivation of the term Flamboyant. The Flamboyant style produced such single masterpieces as the Église St-Maclou in Rouen, the Tour de Beurre of Rouen Cathedral, the belfries of Notre-Dame in Caudebec and La Madeleine in Verneuil-sur-Avre. Civil architecture developed in importance and passed from Flamboyant to Renaissance – a change symbolised in the gables, pinnacles and balustrades of the Palais de Justice in Rouen.

Feudal Architecture

In medieval Normandy permission to build a castle was granted to the barons by the ruling duke, who, prudent as well as powerful, reserved the right to billet his own garrison inside and forbade all private wars.

Over the years the building of castles along the duchy's frontiers was encouraged – Richard Lionheart secured the Seine with the most formidable fortress of the period, Château-Gaillard. Originally only the austere keeps were inhabited, but from the 14C a courtyard and more pleasing quarters were constructed within the fortifications. This evolution can be seen in the castles at Alençon, and Dieppe and some of the Perche manor houses.

A taste for comfort and adornment appeared in civil architecture; wealthy merchants and burgesses built tall houses where wide eaves protected half-timbered upper storeys that overhung stone-walled ground floors. The results were as capricious as they were picturesque: corner posts, corbels and beams were decorated with lively and fantastic carvings.

THE RENAISSANCE (16C)

Georges I d'Amboise, Archbishop of Rouen and patron of the arts, introduced Italian taste and usage to Normandy. The new motifs – arabesques, foliated scrollwork, medallions, shells, urns, etc. – were combined with Flamboyant art. Among the outstanding works of this period is the chevet of the Église St-Pierre in Caen, a masterpiece of exuberance.

Castles, Manor Houses and Old Mansions

The Renaissance style reached its fullest grace in domestic architecture. At first, older buildings were ornamented in the current taste or a new and delicately decorated wing was added (Château d'O and the château at Fontaine-Henry); fortifications were replaced by parks and gardens.

The Classicism rediscovered by humanists took hold so that architects aimed for correct proportion and the imposition of the three Classical Orders of Antiquity.

Imperceptibly the search for symmetry and correctness produced aridity; fantasy was stifled by pomposity.

In Normandy, the Gothic spirit survived, appearing most successfully in small manor houses and innumerable country houses with sham feudal moats, turrets and battlements incorporated in either half timbering or stone and brick.

Norman towns contain many large stone Renaissance mansions. The outer façade is always plain and one must enter the courtyard to see the architectural design and the rich decoration (Hôtel d'Escoville, Caen; Hôtel de Bourgtheroulde, Rouen).

In the 16C, decoration became richer and less impulsive but the half-timbered construction technique remained the same. Many of these old houses have been carefully restored and there are good examples to be found in Alençon, Bayeux, Bernay, Caen, Domfront, Honfleur, Pont-Audemer, Verneuil-sur-Avre and Rouen.

CLASSICAL (17C–18C)

In this period, French architectural style, now a single concept and no longer an amalgam of individual techniques, imposed its rationalism on many countries beyond its borders.

Louis XIII and the "Jesuit Style"

The reign of Henri IV marked an artistic rebirth. An economical method of construction was adopted in which bricks played an important part: it was a time of beautiful châteaux with plain rose and white façades and steep grey-blue slate roofs.

The first decades of the 17C coincided with the Counter-Reformation. The Jesuits built many colleges and chapels – cold and formal edifices, their façades characterised by superimposed columns, a pediment and upturned consoles or small pavilions joining the front of the main building to the sides.

The Grand Siècle in Normandy

The symmetrical façades of the Classical style demanded space for their appreciation as in the châteaux at Cany, Beaumesnil, Balleroy and elsewhere. The Benedictine abbeys, which had adopted the **Maurist Reform** (the Benedictine Congregation of St Maur was founded in 1621), rediscovered their former inspiration. At the beginning of the 18C, the monastery buildings of the Abbaye-aux-Hommes in Caen and at Le Bec-Hellouin were remodelled by a brother architect and sculptor, **Guillaume de la Tremblaye**. The original plan was conserved but the design and decoration were given an austere nobility.

The urban scene was transformed by the construction of magnificent bishops' palaces, town halls with wide façades and large private houses.

CONTEMPORARY (19C–20C)

Following the extensive destruction caused by World War II many towns and villages in Normandy were rebuilt in the mid-20C in accordance with the precepts of modern town planning. A good example of successful reconstruction is Aunay-sur-Odon, with its large and imposing church.

Auguste Perret (1874–1954), the architect who pioneered the use of reinforced concrete construction, was appointed Chief Architect for the reconstruction of Le Havre; his works include the modern district of Le Havre and the Église St-Joseph. His work makes use of textured concrete and is designed to take the best advantage of natural light.

Normandy is a region of innovation as well; in Le Havre, note the **Espace Oscar-Niemeyer**, named after the Brazilian architect, as an example. Two surprising white structures evoke a volcano, and stand out in contrast to the buildings designed by Perret. The Musée des Beaux-Arts André-Malraux, also in Le Havre, resembles a glass ship at anchor. In Rouen, the renovation of place du Vieux-Marché in the 1970s included the construction of the Église Ste-Jeanne-d'Arc, based on a design by Louis Arretche. The roof of the church is in the shape of a boat hull (upside down).

Three of Normandy's bridges are also noteworthy examples of modern architecture: the **Tancarville bridge** was inaugurated in 1959, the **Brotonne bridge** in 1977, and the colossal **Pont de Normandie**, spanning the Seine estuary, opened in 1995. The most recent bridge is not only a boon to travellers, it is also a work of art and a technological feat, a milestone of civil engineering. It is a cable-stayed bridge, more elegant and cheaper to build than a suspension bridge, made of steel and concrete, able to withstand winds of 440kph/274mph. More recently, Michel

Virlogeux again constructed a bridge, Rouen's sixth, known as the Gustave Flaubert bridge.

POPULAR ARCHITECTURE

Normandy is often associated with **half-timbered** houses. The basic box frame is essentially composed of horizontal and vertical beams, but there are very often different local methods of construction. Footings or a base of some solid material is laid to prevent damp from rising.

A wooden sill or horizontal beam is laid along this base to ensure the correct spacing of the upright posts or studs. It is divided into as many sections as there are intervals between the vertical posts. The upper horizontal beam, sometimes known as a summer or bressumer, consists of a single beam. Along the gable ends it is known as a tie-beam. Bricks are often ingeniously used to make attractive patterns between the timbers.

Roofing materials such as thatch, which is so vulnerable to fire, and shingles of sweet chestnut, are becoming increasingly rare. The schist slabs of the Cotentin are a typical part of the landscape. The slate which has been used since the 18C for houses and outbuildings alike has a silver tinge.

A watertight roof depends on the correct hanging of the slates. The appearance of the villages is conditioned by the local materials used and the trades of the various villagers. One well-known building material, **Caen stone**, is quarried from the Jurassic deposits. It can be either friable or durable and varies in colour through grey and off-white to its more characteristic light creamy colour. The ashlar blocks are divided into two groups, one with the grain running vertically for façades, corner stones and gables and the second with a horizontal grain for courses and cornices.

Farms

In the open landscape of the **Caen plain** the typical courtyard farms are surrounded by high walls. A gateway gives access to the courtyard with the one- or two-storeyed farmhouse at the far end. The smaller crofts usually consist of two buildings, one long house for the living quarters and cowshed or barn and another for the stable or byre.

The farm buildings of the **Bessin** stand round a large courtyard that has two entrances, side by side, one for wheeled vehicles and a second for people. The house stands at the far end with the service and outbuildings to the right and left. There is usually a well in the middle. Built of limestone or Jurassic marls, the house has a pristine appearance. The windows are tall and wide; the roofing is either tiles or slates.

The small flat-tiled houses in the **Argentan** area have symmetrical façades. The buildings are usually a harmonious mixture of schist, brick (chimneys and window surrounds) and limestone (the walls). Some are surrounded by walls or a screen of vegetation. Large barns are frequently adjoined by sheds.

Brick and small laminated schist tiles predominate in the **Sées** countryside. Sometimes the buildings fit snugly one against the other, creating a jumble of roofs of varying pitch.

The farms in the region of **Alençon** are built around an open courtyard. The infinitely varied architecture reflects the wide range of rocks: granite, schist, flint, clay and kaolin.

The most common house type in the **Falaise** countryside is akin to those found in the Caen region. The walled courtyard predominates. The brick chimney replaces the rubblework one and tiles are used for roofs in the area bordering the Auge region.

The houses in the **Suisse Normande** are built of schist known as Pont-de-la-Mousse slate quarried near Thury-Harcourt and the settlements often have the rugged appearance of mountain villages. In the Orne Valley the houses huddle closely together on the flats whereas those on the slopes are scattered, even isolated.

The farm courtyard in the **Vire** *bocage* is often planted with apple and pear trees. On either side of the farmhouse are the barns, cattle sheds and outbuildings for

Dovecotes of Normandy

Manoir de Caudemonde

Château de Crèvecoeur-en-Auge

Manoir d'Auffray, Oherville

Dovecote in the hamlet of Petit Veauville,
Héricourt-en-Caux

Château de Betteville

M. Dewynter/MICHELIN

the cider press. Brown or red schist is the main building stone.

Seaside Architecture

In the 19C, the coast became a popular destination and bathing in the sea a novel pastime. Wealthy patrons ordered quirky houses for their holiday pleasures. Sometimes they were built in or near existing fishing villages, and in other places whole resort communities sprang up. Many of these villas are still standing along the coast at Cabourg, Houlgate, Villers, Deauville, Trouville, Villerville, Ste-Adresse, Étretat, Dieppe, Le Tréport, Mers-les-Bains, etc. Generally, they are remarkable for their multicoloured façades, busy with balconies, bow windows, railings, gables and other decorative elements.

A profusion of skylights, projecting eaves and rooftop finials adds to the exuberance. Other models are more reserved and even stately, recalling the Renaissance style. Some are more modestly termed chalets, and are said to be in the Swiss, Spanish or Persian style, depending on their features.

NORMAN DOVECOTES

The practice of keeping pigeons, formerly known as doves, dates back to the earliest civilisations. Although domestication is believed to have originated around 4500 BCE, the practice became widespread some 2 000 years later, in ancient Egypt, where pigeon was appreciated for its succulent flesh, a fact evidenced by the many frescoes of feasts and banquets.

THE CARRIER PIGEON

The carrier pigeon is mostly known for its military role in times of war. News of the conquest of Gaul by Julius Caesar was relayed to the capital by means of pigeons, as was Napoleon's defeat at Waterloo. During the Siege of Paris in 1870, 400 birds helped defend the city by carrying tiny strips of film attached to their claws.

More recently, during World War I, English troops entrusted some 10,000 messages to their feathered friends.

Several warrior birds became legendary figures and some were even awarded a military decoration: The Mocker, Lord Adelaide, Burma Queen, etc. The cities of Brussels and Lille have erected memorials to these worthy messengers.

THE HOMING PIGEON

In the early 19C, a new sport appeared in Belgium – pigeon racing, in which birds are trained to return to their home loft after being released in the wild. The first long-distance race (160km/99.4mi) was held in 1818 and the sport gradually gained prominence in Great Britain, France and the United States. Today, many French villages have their own Pigeon-Fanciers Club (Société Colombophile) and organise races regularly.

FOR THE BIRDS

A familiar sight in Normandy, especially in the Pays de Caux, is the dovecote (colombier). Norman dovecotes are square, polygonal or round; the last type is the most common. The door is at ground level, usually rectangular but sometimes rounded at the top and often surmounted by the arms of the owner. The projecting ledge halfway up (larmier) is designed to prevent the entry of rodents. There are openings for the pigeons all round. The roofs, conical on circular dovecotes and faceted on square or polygonal dovecotes, are often covered with slates. The lead finial may be in the shape of a pigeon or a weathervane.

The interior is lined with pigeonholes (boulins) – one hole for each pair of pigeons – and the number varies according to the wealth of the owner. They are reached by a ladder fixed to an arm attached to a central post which pivots on a hard stone. In some dovecotes only the upper part is intended for pigeons; the lower part may be used as a hen house or a sheep pen. When the two parts are separated by a wooden floor, the door to the upper part is above the stone rat ledge and reached by an external detachable ladder.

There are two kinds of dovecote. The standard or classic type is built of ashlar stone (not common), in an attractive contrast to black flint and white stone (north and northeast of Le Havre), in brick, black flint and ashlar stone (brick tended to replace black flint after the 17C), or in brick and stone (fairly common). The type of dovecote called secondary includes buildings in light coloured flint (a similar shade to ashlar stone), in flint and stone, or in flint, brick and stone.

The first known laws on pigeon breeding were instituted in the Middle Ages. In Normandy, the owners of fiefs were the only ones entitled to build dovecotes. This right, known as the *droit de colombier*, was abolished on 4 August 1789 and very few new dovecotes were built after the French Revolution.

A total of 535 were officially registered in the Seine-Maritime in the early 20C. However, many have been abandoned and are now in a state of neglect. The French government and local authorities have recently taken measures to finance the restoration of these charming buildings, which are an essential part of Normandy's rural heritage.

DECORATIVE ARTS
CERAMICS AND POTTERY

The glazed pavement in the chapter house of St-Pierre-sur-Dives (13C) demonstrates the long tradition of ceramic art in Normandy. In the mid-16C, Masséot Abaquesne was making decorated tiles, which were greatly prized in Rouen, whereas potteries in Le Pré-d'Auge and Manerbe (near Lisieux) were producing "earthenware more beautiful than is made elsewhere". In 1644, **Rouen faïence** made its name with blue decoration on a white ground and white on blue.

By the end of the century production had increased so that when the royal plate was melted down to replenish the Treasury, "the Court changed to chinaware in a week" (Saint-Simon). The so-called radiant style is reminiscent of the wrought-iron work and embroidery for which the town was well known.

The desire for novelty brought in the vogue for chinoiserie. In the middle of the 18C came the Rococo style with its quiver decoration and the famous Rouen cornucopia, a horn of plenty overflowing with flowers, birds and insects. This industry was ruined by the 1786 trade treaty, which allowed the import of English chinaware into France.

NORMAN FURNITURE

Sideboards, longcase clocks and wardrobes – the three most characteristic and traditional pieces of furniture in Normandy – are valued for their elegance, solidity and generous proportions.

The wardrobe, which gradually replaced the medieval chest, first appeared in the 13C; by the beginning of the 17C, the sideboard was already in existence and in the 18C longcase clocks became widespread. The golden age of furniture making in Normandy produced well-proportioned and delicately carved sideboards or kitchen dressers; coffin clocks (broader at the top than at the bottom); longcase clocks characterised by carved baskets of fruit and flowers round the clockface; tall pendulum clocks, with delicately chased dials in gilt bronze, copper, pewter or enamel; majestic oak wardrobes, ornamented with finely worked fittings, in brass or other metals, or with medallions, surmounted with carved cornices of doves, birds' nests, ears of corn, flowers and fruit or Cupid's quiver, etc.

The wardrobe was often part of a young woman's dowry and contained her trousseau; its transfer from her parents' house to her new home was the occasion for traditional celebrations.

PAINTING

Painting took first place among the arts in 19C France. Landscape totally eclipsed historical and stylised painting and Normandy was to become the cradle of Impressionism.

THE OPEN AIR

While the Romantics were discovering inland Normandy, Eugène Isabey, a lover of seascapes, began to work on the still deserted coast. **Richard Bonington** (1801–28), an English painter who went to France as a boy, trained there, and, in his watercolours, captured the atmosphere of the beaches.

In the second half of the 19C artistic activity was concentrated on **Eugène Boudin** (1824–98) round the Côte de Grâce. This painter from Honfleur, named King of the Skies by Corot, encouraged a young 15-year-old from Le Havre, **Claude Monet**, to drop caricature for the joys of real painting and urged his Parisian friends to come and stay in his St-Siméon farmstead.

IMPRESSIONISM

The younger painters, nevertheless, were to outstrip their elders in their search for pictorial light. They wanted to portray the vibration of light, hazes, the trembling of reflections and shadows, the depth and tenderness of the sky, the fading of colours in full sunlight. They – Monet, Sisley, Bazille and their Paris friends, Renoir, Pissarro, Cézanne and Guillaumin especially – were about to form the Impressionist School, which gave France a front rank in the history of painting.

From 1862 to 1869, the Impressionists remained faithful to the Normandy coast and the Seine estuary. After the Franco-Prussian War they returned only occasionally – although it was in Normandy, at Giverny, that Claude Monet set up house in 1881 and remained until he died in 1926.

Impressionism, in its turn, gave birth to a new school, **Pointillism**, which divided the tints with little touches of colour, applying the principle of the division of white light into seven basic colours, to get ever closer to a luminous effect. Seurat and Signac, the pioneers of this method, also came to Normandy to study its landscapes.

In the early 20C, **Fauvism** was born as a reaction against Impressionism and neo-Impressionism. These brightly coloured linear compositions exploded on the canvas.

For half a century, therefore, the Côte de Grâce, the Pays de Caux, Deauville, Trouville and Rouen were the sources of inspiration of a multitude of paintings.

A PLEIAD OF PAINTERS

Numerous artists still came to Normandy in the first half of the 20C, notably Valloton and Gernez (the latter died in Honfleur); Marquet, who had worked in Gustave Moreau's studio in Paris; Othon Friesz, who particularly enjoyed Honfleur, which he portrayed in its many aspects; and Van Dongen, painter of the worldly and the elegant and a frequent guest at Deauville.

Marquet, Friesz and Van Dongen were strongly influenced by Fauvism, whereas **Raoul Dufy**, a native of Le Havre, soon overthrew accepted convention to associate line drawing and richness of colour in compositions which were full of movement.

LITERATURE

Literature and architecture both sprang from the monasteries. It is therefore hardly surprising that Normandy and its abbeys became rich in literary activity from the 13C. Monks and clergymen with a sound knowledge of history and legend, together with travellers and pilgrims, provided the poets with the inspiration needed to create the Christian epics known as the *chansons de geste*.

Such verse appeared chronologically after the early hagiographic literature (lives of saints) but remains one of the first examples of the use of French as a literary mode of expression. In the 12C, the Anglo-Norman **Robert Wace**, who was born in Jersey but brought up in Caen, wrote two notable verse chronicles. *Le Roman du Rou* (1160–74) was commissioned by Henry II of England and is a history of the dukes of Normandy.

17C

Pierre Corneille (1606–84) is often called the father of French Classical tragedy. His main works are known together as the classical tetralogy: *Le Cid* (1637), *Horace* (1640), *Cinna* (1641) and *Polyeucte* (1643).

The dramatist enjoyed a happy life with his extended family in Rouen (he married and had seven children; his brother married his wife's sister and their households were very close), and despite occasional brushes with the authorities, his plays were generally well received. Balzac praised him, Molière acknowledged him as his master and the foremost of dramatists, Racine lauded his talent for versification. From the 20C viewpoint, it is clear that Corneille also had a great impact on the rise of comedy, and in the development of drama in general, in particular in regard to his ability to depict personal and moral forces in conflict.

18C

Born in Le Havre, **Bernardin de St-Pierre** (1737–1814) travelled the world to fulfil his dreams, and spent part of his life on the Indian Ocean island of Mauritius. In Paris, he became the disciple of the Romantic philosopher Jean-Jacques Rousseau. His best-known works are *Paul and Virginie* (1787) and *Studies of Nature* (1784).

19C

The founder of Norman regionalism is **Barbey d'Aurevilly** (1808–99), a nobleman from Cotentin, who was born in St-Sauveur-le-Vicomte. In a warm and bright style, illuminated with brilliant imagery and original phrases, he sought, like the Impressionists, to convey the atmosphere, the quality, the uniqueness of his region. Valognes, the town where he spent most of his adolescence, is mentioned in several of his works (*Ce qui ne meurt pas*, *Chevalier des Touches* and *Les Diaboliques*).

Although born in Paris, **Charles Alexis de Tocqueville** (1805–59) was from an old Norman family. It was during stays at the ancestral home, the Château de Tocqueville, not far from Cherbourg, that he wrote many of the works which were to bring him fame. This political scientist, politician and historian is best-known for his timeless classic *Democracy in America*.

Gustave Flaubert (1821–80), a prime mover of the Realist School of French literature, considered art as a means to knowledge. His masterful *Madame Bovary* (1857), a portrait of bourgeois life in the provinces, took him five years to complete. The French government sought to block its publication and have the author condemned for immorality – he narrowly escaped conviction.

Flaubert greatly influenced **Guy de Maupassant** (1850–93), a family friend born in Dieppe who regarded himself as the older author's apprentice. Maupassant's work is thoroughly realistic, the language lucidly pure and the imagery sharp and precise. The author wrote best-selling novels (*Une Vie*, *Bel-Ami*, *Pierre et Jean*), but his greatest achievement lies in his short stories; many of these works are considered among the finest in French literature. Today, he is one of the most widely read French authors in English-speaking countries.

Octave Mirbeau (1848–1917), from Trévières near Bayeux, was an active participant in the literary and political quarrels of his time, speaking out in defence of anarchist ideas. As a novelist, he was fiercely critical of the social conditions of the time.

Detail of On the Beach (1880) by Eugène Boudin

20C

Maurice Leblanc (1864–1941), born in Rouen, created the gentleman burgler Arsène Lupin. A museum in Étretat is devoted to this still-popular author.

André Maurois (1865–1967), born Émile Herzog in Elbeuf, is known for his war memoires, novels, biographies of literary figures such as Disraeli, Shelley, Victor Hugo, Balzac and Proust, and historical works (*History of England*, 1937, *History of the United States*, 1943).

Alain (1868–1951), made a name for himself by his columns in a Rouen newspaper. A professor of philosophy and author of many essays, he revolted against all forms of tyranny. His works *Remarks on Happiness* (1928) and *Remarks on Education* (1932) are noteworthy.

Jean de la Varende (1887–1959), from the Ouche region, evokes in his novels the Normandy of yesteryear. His work *Par Monts et Merveilles de Normandie* is a description of all he saw and admired in the region.

André Breton (1896–1966), from Tinchebray in the Orne, was a poet, essayist and "Pope" of the Surrealist movement. His work, including *Nadja* (1928), *L'Amour Fou* (1937) and two Surrealist manifestos, stirred up, as intended, intense controversy.

Armand Salacrou (1899–1989), born in Rouen, called his dramatic works a "meditation on the human condition". He experimented with different dramatic styles. Two of his popular successes were *Un homme comme les autres* (1926) and *Boulevard Durand* (1961).

Raymond Queneau (1903–76) was born in Le Havre and achieved distinction as the director of the prestigious *Encyclopédie de la Pléiade*, a scholarly edition of past and present authors. As the author of many poems, novels and plays, Queneau stands out for his quirky style and verbal juggling, revealing the absurdity that underlies our everyday world. One of his best-loved works, *Zazie dans le métro* (1959), was made into a charming film.

MUSIC

Composer of operas and comic operas, **François-Adrien Boieldieu** (1775–1834) was born in Rouen. His work *The Caliph of Baghdad* (1800) earned him a glowing reputation throughout Europe. From 1803 to 1810, he was Director of Music at the Imperial Opera of St Petersburg. His talent was universally recognised with his masterpiece *La Dame Blanche* in 1825. **Camille Saint-Saëns** (1835–1921) was born in Paris, but his father was from Normandy. A brilliant pianist, he composed symphonies, operas, concertos and religious works. He is best known for the *Danse Macabre* (1875) and *Samson et Dalila* (1877).

Arthur Honegger (1892–1955) was born in Le Havre, of Swiss origin. At first he composed melodies to poems by Cocteau, Apollinaire and Paul Fort, then *Pacific 231* (1923) and *King David* (1924). *Joan at the Stake* (1935) and *The Dance of the Dead* (1938) have texts by Paul Claudel.

Born in Honfleur, **Erik Satie** (1866–1925) began as a pianist in the cabarets of Montmartre (The Black Cat), where he met Debussy. Sarcasm and irony permeate his works, his greatest being the symphonic drama *Socrates* (1918) for voice and orchestra based on texts by Plato. Satie exerted an undeniable influence both on his time and on musicians such as Ravel, Debussy and Stravinsky.

CINEMA

One of France's early great directors, **Georges Méliès** (1861-1938) first worked here, and the trend has continued since with names like Malle, Renoir, Truffaut, Chabrol, Lelouch.

Home to the prestigious American Film Festival, in Deauville, Normandy is inextricably linked to the world of cinema.

Nature

Normandy is not a homogeneous geographical unit, rather it is an old province, formerly a dukedom, embracing two large areas with different geological structures, which become progressively younger from west to east. The sandstone, granite and Precambrian schists of the Armorican Massif in the west give way to strata of clay, limestone and chalk dating from the Triassic (beginning 254 million years ago) to the Tertiary (beginning 65 million years ago) periods, which belong to the geological formation of the Paris basin. Normandy can therefore be conveniently divided into two quite distinct regions: Haute-Normandie, which lies northwest of the Paris basin, and Basse-Normandie, which resembles its neighbour Brittany and consists of an eroded foundation of ancient rocks. The administrative region of Haute-Normandie is made up of the Eure (27) and Seine-Maritime (76) *départements*; Basse-Normandie includes the Calvados (14), Manche (50) and Orne (61) *départements*.

REGIONS OF NORMANDY

The inland areas can be divided into two types of regions, **open country** and **woodland**. In the strictest sense, the open country *(campagne)* consists of dry, windswept plains and cultivated fields. The woodland *(bocage)* is typical of the Armorican massif, although to the east it spills over into the Maine, the Perche and the Auge regions. Typical of the countryside, and sometimes confusing for casual ramblers, a network of dense hedges grows on earthen banks, enclosing fields and meadows and forming a sort of labyrinth.

The people living on the farms and hamlets scattered along the sunken roads have for a long time lived in relative isolation. Lastly, the different parts of the **coast** of Normandy also have distinctive characteristics.

OPEN COUNTRY

The **Pays de Caux** is a vast limestone plateau, stretching from Le Havre to Dieppe, covered with fertile silt, ending along the coast in cliffs famous for their hanging valleys *(valleuses)* and bordered to the south by the Seine valley. The area produces wheat and industrial crops such as flax, sugar beet and rape. Cattle here are raised for meat.

Bordered by the valleys of the Epte and the Andelle, the **Vexin normand** is covered by a particularly thick layer of alluvial soil which favours the intensive cultivation of wheat and sugar beet.

The **Plaine du Neubourg** and the **Évreux-St-André** district present a flat landscape of open fields, similar to the area known as **Caen-Falaise**. The fertility of the soil in these areas favours large-scale arable farming coupled with cattle-breeding for the production of meat. Vegetables are grown around Caen.

The **Argentan-Sées-Alençon** country, north of the Sarthe valley and the Alpes Mancelles, is composed of small chalk regions where horses and cattle graze in the open orchards.

TRANSITIONAL REGIONS

The **Roumois** and **Lieuvin** plains, marked by hedges and apple orchards, are separated by the Risle Valley. The **Pays d'Ouche** is more densely forested, whereas the rolling hills of the **Perche normand**, a famous horse-breeding district, form a transition between the Paris basin and the Armorican Massif.

WOODLANDS

The Norman part of the **Pays de Bray** is a vast clay depression, known as the buttonhole, bordered by two limestone heights. It is stock-raising country and has increased its production of meat; it also specialises in fresh dairy produce such as yoghurts and *petits-suisses*.

The **Pays d'Auge**, which contains the river valleys of the Touques and the Dives, differs from the other regions in that the chalk strata have been deeply fissured by streams. High local humidity

Quaternary Era	Alluvial deposits
Tertiary Era	Sedimentary deposits
Secondary Era	Cretaceous limestone
	Jurassic limestone
Primary Era	Granite
	Metamorphic rocks

promotes the growth of grassland and hedges. Apples are turned into cider and Calvados, and milk into Camembert. Horse breeding is also a tradition near the coast and the Perche region.

The **Bessin**, with Bayeux as its capital, lies to the east of the Armorican Massif. Breeding of saddle-horses and trotters is a long tradition, while famed local dairy produce carries the name Isigny.

South of the Bessin is the **Bocage normand**, where meadows, sometimes planted with apple or pear trees, are enclosed by hedges. Dairy farming is still the main activity. In addition to the traditional Normandy cream and butter, farmers produce sterilised milk with a long shelf life and which needs no refrigeration (UHT milk) and a great variety of low-fat dairy produce.

The remote peninsula of **Cotentin**, which lies between the Vire estuary and Mont-St-Michel bay, is part of the Armorican massif. The peninsula itself is divided from the Bocage normand by a sedimentary depression, which is flooded at certain times of the year; there are three distinct areas within the peninsula: the Cotentin Pass, the Val de Saire and Cap de la Hague.

The region is still largely devoted to stock raising except along the coast where vegetables are grown, as they are in nearby Brittany.

THE COAST

The coast of Normandy from the River Bresle west to the River Couesnon is as varied as its hinterland. Erosion by the sea has transferred material from rocky projections and deposited it in sheltered coves. The sea has brought shingle (stones) to the bays and ports of the Pays de Caux and mud to the Seine estuary; it has silted in more than one port (Lillebonne was a sea port in Gallo-Roman times).

The Pays de Caux meets the sea in what is known as the **Côte d'Albâtre** (Alabaster Coast), a line of high limestone cliffs, like the White Cliffs of Dover, penetrated by shingle-bottomed (stony) inlets. The sea beating at the foot of the cliffs has eroded the cliff face, forming hanging valleys where streams once flowed.

The **Côte Fleurie** offers miles of fine sand beaches where the sea may withdraw more than a mile at low tide; it also enjoys a high level of sunshine. The Calvados coast is composed of the low Bessin cliffs, interspersed with sand dunes and salt marshes (Caen area).

To the west are the sand or sand and shingle (stony) beaches of the bracing **Côte de Nacre** (Mother-of-Pearl Coast). The Cotentin peninsula resembles Cornwall and Brittany with its rocky inlets, although sand dunes and beaches stretch along the coast where the continental rock base does not reach the shore. Mont-St-Michel bay is known for its vast sands and mud flats from which the sea seems to withdraw completely at times.

The **lighthouses** along the Normandy coast, which guide navigators in the Channel, also make good vantage points. The Norman engineer **Augustin Fresnel** (1788–1827) replaced the conventional parabolic reflector with compound lenses, which led to great progress in the length of beam projected out to sea. At night, in the more difficult sectors, several lighthouses can be seen at once, each with its own peculiarities: fixed, revolving or intermittent beam.

HORSES: THE PRIDE OF NORMANDY

More than 70 percent of all French thoroughbreds and trotters are bred in Basse-Normandie as well as the most powerful draught horses (Percherons) and some of the best carriage-horses (cobs).

Thoroughbreds are the fastest and the most refined horses, but their racing career does not exceed three years. The sale of yearlings at the end of August in Deauville attracts international racing stable owners. The sale of brood mares and foals is held in late November.

French trotters were developed from Normandy mares and Norfolk-roadster trotters.

French saddle-horses, a term which first appeared in 1958, encompasses almost all French competition horses, particularly for show jumping.

Whether chestnut or bay, the **Norman cob** is strong, compact, likeable, full of energy and has a pleasant way of trotting. Cobs can work in the fields or be harnessed to a carriage.

Percherons, dappled grey or black, are the most sought-after heavy draught horses in the world; the race was developed from cobs and Arabs, some say as far back as the Crusades.

Finally, one can not ignore the **Cotentin donkey**, recognised by the national stud in 1997, which has a soft grey coat, with a cross of St Andrew on its back. These gentle beasts now carry tourists on treks across the Cotentin.

NATIONAL STUD FARMS

As one of the oldest French institutions – the first was founded by Colbert in 1665 – the system of 23 national stud farms works in close collaboration with the Institut National de la Recherche Agronomique to improve breeding techniques. The system also supervises all equestrian activities, horse racing and betting in France.

Normandy has the two of the most beautiful and remarkable stud farms in France: the early 18C Le Pin stud farm is virtually a monument to the horse; while the St-Lô stud farm provides 20 percent of France's production.

Paddleboarding and kayaking at high tide, Mont St-Michel

The region surrounding Rouen is remarkable for being crisscrossed by one of the most beautiful rivers in the world: the Seine. Its meanderings water the land, making for green, lush scenery with that gentle charm typical of the Norman landscape. The inhabitants love this countryside as much as they do their beautiful city of Rouen, and they enjoy life here to the hilt. So whether you love the outdoor life, the arts, sports or architecture, you will find your stay here fulfilling – and convivial.

Highlights

1   A visit to **Notre-Dame Cathedral** in Rouen (p87)
2   A visit to the **Rouen Musée des Beaux-Art** (p93)
3   A drive along the **Boucle de Roumare** (p100)
4   Exploration of **Jumièges abbey** (p110)
5   A bicycle ride in **Brotonne forest** (p112)

The Seine

This river is an integral part of the Rouen landscape. Dividing the Norman capital into two distinct banks, it is also a material link between a great many towns and villages in the surrounding region. Lovely, multifaceted, the Seine offers delight to pleasure-craft enthusiasts and nature-lovers alike. Its economic and industrial impact cannot be overlooked, however; for centuries it has marked the region's history and relief, its quays, towpaths and ports providing tangible proof of its importance for the inhabitants of Rouen and its region.

A place in history

The history of Rouen and its region cannot be evoked without Jeanne d'Arc. She is everywhere here, from the vestiges of the Philippe-Auguste's castle where she was imprisoned and judged, to the museum devoted to her life, a few steps from the square where she was burned alive on 30 May 1431. Yet Rouen is this and much more. From when the Vikings first sailed up the Seine to the brilliance of the city's golden age in 16C to 18C, from its period of economic and social crisis in the early 19C to its phenomenal industrial rise, from emerging from the destruction of World War II to the modern Rouen assuming leadership for its region, the city remains a stage on which history plays and leaves its trace.

Abbaye St-Wandrille

© Bertrand Rieger/hemis.fr

Forêt de Brotonne

© Michael Busselle/age fotostock

Remarkable architecture

Rouen owes its fame in great part to the wealth of its architectural heritage, museums and monuments where culture is often combined with a remarkable setting, from St Wandrille abbey to Elbeuf's circus-theatre. Over 200 sites await you, not only religious and civil buildings, but museums, sites related to Impressionist history, and the lively streets and squares of Elbeuf, Louviers, Caudebec-en-Caux and, of course, Rouen.

The cradle of Impressionism and Post-Impressionism

It was Rouen architecture that became a major element in the history of art. It was here that from 1892–1893 Monet painted the series of 30 paintings of Rouen Cathedral, seen in different lights and from three different viewpoints. His work enthused and influenced celebrated artists such as Renoir, Cézanne, Pissaro and Degas, launching an entire art movement that would change the way both artists and art-lovers see the world around them. In a word: Impressionism.

But it did not stop there. While the Impressionist movement was taking the rest of the world by storm, Rouen went on to become the cradle of the post-Impressionist movement, known today as the Rouen School, including artists such as Lebourg, Fréchon, Delattre or Pinchon, who expressed their deep attachment to their native land by capturing the changing, misty quality of the landscapes on the Seine's banks. Many of the masterpieces that left their trace on art history can be seen today in the fabulous collection at Rouen's Musée de Beaux Arts, while modern ones are in the making here.

Verdant landscapes and outdoor life

Throughout the year you can experience the quiet beauty of the Seine valley's many parks and gardens. The Parc Naturel Régional des Boucles de la Seine Normandie is a place of calm for nature-lovers, but also an outdoor education for families, with its numerous flora and fauna. There are a great many itineraries to take you on a voyage of discovery of the region's marshlands, coastal river, forests and meadows, while sports such as kayaking, canoeing, trekking, cycling and especially horse riding are appreciated and flourish here for visiting enthusiasts to enjoy.

Gourmet treats

Between gourmet pleasures and Rouen regional traditions, food-lovers will be delighted with what is to be found here.

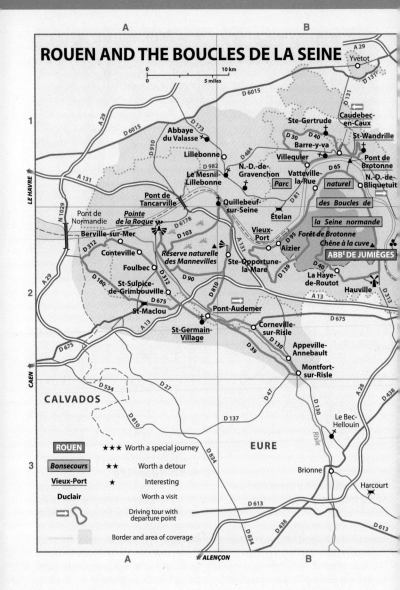

ROUEN AND THE BOUCLES DE LA SEINE

ROUEN	★★★ Worth a special journey
Bonsecours	★★ Worth a detour
Vieux-Port	★ Interesting
Duclair	Worth a visit
	Driving tour with departure point
	Border and area of coverage

The apple reigns, and from apple juice, to cider, from Calvados to pommeau and beer, Rouen and the Seine valley have a great many beverages of renown – and a few surprises in store as well. Yet chocolates, sweets and biscuits await you here too, made with the fresh Normandy cream and butter that makes them a unique taste experience.

Food is taken seriously here, but Norman conviviality has to be there too.

Therefore, visitors will enjoy not only the pleasure of dining in fine restaurants and charming bistros, and shopping for local products at open-air markets; they will also have the fun of gastronomic fairs like the October Fête du Ventre in Rouen.

Try Rouen specialities such as Larmes de Jeanne d'Arc, Cadran du Gros Horloge, Pavé du Vieux Marché, the 100 clochés, caramel apples or sable biscuits, but

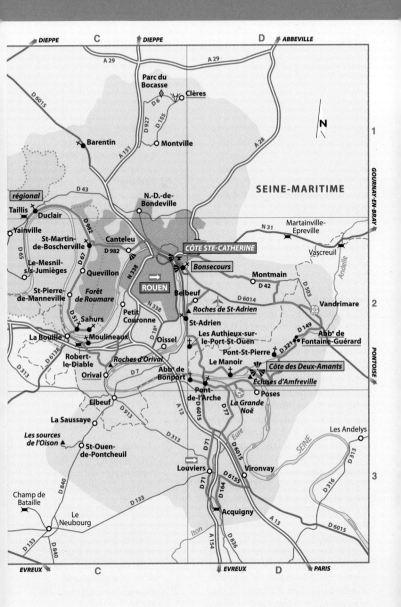

save room for dinner – something à la crème, of course!

Craftsmanship

Rouen is the biggest and most important centre for ceramics in France, its know-how having had considerable influence on French faïence. Production began here in the 16C with apothecary pots, but it was in the 17C that the famous blue decoration inspired by both Italian and Chinese patterns began to develop. At its high point, Rouen had as many as 22 ceramics works.

The history of Rouen and the Seine valley, however, is inextricably linked to that of cloth making, Norman drapers providing 60 percent of French production. In eastern Rouen, it is difficult to miss the close link between the city.

Rouen★★★

Rouen, capital of Upper Normandy, has undergone a remarkable campaign of restoration that has given new life to the old city's network of narrow, winding streets lined with magnificent half-timbered houses. In addition, Rouen is a city of first-rate museums – the Musée de Beaux-Arts alone is worth the trip – and possesses one of the most sumptuous Gothic cathedrals in France. Rouen sits in a lovely valley surrounded by high hills, from which there are extensive views over the city and the Seine.

A BIT OF HISTORY

Rollo the Forerunner – After the Treaty of St-Clair-sur-Epte in the year 911, Rollo, the Viking chief and first Duke of Normandy, was baptised at Rouen, the capital of the new duchy, and took the name Robert. He proved to be a far-sighted planner: he narrowed and deepened the river bed, built up unused marshlands, linked the downstream islands to the mainland and reinforced the banks with quays. His works lasted until the 19C, unrivalled for their efficiency.

Goddons – Rouen was hard hit during the Hundred Years' War: in 1418, Henry V of England besieged the town, which was starved into capitulation after six months. Revolts and plots followed against the Goddons – the nickname for the English derived from their common blasphemous phrase, "God damn". Hope was reborn by the exploits of Joan of Arc and the coronation of Charles VII, then Joan was taken prisoner at Compiègne by the Burgundians. The English threatened the Duke of Burgundy with economic sanctions and through the mediation of Pierre Cauchon, Bishop of Beauvais, Joan was handed over to the English. On Christmas Day 1430, she was imprisoned in the Tower of the Fields in the castle built in the 13C by Philippe Auguste. A strong military presence under Lord Warwick deterred any uprisings.

▶ **Population:** 110 117.
⌚ **Michelin Map:** 304: G-5.
🈶 **Info:** 25 pl.de la Cathédrale. ℘02 32 08 32 40. www.rouentourisme.com.
◗ **Location:** Some 130km/ 81mi NW of Paris, Rouen spreads out along both banks of the Seine.
🅿 **Parking:** Car parks are found on: place du Général-de-Gaulle (Hôtel de Ville), Square Verdrel, Palais, Vieux-Marché, La Pucelle, Charrettes, la Bourse (rue du Général-Leclerc), la Haute-Vielle-Tour, St-Marc, 39e RI and St-Vivien. There are free car parks on the lower quays of the left bank and at Boulingrin, near the train station.
☺ **Don't Miss:** The Gothic splendour of the cathedral and of the churches of St-Maclou and St-Ouen; the lovely half-timbered houses of Old Rouen; the Musée des Beaux-Arts.
🕐 **Timing:** Spend at least one day here: the morning exploring the old streets, reserving the afternoon for museums.
☺ A **Pass en Liberté** for €10 gives discounts in cinemas, hotels, B&Bs, bars, monuments, and much more. Purchase at tourist office, or online (*www. rouentourisme.com/pass-en-liberte*).
👫 **Kids:** Musée Flaubert; Musée d'Histoire de la Médecine; Musée Maritime, Fluvial and Portuaire.

Golden Century – The period between the French reconquest (1449) and the Wars of Religion (1562–98) was a golden century for Normandy and particularly

Joan of Arc

Trial of Joan of Arc – Bishop Cauchon promised a fair trial and opened the first session on 21 February 1431. An amazing dialogue began between Joan and her judges: the Maid replied to all the tricks and subtleties of the churchmen and lawyers. On 24 May, in the cemetery of the abbey of St-Ouen, tied to a scaffold, Joan was pressed to recant; she finally gave in, was granted her life but condemned to life imprisonment. The English were furious and threatened the judges. Cauchon replied, "We will get her yet." On Trinity Sunday the guards took away Joan's women's clothes which she had promised to wear, and gave her men's clothing instead. At noon "for the necessities of the body, she was constrained to go out and indulge in the said habit". She was thus said to have broken her promise and was condemned to the stake. On 30 May, she was burned alive in place du Vieux-Marché. In 1449, Charles VII entered Rouen; in 1456, Joan was rehabilitated and in 1920 she was canonised and made **Patron Saint of France**.

for the city of Rouen. Local dignitaries built sumptuous stone mansions and carved woodwork adorned the façade of burgesses' houses.

Rouen merchants in cooperation with Dieppe navigators traded along all the main maritime routes.

Industrial Upsurge – Industrialisation, launched by textile manufacturing, called for changes in the port: in the 19C docks were constructed, the railway was built; the old city on the right bank spread to the tributary valleys and hillsides.

Modern City – Industrial expansion accelerated at the beginning of the 20C. During World War II, the old districts close to the Seine and the industrial zone on the south bank were destroyed. On the right (N) bank, a series of arching boulevards define the city centre, its old residential districts and historic centre. On the left (S) bank are administrative offices, the Préfecture, modern residential and business districts, and the industrial zone.

Lacroix Island, formerly industrial, has become residential with parks and open spaces.

Port – *Bd Émile-Duchemin, Hangar 13 (on the road to Le Havre from the Pont Guillaume-le-Conquérant)* Rouen is France's fifth-busiest port after Marseilles, Le Havre, Dunkerque and Nantes-St-Nazaire, and the third-biggest river port. Its location between Paris and the sea is a great advantage.

Owing to improved maritime access, modernisation of port equipment and facilities, and the building of silos and new terminals, the growth of the port has been constant. It now stretches from Rouen to Tancarville on the right bank of the Seine and from Rouen to Honfleur on the left bank.

CATHÉDRALE NOTRE-DAME★★★

Allow 1h30. ♿ 🕐*Mon 2–7pm, Tue–Sat 9am–7pm, Sun and public holidays 8am–6pm.* 🕐*1 Jan, 1 May, 8 May, 11 Nov; during Nov–Mar the cathedral is closed noon–2pm and at 6pm.* 👝*No charge.* 𝄞*02 35 71 85 65. www. cathedrale-rouen.net.* ☏*Guided tours (Reservations* 𝄞*02 35 71 51 23;* 👝*€2;) including the baptistry, the Chapel of the Virgin and the crypt, Sat–Sun at 2.30pm (daily during school holidays).*

The cathedral of Rouen is one of the most beautiful examples of French Gothic architecture. Construction began in the 12C, but after a devastating fire in 1200, the building was reconstructed in the 13C. The cathedral took on its final appearance in the 15C under the master builder Guillaume Pontifs and in the 16C under Roulland le Roux. In the 19C it was crowned with the present cast-iron spire. Badly damaged during World War II, the cathedral is open but the enormous restoration work started over 50 years ago continues.

The attraction of Rouen Cathedral lies in its infinite variety, including an immense façade bristling with pinnacles and framed by two totally different towers: the Tour St-Romain on the left and the Tour de Beurre on the right.

West front

This imposing façade was used in a series of paintings by Monet to study the effects of lighting at different times of the day on the same subject. Dating from the 12C, the **Portail St-Jean** *(left)* and the **Portail St-Étienne** *(right)* doorways each have a delicately carved semicircular arch crowned by a small colonnade. The two tympana are 13C. The lattice-work window gallery (1370–1420) above the two portals is in the Flamboyant style; the niches decorated with statues and topped by openwork gables are 14C and 15C.

The **central doorway** (early 16C) is flanked by two powerful pyramid buttresses decorated with statues of the Prophets and Apostles. The tympanum is decorated with a Tree of Jesse, destroyed by the Huguenots and restored in 1626.

The **Tour St-Romain**, to the left, is the oldest tower (12C), and in the Early Gothic style. The sumptuous **Tour de Beurre** (Butter Tower) was thus named in the 17C when it was believed that it had been paid for by dispensations granted to those did not fast during Lent. It never received a spire but was surmounted by an octagonal crown. Inside is a carillon of 56 bells.

South side – The **central lantern tower** with its spire is the tallest in France (151m) and the glory of Rouen. It was started in the 13C and was raised in the 16C. The present spire, in cast iron, replaced in 1876 the wooden spire covered in gilded lead, which dated from 1544. The **Portail de la Calende** (Calende doorway), which opens between two 13C square towers, is a 14C masterpiece.

North side – On skirting the **Cour d'Albane** (Albane Court), closed to the east by the cloister gallery, one can see the north side, the lantern tower and spire and the upper section of the Booksellers' transept.

A little further on the **Cour des Libraires** (Booksellers' Court) is closed by a magnificent stone gateway in the Flamboyant style. At the end of the court is the **Portail des Libraires** (Booksellers' Doorway) (*see Introduction: Religious architecture, p62*), which opens on to the north side aisle.

The tympanum (late-13C) features a Last Judgement depicted in terrifying detail.

Interior

Nave – In the early Gothic style, the nave is made up of 11 bays four storeys high. Dominating the transept crossing is the **lantern tower** rising with incredible boldness 51m on enormous piles which sweep upwards.

CATHÉDRALE NOTRE-DAME

Chapelle de la Vierge

Archbishop's Palace

Ambulatory

CHANCEL

Portail de la Calende

Cour des Libraires

TRANSEPT

NAVE

Cour d'Albane

Tour St-Romain

R. Georges Lanfry

Portail St-Jean

Central Doorway

Portail St-Étienne

Tour de Beurre

West front, Cathédrale Notre-Dame

Transept – In the north arm is the famous Escalier de la Librairie (Booksellers' Stairway); from a charming little balcony rise the two flights of the staircase (the first is 15C, the second 18C).

Chancel – The choir of finest 13C style is the most noble part of the cathedral on account of its simple lines and the lightness of its construction. The high altar is made of a marble slab from the Valle d'Aosta, and dominated by a Christ in gilded lead (18C). Opening off the south arm is the apsidal chapel dedicated to Joan of Arc and embellished with modern stained-glass windows by Max Ingrand.

Crypt, Ambulatory, Lady Chapel – The 11C ring-shaped crypt preserves its altar and its curb stone well (5m deep). The heart of Charles V is preserved in a coffer embedded in the east end wall.

The ambulatory *(access south arm – exit north)*, which is made up of three apsidal chapels, holds the recumbent figures of Rollo, Richard Lionheart (late 13C), Henry (second son of Henry II of England) the Young King (13C), and William Longsword, Duke of Normandy and son of Rollo (14C). Also shown are five 13C **stained-glass windows★**, the bottom one of which, depicting St Julian the Hospitaller, was presented by the Fishmongers' Guild and inspired Flaubert to write a tale.

The Lady Chapel (14C) contains two admirable 16C tombs. To the right, the **tomb of the Cardinals of Amboise★★** of the Early Renaissance (1515–25) was carved after drawings by Roulland le Roux. The two cardinals – Georges d'Amboise *(left)*, minister under Louis XII and Archbishop of Rouen, and his nephew, also Georges *(right)* – are shown kneeling.

On the left, stuck on the recess of the Gothic tomb of Pierre de Brézé (15C) is the **tomb of Louis de Brézé★**, Seneschal of Normandy and husband of Diane de Poitiers, who became the mistress of Henri II after her husband's death. It was built between 1535 and 1544.

The chapel houses 14C stained-glass windows representing the Archbishop of Rouen and a fine picture by Philippe de Champaigne, *The Adoration of the Shepherds*, framed in a 1643 altarpiece.

🐾 WALKING TOURS

OLD ROUEN★★★
Allow about 30min.

▷ Depart from place de la Cathédrale.

Place de la Cathédrale

Opposite the cathedral on the corner of rue du Petit-Salut stands the former **Bureau des Finances** (House of the Exchequer – tourist office), an elegant Renaissance building (1510).

▶ Turn right to enter Rue Saint-Romain.

Rue Saint-Romain★★

One of Rouen's most fascinating streets with its beautiful 15C–18C half-timbered houses and at the end the spire of the Église St-Maclou. Note No. 74, a Gothic house with 15C bay windows.

Archevêché

Next to the Booksellers' Court stands the 15C Archbishop's palace (altered in the 18C). A gable pierced by the remains of a window is all that is left of the chapel where the trial of Joan of Arc ended on 29 May 1431, and where her rehabilitation was proclaimed in 1456. Cross rue de la République to reach **place Barthélemy** bordered with picturesque half-timbered houses where St Maclou's Church stands.

▶ Cross Rue de la République.

Église St-Maclou★★

🕐 Apr–Oct Mon, Sat–Sun 10am–noon, 2–6pm; Nov–Mar 5.30pm;
🕐 1 Jan, 25 Dec. www.rouen.fr/eglise-saint-maclou.

This beautiful church of Gothic-Flamboyant style, built between 1437 and 1517, is remarkable for its homogeneity, despite being finished during the heyday of the Renaissance. Only the spire of the belfry is modern.

The west façade, the finest part of this building, is preceded by a large five-panelled porch set like a fan. Two of the three doorways, the central one and that on the left, are celebrated for their Renaissance **panels★★**.

These panels are divided into two parts: the leaf of the door has charming little bronze heads of lions and other animals and designs in semi-relief of pagan inspiration, whereas the upper panel, which is a little heavy, has a carved medallion.

The medallions on the central door represent the Circumcision on the left and the Baptism of Christ on the right; the upper part of the door represents on the left God the Father before the Creation; on the right, God the Father after the Creation.

The Font Door on the left has only one panel. The medallion represents the Good Shepherd entering the pasture after he has expelled the thieves.

Inside, the **organ case★** (1521) has remarkable Renaissance woodwork. The **spiral stairs★** (1517), magnificently carved, are from the choir screen.

▶ Continue ESE into Rue Martainville.

Rue Martainville★

The street has kept some marvellous 15C–18C half-timbered houses. On the northwest corner of St Maclou's Church is a lovely Renaissance fountain.

Aître St-Maclou★★

184–186 r. Martainville.

This 16C ensemble is one of the last examples of a medieval plague cemetery. The half-timbered buildings which surround the yard were built from 1526 to 1533; the south side was built in 1640 and never served as a charnel house.

The ground floor of these buildings is made up of galleries which were once open – as in a cloister. On the column shafts (formerly door frames) are carved figures (damaged) portraying the Dance of Death.

Above the ground floor, the attic was used as a charnel house until the 18C. These buildings now house the School of Fine Arts (École des Beaux-Arts).

▶ Return to the west end of St-Maclou and turn right.

Rue Damiette★

The street is lined by half-timbered houses and offers a nice vista of the central tower of St Ouen's church. Note on the right the picturesque blind alley of the Hauts-Mariages.

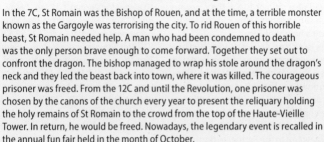

St Romain and the Gargoyle

In the 7C, St Romain was the Bishop of Rouen, and at the time, a terrible monster known as the Gargoyle was terrorising the city. To rid Rouen of this horrible beast, St Romain needed help. A man who had been condemned to death was the only person brave enough to come forward. Together they set out to confront the dragon. The bishop managed to wrap his stole around the dragon's neck and they led the beast back into town, where it was killed. The courageous prisoner was freed. From the 12C and until the Revolution, one prisoner was chosen by the canons of the church every year to present the reliquary holding the holy remains of St Romain to the crowd from the top of the Haute-Vieille Tower. In return, he would be freed. Nowadays, the legendary event is recalled in the annual fun fair held in the month of October.

In place du Lieutenant-Aubert bear left onto rue d'Amiens to the 17C **Hôtel d'Étancourt** and admire its façade embellished with large statues.

▶ Return to place du Lieutenant-Aubert; left onto rue des Boucheries-St-Ouen and right onto rue Eau-de-Robec.

Rue Eau-de-Robec

In this street, lined with old houses boasting recently restored timber framing, flows a little stream, spanned by a series of footbridges. Several of these tall buildings have workshop-attics, where drapers would leave their skeins of cotton and sheets of fabric out to dry.

Musée national de l'Éducation★

185 r. Eau-de-Robec.
&. ⊙Mon and Wed–Fri 1.30–6.15pm, Sat–Sun 10am–12.15pm, 1.30–6.15pm. ⊙1 May, 15 Aug, 1 Nov, 25 and 31 Dec. ⊛No charge. ℘02 35 07 66 61. www.reseau-canope.fr/musee.

The National Museum of Education is housed in a handsome 15C residence known as the **Maison des Quatre Fils Aymon★**. It was once a notorious trysting spot referred to as the House of Marriages on account of the many casual encounters that took place there.

The museum evokes school life from the 16C up to the present day. A 19C classroom has been reconstituted.

On the corner of rue du Ruissel, note the **Pavillon des Vertus**, a fine 16C mansion decorated with statues of women symbolising the cardinal virtues.

▶ Return to rue des Boucheries-St-Ouen and turn right to Rue des Faulx and then into pl. du Gén-de-Gaulle.

Abbatiale Saint-Ouen★★

⊙Apr–Oct Tue–Sun 10am–noon, 2–6pm; Nov–Mar Tue–Sun 10am–noon, 2–5pm. ⊙1 Jan, 25 Dec. ℘02 32 08 32 40. www.rouen.fr/abbatiale-saint-ouen.

Remarkable for its proportions and the purity of its lines, this former abbey church is one of the jewels of High Gothic architecture. The construction, which began in 1318 and slackened during the Hundred Years War, was completed in the 16C.

Exterior – On the south side is the beautiful door named after the wax candle merchants (ciriers) who held their market here. The **east end★★** is beautiful, with flying buttresses and pinnacles and individually roofed radiating chapels. At the transept crossing, the square **central tower★**, flanked by small towers, rises two tiers before ending in a ducal coronet.

The **Porche des Marmousets**, which occupies the lower level, is unusual: its arching leans to one side and appears to end in mid-air, resting not on colonnades but on two false keystones.

Interior – The **nave** (&see illustration in INTRODUCTION, p63), of a light construction, demonstrates elegance and harmonious proportions. Such perfection could be explained by the golden mean, which in this particular case would be a ratio of 1 to 3: the piers are each separated by 11m and the vaults reach a height of 33m.

This slender structure is further enhanced by the warm, radiant light that filters through the large **stained-glass windows★★**. The oldest ones date from before 1339 and are still embedded in the chapels surrounding the chancel. The 16C clerestory windows in the nave are devoted to the Patriarch (north) and to the Apostles (south). The two 15C rose windows in the transept arms illustrate the Celestial Court (north) and a Tree of Jesse (south). The modern Crucifixion adorning the axial bay is by Max Ingrand (1960). The big rosette to the west is the work of Guy le Chevalier (1992).

The chancel is closed off by gilded **grilles★★** (1747) by Nicolas Flambart.

▶ From pl. du Gén-de-Gaulle locate and follow rue de l'Hôpital.

At the corner of rue des Carmes stands the attractive Gothic Crosse fountain (restored), and further on at the corner of rue Beauvoisine and rue Ganterie is a handsome half-timbered house.

▶ Turn right onto rue Beauvoisine, which crosses rue Jean Lecanuet, one of Rouen's most commercial streets.

In rue Beauvoisine note **No. 55**, a carved half-timbered house with courtyard: **No. 57** is a Renaissance house.

▶ Turn left onto rue Belfroy, bordered at the beginning by 15C–16C half-timbered houses, to reach place St-Godard and Rue Jacques-Villain.

Église Saint-Godard★

This late-15C church contains wonderful **stained-glass windows★**, in particular a 16C one on the right side showing the Tree of Jesse. The window of the Virgin, is made up of six 16C panels.

▶ Follow rue Jacques-Villon.

Musée Le Secq des Tournelles★★

🕑*Wed–Mon 2–6pm.* 🕑*1 Jan, 1 May, 1 and 11 Nov, 25 Dec.* ✆*No charge for the permanent collections.* 📞*02 35 88 42 92. https://museeelesecqdestournelles.fr.*

The Wrought Ironwork Museum is housed in old Église St-Laurent, a fine Flamboyant building, and is exceptionally rich (3C–20C).

The nave and transept contain large items, such as balconies, signs, railings, etc., and in the display cabinets, locks, door knockers and keys. Note their evolution from Gallo-Roman times.

The north aisle includes displays of locks, belts and buckles (15–19C).

The south aisle exhibits a large variety of domestic utensils and tools.

The north gallery on the first floor is devoted to accessories such as jewels, clasps, combs and smoking requisites.

A rare 16C–19C collection of professional tools is housed in the south gallery.

▶ Turn back, cross place Restout and head along the edge of square Verdrel to the corner with rue Faucon.

Musée de la Céramique★★

1 r. Faucon or 94 r. Jeanne-d'Arc. 🕑*Daily except Tue 2–6pm.* 🕑*Public holidays.* ✆*No charge for permanent collections.* 📞*02 35 07 31 74. https://museedelaceramique.fr.*

The 17C Hôtel d'Hocqueville houses the Ceramics Museum, which presents a collection of 16C to 18C Rouen faïence. The work of Masséot Abaquesne, Rouen's first faïence maker, who plied his trade around 1550, is represented by paving flags and portrait vases.

After a lull, production resumed with Louis Poterat (1644–1725), whose workshop produced dishes and tiles enhanced with a blue and white décor. The colour red made its first appearance around 1670.

Faïence was to enjoy a surge of popularity in the early 18C. Decors featuring five colours (starch or yellow ochre ground) appeared. In the room devoted to polychrome decoration, note the **celestial globe** by Pierre Chapelle,

Catherine Lancien et Carole Loisel/Musée des Beaux-Arts de Rouen

Detail, View of Rouen *(1892) by Claude Monet, Musée des Beaux-Arts de Rouen*

a masterpiece of faïence making. After 1721, motifs became more varied. Subsequently, around the mid-18C, the Rococo style came into fashion, embellished with varied floral motifs.

▶ Walk around square Verdrel until you get to rue Jean-Lecanuet.

Musée des Beaux-Arts★★★

espl. Marcel-Duchamp.
&.⏰*Daily 10am–6pm.* ⏰*1 Jan, 1 May, 1 and 11 Nov, 25 Dec.* ✆*No charge for permanent collections.*
✆*02 35 71 28 40. https://mbarouen.fr.*
The 19C Museum of Fine Arts, restored between 1989 and 1994, has recovered its original harmonious proportions and gained modern exhibition areas.

15C–17C Painting – One of the most striking canvases is an oil painting on wood, *The Virgin among the Virgins*, by Gérard David (c. 1460–1523), one of the masterpieces of Flemish Primitive painting. Besides the Italian Primitives, you can admire works by François Clouet (*The Bath of Diana*), Lavinia Fontana (*Venus and Cupid*) and Paolo Caliari *(St Barnabus Healing the Sick)* and Michelangelo Merisi da Caravaggio (*The Flagellation of Christ*). Spanish masters include Velásquez and Ribera; Dutch art is represented by Martin de Vos, Van de Velde, N Berchem and Pieter Aertsen *(The Adoration of the Shepherds).* French painters also include Louis de Boullogne *(Cerès :*

Allégorie du mois d'Août), Poussin (*Venus Presenting Arms to Aeneas*), François de Troy, Simon Vouet and Jouvenet.

18C Painting – The rooms dedicated to 18th century art contain paintings by Fragonard *(The Washerwomen)*, Boucher and Hubert Robert, together with sculptures and objets d'art.

19C Painting – This section is the highlight of the museum, in terms of both its size and the high standard of its collection. The museum is the home of France's biggest Impressionist collection outside Paris. Europe's main artistic movements are represented – neo-Classicism, Impressionism or Symbolism – as well as great masters: Ingres, Monet, David, Géricault, Degas, Caillebotte, Corot, Chassériau, Millet, Moreau, Sisley, Renoir and many others. In the Salle du Jubé (Rood Screen Room), Romanticism is represented by five sculptures by Pierre-Jean David d'Angers along with *Justice of Trajan* by Delacroix and *Les Énervés de Jumièges*, a hyper-realist painting by Vital-Luminais.

20C Painting – More recent painters' works exhibited include Modigliani, the Duchamps brothers, Dubuffet, Nemours and others.

▶ On leaving take allée Eugène-Delacroix, then rue Ganterie on the left.

Rue Ganterie★ is a charming street lined with old half-timbered houses.

ROUEN

```
0          100 m
0          100 yds
```

WHERE TO STAY

Auberge de jeunesse.....................③
Bertelière (Hôtel La).....................⑤
Bonaparte (Hôtel le).....................②
Camp du Drap d'or (Hôtel du)...........⑦
Cardinal (Hôtel le).....................④
Cathédrale (Hôtel de la).....................⑧
Dandy (Hôtel).....................⑩
Dieppe (Hôtel de).....................⑫
Vieux Carré (Hôtel le).....................⑱

WHERE TO EAT

Bistrot du Siècle (Le).....................⑥
Couronne (La).....................⑩
Écaille (L').....................⑫
Gill.....................⑭
Maraîchers (Les).....................⑯
Marmite (La).....................⑳
O Boeuf.....................④
Pascaline.....................㉒
P'tits Parapluies (Les).....................㉓
Réverbère (Le).....................㉕
Tavola (La).....................㉗
37 (Le).....................㉙

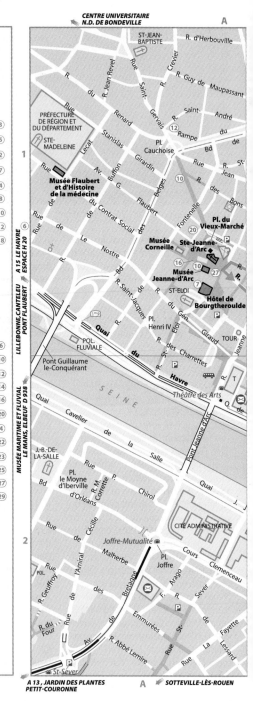

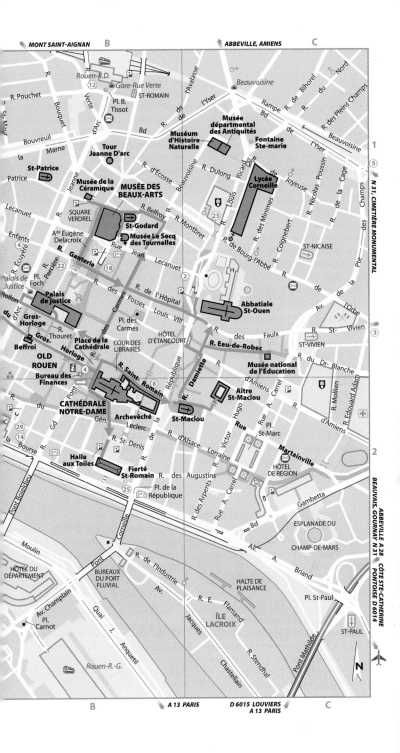

In the other direction, towards place Cauchois, this street is **rue des Bons-Enfants**, where several 15C houses still stand; on No. 22, notice the sculpted figures.

Take rue des Carmes to the right, then turn right again on rue aux Juifs, which runs alongside the Palais de Justice.

Palais de Justice★★

This splendid 15C and early 16C Renaissance building was built to house the Exchequer of Normandy (law courts). Renovated in the 19C, it was badly damaged in August 1944.

The **main court** is flanked by two wings, the **façade**★★ (1508–26) of which is exquisite.

The decoration of the façade, is typical of the Renaissance: the base is quite plain but the ornamentation increases on each floor so that the roof line is a forest of chiselled stone with pinnacles, turrets, gables and flying buttresses.

The left-wing stone staircase leads to the **Salle des Procureurs** (Prosecutors' Room). This large room has a splendid modern panelled ceiling.

Place du Vieux-Marché★

In the Middle Ages the square was the scene of public mockery and executions. On the north, the foundations of the pilleries have been excavated, and on the South, an outline marks the tribune from where the judges of **Joan of Arc** watched her execution.

A cross has been erected at the spot where she was burned at the stake on 30 May 1431.

Église Ste-Jeanne-d'Arc – *pl. du Vieux-Marché*. Completed in 1979, the church is shaped like an upturned ship. Inside are 13 panels of superb **Renaissance stained glass**★★ (16C) from St Vincent's Church, which was destroyed in 1944. This unique ensemble depicts the Childhood of Christ, the Passion, the Crucifixion, the Resurrection, and the lives of St Anne, St Peter and St Anthony of Padua in a variety of rich colours.

Rue du Gros-Horloge★★

Connecting place du Vieux-Marché to the cathedral is the abbreviated rue du Gros-Horloge, a busy commercial street during the Middle Ages and the seat of local government from the 13C to the 18C. With its large cobblestones and attractive 15C–17C half-timbered houses, rue du Gros-Horloge is nowadays one of the city centre's major tourist attractions.

Gros-Horloge – ◷*Apr–Oct Tue–Sun 10am–1pm, 2–7pm; Nov–Mar Tue–Sun 2–6pm;* ◷*1 Jan, 25 Dec;* ◉*€7;.* ℘*02 32 08 01 90; www.rouen.fr/gros-horloge*. The most popular monument in Rouen. The clock, formerly placed in the belfry, was moved to its present location in 1527 when the arch was specially constructed to receive it. In addition to the single hand which gives the hours, there is the central section telling the phases of the moon and the lower inset indicating the weeks.

The small tower is topped by a dome added in the 18C to replace the one removed by Charles VI in 1382 to punish the citizens of Rouen, who had organised a tax revolt, known as La Harelle. Within there is a spiral staircase (1457). Inside are the two bells (13C) which gave the signal for the Harelle uprising: on the right the Rouvel (not operated since 1903); on the left, the Cache-Ribaud, which sounds the curfew every night at 9pm. From the top of the belfry there is a majestic **vista**★★ of the city, its port and the surrounding countryside.

Next to the belfry is the Renaissance loggia, where the Great Clock keeper used to stand, as well as a beautiful 18C fountain.

On the corner of rue du Gros-Horloge and rue Thouret stands the old town hall (1607).

Rue du Gros-Horloge leads back to place de la Cathédrale.

After this long walk around town, you will want to relax in one of the outdoor cafés set up around the square.

▷ From place de la Calende, cross Rue du Général Leclerc into rue de l'Épicerie which leads to the Fierté St-Romain and the Halle aux Toiles.

Fierté St-Romain

This charming Renaissance building is crowned by a stone lantern that used to contain the relics of St Romanus.
The building adjoins the **Halle aux Toiles** (Linen Hall), with exhibit, conference and banquet rooms.

OTHER SIGHTS

Hôtel de Bourgtheroulde

15 pl. de la Pucelle, behind the place du Vieux-Marché. This magnificent building is now home to a 4-star hotel.
This flamboyant 16C mansion (pro-nounced Boortrood), inspired both by Gothic and early Renaissance styles, was built by Guillaume le Roux, Lord Bourgtheroulde. Stand back a little to look at the façade and then enter the inner court.
The end building is pure Flamboyant, with a hexagonal staircase tower. The left gallery is entirely Renaissance with six wide basket-handle arches. It is surrounded by friezes: the upper one, disfigured, shows the Triumphs of Petrarch, the lower, the famous meeting of Henry VIII and François II on the Field of the Cloth of Gold (1520).

Maison natale Pierre Corneille

4 r. de la Pie.
🕐*Jul–Aug Wed–Sun 1.30–5.30pm; Sept–Jun Tue–Fri 1.30–5.30pm, Sat 9am–noon, 1.30–5.30pm, Sun 2–6pm.*
🕐*1 Jan, 1 May, 1 and 11 Nov, 25 Dec.*
🖉*02 76 08 80 88. www.rouen.fr/corneille.*
The French playwright **Pierre Corneille** (1606–84) was born and lived here for 56 years. Considered the father of French Classical tragedy he wrote, among others, *Mélite* (1629; first performed in Rouen), *Le Cid*, *Horace* and *Cinna*.

🏛♿ Musée Flaubert et d'Histoire de la Médecine

51 r. de Lecat.
🕐*Tue 10am–6pm, Wed–Sat 2–6pm.*
🕐*Public holidays.* ✍€4.
🖉*02 35 15 59 95.*
www.chu-rouen.fr/le-chu/culture-et-patrimoine/le-musee-flaubert.
The Hôtel-Dieu (17C–18C) has a Classical façade. This museum devoted to the history of medicine is set in the home where **Gustave Flaubert** (1821–80) was born. His father worked as a surgeon. Souvenirs of Flaubert are on display.

Musée des Antiquités de la Seine-Maritime★★

198 r. Beauvoisine or rue Louis Ricard.
♿🕐*Tue–Sat 1.30–5.30pm, Sun 2–6pm.*
🕐*1 Jan, 1 May, 1 and 11 Nov and 25 Dec.* ✍*No charge for permanent collections.* 🖉*02 35 98 55 10.*
www.museedesantiquites.fr.
A 17C convent houses this museum which displays objects from prehistory to the 19C. From the Middle Ages and the Renaissance are items including stunning religious gold and silver plate (12C Valasse Cross), 12C–13C **enamels★**, 5C–16C **ivories★** (a 14C seated Virgin) as well as a collection of arms and Moorish and Italian majolica. In a long gallery are Gothic and Renaissance **carved façades★** from half-timbered houses in old Rouen. A separate gallery contains the 15C **Winged Deer tapestry★★** and Renaissance furnishings.
The **Gallo-Roman collection★**, famed for its bronzes and glassware, includes the **Lillebonne mosaic★★** (4C, restored 19C), the largest signed and illuminated Roman mosaic in France.
Near the museum gardens stands the large **Fontaine Ste-Marie** by Falguière.

Église St-Patrice

Corner r. St-Patrice and r. de l'Abbé-Cochet. This Gothic church is remarkable for its **stained-glass windows★** made between 1538 and 1625. The windows on the north side of the chancel depict the Triumph of Christ; in the adjoining chapels are St Faron, St Fiacre, St Louis and St Eustache, and an Annunciation

Rouen Faïence

The word ceramics covers all aspects of terracotta (baked clay), whereas faïence is a type of ceramic made of compound clay covered with a tin-based enamel. White in colour, faïence can be decorated. Two types of earth went into the making of Rouen faïence: St-Aubin (from the Boos Plateau), clayey and bright red, and earth from Quatre-Mares (between Sotteville and St-Étienne-du-Rouvray), a light, sandy alluvial soil. Mixed in the right proportions, the result was ground, washed, dried, powdered, sifted and placed in decantation containers. When sufficiently consistent, the mixture was placed near an oven to finish the evaporation process, and then trodden to extract fermentation gases. Sand was then added to form a ceramic compound. Finally there were the different processes of shaping, casting, glazing, painting and curing.

in Italian Renaissance style as well as a Nativity scene. In the north aisle are the stories of St Barbara and St Patrick and Job. An 18C gilt baldaquin crowns the altar.

Le Donjon de Rouen – Tour Jeanne-d'Arc

r. de Bouvreuil.
🕐*May–Jun Tue–Sun 2–4pm.* 🕐*1 Jan, 1 May, 1 and 11 Nov, 25 Dec.* ☎*02 32 08 32 40. www.donjonderouen.com.*
This is the former keep in Philippe Auguste's 13C castle, where Joan was tortured on 9 May 1431. The second floor is devoted to the life of Joan of Arc.

Église St-Romain

r. de la Rouchefoucauld.
The former 17C Carmelite chapel, restored in the 19C and again in 1969, contains Renaissance **stained glass**.

Muséum d'Histoire naturelle

198 r. Beauvoisine.
♿🕐*Tue–Sat 1.30–5.30pm, Sun 2–6pm* 🕐*1 Jan, 1 May, 1 and 11 Nov, 25 Dec.* 🎫*No charge for permanent collections.* ☎ *02 35 71 41 50.*
https://museumderouen.fr
In a 17C former convent, this museum, containing over 400 000 objects, is half-way between a cabinet of curiosities and a futuristic laboratory! Ornithology, ethnography, botany: the collections show-case the history of science (notice especially the dioramas). Nevertheless, the collections are turned to the future; it is

difficult to visit without thinking about biodiversity, respect for the ecosystem and management of natural resources. Close to the museum gardens and over-looking rue Louis-Ricard, the monumental Ste-Marie fountain (C1), sculpted by Falguière, hides a water tower. The lycée Corneille, a school a step away (rue Joyeuse), is in a former Jesuit school (17C–18C) frequented by Corneille and Cavelier de La Salle. Corot, Flaubert, Maupassant, Maurois studied there and the philosopher Alain taught there.

👥 Musée maritime, fluvial et portuaire

Quai E.-Duchemin, Hangar No. 13.
♿🕐*Tue–Sun and public holidays 2–6pm.* 🎫*€5 (child 6–18, €3).*
🕐*1 Jan, 1 Mar, 24–25 and 31 Dec.* ☎*02 32 10 15 51.*
www1.musee-maritime-rouen.asso.fr.
Special documentation makes this maritime, river and port museum very accessible to children.
In an old hangar in Rouen's port, this museum presents the history of the city's river activity, with photos and informative panels as support. It addresses first all professions tied to the sector.
Both voters and mechanics are exhibited as well as models, with a look back at certain legendary ships such as La Combattante. Temporary exhibitions and conferences.

Right bank quay

There is an esplanade on the right bank quays from the Croisière terminal to pont Corneille (B2), going by the quai du Havre (A2) and the quai de la Bourse (B2). A path gives access on foot, bicycle or skates to the old hangars are stored in the 19C.

In Hangar 2, **Espace H2O** (*quai de Bois-Guilbert, Espace des Marégraphes; ○ Mar–Aug Mon–Fri 9am–6.30pm, Sat–Sun 2.30–6.30pm; Sept–Feb Mon–Fri 9am–5.30pm, Sat–Sun 2.30–5.30pm; ⊜€3; ℘02 35 52 95 29; www.metropole-rouen-normandie.fr*) is dedicated to eco-sciences and sustainable development.

Pont Gustave-Flaubert

Constructed upstream of the five current bridges, the Gustave Flaubert is a transporter bridge and the sixth to cross the Seine. The designers include Michel Virlogeux, who designed the Normandy bridge and Millau viaduct. Inaugurated in 2008 at the time of the Armada, the Flaubert bridge is the longest of its type in Europe (670m). Its horizontal deck raises in 12 minutes, to allow passage of cruise ships and yachts returning periodically to Rouen for the Armada.

EXCURSIONS

Jardin des Plantes★

114 av. des Martyrs-de-la-Résistance. 2.5km/1.5mi.
&. ○ *Daily from 8am until Mar–Apr and Sept–Oct 6.45pm; May–Aug 8.15pm; Nov–Feb 5.30pm.* ⊜ *No charge.* ℘02 32 18 21 30.
www.rouen.fr/jardindesplantes.
This beautiful 10ha park, originally designed in the 17C, contains around 3 000 plant species inside the conservatories and **tropical hothouses** and a further 5 000 out in the open air. A star attractions is the **Victoria Regia**, a giant water lily from the Amazon, whose large, flat leaves can reach a diameter of 1m in summer. Its flowers bloom, change colour and die the same day.

Centre Universitaire

5km/3mi. Leave Rouen by rue Chasselièvre NW.
From the road, which ends on the Mont-aux-Malades plateau where the university lies, there is a good **panorama★★** of the city, the port and the curve in the river.

Cimetière monumental

2 km/1.2mi northwest of centre. Leave from place Beauvoisine (C1) and reach place du Boulingrain by bd de l'Yser. Take avenue Georges-Métayer on left by the Saint-Hilaire exit.
The "Père Lachaise" of Rouen, this monumental cemetery is worth going out of your way for, with various architectural styles for the tombs of well-known figures dear to Rouen inhabitants: Gustave Flaubert (1821–1880), François-Adrien Boieldieu (1775–1834), the city's mayors and politicians and major industrialists. Superb panoramic view of Rouen.

Manoir Pierre-Corneille

In Petit-Couronne, 8km/5mi.
From Rouen take avenue de Bretagne, on the map; turn right by the first houses of Petit-Couronne onto rue Pierre-Corneille.
&. ○ *Apr–Sept Wed–Sat 10am–12.30pm, 2–6pm, Sun 2–6pm; Oct–Mar Wed–Sat 10am–12.30pm, 2–5.30pm, Sun 2–5.30pm.* ○ *1 Jan, 1 May, 1 and 11 Nov, 25 Dec.* ⊜ *No charge for permanent collections.* ℘02 35 68 13 89.
www.museepierrecorneille.fr.
The Norman "house in the fields" was bought in 1608 by the poet's father, who died in 1639, leaving it to Corneille. The museum evokes the writer's family life with 17C furniture.

Musée industriel de la Corderie Vallois

8km/5mi NW. Leave Rouen by quai Gaston-Boulet and proceed towards Dieppe; follow N 27 until you reach Notre-Dame-de-Bondeville.
&. ○ *Daily 1.30–6pm.* ○ *1 Jan, 1 May, 1 and 11 Nov, 25 Dec.* ℘02 35 74 35 35.
www.corderievallois.fr.

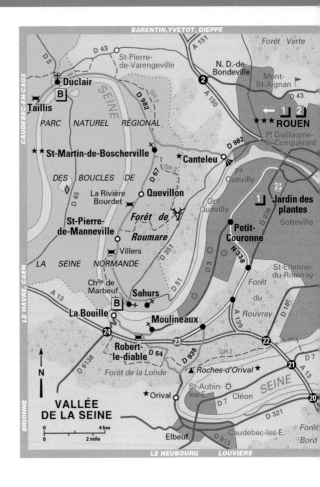

This old factory has retained 19C rope-making machinery in working order. A huge paddle wheel drives the whole complex mechanism.

Forêt Verte
23km/14.3mi.
The road passes through the forest, a favourite spot with the Rouennais.

Barentin
17km/10.5mi NW. Leave Rouen by A 15 or N 15.
Entering Barentin from Mesnil-Roux you see a 13.5 polystyrene Statue of Liberty, made for a film. The town boasts works by Rodin, Janniot, Bourdelle and Gromaire. On place de la Libération is a 17C fountain by Coustou.

The brick railway viaduct, 505m long, which carries the Paris–Le Havre railway line across the Austreberthe Valley, stands in Barentin. The 19C **church** has modern windows depicting the lives of St Martin, St Helier and St Austreberthe.

DRIVING TOURS

① LA BOUCLE DE ROUMARE
Itinerary on map above. 50 km/31mi. 4h30.

Motorway south from Pont Guillaume le Conquerant, then N 138 for Caen, Orival exit by D 938. Before reaching Orival take D 64 (NW) for La

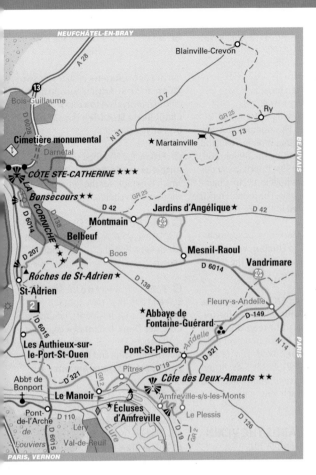

Bouille. Turn right immediately after going under autoroute bridge.

The tour begins with the ruined **Château de Robert-le-Diable** (*only wallwalk open*), which was Robert-the-Devil's 11C Seine fortress.

▷ From the château, take the D 64 to the junction with the D 3, and there turn east to **Moulineaux**, which has a 13C church with attractive **stainedglass windows**★.

▷ From Moulineaux backtrack a short distance and take the D64 to **La Bouille**, Hector Malot's pretty birthplace. From here you can take a small car ferry (*Bac De La Bouille; http://bacsdeseine.over-blog.com*) across the Seine to **Sahurs**, where you catch sight of the 16C Marbeauf chapel (○━ *closed to public*).

Nearby are the **Fôret de Roumare - Parc animalier** (*26ha. Brochure at tourist offices*) and **Eglise de Sahurs**, which enjoys a pretty view.

▷ Take the D 51/D 67 north along the Seine to **St-Pierre de Manneville** and the grand residence and park of **Manoir de Villers** (*www.manoirdevillers.com*). In **Quevillon** is the sumptuous 17C château de la Rivière-Bourdet (○━ *closed to public*).

Further along the D 67 is **St-Martin-de-Boscherville**★★. The **Abbaye St-Georges**★★ (①*Apr–Oct 9am–6.30pm; Nov and Mar 2–5pm.* ①*1 Jan, 1 May, 1* and 11 Nov. €6; 02 35 32 10 82; www. abbayesaintgeorges.fr) was founded by William of Tancarville in 1144 and built where a collegiate church once stood. Concerts are often organised here (ask at the tourist office for details).

The chapter house dates from the 12C, surmounted by a 17C structure. The conventual outbuilding, built in 1690 and partly demolished by the Revolution, was restored in 1994; the chapelle des Chambellans was built in 13C for Chambellans of Tancarville. The formal French **park** was restored in the 17C style.

Leaving St-Martin-de-Boscherville, take the D 982 to **Duclair**, where two trekking paths leave from the tourist office (227 av. du Prés.-Coty).

Duclair also has a 12C–15C church, the **Église Saint-Denis**, as well as the formal English-style **Château du Taillis park** (Interior by arrangement only; Park and museum: Wed–Sun 10am–noon, 2–5pm; 02 35 37 95 46; http://chateaudutaillis.com/programme) and a good World War II museum (€5).

2 TOWARDS THE VEXIN

Itinerary on map pp100–101. 110km/34mi, 4h30.

From place St-Paul in Rouen (C2), take r. Henri-Rivière, then r. du Mont-Gargan; right on r. Annie-de-Pène.

The winding road of the **Côte Ste-Catherine★★★** has a **panoramic view** of the river, Rouen and its surrounding area. Follow the D 95 and then the D 914 to get to **Bonsecours★★** and its neo-Gothic basilica (1840), which has magnificent **panoramic views★★**, as does the cemetery.

Head towards Mesnil-Esnard on D 6014; continue 3km/1mi, then turn right on D7 to park right in front of the 18C château of **Belbeuf**. Belbeuf's pretty church is worth a look while you are here.

Leaving Belbeuf, follow the D 7 then D 6015 to St Adrien.

Roches de St-Adrien★ includes the two **Côteau de St-Adrien** walking routes (info at tourist office) to a rocky spur. The **Chapelle de St-Adrien** is a 13C partly troglodytic chapel.

Follow the N15 then signs to **Les Authieux-sur-le-Port-St-Ouen**, which is notable for the Renaissance window of its church.

From here, take the D13, D 6015, D 321, then D508 to get to **Le Manoir**, which has a fine glass-brick modern church.

From Le Manoir take the D508, D20 and D19, then turn right for Amfreville-sous-les-Monts, where the **Côte des Deux-Amants★★** coastal road begins. There is a magnificent view of the Seine and Eure; the **panorama des Deux-Amants★★**.

Return via Le Plessis and Amfreville-sous-les-Monts to get to the locks, dam and fishery with observation room at the **Ecluses d'Amfreville★** and the musée de la Batellerie (Apr–Sept Tue–Sat 2–6pm. €4).

Follow the D20 initiallty south, then the D508 north to **Pont-St-Pierre** and its 11C–12C church with **sculpted wood★**.

At the 12C **Abbaye de Fontaine-Guérad★** (Sun only May and Sept 2–6pm; Jul–Aug daily except Mon 2–6.30pm; 06 86 08 04 67; www. abbayefontaineguerard.fr) there is an interesting chapter room and dormitory.

Follow D149 and D505 to **Vandrimare**, which has a chateau, park and gardens (mid-Apr–mid-Oct Sat–Mon and public holidays 2.30–7pm; 02 32 49 03 57), then take the D6014 and follow signs to Le Mesnil-Raoul.

Finally, the tour ends further along the D42, en-route to see over 2 000 varieties of rose on display in the gardens at **Montmain.**

Jardins d'Angélique (🕐 *May–Jun 11am–7pm; Jul–mid-Oct Wed–Mon 11am–7pm;* ☞*€7;* ℘*02 35 79 08 12*).

ADDRESSES

🛏 STAY

🛏 **Youth Hostel** – *Le Robec, 3 r. du Tour, route de Darnétal.* ℘*02 35 08 18 50. 108 beds.* In old Auvray dyers installations, typically 18C architecture. At Robec River, home, charming, simple, functional rooms.

🛏🛏 **Hôtel Le Cardinal** – *1 pl. de la Cathédrale.* ℘*02 35 70 24 42. www.cardinal-hotel.fr. 15 rooms.* Near Notre Dame Cathedral, family hotel with distinctive red façade; moderate-sized rooms, modern furnishings. Summer breakfasts on terrace.

🛏🛏 **Hôtel Le Vieux Carré** – *34 r. Ganterie.* ℘*02 35 71 67 70. www.hotel-vieux-carre. com. 13 rooms.* Charming, half-timbered property (1715), modern rooms.

🛏🛏 **Hôtel Bonaparte**– *3 r. Jean-Lecanuet.* ℘*02 35 07 77 07. 33 rooms.* Practical, on boulevard near hôtel de ville. Functional rooms, efficient soundproofing.

🛏🛏–🛏🛏🛏 **Hôtel de la Cathédrale** – *12 r. St-Romain.* ℘*02 35 71 57 95. www. hotel-de-la-cathedrale.fr. 26 rooms.* Beautiful 17C building in a pretty, pedestrian street near cathedral. Rooms comfy, atmosphere delightful. Lovely patio.

🛏🛏🛏 **Hôtel La Bertelière** – *1641 av. Mesnil-Grémichon, 76160 Saint-Martin-du-Vivier.* ℘*02 35 60 44 00. www.laberteliere. com. 44 rooms. Restaurant* 🍽🍽–🍽🍽🍽. Comfy rooms on Rouen heights, wide salons open on gardens. 10 min from downtown Rouen, near A 28. Nice welcome, rooms with access for disabled.

🛏🛏🛏 **Hôtel Dandy** – *93 bis. r. Cauchoise.* ℘*02 35 07 32 00. www.hotels-rouen.net. 18 rooms.* Near Place du Vieux-Marché; tearoom, charming bar. Rooms refined, pretty breakfast room.

🛏🛏🛏 **Hôtel de Dieppe** – *pl. Bernard Tissot (opposite train station).* ℘*02 35 71 96 00. https://hotel-dieppe.fr. 41 rooms.* Run by the same family since 1880. Neat rooms each with own décor. Rouen duck (Canard à la Rouennaise) is restaurant (🍽🍽🍽) speciality.

🛏🛏🛏 **Hôtel de Bourgtheroulde** – *5 pl. de la Pucelle.* ℘*02 35 14 50 50. www. hotelsparouen.com. 78 rooms and suites.* Pleasant, contemporary rooms. Spacious, light. Marble bathrooms, steam bath, sauna, brasserie, upscale restaurant l'Aumale.

🍽 EAT

🍽 **O Boeuf** – *91 r. Ecuyères.* ℘*02 35 15 97 02. Closed Sun–Mon.* A traditional address serving traditional dishes.

🍽 **Pascaline** – *5 r. de la Poterne.* ℘*02 35 89 67 44. www.pascaline.fr. Reservations advised.* Nice restaurant with bistro façade. Brasserie décor, handsome wood counters, long seats, yellow walls. Good fixed-price menus. Book ahead – often full.

🍽🍽 **Le Bistrot d'Adrian - Les Maraîchers** – *37 pl. du Vieux-Marché.* ℘*02 35 71 57 73. www.les-maraichers.fr.* Parisian style in half-timbered house. Improvised cuisine. Norman-style second dining room on ground floor.

🍽🍽 **La Marmite** – *3 r.de Florence.* ℘*02 35 71 75 55. www.lamarmiterouen. com.* Near place du Vieux-Marché. Delicately flavoured traditional cuisine, fresh products, attentively prepared.

🍽🍽 **La Tavola** – *11 pl. du Vieux-Marché.* ℘*02 35 71 46 29.* Also known as 'Le Table de Jeanne' this eclectic restaurant offers Mediterranean dishes as well as traditional French and Normandy creations.

🍽🍽 **Le Bistrot du Siècle** – *75 r. Louis Bourdon, 76480 Duclair (20km/12.4mi NW).* ℘*02 35 37 62 36. Closed Sun and Mon.* Little bistro with fine local reputation. Convivial two dining rooms: one with old poster, other on veranda. Flame-grilled meats, a few dishes from Reunion Island.

🍽🍽 **Le 37** – *37 r. St-Étienne-des-Tonneliers.* ℘*02 35 70 56 65. www.le37.fr. Closed Sun–Mon, and public holidays.* Trendy bistro, casual. Up-to-date cuisine, daily specials.

🍽🍽🍽 **Les P'tits Parapluies** – *46, rue Bourg l'Abbé, pl. Rougemare.* ℘*02 35 88 55 26. www.lesptits-parapluies.com. Closed Sat lunch, Sun dinner, Mon.* 16C former umbrella factory (hence the name). Pleasant, modern, yet with period beams.

⊖⊜🍽 **Reverbère** – *5 pl. de la République.* *℘02 35 07 03 14. https://le-reverbere-rouen.fr. Closed Sat lunch, all day Sun.* A discreet glass front on small square, near river. Modern dining room, small, low-key lounge, wooden staircase to a rustic lounge.

⊖⊜🍽 **L'écaille** – *26 rampe Cauchoise.* *℘02 35 70 95 52.* Seafaring restaurant with blue-green décor, modern paintings, up-to-date fish dishes.

⊖⊜ **La Couronne** – *31 pl. du Vieux-Marché.* *℘02 35 71 40 90. www.lacouronne.com.fr.* Superbly preserved, 1345 home is France's oldest and most beautiful inn. Rustic setting, flower-decked terrace in summer.

⊖⊜🍽🍽 **Gill** – *9 quai de la Bourse.* *℘02 35 71 16 14. www.gill.fr. Closed Sun and Mon.* On the Seine, elegant, comfortable, simple dining room. Inventive cuisine, Normandy ingredients.

NIGHTLIFE

ROUEN

Famed as where Joan of Arc met her end, place du Vieux-Marché is today a lively nightspot; lots of bars and restaurants, many with terraces. Check *The Viking*, a free information brochure distributed locally.

Bar de la Crosse – *53 r. de l'Hôpital.* *℘02 35 70 16 68. Closed Sun, and public holidays.* This small bar has gained its popularity from the relaxed and friendly atmosphere you find here.

Taverne St-Amand – *11 r. St-Amand.* *℘02 35 88 51 34. www.tavernesaintamant.fr. Closed Sun–Mon.* Set up as a restaurant-bar for 32 years, this 17C house has welcomed painters, writers, actors and other artistic habitués.

PERFORMING ARTS

ROUEN

Théâtre de l'Écharde – *16 r. Flahaut.* *℘02 35 89 42 13. Tickets also sold at theatre before performance.* Theatre with 100 seats with shows for young theatre-goers.

Théâtre des Arts – *7 r. du Dr-Rambert, Vieux-Marché.* *℘02 35 98 74 78. www.operaderouen.fr.* A whole host of concerts, plays and operas shown.

Théâtre des Deux Rives – *48 r. Louis Ricard.* *℘02 35 70 22 82. www.cdn-normandierouen.fr.* Classical and modern theatre, with an emphasis on living playwrights.

SHOPPING

ROUEN

Faïencerie Augy-Carpentier – *26 r. St-Romain.* *℘02 35 88 77 47. www.fayencerie-augy.com. Closed Sun–Mon. Tour of the workshop by appointment.* The last hand-made and hand-decorated earthenware workshop in Rouen offers copies of many traditional motifs from blue monochrome to multicoloured

Chocolatier Auzou – *163 r. du Gros-Horloge.* *℘02 35 70 59 31. www.auzou-chocolat.fr.* Located in a half-timbered house, this renowned chocolatier will tempt you with *les Larmes de Jeanne d'Arc* (Joan of Arc's Tears: lightly roasted almonds covered with nougatine and chocolate) or *l'Agneau Rouennais* (a sort of sponge cake) and candied apples.

Maison Hardy – *22 pl. du Vieux-Marché.* *℘02 35 71 81 55. http://maisonhardy.fr. Closed Sun.* This delicatessen occupies a suberb half-timbered house on one of the liveliest squares in Rouen. Specialities include sheep's foot à la rouennaise, *andouilles* with hot peppers and Caen tripe cooked in Calvados and cider. In the afternoons, you can eat in the establishment's restaurant (*Open Mon–Sat lunch*).

ANTIQUES MARKET
Place St-Marc Sun 8am–1.30pm

TRADITIONAL MARKETS –
Place St-Marc– Tue and Fri–Sun.
Place des Emmurées – Tue, Thu and Sat.
Place du Vieux-Marché – Tue–Sun.

LEISURE

ROUEN

The tourist office distributes two useful brochures: *L'Agenda rouennais* (3-weekly) and the *Rouen magazine* (bi-monthly). **Audio-guided Tours** in 6 languages are available, along with **horse-and-carriage tours**, **group tours** and **little train tours** through the city.

CULTURAL EVENTS

ROUEN

Evening light shows – *℘02 32 08 32 40 (Rouen tourist office). Open early Jun–late Sept from about 10pm.* A dozen cathedral pictures inspired by Monet are projected onto the façade of Rouen Cathedral, creating strange forms and colours.

Clères★

One of Normandy's greatest attractions is the animal park at the château of Clères. The original castle, now in ruins, was built in the 11C. The present château consists of a 19C western wing in the neo-Gothic style, and an eastern wing dating from the 15C, which was remodelled towards 1505. In the market square stands the wooden structure and slate roof of an 18C covered market.

SIGHT

♿🐾 Parc Zoologique de Clères-Jean-Delacour★

♿🐾🕐*Daily: Mar and Oct 10am–noon 1.30–6.30pm; Apr–Aug 10am–7pm; Sept 10am–6.30pm; Nov 1.30–5.30pm.* ⊕*€9 (child 3–16, €6.50). ✆02 35 33 23 08. www.parcdecleres.net.* 🕐*The best time to visit is before the end of Jun.*

In an exceptional natural setting, the park of Clères provides a wonderful opportunity to see the birds and mammals collected by the botanist and ornithologist **Jean Delacour** (1890–1985). In the garden are pink flamingos, ducks and exotic geese. Antelope, kangaroos, gibbons, cranes, peacocks and deer roam in partial liberty. Indoor

Parc Zoologique de Clères-Jean-Delacour

© Thomas Pozzo Di Borgo/Dreamstime.com

▶ **Population:** 1 366.

🧭 **Michelin Map:** 304: G-4.

📋 **Info:** 59 av. du Parc. ✆02 35 33 38 64. www.normandie-caux-vexin.com.

▶ **Location:** Clères is 30km/18.5mi N of Rouen, following A 150, A 151 and D 6, or about 50km/31mi S of Dieppe by N 27 and D 6.

👁 **Don't Miss:** The rare birds in the aviary at Clères.

🕐 **Timing:** Give yourself a good 2 hours to tour the zoo.

👨‍👧 **Kids:** After the Clères zoo, visit the amusement park at Bocasse.

and outdoor aviaries are reserved for lesser-known birds, some endangered species: around 2 000 birds.

EXCURSIONS

👨‍👧 Parc du Bocasse

2km/1mi W by D 6. ♿✕🕐*Jul–Aug 10am–7pm; Apr–Jun and Sept–Oct Sat–Sun 10.30am–6pm and at holiday periods: see website for details.* ⊕*€20.50 (child under 12, €17.50). www.parcdubocasse.fr.*

With numerous attractions including mini golf and head-spinning fairgound rides, this place will keep children (and adults accompanying them) amused for hours. You can bring a picnic.

Montville

6km/4mi S on the D 155.

The **Musée des Sapeurs-Pompiers de France** 👨‍👧 (♿🕐*Apr–Oct Mon–Sat 9am–12.30pm, 2–6pm, Sun 2–6pm; Nov–Mar Mon–Sat 9am–12.30pm, 2–5pm, Sun 2–5pm.* 🕐*1 Jan, 1 May, 1 and 11 Nov, 24–31 Dec.* ⊕*€4.50 (child 3–14, €1.80); ✆02 35 33 13 51; www.musee-sapeurs-pompiers.org)* has a fine collection of red fire engines, banners and uniforms, tall ladders and gleaming helmets. The museum retraces the glorious history of the French fire brigades.

Louviers★

Badly damaged in 1940, Louviers has been carefully reconstructed, sparing the remaining old houses and delightful avenues along the River Eure. The old town north of Notre-Dame church has pretty half-timbered houses, such as in rue Tatin, rue du Quai and rue Pierre Mendès-France. Louviers remains an industrial centre, especially in the north of the town.

▶ **Population:** 18 538.
⬥ **Michelin Map:** 304: H-6.
▫ **Info:** 10 rue du Maréchal-Foch. ☎02 32 40 04 41. www.tourisme-seine-eure.com.
◖ **Location:** Louviers is 32km/20mi S of Rouen and 103km/64mi NW of Paris via A 13.
◉ **Don't Miss:** The Flamboyant Notre-Dame church and Acquigny park.
◷ **Timing:** You will need 1hr30min to see the town.

👣 WALKING TOUR

◖ From the Notre-Dame church in the town centre, take rue de la Poste and the rue des Penitents, which cross both branches of the Eure river.

Ancien couvent des Pénitents

All that remains of this Franciscan convent, built in 1646 on a tributary of the Eure, is the inhabited main building together with three small arcaded galleries belonging to the cloister. The western gallery is in a ruinous state and overlooks a square with lawn and trees. **Rue de la Trinité** (on the left) leads into the former manufacturing district and circles north and east to **rue Terneaux**, where the buildings have large attics once used for drying dyed fabrics.

◖ From rue Terneux, turn right into rue Polhomet, then right again on rue du Quai. Pretty half-timbered houses line the street. Rue au Coq, on the left, leads to the museum; rue Pierre-Mendès-France takes you back to the east end of Notre Dame Church.

Musée municipal

♿◷Wed–Mon 2–6pm. 🚫No charge. ☎02 32 09 58 55. http://musee.ville-louviers.fr/le-musee. The museum hosts temporary exhibitions of contemporary art, history, archaeology and heritage, alternating with fine displays of faience, painting and photography. One room is devoted to the clothing industry.

Maison du Fou du Roy

10 r. du Maréchal-Foch.
This half-timbered house in the main street is also the tourist office. It once belonged to Guillaume Marchand, an apothecary, who became Henri IV's jester (Fou du Roy) after the previous incumbant was killed in battle.

Normandy's Literary Ghosts

Many of Normandy's towns, villages, manor houses, coastal and rural scenes were described often under a fictional name by one of the region's celebrated writers.
Cabourg – the Balbec in Marcel Proust's À la recherche du temps perdu.
Ry – the Yonville-l'Abbaye of Gustave Flaubert's Madame Bovary (1857).
Le Havre – Guy de Maupassant's Pierre et Jean (1888).
Inland from Yport – Maupassant's Une Vie (1883).
The Cotentin – Barbey d'Aurevilly's (the Walter Scott of the region) Le Chevalier des Touches, Une vieille maîtresse and L'Ensorcelée.

Église Notre-Dame

© Marek Slusarczyk/Fotolia.com

Église Notre-Dame

Built in the 13C, this church received its famous Flamboyant exterior in the late 15C. Outside, the **porch**★ is stone lacework, but it is especially the south side that shows great Gothic virtuosity. Several interesting **artworks**★ inside.

🚗 DRIVING TOUR

🚗 BETWEEN THE SEINE AND THE EURE

3km/32mi. Allow 2h.

▷ Leave Louviers south on D 71, then left on D 82 to Acquigny.

Acquigny French Gardens

♿🕐*Apr–Oct Sat–Sun and public holidays 2–6pm (mid-Jul–Aug daily 1–7pm).* ☞€8. ✆*02 32 50 23 31. http://chateau-acquigny.fr.*
The formal **French gardens**, lying at the confluence of the River Eure and River Iton, still have long avenues and orangery. Waterfalls, artificial streams and recall the Romantic period.

▷ Cross the Eure to reach the D 164. From the bridge over the river, preview of the late 16C château. Take the D 164 north, then turn right onto the D 6155. At Heudebouville, head northwest to Vironvay on the D 6015.

Vironvay

The **view**★ on approaching extends over the river spanned by the bridge at St-Pierre-du-Vauvray and, further east, the ruins of Château-Gaillard.

▷ Take the D 6015 and later branch right onto the D77 (north). At Le Vaudreuil stay on the D 77 continuing north. Before Les Damps, follow the sign on the right indicating "Base de loisirs de Léry-Poses".

🧍‍♂️🧍 Réserve ornithologique de la Grande Noë

Chaussée de l'Andelle, 27100 Val-de-Reuil. ✆*06 07 27 97 89. http://grande-noe.gonm.org.*
Guided tours of the ornithological reserve in summer; a great many species of migrating birds make a stop here, taking advantage of the wide diversity of environments for refuge.

▷ Return towards Les Damps and take minor road to Pont-de-l'Arche.

Pont-de-l'Arche

On the south bank of the Seine.
The small town, named after the first bridge to be built over the lower Seine, is pleasantly set in a valley. On the south side is Bord forest.
The **Église Notre-Dame-des-Arts** exhibits the Flamboyant Gothic style in the doorway and the ornate south side.

Elbeuf

Elbeuf was once a major cloth-making centre, but the 15C industry begun here declined; today there is manufacturing of chemicals, electrical goods, machinery, metallurgy and automobiles.

▶ **Population:** 16 503.

Michelin Map: 304: G-6.

Info: 28 rue Augustin Henry. ℘02 35 77 03 78. http://tourisme-elbeuf. pagesperso-orange.fr.

Location: Elbeuf is 22.4km/ 14 mi S. of Rouen or 16km/10mi SE of Louviers.

Don't Miss: The old cloth-making neighbourhoods; a River Oison excursion.

Timing: Attractions are more likely to be open in afternoons.

❦ WALKING TOUR

OLD TOWN

Allow 1h.

All that is Viking about Elbeuf now is its name – the Scandinavian suffixes *bo* or *bou* gave *beuf* (from *budh*: "temporary shelter"). The itinerary therefore concentrates more on the town's cloth-making past.

▷ Take rue Augustin Henry.

Église St-Jean-Baptiste

Gothic church, Classical ornamentation and furnishings, 16C stained glass. The oldest and best preserved is in the 1st, 3rd, 4th and 5th north aisle windows and the first south aisle window.

Across from the church, **place St-Jean** and the Puchot district are at the heart of the old town.

▷ Turn left on rue Guyemer.

At **No. 72** rue Guyemer, the large 18C building was the **manufactory of Grandin de L'Epervier.** At **No. 63** was the **Godet manufactory**; an 18C workshop and a old mill (19C) surround the courtyard remains. Note the ostentatious roof on the Maison 1740 in the same street.

▷ Straight along rue Jean-Poulain, first right (r. de Marché) to reach place de la République.

From **place de la République** note the old 19C smokestack; the **Clarenson factory** replaced the Petou manufactory before closing in 1961. The beautiful 18C structure is best seen from the back.

▷ Continue along rue des Echelettes and turn into rue aux Bœufs. Cross rue Boucher-de-Perthes. Go through the gardens to St-Étienne church.

Église St-Étienne

16C stained glass. St Roch is in the south aisle chapel, and a panel shows drapers in work clothes. Carved Louis XV-style rood beam, 13C recumbent Christ; St Stephen and St John flank the chancel.

▷ Continue E along r. de la République. Right into rue Jean-Poulain, left along r. Camille Randoing. Briefly turn right into r. Théodore Chenneviere, then left to continue along r. Camille Randoing to reach cours Gambetta.

Musée intercommunal d'Elbeuf A2

♿ Tue–Sun, 2–6pm. ℘02 32 96 30 40. www.musees-haute-normandie.fr. Housed in the former **Blin & Blin textile factories**, the Seine links the three collections of Elbeuf's natural history, archaeology and industrial heritage.

▷ Continue N on r. du Neubourg and r. Jean Jaurès.

Circus-Theatre B1

2 rue Augustin Henry. ℘02 32 13 10 50. www.cirquetheatre-elbeuf.com.

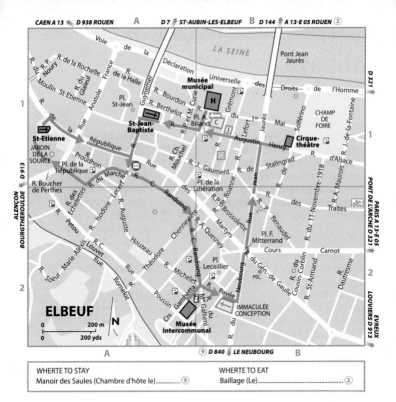

LA SEINE

Pont Jean
Jaurès

Voie de la
Déclaration
Universelle des Droits de l'Homme

D 321

Musée
municipal

H

St-Jean-
Baptiste

St-Etienne

JARDIN
DE LA
SOURCE

Pl. de la
République

République

Pl. de la
Libération

CHAMP
DE
FOIRE

Cirque-
théâtre

ELBEUF

0   200 m
0   200 yds

N

Musée
intercommunal

IMMACULÉE
CONCEPTION

ALENÇON
BOURGTHÉROULDE   D 913

PARIS A 13-E 05
PONT DE L'ARCHE D 321

EVREUX
LOUVIERS D 913

A | ⑨ D 840 ⬆ LE NEUBOURG | B

Restored octagonal building, a remaining examples of 19C circus architecture.

▶ Return by r. Augustin Henry to get to place Aristide Briand.

EXCURSIONS

Saint-Ouen-de-Pontcheuil

8km/5mi S via D 840. Moulin Amour.
♿⏱*Early Apr–mid-Oct Sun and public holidays 2.30–6.30pm.* ⊗€4. ℘*02 35 77 54 44. www.moulinamour.com.*
The **Moulin Amour**, the last official water mill along the River Oison's banks, operates only in demonstrations.

Les Roches d'Orival ★

⏱*See HONFLEUR, p184.*

Château de Robert le Diable★

The castle overlooks the Seine valley. Robert the Devil is vaguely based on Robert the Magnificent, William the Conqueror's father.
Destroyed in 1204, Philippe Auguste rebuilt it before the French again

destroyed it in the 15C to prevent it from falling to the English.

ADDRESSES

🛏 STAY

⊝⊜🏠🏠 **Le Manoir des Saules** – *2 pl. St-Martin, 27370 Saussaye.* ℘*02 35 87 25 65. www.manoirdessaules.com. Closed Mon and Tue.* ♿*. 6 rooms. Restaurant* ⊝⊜🏠🏠*.* Charming welcome in authentic Norman manor with garden. Half-timbering, turrets; beautiful furniture in rooms. Unique dining rooms.

🍴 EAT

⊝🍽 **Le Baillage** – *62 route Pont-de-l'Arche, 76410 Freneuse.* ℘*02 35 87 57 37. www.lebailliage.com. Open 10am until 6pm on Tue, Wed and Sun, and 10pm on Thu–Sat. Closed Mon.* Beautiful, bourgeois house. Traditional cuisine, fish specialities.

⊝🍽🏠 **La Pomme** – *44 r. Eure, 72340 Les Damps, Pont de l'Arche,* ℘*02 35 23 00 46. www.laubergedelapomme.com. Open for lunch and dinner. Closed Sun–Mon.* A pretty Norman cottage on the banks of the Eure.

Abbaye de Jumièges★★★

Jumièges is one of the most impressive ruins in France, occupying a splendid site on the Lower Seine. The history, galleries, south aisle, the nave roof, the transept crossing, the chancel apse and the roofless cloisters are described below.

- ⚓ **Michelin Map:** 304: E-5.
- **Info:** Rue Guillaume-le-Conquérant. ☎02 35 37 28 97. www.abbayede jumieges.fr.
- 🕐 *Daily mid-Apr–mid-Sept 9.30am–6.30pm; mid-Sept –mid-Apr 9.30am–1pm, 2.30–5.30pm.* 🕐*1 Jan, 1 May, 1 and 11 Nov, 25 Dec.*
- ▶ **Location:** Jumièges is located on a graceful meander of the Seine, between the villages of Duclair and Trait, 28km/17.4mi W of Rouen.
- 🦌 **Don't Miss:** Not far from Jumièges, in Mesnils sous Jumièges (*5km/3mi SE*) sits the 13C manor where the lovely and astute Agnès Sorel, mistress of Charles VII, died in 1450.
- 🕐 **Timing:** You may wish to spend time admiring the view and strolling near the Seine.
- 🐾 **Advice:** Jumièges is a ruin and exposed to the elements: dress for the weather.

A BIT OF HISTORY

Jumièges Almshouse – In the 10C Duke William Longsword rebuilt Jumièges on the ruins of the 7C abbey destroyed by the Vikings. The new Benedictine abbey soon became known as the Jumièges Almshouse as well as a centre of learning. The abbey church was consecrated in 1067 in the presence of William the Conqueror.

The last monks dispersed at the Revolution, and in 1793 the abbey was bought by a timber merchant who intended to turn it into a stone quarry and used explosives to bring down the church lantern. A new proprietor in 1852 set about saving the ruins, which now belong to the nation. Many consider these to be the most beautiful ande evocative ruins in France.

THE ABBEY★★★
Église Notre-Dame
The projecting porch is flanked by twin towers (43m high), whose spires were visible until 1830.

The entire nave (27m high) still stands, together with part of the transept and the chancel. At the west end there is a deep gallery overlooking the nave, which is articulated by strong square pillars, quartered by columns, alternating with more slender clusters of columns; the aisles are covered by rib vaulting. Most of the transept was demolished in the 19C.

Only the west side of the lantern has survived, resting on an arch which is impressive for its height and reach. A slim, pepper-pot turret is attached to the NW corner.

Passage Charles-VII – The passage leading to St Peter's Church was named for the visit of King Charles VII (1403–1461) to Jumièges.

Église St-Pierre – The porch and first bays of the nave are Norman Carolingian (oculi and twinned arcades) the remaining ruins date from the 13C and 14C. The arched entrance porch is flanked by two small doors with stairs to the gallery towers behind. The first two bays of the nave are a rare example of 10C Norman architecture.

Chapter house – Between the abbey and St Peter's, the 12C chapter house opens off the cloisters. The square body and apse were covered with some of the earliest ogival vaulting known to have existed.

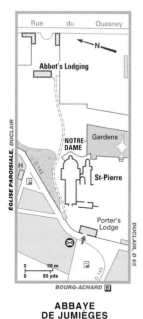

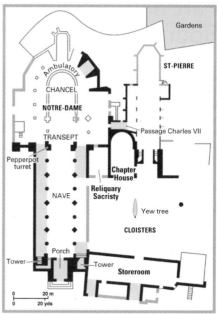

**ABBAYE
DE JUMIÈGES**

Cloisters – In the middle of the cloisters grows an ancient yew tree. The four galleries once consisted of 26 bays. The refectory was on the south side.

Storeroom – The great cellar dates to the late 12C.

Gardens – Beyond a fence, a 17C set of steps leads to a broad terrace and the gardens.

Abbot's Lodging – Beyond the lawn rises the former abbot's lodging, a majestic 17C rectangular building.

Église paroissiale St-Valentin

The parish church, which dominates the village, has an 11C–12C nave and a 16C chancel and ambulatory; inside, altarpieces and 15C–16C stained-glass windows in ambulatory chapels escaped pillaging in the Revolution.

Église Notre-Dame, Abbaye de Jumièges

© Jean-Luc Bohin/age fotostock

111

Parc naturel régional des Boucles de la Seine★★

The Brotonne forest was made readily accessible by the creation of the Parc naturel régional des Boucles de la Seine in 1974 and the construction of the Brotonne bridge in 1977. La Haye-de-Routot is part of the Écomusée de la Basse-Seine (regional open-air museum), which preserves ancient crafts.

- **Michelin Map:** 304: D-5 to E-5.
- **Info:** Maison du Parc, 76940 Notre-Dame-de-Bliquetuit. ℰ02 35 37 23 16. www.pnr-seine-normande.com. ᶜ
- **Location:** The park extends on either side of the Seine below Rouen. Bridges at Tancarville and Brotonne as well as ferries pass from one bank to the other.
- **Don't Miss:** The many marked paths in the forest, as well as Vieux-Port and its surroundings.
- **Timing:** Find lodging outside the park, near Pont-Audemer, and pack a lunch.

🚗 DRIVING TOUR

🚗 FORÊT DE BROTONNE
80km/50mi. About 3h.
Some say that the forest is named after St-Condède, a Breton hermit to whom the Merovingian King Theodoric II gave part of the forest of Arelaune; others say it went to a certain *Burton*. No matter, the **forest roads** offer beautiful views between the beaches, oaks and firs.

Notre-Dame-de-Bliquetuit
Nearby, the Parc naturel des Boucles de la Seine Normande is headquartered in old farm buildings at the **Maison du Parc**.
Discover a conservatory orchard, laid hedge and duck pond while learning about tree species. Two walking routes (8km and 12 km) depart from here.

▶ Leave Notre-Dame-de-Bliquetuit S to join the D 913.

"Chêne à la cuve"
At milestone 11 on D 913, to the right of the road. Four oak trunks from the same roots form a natural bowl 7m across.

▶ Continue on D 313. After having passed the forest, take the D 90 (right).

Moulin de Hauville
⏰*Mid Apr–mid Sept Sun 2.30–6.30pm (Jul–Aug daily). ℰ02 32 56 57 32.*
This 13C grain mill belonged to the Abbey of Jumièges (ᶜ*see Abbaye de Jumièges, p110*). Oak roof beams with reed thatching; works visible in stone tower. There is a small museum in the miller's house.

▶ From Hauville head west and then North on minor roads for La Haye-de-Routout.

La Haye-de-Routot
Two colossal 1 500-year-old **yews**★ – one contains a chapel, the other an oratory – are next to the cemetery surrounding the small **church**.
The wood-burning **bread oven** (⏰*Mar–Sept–Nov Sun and public holidays 2–6pm.* ⏰*1 Jan, 8 May, 1 and 11 Nov, 25 Dec.* ⊚€2, Sun free for under-16s. ℰ02 32 57 07 99) is an 18C structure, demonstrating breadmaking of yore. Exhibition of bakers' tools and fantasy breads.
The **shoe museum** (⏰*Mar–Sept–Nov Sun and public holidays 2–6pm;* ⏰*1 Jan, 8 May, 1 and 11 Nov, 25 Dec.* ⊚€2; ℰ02 32 57 59 67) is in a traditional 17C Roumois house; it presents early tools and techniques.

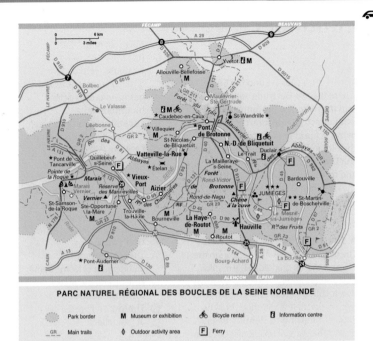

PARC NATUREL RÉGIONAL DES BOUCLES DE LA SEINE NORMANDE

Park border	**M** Museum or exhibition	🚲 Bicycle rental	ℹ Information centre
GR Main trails	◊ Outdoor activity area	**F** Ferry	

Take the D 40 north into the forest. At the D 686 intersection turn left for La Haye-Aubrée. Continue south, then right on D 90 to Bourneville, then northwest on D 89 for Quillebeuf. At Trouville-la-Haule, turn right on D 95.

Vieux-Port★

Charming thatched-roofed village nestles in the greenery alongside the Seine. Two itineraries lead from the esplanade alongside the Seine, the **Parcours historique Portut tutus**" and "**Chemin des sources bleues**".
The first (*2km/1mi*) is about the village's origins, the second (*7.8km/5mi*) reveals beautiful thatched houses in hedged farmland alongside the Seine. A mountain bike itinerary (*22 km/13mi*) also leaves from Vieux-Port.

Continue on the D 95.

Aizier

The stone belltower of the 12C Romanesque church looks very archaic.
Near the church a stone slab covers the remains of a covered alley (2000 BCE).

Continue to Vatteville-la-Rue by the D 95, then the D 65.

Vatteville-la-Rue

In the church's Renaissance nave the walls have an armorial band of black, a trace of a lord's funeral. There is 16C stained-glass in the Flamboyant chapel. Three trekking paths depart from the church to the village centre (5km/3mi), the Seine (10km/6mi) or the forest (17km/10mi).

St-Nicolas-de-Bliquetuit.

Beautiful enclosed gardens and quaint half-timbered houses. A trekking path (5.5km/3mi or 7km/4mi) leaves from the ferry slipway, heading for the Barrey-Va meadows (see p116).

From the village, head for the **Pont de Brotonne★★**; the bridge, which spans the Seine above Caudebec-en-Caux, was opened in 1977.

Caudebec-en-Caux★

Caudebec settles around the Seine where the Ste-Gertrude valley runs into the river. The Brotonne bridge leads directly to the forest of the same name. A fire in 1940 destroyed most of the old buildings, but the Church of Our Lady was virtually undamaged and three old houses to the left of the church give some idea of what Caudebec must once have looked like.

A BIT OF HISTORY

A Short-Lived Prestigious Past – The name Caudebec first appears in the 11C on a charter granted to the monks of St-Wandrille abbey. In the 12C the town was fortified to resist the English who were nevertheless victorious in 1419. After submitting to Henri IV in 1592, during the Wars of Religion, it became a flourishing glove- and hat-making centre. The Revocation of the Edict of Nantes in 1685, which revived the persecution of Protestants, put an end to this period of prosperity.

WALKING TOUR

2km/1mi. About 1h starting from the tourist office on place du Général de Gaulle. Take rue de la Vicomté.

The Sentier de la Gribane (signposted and dotted with explanatory panels) provides an interesting itinerary for visiting the city.
The promenades of La Vignette and Mont-Calidu offer lovely vistas of the town. On the right , the old prison is set in the 14C ramparts.

▶ Continue along rue de la Vicomte and turn right into rue Thomas-Bazin.

Maison des Templiers

The Templars' House is a precious specimen of 13C civil architecture which has retained its two original gable walls.

○ **Michelin Map:** 304: E-4.

ℹ **Info:** Place du Général De Gaulle, Bord de Seine. ℰ02 32 70 46 32. www.normandie-caux-seine-tourisme.com.

▶ **Location:** Midway between Rouen (48km/30mi E) and Le Havre (52km/32.5mi W), Caudebec is on the banks of the Seine.

🅿 **Parking:** Public parking on place du Marché (except Saturday mornings), place Henri-IV and place d'Armes.

☺ **Don't Miss:** The Flamboyant architecture of Notre-Dame church, and the pretty town of Villequier.

🕐 **Timing:** You need a day at Caudebec.

▶ Follow cours de la Ste-Gertrude to reach rue des Tanneurs. You walk by two towers: **Tour des Fascines** and **Tour d'Harfleur**.

▶ Continue along rue de la Tour d'Harfleur to reach rue du Havre. Turn left, and then left into rue Planquette. Go along rue du Huit-Mai.

Église Notre-Dame★

Place du Parvis.
This fine Flamboyant edifice (○*see illustration in Introduction: Religious architecture, p62*) which Henri IV described as "the most beautiful chapel in the kingdom" was built between 1425 and 1539.

Exterior – The belfry (53m high) adjoining the south wall has a delicately worked upper part surmounted by a stone crown spire. The west face is pierced by three beautiful Flamboyant **doorways** – the larger of the two is said to portray 333 different characters – and by a remarkable rose window surrounded by small statues.

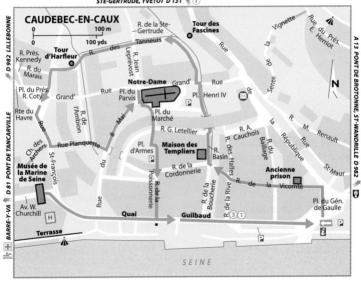

WHERE TO STAY	
Marine (Normotel la)	①
Normandie (Hôtel le)	③

WHERE TO EAT	
Rendez-Vous des Chasseurs (Au)	①

Interior – There is no transept. The triforium and tracery are the most characteristically Flamboyant features.

The 17C **font** is decorated with intricately carved panels. The **great organ★** (early 16C – 💿 see illustration in Introduction: Religious architecture, p63) was restored in 1972; it has 3 345 pipes of repoussé pewter.

Chapelle du St-Sépulcre – The chapel inspired Fragonard to sketch it. Beneath the 16C baldaquin a recumbent Christ, carved in incredible detail, faces some very large stone statues – all from Jumièges abbey. The Pietà between the windows is 15C.

Chapelle de la Vierge – The Lady Chapel is famous for its **keystone★**, a 7t monolith supported only by the dependent arching and forming a 4.3m pendentive. The architect of this feat, Guillaume Le Tellier, lies buried in the chapel and is commemorated in a plaque beneath the right window.

▶ Head for place du Marché, on the south side of the church, and take rue des Belles femmes and rue de la Poissonnerie south towards the river. Turn right on Quai Guilbaud towards avenue Winston Churchill.

Muséoseine – Musée de la Marine de Seine

av. Winston-Churchill. 🕐Tue–Sun Feb–Nov 1–6.30pm (Jul–Aug 10am–6.30pm). 💶€5. 📞02 35 95 90 13; www.museoseine.fr.

The museum is devoted to the history of navigation along the River Seine: ports, commercial exchanges, shipbuilding, crossings. Visitors can learn about a bygone phenomenon, the **tidal bore,** which used to rip down the Seine.

▶ Return along the quai Guilbaud.

🚗 DRIVING TOURS

🚗 AROUND ST-WANDRILLE
Round-trip of 8km/5mi.

▶ Leave Caudebec by rue St-Clair and follow chemin de Rétival keeping to the right.

The road runs along the top of a small escarpment with tantalising glimpses of the bend in the river.

▶ At the bottom of a steep descent take D 37 on the left.

The road goes up a delightful little **valley★** with thatched farmhouses scattered here and there.

◉ Before reaching Rançon, turn right on D 33 to St-Wandrille.

Abbaye de St-Wandrille★
♿ *See Abbaye de St-Wandrille, p117.*

◉ Take D 22 towards Caudebec.

Latham-47 Monument
This commemorates the polar explorer **Roald Amundsen** and his companions, who disappeared in the Arctic in 1928.

◉ Continue on D 22, then D 982 to return to Caudebec.

🚗 AROUND BARRE-Y-VA
Round-trip of 21km/13mi. Allow 1h.

◉ Leave Caudebec to the north on the Yvetot road and turn left onto the D 40.

Ste-Gertrude
The small **church** stands in attractive surroundings. It was consecrated in 1519 and is Flamboyant in style.

◉ Head west on D 40, then D 30. Turn south on D 440 towards Anquetierville. At the junction with D 982 turn left, then at St-Arnoult right onto D 440. Turn right onto D 281 and almost immediately left down a steep hill to Villequier.

Villequier★
Villequier occupies a beautiful **site★** on the banks of the Seine at the foot of a wooded height crowned by a castle. In 1843, six months after their marriage, Charles Vacquerie and his wife, Léopoldine Hugo, the daughter of the novelist and poet Victor Hugo, were drowned in the Seine at Villequier. 🚶 Walking paths with magnificent panoramic views of the Seine have been created in the neighboring forest. When you leave the town, on the D 81 heading southwest, there is a 🚲 bicy-

cle route 12km/7mi long, waiting to be enjoyed by foot, by bicycle or on roller skates. It follows the towing path as far as Petiville.

Musée Victor-Hugo – Maison Vacquerie★ – *Access through the rue Ernst-Binet.* ♿ ⏰ *Daily except Tue: Apr–Sept 10am–12.30pm, 2–6pm, Sun 2–6pm; Oct–Mar 10am–12.30pm, 2–5.30pm, Sun 2–5.30pm.* ⏰ *1 Jan, 1 May, 1 and 11 Nov, 25 Dec.* ⊛ €4. ☎ 02 35 56 78 31. www.museevictorhugo.fr. A house once owned by the Vacquerie family, rich boat builders from Le Havre.

◉ Take D 81 back towards Caudebec.

Barre-y-Va
This tiny hamlet is named after the tidal wave or bore *(barre)* which used to swell upstream along the Seine. There is an oratory and a small **chapel** perpetuating the memory of pilgrimages; there are also votive offerings that sailors used to express their gratitude and thanks for their safe return.

◉ Return to Caudebec via D 81.

ADDRESSES

🛏 STAY

⊜ ⊜ **Hôtel Le Normandie** – *Quai Guilbaud.* ☎02 35 96 25 11. www.le-normandie.fr. *15 rooms.* 🅿. On road along Seine, small, simple hotel. Some rooms wth balconies. *Restaurant* (⊜⊜) serving traditional Norman cuisine.

⊜ ⊜ **Normotel La Marine** – *18 quai Guilbaud.* ☎02 35 96 20 11. www.normotel-lamarine.fr. *31 rooms.* 🅿. *Restaurant*⊜⊜. On the quai along the Seine, best rooms have balconies over river.

🍴 EAT

⊜ ⊜ **Au Rendez-Vous des Chasseurs** – *1040 route de Ste Gertrude, 76490 Maulévrier Ste-Gertrude.* ☎02 35 96 20 30. www.aurendezvousdeschasseurs.fr. *Closed Tue–Wed and Sun evening.* Half-timbered building with pretty garden terrace, and regional cuisine.

Abbaye St-Wandrille★

St-Wandrille abbey, like Le Bec-Hellouin, is a moving testimony to the continuity of the Benedictine Order in Normandy. Today, the monks earn their living mainly from the manufacture of furniture polish and household products.

A BIT OF HISTORY

God's Athlete (7C) – King Dagobert's court was celebrating the marriage of Count Wandrille, who seemed destined for a brilliant career, when, to general surprise, the bride entered a convent and Wandrille joined a group of hermits. The king ordered Wandrille to return to court but, enlightened by a miracle, accepted the choice. Wandrille's saintliness and magnificent physique earned him the nickname of God's Athlete.

Valley of the Saints (7C–9C) – In 649, Wandrille founded Fontanelle monastery, "where saints flourish like rose trees in a greenhouse".

Benedictine Continuity – In the 10C, monks began to rebuild the abbey, destroyed by Vikings. It survived the Wars of Religion, but the Revolution scattered the monks and the buildings fell into ruin. In 1931, the Benedictines returned permanently.

Abbaye★

Guided tours: Late Mar–Jun and Sept–early Nov at 3.30pm (+11.30am on Sun); Jul–Aug at 11.30am, 3pm, 4pm.
The entrance to the abbey is through a 15C door surmounted by a symbolic pelican. The porter's lodge and its twin are 18C. The imposing 18C Porte de Jarente leads to the main courtyard, accessible on guided tours only. The only parts of the abbey church still standing are the tall columns.

- **Michelin Map:** 304: E-4.
- **Info:** 2 Rue Saint-Jacques, 76490 Saint-Wandrille-Rançon. ✆02 35 96 23 11. www.st-wandrille.com.
- **Location:** The village and abbey lie on D 982, 4km/2.5mi E of Caudebec and 51km/32mi W of Rouen.
- **Don't Miss:** The cloister, the only part of the abbey still intact.
- **Timing:** Visit on Sunday morning or, on other days, in the afternoon.

Cloisters★

The 14C south gallery, parallel with the nave, was linked to it by a door surmounted by a now mutilated tympanum illustrating the Coronation of the Virgin. A niche in the 13C church wall contains the graceful 14C statue of Our Lady of Fontenelle.

Èglise

The church is an old 13C tithe barn, the Canteloup Barn, which was transported in 1969 from La Neuville-du-Bosc in the Eure and re-erected at St-Wandrille.

Chapelle St-Saturnin

Closed to the public.
By car, follow the signs; on foot about 45min there and back. Leave the abbey and take the path downhill (right); note the 16C Entombment in a niche. Skirt the wall for 150m; go around a field and take the path beside the abbey wall.
This small 10C oratory was probably built on Merovingian foundations. The façade was remodelled in the 16C.

Lillebonne

The small industrial town of Lillebonne was once a Roman military camp named Juliobona, after Julius Caesar. With the arrival of several textile factories towards the end of the 19C, the Lillebonne-Bolbec valley came to be known as the Golden Valley.

▶ **Population:** 8 927.
◊ **Michelin Map:** 304: D-4.
🄸 **Info:** Place Félix Faure, 76170 Lillebonne. ℘02 32 70 46 32. www.normandie-caux-seine-tourisme.com.
◐ **Location:** Lillebone is 67km/41.6mi W of Rouen and 37km/23mi E of Le Havre via D 982.
🄰 **Don't Miss:** The Roman theatre and artefacts at the museum.
◔ **Timing:** Allow at least half a day.

SIGHTS

Théâtre romain

🕐 *Mon–Fri 9.30am–noon, 1.30–5pm, Sat–Sun (Apr–Oct 1.30–5.30pm).*
🕐 *Dec–Mar. ℘02 35 15 69 11. www.theatrelillebonne.fr.*
From place de l'Hôtel-de-Ville it is possible to see the general layout of this Roman amphitheatre, built in the 1C and 2C. The central arena follows the usual plan of amphitheatres in north-west Gaul, where all kinds of spectacles were held (mythological scenes, gladiator fights, performing animals, hunts with small game). The crowd watched on from the **cave★**, a series of stands probably made of wood.

Château

Access by 46 r. Césarine.
Contact tourist office for visiting hours.

Little remains of the fortress (rebuilt in the 12C and 13C), where William the Conqueror assembled his barons before invading England: one wall of an octagonal tower and, on the left, a round three-storey keep.

Église Notre-Dame

rue Sadi-Carnot.
This 16C church has a sweeping spire (55m) rising above a square tower. Inside, a stained-glass window tells the story of John the Baptist. The stalls were originally from the Abbaye du Valasse.

Théâtre-Amphithéâtre romain

Juliobona, musée gallo-romain
pl Félix-Faure.
🕐*Feb–Nov Wed, Sat–Sun 1.30–5.30pm; check website for school holiday periods.* ✆€5. *02 32 84 02 07.*
https://musee-juliobona.fr.
Exhibition of the town in the Gallo-Roman period, with local archaeological collections: incineration tomb, pottery, 1C–3C ironwork. Displays include nearly 300 pieces of Gallo-Roman heritage and new objects from the reserves of the Museum of Antiquities in Rouen.

EXCURSIONS
👥 L'Abbaye du Valasse at Le Parc Eana
6km/3.7mi NW by D 173, turn left at Le Becquet.
Since 2009, the site has operated as a **leisure park**, with access to the abbey, gardens and park. The foundation of the abbey resulted from two vows; the first one was made by Waleran de Meulan for having escaped from a shipwreck, and one made by Empress Matilda, William the Conqueror's granddaughter. In her case it was for having survived the difficult struggle she undertook for the throne of England against her cousin Stephen of Blois.
The abbey, consecrated in 1181, prospered until the 14C, when the Hundred Years' War and the Wars of Religion brought ruin. The building was sold at the Revolution, converted into a château, then sold to a dairy; in 1984 it was bought by the municipality of Gruchet-le-Valasse.
The main façade is an elegant 18C composition with two return wings. The central pediment bears the arms of Empress Matilda: three Norman leopards (from William the Conqueror) and an eagle (from her husband, the German Emperor Henry V).

Le Mesnil-sous-Lillebonne
2km/1mi S.
The extremely ancient parish **church** presents a display of religious art and a collection of fossils and minerals.

Notre-Dame de Gravenchon B1
Interesting modern church, with St George and the Dragon on the façade in lead and brass. Abstract stained glass by Max Ingrand.

Château d'Etelan
15km/9mi by the D 51 and, at Norville, take the D 281 on the right to St-Maurice-d'Etelan.
🕐*Jun–Sept: self-guided visits, gardens and chapel only 11am–1pm* ✆€5: *guided tour including chateau, 3–7pm.* ✆€7.; *check website for opening days, which vary seasonally.* *02 35 39 91 27.*
www. chateau-etelan.fr.
Built in 1494 on the site of a former fortress, this Flamboyant château overlooks the valley. An elegant stairway tower lit by nine bays announces "the first Norman Renaissance". In the restored chapel, interesting 16C murals and beautiful carved wood panels. Some rooms are furnished and inhabited, while others are for exhibitions and concerts.
View from chateau terrace: marshlands of St-Maurice-d'Etelan and Norville, Brotonne forest, as well as unexpected show of boats sailing up and down the Seine. Take a stroll in the former vegetable garden, recently restructured; beautiful collection of squashes and melons, as well as herbs. There is also a "vine terrace" in a pergola nearby.

Tancarville
9km/5.5mi southwest.
Standing on the chalky protrusion of cliffs before the estuary spreads out, the castle overlooks the Seine's right bank; it is also from here that the suspended bridge springs over the river.
Feudal castle – *02 35 39 75 12. http:// tancarville.free.fr.* This was part of the overall strategy controlling the Seine estuary. In the 11C, William the Conqueror granted privileges in the person of Raoul de Tancarville, his advisor. The oldest parts date to the 10C; only the Tour de l'Aigle (15C), shaped like a spur, remains intact. Of square residential tower (12C) rise on the other side of the terrorists. Two round towers flank

the small entrance castle. Ruins of the main building remain in the court-yard, opened by three pointed arches. **Road bridge★** Until 1959, when the bridge was inaugurated, ferries ran between the two banks. Today two 125m pylons support the suspended deck at 48m. 1 400m long, it has 960m of metal bays. It offers a **view★** of the Seine estuary (*leave the car at the end of the bridge*): in the foreground, the Tan-carville canal, and more downstream, the Pont de Normandie.

Sentier du Vivier 🐾 *From Place de Tancarville-Bas. Way marked to the right, behind the bakery*. This path, part of the regional nature park, takes you on a 12-part stroll along the river.

Saint-Jean-d'Abbetot

16km/10mi west, going through Tancarville and heading for St-Romain-de-Colbosc. Go for 4km/2.5mi on the D 39 and then turn left for the D 112. In the 11C **church** crypt there are several 12C, 13C and 16C **frescoes★**.

Pont-Audemer★

This quaint town of 16C houses is sometimes called the Venice of Normandy, its canals once serving a prosperous tanning trade.

WALKING TOUR

OLD TOWN
Allow 45min.

▶ Start from place du Général de Gaulle. Take rue des Carmes, then rue de la République on left. 100m, then left again into Impasse de l'Epée; come out, turn left into parallel Impasse St-Ouen alongside Église St-Ouen.

Église St-Ouen – 11C–16C. Renaissance **stained-glass★** in side chapels.

▶ Return to rue de la République, turn left and then continue into rue Thiers.

Pretty view from **Risle River bridge**.

▶ From place Victor-Hugo, go to Place Louis-Gillain, right, and into rue des Cordeliers.

A turreted, half-timbered house with a stone ground floor, rises on the corner of rue des Cordeliers. Note the sculpted doorways (*Nos. 8, 16, 18, 20 and 27 bis*).

▶ **Population:** 10 436.
⬧ **Michelin Map:** 304: D-5.
🛈 **Info:** 2 Place du Général de Gaulle. ℰ02 32 41 08 21. www.tourisme-pontaudemer-rislenormande.com.
▷ **Location:** 24km/15mi E of Honfleur and 58km/36mi W of Rouen.
🅿 **Parking:** Car park on place Général de Gaulle.
👁 **Don't Miss:** Compass cards painted on the ground, let you explore the town at your own pace.

▶ Take rue Sadi Carnot. **Rue Place-de-la-Ville** (*right*) crosses a small bridge into rue de la République, at St-Ouen.

▶ Go up rue de la République and take the first passage right, after rue des Carmes.

Cour Canal has lovely half-timbered houses.

Musée Alfred-Canel
Former mayor, Alfred Canel initiated the creation of the municipal library in 1834 and began to build museum col-lections at the end of his life. He died in 1879, bequeathing his house, his books and some pieces of furniture to the city

Pont-Audemer

© Günter Gräfenhain/Sime/Photononstop

of Pont-Audemer. Today, the building houses temporary exhibitions: consult the website for details: www.ville-pont-audemer.fr/culture/musee-alfred-canel/le-musee.

🚗 DRIVING TOUR

🚗 THE RISLE VALLEY
Pont-Audemer to Montfort-sur-Risle. 50km/32mi. About 1h30.

Corneville-sur-Risle
The 12-bell **chimes** in the Hôtel Les Cloches were made following the incredible success of an 1877 operetta by Robert Planquette, *The Bells of Corneville.*

Appeville-Annebault
In the 16C the Admiral d'Annebault, Normandy's governor, conceived the plan to make Risle navigation possible; he also had built the large church while preserving its 14C chancel. Note the keystones

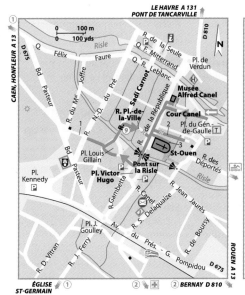

and beautiful staffs of the charitable brotherhoods.

Montfort-sur-Risle

This charming municipality is next to the Montfort forest hills and dales, and enjoys a river. A club offers Risle canoeing and kayaking (*a day or half-day, with or without guide*), a relaxing moment with verdant scenery.

Castle – *By car from town centre; take rue de l'Ecu, follow signs; reached on foot, 231 steps behind the church.* Only ruins remain of the 11C castle, still extending over 4.5ha. An itinerary helps envision the original fortress the English dismantled. Vegetation invades the pretty setting; wonderful view of Montfort and the Risle valley.

"Les Catellers" – *Leave Montfort-sur-Risle by D 91 east; about 1.5 km/1mi into the forest you reach Beuvron roundabout, take Chemin de la Mare Votret (head for "Les Catellers").*
A 2.7km/1.5mi path signposted with black leaves on white teaches about Montfort state forest trees. *Brochure from Montfort-sur-Lisle tourist office.*

▶ Cross the Risle by the D 47, then Pont-Audemer by the D 39.

The Risle estuary

▶ Take D 675 to Toutainville exit, turn right into the D 312.

Saint-Sulpice-de-Grimbouville

Medieval House – *www.normandie-accueil.fr.* ♿. Lovely corbelled-out gatehouse (*timberwork*). Also: 15C thatched cottage, 19C building, two old washhouses (perhaps paleo-Christian baptistry); dolmen.

"Le sentier de l'Anguille" – *Starts at the mairie – 4.2 km/2.5mi, blue waymarking. Brochure in region's tourist offices.* Wear boots. An educational walk to the Risle coastal river marshlands, to learn about sources and biodiversity.

"Le sentier de la Risle maritime" – *Starts at the mairie – 12.5km/7.5mi. Brochure in region's tourist offices.* Sign-posted walk through peat marshes by an old towpath; pretty, typically Norman houses.

▶ Continue on the D 312 to Foulbec.

Foulbec

"Le sentier de la Brûlette" – *Starts at Place de la Maison-du-Village – 8km/5mi. Brochure in the tourist offices.* Signposted walk with nice panorama of Brûlette coastline; walk in woods.

▶ Continue on the D 312 until Conteville.

Conteville

"Le sentier des hameaux et du Marais" – *Starts at the church – 12.5 km/7.5mi. Brochure in the region's tourist offices.* Pretty, signposted, for discovering the Risle coastal river marshland while overlooking the valley.

▶ D 312 to Berville-sur-Mer.

Berville-sur-Mer

"Le sentier à fl'Eure de l'eau" – Footpath 2.3 km/1.5mi long, organised to permit discovery of the village's history and the estuary's aquatic environments.
"Le sentier des Voiles de la liberté" – *Leaves from the esplanade - 13km/8mi or 18km/11mi. Brochure in tourist offices.* Pretty walk and panoramic views of estuary, goes through forest.

▶ West to Pont-Audemer by the D 180, heading for La-Rivière-St-Sauveur.

The Vernier marshlands

55km/34mi, 1h30. Leave Pont-Audemer heading north on the D 810.
Perhaps you'll meet the "marshlands clown", a spaniel so called because he loves hunting in the marshlands.

Ste-Opportune-la-Mare

Follow the signs *Panorama de la Grande Mare* to viewpoint over Great Marsh and beyond to the reclaimed Marshland.

> To drive here, take a little road in Ste-Opportune to the Vernier marshland, turn left

Réserve naturelle des Mannevilles
Guided tours (3h) from Ste-Opportune-la-Mare. www.pnr-seine-normande.com. Wear boots.
Flora and fauna of the marshlands, visit with Camargue horses, Scottish highland cattle.

> D 810 to the Seine, then D 87.

Quillebeuf-sur-Seine
Until the 19C captains waited here for high tide, to sail its dangerous channel. Today, the old port is has many oil refineries and petrochemical installations in Port Jérôme. The town still feels authentic, and has an excellent view of Port Jérôme from the lighthouse. Église Notre-Dame-de-Bon-Port has a fine but incomplete Romanesque tower.

Pointe de Quillebeuf – This is the tip of a promontory separating the Vernier marshland meander from that of Vieux-Port. Small lighthouse, good view of river, Port-Jérôme, Shea's and Tancarville bridge.

Two mountain bike itineraries *(13km/8mi and 32km/20mi)* starting from lighthouse at the end of the quay.

Église Notre-Dame-du-Bon-Port - Incomplete but lovely Romanesque tower; 12C portal. Purely Romanesque nave with archaic capitals, 16C chancel. Boat models and sailors' graffiti recall port's role in Seine navigation.

> Take the D 103 across marshland, to Pointe de la Roque.

Pointe de la Roque★
From lighthouse, **panorama** of Seine estuary to Cap de la Hève, Côte de Grâce. Tancarville cliffs and bridge to the right.

ADDRESSES

🛏 STAY

🛌 **Camping Les Etangs Risles-Seine** – *19 route des Etangs.* ℘02 32 42 46 65. *www.camping-risle-seine.com.* Spend one or several nights in protected natural site next to Pont Audemer ponds.

🛌🛌 **Chambre d'hôte La Venise Normande** – *9 r. Sadit-Carnot.* ℘02 32 56 82 53 or ℘06 87 76 49 63. *www.venise normande.com. 3 rooms.* A former 17C–18C butcher's converted into charming B&B.

🛌🛌🛌 **Chambre d'hôte Le Prieuré des Fontaines** – *140, Côte du Mont Morel, 27500 Les Préaux (5km/3mi SE by D 139).* ℘06 13 17 87 02. *www.leprieuredesfontaines.fr.* This 17C building has spacious, comfortable rooms.

🍴 EAT

🍽🍽 **Auberge du Cochon d'Or** – *64, rue des Anciens d'Afrique du Nord, 27210 Beuzeville (14km/8.7mi W via D 675).* ℘02 32 57 70 46. *www.le-cochon-dor.fr.* Locals appreciate the changing menus.

🍽🍽🍽 **Le Petit Coq aux Champs** – *400 chemin du Petit Coq, 27500 Campigny (6km/3.7mi S via D 810 and D 29).* ℘02 32 41 04 19. *www.lepetitcoqauxchamps.fr. Reservations required.* This beautiful thatched cottage houses a restaurant and 12 guest rooms.

COTE D'ALBÂTRE *and Pays de Caux*

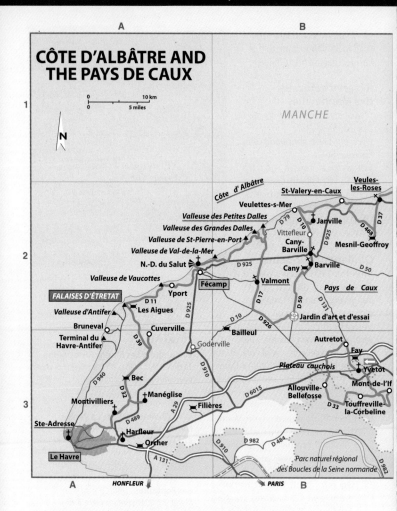

CÔTE D'ALBÂTRE AND THE PAYS DE CAUX

0 — 10 km
0 — 5 miles

N

MANCHE

Côte d'Albâtre

St-Valery-en-Caux

Veules-les-Roses

Veulettes-s-Mer

Janville

Valleuse des Petites Dalles

Vittefleur

Valleuse des Grandes Dalles

Mesnil-Geoffroy

Valleuse de St-Pierre-en-Port

Cany-Barville

Valleuse de Val-de-la-Mer

N.-D. du Salut

Cany

Barville

D 925

Valleuse de Vaucottes

Fécamp

Valmont

Pays de Caux

FALAISES D'ÉTRETAT

Yport

Valleuse d'Antifer

Les Aigues

D 11

D 925

D 10

D 17

D 50

D 131

Jardin d'art et d'essai

Bruneval

Cuverville

Bailleul

D 926

Autretot

Terminal du Havre-Antifer

Goderville

Fay

D 39

Plateau cauchois

Yvetot

Bec

D 910

Allouville-Bellefosse

Mont-de-l'If

Montivilliers

D 31

Manéglise

Filières

D 6015

D 33

Touffreville-la-Corbeline

A 29

Ste-Adresse

D 489

Harfleur

Orcher

D 910

D 982

D 484

Le Havre

A 131

Parc naturel régional des Boucles de la Seine normande

HONFLEUR   PARIS

The Pays de Caux, lying between Rouen and Le Havre, has a charming, intimate feel to it, ideal for a family excursion, a romantic getaway or simply getting a break. The Seine meanders through a lovely, forested landscape dotted with small villages on its way to the sea: ideal for exploring on a bicycle, on horseback or by foot. In sharp contrast is the land that will appeal to more intrepid walkers, the Alabaster Coast with its cliff views and the sight of the endless sea and sky.

Highlights

1 **Maison de l'Armateur** (p130)

2 **Etretat** cliff walks (p133)

3 **Palais Bénédictine** (p137)

4 **Alabaster Coast** drive (p140)

5 **Dieppe castle-museum** (p151)

The Pays de Caux is a mosaic ranging from city to river, while the Alabaster Coast has the pure, wild beauty of the sea crashing against chalky cliffs. Le Havre, a deep-water port at the mouth of the Seine, suffered grievously during World War II; from ruins, it is today a model of city planning. Dieppe, an old fishing port, hideout of privateers and a

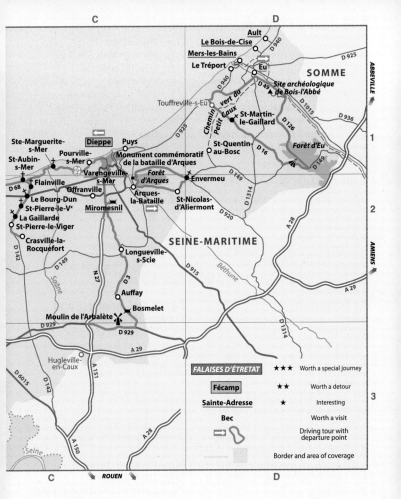

redoubt against the English, has both a sturdy castle and lovely beaches, and is France's oldest seaside resort. The city suffered in the 1942 Dieppe Raid, but still has its attractive old quarter.

At the charming seaside resort of Varengeville-sur-Mer visitors may enjoy the intimate feel of an English-style garden before their nature walk. Eu's collegiate church and château offer architectural heritage, while the pretty little port of Le Tréport takes pride in its church and calvary. Walks along the cliffs at Étretat are absolutely not to be missed, giving breathtaking views over the beaches and headlands. Walkers will want to explore its famous *valleuses* (valleys giv-

ing access to the sea) as well. Fécamp, from which intrepid fishermen sailed to Newfoundland for cod, has a magnificent ducal church and a 19C Benedictine palace, where the well-known liqueur is made.

The region around the seaside resorts of Veules-les-Roses, St-Valéry-en-Caux and Veulettes-sur-Mer offers driving itineraries taking in pretty little villages and stately châteaux, ancient churches and hedged farmland, and even a chance to learn how linen is made.

Last, a visit to the Caux Plateau will include not only the oldest oak in all of France, but also manors and a church with stained glass by Max Ingrand.

Le Havre★★

In 1945, Le Havre was Europe's most badly damaged port; today the town, including the residential area of Ste-Adresse and the old port of Harfleur, is a remarkable example of large-scale reconstruction and successful town planning. Le Havre's university is new, it opened here in 1986.

▶ **Population:** 170 352.
◉ **Michelin Map:** 304: A-5.
▣ **Info:** 186 boulevard Clemenceau. ℘02 32 74 04 04. www.lehavretourisme.com.
◑ **Location:** 197km/122.4mi from Paris and 90km/56mi from Rouen. Car ferries operate to England and Ireland.
◷ **Timing:** The best time to visit is Wednesday or weekends, when all sites are open.
👥 **Kids:** The Malraux museum has a tour map for children.

A BIT OF HISTORY

A Judicious Choice – In 1517, **François I** ordered the construction of a new port, called Havre-de-Grâce, to replace Harfleur, which had silted up. The marshy site chosen by Bonnivet, Grand Admiral of France, had the crucial advantage of a high tide that lasted for over two hours.

An Ocean Port – The career of Le Havre as a trading and transatlantic port began during the American War of Independence when supplies for the rebels were shipped from Le Havre.

Le Havre bustled in the 19C when great transatlantic passenger liners reduced the journey time in New York.

Le Havre during the War – Le Havre suffered 146 raids, in which more than 4 000 were killed. The siege of the town began on 2 September 1944 – the Battle of Normandy was over and Paris liberated, but Le Havre was still occupied.

Allied air raids went on ceaselessly for eight days from 5 September; the Germans were determined to blow up any port installations still in existence. On 13 September 1944, Le Havre was liberated. It took two years to clear the destruction and reconstruction began only in 1946.

🐾 WALKING TOUR

THE MODERN TOWN★

The old town was virtually wiped out in 1944. A new town was planned by **Auguste Perret** (1875–1954), the pioneer of reinforced concrete construction, who achieved

remarkable architectural unity.
◉See map, p128.

Bassin du Commerce and Espace Oscar-Niemeyer

The commercial dock is the focal point of the new district accessible by an elegant footbridge, designed by the architects Gillet and Du Pasquier.

At the west end, facing the war memorial, is the **Espace Oscar-Niemeyer** complex on place Gambetta. The main pavilion (Grand Volcan) has a large theatre, a cinema and exhibition rooms.

Appartement-témoin Auguste-Perret★

🐾Guided tours only: Generally 11am, 2.30pm, 3.30pm, 4.30pm, but only daily in Jul–Aug, and with several seasonal variations: check website for details.
◉1 Jan, 25 Dec. ⊘€5 (under 26, no charge), no charge 1st Sat of month. ℘02 35 22 31 22. http://unesco.lehavre. fr/fr/decouvrir/lappartement-temoin-perret.

A beautiful recreation of the model apartment Auguste Perret first presented at the 1947 World Exhibition, then again two years later to Le Havre, which was to be rebuilt. The tour gives a good idea of the architect's vision, which called for well thought-out, flexible space.

The clean-lined, functional furniture by designers such as René Gabriel, Marcel

Town, beach and the Église Saint-Vincent-de-Paul viewed from the sea

Gascoin or André Beaudoin, as well as the many day-to-day objects, create a lively environment, while giving a glimpse of post-war social changes.

Place de l'Hôtel-de-Ville★

The square, which was designed by Auguste Perret, is bordered by three-storey buildings, punctuated by taller ten-storey blocks. The open space is laid out with fountains, lawns, arbours and yew hedges. The **hôtel de ville**, an austere building, is distinguished by a great tower (72m high) in concrete.

Leave the square E and walk along Avenue Foch.

Avenue Foch★

The central roadway is bordered by lawns shaded by trees; the Porte Océane marks the west end of the street on the seafront.

North dyke and the beach★

The north breakwater that serves to reinforce the jetty, encloses the marina. The Le Havre and Ste-Adresse beach stretches from the north breakwater to the Hève Cape.

There are views of the Seine estuary from the dyke walk (*boulevard Clemenceau*). Note the turn-of-the century **villas** spared the 1944 bombings, especially the exquisite Villa Maritime at No. 66. Summer restaurants and greenery are found along the pleasant 4km/2mi walk. In season some 600 beach huts dot the

beach; they were authorised in 1910 for a sense of propriety and to protect visitors from the chill.

When you reach the "Porte Océane", head S along bd Clemenceau, which runs alongside anse des Régates and anse de Joinville. Turn left down rue Frédérick Lemaître where you have a pretty view of the pleasure port.

Église St-Joseph★★

Bd François 1er.

This sober **church** typical of Auguste Perret's style was built of concrete between 1951 and 1957. It is surmounted by an octagonal lantern-belfry (109m high). The **interior★★** is monumental and impressive.

Return to bd Clemenceau. Follow it to the museum.

Musée d'Art Moderne André-Malraux★★

2 bd Clemenceau.

⚫*Tue–Fri 11am–6pm, Sat–Sun 11am–7pm.* ⚫*1 Jan, 1 May, 14 Jul, 11 Nov, 25 Dec.* ⚫*€7 (no charge 1st Sat of month or for under-26 years old).* 📞*02 35 19 62 62.* *www.muma-lehavre.fr.*

The glass and metal building looks out to the sea through a monumental concrete sculpture known locally as Le Signal. The roof, designed to provide the best possible light to the galleries

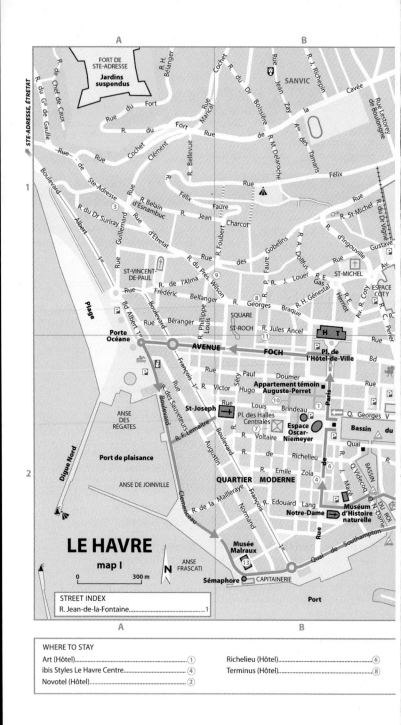

LE HAVRE

map I

0   300 m

STREET INDEX
R. Jean-de-la-Fontaine..1

WHERE TO STAY

Art (Hôtel)...①   Richelieu (Hôtel)....................................⑥

ibis Styles Le Havre Centre..................④   Terminus (Hôtel)....................................⑧

Novotel (Hôtel)...................................②

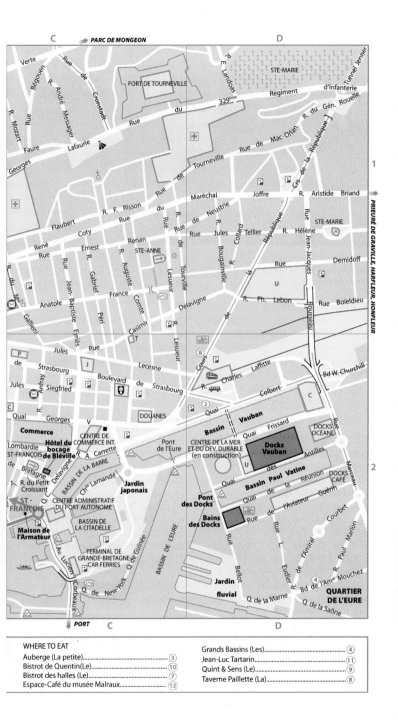

WHERE TO EAT

Auberge (La petite)..③	Grands Bassins (Les)...④
Bistrot de Quentin(Le)....................................⑩	Jean-Luc Tartarin...⑪
Bistrot des halles (Le)......................................⑦	Quint & Sens (Le)..⑨
Espace-Café du musée Malraux......................⑬	Taverne Paillette (La)..⑧

Musée d'Art Moderne André-Malraux

inside, consists of six sheets of glass covered by an aluminium sun blind. The museum presents a fine **collection★** of works by **Raoul Dufy** (1877–1953), who was born in Le Havre, and **Eugène Boudin** (1824–98), a native of Honfleur.

Sémaphore

The view from the end of the pier embraces the harbour entrance and the long southern breakwater protecting the outer harbour.

▷ Continue along the seafront and take quai Southampton up to Maison de l'Armateur.

Musée Maison de l'Armateur★★
3 quai de l'Île.
🕑*Daily except Tue: Apr–Oct 10am–12.30pm, 1.45–6pm; Nov–Mar 10.30am–12.30pm, 1.45–5.30pm.*
🕑*1 Jan, 1 and 8 May, 14 Jul, 11 Nov, 25 Dec.* ✆€7 *(under 26, no charge).*
✆*02 35 19 09 85. www.lehavre.fr.*
This late 18C house is a rare survivor of the 1945 bombings. Built for the personal use of the city's architect and fountain-builder, M. Thibault, a shipowner bought it in the early 19C – hence its name (the "Shipowner's House").
Five circular levels embellished with carved wood fit around a remarkable octagonal light well. All the rooms have been re-created to showcase the aes-

thetics of the elite: stables, bedrooms, trade office, cabinets of curiosities and an observation room.

▷ Take rue du Général-Faidherbe on the left, then the Notre-Dame Bridge. Take the quay Videcoq on the right, then head up rue des Drapiers on the left. Just before getting to the cathedral you will see the Museum of Natural History on the right.

Muséum d'histoire naturelle
place du Vieux-Marché.
🕑*Tue–Sun 10am–noon, 2–6pm, Thu 2–6pm.* 🕑*1 Jan, 1 and 8 May, 14 Jul, 11 Nov, 25 Dec.* ✆€5. ✆*02 35 41 37 28. www.museum-lehavre.fr.*
The Natural History Museum is housed in the old 18C law courts. One of the rooms displays works by the naturalist painter **Charles-Alexandre Lesueur** (1778–1846).

Cathédrale Notre-Dame
Rue de Paris.
Built between 1575 and 1630, the cathedral is a combination of Gothic and Renaissance styles and bristles with buttresses decorated with gargoyles. The organ (1637) was presented by Richelieu and bears his arms.

▷ Rue de Paris takes you to place du Général-de-Gaulle.

ADDITIONAL SIGHTS
Quartier de l'Eure
The 19C **Vauban docks** were recently redone to offer a large commercial gallery with the major names in culture, fashion and leisure.

There is a nice walk beyond the Paul-Vatine Basin with its surprising moveable bridge. The **Bellot Esplanade** and canal gardens will be part of a 9ha/22 acre city park that strollers, skaters and cyclists may enjoy.

Les Bains des Docks – *quai de la Réunion. 02 35 12 41 41. www.vertmarine.com.* This development won the architectural award, the Pritzker Prize, in 2008, bringing prestige to one of Le Havre's major installations. Inspired by Roman thermal baths, this nautical complex of 5 000sq m plays on light, lines, openings and volumes. The noon sun accentuates the sense of calm and well-being that pervades the space. Numerous basins, for various ages and various users. Balneotherapy, cardiotherapy spaces, fitness rooms, Olympic pools and areas just to have fun.

The Port★★
Le Havre is a deep-water port situated in the Seine estuary; it ranks first among French ports for exports and container traffic, and fourth in Europe for total traffic. Le Havre also has frequent car-ferry links with Great Britain (Le Havre–Portsmouth) and Ireland (Le Havre–Rosslare, Le Havre–Cork). Each year 7 000 merchant ships dock in Le Havre, including 2 250 container ships.

EXCURSIONS
Sainte-Adresse★
Allow 1h.
This a pleasant district extends from the edge of Le Havre towards the Hève Cape and consists of a seaside resort and the old town of Ste-Adresse.
Boulevard Albert-1er runs alongside the beach to place Clemenceau and the statue of Albert I, King of the Belgians from 1909 to 1934.

Follow the signs for Pain de Sucre and Notre-Dame-des-Flots.

After a few bends in the road you arrive at the **Pain de Sucre**. A little higher up on the right the **Chapelle Notre-Dame-des-Flots** contains sailors' votive offerings.

Turn left onto route du Cap.

The road passes in front of the École Nationale de la Marine Marchande (Merchant Navy College).

Cap de la Hève
Continue to the lighthouse.
Allow 15min on foot there and back.
This rocky site overlooks the mouth of the Seine. Boulevard du Président-Félix-Faure, to the right and facing the ocean, offers an extensive **view★**.

Return to place Clemenceau.

Harfleur
Église St-Martin
Access by rue Aristide-Briand and rue de Verdun following the direction of Rouen.
The 15C belltower (83m) of the Église St-Martin is famous in the Caux region. Take rue des 104 and rue Gambetta, right, to the **bridge** over the Lézarde from which there is a good view.

Montivilliers
8km/4mi. Leave Le Havre by the D 489.
Following over 20 years of works, the Abbey St Philibert, founded in the 7C, now stages the historical retrospective "**Cœur d'Abbayes★**" (*Partially closed during 2019 for restoration; check website for updates; 02 35 30 96 66; www.abbaye-montivilliers.fr*).
Église St-Sauveur★ – Walk round on the left to see the transept's 11C lantern tower. The Romaneque tower's spire was redone in the 19C. Two naves: the larger, Romanesque, has a carved oak pulpit; the Gothic side nave was added in the 16C. Flamboyant organ-loft behind the belltower.
Aître de Brisegaret – *Reached by route de Fécamp (left before monumen-*

tal mason's). Only a 16C wood-vaulted gallery remains of this old ossuary. Pillars with skeletons, faces, shields, etc.

Château de Filières
20km/12.4mi NE via N15; D 31 left after St-Romain, then D 80 to the right.
🕐*Jul–Aug daily 2–6pm (🚶‍♂️Guided tours (30min) at 2.30pm, 3.30pm, 4.30pm and 5.30pm); Jun–Sept Sun 2–6pm.* ♿*€7.* 📞*02 35 20 53 30. www. chateaux-france.fr/chateau-de-filieres.* The château, in a fine park, is in white Caen stone after designs by Victor Louis. The late 16C wing is to the left, and the 18C central pavilion has a Classical façade and the Mirville family arms. Ancestors of today's owners, they built the château. In the park, west of the château, are seven rows of magnificent beech trees, known as the **Cathedral★** as their branches meet overhead to form a living vault.

ADDRESSES

🏠 STAY
🛏️ **Hôtel Richelieu** – *132 r. de Paris.* 📞*02 35 42 38 71. www.hotellerichelieu.fr.* *19 rooms.* Simple hotel in a busy street, edged with a great many shops.

🛏️ **Inter Hôtel Terminus** – *23 cours de la République.* 📞 *02 35 25 42 48.* *42 rooms. Restaurant* 🍽️. In the centre of Le Havre, across from the train station, this address has up-to-date, functional rooms. The discreet lounge-bar has a billiard table.

🛏️ **Art Hôtel** – *147 r. Louis-Brindeau.* 📞*02 35 22 69 44. www.art-hotel.fr.* *31 rooms.* Across from the Oscar-Niemeyer space, this 1950s building (classified façade) gives pride of place to modern architecture and art: luminous rooms with clean lines; exhibitions.

🛏️ **ibis Styles Le Havre Centre Auguste Perret Hotel** – *121 r. de Paris.* 📞*02 35 41 72 48. www.accorhotels.com.* *37 rooms.* On the boulevard leading to the port, this hotel's rooms are rather large and functional. A good address to combine business and tourism.

🛏️ **Novotel Le Havre Centre Gare Hotel** – *20 cours Lafayette.* 📞*02 35 19 23 23. www.accorhotels.com. 134 rooms.* Contemporary architecture close to the station, sitting on the banks of the Vauban basin. Trendy seasonal cuisine served in a dining room with windows opening on for garden. Summer outdoor dining.

🍴 EAT
🍽️ **Le Bistrot des Halles** – *7 pl. des Halles Centrales.* 📞*02 35 22 50 52. Closed Sun evening.* Dining room covered with enamel advertising signs and old posters, where stylish waitresses officiate.

🍽️ **La Petite Auberge** – *32 r. Ste-Adresse.* 📞*02 35 46 27 32. www. lapetiteauberge-lehavre.fr. Closed Wed noon, Sun evening, Mon.* In this small inn, formerly a way station, tasty country cuisine is to be had at good prices. Cared-for Norman façade.

🍽️ **La Taverne Paillette** – *22 r. Georges-Braque.* 📞*02 35 41 31 50. www.taverne-paillette.com.* Authentic brasserie setting for this Le Havre institution; choose between traditional dishes such as sauerkraut or *cassoulet*, seafood platters and fish recipes.

🍽️ **Le Quint & Sens** – *98 r. Prés.-Wilson.* 📞*02 35 41 18 28.* Warm and simple bistro décor, convivial atmosphere and charming welcome characterise this popular restaurant on a little square. Traditional cuisine.

CAFÉS
Le Clapoutis – *Sente Alphonse-Karr, 76310 Ste-Adresse.* 📞*02 35 49 09 17. www. le-clapotis.fr.* This establishment overlooks the sea. On the terrace in summer, large glass windows in winter. Seafood and fish on the menu. Café-tea room.

SHOPPING
Les Gobelins – *R. du Prés.-Wilson. Mon, Wed and Fri 7.30am–1.30pm.* Modest market right in the centre of town, on a big avenue next to the mairie. Numerous sellers of spring vegetables, butchers, specialised pork butchers and fishmongers offering products of excellent quality.

Les Halles Centrales – *Close Sun and holidays.* Stalls well-maintained, often by the best sellers in town. About 30 food stands.

Falaises d'Étretat★★★

The elegant resort of Étretat is renowned for its magnificent setting. The grandeur of the high cliffs and crashing waves has inspired many writers, artists and film directors. Maurice Leblanc described the Aiguille Creuse through his famous character, Arsène Lupin. Maupassant spent his childhood here, "leading the life of a wild foal". Other famous habitués included Alexandre Dumas, André Gide, Victor Hugo, Gustave Courbet, Jacques Offenbach and Claude Monet.

ÉTRETAT

Étretat's setting is a magnificent land-scape that is unforgettable no matter the season in which it is seen. With a **dyke-walkway** running along its edge, the pebbled **beach** is framed by the famous white-chalk **cliffs.** The view is so spectacular it is almost hard to believe it is real: to the right, the Amont cliff with the little chapel of Notre-Dame-de-la-Garde and the monument to the lost aviators Nungesser and Coli; to the left, the Aval cliff with its natural monumental arch, the Porte d'Aval. The Aiguille, 71m high, stands a little further off, a lonely needle of rock among the waves. The quaint thatched *caloges,* former fishing boats converted to store fishermen's equipment, have disappeared – three recreated *caloges* stand there today.
Halles – This wooden covered market in place du Maréchal-Foch is a reconstruction.
Église Notre-Dame – *rue Notre-Dame at corner of rue Nungesser et Coli* – This church has a Romanesque doorway with a 19C tympanum. The rest of the building is 12C. Go to the transept crossing to admire the 13C lantern turret.
Le Clos Lupin★ – *15 r. Guy-de-Maupassant.* ◷*Apr–Sept daily except Mon 10am–12.30pm, 1.30–6pm; Oct–Mar Sat–Sun and school holidays (except Mon) 10am–12.30pm, 1.30–5.30pm.* ◷*1 Jan,*

▶ **Population:** 1 339.
⚙ **Michelin Map:** 304: B-3.
🛈 **Info:** Place Maurice-Guillard, Étratat. ℘02 35 27 05 21. www.etretat.net.
◗ **Location:** This seaside resort is located 47km/29.2mi N of Honfleur, 90km/56mi NW of Rouen and 219km/136mi from Paris.
🅿 **Parking:** place du Général-de-Gaulle (fee). Free car parks: the Grand Val (rue Guy de Maupasssant, 300m from the centre), the route du Havre to the S and near the former train station to the N.
☺ **Don't Miss:** Panoramic view from the cliffs of Aval and Amont.
👪 **Kids:** The Tourist Train between Étretat and Les Loges.

25 Dec. ⬤€7.50. ℘*02 35 10 59 53. www. etretat.net.* Arsène Lupin is a gentleman burglar; a character created by author Maurice Leblanc. The museum, in a vast Norman family home, mingles mementos of the two.

CLIFF WALKS

Falaise d'Aval★★★

🚶 *Allow 1h on foot there and back. From the west end of the promenade climb the steps (180 steps, handrail) to the path which scales the cliff face. Walk along the edge of the cliff as far as the ridge of Porte d'Aval.*
Magnificent view: the massive Manneporte arch (left), the Aiguille opposite and Amont cliff on the bay's far side.

Falaise d'Amont★★

🚶 *Allow 1h on foot there and back. From the east end of the promenade take the steps cut into the chalk cliffs and the path to the clifftop. Access by car: take D 11 Fécamp par la Côte; just before the sign indicating the*

Falaise d'Aval with the Aiguille

© Perszing1982/iStockphoto.com

end of the built-up area, turn sharp left onto a steep and narrow uphill road. Park near the monument.

From **Notre-Dame-de-la-Garde** there is a magnificent **view★** of Étretat and its surroundings, with the long shingle beach from Aval arch to Aiguille. Behind the chapel an immense spire points skyward, memorial to Nungesser and Coli. These French aviators made the first attempt to fly the Atlantic on 8 May 1927, their craft, *Oiseau Blanc*, was last seen here.

Château des Aygues – *D 940, Etretat exit to Fécamp.* ⏱*Jul–Sept Wed–Mon 2–6pm.* €8 (child 12–18, €6). *Guided tours.* ⏱*15 days in Aug.* ℘*02 35 28 92 77. www.chateaulesaygues.com.*

Built in 1866, this was the summer residence of the queens of Spain, Maria Cristina of Bourbon and Isabella II. It welcomed famous guests such as Jacques Offenbach and Alexandre Dumas. A beautiful collection of Chinese ceramics and porcelains pay homage to Isabella II.

EXCURSIONS
Terminal du Havre-Antifer
15km/9mi S. Leave Étretat on avenue George-V, D 940.
⚠ *The cliffs can collapse without warning. Do not walk directly beneath them; beware of tides.*

Valleuse d'Antifer – *From Tilleul take rue de Mer, across from the church portal; take rue d'Antifer, right, which takes you to a car park; take the pretty path down through woods and meadows for about 20min.* This cliff hollow (*valleuse*) is an effort to reach, but worth it. You may not be alone when you reach the beautiful, famous view!

⚠Two local conservation associations protect the *valleuse* and offer summer nature walks. *Contact Étretat tourist office.*

Bruneval – *Return to the D 940 and 800m after Le Tilleul, take the D 111 towards La Poterie-Cap-d'Antifer.* An Allied raid on the night of 27–28 February 1942 was aimed at the German radar installation near the beach. Three British parachutist detachments destroyed the position, re-embarking almost without loss.

Terminal du Havre-Antifer – *Between Bruneval and St-Jouin, the road leads through pretty countryside to the oil terminal.* Le Havre-Antifer port was created in 1976 to receive oil tankers too big for the facilities at Le Havre. On the way back to St-Jouin, a narrow road on the right (signalled Port du Havre/Antifer/Belvédère), leads to a belvedere with a fine **view**.

ADDRESSES

🛏 STAY

🍽🛏 **Hôtel La Résidence** – *4 Boulevard Président René Coty. ☎02 35 27 02 87. 15 rooms.* This downtown mansion was built in the 14C. Pleasant rooms with amusing, eclectic furniture. Cycle hire.

🍽🛏🛏 **Le Donjon Domaine Saint Clair** – *Chemin de Saint Clair. ☎02 35 27 08 23. www.hoteletretat.com. 21 rooms.* Nestled on the heights of Etretat, directly below the seaside resort, the hotel enjoys a dominant position, in the heart of a beautiful green park overlooking the sea. Gastronomic restaurant (🍽🛏🛏).

🍴 EAT

🍽 **Lann Bihoué** – *45 r. Notre-Dame. ☎02 35 27 04 65. Closed Tue exc. during school holidays and Wed.* To make a change from Norman cuisine, try this crêperie near the town centre.

🍽🛏 **Le Clos Lupin** – *37 r. Alphonse-Karr. ☎02 27 30 19 33. www.leclos-lupin. com. Open Tue–Sat for lunch and dinner.*

Reservations required. Behind the stylish painted façade and lace trimmings, you'll find a long dining room in the heart of town. The sesonally changing menu features classic fare at reasonable prices.

🍽🛏🛏 **Le Galion** – *bd René-Coty. ☎02 35 29 48 74. Closed Tue–Wed except school holidays.* Situated in the town centre, this house, built with materials taken from an old Lisieux residence, has a noteworthy 14C ceiling of carved beams.

LEISURE

👥👤 🚲 **Étretat Tourist Train – Vélorail.** At the train station (*6km/3.7mi east of Étretat via D 940, 76790 Les Loges*). ☎02 35 29 49 61. www.lafrancevuedurail.fr/ttepac. *Apr–Oct weekends, departure from Les Loges and from Étretat (departure schedule varies by month). Round trip €7 (child 4–14, €4).* Across the green countryside between Étretat and Les Loges. You can also pedal the vélorail (a bicycle on train tracks) from Loges.

Fécamp★★

Fécamp is a fishing port as well as a centre for pleasure boats. The town is also the home of Benedictine liqueur – a link with its monastic past. Guy de Maupassant was one frequent visitor to the town, which features in several of his works.

A BIT OF HISTORY

As early as the 7C there was a monastery in Fécamp with a relic of the Precious Blood. Richard II, Duke of Normandy from 996–1027, established a Benedictine community here. Before the rise of Mont-St-Michel, this was the foremost place of pilgrimage in Normandy.

TOWN

Until 1863, **Guy de Maupassant** often came to his maternal grandmother's home in Fécamp. *La Maison Tellier* and various episodes in his tales are situated

- ▶ **Population:** 18 900.
- 🧭 **Michelin Map:** 304: C-3. Local map, 🔖see *Pays de Caux, p140.*
- ℹ **Info:** Quai Sadi-Carnot. ☎02 35 28 51 01. www.fecamptourisme.com.
- ◐ **Location:** Fécamp is 43km/ 26.7mi NE of Le Havre and 72km/44.7mi NW of Rouen.
- 😊 **Don't Miss:** The rich collections of the Benedictine palace, the abbey of La Trinité and the superb view from Cap Fagnet and Valmont abbey.
- 🕐 **Timing:** Fécamp and its surroundings will take up a day.
- 👥👤 **Kids:** The museum of Terre-Neuvas et de la Pêche.

Palais
Bénédictine

© Günter Gräfenhain/Sime/Photononstop

in this port town; little remains of that time, aside from the abbey church of La Trinité at place des Halettes. Fécamp's heart is however forever in its port. The "*Bout menteux*" (Liars' Corner), between quays Vicomté and Bérigny, a former sea dog lair, is just as lively today as it was in the past. The beach stretches from the channel entrance to the casino. As for the Gayant causeway crossing the inner harbour (moveable bridge), it connects with the north cliff and Côte de la Vierge; the Notre-Dame-de-Salut chapel can be made out against the horizon *(see Excursions)*.

The Port

The Freycinet handles commercial traffic. Verdun quay receives vessels loaded with gravel, sand for glass-making, salt from the Salins du Midi and logged or sawn wood.

Abbatiale de la Trinité★

pl. des Ducs Richards.
The abbey church built by Richard II was struck by lightning and burned down. The subsequent building (12C–13C) was modified several times between the 15C and 18C.

Exterior – The cathedral is one of the longest (127m) in France. The Classical façade does not accord with the rest of the building and the nave walls are aus-

tere. Skirt the south porch: the tympanum above the door is a good example of Norman Gothic decoration. Above the transept crossing rises the square lantern tower (65m high), designed in the typical Norman style.

Interior – The south transept contains a beautiful late 15C **Dormition of the Virgin★**. On the right of the the altar is the Angel's Footprint. In 943, when the reconstructed church was being consecrated, it is said that an angel appeared and left his footprint on the stone.

The chancel's dimensions make it magnificent. The stalls, baldaquin and high altar are all good 18C works by the Rouen artist De France. A Renaissance altar stands behind the high altar. In the centre of the sanctuary is an ancient shrine adorned with low-relief sculptures dating from the 12C. The chapels off the chancel aisles and radiating chapels were embellished with wonderful **carved screens★** in the 16C. In the fourth chapel, on the right, is the **tomb★** of Abbot Thomas of St-Benoît, who died in 1307; the tomb is decorated with scenes from the abbey's history on its base.

The 15C **Lady Chapel★** forms a separate group in the Flamboyant style. The wood medallions are 18C; the windows are 13C, 14C and 16C. Facing the chapel is the white-marble **tabernacle★** of the

Precious Blood. The 17C tomb in the chapel of the Sacred Heart belongs to **Guglielmo da Volpiano**, first abbot of Fécamp, who died in 1031.

Palais Bénédictine★★

110 r. Alexandre-le-Grand.
◷*Early Apr–early Jul and Sept–early Nov 10am–1pm, 2–6.30pm; Early Jul–Aug 10am–6.45pm.* ◷*1 Jan, 1 May and 25 Dec.* ◐€12. ✆*02 35 10 26 10.*
www.benedictinedom.com/ flamboyant-palais.

The building, designed by Camille Albert in the late 19C, is a mixture of neo-Gothic and neo-Renaissance styles. The **museum** displays a large collection of objets d'art: silver and gold work, ivories, Nottingham alabasters (late 15C), wrought-iron work, statues and many manuscripts.

The Gothic Room is covered by a fine pitched roof made of oak and chestnut, shaped as the upturned hull of a ship; it houses the library: 15C Books of the Hours with fine **illuminations**, numerous **ivories**, a collection of **oil lamps** dating from the early days of Christianity and a Dormition of the

Virgin, a painted low-relief wooden carving of the German School.

The Alexander Le Grand Room, named after the Fécamp merchant who first marketed the Benedictine liqueur in 1863, displays objects and documents relating to its history.

Musée des pêcheries★

3 Quai Capitaine Jean Recher.
♿◷*May–mid-Sept daily 10am–6pm; mid-Sept–Dec daily except Tue 10am–6pm.* ◷*1 Jan, 1 May, 25 Dec.* ◐€7. ✆*02 35 28 31 99.*

This Fishing Museum, opened in 2017, accommodates the collections formerly housed in the Musée des Terre-Neuvas et de la Pêche. It evokes memories of the Fécamp fishing industry. The lower gallery explores the great adventure of the cod fishermen on the Newfoundland banks in the days of the sailing ship and the dory, a flat-bottomed craft rising at bow and stern.

There are also rich collections of Fine Arts, and regional collections of cabinets, costumes and Norman jewellery. Breathtaking 360° **view★★** of the city and the port.

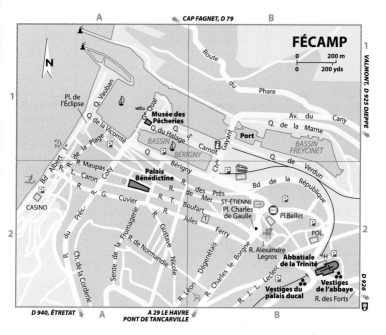

Deep-Sea Fishing, an Old Tradition

The herrings of Fécamp have been renowned since the Middle Ages. During the Renaissance ships sailed from Fécamp to Newfoundland to fish for cod. Fishing techniques did not change much for nearly 400 years: the fish was caught with a ground line by two men aboard a 5m-long flat-bottomed boat called a doris. The fish was then gutted, cleaned, boned, salted and stored in the hold; this was called fishing for green cod. Fishing for dried cod meant fishermen had to settle during the season on the coast of Newfoundland, where they would build drying racks for their catch.

During the 1970s, 15 huge trawlers with a crew of 900 men salted and froze 21 000t of cod in the icy waters of the North Atlantic. Today, pleasure boats have replaced trawlers, but until recently one could still meet old fishermen recalling their memories at the Bout Menteux (Liars' Corner, situated between quai Vicomté and quai Bérigny).

EXCURSIONS

Cap Fagnet

On the cliff north of Fécamp's port.
The cape has been home to five wind turbines since 2005. The place is worth a visit for the pretty little 11C **Notre-Dame-du-Salut** chapel built to protect sailors (votive offerings). A magnificent panoramic view may be found here.
⚠️*Hollows (valleuses). Respect safety measures! Watch children and avoid clifftops; rare landslides do happen.*

Vaucottes

9km/5mi SW of Fécamp, from Yport or Vattetot (12 km/7mi SW of Fécamp via D 940 and D 11) by a pretty road from Les Hogues or from Yport by a beautiful coast road.
This *valleuse* belongs to Vattetot-sur-Mer, its church steeple is a sailors' seamark. The site is restricted, with a path down to sea to pretty, early-20C villas.

Val-de-la-Mer

At Senneville-sur-Fécamp (5km/3mi NE by D 925), take r. du Val-de-Mer, after church on left.
These impressive cliffs are especially favoured by birdwatchers. There are stairs, but you may prefer to enjoy the view from top of the steps because of the risk of frequent cliffslides.

St-Pierre-en-Port

13km/8mi NE from Fécamp by D 925 and D 79.
This old port at end of a *valleuse* today has pretty, familial beach and a magnificent view.

Les Grandes Dalles

Just NE of St-Pierre-en-Port.
This early fishing village is set in a cliff hollow and is easily reached. There is a little pebbled beach with a superb view.

Les Petites Dalles★

NE of St-Pierre-en-Port, 1.5k/1mi from Sassetot-le-Mauconduit.
Late 19C homes combine with a delightful setting and a magnificent sea view, enjoyed by some leading lights of history including Monet, Pissarro, Delacroix and, **Sissi**, Empress of Austria. Almost carried off by the currents, Sissi granted her rescuer a gold watch. In 1940 **Rommel** and his men forced through here to separate the French and English troops. They celebrated afterwards with a swim.
The Petites Dalles **cavern** (🔊*guided tour (1h) by arrangement with tourist office ☎02 35 27 87 98; www.les-petites-dalles.org*) was discovered in 1966. It eroded itself into existence about 800 000 years ago.

A **walking route** (3h30 round trip, take southern coastal path (GR 21) from small car park over the beach; picnic areas on path, among pastures and cliffs) links Les Petites Dalles, Les Grandes Dalles, St-Pierre-en-Port and Sassetot-le-Mauconduit in a ring. There are beautiful panoramic views of the sea, the *valleuses*, and the Château de Sassetot park. The trip down to Les Petites Dalles from Sassetot, through a forest and to a chapel in a hamlet, is magical.

Château de Bailleul
10km/6mi SE by D 73.
This elegant 16C château (*closed to the public; https://chateaudubailleul.com*) consists of a central square building flanked by four pavilions. The medieval side façades are almost blind. A chapel stands in the wooded park.

Valmont
11km/7mi E via D 150.
Located in the very heart of the Pays de Caux and dominated by a castle built on a rocky spur, the village of Valmont is known for the ruins of its Benedictine abbey.
Abbey★ – *Church only: daily 11am–noon, 2.30–5pm. 1 Jan, Easter Sun, Pentecost Sun, 1 Nov, 25 Dec. 02 35 27 34 92. www.abbaye-valmont.fr.* Founded in the 12C, the Benedictine abbey of Valmont was rebuilt in the 14C following a fire and was radically altered in the 16C. After the Revolution the abbey became a private residence The **Chapelle de la Vierge★**, or Six o'clock Chapel (the monks celebrated Mass at this time every day), which has remained intact among the ruins, has an overall effect of great grace. Above the altar is a tiny room which has exquisite decorations and also a picture of the Annunciation attributed to Germain Pilon.
Château – *Closed to the public* – Property of the Estoutevilles, lords of Valmont, this former military fortress preserves a Romanesque keep flanked by a Louis XI wing, crowned by a covered watch-path, and a Renaissance wing.

ADDRESSES

🛏 STAY
Chambre d'hôte La Marnière – *2 rue Vallée, 76110 Daubauf-Serville (13km/8mi SE of Fécamp, via D926 dir. Caudebec). 02 35 29 38 80. 5 rooms.* This charming farmhouse is only 10 mins from the sea in a wooded setting with a large garden. Guest rooms are traditionally furnished and comfortable.

Hôtel de la Plage – *87 r. de la Plage. 02 35 29 76 51. https://hotel-fecamp.com. 20 rooms.* Situated close to the waterfront, this very simple family hotel is a modest stopover. Rooms are spic-and-span and the breakfast room is picturesque with its marine décor and counter shaped like a ship's hull.

🍴 EAT
Chez Nounoute – *3 pl. Nicholas-Selle. 02 35 29 38 08. www.cheznounoute.com. Closed Sun evening (except school holidays), and all day Wed. Reservations advised.* Occasionally you like to find an unusual place, managed by a rather special but friendly owner. Here you find seafood choucroute and fresh fish wonderfully cooked.

La Matelotte – *2 pl. Nicolas-Selle. 02 27 30 44 21. www.restaurant lamatelotte.fr.* This restaurant situated in the marina offers seafood from the fisheremonger directly opposite, as well as local, seasonal meat dishes.

Le Vicomté – *4 r. du Prés.-René-Coty. 02 35 28 47 63. Closed Wed eve, Sun, holidays.* Near the great Benedictine palace, where a celebrated liqueur is produced, this small bistro is decorated with old engravings. The chef uses ingredients sourced from local markets to make delicious dishes.

LEISURE
Tourisme et loisirs maritimes – *15 r. Vicomte. 06 16 80 24 10. Aug excursions Fécamp–Etretat; Sept–Jul: tour of Le Havre port – sea excursion and port tour.* A variety of excursions on boats along the Norman coast are proposed, including fishing expeditions, from Fécamp and Le Havre.

The tourist office has suggestions for bicycle excursions and walks in the area.

Pays de Caux★

The Caux is mainly known for its impressive coastline. Visitors delight in the natural beauty of the area, returning each year to the vast beaches below the splendid chalk cliffs. The surrounding countryside offers a swathe of remarkable churches, castles and manor houses.

GEOLOGY

Côte d'Albâtre – Along the Alabaster Coast the chalk cliffs, with alternate strata of flint and yellow marl, are worn away ceaselessly by the action of the tides and the weather.

The Étretat needle rocks and underwater shelves 1.6km/1mi from the shore indicate the former coastline. At the particularly exposed point of **Cap de la Hève**, erosion carves away 2m a year; the water is milky with chalk, and flints are pounded endlessly upon the beaches. The hollows *(valleuses)* cut into every clifftop as far as the eye can see are dry former river valleys, truncated by the retreating coastline. Some rivers were powerful enough to carve valleys right down to the coastline, and that is where ports and resorts have appeared.

Caux Farmsteads – The farms appear as green oases surrounded by 2m-high windbreaks topped by a double row of oaks, beeches or elms.

The **farmstead** comprises a meadow planted with apple trees in which stand the half-timbered farm buildings. The entrance is often through a monumental gateway. In spring, cattle and horses are tethered to a post *(tière)* and each animal marks out its territory in the form of a perfect circle. Milk production is the chief source of income.

🚗 DRIVING TOURS

🚗 ① CÔTE D'ALBÂTRE★
From Dieppe to Étretat, 77km/48mi. Allow about 2h30.

▶ Leave Dieppe by D 75 (🕮 *see Dieppe, p149*).

- 🦽 **Michelin Map:** 512 folds 7-10, 19-22.
- ▦ **Info:** Several villages have their own tourist offices. Those of Dieppe, Étretat, Le Havre and Caudebec-en-Caux also serve the wider Caux region.
- ◐ **Location:** The Pays de Caux is bounded on the S by the Seine valley, on the W and N by the Alabaster Coast and on the E along a line extending between Dieppe and Rouen.
- 👁 **Don't Miss:** The resorts and little villages of the Alabaster Coast, as well as the charming villages of the interior and the Parc des Boucles de la Seine.
- 🕐 **Timing:** You will need several days to tour this region.
- 👪 **Kids:** The outdoor centre on Lac de Caniel offers sports and games.

Glimpses of the sea and cliffs and pleasant views of resorts are the main features of this drive, which is at its best in the morning.

Pourville-sur-Mer

This seaside resort, pleasantly situated near jagged cliffs, has risen from the ruins of the Dieppe commando raid of 19 August 1942; the Cameron Highlanders and a Canadian Regiment, the South Saskatchewan, landed to the sound of bagpipes and inflicted severe damage on the enemy. Under cover of the Navy and sacrificing their rearguard, they re-embarked early in the afternoon. A commemorative stele of pink marble stands on the seafront.

▶ Continue west on D 75 through **Varengeville-sur-Mer**⚓ (🕮 *see Varengeville-sur-Mer, p147*).

Cliffs of the Côte d'Albâtre near Fécamp

© Musat/iStockphoto.com

Ste-Marguerite-sur-Mer
The 12C church, which has no transept, was considerably remodelled in the 16C. Inside, four of the original **arches★** remain on the north side; those on the south date from 1528. The high altar dates from 1160 and is one of the very few remaining of this period.

Saint-Aubin
The pretty 16C **church** still betrays numerous traces of the Romanesque period, such as the portal and the tower in flint. The **town**, standing at its post at the mouth of the Dun river, is a sort of entranceway to the pretty **valley** of the same name, 10km–12km/6mi–7mi long and on the list of Seine-Maritime's beautiful sites. It is also know as the "linen valley" owing to the chateaux, manors, farms and thatched homes of drapers that are all part of the region's rich architectural heritage.

The valley offers numerous options for excursions by foot or bicycle. Contact the Bourg-Dun tourist office (see below). Bicycles can be rented there.

▶ Take the D 237 on the left.

Flainville
Halfway between St-Aubin-sur-Mer and the Bourg-Dun, on the left.
Beautiful Renaissance frescoes can be found inside the 16C **chapel of St Julien**. The recently restored **bread oven**, presents all the bakers' tools of yesteryear.

▶ Take the D 237 south.

Le Bourg-Dun
Office de Tourisme, 2 Route de Dieppe. ℰ02 35 84 19 55.
www.plateaudecauxmaritime.com.
Notre-Dame-du-Salut is a vast composite church, remarkable for its **tower★**, built on a massive square 13C base. The hatchet-shaped roof is 17C. A Renaissance door opens into the south aisle. Beneath Flamboyant vaulting in the south transept are a Renaissance bay and piscina; three arches in the chancel open into the beautiful south aisle, added in the 14C. The font in the north aisle is Renaissance.

▶ Continue on the D 237.

Saint-Pierre-le-Vieux
The 12C and 13C **church** has its Romanesque-style belltower and Gothic and neo-Gothic elements from the 14C and 16C. Note the **dial** at the foot of the church; the road-mender used it in the past to show which direction he had gone to work in.

▶ Continue on the D 237.

La Gaillarde
The pretty **St Margaret's chapel** is remarkable for the finesse of its sculpted Romanesque porch, especially the heads forming the column capitals. There is an old bread oven in the centre of the village.

▶ Continue on the D 237.

Saint-Pierre-le-Viger

Two Friday afternoons a month you can visit the "**Terre de lin**" factory (*information at the Plateau de Caux maritime tourist office; www.terredelin.com.* ℘*02 35 84 19 55*), one of France's largest linen-making cooperatives. Here you can learn about the various stages required to convert the plant into a textile fibre. There is a pretty limestone **manor** alongside the Dun, dating 16C and 17C.

▷ Take the D 142 S then the D 108 on the left.

HONFLEUR

Crasville-la-Rocquefort

The **St-Cosme Chèvrerie** 👤👤 is in an enclosure, surrounded by a windbreak of beeches and fields of wheat, beets and flax. The family organises farm visits in a warm and friendly atmosphere, a chance to discover the goat cheese dairy, the pigs, turkeys, cows and rabbits. A variety of cheeses are on sale here, including the house creation and speciality, the galet d'Albâtre.

▷ Return to St-Aubin and head SW on the D 68.

Veules-les-Roses★

The seaside resort, sheltered in a small valley, has pretty surroundings, notably windmills and picturesque villas dating from the 19C, when the town attracted fashionable Parisians. **St-Martin**, in the town itself, is a 16C–17C church with a

13C lantern. A timber-framed roof covers the nave and aisles. Inside are five 16C twisted limestone columns and ancient statues.

Veules-les-Roses on a winter morning

© I. Lainey/MICHELIN

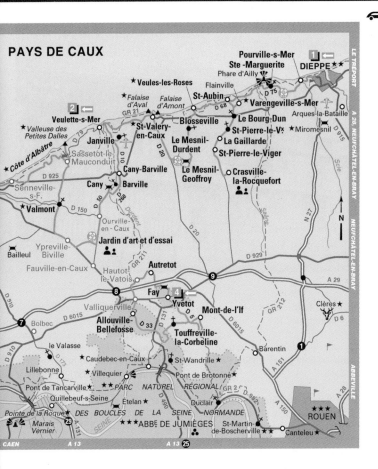

PAYS DE CAUX

A walking route takes you past mills, villas and homes built of brick and flint. Some spots are very pretty, especially near the watering trough where watercress is grown (*Mairie de Veules les Roses, 7 avenue du Docteur Michel. ℘02 35 97 64 11; www.veules-les-roses.fr*).

▶ Briefly turn right onto D 925, then turn left onto D 37.

Église de Blosseville
The church, surmounted by a 12C belfry, possesses beautiful Renaissance stained-glass windows and some old statues.

▶ Continue on D 37 towards Ermenouville.

Château du Mesnil-Geoffroy
May–Sept Wed–Sun 2–6pm. ⌖€7 (*guided visit of chateau €9*). ℘06 71 07 22 50. www.chateau-mesnil-geoffroy.com.
Surrounded by a 9ha formal French park with a famous rose garden (2 500 species), this 17C and 18C château is an interesting testimony to the gentle art of living under Louis XV.

▶ On leaving the château, turn right on the D 70, and then minor roads.

Mesnil-Durdent
Make sure you visit this charming village and its wild garden, the **Jardin communal d'Amouhoques**, an irregular plot of land with many paths and embankments, planted with all

143

*Maison d'Henri IV,
Saint-Valery-en-Caux*

© H. Payelle/Michelin

manner of herbs carrying quaint, old-fashioned names.

▶ Take the D 75 to Angiens, then D 468 NW until you reach St-Valery-en-Caux.

Saint-Valery-en-Caux★

St-Valery is both a popular seaside resort, with a promenade overlooking the long shingle beach, and a fishing and coastal trading port.

The **Falaise d'Aval★** (West Headland) *(access on foot via sentier des Douaniers and steps)* is crowned by a monument commemorating the battles of June 1940 (51st Highland Division and the French 2nd Cavalry Division).

The view embraces the Ailly lighthouse and, on a clear day, Dieppe. The **Maison d'Henri IV** *(quai du Havre)* is a beautiful Renaissance house with carved beams. On the **Falaise d'Amont** (East Headland) *(access by steps)* stands the 51st Highland Division Monument overlooking the town, harbour and beach. The more modern monument nearby was erected in memory of Coste and Bellonte, who in 1930 made the first flight from Paris to New York.

🚶 The area around St-Valery-en-Caux offers many pleasant walks (🚻*Tourist Office, Quai d'Amont. ☎02 35 97 00 63).*

Veulettes-sur-Mer

The 11C and 13C church stands halfway up a hill overlooking the seaside resort, which has a 2.5km/1.5mi beach. The finest **panorama★★** is between Senneville *(narrow road)* and Fécamp, near the **Chapelle Notre-Dame-du-Salut** (sailors' pilgrimage). The cliffs to the west of Fécamp stretch as far as Étretat.

🚘 ② VALLÉE DE LA DURDENT

52km/32mi. Allow 3h.

▶ Leave Veulettes on the D10 south. At Paluel take the D68 left.

La Durdent wends its way to lazily spill out at Veulettes-sur-Mer, having worn a wide green valley through the open spaces of the Caux plateau.

Chapelle de Janville

This pilgrimage church has an attractive wrought-iron grille in the chancel.

▶ Return to Paluel. Turn left (S) onto D 10.

Cany-Barville

☞*Guided tours on request from Tourist Office, Place Robert Gabel. ☎02 35 57 17 70.*

The **church** on the west bank, rebuilt in the 16C, has a 13C belfry. On the high altar (18C) stands a Christ in Majesty made of over 80 angels in relief work. The **Ecomusée Moulin St-Martin** (⏱*Apr–Oct, by appointment;* 📞*02 35 97 59 71*) is in the old mechanics workshop next to the 15C wheat mill. It contains a rich collection of old tools and objects.

▶ Take the D 268.

Barville
The small church has a delightful **setting★** between two arms of the River Durdent.

▶ Continue on D 268.

Château de Cany
🕑*Guided tours Jul–Aug Sat–Thu 10am–noon, 3–6pm.* 📞*02 35 97 04 60.*
Surrounded by moats fed by the River Durdent stands an imposing stone and brick château built in 1640, the Louis XIII era. The apartments contain fine 17C and 18C furnishings. In the basement, a kitchen contains utensils, crockery and costumed figures.

▶ Continue on the D 268, then take the D 131 on the right, then the D 50 on the left. Go past Ourville-en-Caux. When you get to Normanville, leave the village on your right and go a little further, following the signs indicating the garden on the right.

👥 Jardin d'Art et d'Essais★
D 50, rte de Fauville, Normanville.
♿⏱*Early May–Oct daily except Wed 11am–1pm, 3–8pm.* ⏹€6 *(child €3).*
⏱*1 Jan, 25 Dec.* 📞*02 35 29 62 39.*
http://aisthesie.free.fr.
An organic garden of unusual plants, superb trees, meandering waters and beautiful bamboo. A walk that will wake all five of your senses!

▶ Continue NW on the D 33 after leaving Normanville; head for Sorquainville and get to Ypreville-Biville by the D 75. Take the D 926

heading for Fécamp and after 2km/1mi turn right onto the D 17.

Valmont
ⓘ*See VALMONT, p139.*

▶ Continue north on the D 17 to head for Thérouldeville, then Sassetot-le-Mauconduit. In crossing the village, take a look to the left to admire the Château de Sassetot, then continue on D17. Cross the D 925. Pass through Sassetot-le-Mauconduit, and then follow the D 5 until you reach Petites Dalles.

Les Petites Dalles★
ⓘ*See Les Petites Dalles, p138.*

▶ Return to Sassetot-le-Mauconduit and take the D 79 along the coast in the direction of Senneville. Head along the cliff to reach Fécamp.

The most beautiful **panoramic view★★** of the itinerary is between Senneville and Fécamp, close to the **chapelle de N.-D.-du-Salut** (sailors' pilgrimage), where there is a viewpoint.

🚗 ③ VALLÉE DE LA LÉZARDE
33km/21mi. Allow 1h.

▶ Leave Fécamp on the D940.

Yport
Yport, a seaside resort tucked away in a valley, had a fishing fleet until 1970.

Étretat★★★
ⓘ*See FALAISES D'ÉTRETAT, p133.*

▶ Leave Étretat by D 39 (SE). At Criquetot-l'Esneval turn acutely left onto D 239.

Cuverville
The writer André Gide (1859–1951) is buried in the small cemetery, under a simple gravestone at the fromt of the church. The author of the *Nourritures*

terrestres spent long periods at Cuverville on the property of his cousins, the Rondeaux.

⬡ Return to Criquetot-l'Esneval and take D 79 (SW) through the pleasant Lézarde valley.

Château du Bec
⚫⃛ *Not open to the public.*
The 12C–16C castle has an enchanting setting of trees and still waters (*http://chateaudubec.com*).

⬡ In Épouville turn left onto D 925 and then right onto D 52.

Manéglise
The small church is a graceful example of Romanesque architecture.

⬡ Return to Épouville; continue SW.

Montivilliers
An 11C lantern tower above the transept crossing and a Romanesque belfry surmounted by a spire (restored in the 19C) identify the **Église St-Sauveur★**.

⬡ The road leaves the Vallée de la Lézarde via Rouelles, just outside Le Havre. The road skirts the edge of Montgeon forest, and leads to the Jenner tunnel, which leads to the town centre.

🚗 4 PLATEAU CAUCHOIS★
Round trip starting from Yvetot. 50km/32mi. Allow 1h30.

Yvetot
The town, made famous in a song as the capital of an imaginary kingdom, is in fact a large market town on the Caux plateau. The **Église St-Pierre**, built in 1956, contains remarkably large **stained-glass windows★★** by Max Ingrand, which produce a dazzling effect; other windows show founders of religious orders, saints of the Rouen diocese and the saints of France. The Lady Chapel *(behind the altar)* windows depict episodes in the life of the Virgin.

⬡ Leave Yvetot by heading for Ste-Marie-des-Champs on the D 37. After the Yvetot exit, turn left at the roundabout. Take the minor road, rue du Vieux-Ste-Marie, to the Manoir de Fay.

Manoir de Fay
This pretty 17C manor (*not open to the public*), in brick with pale stone wall ties and toothing, apparently once welcomed the uncle of French literary luminary Pierre Corneille.
The property has an immense **orchard and walled vegetable garden** (*Parc-Verger*) which is pleasant for a wander (🕐*Apr–Sept 8.30am–8pm; Oct–Mar 8.30am–5.30pm; www.manoirdufay.com*).

⬡ Continue on rue du Vieux-Ste-Marie then take route de La-Linerie on the left to get to D 131 on the right, to be taken N to Autretot.

Autretot
A pretty village typical of the Caux region, which prides itself on its flowers – close to 20 000 are planted every year to brighten the centre of Autretot.

⬡ On leaving Autretot, just before the water tower, take the D 110 on the left and follow it to Allouville-Bellefosse; you will pass through Veraval, Hautot-le-Vatois, Écretteville-lès-Baons and Valliquerville.

Allouville-Bellefosse
The village is known for the **oak tree** (*chêne*) which grows in front of the church; it is believed to be more than 1 300 years old, one of the oldest in France and the most famous tree in Normandy.

⬡ Leave Allouville on the D 33 to join the D 104 (E).

Touffreville-la-Corbeline
Touffreville has an 18C church with 12C belltower. The tomb here is of the Bossières brothers, explorers of southern climes. Moving on from here, you find pretty farms along the roadside.

▶ Continue on the D 104, then take successively the D 89 on the left, the D5 on the right and then D 304 on the left to Mont-de-l'If.

Mont-de-l'If
There are two manors in this village; church with 11C vestiges.

▶ Return on the D 304 then follow the D 5 to return to Yvetot.

ADDRESSES

🛏 STAY

🍽🍽 **Chambre d'hôte Le Château de Grosfy** – *61 r. du Calvaire, 76570 Hugleville-en-Caux.* ☎*07 82 06 57 52. 4 rooms.* A lovely alley of lime trees leads to this 18C–19C family home, formerly a hunting lodge. Both rustic and reproduction antique furniture in the large, peaceful guest rooms. Large park with a little wood.

⁑ EAT

🍽 **La Boussole** –*1 r. Max-Lerclec, 76460 St-Valery-en-Caux.* ☎*06 26 98 36 36. Closed Tue.* Prettily set in a navy blue half-timbered house, this restaurant opposite the port is entirely devoted to seafood. Two cosy rooms with bistro chairs and wooden tables. Shellfish platters in summer and many fish specialities.

🍽🍽 **Le Belvédère** – *76280 St-Jouin-Bruneval (10km/6mi S of Étretat via D 940 then D 111).* ☎*02 35 20 13 76. www. restaurant-lebelvedere.com.* A curious blue building perched upon the cliffs of the Pays de Caux. The comfortable dining room offers an exceptional view of the sea. Enjoy fish, mussels and other shellfish while gazing over the deep blue sea.

LEISURE

👫 **Parc de Loisirs - lac de Caniel** – *R. du Dessous-des-Bois (between St-Valery-en-Caux and Fécamp), 76450 Vittefleur.* ☎*02 35 97 40 55. www.lacdecaniel.com. Open daily from noon.* A great many water sports: water skiing, boating, canoeing, kayaking, summer sledding, pedal boats, boats with lifeguards (*Jul–Aug*). Playing field, bowling, mini golf, billiards and restaurant.

Varengeville-sur-Mer★

The resort consists of a series of hamlets in a charming landscape of hedges and half-timbered houses. The church stands on an attractive site★ overlooking the sea. The stained-glass window in the south aisle depicting the Tree of Jesse is by 20C abstract artist Georges Braque, who is buried in the graveyard.

SIGHTS

Église
The church site★ overlooks the sea. The tombs of artist **Georges Braque** (1882–1963) and musician and composer **Albert Roussell** (1869–1937) are found here. Braque's stained-glass Tree of Jesse is in the south nave.

▶ **Population:** 971.
⏱ **Michelin Map:** 304: F-2.
🅸 **Info:** Office de Tourisme de Quiberville-sur-Mer, 12 Rue de la Saâne, 76860 Quiberville. ☎02 35 04 08 32. www.quibervillesurmer-auffay-tourisme.com.
▶ **Location:** The pretty coastal road D 75 leads to Varengeville, which is 4km/2.5mi W of Dieppe, between Pourville-sur-Mer and Vasterival.
👁 **Don't Miss:** The beautiful view from the church; the garden at the Bois des Moutiers, designed by Gertrude Jekyll.
🕐 **Timing:** Take 1h to see the garden.

Manoir d'Ango with its dovecote
© Bertrand Rieger/hemis.fr

♣♦"Les Bruyères" nature walk
1hr. Take route de l'Aumône across from the mairie and follow bois des Communes

This 500m-long path is waymarked with panels explaining the geology, flora and fauna of the Bois des Communes moors.

Parc floral du Bois des Moutiers★
🕐 *Mid-Mar–mid-Nov daily 10am–8pm.* ⊗€11. ℘02 35 85 10 02.
www.boisdesmoutiers.com.

In a valley facing the sea is a lovely English-style garden (9ha/22 acres). The **house** (1898) was designed by the renowned English architect Sir Edwin Luytens and the **garden** by his frequent collaborator, Gertrude Jekyll.

Chapelle St-Dominique
On the outskirts of Varengeville, on the left side of the road to Dieppe.

There is more **stained glass** by Braque as well as a painting by 20C artist Maurice Denis.

EXCURSIONS
Phare d'Ailly★
1km/0.6mi on D 75A off D 75.

A modern lighthouse has replaced the two older ones (18C–19C), lost in 1944.

Manoir d'Ango
Follow the signs from D 75 onto a little road, and turn right a bit further on a drive to car park.

🕐 *10.30am–noon, 2–6pm: May–Sept daily; Apr and Oct–early Nov Sat–Sun and public holidays.* ⊗€5.50.
℘02 35 04 19 94. www.manoirdango.fr.

This was the lovely Renaissance home of **Jean Ango**, the great 16C navigator, fleet-owner, governor of Dieppe and naval adviser to François I.

With a large inner courtyard, it also has an Italian-style **loggia**. Typically Renaissance, there are many sculpted ornaments forming foliage, seashells and medallions.

Valleuses
In the direction of the Ailly lighthouse.

The very beautiful Petit-Ailly and Vasterival are among the most typical of these hanging valleys. Garden-lovers will enjoy the **Jardins du Vaserival** (👁*Guided tours Apr–Oct Mon–Fri at 11am* ⊗€15); ℘02 35 85 12 05; www.vasterival.fr).

ADDRESSES

♐ EAT
⊖⊖ **La Maison des Jules** – *Pl. des Canadiens.* ℘02 35 84 28 97. www.lamaisondejules.com. Closed Wed. A former butcher's is converted into a tea room, wine bar and gallery. A warm décor with stove, club chairs and exposed beams. In summer, small terrace set up outdoors. Platters of fresh food, oysters, quiches, pastries, etc.

Dieppe★★

Dieppe is home to Paris's closest beach and is thus France's oldest seaside resort. The harbour is modern but many old corners and alleys remain, along with churches, a castle and a museum. In the square du Canada stands a monument commemorating the men of Dieppe who explored Canada in the 16C, 17C and 18C, a reminder of more than 350 years of common history. A plaque recalls the Commando Raid in 1942.

A BIT OF HISTORY

Jean Ango and the Privateers' War (16C) – When the Portuguese decided to treat any vessel found off the African coast as a pirate ship, François I riposted by issuing letters of marque. The seamen of Dieppe took the lead. **Jean Ango**, shipbuilder and naval adviser to François I, produced a fleet of privateers, "which would make a king tremble". Among his captains was **Verrazano** from Florence who discovered the site of New York (1524). Within a few years Ango's ships had captured over 300 Portuguese vessels. Fearing ruin, the King of Portugal forced Ango to give up his letter of marque. The captain built himself a splendid mansion in Dieppe and a country residence in Varengeville. In 1535, he was appointed Governor of Dieppe. In 1551, he was buried in a chapel of St James' Church.

Dieppe Spa – According to the chronicler Pierre de l'Estoile, in 1578 Henri III, who was suffering from scabies (a skin disease), was advised by his doctors to bathe in the sea at Dieppe.

Later Madame de Sévigné mentioned in her letters that some of the court ladies went to Dieppe. She wrote of one of them, "The sea received her bare naked and thus was made proud; I mean to say the sea was proud, for the lady was greatly embarrassed."

Throughout the 19C the baths and casinos of Dieppe attracted extravagant people showing off their fine clothes, as well as celebrities such as King Louis-Philippe, Napoleon III, Eugène Delacroix, Camille Saint-Saëns, Alexandre Dumas and Oscar Wilde.

Canadian Commando Raid in 1942 – On 19 August 1942, Operation Jubilee was launched; it was the first Allied reconnaissance expedition on Europe's coast. Dieppe was the primary objective. Seven thousand men, mostly Canadians, landed at eight points between Berneval and Ste-Marguerite, but the Churchill tanks floundered hopelessly on the beach under intense fire. Five thousand men were killed or taken prisoner; the Allies learned from this raid that German

▶ **Population:** 29 606.

🚗 **Michelin Map:** 304: G-2 – Local map, *see Pays de Caux, p140*.

🪧 **Info:** Pont Jean-Ango. ✆02 32 14 40 60. www. dieppetourisme.com.

◐ **Location:** Dieppe is 65km/40.5mi N of Rouen and 108km/67.5mi from Le Havre. The city is cut in two by the River Béthune, with the picturesque old districts on the right bank and the commercial and government buildings on the left bank around the Grande-Rue and the rue de la Barre.

🅿 **Parking:** Look for free parking along the seafront (bd de Verdun), along the quai de Bérigny (cultural centre) and behind the train station. The car park opposite the town hall (Mairie) on Maréchal-Joffre is paying.

👁 **Don't Miss:** The 18C buildings along rue de la Barre and the wonderful view of the city from the château museum.

🕐 **Timing:** You need a day to see Dieppe, and half a day to tour the Forest of Eawy.

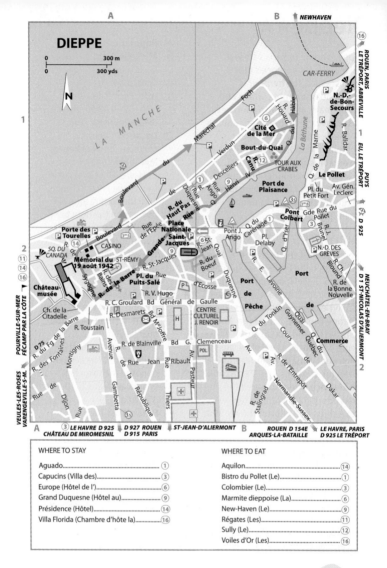

DIEPPE

0 ____ 300 m
0 ____ 300 yds

N

LA MANCHE

NEWHAVEN

ROUEN, PARIS
LE TRÉPORT, ABBEVILLE

CAR-FERRY

N.-D.-
de-Bon-
Secours

Cité
de la Mer

Bout-du-Quai

TOUR AUX
CRABES

Le Pollet

EU, LE TRÉPORT

PUYS

R. de la Marne

R. Baldar

Port de
Plaisance

Pl. du
Petit Fort

Gde Rue du
Pollet

Pont
Colbert

D 925

Porte des
Tourelles

Place
Nationale
Saint-
Jacques

R. du
Haut Pas

Pont J.
Ango

Pl.
Delaby

N.-D. DES
GRÈVES

NEUCHÂTEL-EN-BRAY
D 1 ST-NICOLAS D'ALIERMONT

CASINO

ST-RÉMY

Quai
St-
Jean

R. du
Boeuf

Port

de

R. de
la Bonne
Nouvelle

Mémorial du
19 août 1942

Pl. du
Puits-Salé

R. V. Hugo

d'Écosse

Port
de
Pêche

Commerce

Château-
musée

Ch. de la
Citadelle

R. C. Groulard

R. Desmarets

R. Toustain

Bd Général de Gaulle

CENTRE
CULTUREL
J. RENOIR

Q. du Tonkin

Q. de Québec

Quai

Dakar

POURVILLE-SUR-MER
FÉCAMP PAR LA CÔTE

D 75

R. du Fg de la Barre

R. des Fontaines

Montigny

Avenue

R. de Blainville

Bd G. Clemenceau

POL

H

VEULES-LES-ROSES
VARENGEVILLE-S-M.

Rue de Dijon

Gambetta

Rue Jean

Rue

Ribault

Pasteur

République

Thiers

A

B

LE HAVRE D 925
CHÂTEAU DE MIROMESNIL

D 927 ROUEN
D 915 PARIS

ST-JEAN-D'ALIERMONT

ROUEN D 154E
ARQUES-LA-BATAILLE

LE HAVRE, PARIS
D 925 LE TRÉPORT

WHERE TO STAY		WHERE TO EAT	
Aguado	①	Aquilon	⑭
Capucins (Villa des)	③	Bistro du Pollet (Le)	①
Europe (Hôtel de l')	⑥	Colombier (Le)	③
Grand Duquesne (Hôtel au)	⑨	Marmite dieppoise (La)	⑥
Présidence (Hôtel)	⑭	New-Haven (Le)	⑨
Villa Florida (Chambre d'hôte la)	⑯	Régates (Les)	⑪
		Sully (Le)	⑫
		Voiles d'Or (Les)	⑯

defences were concentrated round the ports and, as naval losses were small, that amphibious operations on a larger scale might be successful; the Germans, however, concluded that future Allied attacks would be directed particularly at the ports.

They were wrong; the Allies developed artificial ports, the famous Mulberries, which they towed across the Channel for the Normandy Landings, avoiding highly defended ports.

WALKING TOURS

Downtown and the Beach

About 1h30 from the parking spot at place Nationale, near St-Jacques.

Place Nationale

In the centre of the circle stands a statue of Abraham Duquesne (1610–88), famous for defeating the Dutch navy and for hunting down and disarming pirate ships in the Mediterranean. Two of the buildings on place Nationale (Nos. **18** and **24**) date from the early 18C.

Église St-Jacques★

Begin by going round the outside of the church, which has been considerably rebuilt over the centuries. Over the 14C central doorway is a fine rose window; the façade tower is 15C, the east end and radiating chapels are 16C; the unrenovated south transept, on the other hand, is a good example of early Gothic.

Interior – The well-proportioned nave, which is 13C, was ornamented in the 14C with a triforium and given tall windows a century later. The first chapel in the south aisle, the Chapel of the Holy Sepulchre, is 15C. The transept, the oldest part of the church, supports the dome, which was rebuilt in the 18C. A fine 17C wooden statue of St James stands above the high altar. The Sacred Heart Chapel on the right facing the high altar has original Flamboyant vaulting; the centre chapel is known for carved organ consoles (1635). Left, above the sacristy door, is a frieze of Brazilian Indians that recalls the voyages of Dieppe explorers.

Grand-Rue

Many of the houses in white brick date from the reconstruction of Dieppe after the British naval bombardment of 1694. No. **21** (now the Globe Café) was once the home of the dreaded pirate Balidar, terror of the English Channel. In the courtyard of No. **77**, there is a fountain dating from 1631. At No. **186**, an apothecary's old sign on the first floor illustrates three elements of nature: an obelisk (mineral), a palm (vegetable) and a sun (fire).

Place du Puits-Salé

At the junction of six roads, this is the liveliest quarter of Dieppe. The name recalls an old salt-water well (the current well is purely decorative). The large white façade of the early 18C Café des Tribunaux has a clock from 1709.

Dieppe port

© Musat/iStockphoto.com

Rue de la Barre

The pharmacy at No. **4** was founded in 1683. Voltaire lodged here when he returned from exile in England, at the home of his friend the apothecary **Jacques Féret**. The houses here are once again early 18C, with period balconies (Nos. **40**, **42**, **44**). The Protestant church at No. **69** was once the chapel of a Carmelite convent (1645).

Château-musée★

From the east end of **boulevard de la Mer**, there is a magnificent **view★** of the city and the beach. Dieppe Castle was built round a massive circular tower which formed part of the earlier, 14C, town fortifications. Note the 17C curtain walls linking the castle to the square St-Rémy Tower. Formerly belonging to the governors of the town, it now houses the Municipal Museum.

Museum★ – *Within château.* ○*Wed–Sun: Jun–Sept 10am–6pm; Oct–May 10amnoon, 2–6pm).* ○*1 Jan, 1 May, 1 Nov, 25 Dec.* ⊛€4.50. *℘02 35 06 61 99.* The collections centre on two themes: the navy and ivory. At the entrance is a display of ship models, maps and navigational tools. On the first floor, several rooms are devoted to Dutch painting and furniture – many seascapes and still-life pictures of fish (Pieter Boel, 17C) – as well as to 19C and 20C French and international painting: Isabey, Noël, Boudin, Renoir, Pissarro, Mebourg, Sisley, Jacques-Émile Blanche and Walter Sickert. There is an important collection of Pre-Columbian (Peruvian) pottery. On the first floor is an incomparable collection of **Dieppe ivories★**. The craftsmanship is meticulous: model ships and navigational instruments, as well as religious items and secular pieces (toilet articles, sewing requisites, fans, snuff boxes, etc.).

A small workshop has been reconstituted to show the tools of local craftsmen who carved ivory imported from Africa and the Orient. In the 17C, there were 350 ivory carvers in the town.

Mémorial du 19 août 1942

A monument in the **square du Canada** recalls the 350 years of history uniting Dieppe and Canada, starting with the 17C colonists who left for Québec and continuing through the raid of 19 August 1942. In the summer, you can enter the château-museum from the square.

Boulevard de Verdun leads to the beach through the monumental gate **Les Tourelles**, the only survivor of five gates (15C) in the old fortifications. Continue along quai du Hâble in the neighbourhood known as **le Bout du Quai**. The little streets off place du Moulin-à-Vent have traditionally been home to local fishermen. The **Maritime Museum** (Estran-Cité de la Mer Museum, see below) is on the north side. Just before the corner of rue de la Rade and quai du Hâble, are the vestiges of a 14C tower (Tour aux Crabes). Follow quai Henri IV along the marina.

Estran-Cité de la Mer★

37 r. de l'Asile-Thomas. ♿ ◷*Mon–Fri 9.30am–6pm, Sat–Sun 9.30am– 12.30pm, 1.30–6pm.* ◷*1 Jan, 25 Dec.* ◉*€7.50.* ✆*02 35 06 93 20. www.estrancitedelamer.fr.*

Situated at the heart of an old fishermen's district, this museum is devoted to maritime industry and to the ecosystem of the eastern Channel.

The Port, le Pollet and the Cliff

⏱ *2h, starting from the tourist office. Go up the cliff from the fishermen's neighbourhood, Le Pollet, for a view.*

Avant-Port

Tall, dark stone buildings surround the basin where the Newhaven–Dieppe ships used to moor.

A yachting marina designed to accommodate up to 400 boats was recently built following the 1994 transfer of the car ferry terminal onto the new outer port. To reach the terminal on foot, cross two bridges, Pont d'Ango and Pont Colbert, built in 1889 from designs by Gustave Eiffel. They lead to the Pollet district. Follow along the base of the cliffs, where you can see *gobes*, former cliff dwellings, now walled up.

▶ Go back to the Colbert Bridge and take ruelle des Grèves (next to a butcher's shop). From rue Guerrier, take rue du Petit-Fort, which ends in a stairway to the top of the cliffs.

Le Pollet and Cliff

There is a very old street leading off rue Guerrier, rue Quiquengrogne; the strange name was a rallying cry of pirates on the Channel in the 15C.

Next to No. 3 rue du Petit-Fort, a tiny fisherman's cottage, its roof caved in, predates the 1694 bombardment of Dieppe by the English.

On top of the cliff stands the **Chapelle Notre-Dame de Bon-Secours**, built in 1876. The military light signal is operational 24hr. Step away from the mast for an extensive **view★** of the city and harbour.

Port de pêche (bassin Duquesne)

Dieppe has a large fishing fleet which goes out to sea on shortish expeditions (one to five days), bringing back fish and seafood for auction. The early-morning fish market is a colourful sight. Dieppe is France's leading source of scallops (coquilles St-Jacques), as well as of sole and other fine fish.

Port de commerce (arrière-port)

The fruit trade continues to be very important at this port, with deliveries of Ivory Coast bananas, pineapples and mangoes, and Morocco citrus fruits, potatoes and spring vegetables. Oils, cereals, crabs, and wood also count among the imports here.

ⓘ You can buy fish and shellfish from the fishermen stalls in front of the tourist office.

🚗 DRIVING TOUR

🚗 LE LONG DE LA SCIE

55km/34mi circuit. Allow 3h.

Leave Dieppe on the D 915, then take the N 27 for St-Aubin-sur-Scie and continue to Sauqueville to see the **Château de Miromesnil★** (&.⏱Apr–Oct daily 10am–noon, 2–6pm; ⊜€10, €7 garden and park. 𝒫02 35 85 02 80. www.chateaumiromesnil.com), where Guy de Maupassant was born. The château has a monumental Louis XIII façade. The south front is in the Henri IV style, in brick with stone trim. Note the 16C chapel, part of an earlier château. Rich interior decoration from 1780. The flowery gardens and **vegetable plots★** are surrounded by brick walls supporting espaliered fruit trees. The 16C **chapel**, richly decorated inside, is all that remains of the fortress destroyed in 1589.

▶ Take the D 3 at Sauqueville, then head south to **Auffray** via Longueville-sur-Scie.

At Auffay you can see the famous **bell-strikers** in the imposing late 11C collegiate church. Also, enjoy the 120km/74mi of marked footpaths around Auffay. Ask at the tourist office for more details.

ADDRESSES

🛏 STAY

⊜⊜ **Aguado** – 30 bd de Verdun. 𝒫02 35 84 27 00. www.hoteldieppe.com. 55 rooms. The building is on a street leading to the seafront. The rooms on the promenade

side or overlooking the town and harbour have efficient soundproofing.

⊜⊜ **Hôtel au Grand Duquesne** – 15 pl. St-Jacques. 𝒫02 32 14 61 10. 12 rooms. Restaurant ⊜⊜. Budget-friendly and close to restaurants and attractions.

⊜⊜🍽 **Chambre d'hôte La Villa Florida** – 24 ch. du Golf. 𝒫02 35 84 40 37. www.lavillaflorida.com. 4 rooms. This hotel's rooms are modern and stylish; each with a terrace.

⊜⊜🍽–⊜⊜🍽⊜ **Mercure Dieppe La Présidence** – 1 bd de Verdun. 𝒫02 35 84 31 31. www.accorhotels.com. 81 rooms and 4 suites. Restaurant ⊜⊜🍽. This luxury hotel's rooms were entirely renovated in 2008. Ideally located near the beach. Pleasant bar and lounge area.

⊜⊜🍽 **Villa des Capucins** – 11 r. des Capucins. 𝒫02 35 82 16 52. https://villadescapucins.jimdo.com. 4 rooms. In the old Pollet quarter, this villa is set in splendid surroundings. Pretty rooms.

⊜⊜🍽⊜ **Hôtel de l'Europe** – 63 bd de Verdun. 𝒫02 32 90 19 19. www.hotel-europe-dieppe.com. 60 rooms. A bland façade belies an interior with touch of class. Rooms are of a good size.

🍴 EAT

⊜⊜ **Restaurant l'Aquilon** – 128 Rue des Verts Bois, section Pourville sur mer, 76550 Hautot-sur-Mer (5km/3mi W of Dieppe via the D 75). 𝒫02 35 84 59 84. www.restaurantlaquilon.fr. Closed all day Mon, Thu evening and Sun evening. This inn overlooks the beach on which the Canadians disembarked in 1942 as part of the "Jubilee" operation. On the menu: traditional French cuisine.

⊜⊜ **La Marmite dieppoise** – 8 r. St-Jean. 𝒫02 35 84 24 26. https://marmitedieppoise.fr. Closed Sun evening and all day Mon. This small restaurant is well-known to the Dieppe regulars. Seafood and Dieppe *marmite*, the house speciality.

⊜⊜ **Le Bistrot de Pollet** – 23 r. Tête-de-Bœuf. 𝒫02 35 84 68 57. Closed Sun and Mon; only by reservation. A nice little ocean bistro with a convivial atmosphere on the Pollet harbour island. The cuisine varies with the market offerings.

⊜⊜ **Le Colombier** – R. Loucheur, 76550 Offranville, 6km/3mi SW of Dieppe. 𝒫02 35 85 48 50. www.lecolombieroffranville.fr.

Closed Tue, Sun evening and Wed. This venerable Norman house (1509) is the dowager of the town. Yellow walls, restored beams, beautiful early fireplace and old roasting-spit in the dining room. Contemporary cuisine.

⊜⊜ **Le New-Haven** – *53 quai Henri-IV. www.restaurantdieppe.fr. ℘02 35 84 89 72. Closed Tue evening, and all day Wed (except Jul–Aug).* A nice and simple restaurant with veranda windows opening on to the pleasure port.

⊜⊜ **Le Sully** – *97 quai Henri-IV. ℘02 35 84 23 13. Closed Tue evening and Wed. Reservations advised at weekends.* A family restaurant with three different dining rooms: the first in the "retro" style with its port-side veranda; the second contemporary, the last rustic, embellished with stonework and

exposed beams and a collection of copper pieces. Seafood has pride of place on the menu.

⊜⊜ **Les Régates** – *30 r. du Casino , 76550 Pourville-sur-Mer (5 km/3mi W of Dieppe by the D 75). ℘02 35 84 11 33. www. restaurantlesregates.com.* Don't miss this little place to taste mussels and chips and salads, with a view of the sea. Stop here for a before-dinner drink at sunset, surrounded by the many Dieppe regulars for whom this is a tradition.

⊜⊜⊜ **Les Voiles d'Or** – *2 chemin de la Falaise. ℘02 35 84 16 84. www.lesvoiles dor.fr. Closed 16 Nov–1 Dec, Sun evening, Mon–Tue. Reservations advised.* Fine-dingin restaurant offering up-to-date cuisine, perched on a Pollet cliff; near the chapelle Notre-Dame-de-Bon-Secours and the lighthouse.

Arques-la-Bataille

Arques lies under a massive medieval fortress where the future Henri IV won a celebrated battle. A nearby château, Miromesnil, was the birthplace of writer Guy de Maupassant.

A BIT OF HISTORY

When **Henri IV** (1553–1610) was still a king without a kingdom, he possessed the formidable fortress of Arques, where he dug in, with 7 000 men, to await the arrival of 30 000 soldiers under the Duke of Mayenne. The battle fell on 21 September 1589. A fog delayed artillery but finally Henri's cannon thundered into the besiegers. Mayenne had to beat a hasty retreat.

SIGHTS
Château
Allow 30min. From place Desceliers, where the town hall (Mairie) is located, take the second road to the right, uphill to the castle entrance, about 45min; the road is very narrow, steep and winding. ⚬⇥*Closed for safety reasons.* ⚏*Château grounds, no charge.*

> ▸ **Population:** 2 573.
> ⚲ **Michelin Map:** 304: G-2.
> ▷ **Location:** Arques is 8km/5mi SE of Dieppe, near the confluence of the rivers Varenne and Béthune. The Forest of Arques lies to the NE.
> ☺ **Don't Miss:** The medieval fortress offers a magnificent view of the countryside; the gardens of Miromesnil are splendid.
> ⏱ **Timing:** You can visit only the exterior of the fortress, which takes 30min. Plan at least 1hr30min for the Miromesnil château.
> ⚎ **Kids:** Cool off the kids at the waterpark.

The 12C keep occupies the highest point, with the earliest part from 1038–1043. In 1053, William the Conqueror attacked and Henri I rebuilt in 1123; the 14C brought two new towers. Vital in the late 16C wars of religion, Protestant forces under the future Henri IV repelled the Catholic League in 1589. On the last of the triple doors to the castle, a carved low relief depicts Henri IV at the Battle of Arques. Follow the old sentry path along the moat to enjoy a view of the Arques valley.

Église Notre-Dame-de-l'Assomption

Rue des Bourguignons.
Rebuilt around 1515, the church belfry is 17C. The nave with wood cradle vaulting and apse windows are 16C. A chapel right of the chancel has a small bust of Henri IV. 15C *Pietà* in south chapel.

Varenne Plein Air⛸

Base de Loisir, 76510 St-Aubin-le-Cauf. ⏱*Jul–Aug Mon–Fri 9am–noon, 1.30–6.15pm, Sat–Sun 2–6pm; Apr–Jun and Sept Mon–Fri 9am–noon, 1.30–5.30pm, Sat–Sun 2–6pm.* ✆*02 35 85 69 05. www.varennepleinair.fr.*
On the edge of a lake near Arques, this recreational centre offers facilities for water sports.

🚗 DRIVING TOUR

🚗 LA FORET D'ARQUES

30km/18mi circuit. Allow 1h.

▶ Leave Arques heading E on the D 56.

This beech forest tops a spur surrounded by the Eaulne and Béthune, which join at its feet to form the Arques. The D 56 crosses the river of the forest while running along an old Roman way.

Saint-Nicolas-d'Aliermont

Like the other villages stretching along the D 56 on the narrow Aliermont plateau, this town is an example of a "street village", typical of 12C and 13C colonisation developing along travel routes.
Musée de l'Horlogerie★ – *48 r. Édouard-Cannevel.* ⏱*Jun–Sept Tue–Sat, 10am–noon, 2–6pm; Oct–Dec and mid Feb–May Wed–Sun 2.30–6pm.* ⏱*1 May, 1 and 11 Nov, 25 Dec.* ☞€5 *(child 14–18, €2.50).* ✆*02 35 04 53 98. www.musee-horlogerie-aliermont.fr.* At the heart of the watch-

making and clockmaking industry for close to three centuries, Saint-Nicolas-d'Aliermont reopened its museum in 2007. The collections, presented chronologically, highlight local history and the evolution of techniques. A workshop in the museum lets you observe a watch-maker conducting his precise work.

▶ On leaving St-Nicolas, turn left onto the D 149.

Envermeu

The **church** in this village, in the Gothic style with Renaissance motifs, remains unfinished. Note the barley-sugar columns, carved wood pulpit, canopy, majestic **chancel**★ and apse.

▶ From Envermeu, take the D 920, to the west, then the D 54 taking you to Martin-Église.

The village of **Martin-Église**, at the forest's edge, is known for trout fishing.

▶ Take the D 1 to Arques.

Immediately after a beautiful wooden house (hotel) and a bridge over the Eaulne, take a narrow road on the left. 600m further, before a house, turn right into the forest road of **Bivouac**, which remains very close to the forest edge; you will have some beautiful glimpses of the Arques valley.

Monument commémoratif de la bataille d'Arques

🚶🚗*15min return. Leave the car in the curve on the left (grassy lot on the right).* You will see a path to the obelisk, which was raised during the Restoration, commemorating Henri IV's victory here. Arques-la-Bataille and its castle can be seen on the valley's other side. The road then heads deep into the forest.

▶ After the Henri IV roundabout, after going straight, turn right into the Sully forest road.

The road crosses another part of the forest. The D 56, right, leads to Arques.

Eu★

Eu is a small town on the River Bresle, set between the sea and the forest from which it takes its name. The town centres around its beautiful 11C collegiate church. It was in Eu that the two Anguier brothers, François (1604–69) and Michel (1612–86), were born: these Baroque sculptors contributed to the building of the Louvre and the Val de Grâce in Paris.

SIGHTS

Collégiale Notre-Dame et St-Laurent★

pl. Guillaume-le-Conquérant.
⊙*Daily Apr–Sept 9.30am–12.30pm, 2.30–5.30pm; Oct–Mar 9.30am –12.30pm, 2–4.30pm.* ⊙*1 Jan, Sun and public holidays.* ☜*No charge.* ✆*02 35 86 04 68.*

The collegiate church was erected in the 12C and 13C in the Gothic style. In the 15C the apse was remodelled and in the 19C Viollet-le-Duc, the architect and restoration specialist, undertook a general restoration of the building. The church is dedicated to the Virgin Mary and St Lawrence O'Toole, Primate of Ireland who died in Eu in 1180.

The **interior** is striking for its size and harmonious proportions. Beneath a Flamboyant canopy in the second ambulatory chapel on the right, the

- ▶ **Population:** 6 995.
- ⊙ **Michelin Map:** 304: i-1.
- ▯ **Info:** Mairie de Eu, 1, rue Jean Duhornay. ✆02 35 86 44 00. www.ville-eu.fr.
- ◯ **Location:** Eu is 4km/2.5mi E of Le Tréport by D 1915 and 34kim/21mi NE of Dieppe by D 925.
- ▯ **Parking:** There is parking on the square between the château and the church.
- ◉ **Don't Miss:** The château and its museum; the historic centre of town for its lively pedestrian streets.
- ◯ **Timing:** Spend the morning seeing the city, then head towards the pretty forest of Eu.
- ▮▮ **Kids:** Take them to the archaeological site at Bois-Abbé and the Glass-Making Museum.

Chapel of the Holy Sepulchre, is a 15C **Entombment★**; opposite is a magnificent head of Christ in Sorrow, also 15C.

Crypt

The crypt, which is beneath the chancel, was restored in 1828 by the Duke of Orléans, who reigned as King Louis-

Collégiale Notre-Dame et St-Laurent

© Angelo D'Amico/iStockphoto.com

Château d'Eu

© Alonbou/Fotolia.com

Philippe from 1830 to 1848. The 12C–13C recumbent statue of St Lawrence O'Toole is believed to be one of the oldest in France.

Château★

Nothing remains of the original castle where William the Conqueror married Matilda of Flanders in 1050. It was destroyed in 1475 on the orders of Louis XI. The present château, a huge brick and stone building begun by Henri of Guise and Catherine de Clèves in 1578, has been restored several times since. It passed to the Orléans family and became one of the favourite residences of Louis-Philippe, who received Queen Victoria there twice. Viollet-le-Duc was commissioned to redecorate it between 1874 and 1879 for the Count of Paris, grandson of the king. The château, which now belongs to the town of Eu, is occupied by the town hall and the communal archives, and houses the **Louis-Philippe Museum**.

Musée Louis-Philippe

&🕐*Mid-Mar–early Nov Wed–Thu and Sat–Mon 10am–noon, 2–6pm, Fri 2–6pm.* 👓€5. 📞*02 27 28 20 76. www.chateau-eu.fr.*
On the ground floor visitors are shown the grand staircase and the Duchesse d'Orléans' suite, redecorated by Viollet-le-Duc in 1875, as well as the two salons and the bedroom where Queen Victoria and Prince Albert slept in 1843

and 1845, embellished with a superb inlaid parquet floor made under Louis-Philippe.

In the restored portico overlooking the garden, note the dazzling **wall of light** conceived by Viollet-le-Duc and master-glazier Oudinot.

On the first floor you can visit the 19C bathroom, the gold bedroom with its pretty green and gilt wainscoting bearing the monogram of the Grande Demoiselle (Princesse Anne Marie Louise d'Orléans, 1627–1693, who once lived here), the Louis-Philippe **dining hall** with its lovely 17C coffered ceiling, the Black Salon, with its strange pink and black colour scheme, and the vast **Galerie des Guise**, currently being renovated to house 145 family paintings purchased in 2000. The gallery contains 10 000 volumes, including books from Eu's Jesuit College and those belonging to the last Comte d'Eu.

The south wing of the first floor, which once housed the private suites of Louis-Philippe and Marie-Amélie, is being restored to its former glory.

The Park

Most of the trees are beeches, one of which, known as the Guisarda, was planted in 1585.

Chapelle du Collège★

The Jesuit college now bears the name of the 17C Anguier brothers, who studied here. The chapel was commissioned in

1624 by Catherine de Clèves, widow of Henri de Guise, to whom she brought the County of Eu as a dowry in 1570.

The Louis XIII **façade★** is quite remarkable. The beautifully restored brick and stone masonry lends both warmth and harmony to the whole ensemble.

👤👤 Musée des Traditions Verrières

r. Semichon, follow the signs from the Salle Audiard.

♿🕐*Apr–Jun Tue, Sat–Sun 2–5.30pm; Jul–Sept Tue–Wed and Sat -Sun 2–5.30pm; Oct Tue and Sat 2–5.30pm.* 🎫€5 (child 12–18, €4). 📞02 35 86 21 91. www.traditions-verrieres.com.

The former stables of the Bresle cavalry house this museum devoted to glass-making techniques.

The Forêt d'Eu

This beech wood covers three isolated massifs with beautiful beech glades: St Martin's Priory Chapel (pretty doorway); **St Catherine's Viewpoint** (a 45min walk leads up to a view of the Yères valley); **La Bonne Entente** (an oak and a beech growing intertwined); **St-Martin-le-Gaillard** (13C **church**).

The interior has cornices carved with humorous human figures; 18C Virgin and Child. Note that that Baby Jesus is receiving a fig.

ADDRESSES

LEISURE

Cycles Joostens – *1 r. Charles Morin. 📞02 35 86 22 24. Bike rentals. Tourist offices has maps for some marked trails.* If you dislike dirt paths, head for the Bois de Cise (before Ault and N of Mers), where the trails are paved and lead you to a little-frequented beach. The Hyères valley circuit (50km/31mi), starting from the beach at Mesnil-Val, passes through lovely countryside but you need to be in shape. There's an alternative, more relaxed circuit of only 25km/15.5mi.

Le Tréport

Fishing boat leaving Le Tréport harbour

Set at the mouth of the Bresle near the border with Picardy, Le Tréport is a small fishing port and seaside resort, popular for its close proximity to Paris.

During the summer lively crowds throng the harbourside as the town hosts a fair. The long shingle beach, backed by tall cliffs, is packed with visitors on weekends. Mers-les-Bains, on the right bank of the Bresle, is less commercial than Le Tréport and has many devotees, as has Ault, a beach further north.

© Peter Hermus/iStockphoto.com

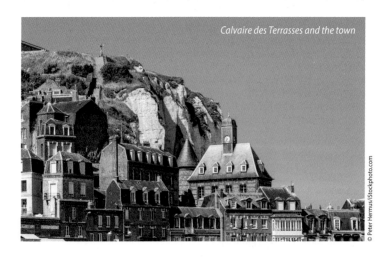
Calvaire des Terrasses and the town

© Peter Hermus/iStockphoto.com

- ▶ **Population:** 4 895.
- ⏱ **Michelin Map:** 304: I-1.
- 🛈 **Info:** Quai Sadi-Carnot.
  ℘02 35 86 05 69.
  www.destination-letreport-mers.fr.
- 🕒 **Location:** Le Tréport is
  93km/57.8mi from Rouen
  and 30km/18.5mi NE of
  Dieppe by D 925, on the
  border of Picardy.
- ⊘ **Don't Miss:** The view from
  the Calvaire des Terrasses.
- 🕐 **Timing:** Spend the
  morning in Le Tréport, then
  see the pretty resort of
  Mers-les-Bains.

SIGHTS

Calvaire des Terrasses★

🚶 *Allow 30min round-trip on foot.
Access by car via rue de Paris, rue
St-Michel and boulevard du Calvaire.*
A flight of stairs (*378 steps*) leads up
from the town hall to the Calvary on
the clifftop. From the terrace, there is a
view★ over the town, extending north
beyond the Caux cliffs to Hourdel Point,
the Somme estuary and inland, along
the Lower Bresle Valley to Eu and the
lower town's slate roofs, beach and
harbour.

Église St-Jacques

The church, which stands halfway up
the hill, dates from the latter half of the
16C, but was extensively restored in
the 19C. The modern porch shelters a
Renaissance doorway. Inside, at the far
end of the church, stands a fine statue
of the Virgin of Tréport. The chapel of
Notre-Dame-de-la-Pitié (Our Lady of
Mercy) holds a 16C *Piéta*. A low relief
over the altar shows a Virgin surrounded
by Biblical emblems.

ADDRESSES

🛏 STAY

🍽 **Golf Hôtel** – *102 rte de Dieppe.*
℘*02 27 28 01 52. www.hotels-treport.com.*
15 rooms. 🅿. At the entrance to the
campsite, turn left. An alley of trees takes
you to this beautiful half-timbered 19C
house. The rooms, non-smoking, are all
different and well-equipped. Pleasant
welcome. A small charming hotel at a
reasonable price.

🍷 EAT

🍽🍽 **Le Saint-Louis** – *43 quai François-ler.*
℘*02 35 86 20 70.* Fish and seafood
restaurant offering a view of the fishing
port. Brasserie style décor, with moleskin
-upholstered benches and cosy booths
under a colourful glass roof.

VEXIN NORMAND *and Pays de Bray*

The Vexin Normand has a rich history closely tied with that of Normandy itself. Richard the Lion Heart and Philippe Auguste shaped history here as they fought to possess these lands between the Duchy of Normandie (the Vexin Normand) and the Kingdom of France (the Vexin Français). The Pays de Bray is a place of beautiful, greatly varied landscapes, the irregularity of clay-rich soil and erosion explain this diversity which even created the remarkable geological event known as the "buttonhole". It is therefore not surprising to find here a long tradition of pottery, ceramics and brick and tile craftsmanship.

Highlights

1 William II's 11C château fort at **Gisors** (p162)

2 Monet's atmospheric gardens at **Giverny** (p166)

3 Richard the Lionheart's stronghold, **Château Gaillard** (p168)

4 A drive through the **Forêt de Lyons** (p171)

5 A visit to **Eawy forest** (p180)

villages and country churches. The history of the region, however, can be understood at sites such as Les Andelys and especially the Château Gaillard, which today is a silent witness to the struggle between Richard the Lion Heart and Philippe Auguste to control the Seine and the route to Rouen.

But for nature lovers today the Vexin Normand, surrounded by the Lyons Forest, the Seine, the Andelle and the Epte, is a real haven of peace for exploration by foot, bicycle or on horseback – or to enjoy with a fishing rod in hand.

The Vexin Normand

This is the countryside that inspired painters Poussin, Pissarro, Monet, and Picasso, and writers Michelet and Flaubert, an artistic heritage continuing today with everything from mosaic to glass being worked here.

Yet the Vexin Normand remains rural, with majestic fortresses, châteaux and abbeys rising alongside charming little

The Pays de Bray

To the east of the Seine-Maritime region, the Pays de Bray consists of green meadows and hedged farm land. Above all a region for lovers of the great outdoors, it is here that lies the magnificent Eawy forest, which together with Lyons is the most beautiful beech forest in Normandy.

Forêt d'Eawy

© Francis Cormon/hemis.fr

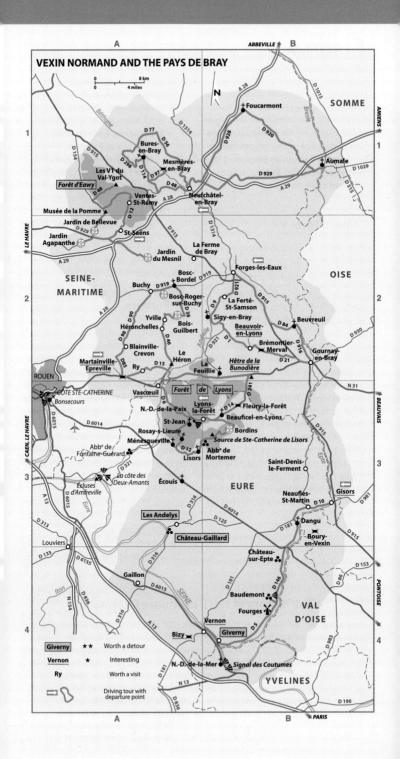

VEXIN NORMAND AND THE PAYS DE BRAY

Gisors★

Gisors is the capital of the Norman Vexin: it was once a frontier town belonging to the dukes of Normandy. The town owes its origins to the castle, which formed part of a line of defence running from Forges-les-Eaux to Vernon and included the castles of Neaufles-St-Martin and Château-sur-Epte.

VISIT

Château Fort★★

Pl. Blanmont.
Park: Apr–Sept 9am–7.30pm; Oct–Mar 9am–5pm. *Guided tours of the fortress Apr–Sept daily 10am, 2pm, 3.15pm, 6.15pm; Oct–Mar Mon–Fri 10am, 2pm and 3.15pm.* Dec and public holidays. €5 (child 6–17, €4). ℘02 32 27 60 63.

The castle was built as early as 1097 by William II of England, son of the Conqueror. In 1193 it was taken by Philippe Auguste of France. During the Hundred Years' War the castle changed hands several times before returning to the French crown in 1449.

The 11C **keep**, on its 20m artificial mound in the centre of the fortified perimeter and surrounded now by a public garden, is flanked by a watch-tower. A staircase leads to the top from where there is a fine **view** over the surrounding woodland.

▶ **Population:** 11 918.
◉ **Michelin Map:** 304: K-6.
🛈 **Info:** 1 Passage du Monarque. ℘02 32 27 60 63. www.tourisme-gisors.fr.
▶ **Location:** Gisors is 76km/47mi NW of Paris and 64km/40mi NE of Rouen.
◉ **Don't Miss:** The château and the Tree of Jesse in St-Gervais-et-St-Protais.
◕ **Timing:** See Gisors in the morning, then tour the Epte valley.

Église St-Gervais-et-St-Protais★

r. de Vienne.

The oldest parts of the church date back to the 12C, but construction continued to the end of the 16C, as is evident both outside and inside. The Gothic chancel was completed in 1249; the side chapels adjoining the ambulatory were added in 1498 and 1507. The transept doors are 16C and Gothic, as is the very tall nave. The monumental west front is Renaissance: the doorway is flanked by two towers, that on the north being built in 1536, that on the south left unfinished in 1591.

In spite of the mixture of architectural styles the church as a whole appears perfectly harmonious.

The large monochrome window in the chapel on the right of the choir dates

---

The History of the Dukedom of Normandy

It was at St-Clair-sur-Epte in 911 that Charles the Simple – a nickname meaning honest and straightforward – met with Rollo, the ruler of the Vikings. Dudon de St-Quentin, Normandy's first historian, recounts that, to ratify the agreement creating the Dukedom of Normandy, the Viking placed his hands between those of the French king. This informal deal, concluded in the manner of tradesmen, carried the same legal weight as a formal exchange of seals and signatures, for a written treaty was never signed. The dukedom is bordered by the River Epte north of the River Seine and by the River Avre to the south. Normandy's boundaries were often fought over throughout history by the kings of France and the dukes of Normandy, who became the kings of England in the 11C.

Château Fort

from the 16C. The chapel below the South Tower contains a charming spiral staircase by Jean Grappin and a huge late 16C Tree of Jesse.

ADDITIONAL SIGHT
Saint-Denis-le-Ferment
7km-4mi NE. Leave Gisors by the D 915, then turn left on the D 16.

The mill of Saint-Paër and its fish farm mark the entrance to this quiet town crossed by the Levrière. In its centre, the church, château and manor are all charmingly authentic. A path (*9km/5mi, 3h*), the GR 125, runs along the left bank of the Lévrière, taking you to Hébecourt. It then links, running through woods and fields, the **Château de La Rapée**, **Saint-Paër**, **Bézu-St-Éloi** and then **St-Denis-le-Ferment**. Queen Blanche d'Evreux (also known as Blanche de Navarre), Princess of Navarre, withdrew in 1364 to the Château de Neaufles-Saint-Martin after the death of her husband Philippe VI of Valois.

🚗 DRIVING TOUR

🚗 EPTE VALLEY
41km/25.5mi. Allow 2h.

The road from Gisors to Vernon follows the shady west bank of the Epte, which contrast with the bare slopes hewn out of the chalk bed of the Vexin plateaus.

▶ From Gisors take D 10 W.

Neaufles-St-Martin
The village is dominated by a keep standing upon a perfectly preserved artificial mound.

▶ At roundabout turn left onto D 181.

Dangu
The main features of the Gothic **church** are the 18C woodwork and painted panelling in the chancel and the 16C Montmorency chapel.

▶ Take the D 146 south into the valley.

Château-sur-Epte
Standing on an artificial mound surrounded by a moat are the remains of a massive keep built by William Rufus, King of England from 1087 to 1100, to protect the Norman frontier.

▶ Return on the D 146. At Bray-et-Lu, turn right.

Château de Baudemont
From the ruins of the 11C fortress, standing on its artificial mound, there is a pretty **view** of the valley.

▶ Continue on the D 5.

Moulin de Fourges
Built on the banks of the Epte in 1750, the mill has an imposing wheel, which still functions today, turned by the force of the river's waters.

▶ Continue via Gasny to Giverny on the D 5.

Giverny★★
See GIVERNY, p166.

Drive on to Vernon. Return to Gisors on the D 181 and D 10.

ADDRESSES

STAY
Hôtel Moderne – *1 pl. de la Gare.* *02 32 55 23 51. www.hotel-moderne-gisors.com.* *30 rooms.* Family hotel at train station, good for a brief stay.

EAT
Le Cappeville – *17 r. Cappeville.* *02 32 55 11 08. www.lecappeville.com. Closed Wed and Thu.* Dining room in bright lively colours; still has its beams and fireplace. Up-to-date cuisine with authentic accents.

Vernon★

Vernon, which is close to the forest of the same name, was created by Rollo, first Duke of Normandy, in the 9C. It became French early in the 13C and is now an extremely pleasant residential town.

WALKING TOUR

Park near the Clemenceau bridge (access from boulevard du Maréchal-Leclerc or rue de la Ravine).

Bridge Viewpoint
From the bridge there is a view of Vernon, the wooded islands in the Seine and the ruined piles on which the 12C

- **Population:** 23 705.
- **Michelin Map:** 304: I-7.
- **Info:** 12 Rue du Pont. 02 32 51 39 60. www.cape-tourisme.fr.
- **Location:** Vernon is 65km/40.4mi SE of Rouen on A 13.
- **Parking:** Two car parks are located at each end of the Clemenceau bridge.
- **Don't Miss:** The Église Notre-Dame and the park of the Château of Bizy.
- **Timing:** Guided tours of the Château de Bizy take 45min. The park can be seen in 30min.

Mill and the old bridge over the Seine

© ADT de l'Eure, M. Aubry

Château de Bizy

© Mel Longhurst/age fotostock

bridge stood. On the right bank are the towers of Tourelles Castle, which formed part of the defences of the old bridge.

▶ Turn left and walk along the Seine.

The walk takes you by the 18C Bourbon-Penthièvre house, named for the last Duke of Vernon. The street of the same name leads into the **old town**. Notre-Dame Church stands at the end of the pretty street with some half-timbered houses. Note the 16C façade embellished with Gothic sculptures at no 15.

Musée de Vernon

12 rue du Pont. ♿⏰*Apr–Oct Tue–Sun 10.30am–6pm; Nov–Mar Tue–Fri 2–5.30pm, Sat–Sun 2.30–5.30pm.* ⏰*1 Jan, 1 May, 14 Jul, 15 Aug, 1 and 11 Nov, 25 Dec.* ⊛€5. ✆*02 32 21 28 09.*

A wrought-iron gate that comes from the castle of Bizy leads you into the museum's courtyard, housed in restored buildings from a variety of different eras (15C–18C).

The collections focus on painting, drawing and sculpture. The collection includes works by Monet, Rosa Bonheur, Maurice Denis, Pierre Bonnard, Vuillard and Steinlen (1859–1923). Do not miss two works by Claude Monet: Water Lilies and Cliffs at Pourville. The cartoons humorising French society also deserve a look.

Église Notre-Dame★

1 r. du Chapitre.

This 12C collegiate church was remodelled several times before the Renaissance. The 15C west front has a beautiful rose window flanked by galleries. The choir triforium and the clerestory windows combine beautifully. The organ loft and beautiful stained glass windows of the second chapel on the right aisle also date from the 16th century. The organ is 17C.

In rue du Chapitre, on the right side of the church, is a 17C house (Nos. 3-5). It is one of the oldest houses in Vernon and also serves as the tourist office. There are other interesting old houses in rue Carnot and rue Potard, in particular.

Côte St-Michel★

From Vernonnet (north); rue J.-Soret to the church, turn right; follow signs. Allow 1hr round-trip on foot.

From the top of the hill there is a good view of Vernon and the Seine valley.

EXCURSIONS
Château de Bizy★

2km/1mi W of Vernon by D 181. Avenue des Capucins. ♿⏰*Late Mar–early Nov daily except Mon, 10am–6pm. Chateau:* ☞*guided tours only (45min) at 10.30am, 11.15am, 2pm, 3pm, 4pm and 5pm.* ⊛€9 (gardens only €5). ℘02 32 51 00 82. www.chateaudebizy.com.

Begun in 1740 by Coutant d'Ivry for the Duke of Belle-Isle, Marshal of France, the château was remodelled several times by successive owners. These included the Duke of Penthièvre, General Le Suire, King Louis-Philippe and Baron Schickler. It is now owned by the family of Albufera.

A Classical colonnaded façade faces the park. Inside, the rooms are accented with beautiful Regency woodwork, 18C Gobelins tapestries woven for Louis XIV, and Empire furniture. The 18C **park** was redesigned in the English style by King Louis-Philippe. Renovation work has restored the splendid chemin d'eau.

Signal des Coutumes

8km/5mi from Vernon. Take N 15 out of town and after 5km/3mi, just before Port-Villez, turn right on D 89.

Notre-Dame-de-la-Mer – From the **look-out point★** there is a view of the river between Bonnières and Villez. Carry on along D 89; left at the mairie of Jeufosse and leave the paved road on the right. Outside the hamlet of Les Cou-

tumes, take a paved road to the right, which leads to the edge of the woods. **Signal des Coutumes** – There is a lovely, broad **view★** over the Bonnières meander.

ADDRESSES

🛏 STAY

😑😑😑 **Hôtel Normandy** – 1 av. Pierre Mendès France. ℘02 32 51 97 97. https://normandy-hotel.fr. 🅿 50 rooms - Restaurant 😑😑. Central; good rooms, functional furniture, cosy lounge and bar.

🍴 EAT

😑😑 **Le Bistro des Fleurs** – 73 r. Sadi Carnot. ℘02 32 21 29 19. Closed Sun and Mon. This old bar has daily specials of traditional dishes and wine by the glass.

😑😑 **Restaurant l'Estampille** – 6 place de Paris. ℘02 77 19 00 12. www.restaurantlestampille.fr. Closed Sun evening. Serving modern cuisine in a cosy atmosphere, this restaurant is close to the quais de Seine. Lovers of Impressionist painting might try the Menu Claude Monet.

Giverny★★

Claude Monet lived in this village from 1883 until his death in 1926, and attracted many other artists to the area. It was here that he painted the huge canvases of water lilies that can be seen in Paris at the Orangerie Museum and the Marmottan Museum.

VISIT

Maison de Claude Monet★

84 rue Claude-Monet. ✂🕐Late-Mar–1 Nov daily 9.30am–6pm. ⊛€9.50 (due to the many groups and crowds, the best time to visit is from end Apr to early Jun, especially late afternoon or lunchtime. ℘02 32 51 28 21. www.fondation-monet.com.

▶ **Population:** 502.
🕐 **Michelin Map:** 304: J-7 – 2km/1mi SE of Vernon.
◗ **Location:** Giverny is 2km/1mi SW of Vernon, which is (69km/43mi) from Rouen via D 313/D 5.
🅿 **Parking:** Car parks (free) are found on both sides of D 5.
☺ **Don't Miss:** The home of Claude Monet and the Impressionist Museum.
🕐 **Timing:** Give yourself 2hr for each of the museums.

Claude Monet's garden

© James Metcalf/iStockphoto.com

Claude Monet's **garden** (&,*only partially accessible*) slopes gently to the banks of the River Epte. The house displays reproductions of his greatest paintings; the originals hang in musems in Paris and around the world. The tour includes the blue salon, the bedroom with the roll-top desk, the old studio, the yellow dining room with its painted wooden furniture and the tiled kitchen.

The walled garden *(clos normand)*, is planted according to Monet's own design, and *(via a tunnel to the other side of the road)* the Japanese-inspired water garden is fed by the River Epte.

Despite Monet's love for the village, Giverny's inhabitants did not always make work easy for Monet; they required hefty fees before permitting him to paint their haystacks.

Musée des Impressionismes Giverny★

90 rue Claude-Monet.

&✗⊙*Late-Mar–early Nov daily 10am–6pm.* ⊕€7.50 (child 7–11, €3.50; 12–17, €5); €17 (including Maison de Claude Monet). No charge 1st Sun of month). ⊙During change of exhibitions; check website for details. ✆02 32 51 94 65. www.mdig.fr.

This museum, opened in May 2009 in the former premises of the Musée d'Art Américain, holds temporary exhibits on the subject of Impressionist art.

The museum gardens, composed of sections separated by hedges, burst with bright colour.

Designed as a cultural centre, in addition to the collections there are also three galleries and a large auditorium.

ADDRESSES

🏠 STAY

⊖⊜ **Chambre d'hôte Au Bon Maréchal** – 1 r. du Colombier. ✆02 32 51 39 70. *3 rooms.* A former venue for meetings between Monet and his artist friends. Cosy, comfortable rooms.

⊖⊜ **La Musardière**– 123 r. Cl.-Monet. ✆02 32 21 03 18. www.lamusardiere.fr. *11 rooms. Restaurant* ⊖⊜⊜. An old, rustic house (1880s) in the middle of a peaceful garden.

🍽/EAT

⊖⊜ **Restaurant Baudy** – 81 r. Claude-Monet. ✆02 32 21 10 03. www. restaurantbaudy.com. Open Apr–Oct. The former hotel residence of Impressionist painters. Specials and salads. Old rose garden.

⊖⊜⊜ **Le Moulin de Fourges**– 38 r. du Moulin, 27630 Fourges, 11km/7mi NE. ✆02 32 52 12 12. www.moulindefourges.com. *Closed Nov–Mar.* A former 18C watermill on the Epte; a place Monet would have loved. Enjoy your meals on its large heated terrace at the foot of the river.

Les Andelys★★

Les Andelys, dominated by the impressive ruins of Château-Gaillard, lies in a lovely setting along the Seine. It once consisted of two distinct areas, Le Petit Andely to the west and Le Grand Andely to the east. The latter was the site of a 6C monastery founded by Clotilde, who converted her husband, King Clovis, to Christianity. At a fountain at 29 rue Ste-Clotilde, she is said to have turned water into wine for workmen building the monastery chapel.

A BIT OF HISTORY

In 1196, **Richard the Lionheart**, King of England and Duke of Normandy, decided to bar the King of France's way to Rouen along the Seine valley by building a massive fortress on the cliff commanding the river at Andely. Within the year Château-Gaillard was erected and Richard cried "See my fine yearling!" **Philippe Auguste**, King of France, did not at first dare attack so formidable a redoubt. But when the vacillating King John succeeded Richard in 1199, the French beseiged the castle, filled in the moat, mined the walls and took the castle by storm on 6 March 1203.

▶ **Population:** 8 098.
◔ **Michelin Map:** 304: I-6
🚩 **Info:** 2 Rue Grande, 27700 Les Andelys. ℘02 32 21 31 29.
◗ **Location:** The two Andelys are linked by avenue de la République and rue du Maréchal-Leclerc. Paris is 100km/62mi away, and Rouen 40km/25mi.
◉ **Don't Miss:** The view of the Seine valley from the heights of the château.
◕ **Timing:** Visit the château in the morning, then enjoy Les Andelys and its surroundings.
🧒 **Kids:** Children will be thrilled by the massive fortress.

Château-Gaillard★★

Allow 1h. To reach the château by car: from Grand Andely, follow the signs from rue Louis-Pasteur. On foot (allow 30min ascent): from Petit Andely, follow rue Richard-Cœur-de-Lion, near the tourist office.
◕*Apr–early Nov Wed–Mon 10am–1pm, 2–6pm.* ◕*1 Nov.* ◓€3.50. ℘*02 32 54 41 93.*
From the car park there is a **view★★** of the castle, the Seine and Les Andelys.

Le Petit Andely by the Seine viewed from Château-Gaillard
© José Antonio Moreno/age fotostock

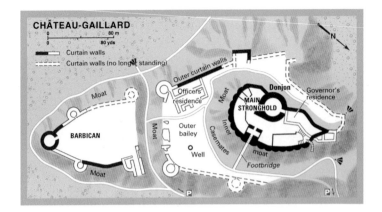

CHÂTEAU-GAILLARD

0   80 m
0   80 yds

■ Curtain walls
--- Curtain walls (no longer standing)

N

Outer curtain walls

Officers' residence

Moat

BARBICAN

Moat

Moat

Outer bailey

Well

Moat

Casemates

Inner moat

MAIN STRONGHOLD

Donjon

Governor's residence

moat

Footbridge

P   P

Barbican

The redoubt, separated from the main castle by a deep moat, possessed five towers of which only one, the barbican, remains, encircled by a narrow path.

Castle

The outer ward, the esplanade, is situated between the redoubt and the castle. Around the wall to the left are the foundations of the keep, which rises from the natural rock. At the far end of the wall there is a fine **viewpoint**. Returning along the bottom of the moat, you pass the casemates (*right*) hollowed out of the rock to store the garrison's food. The keep is round (8m in internal diameter) with thick walls (5m). Adjoining (*right*) are the ruins of the Governor's residence.

Outside the perimeter wall, a path leads to the edge of the rocky escarpment, which provides an extended view of the Seine valley.

▶ Take the one-way descent to rue Richard-Cœur-de-Lion to return to the town.

ADDITIONAL SIGHTS
Collégiale Notre-Dame★
Grand Andely.
🕘*Daily Jun–Sept 9am–7pm; Oct–May 9am–noon, 2–5.30pm.* ☎*02 32 54 12 70.*
A well-balanced façade of twin towers flanked by a square staircase tower fronts the church. The 16C south side is in the Flamboyant style and the 16C and 17C north side is Renaissance in style with round arches, Ionic pilasters, balustraded roofs, caryatids and antique-style statues.

Inside, the nave is 13C; the delicately ornamented triforium was remodelled in the 16C and the windows enlarged; the **organ and loft★** are Renaissance. In the north transept and a nearby chapel are two lovely paintings by Quentin Varin, teacher of Les Andelys native Nicholas Poussin (1594–1665). The Entombment in the south aisle beneath the tower is 16C, the Christ in the Tomb is 14C.

Collégiale Notre-Dame

© JavierGil1000/iStockphoto.com

Village of Gaillon with the turrets of the castle

© JONATHAN/Fotolia.com

Musée Nicolas-Poussin

R. Ste-Clotilde. Close to the Fontaine Ste-Clotilde, in a street of the same name. ⏱May–Sept Wed–Mon 2–6pm. 📞02 32 54 31 78. www.ville-andelys.fr/musee-nicolas-poussin.

The famous Classical painter Poussin (1594–1665) was born in Villers, not far from Andelys. This museum devoted to Poussin is in an 18C residence, where copies and a painting by the master, *Coriolanus supplicated by his Mother*, may be found. There is also a 3C mosaic, a few art objects including a beautiful Virgin with Child in painted stone (14C) and a few traditional 17C and 18C pieces of furniture.

Église St-Sauveur

pl. St-Sauveur, Petit Andely.
St Saviour's floorplan is a Greek cross and Gothic in style; the chancel is late-12C, the nave early 13C. The wooden porch stands on an early 15C stone foundation. Inside there is an organ dating from 1674.

EXCURSION

Château de Gaillon

12km/9mi S by the D 316. Allée du Chateau , Gallion.
⏱*Daily except Tue Apr 7–Oct 10am–noon, 2–5.30pm.* ♿€5. 📞02 32 53 86 40. www.ville-gaillon.fr/lechateau.

The property of Rouen's archbishops since St Louis, Gaillon was remodelled by Georges d'Amboise, the first great cardinal-minister, in the new Italian style (1497–1510). The structure was the avant-garde monument of its time, bringing the Renaissance to Normandy. The access ramp is to the right, at the top of the D 6015's rise to Rouen. The entrance pavilion with its towers has Renaissance décor.

ADDRESSES

🛏 STAY

😊😊 **Chambre d'hôte La Haye Gaillard** – Côte de Cléry, 27700 Les Andelys. 📞02 32 51 66 23. www.fermedelahayegaillard.com. 🗏. *3 rooms.* Farm with comfortable rooms, one in a cleverly-restored dovecot.

🍽EAT

😊😊 **Hotel de Paris** – 10 av. de la République. 📞02 32 54 00 33. www.hotel-andelys.fr. Attractive early 20C restaurant. Simple **rooms** are available.

😊😊😊 **La Chaîne d'Or** – 25 r. Grande. 📞02 32 54 00 31. www.hotel-lachainedor.com. Open every day except Wed, and from the middle of October to the middle of April, on Sunday evenings, on Tuesdays and Wednesdays. Lovely views of Seine. Renowned cuisine. **Rooms** available.

Lyons-la-Forêt★

The half-timbered houses, old brick buildings and woodland setting in the heart of the Forêt de Lyons create a picture-book vision of Normandy. Unusually in the French language, the final "s" of Lyons is pronounced, indicating the town's Scandinavian origins.

THE VILLAGE
Halles
pl. Benserade.
The old covered market in the centre of place Benserade was used for scenes in Jean Renoir's film *Madame Bovary*. The fountain appeared in Claude Chabrol's 1990 version of the same novel.
Pretty half-timbered houses surround the square. In the steep street west of the square, **Maurice Ravel** composed *Le Tombeau de Couperin* and completed the orchestration for Moussorgsky's *Pictures at an Exhibition*.

Église St-Denis
r. Bout-de-Bas leads to St-Denis Church, at the edge of the village, on the riverside.
The 12C church was completely renovated in the 15C. The stonework and the timber belfry are admirable, and in the chancel the statue of St Christopher carrying the infant Jesus dates from the 16C.

🚗 DRIVING TOUR

🚗 FORÊT DE LYONS★★
70km/43.5mi. Allow one day.

The forest covers 10 700ha and is known for its glorious beech trees. You can also admire an old abbey and two interesting châteaux.

🚗 ①LYONS TO LES BORDINS

▷ Leave Lyons to the W via D 6.

- ▶ **Population:** 729.
- ⚙ **Michelin Map:** 304: I-5.
- ℹ **Info:** 25 bis place Isaac Benserade. ✆02 32 49 31 65. www.lyons-andelle-tourisme.com.
- ▷ **Location:** Lyons-la-Forêt is 43km/27mi E of Rouen and 20km/12.5mi N of Andelys.
- ☞ **Don't Miss:** The château of Vascœuil and the beautiful Forêt de Lyons.

Notre-Dame-de-la-Paix
From this statue there is a fine view of the town of Lyons.

▷ Take D 169 left.

Chapelle St-Jean
Behind the 17C chapel a path leads to the Chêne St-Jean (St John's Oak) which has a circumference of 5m at a height of 1.30m from the ground.

▷ Turn left onto the D 11 for Rosay.

Rosay-sur-Lieure
The **church** and churchyard are in a pleasant setting.

▷ D 11 goes on to Ménesqueville.

Ménesqueville
The small 12C country **church,** skilfully restored, contains some very old statues. The stained-glass windows by contemporary artist F E Décorchemont portray the Song of Songs.

▷ From here, D 12 goes SE along the pretty Fouillebroc valley as far as Lisors.

Lisors
The church contains a 14C crowned Virgin which was found buried in 1936.

▷ Take D 715. On the right, you will see the ruins of the abbey.

Place Isaac Benserade, Lyons-la-Forêt

© Hervé Lenain/hemis.fr

Abbaye de Mortemer
🕐*Unaccompanied access to park
Apr–Aug 11am–6pm; rest of year, see
website.* 👥*Guided visits Apr–Aug
daily 1.30–6pm.* 🏛*Park and museum
€9. Park alone €5.* 📞*02 32 49 54 34.
www.abbaye-de-mortemer.fr.*
In the forest stand the ruins of the 12C–
13C Cistercian abbey. A **museum** below
the conventual building, reconstructed
in the 17C, explains monastic life and
evokes the various legends connected
with the abbey.

▶ Across from the abbey, on the N
side of D 715, a short path leads to the
Croix-Vaubois crossroads.

Carrefour de la Croix-Vaubois
The monument erected here recalls the
foresters who died in the Resistance.

▶ As you continue along D 715, look
for two springs (sources) off to the left.

Fontaine de Ste-Catherine
A footbridge spanning the Fouillebroc
leads to an oratory, traditionally visited
by young girls in search of a husband.

Source du Fouillebroc
This spring is set in pleasant forest
surroundings.

Les Bordins Arboretum
Visit year round. 📞*02 32 49 04 09.*
Opened in 1994, this 4 451.5ha area
abounds with trees from across the
world, grouped by continent.

🚗 **2 NORTH OF THE FOREST**
60km/37mi. Allow about 2h30.

▶ Leave Lyons to the E via D 14.

Beauficel-en-Lyons
The **church** is preceded by a 17C porch
and contains beautiful statues, including
a 14C virgin in polychrome stone.

▶ D 14 runs alongside Fleury-la-
Forêt Castle (to the right).

Château de Fleury-la-Forêt
📞*02 32 49 63 91.*
www.chateau-fleury-la-foret.com.
Beyond a wrought-iron gate, an avenue
of lime trees leads to the 17C château
built of red brick, flint and sandstone.
The interior contains interesting displays
of dolls, toys and furniture. There is also
a huge, richly decorated kitchen.

▶ Turn left after Fleury-la-Forêt and
follow D 14e and then D 241.

Hêtre de la Bunodière★
Indicated by a signpost on the right as
you approach the N 31, this magnificent
beech, at 40m tall, stands near the
Câtelier Reserve. Its circumference
measures 3.3m.

▶ N 31 leads back to La Feuillie.

La Feuillie
At 54m, the slender church **spire★** is a
bold piece of carpentry.

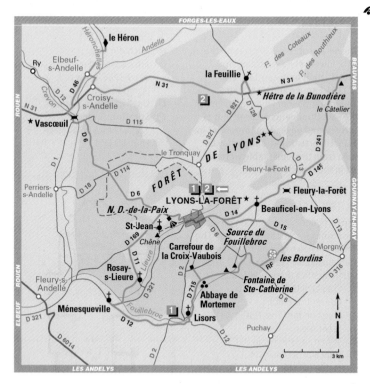

Le Héron

This pleasant tree-shaded area was designed by La Nôtre.

▶ Continue on N 31 to Vascœuil.

**Château de Vascœuil –
Centre d'Art et d'histoire★**

🕓Jul–Aug 11am–6.30pm; Apr–Jun and early Sept–end Oct Wed–Sun and holidays 2.30–6pm; Nov Sat–Sun and public holidays 2–5pm. ⌧€10 (child 12–19, €7.50). ℘02 35 23 62 35. www.chateauvascoeuil.com.

The château is a known cultural centre associated with the memory of Jules Michelet. The **Michelet museum** presents portraits, posters and writings related to the historian and his family, as well as his re-created study. Jules Michelet (1798–1874) wrote a part of his famous *Histoire de France* at Vascœuil. A fierce defender of democracy, he also wrote l'*Histoire de la Révolution*.

The Crevon waters the gardens, now a **sculpture park**: Volti's well-endowed women, Pompon's pigeon, Dali's *Freedom's Victory*, the exuberant *Ludivine* by Coville, ceramics and mosaics by Léger or Vasarely. Contemporary art exhibitions are held in the 14C–16C **château** and superb 17C **dovecote.**

ADDRESSES

🛏 STAY

⌧⌧ **Hôtel Les Lions de Beauclerc–** 7 r. de l'Hôtel-de-Ville. ℘ 02 32 49 18 90. www.leslionsdebeauclerc.com. 6 rooms. Restaurant ⌧⌧. Close to the market; modern comfort and old antiques (adjoining shop). Restaurant and tea room.

🍽/EAT

⌧⌧ **Café du Commerce** – 19 pl. Benserade. ℘02 32 49 49 92. Closed Mon. Overlooks the 200-year-old market; café-restaurant with outdoor tables.

Écouis★

The village of Écouis centres on the twin towers of its old collegiate church, built between 1310 and 1313 by Enguerrand de Marigny, Superintendant of Finances to Philip the Fair. Opponents accused him of sorcery, and he died on the gibbet in 1315. His artistic patronage may be seen from the remarkable works of art in the church.

COLLÉGIALE NOTRE-DAME★

The brick and stone vaulting replaced roof timbers in the late 18C. The immense choir has beautiful furnishings and remarkable **statues**★ (14C–17C); it terminates in a three-sided apse.

1) Chapel of the Immaculate Conception (16C).
2) Christ on the Cross (13C).
3) St Nicaise.
4) St Ann and the Virgin (14C).
5) Our Lady of Écouis (14C).
6) Statue of St Margaret (14C).
7) Statue of Jean de Marigny, brother of Enguerrand, who was Archbishop of Rouen when he died in 1351.
8) St John Chapel – The wooden vault is a trace of the nave's former vault. Statue of Alips de Mons, wife of Enguerrand de Marigny. Stained glass (14C) of Crucifixion with St John and Mary at the Cross.
9) 14C choir stalls; 16C doors and woodwork.
10) Door of former rood screen.
11) Christ and his Shroud (16C).
12) North side chapel: St Martin, St Francis, St Laurent (14C), St Cecilia.
13) Madonna of the King (14C).
14) St Agnes (14C).
15) St Veronica (14C).
16) Ecce Homo in wood (15C).
17) Annunciation (15C) – The statue of the Virgin is supported by a charming group of small angels reading prophecies relating to the mystery of the Incarnation. The hands and face of the Virgin, together with the face of Archangel Gabriel, are in marble set into the stone.

▶ **Population:** 822.
⚙ **Michelin Map:** 304: I-6.
▣ **Info:** 6 place du Cloître. ℰ 02 32 69 43 08. www.collegiale-ecouis.asso.fr.
◷ Open daily 7am–7pm.
◑ **Location:** Écouis is 12km/7.4mi S of Lyons-la-Forêt via D 2.

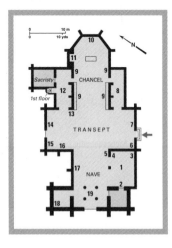

18) St John the Baptist (14C).
19) Organ case (17C).

In a **room** on the first floor beautiful works of art are displayed including a cope chest and the chalice of Jean de Marigny (14C).

EXCURSION

Abbaye de Fontaine-Guérard★

12km/7.4mi NW via N14. Just before Fleury-sur-Andelle, take D 321 left, then the second road on the right. Allow 30min to visit.

The ruins of the 12C abbey, on the north bank of the Andelle, are both evocative and moving, owing to their isolation and the threat of flooding. Beside the path stands the 15C St Michael's Chapel (left). The abbey church dates from 1218; the square chevet and some apsidal vaulting have survived. The **chapterhouse** (right) is a fine example of early 13C Norman architecture.

Château de Martainville★

This magnificent First Renaissance château is home to a remarkable ethnological musuem devoted to Norman arts and traditions. It offers a complete look at how regional furniture developed from the late MIddle Ages to the Second Empire. The visit is even more fascinating in that the presentation includes all aspects of Normandy's rich culture.

- **Michelin Map:** 304: H-4.
- **Location:** Blainville-Crevon is 20km/12.4mi NE of Rouen via N 31, then D 7.
- **Don't Miss:** The church; the "Emma Bovary" tour. Map in area tourist offices.
- **Timing:** Allow 1hr; marked tour of village (60km/ 37.2mi itinerary). around Ry lets you pass time with Emma Bovary.

VISIT

Daily except Tue: Apr–Sept 10am–12.30pm, 2–5.30pm, Sun 2–6pm; Oct–Mar 10am–12.30pm, 2–5pm, Sun 2–5.30pm. *1 Jan, 1 May, 1 and 11 Nov and 25 Dec.* ☞€4. ℘02 35 23 44 70. www.chateaudemartainville.fr.

The elegant brick and stone château, little changed since its construction in 1485–1510, has a massive dovecote (16C) and a half-timbered cart shed (18C).

The château houses the **Musée Départemental des Traditions et Arts Normands★**, with displays of furniture from Rouen and the Pays de Caux, chests, 17C buffets, 18C cupboards, earthenware and pottery, glass, pewter and copper, regional ceramics and costumes.

🚗 DRIVING TOUR

🚗 MARTAINVILLE TO CREVON

Tour of 50km/31mi, about 1h30.

▶ Leave Martainville E along the D 13.

Ry is a village of half-timbered and brick houses thought to be Yonville-l'Abbaye, where **Gustave Flaubert** (1821–80) set *Madame Bovary* (1857).

Look at the 12C **church** with its Renaissance oak **porch ★** before driving towards Elbeuf-sur-Andelle; you'll turn left on the D 46. This takes you to **Le Héron** with its château and Le Nôtre park; Flaubert is said to have discovered sophisticated society here.

Head north on the D 46, to come to **Héronchelles**, a pretty village with a 16C riverside manor. Continuing on the D 46 to **Yville**; you will admire the beautiful oversized thatched roofs here. Drive even further on the D 46, and take the next right to **Bois-Guilbert**. Right after you enter the village, you will see a grand estate on the left, Bois-Guilbert; it has 7ha of park, the **jardins de Bois-Guilbert**. The 17C–18C setting inspired sculptor and landscaper Jean-Marc de Pas to blend unspoiled nature and landscaping to create the Cosmos garden, the Four Elements garden, the Sun garden and the Four Seasons garden. Over 60 sculptures, most in bronze (*Four Seasons, Abbé Pierre, African Woman*, etc.) decorate the park's various green spaces.

Back in your car, you soon join the D 38, which you follow by turning left after Bois-Guilbert to head north. At **Bosc-Bordel** there is a small 13C church with a 16C wood porch.

Now drive W on the D 919 heading for Buchy, but taking the D 96 on the left. At **Bosc-Roger-sur-Buchy**, there is a pretty English-style garden, the **Jardin de Valérianes** (*mid-May–Sept Wed–Sun and holidays 1.30–6.30pm;* ☞€8; ℘06 85 48 26 76; http://jardindevalerianes.e-monsite.com), with 4ha planted with over 1 000 botanical varieties. Continue on the D 919 to stop off in **Buchy** to visit **Notre-Dame church** with its Renaissance stained glass. Leave Buchy by the D 7. At the intersection take the D 90 for St-Germain-des-

Château de Martainville

© milosk50/Shutterstock

Essort, which you cross for a pleasant drive along the Crevon river to Blainville. The small village of **Blainville-Crevon**, in the river valley, is also the birthplace of artist **Marcel Duchamp** (1887–1968). Many artists from the School of Rouen stayed in this town, including Gustave Flaubert (1821–80). Today Blainville-Crevon hosts the annual Archéo-Jazz Festival (*www.archeojazz.com*) with dance, cinema, theatre and music.

You won't want to miss the **collegiate church of St. Michael**. Founded in 1488, it has chequered sandstone and silex facing; the interior is Flamboyant. Have a look at the left transept at the monumental late 15C painted wood statue of **St Michael slaying the dragon**. While you are here you should also visit the **castle** (🚶*Tours for groups only by arrangement; ℘02 35 34 24 82; www. chateau-blainville-76.com*).

The remodelling work going on since 1968 on the medieval castle ruins has unearthed a staircase buried in an artificial mound dating from the 11C, along with about 100m of curtain wall 5–8m high, dry moats and two towers with well-preserved lower floors belonging to 14C and 15C constructions.

Forges-les-Eaux

In the green heart of the Pays de Bray, Forges-les-Eaux is a spa resort with iron-rich waters reputed to be both refreshing and stimulating.

SIGHTS
Collection Faïence de Forges
🕐*Tue–Fri, only by appointment via tourist office.* 👛*€2.50.* ℘*02 35 90 52 10.* A hundred or so examples of Forges faïence, manufactured until the 19C, are displayed at the town hall.

▶ **Population:** 3 804.
⌖ **Michelin Map:** 304: J-4.
🛈 **Info:** Rue Albert-Bochet. ℘02 35 90 52 10. https:// fr.forgeseseaux-tourisme. com.
▶ **Location:** Forges-les-Eaux is 60km/37mi NE of Rouen.
👁 **Don't Miss:** Excursions into the Pays de Bray to see the pretty villages.
🕐 **Timing:** After a morning in town, see the Pays de Bray.

Musée de la Résistance et de la Déportation

r. du Marechal-Leclerc.

🕐*Daily 2–6pm.* 📞*02 35 90 64 07*
Insignia, arms and uniforms as well as documents recount the dark days of the Occupation in Haute Normandie.

The Spa

Rue de la République boasts some half-timbered façades (17C–18C), and leads onto avenue des Sources, where it passes under the old railway line (now a footpath).

The resort grounds and casino are to the left, just after the bridge. The **park** and spa are managed by the Club Méditerranée in an elegant setting.

Parc Montalent and Épinay Forest

On the other side of avenue des Sources, four pleasant and well-marked **nature trails** wind among the ponds and into the woods.

EXCURSION

La Ferme de Bray

Leave Forges via D 915 NW; after 8km/5mi, turn left before Sommery and follow the signs. 281 Chemin de Bray.
♿🕐*2 –6pm; Easter –Oct Sat–Sun and public holidays, and daily Jul–Aug.*
📞*02 35 90 57 27.*
http://ferme.de.bray.free.fr.
On the banks of the Sorson, this restored site shows what a prosperous 17C–18C farm was like. The bread oven, the cider press and the mill are in use. There are regular exhibits in the main house, a spacious 16C building whose façade was redone in the 17C.

🚗 DRIVING TOUR

🚗 LE PAYS DE BRAY

60km/37mi. Allow 2h.

The Pays de Bray is a lush strip at the centre of the vast bare stretches of the **Caux plateau**. It owes its chief characteristic, known as the Bray "Buttonhole", to a geological accident, which created a hollow in the surrounding chalk. Running parallel to the valley of the River Seine, the region is a sparsely inhabited patchwork of vales, limestone bluffs, hills, meadows and forests.

▶ Leave Forges-les-Eaux south on the D 921 and deviate to **La Ferté-St-Samson**. This village is perched just before the main edge of the Bray Buttonhole and from the approach to the church there is an extended view of the depression with its clearly defined rim. In the main square is the 16C house of Henri IV.

▶ From La Ferté take the D9 south. **Sigy-en-Bray** has an abbey church is all that remains of Sigy abbey, founded in the 11C by Hugh I. It has kept its 12C chancel and seven-sided apse, a 13C portal and the nave vaulting, restored in the 18C. The 15C belltower overlooks a cemetery with a late 15C sandstone calvary.

▶ Take the D 41 east to Argueil, the D 921 south to Fry, then turn left onto the D 1 before the church. The road runs along the southwest Bray escarpment of massive bare mounds crowned with beech trees, called Mont Robert. From the east end of **Beauvoir-en-Lyons★** (🅿*park beyond the mairie; walk up the street on the left to the church*) there is a **view★** of the green Bray valley cutting away in a straight line southeast. In clear weather Beauvais cathedral is visible.

▶ Return to your car and continue on the D 1; at a crossroads, turn left downhill onto the D 57 for open views of Bray. Pass Elboeuf-en-Bray and then head left for **Brémontier-Merval**. The beautiful 17C Château de Brémontier-Merval is home to an agricultural school; its 100ha grounds are open to all. Over 500 varieties of apples are grown here.

▶ Return towards Elbeuf-en-Bray and head for **Gournay-en-Bray** and **Ferrières**, the busiest towns in the Pays de Bray. The local dairy industry supplies most of the fresh cheese con-

177

sumed in France. Collégiale St-Hildevert, a collegiate church, is largely 12C; it has withstood several wars but the late 12C doors have suffered from excessive restoration. Inside, the massive columns are surmounted by carved capitals. The oldest and most worn, at the end of the south aisle, are among the earliest examples of attempts at human portrayal during the Romanesque period.

▷ Take the D 916 north and continue straight on the D8; at St-Etienne, turn left onto the D 84 for **Beuvreuil**, which has a small 11C country **church** with a wooden porch. The building is decorated with enamelled bricks. Inside are an 11C font stoup, a 15C holy-water stoup, Gothic statues, a 15C altarpiece and a 16C lectern.

▷ Return to Forges by the D 915.

Neufchâtel-en-Bray

The former capital of the Pays de Bray is today the capital of "bondon", a cylinder-shaped cheese. The other local stars are the "petit-suisse", invented near Gournay-en-Bray, and the *fromage de Neufchâtel*, a farm cheese produced in several shapes.

▸ **Population:** 4 722.
⚙ **Michelin Map:** 304: I-3.
▯ **Info:** 6 place Notre-Dame. ℰ02 35 93 22 96. http://brayeawy.fr.
▷ **Location:** This village is 45km/28mi SW of Dieppe, 50km/31mi NE of Rouen.
◈ **Don't Miss:** Église St-Pierre -et-St-Paul (in Aumale).
◐ **Timing:** Count on a good half-day to see Neufchâtel and its pretty countryside.

VISIT
Église Notre-Dame
The doorway dates from the end of the 15C; the early 16C nave contains Renaissance capitals. The eight windows in the aisles depict local saints: St Radegonde, St Vincent, St Anthony. In the 13C chancel round columns support the pointed vaulting; against a pillar is a gilt wood Virgin crowned.

Musée Mathon Durand – Musée des traditions et arts populaires
◐*Mid-Jun–mid Sept Tue–Sun 2–6pm; Apr–mid-Jun and mid-Sept–Oct Sat–Sun and public holidays 2–6pm.*
◐*1 Jan, 1 and 11 Nov, 25 Dec.* ⊜€4. ℰ*02 35 93 06 55.*

The Bray Buttonhole

The movement of the earth's crust during the Tertiary era (64–1.8 million years ago), which brought about the raising of the Alps some 12 million years ago had repercussions as far as the Paris basin. The shocks formed wide, deep undulations in a southeast/northwest direction and subsequently, in the area we call Bray, one of these swelled into a large dome with a steep northeast face.

Erosion relentlessly ate into the limestone surface of the dome, exposing clay laid down in the upper Jurassic Period some 160 million years ago. This elliptical cut, with its clearly defined rim, is known to geologists as a buttonhole, hence the term Bray Buttonhole (⚲*see Forges-les-Eaux*).

Continued erosion has given the area irregular, varied landscapes of marshes, *bocage* country, cultivated fields, orchards and great forests.

Musée Mathon-Durand

© Franck Guiziou/hemis.fr

This museum is set in a half-timbered house built after the destruction of 1940. Its collections are devoted to the Pays de Bray folk art and traditions, smithing and ironwork. An apple mill (1746) is in the garden, along with a press (1837), typical of the region.

🚗 DRIVING TOUR

🚗 NORTHERN PAYS DE BRAY
46km/28mi. About 1h30.

▷ Leave Neufchâtel on D1314 to the north.

From the road, which runs through the so-called Bray Buttonhole formation, there are extensive views of the Béthune valley *(left)* and Hellet Forest *(north)*.

▷ At a junction turn left on D 56 to Croixdalle.

The road crosses Hellet forest.

▷ From Croixdalle, D 77 *(left)* down the Béthune valley to Osmoy-St-Valery; it climbs southwest and passes through a gap. The view is of Nappes forest. On leaving the Mesnil-Follemprise valley, Bures-en-Bray's belltower appears with Hellet forest and the Château of Mesnières.

Château de Mesnières
Institution Saint Joseph, 76270 Mesnières-en-Bray. The château is occupied by a private agricultural school.
🕐 *Jul–Aug daily except Tue 2.30–6.30pm.* ✆€6. ☎02 35 93 10 04. *www.chateau-mesnieres-76.com.*
This majestic Renaissance château, begun in the late 15C on the site of a medieval castle, lies at a strategic crossing of two royal roads, Paris–Dieppe and Abbeville–Rouen. The beautiful park was designed by Le Nôtre.

Bures-en-Bray
The **church**, partly 12C, has a modern brick façade with porch and a bold twisted wooden spire. In the north transept are an Entombment, a 16C stone altarpiece and a 14C Virgin and Child.

▷ Uphill after the church take the first road, D 114, left near the café-tobacconist.

The road follows a terrace at the foot of the southwest face on which the villages have been built.

▷ At Fresles turn left onto D 97, and later right on the D1 back to Neufchâtel.

Forêt d'Eawy★★

The Eawy forest (6 600ha), together with the Lyons forest, is the most beautiful beech forest to be found in Normandy.

🚗 DRIVING TOUR

🚗 EAWY FOREST
35km/21mi from St-Saëns. About 4h30.

St-Saëns
This small forest town lies next to the Varenne. The church is 19C.

▷ Take the D 12 NE for Pommeréval.

👫 Ventes-St-Rémy
A signposted path teaches visitors about the forest's trees. There are three itineraries (*tourist office brochure*): local species; forest management and swamps; and conifers and "carcahoux".

▷ Continue on the D 12, turn left on the D 97, then right to Val-Ygot.

Les V1 du Val-Ygot
Panels explain the 13 concrete buildings, re-created V-1 launchpad (the V-1 flying bomb was the world's first guided missile) and monument to victims of Hitler's secret weapons. There were 117 V-1 sites in Seine-Maritime.

▷ Take D 99 to Bellencombre.
At the town entrance, left and head for Rosay.

Musée de la Pomme, du Cidre et des Métiers traditionnels
1 route de la Forêt d'Eawy, Rosay,
🕐*Easter–Oct Sun and public holidays 2.30–6pm; mid-Jul–mid-Aug 2.30–6pm daily.* 📞*06 46 77 32 08.*
http://musee-cidre-metiers.com.
An eco-museum on traditional professions, and the production of cider.

▷ From Rosay, take the D 97 to Beaumont-le-Hareng.

- 🕭 **Michelin Map:** 304 H3
- 🛈 **Info:** 📞02 35 34 57 75. www.normandie-tourisme.fr.
- ▶ **Location:** About 12km/7mi W of Neufchâtel-en-Bray
- 🐾 **Don't Miss:** The Christmas rose collection at the Bellevue gardens.
- 👫 **Kids:** Ventes-St-Rémy

Jardins de Bellevue★
Cross Beaumont-le-Hareng; left at bend at church.
👫🕐*Thu–Sun 10am–6pm (Jul–Aug daily).* ✏️€8. 📞*02 35 33 31 37. http://jardin-de-bellevue.e-monsite.com.*
A 6ha array of flowers, especially Christmas roses. Superb view at end.

▷ D 97; at Beauzeville-la-Giffarde, takes the D 225 to Grigneuseville.

Jardins Agapanthe★
1, impasse Agapanthe, 76850 Grigneuseville.
🕐*May–Sept Fri–Sun and public hollidays 2–7pm (and Thu Jun–Aug)*
🕐*1 Jan, 11 Nov and 25 Dec.* ✏️€10 *(child 6–15, €5).* 📞*02 35 33 32 05.*
www.jardins-agapanthe.com.
A delightful garden of varied intimate spaces; pools, gazebo, tables, seats.

▷ Continue on D 225 to Biennais, then right for Etaimpuis. Return to D 225 to Beuzeville-la-Giffarde, then D 929 and D 1029 to St-Martin-Osmonville, then D 38 to Montérolier.

Jardin du Mesnil
25 route du Mesnil, Montérolier.
🕐*End Apr–early Nov Fri–Sun 2–6pm.* ✏️€8. 📞*06 77 35 83 62.*
www.jardin-du-mesnil.com.
Flowers, rare bushes, maples, hydrangeas.

▷ Head back to St-Martin-Osmonville and return N to St-Saëns by the D 38.

The Côte Fleurie or "Flowering Coast" runs from the Pays d'Auge to the east of Calvados, the name evoking Belle Epoque Parisians "summering" at Honfleur or Deauville. Today the vast beaches of fine sand still delight holiday-makers and movie stars alike; the Pays d'Auge itself, straddling Calvados and Orne, produces wonderful dairy products. Camembert is made here, but also Livarot and Pont l'Évêque – fine cheeses, but also the names of the villages making them. Producing apples as well, the Pays d'Auge achieved Appellation d'Origine Contrôlée status for its Calvados in 1942, and for its cider, in 1996.

Côte Fleurie: Subdued chic

The Deauville American Film Festival, considered here to be second only to Cannes, creates a certain image of movie stars and paparazzi. While it is true that there are all-night casinos, elegant seafood restaurants, celebrity homes and artistic history, the Côte Fleurie is only two hours from the French capital, and is also simply a summer home to many Parisians, who come to appreciate its golden sands and local cuisine. Glamour is here, but it is kept discreet; local obsessions do include horses and yachts, but Calvados is drunk more than champagne, and while art galleries abound, there are just as many Sunday painters. The beautiful people – and holiday-makers – are here to relax and rejuvenate, not to be seen.

Pays d'Auge: Authenticity

The Pays d'Auge has long cultivated its verdant countryside to produce Calvados and pommeau from apples, while cider has been the drink of the people since the Middle Ages, although Louis

Highlights

1 A platter heaped with seafood in **Honfleur** (p184)
2 A drive along the south bank of the **Seine** (p190)
3 Exploring contemporary art in a **Trouville** art gallery (p194)
4 Strolling on the Planches in **Deauville**, with sunglasses (p195)
5 Treasure hunting with the kids at **Château de Crèvecoeur** (p211)

XVI sang its praises. Dairy farming is important here too, close to 50 per cent of the milk production making celebrated Auge cheeses: Camembert, Pont l'Évêque and Livarot, formerly called "the worker's meat". Yet the Pays d'Auge is more than taste treats: preserved villages with half-timbered old quarters, châteaux, Belle Epoque residences, beautiful parks and gardens and places of pilgrimage, all await the visitor.

Apple orchard in spring, Pays d'Auge

© Loïc Durand/Calvados Attractivité

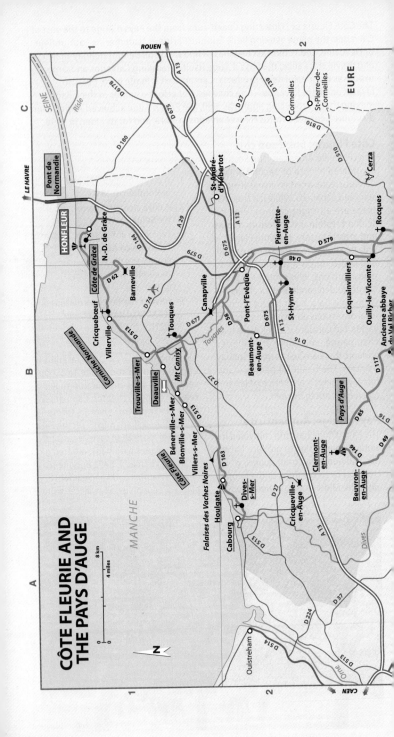

CÔTE FLEURIE AND THE PAYS D'AUGE

N

0   4 miles
0   8 km

ROUEN

SEINE

Risle

EURE

LE HAVRE

Pont de Normandie

HONFLEUR

Côte de Grâce

N.-D. de Grâce

Criquebœuf

Villerville

Corniche Normande

Trouville-s-Mer

Deauville

Mt Canisy

Bénerville-s-Mer

Blonville-s-Mer

Villers-s-Mer

Côte Fleurie

Falaises des Vaches Noires

Houlgate

Dives-s-Mer

Cabourg

Criqueville-en-Auge

Ouistreham

CAEN

MANCHE

Barneville

Touques

Canapville

Touques

Pont-l'Évêque

St-André d'Hébertot

St-Hymer

Beaumont-en-Auge

Pierrefitte-en-Auge

Coquainvilliers

Ouilly-le-Vicomte

Ancienne abbaye du Val Richer

Cormeilles

St-Pierre-de-Cormeilles

Cerza

Rocques

Clermont-en-Auge

Beuvron-en-Auge

Pays d'Auge

Dives

Orne

D 678
D 180
D 27
A 13
D 675
D 139
D 810
D 510
D 144
A 29
D 579
D 62
D 74
D 513
D 677
D 579
D 675
D 58
A 13
D 48
D 16
D 117
D 85
D 146
D 49
D 27
A 13
D 163
D 513
D 513
D 27
D 37
D 324
D 514
D 27 G

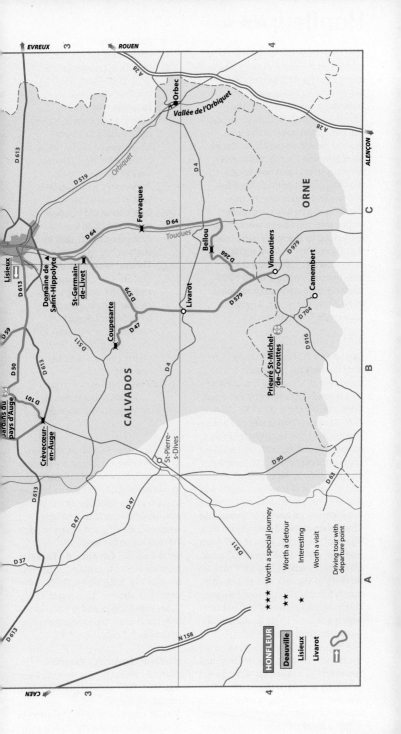

EVREUX 3
ROUEN
A 28
Orbec
Vallée de l'Orbiquet
A 28
ALENÇON
D 613
Orbiquet
D 519
D 4
D 64
Touques
Fervaques
ORNE
D 64
Bellou
Lisieux
D 613
Domaine de Saint-Hippolyte
St-Germain-de-Livet
D 579
D 268
Vimoutiers
D 979
Camembert
D 59
Coupesarte
D 47
Livarot
D 579
D 704
D 916
Prieuré St-Michel-de-Crouttes
D 50
D 511
D 613
CALVADOS
D 4
Jardins du pays d'Auge
D 101
Crèvecoeur-en-Auge
St-Pierre-s-Dives
D 90
D 63
D 613
D 47
D 47
D 37
D 511
A
B
C
N 158
D 613
CAEN 3
4

HONFLEUR
Deauville
Lisieux
Livarot

★★★ Worth a special journey
★★ Worth a detour
★ Interesting
Worth a visit
Driving tour with departure point

183

Honfleur★★★

The lovely town of Honfleur is located on the Seine estuary. The impressive Pont de Normandie has made it easier to get to and from the town, and to visit the Pays d'Auge and the Côte de Grâce. You can spend hours wandering around the old dock (Vieux Bassin), Ste-Catherine Church, the narrow winding streets and port where the fishing fleet unloads fresh fish and shellfish every day. Today, Honfleur can rightly claim to be both a river port and a seaport, as evidenced by the many large liners that choose the welcoming city as a stopover: 220m-long ships, able to accommodate up to 1 200 passengers in optimal conditions, glide along the quays, where the waters are 7.5–9.5m deep.

A BIT OF HISTORY

Canada, a Norman Colony – Ever since the early 16C, navigators had been anchoring briefly along the coast of a land named Gallia Nova by Verrazano, the discoverer of the site of New York. In 1534, **Jacques Cartier** stepped ashore and claimed the territory for France, naming it Canada. François I was less than impressed with the explorer on his return as he brought back no spices, gold or diamonds. Canada was thus left unexplored until the 17C when the experienced navigator **Samuel de Champlain** received orders to colonise this vast territory. He set sail from Honfleur, and in 1608 founded Quebec. On Colbert's advice Louis XIV took an interest in Canada and the country rapidly became a Norman and Percheron colony settled by over 4 000 peasants who made their living by agriculture, fishing, hunting and fur trading.

The Iroquois Indians bitterly opposed the French colonists, who by 1665 had to appeal to France for aid against mounting attacks. A thousand soldiers arrived; simultaneously a decree was issued compelling each man to marry, within a fortnight upon her arrival, one

> ▶ **Population:** 7 728.
> ◔ **Michelin Map:** 303: N-3.
> ▤ **Info:** Quai Lepaulmier. ☎02 31 89 23 30. www.honfleur-tourism.co.uk.
> ◖ **Location:** The city, 25km/15.5mi from Le Havre and 91km/56.5mi from Rouen, lies on the left bank of the Seine, 3km/2mi from the Pont de Normandie.
> ▣ **Parking:** Park on quai de la Tour in the old city.
> ◉ **Don't Miss:** Old Honfleur and the wooden Ste-Catherine Church, built by shipwrights.
> ◕ **Timing:** Allow a full day. Visit Ste-Catherine Quay early in the morning to capture the elongated reflections of the old houses in the still water. In the evening, sunset lights up the *greniers à sel* just opposite.
> ⮛ **Kids:** Naturospace offers hundreds of butterflies in an immense greenhouse.

of the women, known as the king's daughters (*filles du roy*), who were sent out from France to help increase the sparse population. The queen took an interest in the selection of the young women, who were to be "not ugly... not repulsive... healthy and strong enough for working on the land".

From Canada, **Cavalier de La Salle** journeyed south to explore and colonise Louisiana in 1682. He established the communication route along the Ohio Valley which was to lead to war with the British and finally the loss by the French of Canada in 1760.

Honfleur, an Artist's Paradise – The character and atmosphere of Honfleur has inspired painters, writers and musicians.

Musset came to stay in St-Gatien in the period when the Normandy coast

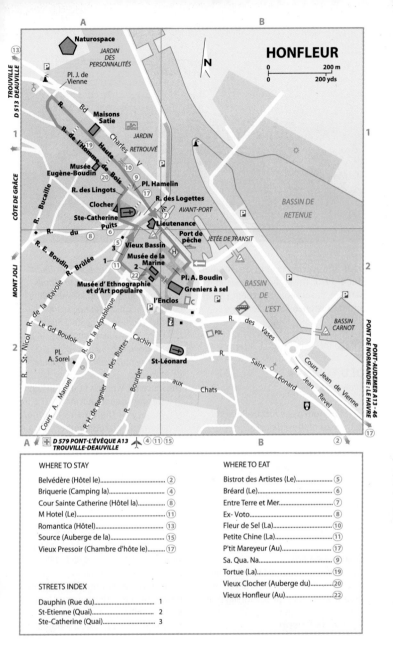

HONFLEUR

0   200 m
0   200 yds

WHERE TO STAY

Belvédère (Hôtel le)	②
Briquerie (Camping la)	④
Cour Sainte Catherine (Hôtel la)	⑧
M Hotel (Le)	⑪
Romantica (Hôtel)	⑬
Source (Auberge de la)	⑮
Vieux Pressoir (Chambre d'hôte le)	⑰

STREETS INDEX

WHERE TO EAT

Bistrot des Artistes (Le)	⑤
Bréard (Le)	⑥
Entre Terre et Mer	⑦
Ex- Voto	⑧
Fleur de Sel (La)	⑩
Petite Chine (La)	⑪
P'tit Mareyeur (Au)	⑰
Sa. Qua. Na.	⑨
Tortue (La)	⑲
Vieux Clocher (Auberge du)	⑳
Vieux Honfleur (Au)	㉒

was fashionable with the Romantics. Honfleur began to fill with painters – not only those who were Norman-born such as Boudin, Hamelin and Lebourg, but also Paul Huet, Daubigny, Corot and others from Paris and foreigners such as Bonington and Jongkind.

It was in the small St-Siméon Inn – "chez La Mère Toutain" – that the Impressionists first met. Ever since artists have continued to visit Honfleur. Baudelaire, who stayed in the town with his mother in her old age, declared, "settling in Honfleur has always been the dearest of my dreams" and while there wrote his *Invitation au Voyage*.

Other Honfleur citizens include the composer Erik Satie (1866–1925), the

Vieux Bassin

poet and novelist Henri de Régnier (1864–1936), the author Lucie Delarue-Mardrus, the economist Frédéric Le Play and the historian Albert Sorel.

👣 WALKING TOUR

OLD TOWN★★
Allow 1h30.

▶ Start from place Arthur-Boudin to the east of the old dock.

Old slate-shingled houses stand around the square; No. 6 is a Louis XIII house with stone and flint chequered decoration. The Saturday-morning flower market brings colour and life to the area.

▶ Turn right into rue de la Ville.

Greniers à sel
These tile-covered stone buildings were constructed in the 17C in order to store the salt required by the cod fishing fleet.

Rue de la Prison
Opposite the Greniers à sel.
Very picturesque with its line of old timber-framed houses. At the end of the street, on the right, is the former church of St-Étienne, its bell-tower rising up above the old port.

Musée de la Marine
quai St-Étienne.

♿🕐*Daily except Tue: Apr–Sept 10am–noon, 2–6pm (Jul–Aug 10am–6pm); Oct–Mar 2.30–5.30pm, Sat–Sun 10am–noon, 2.30–5.30pm (during school holidays 10am–noon, 2.30–5.30pm).* 🕐*25 Dec–early Jan, 1 Feb, 1 May, 14 Jul.* ☞*€8 (during exhibitions).* 📞*02 31 89 14 12. www.musees-honfleur.fr/musee-de-la-marine.*
The museum, which is housed in Église St-Étienne (deconsecrated), traces the history of the port of Honfleur and contains a large number of scale models and topographical information on the town.

Musée d'Ethnographie
r. de la Prison.
🕐*Apr–Sept 10am–noon, 2–6pm; mid-Feb–Mar and Oct–Nov Mon and Wed–Fri 2.30–5.30pm, Sat–Sun 10am–noon, 2.30–5.30pm.* 🕐*Dec–mid-Feb, 1 May, 14 Jul.* ☞*€4.20.* 📞*02 31 89 14 12. www.musees-honfleur.fr.*
Nine Normandy interiors have been reconstructed in this museum located in 16C residences. Note particularly the timbered manor house, the bourgeois dining room, the weavers' and printers' workshop, the bedroom and a shop on the ground floor.

Vieux Bassin★★
The quaysides of the old dock – designed by Duquesne on the orders of Colbert – are picturesque, enhanced by the pleasure boats alongside. The contrast is striking between **St-Étienne Quay,** with its splendid two-storey

stone dwellings, and **Ste-Catherine Quay**, where the tall – rising up to seven storeys high – slender houses are faced with slate and timber. The Governor's House (La Lieutenance), next to the swivel bridge, completes the scene.

La Lieutenance

Only a relic now remains of the 16C house in which the king's lieutenant, Governor of Honfleur, once lived. The façade facing the square now incorporates, between two bartizans, Caen Gate, one of the two main entrances to the city in the Middle Ages. From the corner of the passenger quay you get a good view of the house, the old dock and, on the other side, the outer harbour.

Rue de Logettes, a reference to the numerous wooden stalls that once lined the street, leads to place **Ste-Catherine**, in the heart of the neighbourhood of the same name. In addition to the pretty street and half-timbered houses, the neighbourhood is famous for its unique church and belltower.

Église Ste-Catherine★★

This church is a rare example in western Europe of a building constructed, apart from the foundations, entirely of wood. After the Hundred Years' War all masons and architects were employed on the inevitable post-war reconstruction,

but the Honfleur axe masters from the local shipyards determined to thank God immediately for the departure of the English and built a church with their own skills.

The interior has twin naves and side aisles, the timber roof over each nave being supported by wooden pillars. The carved panels ornamenting the gallery are 16C, the organ 18C. There are also many wooden statues.

Clocher de Ste-Catherine★

⏱ *Same hours as Musée Eugène-Boudin (p188), but additionally closed Nov–Easter.* ℘ *06 02 17 75 82.*

The massive oak belfry, a building covered in chestnut wood, stands apart from the church on a large foundation which contained the bell-ringer's dwelling. Today it is used as an extension of the Musée Eugène-Boudin and contains religious works.

Rue des Lingots, narrow and winding, goes around the tower; the old cobblestones lead to **rue de l'Homme-de-Bois**, named after a covered wooden head on the house at No. **23**.

▷ Turn left onto rue de l'Homme-de-Bois; 400m further on, across from the Hôtel-Dieu Chapel, take rue du Trou-Miard to the right, then turn right again onto rue Haute.

Église Ste-Catherine

© Arnaud Guérin/Calvados Attractivité

The hospital's old lighthouse, on place Jean-de-Vienne, is now mostly used by seagulls. **Rue Haute**, formerly a pathway outside the fortifications, was home to many local shipbuilders. The composer Erik Satie was born at No. **88**, where the timbers are painted red; inside there is an unusual museum.

▶ Continue onto **place Hamelin**, birthplace of Alphonse Allais (No. **6**), a French humourist of the late 19C.

▶ End your tour of Honfleur by walking straight on (quai de la Lieutenance and quai de la Quarantaine) to return to place Arthur-Boudin on the right. Or turn and go through the public garden, walking as far as the Seine along the digue de l'Ouest, where a pleasant pedestrian path has been created on the jetty.

SIGHTS

Musée Eugène-Boudin
r. de l'Homme-de-Bois.
🕐*Daily except Tue: Apr–Sept 10am–noon, 2–6pm (Jul–Aug 10am–6pm); Oct–Mar 2.30–5.30pm, Sat–Sun 10am–noon, 2.30–5.30pm (during school holidays 10am–noon, 2.30–5.30pm).*
🕐*25 Dec–early Jan, 1 Feb, 1 May, 14 Jul.* ⊕€8 *(during exhibitions).* ⊕€8. ✆*02 31 89 54 00.*
www.musees-honfleur.fr.
An old Augustinian chapel and a more recent building house this museum, which is chiefly devoted to the painters of Honfleur and of the estuary.
On the first floor is a rich collection of household items from 18C and 19C Normandy. The second and third floors display works by 20C artists who, for the most part, worked in the region: Dufy, Marquet, Friesz, Villon, Lagar, Grau-Sala, Saint-Delis, Gernez, Driès, Herbo, Vallotton, Bigot, etc.
Galleries adjoining the chapel feature 19C paintings by Eugène Boudin (the museum possesses 89 of his paintings and drawings) and by Monet, Jongkind, Dubourg, Isabey, Pécrus, Courbet, Cals. A second holds the Hambourg-Rachet bequest of some 300 canvases (19C–

20C) by Derain, Foujita, Garbell, Marie Laurencin, Van Dongen and Hambourg. The third is a drawings room in which about 100 works are rotated each year.

Maisons Satie★
Entrance at 67 bd Charles-V (running parallel to r. Haute).
🕐*Daily except Tue: May–Sept 10am–7pm; Oct–Apr 11am–6pm.*
🕐*Jan–mid-Feb, 1 May, 14 Jul and 25 Dec.* ⊕€6.30. ✆*02 31 89 11 11. www.musees-honfleur.fr/maison-satie.html.*
Wearing headphones, you are guided through a series of stage-like settings recalling the career of Erik Satie (1866–1925) – "born young in an old world". The museum offers the opportunity to hear the music and understand more about the life of the man who came out with such conversational pearls as: "Give me a minute to get my skirt on, and I'll be right with you!"; "Although our information is false, we cannot guarantee it"; "What do you prefer, music or cold-cuts?"; "The piano is like money, it's only pleasant when you've got your hands on it."

Église St-Léonard
S of the Vieux-Bassin, take the rue de la République, then left into the rue Cachin, which leads to the place St-Léonard.
The façade of this church is a bizarre combination of an ornate Flamboyant doorway and a 17C belfry tower.
Inside are two immense shells which have been converted into fonts.
At the entrance to the chancel stand statues of Our Lady of Victory and St Leonard with two prisoners kneeling; note in the chancel the wooden statues of St Peter, St Paul and the four Evangelists. The narthex is furnished with an 18C copper lectern from Villedieu-les-Poêles.

🚹🚹 Naturospace★
Opposite the hospital lighthouse, bd Charles V.
♿🕐*Daily Apr–Sept 10am–6.30pm; Feb–Mar and Oct–mid-Nov and*

Christmas period 10am–5pm. ⏱*Mid-Nov–mid-Dec–Jan.* ⏤*€9 (child 3–14, €7).* ☏*02 31 81 77 00.*
www.naturospace.com.

Inside an enormous greenhouse, 60 species of butterflies from six continents float gracefully in perfect freedom. Surrounded by the whispering of their wings, you stroll among tropical plants and observe cocoons from which, early in the morning, a few caterpillars emerge. Good explanations and special exhibits.

ADDITIONAL SIGHTS

Pont de Normandie★★
3km/2mi E via the D 580.
🅐 *There is a toll for cars, but no charge for pedestrians, cyclists and motorcyclists. www.tolls.eu/france.*
🅐 *Watch out – the wind can be very strong!*

The bridge was started in 1988 and officially opened in January 1995; it is the third largest bridge to span the Lower Seine after the Pont de Tancarville and the Pont de Brotonne. Its impact on the economy is three fold: it brings Le Havre and Honfleur closer together by removing the detour via Tancarville Bridge (24km/15mi instead of 60km/37.2mi); it is one of the major motorway links between the Channel Tunnel and the west and south-west of France; and it represents one of the many connections in the so-called **Estuaries Route**, which ties together northern and southern Europe without going through Paris.

The Pont de Normandie, a truly remarkable work of art and a technological feat, was seen as a milestone in the history of civil engineering, since it established the record of the longest cable-stayed bridge (more elegant and cheaper to build than a suspension bridge). Although Lisbon's Vasco da Gama Bridge (1998) is now the longest in Europe, the Pont de Normandie is higher.

This steel and concrete mass, which seems to defy the laws of gravity, is surprisingly light and extremely stable. Careful attention was devoted to the subject of safety: the bridge is designed to withstand winds of up to 440kph/274mph; it can resist shocks caused by the largest cargo boats, which could only collide with the north tower, protected by 9m of concrete; the road surfacing has in-built sensors triggered off by the presence of black ice; tollbooth operators can monitor traffic continually thanks to surveillance cameras.

Besides the standard lighting for road traffic, the Breton architect **Yann Kersalé** conceived a sophisticated lighting system called *Rhapsody in Blue and White* – a bi-coloured display of static lights outline the two towers (blue on the underside, white on the outside), whereas a row of blue twinkling lights run underneath the deck.

Côte de Grâce★★
This famous hillside, appreciated by all Honfleur enthusiasts, has a peaceful beauty.

Calvaire★★
Telescope.
From the cross there is a good **panorama** of the Seine estuary, the Le Havre roadstead, to the right, the Pont de Normandie and, in the distance, Tancarville Bridge.

Chapelle Notre-Dame-de-Grâce
In the centre of the esplanade beneath tall trees stands the small chapel of Our Lady of Grace and within it the statue after which it is named. This graceful

Chapelle Notre-Dame-de-Grâce

© Arnaud Guérin/Calvados Attractivité

17C building has replaced a sanctuary said to have been founded by Richard II, 4th Duke of Normandy. It was here that navigators and explorers came to pray before leaving on journeys of discovery or colonisation to the North American continent; a borough of Montréal bears this name. The north transept chapel is dedicated to all Canadians of Norman origin. There are numerous small, ex-voto vessels.

Mont-Joli viewpoint
The view complements the one from Calvaire: in the foreground are the town, the port and the coast; to the east is the semicircle of hills. Tancarville bridge can be seen in the distance.

🚗 DRIVING TOUR

🚗 SOUTH BANK OF THE SEINE –HONFLEUR TO ROUEN★★
130km/81mi. Allow 5h.

This charming drive takes you through forests and along roads overlooking the river below.

▷ Leave Honfleur via cours Jean-de-Vienne and take D 312 towards Berville. The road follows the lower Risle valley.

Beyond Berville, there are many fine views of the estuary. In the spring, the blooming apple orchards turn the landscape into a wonderland.

▷ Stay on D 312 through Foulbec and Toutainville, and then take D 675.

Pont-Audemer★
See PONT-AUDEMER, p120.

▷ Take D 810, N.

Ste-Opportune-la-Mare
See Quilleboeuf-sur-Seine, p123.

▷ Take D 95, E.

After a section on a crest road, between Val-Anger and Vieux-Port, the Seine valley comes into view again.

Vieux-Port★
The thatched cottages are half hidden by their orchards.

Aizier
The stone bell tower of the 12C church looks very old. Near the church there is a manhole slab – the remains of a covered way dating from around 2 000 BCE.

▷ From Aizier to Quesney, D 95 and D 65 follow the edge of Brotonne forest.

Vatteville-la-Rue
The nave of the church dates from the Renaissance; it bears a black mourning band which was painted on the wall for the funeral of the lord of the manor. The Flamboyant chancel is lit by 16C stained-glass windows.

▷ Keep following the D 65, which leads to La Mailleraye (ferry).

Running alongside the Seine, the road offers views of typical Norman thatched cottages half hidden by trees.

After Notre-Dame-de-Bliquetuit, you can see the two ferries which cross at Yainville and Jumièges.

Viewpoint★
Picnic area. Viewing table.
To the right can be seen the towers of Jumièges abbey, particularly impressive at sunset, and to the left the Seine valley.

▷ 300m further on, stop on the right in the La Mailleraye lay-by.

Chêne à la Cuve
100m from D 913.
Four oak trunks growing from a single bole form a kind of natural vat, 7m in circumference.

▷ Take D 313 towards Bourg-Achard and turn right on D 90.

Moulin de Pierre, Hauville
Easter to late Sept Sun 2.30–6.30pm (Jul–Aug daily 2.30–6.30pm). €2.50. 02 32 56 57 32.
This 13C windmill is one of the few surviving stone mills in Upper Normandy and once belonged to the monks of Jumièges abbey. Its cap can be orientated according to the direction of the wind and is supported by oak beams. The stone tower and large sails are most impressive. If weather allows, you can see the mill in operation.

▷ Take D 101 in the other direction and turn left on D 712. Going down the hill, turn onto D 45 (nice views of the forest and the river), then take D 265, which crosses Mauny forest, then D 64 towards La Bouille. Between La Ronce and La Bouille, the road goes along the river's edge.

La Bouille
La Bouille, in a lovely site at the foot of the wooded slopes of the Roumois plateau, has always attracted artists, writers, poets and painters. In the old days, people from Rouen would come here to sample eels stewed in cider, La Bouille cheese and *douillons aux pommes* (apples filled with butter, wrapped in pastry and baked).
Today the village still offers a charming combination of terraces, inns and avenues. Painters set up their easels and sketch the quaint streets and surrounding countryside.
On the quayside, a plaque on one of the houses recalls the critic and novelist **Hector Malot** (1830–1907), born here.

Moulineaux
The **church** with its slender spire dates from the 13C. Inside there is an attractive woodwork group formed by the pulpit and rood screen (one side of which is Gothic and the other Renaissance). In the apse is the 13C **stained-glass window★**, a gift of Blanche de Castille. Note the 16C tableau of the Flemish School depicting the Crucifixion and a monk in prayer. There is a far-reaching view of the Seine valley from the cemetery.

▷ Take D 3, a steep hill.

Monument Qui Vive
At the crossroads of D 64 and D 67A.
There is a remarkable view of the Seine as it curves round to encircle Roumare forest.
Road D 64 goes down to the Seine so that one gets a view of the river bend commanded by Robert the Devil's castle and the Rouen industrial suburbs.

Château de Robert le Diable★
See Elbeuf – Excursions, p109.

▷ Go back to D 64 up a steep climb. Take D 64 right through Londe forest. At the crossroads known as Le Nouveau Monde, follow D 938 to Orival, to the south.

Orival★
From Oissel to Orival the road is overhung by curious rocks which are part of the chalk escarpment. Orival church is an unusual semi-troglodytic 15C building.

▷ Return to Le Nouveau Monde.

Roches d'Orival★
Park on D 18 by the sign Sentier des Roches; 1hr on foot there and back by a steep path which is slippery when wet. At the top turn right onto a path which passes in front of some caves hollowed out of the rocks.
The path follows the cliff. By a grassy knoll (300m) there is a **view** of the Seine and of the rock escarpment, broken by a grassy corniche on which the path continues.

▷ Follow D 18 along the Seine.

Oissel
Pleasant public garden.

▷ To return to Rouen, take D 13, then N 138 to the right.

The pine forest of Rouvray is an oasis of calm, reminiscent of the Landes of southwest France.

ADDRESSES

🛏 STAY

🍽 **Camping La Briquerie** – ℘02 31 89 28 32. www.campinglabriquerie.com. Open Apr–Sept. 430 sites. Set on the edge of a forest, this campground has sites separated by hedges of shrubs or flowers. Some small but well-kept self-catering cottages. Large swimming pool, games-room and miniature golf. Restaurant-bar (🍽) with meals in season.

🍽🍽 **Chambre d'hôte Le Vieux Pressoir** – 1023 Rue du Potier, 27210 Conteville (13.5/8.5mi from Honfleur via D 580, rte de Pont-Audemer then left on D 312). ℘02 35 57 60 79. www.la-ferme-du-pressoir.com. Restaurant 🍽🍽. Set in the countryside, this 18C half-timbered farm will delight those who appreciate calm and simplicity. Every room contains 19C and 20C objects and furniture. Flower garden, duck pond and 300-year-old cider press add to the charm.

🍽🍽 **Le M Hôtel Restaurant Spa** – 62 cours A.-Manuel. ℘02 31 89 41 77. www.lemhotelhonfleur.com. 50 rooms. 🅿. Restaurant 🍽🍽. At a distance from the city centre, this hotel offers rooms at reasonable prices. Small and functional, they make for an agreeable stay. A garden and a terrace let you bask in the gentle Norman sun.

🍽🍽 **Hôtel Romantica** – ch. Petit-Paris, 14600 Pennedepie, 8km/5mi NE of Honfleur. ℘02 31 81 14 00. www.romantica-honfleur.com. 35 rooms. Restaurant 🍽🍽. Perched high in the village, this hotel offers peace and comfort. There is a fine view over the sea from the restaurant. Two swimming pools.

🍽🍽🍽 **Chambre d'hôte Cour Ste-Catherine** – 74 r. du Puits. ℘07 87 04 49 16. www.coursaintecatherine.com. 5 rooms. Housed in a 17C convent, this pleasant inn offers five elegant guest rooms, opening onto a flower garden. In the lounge there is some pretty furniture and a fireplace. Breakfast is served in the old cider-press.

🍽🍽🍽🍽 **Auberge de la Source** – 14600 Barneville-la-Bertran (5.5km/3.4mi SW of Honfleur). ℘02 31 89 25 02. www.auberge-de-la-source.fr. 16 rooms. Set in the countryside, this beautiful half-timbered farmhouse has a lovely garden with apple orchards.

🍴 EAT

🍽 **La Petite Chine** – 14-16 r. du Dauphin. ℘02 31 89 36 52. Wed–Mon 10am–7pm. This pretty tea room and pastry shop overlooks the port. 120 types of tea.

🍽🍽 **Ex-Voto** – 8 pl. Albert-Sorel. ℘02 31 89 19 69. Closed Wed, 1 Nov, 25 Dec. Reservations advised. 🍽. One of the few inexpensive yet good-value restaurants in town, this place will make you nostalgic for the neighbourhood bistro. Special dishes and short orders from fresh market produce. Very few tables, best to reserve.

🍽🍽 **Auberge du Vieux Clocher** – 9 r. de-l'Homme-de-Bois. ℘02 31 89 12 06. Closed Mon and Tue. Small dining rooms are panelled in wood, with touches of pastel colours, and old plates decorate the walls. Traditional cuisine, with an accent on seafood.

🍽🍽 **Restaurant Le Belvédère** – 36 r. Émile-Renouf. ℘06 63 41 26 31. Closed Jan. This old town restaurant gets its name from the view from its incomparable view over the Normandy bridge. Pretty garden and good restaurant.

🍽🍽 **La Tortue** – 36 r. de l'Homme-de-Bois. ℘02 31 81 24 60. www.restaurant latortue.fr. In a little street of old Honfleur, this regional restaurant has daily specials depending on the catch of the day.

🍽🍽 **Le Bistrot des Artistes** – 14 pl. Berthelot. ℘02 31 89 95 90. Closed Tue and Wed. Antiques, paintings of the sea, photos of Honfleur and leather seating make up the décor of this restaurant with a Parisian bistro flair. Tables near the window have a lovely view of the Vieux Bassin. On the menu: salads and slices of bread with various toppings.

🍽🍽🍽 **Entre Terre et Mer** – 12 pl. Hamelin. ℘02 31 89 70 60. www.entreterreetmer-honfleur.com. Two pleasant, modern dining areas. One is rustic with wooden beams and rush flooring, the other has tiled floors and is decorated with photographs of Normandy. Serving modern cuisine including both meat and seafood dishes. Hotel has 14 **rooms**.

🍽🍽🍽 **Au P'tit Mareyeur** – 4 r. Haute. 02 31 98 84 23. Closed Tue and Wed. Reservations required. This tiny restaurant near Honfleur's fishing port is ideal for an intimate meal. Maritime touches add

Market on Place Ste-Catherine, Honfleur

© Loïc Durand/Calvados Attractivité

to the cosy feel. Fish and seafood are recommended here.

🍽🍷🛏 **Au Vieux Honfleur** – *13 quai St-Étienne. ☏02 31 89 15 31.* This restaurant by the old harbour extends its terrace along the quay when the weather is fine. Savour Norman dishes and seafood while gazing upon the splendid port.

🍽🛏 **La Fleur de Sel** – *17 r. Haute. ☏02 31 89 01 92. www.lafleurdesel-honfleur.com.* The two small dining-rooms with neo-rustic décor at this gourmet restaurant serve good meat and seafood dishes.

🍽🛏 **Le Bréard** – *7 r. du Puits. ☏02 31 89 53 40. www.restaurant-lebreard.com. Closed Mon lunch, and Wed–Thu.* Near Ste-Catherine Church, this restaurant has a green façade and two dining rooms. Modern cuisine.

🍽🍷🛏 **SaQuaNa** – *22 pl. Hamelin. ☏02 31 89 40 80. www.alexandre-bourdas.com. Closed Mon–Wed.* 🍴. SaQuaNa stands for "savours, quality, nature". Surprising cuisine, both technical and intuitive. Modern décor. Specialities.

NIGHTLIFE

Evenings in Honfleur, the Old Port comes alive. Restaurants, brasseries and bars are clustered on the quais Ste-Catherine, La Quarantaine and St-Etienne. Terraces remain open until 2am in summer.

Pomme'cannelle – *60 quai Ste-Catherine. ☏02 31 89 55 25. Closed Dec–Jan.* These ice creams and sherberts must absolutely be tasted: licorice, cinnamon apple, apricot, salty-butter caramel, etc.

SHOPPING

HONFLEUR

Markets – *pl. Ste-Catherine.* Antique market 2nd Sun of each month. Weekly market Sat am featuring local produce and fish. Organic produce market Wed. Evening market Wed in Jul–Aug. Flower market Sat am on place Arthur-Boudin.

Griboulle – *16 r. de l'Homme-de-Bois. ☏02 31 89 29 54. www.gribouillehonfleur. com.* M. Griffoul, nicknamed Gribouille, is an unforgettable local character. He sells Norman shortbread, milk, jam, potted rabbit, preserved pork, cider products, etc. Sample the *pommeau* or Calvados.

La Cave Normande – *13 r. de la Ville* and *12 quai Ste-Catherine.* This is where you will find top-quality Calvados as well as cider, perry and *pommeau.*

LEISURE

Centre équestre du Ramier – *ch. du Ramier, 14600 Equemauville (3.6km/2.2mi SW of Honfleur). ☏02 31 89 49 97.* This pretty riding centre has 15 training horses available. Rides last for 1h–1h30.

GUIDED TOURS

Honfleur's tourist office offers tours around the town. A tour is the best way to see the famous *greniers à sel* (salt stores). Contact the tourist office.

Trouville-sur-Mer★★

At Trouville, the cliffs of the Normandy corniche slope away at the mouth of the River Touques, to be replaced by a wonderful beach of fine golden sand. Although modern, the town retains its charm; at the start of the Second Empire (1852), Trouville launched the Côte Fleurie. As in Deauville, the wooden plank promenade *(planches)* runs the full length of the beach. Owing to the comings and goings of the fishermen and the small resident population, Trouville is worth visiting even out of season.

▶ **Population:** 4 642.
◔ **Michelin Map:** 303: M-3.
🛈 **Info:** 32 quai Fernand-Moureaux, 14360 Trouville-sur-Mer. ℘02 31 14 60 70. www.trouvillesurmer.org.
◑ **Location:** Trouville extends along the north side of the estuary, opposite Deauville, 94km/58.4mi E of Rouen.

VISIT

Corniche★

Make for the corniche road to the north by way of boulevard Aristide-Briand and a left turn.

On the way down there is a magnificent **view** of the Trouville and Deauville beaches and the Côte Fleurie. From the Calvaire de Bon-Secours the view is breathtaking.

Musée Villa Montebello

64 rue du Général-Leclerc.
◔*Jun–Sept Wed–Sun 10am–noon, 2–5.30pm; Oct–May Wed–Fri 2–5.30pm,*
Sat–Sun and holidays 10am–noon, 2–5.30pm. ◔*1 Jan, 25 Dec.*
℘*02 31 88 16 26.*
This villa is a fine example of seaside architecture during the Second Empire (1852–70). The museum shows work by artists who brought fame to the town.

Galeries d'exposition

In the town hall.
♿◔*Mon–Fri 9.30am–noon, 1.30–5pm.*
℘*02 31 14 41 41.*
This gallery hosts temporary art exhibitions throughout the year.

Library beach

Les Planches "Promenade Savignac"
◔*Jul–Aug Mon–Fri.*
The library moves to the beach to provide free access to books and magazines, and to arrange story-telling sessions.

Beach, Trouville-sur-Mer

© Bertl123/iStockphoto.com

ADDRESSES

🛏 STAY

🍴🛏 **Hôtel La Petite Cour** – *15 r. Paul-Besson. ☎02 31 88 10 66. www. trouville-hotel.com. 17 rooms.* Away from traffic, this hotel offers simple, practical accommodation. Close to the casino and beach.

🍴🛏 **Hôtel Le Trouville** – *r. Thiers. ☎02 31 98 45 48. www.hotelletrouville.com. 15 rooms.* If the façade is a bit tired, the interior is bright and clean. The rooms, two of them for families, have complete bathrooms and new beds. Good value for money.

🍴🛏🛏 **Hôtel Le Fer à Cheval** – *11 r. Victor-Hugo. ☎02 31 98 30 20. www. hotel-trouville.com. 34 rooms.* These two old villas at the centre of the resort, near the beaches, offer functional rooms. The proprietor, a former baker, offers delicious croissants and pastries at breakfast and afternoon tea.

🍴 EAT

🍴🛏 **La Petite Auberge** – *7 Rue Carnot. ☎02 31 88 11 07. Closed Tue–Wed.* In the centre of town, a charming little eatery serving traditional cuisine of the region, with the freshest of produce at chef's door.

Deauville★★

Deauville, a popular resort since the mid-19C, is known for the luxury and refinement of its various establishments and the elegance of its entertainments. Events of the the summer season include racing (including the Grand Prix), the polo world championship, regattas, tennis and golf tournaments, galas, and the international yearling fair. Every year, in early September, the city hosts the prestigious American Film Festival.

VISIT

The Resort

The season in Deauville opens in July and ends with the Deauville Grand Prix on the fourth Sunday in August and the Golden Cup of the international polo championship. Horse racing takes place alternately at La Touques (flat racing) and Clairefontaine (flat racing and steeplechasing) and the international yearling sales are held in Deauville in August. Out of season the resort accommodates numerous conventions as well as seminars.

The coming and going on the **Planches** – a wooden plank promenade running the whole length of the beach – is the most distinctive feature of beach life in Deauville. Lined with elegant buildings such as the Pompeian Baths and the Soleil Bar, where stars and celebrities

▶ **Population:** 3 678.
⚬ **Michelin Map:** 303: M-3 – Local map, ⚬see Pays d'Auge, p181.
ℹ **Info:** Quai de l'impératrice Eugénie. ☎02 31 14 40 00. www.deauville.org.
▶ **Location:** Located 94km/59mi from Rouen and 43km/27mi from Le Havre, Deauville lies on the Côte Fleurie. The Touques estuary separates Deauville from the older resort, Trouville.
☺ **Don't Miss:** The pretty villas as well as the view from Mont Canisy and the coastal road from Honfleur to Cabourg.
🕐 **Timing:** Try to see Deauville in the morning; afternoons bring crowds.

like to be seen, the Planches draws fashionable strollers. Between the casino and the Planches, the Centre International de Deauville (C.I.D.) is a remarkable ensemble of suspended gardens, fountains and transparent façades which welcomes all kinds of professional, cultural and festive events. A walk along the seafront boulevard Eugène-Cornuché will prove that

Planches and the beach of Deauville

© lamax/Fotolia.com

Deauville is not called the "beach of flowers" (plage fleurie) for nothing. The yacht marina on the Touques and the Yacht Club strike an elegant note. A little **tourist train** will take you on a guided tour of the city (with commentary), and the tourist office has information about walking tours and bicycle trails.

Deauville Port

The port is enclosed on the west side by a breakwater extending from the beach to the mouth of the Touques and on the east by a jetty marking the port entrance to the channel. The deep access channel means that the port is accessible 80 percent of the time. It consists of three docks, entered through a double lock, which provide deep water moorings and ample capacity: 800 berths along 4 000m of quays. At the centre are the slate-roofed marinas, the Deauville harbour master's office, an annexe of the Marina Deauville Club (quai des Marchands, near the lock) and space for shops and hotel services.

DRIVING TOURS

The mileages given on the following tours are calculated from the Pont des Belges, linking Deauville to Trouville.

In summer, the coast between Honfleur and Cabourg is one of the busiest in France, but is lovely despite the crowds.

LE MONT CANISY★
Round-trip of 25km/15mi (about 1h).

▷ Leave Deauville to the SW by the D 513.

Bénerville church stands overlooking a crossroads.

▷ Turn left before the church. 200m further, at the town hall, go straight and turn left at the crossroads. Continue for 1km/3/4mi.

Parc des Enclos Calouste Gulbenkian

⏱May–mid-Oct. 🚫Public holidays. www.indeauville.fr/le-parc-calouste-gulbenkian.
This very pretty park was designed in the 1930s for petroleum magnate Calouste Gulbenkian. Sheltered from northern winds and with no buildings facing it, it extends over more than 33ha. At the entrance, an avenue edged with boxwood and flower beds leads to a wide lawn with ancient trees, opening onto the Auge *bocage*. Don't hesitate to stroll around to get a good idea of the various perspectives and landscapes: Cross-shaped spits symbolise the four rivers of Islam, the fruit garden, vegetable garden and groves of southwest pines. In summer, there are exhibitions and classical music concerts.

▷ Return to the church and take the street on the right. When you get

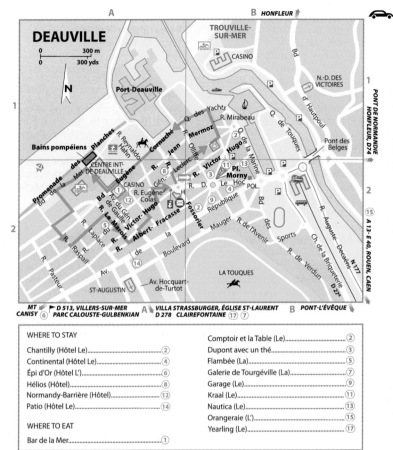

to the top, turn right towards Mont Canisy. Leave your car in front of the barrier.

The path leads to the block house where the view extends from the Cap de la Hève to the Orne estuary. The Conservatoire national du littoral offers tours to discover this protected natural site.

▷ Return to your car and take the road on your right.

After crossing the modern town of Canisy, the road heads down sharply; views of the Touques valley.

▷ At the St-Arnoult crossroads, go forward.

Touques

At the mouth of the river of the same name, the old port of William the Conqueror, the village still has old houses along the Les Ouies stream. The church of St Thomas (12C) owes its name to a visit from St Thomas Becket. The 11C **église St-Pierre** holds exhibitions.

THE CORNICHE NORMANDE: FROM DEAUVILLE-TROUVILLE TO HONFLEUR★★
21km/13mi. Allow 1h.

▷ Leave Deauville-Trouville to the NE by D 513.

This pleasant tour passes through magnificent scenery and affords views over the Seine estuary between gaps in the hedges and orchards.

Handsome properties are scattered along the road. Just before Villerville there is a fine view of the oil refineries on the estuary. To the left Le Havre can be recognised by its thermal power station and the belfry of St Joseph's Church.

Villerville⌂

This lively seaside resort, with its nearby meadows and woods, has kept its rural character. Notice the Romanesque belfry on the local church. From the terrace overlooking the beach there is a view of Le Havre and Cap de la Hève. The road is thereafter narrow with hidden bends.

Cricquebœuf

The 12C **church**, with its ivy-covered walls, is a familiar feature on travel posters. The countryside around, with its apple orchards, grazing cows and tranquil ponds, adds to the emblematic beauty.

▷ In Pennedepie, take D 62; after 2.5km/1.5mi turn right onto D 279.

Barneville

The church, tucked away in the greenery, is backed by the magnificent park of the 18C château.

▷ Take D 279 N; after 4km/2.5mi turn left by a château to reach Honfleur via the Côte de Grâce.

Côte de Grâce★★

See HONFLEUR – Additional Sights, p189.

Honfleur★★

See HONFLEUR, p184.

⌕ THE CÔTE FLEURIE: FROM TROUVILLE-DEAUVILLE TO CABOURG⌂⌂

To Cabourg: 19km/12mi.

▷ Leave Deauville to the SW by D 513.

Bénerville-sur-Mer and Blonville-sur-Mer

The hillsides are dotted with villas overlooking a long sandy beach.

Blonville-sur-Mer

Blonville-sur-Mer's sweeping sandy beach stretches to the slopes of Mont Canisy. At Blonville, there is an amusement park near the sea, as well as extensive sports facilities. The Chapelle Notre-Dame de l'Assomption houses some modern frescoes, the work of the artist **Jean-Denis Maillart**.

Villers-sur-Mer⌂⌂

This elegant seaside resort with casino and excellent sports facilities is known for its large beach and its wooded hilly countryside criss-crossed with small paths leading down to the town centre. The beachside promenade incorporates a signpost indicating the passage of the Greenwich meridian.

The **Musée Paléontologique** (⌂⌖*Mid-Feb–Sept 10am–6pm (Jul–Aug 7pm); rest of year, check website for details.* ⌂€8 *(child 5–14, €5.90).* ⌕02 31 81 77 60. *www.paleospace-villers.fr*) has exhibits of fossils and stuffed birds from the area together with a stone armchair and seashells which belonged to Ferdinand Postel, artist and photographer who lived in Villers from 1880 to 1917 and who collected fossils along the area's limestone cliffs.

Just before Houlgate, on a downhill hairpin bend, a viewing table offers a **panorama** from the mouth of the River Dives to the mouth of the River Orne.

Falaise des Vaches Noires★

⌖ Between Villers-sur-Mer and Houlgate, the Auberville plateau ends in a crumbling and much-eroded cliff face. It is best to walk along the beach at low tide (⌖ *about 2h on foot round-trip*) to enjoy the panorama, which extends from Trouville to Luc-sur-Mer and over most of the Seine bay.

In places large pieces of limestone have broken away from the cliff top and piled up at the base where they have been colonised by seaweed to form fantastic shapes; these are the Black Cows (Vaches Noires). Fossils found on these cliffs form a large part of the collection at the Villers-sur-Mer museum.

Houlgate� glyph

Houlgate is set in the verdant Drochon Valley; the shady avenues and the late-19C houses and gardens, in excellent states of conservation, add to the overall charm of this resort, one of the first to appear on the Côte Fleurie, in 1851.

The promenade Rolland-Garros overlooks the fine sandy beach, which is popular for bathing, and continues to the east towards the cliffs of the **Vaches Noires**. The road runs along the coast and, before Dives-sur-Mer, passes in front of a monument commemorating the departure of **Duke William** for the conquest of England.

Dives-sur-Mer★

ⓒ See DIVES-SUR-MER, p202.

Cabourg⚝⚝

ⓒ See CABOURG, p200.

▶ Head to Cabourg via D 45.

ADDRESSES

🛏 STAY

🍽🍽 **Hôtel Le Patio** – *180 av. de la République.* ℘02 31 88 25 07. *www. hotel-lepatio.fr. 12 rooms.* The name tells it all: this century-old edifice with an immaculate façade possesses an enticing, flower-filled patio where breakfasts are served as soon as the weather warms up.

🍽🍽 **Hôtel Ibis Styles Deauville Centre** – *10 r. Fossorier.* ℘02 31 14 46 46. *www. accorhotels.com. 45 rooms.* A practical address at resort centre. Simple rooms freshened up and a small apartment appreciated by families.

🍽🍽 **Hôtel Le Chantilly** – *120 av. de la République.* ℘02 31 88 79 75. *www. hotel-deauville-le-chantilly.fr. 17 rooms.* This townhouse near the hippodrome has well-looked after rooms. Breakfast in a small dining room.

🍽🍽🍽 **Les Manoirs des Portes de Deauville** – *30 Le Lieu God, D 677, 14800 Canapville.* ℘01 47 64 21 44. *www. hotel-normand.com. 27 rooms.* Set a short distance from Deauville, in a stunning 2ha park, this new hotel, opened in 2019, includes the main manor house, nine cottages, an orchard and a pond, a relaxation area with a pool house, an outdoor heated pool, a sauna and a jacuzzi.

🍽🍽🍽 **Inter-Hôtel Continental Perrot** – *1 r. Désiré-Le-Hoc.* ℘02 31 88 21 06. *42 rooms.* This hotel, built in 1880, is close to the station. Small, nicely furnished rooms. Pleasant breakfast room.

🍽🍽🍽🍽 **Hotel Barrière Le Normandy Deauville** – *38 r. Jean-Mermoz.* ℘02 31 98 66 22. *259 rooms.* This elegant timber-framed manor house dating from 1912 is situated in the liveliest part of town: facing the sea, near the casino and the shopping district. A sumptuous hotel that will cater to your every desire.

🍴 EAT

🍽 **Dupont avec un thé** – *20 pl. Morny.* ℘02 31 88 20 79. *www.dupontavecunthe.fr.* This shop offers wonderful desserts such as lemon-scented sugar biscuits and coffee-flavoured macaroons. Light meals and a hearty breakfast menu.

🍽 **Bar de la Mer** – *Casino Barrière de Deauville.* ℘02 31 88 27 51. *www. casinosbarriere.com/fr/deauville/le-bar-de-la-mer.html.* This restaurant, located right on the famous boardwalk, offers a pleasant dining room, an enormous terrace on the beach and a splendid view of the ocean. On the menu: shellfish, grilled meat and salads.

🍽🍽 **Le Comptoir et la Table** – *1 quai de la Marine.* ℘02 31 88 92 51. *www. lecomptoiretlatable.fr.* Wonderful conviviality in this marina restaurant; wood counter and Trouville painting (1947) on the ceiling. Bistro food and great wines.

🍽🍽 **Le Garage** – *118 bis av. de la République.* ℘02 31 87 25 25. *www. restaurant-garage-deauville.fr.* This former garage is now a brasserie.

🍽🍽 **Brasserie L'Odyssée** – *2 rue Désir.-Le Hoc.* ℘02 31 88 03 27. *http:// lodyssee-deauville.fr.* This brasserie near the train station specialises in fish and grilled meats.

🍴🍴 **Le Yearling** – *38 av. Hocquart de Turto.* ☎*02 31 88 33 37. www.le-yearling. fr.* Serving typical French cuisine, its speciality is the grilled Breton lobster served in a *beurre blanc* sauce.

🍴🍴🍴 **La Flambée** – *81 r Gén.-Leclerc.* ☎*02 31 88 28 46. www.laflambee-deauville.com.* Grilled steaks and chops are prepared in the vast open hearth, right before your eyes.

🍴🍴🍴 **Le Kraal - La Table d'Auge** – *Pl. du Marché.* ☎*02 31 88 30 58. Reservations advised summer. Closed Sun.* Fresh shellfish, delicious, authentic regional recipes.

ON THE TOWN

Casino Barrière – *R. Edmond-Blanc.* ☎*02 31 14 31 14. www.casinosbarriere.com/fr/ deauville.html.* Slot machines, roulette, poker, and more.

Martine Lambert – *76 bis r. Eugène-Colas.* ☎*02 31 88 94 04. www.martine-lambert. com.* Made from Norman cows' milk, Martine Lambert's ice cream is subtle and delicious.

LEISURE

👥 **Le Circuit de Deauville** – *Chemin du Moulin, 14800 St-Arnoult (4km/2.5mi S ofDeauville).* ☎*02 31 81 31 31. www. dupratconcept.com.* Sizeable amusement park specialising in motor sports: go-carting. speed boats and jet skis, safety driving courses and more.

CALENDAR OF EVENTS

Jun – International Sailing Week and Jumping International. Opening of the horseracing season.
Aug – Musical August (Août musical) music festival, polo championship, horse races, sale of yearlings.
Sept – Festival of American Cinema.

Cabourg 🏖🏖

The large seaside resort of Cabourg, created at the time of the Second Empire (1852–70), centres on the casino and Grand Hôtel on the seafront, from which streets radiate inland, intersecting with two semicircular avenues. Many avenues and streets are lined by attractive houses set in shaded gardens.

A BIT OF HISTORY

Cabourg is famous as the place from which William the Conqueror successfully forced Henry I's troops back into the sea. The holiday towns of Dieppe, Deauville and Trouville are joined by Cabourg, which, benefiting from a rail link, became a tourist destination of choice. By the 1880s, hotels and villas had sprung up around the **Grand Hôtel** on the seafront; Cabourg was truly established.
Marcel Proust went to Cabourg for the first time in 1881, when he was 10. The coastal climate was beneficial to his health (he suffered from asthma), while the town's charm and memories of his

- **Population:** 3 657.
- **Michelin Map:** 303: L-4 – Local map, see *Pays d'Auge, p181.*
- **Info:** Jardins de l'Hôtel de Ville. ☎*02 31 06 20 00. www.cabourg-tourisme.fr.*
- **Location:** Take D 513 from Caen (33km/20.6mi to the SW), Deauville (19km/12mi) and Honfleur (51km/31.7mi) to the E; take D 45 from Lisieux (30km/18.6mi to the SE).
- **Don't Miss:** Magnificent view from promenade Marcel-Proust.
- **Timing:** Explore in the morning to avoid crowds.

childhood drew him to visit frequently as an adult, when he would stay at the Grand Hôtel. *Within a Budding Grove (À l'Ombre des jeunes filles en fleurs)* was a vivid portrayal of the customs of Cabourg and of life in a seaside resort at the turn of the 20C.

© Franck Guiziou/hemis.fr
Cabourg houses

EXCURSIONS
Merville-Franceville-Plage
6km/3.7mi W of Cabourg by D 514.
When the Allies landed in June 1944, the strongest point in the defences was the Merville Battery.
It was captured by the 6th British Airborne Division. One of the casemates has been converted into a museum, the **Musée de la Batterie** (&⊙*daily mid-Mar–Sept 9.30am–6.30pm; Oct–mid-Nov 10am–5pm; ⊗€8; ☎02 31 91 47 53. www.batterie-merville.com*).

Ranville
8km/5mi S of Merville-Franceville-Plage on D 223.
Ranville was captured at 2.30am on 6 June 1944 by the 13th Battalion of the Lancashire Fuseliers of the 6th British Airborne Division; it was the first village to be liberated on French territory. A war cemetery commemorates these events.

ADDRESSES

⌂ STAY
⊜⊜ **Hôtel de Paris** – *39 av. de la Mer. ☎02 31 91 31 34. www.hotel-paris-cabourg. com. Closed Jan.* 🅿. *24 rooms.* Hotel on the city's busiest street, two minutes from the ocean. Bar with outdoor tables.

♀/ EAT
⊜ **Dupont avec un Thé** – *6 av. de la Mer. ☎02 31 24 60 32.* A tea salon offering a range of delicious cakes and sweets, notably chocolate and caramel.

⊜⊜ **Le Champagne-Ardennes** – *11 pl. du Marché. ☎02 31 91 02 29. www. lachampagne-ardenne-cabourg.com.* Opposite the market, this modest hotel-restaurant is both convenient and well managed. An elegant dining room with a menu specialising in seafood. Upstairs, comfortable guest rooms.

ON THE TOWN
Le Grand Hôtel Cabourg-MGallery – *Les Jardins du Casino . ☎02 31 91 01 79.* The Grand Hôtel, with its Belle époque style, huge chandeliers and full draperies, is a monument to nostalgia. You needn't be a guest to have tea here, or better yet, enjoy a snifter of 40-year-old Calvados, while gazing out to sea.

Casino De Cabourg Le Kaz – *prom. Marcel-Proust. ☎02 31 28 19 19. https://casino-cabourg.partouche.com.* Everything you would expect of a grand casino, plus a panoramic restaurant facing the ocean. Terrace by the sea.

LEISURE
Pôle Equestre de Cabourg - La Sablonnière – *av. Guillaume-le-Conquérant, rte de Caen, opposite the Vert Pré campsite. ☎02 31 91 61 70. www.pole-equestre-cabourg.fr. Open Fri–Wed (daily during school holidays).* This club organises horseback rides on the beach and in the hinterland for all levels of experience.

Église Notre-Dame de Dives

© Fabien Mahaut/Calvados Attractivité

Dives-sur-Mer★

If Cabourg is known as a holiday resort, its sister city Dives tends to be associated with history, for it was from here that William the Conqueror, Duc de Normandie, set out to invade England in the 11C.

SIGHTS

Halles★

The magnificent oak frame of the covered market (15C–16C) is in very good condition. Wrought-iron signs identify the stalls of the merchants. On the other side of place de la République stands the 16C Bois-Hibou Manor.

▶ **Population:** 5 702.
⚹ **Michelin Map:** 303: L-4 – Local map, *see Pays d'Auge, p180.*
▯ **Info:** 2 Rue d'Hastings. ✆02 31 91 24 66. www.dives-sur-mer.fr.
▶ **Location:** Dives lies across the estuary of the River Dives from Cabourg.
⚘ **Don't Miss:** The old market place (Halles).
◕ **Timing:** Give yourself a couple of hours to enjoy the town...and a coffee.

Entrance, Village Guillaume-le-Conquérant

© Arnaud Guérin/Calvados Attractivité

Église Notre-Dame de Dives

This massive church, a centre of pilgrimage until the Religious Wars, is 14C and 15C, except for the transept crossing, a remnant of an 11C sanctuary. Inside, the elegant 15C nave contrasts sharply with the massive pillars and plain arches of the Romanesque transept crossing.

The transepts themselves, the chancel and the Lady Chapel, were built in 14C Rayonnant Gothic style.

Village Guillaume-le-Conquérant

This pleasant enclave of art and craft shops is located within the precincts of the old inn of the same name, dating from the 16C.

Lisieux ★

Sitting on the east bank of the Touques, Lisieux has become the most important commercial and industrial town in the prosperous Pays d'Auge. The town is renowned for St Theresa of Lisieux and is the second-most important pilgrimage site in France after Lourdes.

▶ **Population:** 20 301.
🜲 **Michelin Map:** 303: N-5 – Local map, *see Pays d'Auge, p203.*
ℹ️ **Info:** 11 rue d'Alençon. ☎02 31 48 18 10. www.lisieux-tourisme.com.
▶ **Location:** 73km/45.4mi E of Evreux via N13 and 36km/22mi S of Honfleur.
🅿 **Parking:** There is ample parking near the basilica.
🜲 **Don't Miss:** The cathedral of St-Pierre and the CERZA zoo.
🕐 **Timing:** Visit Lisieux in the morning, then tour the countryside in the afternoon.
🜲 **Kids:** The popular game reserve CERZA.

A BIT OF HISTORY

Thérèse Martin was born on 2 January 1873 to a well-to-do and very religious family in Alençon; she was an eager and sensitive child who soon showed intelligence and will-power. On the death of his wife, M. Martin brought the family to Lisieux where they lived at Les Buissonnets. At nine years old, Thérèse felt the call of the Church.

The authorities considered her too young and it was only in April 1888, after a pilgrimage to Rome and a request to the Holy Father, that she entered the Carmelite Order at the age of fifteen and three months. As Sister Theresa of the Child Jesus, she resolved "to save souls and, above all, to pray for the priests". Her gaiety and simplicity cloaked a consuming energy. She wrote the story of her life, *History of a Soul*, finishing the last pages only a few days before entering the Carmelite hospital in which, after an agonising illness, she died in 1897. She was canonised in 1925.

On 19 October 1997, Pope Jean-Paul II proclaimed her a Doctor of the Church, an exceptional honour bestowed on saints of great spiritual influence.

THE PILGRIMAGE
Les Buissonnets
🕐*Easter Mon–early Oct 10am–12.30pm, 1.30–6pm; early–end Oct 10am–12.30pm, 1.30–5pm; Nov–Feb 10am–noon, 2–4pm; Mar 10am–12.30pm, 1.30–5pm.* 🕐*1 Jan, 25 Dec.* 🜲*No charge.* ☎*02 31 48 55 08. www.therese-de-lisieux.catholique.fr.*
This house is where Thérèse Martin lived from the age of 4 to 15. The tour includes the dining room, Thérèse's bedroom, her father's bedroom and a display of mementoes from her childhood days.

Chapelle du Carmel
🕐*Daily: mid-Mar–Oct 7.15am–7pm; Nov–mid-Mar 7.15am–6.30pm;* 🜲*No charge.*
The saint's shrine, a recumbent figure in marble and precious wood, is in the chapel on the right and contains her relics.

Basilique Ste-Thérèse
🕐*Apr–Oct 9am–7pm; Nov–Mar 9am–5.30pm.*
This impressive basilica was consecrated on 11 July 1954 and is one of the biggest 20C churches. The **dome** is open to visitors (*Jul–Aug 1–6pm*). The construction of the belltower was interrupted in 1975; it ends in a flat roof and contains the great bell, three other bells and a carillon of 44 bells. Notice on the tympanum of the door the carvings by Robert Coin depicting Jesus teaching the Apostles and the Virgin of Mount Carmel. The immense nave is decorated with marble, stained glass and mosaics by Pierre Gaudin, a pupil of Maurice Denis. In the south transept stands a reliquary

Basilique Ste-Thérèse
© isogood/iStockphoto.com

offered by Pope Pius XI containing the bones of the saint's right arm. The **crypt** (entrance outside, beneath the galleries) is decorated with mosaics (scenes from the life of St Theresa).

Musée-Diorama: Histoire de Sainte-Thérèse

Beneath the north cloister of the basilica. ♿🔊*25min audio tour.* 🕐*Easter–Oct daily 1.30–5pm.* 📞*02 31 48 55 08. www.lisieux-tourisme.com.*
This diorama depicts a dozen episodes in the life of St Theresa.

Cathédrale St-Pierre★

🕐*Daily 9.30am–6.30pm.*
The cathedral was begun in 1170 and completed only in the mid-13C.
Exterior – The façade, raised above the ground on stone steps, is pierced by three doors and flanked by towers. Walk round the church by the right to the south transept's Paradise Door. The massive buttresses linked by an arch surmounted by a gallery are 15C.
Interior – The transept is extremely simple with the lantern rising in a single sweep at the crossing. Walk round the 13C chancel, to the huge central chapel which was remodelled in the pure Flamboyant style on the orders of Pierre Cauchon, Bishop of Lisieux, after the trial of Joan of Arc.

It was in this chapel that Thérèse Martin attended mass. Note the series of 15C carved low-relief sculptures.

Musée d'Art et d'Histoire

🕐*Daily: Jul–Aug Mon–Fri 1–6pm, Sat–Sun 11am–1pm, 2–6pm; rest of year Mon–Fri 2–6pm, Sat–Sun 11am–1pm, 2–6pm.* 🕐*1 Jan, 1 May, 14 Jul, 25 Dec.* 🎫*No charge.* 📞*02 31 62 07 70.*
Set up in a handsome 16C half-timbered house, a collection of documents and images explains the history, arts and crafts of Lisieux and the Pays d'Auge.

ADDITIONAL SIGHT

👥 CERZA★

12km/7.4mi NE. Leave Lisieux by D 510, E on the plan; 3km/2mi after Hermival-les-Vaux turn right onto D 143.
🕐*Daily Jul–Aug 9.30am–7pm; Apr–Jun and Sept 9.30am–6.30pm; Oct–Nov and Feb–Mar 10am–5.30pm.* 🎫*€21 (child 3–11, €14.50).* 📞*02 31 62 17 22. www.cerza.com.*
The **Centre d'Élevage et de Reproduction Zoologique Augeron (CERZA)** provides a pleasant, natural setting for endangered animal species. 52ha offer interesting topographical contrasts – valleys and plains, meadows and forests, barren stretches and lush pockets of vegetation, charmingly dotted with small ponds and burbling streams. Sign-

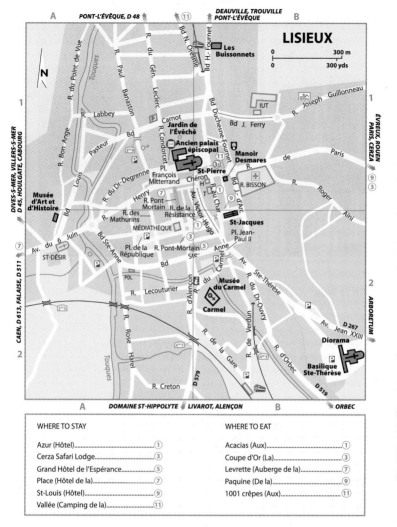

LISIEUX

0   300 m
0   300 yds

WHERE TO STAY		WHERE TO EAT	
Azur (Hôtel)	①	Acacias (Aux)	①
Cerza Safari Lodge	③	Coupe d'Or (La)	③
Grand Hôtel de l'Espérance	⑤	Levrette (Auberge de la)	⑦
Place (Hôtel de la)	⑦	Paquine (De la)	⑨
St-Louis (Hôtel)	⑨	1001 crêpes (Aux)	⑪
Vallée (Camping de la)	⑪		

posted routes will take you through the **African Reserve** (a vast area set aside for rhinoceroses, zebras, watussi, ostriches and giraffes) or on a tour of the valley. A great many primates as well as lemurs live in semi-freedom.

EXCURSIONS
Orbec
Orbec is 18km/11mi southwest of Bernay via D 131 and 20km/12.4mi south of Lisieux via D 516.
Orbec is a small and lively town with a long history, as witnessed by the many old half-timbered houses in the busy

shopping street, rue Grande. The town stands quite close to the source of the River Orbiquet in one of the most pleasant valleys in the Auge region. At the entrance to the town stands the famous Pierre Lanquetot factory, which has been producing its delicious Camembert cheeses for the past century.

The **Musée municipal** (*107 r. Grande.* ⏰*Apr–Sept Wed–Sun 2–6pm;* ⏰*Public holidays;* 📞*02 31 32 58 89*) is located in a beautiful 16C timber-framed house, the **Vieux Manoir★**, built for a rich tanner. Carved figures and geometric patterns decorate the exterior.

Half-timbered house, Orbec

© Loïc Durand/Calvados Attractivité

GR 26 Walk

4.5km/2.8mi S of Orbec

A small road *(chemin de la Folletière-Abenon),* follows alongside the Orbiquet river. Leave the car by the bridge and take a path on the left. The GR 26 itinerary (signposted in red and white) leads you on a tour of one of the prettiest valleys in the Pays d'Auge.

ADDRESSES

🛏 STAY

Camping de la Vallée – *Route de la Vallée.* ☎*02 31 62 00 40. OPen Apr–early Oct. Reservation advised. 73 sites.* North of Lisieux, 1.5km/1mi from town centre, this campsite is ideal for visiting Lisieux and surrounding area. Weekend bungalow rentals.

Hôtel St-Louis – *4 r. St-Jacques.* ☎*02 31 62 06 50. www.hotelsaintlouis-lisieux.com. 12 rooms (over 3 floors, no lift) and 1 apartment.* Family hotel with a little garden.

La Coupe d'Or – *49 r. Pont-Mortain.* ☎*02 31 31 16 84. www.la-coupe-dor. com. 16 rooms. Restaurant ☕☕ serving Normandy cuisine.* Although in a busy downtown street, calm reigns in this hotel-restaurant. French billiards and office with Internet access. Decent prices.

Hôtel de la Place – *67 r. Henry-Chéron.* ☎*02 31 48 27 27. www.lisieux-hotel-delaplace.com. 30 rooms.* The rooms are of varying sizes, bright and modern.

CERZA Safari Lodge – *CERZA zoological park, D 143, 14100 Hermival-les-Vaux.* ☎*02 31 31 82 30. www.cerza safarilodge.com. Closed Dec–Mar. Safari lodges, tents and 'Zoobservatories'.* Save on the airfare for an African safari and replace it with this unusual stay in Normandy in a zoological park. Functional but comfortable.

Grand Hôtel de l'Espérance – *16 Boulevard Sainte-Anne.* ☎*02 31 62 17 53. www.lisieux-hotel.com. 87 rooms.* Large hotel in pure Norman style in town centre. Traditional beams and balconies. Decent rooms, fine dining.

🍴 EAT

Auberge de La Levrette – *48 Rue de Lisieux, 14140 Mézidon Vallée d'Auge (20km/12.4mi SW of Lisieux).* ☎*02 31 63 81 20. Closed Sun eve, Mon except public holidays.* Half-timbered house (1550), mechanical music museum. Traditional food.

Aux Acacias – *13 r. de la Résistance.* ☎*02 31 62 10 95. Closed Sun evening and all day Wed.* Pleasant restaurant with Provençal atmosphere. Traditional cuisine; Normandy ingredients.

Pays d'Auge★★

With its pastures, thatched cottages, manor houses, apple orchards and winding hedgerows, the Pays d'Auge provides a picturesque transition to the beaches of the Côte Fleurie. The heart of traditional rural Normandy, the Auge region is partially covered in original woodland, with a chalk escarpment (30m high), known as the Côte d'Auge, overlooking the Dives valley and the Caen area.

🚗 DRIVING TOURS

🚗 CÔTE D'AUGE
66km/40mi. Allow 2h.

Lisieux★★
See LISIEUX, p203.

▷ From Lisieux take D 613 west. In La Boissière turn right onto D 59.

Ancienne Abbaye du Val Richer
Closed to the public.
Following the destruction of the Cistercian abbey during the Revolution, only the 17C hospice remained. François Guizot (1787–1874), a historian and leading politician during the reign of Louis-Philippe (1830–48), retired here after the 1848 revolution until his death in 1874. The Schlumberger brothers,

Michelin Map:
303: M-4–N-6.

Info: 100, avenue Guillaume le Conquérant, 14107 Lisieux. ℘02 31 61 55 88. www.pays-auge.fr.

Location: The Pays d'Auge, between the River Dives on the west and the River Touques on the east, surrounds Lisieux, 36km/22.5mi S of Honfleur.

Don't Miss: The beautiful château of Crèvecoeur-en-Auge, with its half-timbering typical of the region.

Timing: Give yourself 2hr to visit the Manoir des Évêques de Lisieux, 2hr for the Château de Crèvecoeur and some extra time to see the gardens.

early 20C petroleum engineers, worked here on inventions that would transform the industry (*see Crèvecoeur-en-Auge, below*).

▷ At the crossroads turn left onto D 101 and bear right onto D 117. At the next crossroads turn left onto D 16 and right onto D 85.

Beuvron-en-Auge
© Loïc Durand/Calvados Attractivité

Jardins du pays d'Auge

© Loïc Durand/Calvados Attractivité

Clermont-en-Auge★
Follow the signs Chapelle de Clermont – Panorama.
Leave the car at the start of the avenue leading to the **chapel** *(15min round-trip)*. From the east end there is an extensive **panorama★** of the Dives and Vie valleys; in the distance stretches the Caen countryside, bounded by the dark line of the *bocage* hills. The church contains statues of St Marcouf and St Thibeault in polychrome stone in the chancel and on either side of the altar St John the Baptist and St Michael.

Continue on the D 146.

Beuvron-en-Auge★
This charming village has kept around 40 lovely old timber-framed houses set around the central square. The former covered market is now a shopping centre. There is a very pretty manor at the south exit from the village, decorated with woodcarvings.

Take D 49 southwest. Turn right on the D 16 and on reaching the D 613 continue SW.

Crèvecoeur-en-Auge
The **château** (*www. chateaudecrevecoeur.com*) completed in 1584, and its three main buildings with vast roofs, are typically medieval, whereas its chequered stone and brick decoration are Norman. *See also Crèvecoeur-en-Auge, p211.*

Take D 101 NE to Cambrener.

Jardins du pays d'Auge★
May–Sept 10am–6.30pm. €8.50 (child 6–14, €5). 06 08 92 99 07. www.lesjardinsdupaysdauge.com.
These beautifully themed gardens are planted on close to 3ha/7acres, with perennials, rare plants and bamboos. The names are evocative as well: the Garden of Scents, the Garden of the Sun, the Garden of the Moon, the Garden of Angels and the Garden of Water... In all about 30 spaces co-exist here, marked out with beautiful constructions typical of the Auge region, which the owners transported here one by one.

Return to Lisieux on D 85, D 50 and D 613.

TRADITIONAL NORMANDY: VALLÉE DE LA TOUQUES
60km/37mi. Allow 2h.

Leave Lisieux via boulevard Herbert-Fournet, D 579 north; right onto D 263.

Rocques
The village **church** in the centre of its old burial ground has two wooden porches. The chancel and the tower date from the 13C. Inside note the torches and painting of the Brothers of Charity and several polychrome wooden statues.

▷ Take D 262 NW back to D 579.

Pont-l'Évêque

Since the 13C Pont-l'Évêque has been famous for its cheese. Only a few old houses remain, mostly in rue St-Michel and rue de Vaucelles. The Aigle d'Or Inn *(68 r. de Vaucelles)* was a post house in the 16C and has retained the Norman courtyard of the period.

The **Église St-Michel** is a church in Flamboyant style flanked by a square tower. The modern stained-glass windows (1963–64) are by François Chapuis.

An interesting wooden balcony decorates the old **Dominican Convent**, a 16C half-timbered building beside the Law Courts (Tribunal). The **Hôtel Montpensier**, a building in the Louis XIII style has two corner pavilions.

The 18C Hôtel Brilly (restored) now houses the town hall and the Tourist Information Centre.

While in Pont-l'Évêque visit the **Calvados Experience** (*Route de Trouville.* ⌖ ◔*Apr–Sept 9.30am–7pm; Oct–M 10–1pm, 2–6pm.* ✺*€12.50.* ◔*Jan and 25 Dec.* ✆*02 31 64 30 31; www. calvados-experience.com*) and get to know this delicious tipple.

▷ Continue NW on A 132 and D 677 to Canapville.

Canapville

The 13C–15C **Manoir des Évêques de Lisieux** (⌖ ☛*Visit by guided tour only Jul–Aug Wed–Mon 2–8pm.* ✺*€7.* ✆*02 31 65 24 75. www.manoirdeseveques.fr*) is one of the most charming country houses in the Pays d'Auge. It consists of the large manor, with three monumental stone chimneys, and the small manor with a bishop's head carved on the entrance post. The 18C ground-floor rooms display Chinese porcelain.

▷ Take the D 677 SE towards Pont-l'Évêque, but soon turn right to rejoin D 58.

Beaumont-en-Auge

This small town, remarkably situated on a spur commanding the Touques valley, was the birthplace of the mathematician and physicist Pierre **Simon, Marquis de Laplace** (1749–1827). His house and statue are on place de Verdun.

▷ D 58 south; left on D 675; right on D 280a (*not* the D 280) and pass under the autoroute.

St-Hymer

Pleasantly set in a valley, the village has a 14C **church** with traces of Romanesque in its style. Its belfry is a replica of that of Port-Royal-des-Champs, the famous Jansenist abbey south-west of Paris.

Pierrefitte-en-Auge

In the 13C **church** the nave arches are decorated with cameo paintings of landscapes. There is a fine 16C rood beam.

▷ Take the D 46 S through Coquainvilliers and on D 159.

Ouilly-le-Vicomte

The **church** standing beside the road which spans the Touques is one of the oldest in Normandy, dating from the 10C and 11C.

Parc du château de Bout(t)emont

◔*Easter to early Nov Wed, Sat–Sun and public holidays 10am–12.30pm, 2.30–6.30pm (Jul–Aug daily).* ☛*Guided tours hourly from 11am.* ✺*€10 (child 6–12, €4.50).* ✆*02 31 61 12 16. www.chateau-de-boutemont.com.* This pretty French-style park is set around a château built 14C–16C. Both are registered as Historical Monuments. The château is surrounded by dry moats and consists of a postern, a drawbridge and four corner towers. There is a beautiful view of both château and park from the pretty chapel on the heights behind them.

▷ Return to Lisieux on D 98 and D 579.

Château de St-Germain-de-Livet

🚗 HAUTE VALLÉE DE LA TOUQUES

75km/46mi. Allow 3h round-trip from Lisieux – 🚶*see Lisieux, p203.*

▷ Leave Lisieux via D 579, turn left onto D 64.

Fervaques

Château. Only the exterior can be visited; call for times. 📞*02 31 32 33 96.*
The 16C and 17C **château** overlooking the Touques is a vast building of brick and stone. Fervaques was the retreat of Delphine de Custine, a friend of the author Chateaubriand (1768–1848).

▷ Continue on D 64. In Les Moutiers-Hubert take D 110.

Bellou

In the village centre stands Manoir de Bellou, a pleasant 16C timber-framed manor house. The road (D 110) runs southeast through the Moutiers-Hubert forest and passes the Manoir de Cheffreteau.

▷ Continue on D 110 to junction with D 268. Turn left to Lisores. Continue to D 979 and turn left to Vimoutiers.

Vimoutiers

🚶*See VIMOUTIERS, p213.*

▷ Take D 979 north and continue along D 579.

Livarot

Home of the cheese of the same name, this village has some beautiful houses.

▷ Continue north on D 579. At Le Mesnil-Durand turn left onto D 47.

Manoir de Coupesarte★

🚶*See p212.*
This beautiful residence, surrounded by water on three sides, is the main building of the farm.

▷ Return to D 579 and turn left.

St-Germain-de-Livet★

Château. 🔍*Guided tours only:*
🕐*1 May.* 🎫*€7.50; no charge 1st Sun of month.* 📞*02 31 31 00 03.*
This delightful **château** consists of a 16C wing, decorated in a highly original stone and brick check pattern, adjoining a 15C half-timbered structure.
The 15C wing contains the guard-room, decorated with 16C **frescoes** (battle scene; Judith bearing the head of Holofernes), and a dining room with Empire-style furniture. On the first floor of the 16C wing are two rooms beautifully tiled in terracotta from the Pays d'Auge, the so-called bedroom of the painter Eugène Delacroix (1798–1863), the gallery with paintings by the Riesener family (19C) and a small round Louis XVI salon.

▷ Return to Lisieux on D 579.

ADDRESSES

🏠 STAY

🛏🛏 **Domaine Les Marronniers** – *4235 route d'Englesqueville, 14340 Cambremer. ℰ02 31 63 08 28. www.les-marronniers.com. 5 rooms.* This charming 17C residence, surrounded by a flower garden, has a superb view over the Dives valley. The guest rooms are spacious, and breakfast is served on a pleasant terrace.

🍷 EAT

🍴🍴 **Auberge des Deux Tonneaux** – *14130 Pierrefitte-en-Auge. ℰ02 31 64 09 31. Closed Sun evening and Mon except school holidays.* Beautiful 17C half-timbered house with a thatched roof and terrace overlooking the Touques valley. Dishes typical of the Pays d'Auge.

Crèvecoeur-en-Auge

Crèvecoeur is a pleasant town situated in the Auge valley. Some 500m to the north and to the right of D 613 is the Château de Crèvecoeur.

SIGHTS

👥 Château★

♿🕐*Apr–Sept daily 11am–6pm (Jul–Aug 11am–7pm); Oct Sun 2–6pm. ⊗€8 (child 7–18, €5). ℰ02 31 63 02 45. www.chateau-de-crevecoeur.com.* Encircled by trees and moats, the timber-framed buildings of the **château** – its motte was erected in the 11C – were transformed in the 15C and

- 🕐 **Michelin Map:** 303: M-5 – Local map, ♿*see Pays d'Auge, p180.*
- ℹ️ **Info:** Consult tourist offices in Lisieux and the Pays d'Auge.
- ▶️ **Location:** Crèvecoeur is on N 13 between Caen (43km/26.7mi W) and Lisieux (20km/12.4mi E).
- 🔍 **Don't Miss:** The wonderful dovecote at the château.
- 🕐 **Timing:** As the château opens only at 11am, use the early morning to see the manor of Coupesarte.

Château de Crèvecœur-en-Auge

Manoir de Coupesarte

© Grégory Wait/Calvados Attractivité

restored in 1972. They now form a highly picturesque sight: an outer bailey and feudal motte surrounded by a filled-in moat. The 16C gatehouse used to stand beside the former Château de Beuvilliers near Lisieux.

The 16C barn and 15C manor are home to the collections of the **Musée Schlumberger**, named after two Alsatian brothers Conrad and Marcel; in 1928 these geophysicists and petroleum engineers invented the continuous electric logging of boreholes, a technique that was to be extended to countries all over the world.

The museum displays equipment used in oil drilling and prospecting. The **dovecote**, a remarkable construction, is square shaped. Note the projecting eaves formed by the shingled roofing, visible on all four sides of the building. On the side facing winds, is a shelf from which the pigeons are released. The interior woodwork is pierced with 1 500 pigeon-holes (boulins).

The 12C **chapel** features oak framework in the shape of an upturned hull, as well as fragments of a medieval wall painting. The farm buildings contain the second part of the museum, devoted to **Normandy architecture**, which presents examples of traditional timber-framed architecture from the Pays d'Auge. The History Room (Salle d'Histoire) displays miscellaneous objects retracing the history of Crèvecoeur-en-Auge over the centuries. ☺If not about in the poultry yard, ask to see the **Crèvecoeur hens**. Feathers ruffled, sporting a pretty crest, these rare birds are the last of a local race.

EXCURSION
Manoir de Coupesarte★
15km/9mi SE. Leave Crèvecoeur-en-Auge by D 16 towards St-Pierre-sur-Dives. Near Mesnil-Mauger, turn left onto D 47. Cross Authieux-Papion, then left on D 511 to St-Julien-le-Faucon. Turn right onto D 47. Coupesarte is 1.5km/0.9mi further. ◷Grounds open daily 9am–8pm. ☜No charge. ℘02 31 63 82 12.

This charming half-timbered residence (⚷ *interior closed to the public*) surrounded by water on three sides is the main house of a farm. The construction goes back to the end of the 15C or beginning of the 16C. Its gracious half-timbered façade has two corner turrets. From the field on the left beyond the small lock there is a good view of the half-timbered façade with its two corner turrets reminiscent of watchtowers.

Vimoutiers

The small town of Vimoutiers is tucked away in the valley of the River Vie between hills covered with apple trees that supply the local cider factories. Vimoutiers has close ties with Marie Harel, who gave us the famous Camembert cheese. A statue to her memory, offered by an American cheesemaker, stands on the town hall square.

▶ **Population:** 3 427.
◔ **Michelin Map:** 310: K-1.
🇮 **Info:** 21 Rue de la Renaissance.
  ℘02 33 67 49 42.
  www.vimoutiers.fr.
◔ **Location:** Vimoutiers is 28km/17.5mi S of Lisieux via D 579, and 45km/28mi SW of Bernay.

VISIT
Musée du Camembert

&ⓒ*Apr–early Nov daily 2–6pm (Jul–Aug 10am–6pm).* ☞€3. ℘*02 33 39 30 29. www.museeducamembert.fr.*
The exhibition describes the history and manufacturing process of Camembert. Note the collection of Camembert labels. The legend has it that, during the French Revolution, Marie Harel protected a fugitive priest who, in compensation, revealed to her his secret cheese recipe.

EXCURSIONS
Camembert

Maison du Camembert – &ⓒ*Mar–Apr and Oct Wed–Sun 10–11.30am, 2–4.30pm; May daily 10–11.30am, 2–4.45pm; Jun daily 10–11.30am, 2–5.45pm; Jul–Aug 10–11.45am, 2–5.45pm; Sept daily 10–11.30am, 2–4.30pm.* ☞*No charge.* ℘*02 33 12 10 37. www.maisonducamembert.com.* This modern museum (1992), shaped like an open Camembert cheese box, lies at the heart of this tiny village, facing the 13C church. Information on the famous cheese and where it is made is displayed. It is also possible to visit a few farms where the cheese is made according to traditional methods.

Prieuré St-Michel de Crouttes★

5km/3mi W via the D 916, then take the third road to the right.
The origin of this monastic house (*www.prieure-saint-michel.com*) dates from the 10C. The noble rustic architecture of the buildings is admirably set off by an orchard, gardens and water. Beyond the 18C dairy is the 13C **tithe barn**, the 18C prior's lodging, the chapel (13C) and the bakery, an 18C timber-framed building. The priory is operated as a **bed-and-breakfast**, with reception rooms and tea room.

Maison du Camembert

© Orne Tourisme

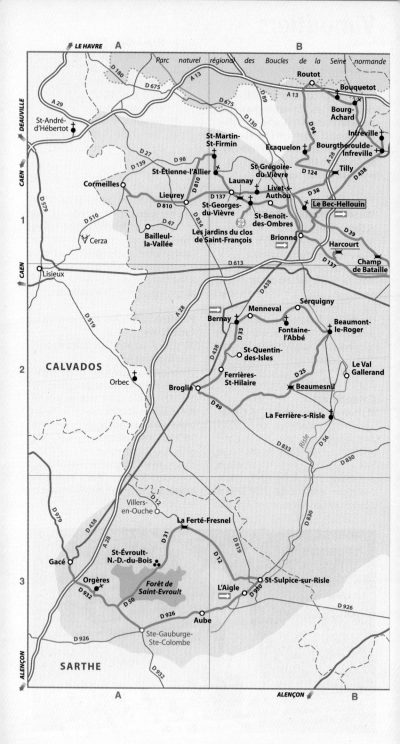

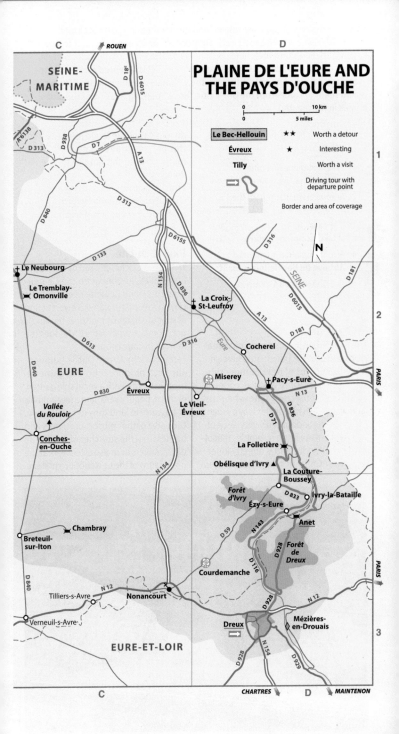

PLAINE DE L'EURE AND THE PAYS D'OUCHE

0		10 km
0	5 miles	

Le Bec-Hellouin	★★	Worth a detour
Évreux	★	Interesting
Tilly		Worth a visit
⇨		Driving tour with departure point
		Border and area of coverage

N

ROUEN

SEINE-MARITIME

D 181
D 6015
A 6138
D 313
D 938
D 7
A 13
D 313
D 6155
D 840
D 133
SEINE
D 316
D 6015
D 181

+ Le Neubourg
Le Tremblay-Omonville
N 154
D 836
+ La Croix-St-Leufroy
A 13
D 181
D 613
D 316
Eure
Cocherel
EURE
D 830
Évreux
Miserey
+ Pacy-s-Eure
D 840
Le Vieil-Évreux
N 13
Vallée du Rouloir
D 836
Conches-en-Ouche
D 71
La Folletière
Obélisque d'Ivry ▲
N 154
La Couture-Boussey
Forêt d'Ivry
D 833
Ivry-la-Bataille
Ézy-s-Eure
Chambray
D 59
N 143
Anet
Breteuil-sur-Iton
D 928
Forêt de Dreux
D 840
D 116
Courdemanche
Tilliers-s-Avre
N 12
Nonancourt
D 928
N 12
Verneuil-s-Avre
Mézières-en-Drouais
Dreux
⇨
EURE-ET-LOIR
D 928
N 154
D 929

CHARTRES MAINTENON

PARIS
PARIS

C D

This region is one of the least-known and most endearing parts of Upper Normandy. Time is suspended here. Only twenty years ago it was still common to see men ploughing their fields by hand and donkeys carrying loads of milk. Hedges enclose and protect little farms, where land is laboured over and crops are dearly earned. Ancient, authentic, the very name of this country, "Ouche", would seem to come from the pre-Celtic "Utica", making this one of the oldest names in Normandy.

Highlights

1 Dream at Diane de Poitier's beloved Château **d'Anet** (p220)

2 Admire craftsmanship of the 13C **St Taurin** reliquary (p224)

3 See cave mushroom cultivation at **La Champignonnière** (p232)

4 A contemplative moment at **Abbaye du Bec Hellouin** (p233)

5 The **Château du Champ-de-Bataille** gardens (p235)

Ancient fields

The Eure plain holds fields of cereal crops and pasture, punctuated here and there by curtains of trees or more substantial hints of forest at valley edges. It is difficult to precisely date when the land was first shaped in this way by man, although it is undoubtedly very ancient. The layout of the farms resembles that of Roman latifundia, and is directly inherited from Gallo-Roman villas. Traces do remain and are found regularly from this period, and it is known that the roads crossing this land lie on the old Roman ways.

The French who know Normandy cherish this countryside, which certainly explains the peppering of second homes to be found here.

Pays d'Ouche

The Pays d'Ouche, crossed by the Upper Risle valley, lies between the Charentonne, Iton and Rouloire rivers. With its clayish soils and calcareous layers acting as sponges to retain moisture, the land is grassy and crisscrossed with hedges: the famous *bocage* country.

Farmers in the Pays d'Ouche traditionally both produce food and gather it. In other words, with a vegetable garden, orchard, poultry yard, and a few animals at pasture on land they generally own, they also gather mushrooms, nuts and berries from the stretches of forest. The day labourers here also often work at the great farms of the Le Neubourg plateau.

Château du Champ-de-Bataille

© Francis Cormon/hemis.fr

Dreux★

Dreux is set on the boundary between Normandy and Île-de-France; it is a lively regional market town earning its living from diverse industrial activities. The town is the final resting place of members of the Orléans family, one of France's royal lines; they can be viewed in the crypt of the Royal Chapel of St-Louis where their tombs comprise an impressive collection of 19C sculpture. Nearby, the Eure valley contains lovely surprises, notably the château of Anet.

▸ **Population:** 30 977.
◔ **Michelin Map:** 311: E-3.
🄸 **Info:** 9 Cour de l'Hôtel-Dieu. ℘02 37 46 01 73. www.ot-dreux.fr.
▶ **Location:** Dreux is 85 km/52.8mi W of Paris via N 12, and 48km/29.8mi E of l'Aigle. The historic centre is on the left bank, and the Grande-Rue (rue Maurice-Violette) is the liveliest street.
☺ **Don't Miss:** The Royal Chapel and the Renaissance Château d'Anet.
🕐 **Timing:** You'll need 2hr to see the town, and another 2hr for Château d'Anet. Make time for a picnic in the château grounds.
👫 **Kids:** The Musée Marcel-Dessal has a children's itinerary.

A BIT OF HISTORY

Dreux rose to importance when the Normans settled west of the River Avre and Dreux castle defended the French frontier against a belligerent neighbour. The castle, which stood on the hill now occupied by St Louis' Chapel, was besieged many times. It was dismantled on the orders of Henri IV, who razed the town in 1593 after a three-year siege.

In 1556, the Paris Parliament decided that the County of Dreux should in the future be the exclusive property of the French royal family. In 1775, Louis XVI ceded Dreux to his cousin, the Duc de Penthièvre, son of the Comte de Toulouse. Eight years later, when at the king's insistence the duc was forced to give up his magnificent property at Rambouillet, he arranged for the family tombs in the parish church of Rambouillet (subsequently destroyed) to be transferred to the collegiate church adjoining Dreux Castle. When the duc's daughter married Louis Philippe d'Orléans, known as Philippe Égalité, her dowry included the County of Dreux. It was thus that Dreux, which until the Revolution had been a simple family burial place, became the mausoleum of the Orléans family.

SIGHTS

Belfry★

Tourist office: ℘02 37 46 01 73.
At the end of the old Grande-Rue (Maurice-Violette) rises the ornate façade of the Hôtel de ville (town hall), which was built from 1512 to 1537. The ground and first floors are decorated in the Flamboyant style; the Renaissance second floor shows the skill of a young architect from Dreux, **Clément Métézeau** (1479–1555).

Église St-Pierre

Built in the early 13C and partly damaged during the Hundred Years' War, St Peter's Church was heavily remodelled from the 15C to the 17C.

The façade dates from the 16C. Of the two towers designed to flank it, only the left one was completed. The gate, chancel and left arm of the transept are 13C. The right arm of the transept dates from the 16C to the 17C. The church interior is notable for its fine 15C and 16C **stained-glass windows**, especially in the side chapels and apsidal chapel. The outstanding organ case (1614) is the work of the local cabinetmaker Toussaint Fortier.

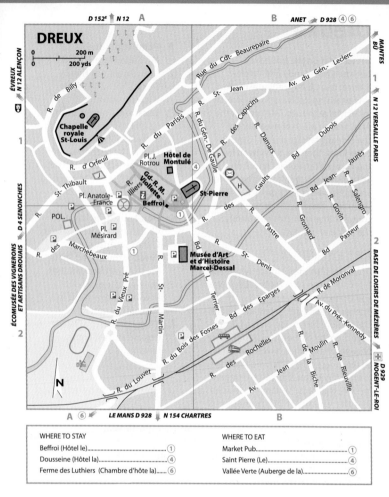

WHERE TO STAY	
Beffroi (Hôtel le)	①
Dousseine (Hôtel la)	④
Ferme des Luthiers (Chambre d'hôte la)	⑥

WHERE TO EAT	
Market Pub	①
Saint Pierre (Le)	④
Vallée Verte (Auberge de la)	⑥

Grande-Rue

The former Grande-Rue, now rue Maurice-Violette, hums with activity most days of the week, particularly during summer festivals. Note at the corner of rue Illiers two 15C half-timbered houses whose upper storeys extend over the street.

Hôtel de Montulé – Maison des Arts

15 rue Godeau.
Daily except Tue 2–6pm.
No charge. 02 37 38 87 51.
This townhouse built during the reign of Henri IV was a prison under the Revolution; it is today a major art centre, and offers temporary exhibitions.

Chapelle royale St-Louis

2 sq. d'Aumale.
Daily except Tue: Apr–Jun and Sept 9.30am–noon, 1.30–5.30pm; Jul–Aug 9.30am–6pm. Oct–Mar. €9.
02 37 46 07 06.
www.chapelle-royale-dreux.com.
Before the Revolution this site was occupied by the Collegiate Church of St Stephen (St-Étienne). In 1783 it received the remains of members of the Toulouse-Penthièvre families.
In 1816 the dowager Duchess of Orléans, widow of Philippe Égalité, erected a chapel in the Neoclassical style. It was enlarged by her son Louis-Philippe (1773–1850) when he became king, and the exterior was embellished with

Chapelle royale St-Louis

© Leroy Arthur/age fotostock

bell turrets and Gothic pinnacles. The building as a whole is a monument to the 19C for both the quality of its architecture and the work of talented artists.

The side windows make it possible to admire the stained-glass representations of the patron saints of France and the royal family: St Philip, St Amelia, St Ferdinand (the heads are portraits). The stained glass in the apse illustrates the life of St Louis.

The main crypt contains the tombs of the Princes of Orléans; the recumbent figures form a little museum of 19C statuary by Mercié, Pradier, Dubois, Chapu, Millet, Lenoir, etc.

On the lower level, five extremely rare **glass panes painted with enamels**★★ catch the visitor's attention. They were made in the Sèvres workshops, as was the other glasswork.

The park contains several remains of old fortifications. A fine **view** can be had of the town.

Musée d'Art et d'Histoire

Place du Musée.

🕑*Wed–Fri and Sun–Mon 3–6pm.*

🕑*Public holidays and Dec school holidays.* ✺€4 (no charge on Sun). ℘02 37 38 55 75. www.dreux.com/le-musee.

The museum offers visitors an encyclopaedic collection in which painting holds pride of place.

In the historic centre of Dreux, the museum presents an overview of the art of the 18C, 19C and 20C and houses some great masters such Granet, Vlaminck and Monet.

The Drouais past is also illustrated by archaeological collections, stunning stained glass windows and medieval capitals, and the memories of the Orleans family and the Royal Chapel.

Écomusée des Vignerons et Artisans Drouias

68 rue St-Thibault.

🕑*Mon–Fri 9am–noon, 2–6pm, Sat 2–6pm, Sun 3–6pm.* ✺€5. ℘02 37 42 62 81. www.museedudrouais.com.

This eco-museum renders homage to Dreux winegrowing: tools, cellars, etc. Medieval garden behind museum is fun for kids; wine appreciation course at nearby Clos St-Thibault.

EXCURSIONS

From Dreux, go 6km/3mi southeast to **Mézières-en-Drouais** for the ♟♟**Lac de Mézières-Écluzelles**, a lake and bird-watching area.

If you go 13km/8mi northwest instead, you come to ♟♟**Courdemanche** and the English-style **Rosemary's Garden** (*La Vallée, 10 rue des Ifs, 27320 Courdemanche,* ℘02 37 48 14 59).

Finally, 16km/9mi west by the N12 takes you to **Nonancourt** and its 12C fortress; also see the Flamboyant Gothic **Église St-Martin** (*Maison Mouret Grande-Rue, 27320 Nonancourt*; ℘*02 32 58 28 74*). Just 1km/6mi S from Nonancourt by the D11 is the **Église St-Lubin-des-Joncherets**.

🚗 DRIVING TOUR

🚗 DREUX AND IVRY FORESTS
80km/49mi. Allow 3h (including château visit).

▶ Leave Dreux via D 928 north and take D 161 to the left. Later D 143.

Outside Dreux, the aqueduct crosses the valley, carrying water from the Avre to Paris. Off to the right, you can see the church in the little town of Montreuil as you drive by, and Dreux forest off to the left. In Ézy-sur-Eure, an old humpback bridge (Pont St-Jean) crosses the river to Saussay.

Ivry-la-Bataille
The town name refers to a battle on 14 March 1590, when Henri IV defeated the Duc de Mayenne and the Catholic League in the Wars of Religion (1561–98). There are a few quaint timber-framed houses; one (*No. 5 rue de Garennes*) may have lodged Henri IV in 1590; the 11C doorway (*end of rue de l'Abbaye*), has three sculpted key stones (renovated), and may have been part of Ivry abbey, destroyed in the Revolution. Diane de Poitiers founded **Église St-Martin**, a 15C–16C church, partly attributed to the famous architect, Philibert Delorme.

▶ Take D 833 towards St-André-de-l'Eure.

In the little village of **Couture-Boussey**, a centre of woodwind manufacture since the 16C, is a **Musée des Instruments à Vent** (🕐*Feb–early Dec Tue–Sun 2–6pm;* 🕐 *1 Jan, 1 May.* ℘*02 32 36 28 80; www. lacoutureboussey.com*).

▶ Return to Ivry via D 833, continue north on D 836.

Between Neuilly and the Merey mills, the 16C **Château de la Folletière** (•━ *closed to the public*) can be seen through the foliage in a park.

▶ From Chambine to Pacy, D 836 rises above Eure; nice views upstream.

Pacy-sur-Eure
There is a monument to Aristide Briand; the beautiful early 13C **Église St-Aubin**, reworked in the 16C, has modern artworks and 16C–17C stone statues. The kids will like the tourist railroad, the **Chemin de fer touristique à la découverte de la vallée de l'Eure** 👥 – (*Gare de Pacy-sur-Eure.* ℘ *02 32 36 04 63.www. cfve.org. Ask for info, regular trains Jul–Aug, Tue–Wed and Sun early Sept–early Oct, €10 (child 4–15, €7*).

▶ Take the right bank for the D 836 to head along the Eure to Anet. D 62, D 16, D 928.

Château d'Anet★
🐾 *Guided tours only: Apr–Oct Wed–Mon 2–6pm; Nov and Feb–Mar Sat–Sun 2–5pm.* ⊗€*9.40.* ℘*02 37 41 90 07. www.chateaudanet.com.*
Successive owners since 1840 have endeavoured to maintain Anet's original ornate appearance.
When widow **Diane de Poitiers** (1490–1566) came to court she caught the eye of François I's second son, Henri. At 32 she was beautiful, intelligent and 20 years older; she still fascinated him when he became King Henri II. When in 1559 Henri died in a tournament, Diane had reigned 12 years over king, court, artists and royal finances. She rebuilt Anet, symbol of her power and taste, from 1548 with architect **Philibert Delorme**. Henri's widow Catherine de' Medici took Chenonceau but left her Anet, where Diane died in 1566. The greatest artists embellished the château: sculptors Goujon, Pilon; silversmith Cellini; enameller Limosin; the Fontainebleau tapestry makers.

Entrance Gate – The work of Philibert Delorme. Above the central arch, the tympanum is a casting of Benvenuto Cellini's bronze low relief now in the Louvre *(Diane Recumbent)*. Above the door is a clock, with a stag held at bay by four dogs; the dogs formerly barked and the stag moved to tell the time. The outlying buildings' chimneys bear coffins to evince Diane's constant mourning.

Left Wing of the Main Courtyard – The visit begins on the first floor with Diane's bedroom. The main attraction is the Renaissance bed, decorated with Diane's three crescents. The stained-glass windows include fragments of the original *grisailles*, a discreet grey element in keeping with Diane's mourning.

The **main stairway**, added by the Duke of Vendôme in the 17C, affords views of both lake and park. The vestibule, also 17C, leads to the Salon Rouge with its French and Italian Renaissance furniture. The Faïence Room, with part of its original tiling, leads to the dining room where two huge atlantes by Puget support the fireplace mantelpiece. Note the central Jean Goujon medallion of Diane snaring the royal stag.

Chapel – Built in 1548 by Philibert Delorme, its layout is a Greek cross. A dome and lantern cover the circular nave, one of the first to be built in France. The skilfully executed diamond-shaped drawing on the coffers produces a surprising optical illusion, the whole cupola seeming to be drawn upwards. The design of the floor tiling recalls this geometrical subtlety. Diane de Poitiers used to attend Mass from the gallery, which communicated with her rooms in the right wing *(demolished)*.

Chapelle funéraire de Diane de Poitiers – *Entrance from place du Château, left of the main entrance.*

The chapel designed by Claude de Foucques, architect to the princes of Lorraine, was begun just before the death of Diane in 1566 and completed in 1577. The white-marble **statue★** representing Diane kneeling on a tall sarcophagus in black marble, is attributed to Pierre Bontemps; so too is the altarpiece. Since the spoiling of the tomb in 1795, Diane's remains are at rest at the chevet of the Anet parish church.

ADDRESSES

🛏 STAY

Hôtel La Dousseine – *47 route de Sorel, 28260 Anet (20km/12mi N of Dreux). ✆02 37 41 49 93. www.dousseine.com. 20 rooms.* Charmingly discreet location for this hotel; all rooms have views of park; half of the rooms are on the ground floor at garden level.

Hôtel Le Beffroi – *12 pl. Métezeau. ✆02 37 50 02 03. www.hotelbeffroi.fr. 15 rooms.* To visit the belltower and church of St Peter, you have a front row seat here. Rooms simple but functional; quieter next to the river.

La Ferme des Luthiers – *12 rue Hottetere , 27750 La Couture-Boussey (26km/16mi N of Dreux). ✆02 32 36 26 23. www.lafermedesluthiers.com. 4 rooms.* Pretty B&B in what was a sheepfold in the 18C; rustic but comfortable. Family-style Norman cuisine.

🍴 EAT

Market Pub – *19 r. Mérigot. ✆02 37 46 18 44. www.restaurant-marketpub.fr.* A step away from the market, modern décor and innovative cuisine with top-quality ingredients. Great view of the old town from second-floor.

Le Saint-Pierre – *19 r. Sénarmont. ✆02 44 10 10 87. www.lesaint-pierre.com. Open daily for lunch and dinner.* Tucked into little street near church of St Peter. Three dining rooms and pretty pastel colours, bistro furniture. Warm welcome, traditional cuisine, nice price.

Auberge de la Vallée Verte – *6 r. Lucien-Dupuis, 28500 Vernouillet (2km-1mi S of Dreux by D 311). ✆02 37 46 04 04. www.aubergevalleeverte.fr. Closed Sun and Mon. 15 rooms.* Exposed beams, fireplace and paintings; traditional cooking. Impeccable rooms, bigger in the annex, embellished with a garden.

Évreux★

Évreux, on the River Iton, is the Eure's religious and administrative capital. The city centre was rebuilt after 1945; the town ramparts, former bishop's palace, cathedral and 15C belfry survived. Pleasant stroll in flower gardens along Iton.

A BIT OF HISTORY

5C – Vandals sack the market town.
9C – Vikings destroy the Roman fortified town on present site on Iton.
1119 – Henry I burns the town.
1193 – Philippe Auguste also burns it.
1356 – Jean the Good burns Évreux.
1379 – Charles V's siege.
June 1940 – German air raids.
June 1944 – Allied air raids raze district round the station.

●●● WALKING TOUR

3km/2mi. 1h30m (not including the cathedral and the museum). **P** *Park at place Clemenceau (see map). Begin at place du Général de Gaulle.*

Place du Général de Gaulle
A castle once stood on this square. Today, there is a fountain that represents the Eure as a woman holding an oar and the city's coat of arms.

Tour de l'Horloge
The elegant 15C clock tower stands on the site of a tower which flanked the town's main gateway.

Promenade des remparts
The walk runs beside the River Iton.

Cathédrale Notre-Dame★★
⏱*Mon–Sat 8.45am–7pm, Sun 9am–6.30pm.* ℘*02 32 33 06 57.*
The nave's great arches are all that is left of the original church, rebuilt 1119-1193; the choir is from 1260, the chapels are 14C. The lantern tower and Lady Chapel came after the 1356 fire. Note the magnificent 16C north transept façade and doorway. In the 1940 fires,

▶ **Population:** 49 899.
⚙ **Michelin Map:** 304: G-7.
▤ **Info:** 11 Rue de la Harpe. ℘02 32 24 04 43. www.grandevreux tourisme.fr.
◐ **Location:** Évreux is 96km/60mi W of Paris, 58km/36mi S of Rouen and 48km/30mi NE of Dreux.
🅿 **Parking:** Parking (fee) behind cathedral, near tourist office, near Cloître des Capucins public garden.
◈ **Don't Miss:** The Flamboyant beauty of Notre-Dame Cathedral and the rich collections of the museum.
🕓 **Timing:** Allow yourself 2h to see the museum.
👥 **Kids:** The Roman ruins at Gisacum will interest them as will the train through the valley of the Dure.

the silver belfry melted; the west towers lost their crowns.
Exterior – *Walk along the north side.* The aisle windows were redesigned in the 16C in the Flamboyant style of which the north door is a perfect example.
Interior – View the ambulatory chapels' **stained glass★** (⚙ *see Introduction: Religious architecture, p64*) and **carved wood screens★** from the transept, between the lantern tower pillars.
Beautiful 18C wrought-iron grill on choir, and the apse windows are perhaps the 14C's most beautiful. Fine Renaissance wood screens at ambulatory entrance. The 15C Treasury chapel is quite unique: closed off by wrought-iron bars and iron frame.
The fourth chapel **screen★** is a masterpiece of imagination and craftsmanship; note the lower figures; the chapel glass is early 14C. The central chapel gifted by Louis XI, has 15C windows of considerable documentary interest.
The upper parts depict France's peers at Louis XI's coronation; he is two windows further on.

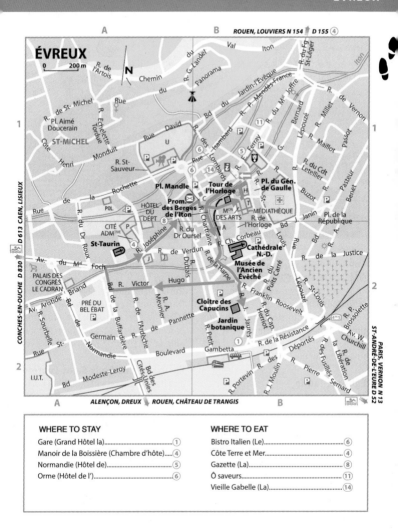

ROUEN, LOUVIERS N 154 D 155 ④

ÉVREUX

WHERE TO STAY	
Gare (Grand Hôtel la)........................①	
Manoir de la Boissière (Chambre d'hôte).....④	
Normandie (Hôtel de).........................⑤	
Orme (Hôtel de l')..............................⑥	

WHERE TO EAT	
Bistro Italien (Le)................................⑥	
Côte Terre et Mer...............................④	
Gazette (La)..⑧	
Ô saveurs..⑪	
Vieille Gabelle (La).............................⑭	

Musée d'Évreux★★ – Musée d'Art, Histoire et Archéologie

6 rue Charles-Corbeau. 🕐*Tue–Sun 10am–noon, 2–6pm.* 🕐*1 Jan, 1 May, 1 and 11 Nov, 25 Dec.* ⊗*No charge.* ℘*02 32 31 81 90.*

The 15C former bishop's palace looks onto the cathedral; Flamboyant, it has dormer windows, ornamented window pediments and a staircase tower. The municipal museum is inside. The ground floor's first two rooms concern the Eure region and town history and geography. The former chapter house (Room 3) has a monumental fireplace and medieval and Renaissance collections. Note the

17C Aubusson tapestries on the Prodigal Son. Room 4 has medieval exhibits: tomb inscriptions in engraved stone, capitals.

The **Archaeological Room★** in Gallo-Roman rampart ruins, displays domestic and religious objects from the Palaeolithic Age (up to 9000 BCE) to the Gallo-Roman era (1C–4C).

17C and 18C paintings on first floor, and decorative items such as Évreux Hospital apothecary jars in Nevers and Rouen faïence. Contemporary art exhibitions and 19C paintings and objects (Lebourg, Jongkind) on second floor, 20C art on the third, including Hartung and Soulages.

Cathédrale Notre-Dame, Évreux

Couvent des Capucins

96 rue de Panette. ◷*Mon–Fri 10am–12.30pm, 1.30–4pm.* ◈*No charge.* ✆*02 32 31 81 90.*

Former Capuchin cloisters with four timber-roofed galleries; monolithic columns; moral texts on walls. Converted to a school of music in 1996.

Église St-Taurin

This former abbey church established in 660 and dedicated to the first Bishop of Évreux dates back to the 14C and 15C. The well-proportioned 14C chancel is lit by superb 15C windows. Three windows in the apse trace the life of St Taurinus.

Châsse de St-Taurin★★ – This masterpiece of 13C French craftsmanship in the north transept was given to the abbey by St Louis to contain St Taurinus' relics and was probably made in the abbey workshops. The silver gilt reliquary enriched with enamel is in the form of a miniature chapel and even shows St Taurinus with his crosier.

EXCURSIONS

▷ Take the N 13 for Paris 9km/5mi east, then the road on right for **Vieil-Évreux** and ♟♟ **Gisacum - Jardin archéologique** – (◷*Mar and Oct–Nov daily except Tue 1–5pm; Apr–Jun and Sept daily 1–6pm; July–Aug daily 10.30am–6.30pm;* ◈*no charge;* ✆*02 32 31 94 78; www.gisacum-normandie.fr),* a garden and 1C archaeological dig.

See **Miserey**'s 18C château, 7km/4mi east by the N 13 (towards Paris), then the D 650 on the left. The park includes Dante-inspired **themed gardens** (◷*daily Apr–mid-Aug Sat–Mon and public holidays 2.30–6pm; Sept–Oct Sun only;* ◈*€6.50;* ✆*02 32 67 00 21).*

▷ To reach **La Croix-Saint-Leufroy** and its **church,** head 17km/10mi north of Evreux, then take the D 316 towards Eure; cross the river and take the D 836 on the left for Louviers.
The church has carved Renaissance baptismal fonts and paintings from the old Croix-St-Ouen abbey.

▷ The last excursion is to the village of **Cocherel**. Drive 25km/15mi northeast of Évreux. Initially take the D 155, then the D 316 and after the Eure, turn right onto the D 836.

It was in Cocherel that the French statesman **Aristide Briand** (1862–1932) acquired his estates. The "Pligrim of Peace" rests today in the church cemetery *(take the way up off the road leading into hamlet).* His tomb is marked by a soot-coloured granite slab. A statue in his memory also stands on the other side of the Eure bridge. Along the D 57, the Jouy-sur-Eure road, a pyramid recalls Bertrand Du Guesclin's victory at the Battle of Cocherel in 1364, over the forces of Charles II of Navarre.

ADDRESSES

🛏 STAY

🍽🍽 **Chambre d'hôte Manoir de la Boissière** – *Hamlet "La Boissaye", 27490 La Croix-St-Leufroy (16km/10mi NE).* ☎02 32 67 70 85. www.chambres-giteslaboissiere.fr. *5 rooms.* This 15C manor is a working farm. The rooms are all different, with family furniture. Pretty duck pond and veranda.

🍽🍽 **Grand Hôtel de la Gare** – *61, boulevard Gambetta.* ☎02 32 38 67 45. www.hotelgare-evreux.fr. *Restaurant🍽🍽. 29 rooms.* Just 2 min from the town centre, rooms here offer a reasonable degree of comfort. The restaurant serves traditional food.

🍽🍽 **Hôtel de l'Orme** – *13 r. des Lombards.* ☎02 32 39 34 12. www.hotel-de-lorme.fr. *39 rooms.* In the town centre, this hotel has functional rooms.

🍴 EAT

🍽🍽 **Le Bistro Italien** – *29 r. St-Thomas.* ☎02 32 58 73 43. www.lebistroitalien.fr. Reservation advised.* Franco-Italian specialities.

🍽🍽 **Côté Terre Et Mer** – *3 Rue Joséphine.* ☎02 32 38 71 27. https://restaurant-coteterreetmer.fr.* Seafood and local produce dishes.

🍽🍽 **La Vielle Gabelle** – *3 r. de la Vieille-Gabelle.* ☎02 32 39 77 13. www.restaurant-la-vieille-gabelle-27.fr.* Half-timbered façade; two dining rooms, modern cuisine.

🍽🍽–🍽🍽🍽 **La Gazette** – *7 rue St-Sauveur.* ☎02 32 33 43 40. www.restaurant-lagazette.fr. Open Tue lunch to Sat dinner (except Sat lunch).* Well looked-after establishment; modern furnishings.

🍽🍽🍽 **Ô Saveurs** – *1 rue du Maréchal-Joffre.* ☎02 27 34 72 43. https://osaveurs.wixsite.com/osaveurs-evreux. Closed Sun evening, Tue evening and all day Wed. Reservation advised.* Traditional Norman cuisine. Two dining rooms, very pleasant terrace.

SHOPPING

Chocolatier Auzou – *34 rue Chartraine.* ☎02 32 33 28 05. www.auzou-chocolat.fr.* This confectioner's produces several house specialities: Zouzous d'Auzou and macaroons of Grand'Mère Auzou.

Conches-en-Ouche★

The town of Conches, on the edge of the woodlands that mark the northern limits of the Pays d'Ouche, is remarkably situated on a spur encircled by the River Rouloir. There is a particularly good view of the town if it is approached along the Rouloir valley (from Évreux). The keep of the ruined castle is illuminated from April to September.

A BIT OF HISTORY

From Rouergue to the Pays d'Ouche – On his return from the *Reconquista de Iberia* (1034), **Roger de Tosny** made a pilgrimage to Conques, in Rouergue (southwest France) and brought back relics of Ste Foy. This may be the origin of the town's name. Roger dedicated a church to **Ste Foy**; at the end of the 15C it was replaced by the present building.

▶ **Population:** 5 033.

⊙ **Michelin Map:** 304: F-28.

ℹ **Info:** Place Aristide-Briand. ☎02 32 30 76 42. www.conches-en-ouche.fr.

▶ **Location:** From Aigle (30km/18.5mi SW) or Évreux (14km/8.5mi NE) take D 830. From Bernay (30km/18.5mi NW) take D 140, and from Rouen (50km/31mi N).

👁 **Don't Miss:** The beautiful windows of the Ste-Foy Church.

🕐 **Timing:** Visit Conches in the morning, then stroll along the many paths in the area.

SIGHTS

Jardin de l'Hôtel de Ville

The Gothic doorway of the town hall – entrance to the former castle – leads to a garden in which stands the

Jardin de l'Hôtel de Ville

© Franck Guiziou/hemis.fr

☺ Walking Tours ☺

Pick up a walking guide to the area from the tourist office called *Les Circuits Touristique*; also shows bike and horse riding trails.

ruined keep of the lords of Tosny, surrounded by 12C towers.

From the terrace there is a fine view of the Rouloir valley and the elegant Flamboyant apse of Ste-Foy church. Below another terrace offers a similar view.

Rue du Val

There are two interesting buildings here. One is the 16C half-timbered **maison Corneille**, home to the family of the famous dramatist (1606–84). At the end of the street, the **hospital** stands on the site of the abbey; the vaulted cellars are open to visitors.

Église Ste-Foy★

The south tower is crowned by a tall spire of wood and lead, a copy of the one blown down in a storm in 1842. The fine carved panels of the façade doors are early 16C. Notice the many gargoyles. Inside there are some beautiful statues including that of St Roch (17C) in the south aisle and near the great organ.

Stained-Glass Windows★ – The Renaissance windows, dating from the first half of the 16C, have retained their unity in spite of restoration. Those in the north aisle depict the life of the Virgin. The seven windows (10.5m) in the chancel are divided into two, the upper part illustrating the Life of Christ, the lower to that of Ste Foy and portraits of the donors.

The windows in the south aisle were made in either Île-de-France or at Fontainebleau. The Mystical Wine Press (fifth window) is the best known.

The houses facing the church are 15C and 16C. The vaulted cellars (11C–12C) are open to visitors.

Musée du Pays de Conches

r. Paul-Guilbaud.

🕐Jun–Sept Wed–Sun 2–6pm. 🚫Public holidays except 14 Jul and 15 Aug. ✆€3. ✆02 32 37 92 16.

Old farming tools and recreated workshops.

Musée du Verre

rte de Ste-Marguerite.

♿🕐Mar–Nov Wed–Sun 2–6pm. 🚫Public holidays except 14 Jul and 15 Aug. ✆€3 ✆02 32 30 90 41. *http://museeduverre.fr.*

Glass objects by the "sorcerer of Conche", François Décorchement (1880–1971).

EXCURSIONS

Head 14km/8.5mi S by the D 840 to **Breteuil-sur-Iton.** It is east of Breteuil Forest; the Iton loops here into a lake in the castle's public gardens. William the Conqueror's daughter wed in the **church**. Now head 4km/2mi E to the 👥 **Château de Chambray**, knowing that only the park is open to the public. Leaving Conches by the Évreux road, the D 830, you can take 10km/6mi of narrow roads to explore the **Rouloir valley**. At 3km/1.5mi turn left onto a sharp road down through underbrush.

After La Croisille, left on first paved road (D 167). Go 1km/6mi; left at crossroads and down to valley bottom at church of St-Elier in a nice setting. Follow river and you return to see Conches at its prettiest angle.

If you take the D 140 W for 14km/8mi W from Conches, you get to **La Ferrière-sur-Risle** with its 13C–14C **church** and beautiful former **tanneries**. Take the D 23 N to the verdant Risle valley, the **Val Gallerand**, skirting the Beaumont Forest; you will see superb old Norman farm buildings in the greenery.

L'Aigle

Visit L'Aigle on Tuesday, when it holds France's third-largest market. A major town, L'Aigle is a centre for metalwork, producing pins, needles and more. The historic centre is place St-Martin, with its church.

CHÂTEAU

The château, home to the town hall and **two museums**, was built in 1690 on the site of an 11C fortress, by Fulbert de Beina, Lord of L'Aigle.
Legend says he found an eagle's nest here, hence the town name. Mansart (Jules Hardouin 1646–1708) designed this and the Château of Versailles for Louis XIV.

Musée des Instruments de Musique

Pl. Fulbert-de-Beina. 🕐*Mon–Thu 8.30am–noon, 1.30–5.30pm; Fri 8.30am–noon, 1.30–4.45pm.* 🎫*No charge.* 📞*02 33 84 44 44. www.ouche-normandie.fr.*
Double spiral staircase leads to the first floor to see a collection of musical instruments, the gift of a former bandmaster: wind instruments, string instruments, and more exotic ones such as the serpent, a bass wind instrument descended from the cornett and a distant ancestor of the tuba.

▶ **Population:** 8 075.

🖲 **Michelin Map:** 310: M-2.

ℹ **Info:** Place Fulbert-de-Beina. 📞02 33 24 12 40. www.ouche-normandie.fr.

◖ **Location:** L'Aigle lies between the Pays d'Ouche and the Perche, on the road linking Dreux, 59km/37mi to the E, to Argentan. Lisieux is only 56km/35mi NW on D 519.

🅿 **Parking:** You will find parking on the public squares: de la Halle, de l'Europe, de Verdun and de Bois-Landry.

👁 **Don't Miss:** The Tuesday market; the museum of La Grosse Forge at Aube.

🕐 **Timing:** Give yourself half a day at L'Aigle before visiting the museums at Aube.

👥 **Kids:** The museum of the Comtesse de Ségur (1799–1874), France's most famous children's author.

Musée "Juin 44"

Pl. Fulbert-de-Beina. 🕐*Apr–Sept Tue–Wed and Sat–Sun 2–6pm.* 🕐*1 Jan, 1 and 11 Nov and 25 Dec.* 🎫*€3.60.* 📞*02 33 84 44 44. www.ouche-normandie.fr.*
The Battle of Normandy Museum has wax figures of De Gaulle, Churchill, Leclerc, Roosevelt, Stalin, etc. and their recorded voices. The battle is on a 36sq m relief

map, events traced on dioramas. A small **archaeological museum** has some interesting objects; there is also an exhibition of a **meteorite** that fell on L'Aigle on 26 March 1803.

SIGHTS
Église St-Martin

An elaborate late 15C square tower contrasts with a small 12C one built of red iron agglomerate *(grison)* and surmounted by a more recent spire. Beautiful modern statues stand in niches between the windows of the south nave, added in the 16C.

Above the high altar (1656) is a beautiful carved wooden altarpiece, consisting of four twisted columns capped by Corinthian capitals and decorated with vine leaves, bunches of grapes and cherubs.

🚗 DRIVING TOUR

🚗 PAYS D'OUCHE
75km/46mi. Allow 4h.

▶ Drive NE from L'Aigle on the D 930.

St-Sulpice-sur-Risle

The **church** adjoins the 13C priory, which was partially rebuilt in the 16C. Among its artworks are a 16C tapestry, a 17C painting of St Cecilia, a statue of St Anne and two stained-glass windows from the 13C and 14C.

▶ Take the road facing the mairie for about 1.5km/1mi; go under the D 918 and continue about 100m (megaliths on right).

▶ Return to L'Aigle by the D 930; take D 12 NW to La Ferté-Frênel at 11km/6mi, where you will see a château.

▶ Leave La Ferté-Frênel S by the D 14 for 1km/0.6mi; then left on D 31 to Saint-Evroult-Notre-Dame-du-Bois.

Saint-Évroult-Notre-Dame-du-Bois

The ruins of this abbey, a great centre of intellectual life in the 11C and 12C, are set in a lovely valley, through which the River Charentonne flows.

Destroyed in the 10C by wars, the Romanesque abbey of Ouche revived in the 11C. It was rebuilt in the 13C in the Gothic style, but little remains.

In front of the main entrance stands a monument to Orderic Vital (1075–1142), an English historian whose work described the abbey in its heyday.

▶ Leave St-Evroult W by the D 13 to Gacé.

Gacé

Musée de la Dame aux camélias – *pl. du Château.* ◷*Mid-Jun–mid-Sept Tue–Sat 2–6pm.* ∞€4. ☎*02 33 67 08 59.* A museum with a modest collection of memorabilia recalling the woman who inspired Verdi's opera, *La Traviata.*

▶ Go S on the D 932 to Orgères.

Orgères

In this **church** to St George, an altarpiece and painting, *The Adoration of the Shepherds* is listed as an Historic Monument.

▶ Continue on the D 932 to Ste-Gauburge-Ste-Colombe, then take the D 926 E to Aube.

Aube

The **Château des Nouettes**, now a medico-pedagogical institute, was once the residence of Countess Eugène de Ségur. 🚶A **"Comtesse de Ségur"** walking itinerary 9km/5mi long begins from Aube's central square.

👥 Musée de la Comtesse de Ségur

7km/4.3mi SW of L'Aigle by N 26. 3 r. de l'Abbé-Derry. ◷*Late Jun–late Sept Wed–Mon 2–6pm; rest of year by appointment.* ◷*Public holidays.* ∞€4 *(under 18, no charge). Ticket combined with Grosse Forge €6 (children, no charge).* ☎*02 33 24 14 93.*

www.musee-comtessedesegur.com.
The Russian-born countess (1799–1864),
languishing in the country while the
count enjoyed other society, produced
very late in life a series of tales for
her grandchildren. The books met
with great success and are still cited,
especially *Les Malheurs de Sophie*,
but mostly as examples of tedious
moralising. The museum's considerable
charm lies in its lovely rural setting and
frequently changing exhibits evoking
19C children's pastimes as well as
aristocratic life and attitudes.
The Musée de la Comtesse de Ségur is
in the former presbytery at the foot of
the church. It contains exhibits evoking
the life and literary career of the
countess. Characters from the writer's
novels are represented by a collection of
dolls and exhibits (toys, games, books,
furniture, etc.).

🚹🚹 Musée de la Grosse Forge d'Aube

r. de la Vielle-Forge. 🕐*Late Jun–late
Sept daily 2–6pm.* 🕐*Public holidays.*
🔊*Guided tours (45min) 15min past
every hour.* 💶€4 (under 18, no charge).
*Ticket combined with Musée de la
Comtesse de Ségur* €6 (children no
charge). 📞*02 33 34 14 93.*
www.forgeaube.fr.
On the River Risle, as you leave Aube
towards L'Aigle, stands the Musée de la
Grosse Forge d'Aube, which retraces five
centuries of metallurgy. This museum
has changed very little since the 17C.
Note the furnace for refining metals,
the massive camshaft hammer and
the wooden bellows (a 1995 replica)
operated by a paddle wheel.
There are beautiful models making
it possible to better understand the
history of metallurgy.

▷ Return to L'Aigle via the N 26.

Bernay

Bernay developed rapidly around
an abbey founded early in the 11C
by Judith of Brittany, wife of Duke
Richard II. The town, which nestles
in the Charentonne valley, has a
number of interesting, renovated,
half-timbered houses.

SIGHTS

The principal streets are rue Thiers and
du Générale-de-Gaulle, along which the
abbey, the museum and the Ste-Croix
Church are clustered.

Boulevard des Monts★

This lovely hillside road north of the
centre commands good views of the
town and the Charentonne valley.

Hôtel de ville★

The 17C town hall buildings, which were
formerly Bernay Abbey, are in the style
of the Maurists, a Benedictine order.

▶ **Population:** 10 392.
👓 **Michelin Map:** 304: D-7.
🛈 **Info:** 29 rue Thiers.
  📞02 32 43 32 08.
  www.bernaytourisme.fr.
▷ **Location:** Bernay lies at
  the junction of the
  Charentonne and the
  Cosnier rivers. Take D 438
  from Rouen (65km/40.5mi
  NE) or Alençon (92km/57mi
  SW), or the D 613 from
  Lisieux (34km/21mi NW) or
  Évreux (52km/32mi SE).
😀 **Don't Miss:** The view from
  boulevard des Monts,
  the municipal museum,
  and the lovely château de
  Beaumesnil.
🕐 **Timing:** Spend a morning
  in town, then drive along
  the Risle river.
🚹🚹 **Kids:** The museum has
  activities for children.

Ancienne église abbatiale

The abbey church was begun in 1013 by **Guglielmo da Volpiano**, summoned from Fécamp by Judith of Brittany. In the 15C the semicircular apse was replaced by a polygonal one. Note the carved capitals above the nave and the twin bays in the galleries. The north aisle, rebuilt in the 15C, has diagonal vaulting.

♟♟ Musée des Beaux-Arts

pl. Guillaume-de-Volpiano
🕐Jun–Sept Tue–Sun 11am–6pm; rest of the year 2–5.30pm. 🕐1 Jan, 1 May, 25 Dec. ⬤⬤€4 (no charge Wed and 1st Sun of month). 🖋02 32 46 63 23.
The museum is housed in the 16C abbot's lodge. Exhibits include a fine collection of Rouen, Nevers and Moustiers faïence and old Norman furniture.

Église Ste-Croix

Started in the 14C, the church is heavily restored and contains fine works of art from Le Bec-Hellouin. The remarkable **tombstone** of Guillaume d'Auvillars, Abbot of Bec (1418), stands at the entrance to the sacristy. Sixteen great statues of Apostles and Evangelists from the end of the 14C are in the nave.

Detail on a half-timbered house, Bernay

Basilique Notre-Dame-de-la-Couture

Access by rue Kléber-Mercier, about 1km/0.6mi S of town centre.
🕐Sat 2–6pm. 🖋02 32 43 06 82.
The interior of this 15C church, established as a basilica in 1950, has wooden vaulting; the statue Notre-Dame de la Couture (16C), highly venerated by pilgrims is placed on a modern altar in the north transept.

🚗 DRIVING TOUR

🚗 ALONG THE RISLET AND CHARENTONNE RIVERS

65km/40mi. Allow 3h.

Near L'Aigle, the pretty, fish-filled **Risle** and the **Charentonne** rivers run almost parallel. There were many watermills in the past, but today only some of them remain, no longer in working order.

▷ Leave Bernay E by the D 133.

Menneval

Delightful country church with renovated façade. The local Brotherhood of Charity dates from 1060.

▷ Continue on the D 133. Less than 2km/1mi after Camfleur, right on D 42.

Fontaine-l'Abbél

A pretty Norman village with a Louis XIII château and a **church** (⚷ *closed to the public*). Inside are displayed the banners of the local Brotherhood of Charity.

▷ Come back to the D 133 and turn right to Serquigny.

Serquigny

The church façade, chequered in blank flint and white stone, has a Romanesque doorway. Inside, the chapel *(left)* and stained-glass windows are Renaissance.

▷ Continue on the D 133 SE, along the Risle.

Château de Beaumesnil

© Arnaud Chicurel/hemis.fr

Beaumont-le-Roger

The ruins of the old 13C priory to the Trinity has imposing buttresses visible from the road. The 14C–16C **church** to St Nicholas, badly damaged by the bombings, has been restored; it has both early 15C–16C and modern stained glass.

Seven trekking paths permit discovery of Beaumont-le-Roger's surrounding area (*Contact the tourist office, 6 Place de l'Église* ℘*02 32 44 05 79*).

Leave Beaumont SW by the D 25.

Château de Beaumesnil★

13km/8mi SE by D 140.
Jul–Aug daily 10am–6pm; May–Jun and Sept Sat–Sun 2–6pm. ✕ €8.50.
℘*02 32 44 40 09.*
www.chateaubeaumesnil.com.
The château, a masterpiece of the Louis XIII style, is built of brick and stone. The formal gardens and the 60ha **park** echo the sumptuous lines of the château.

The Beaumesnil canton has 17 walking itineraries (*ask at Bernay or Beaumesnil tourist office*).

Leave Beaumesnil SW for La Grimoudière, then by minor roads W to Landepeureuse. Then head for Menhir to SW to take the D 49, right, for Broglie.

Brogile

The 18C **château** (*private*) is built around a medieval fortress.
The pillars and the choir of the **church** are Romanesque; the rest is 15C and 16C.

Jardin aquatique

Daily. No charge.
℘*02 32 44 60 58.*
This charming little water garden is irrigated by the River Charentonne.

Head alongside the Charentonne in the direction of Bernay, by the D 33.

Étang Saints-Pères

Open daily. No charge.
℘*02 32 44 60 58.*
The banks of this little pond offer picnic tables, pedal-boats, walks and recreation facilities.

Ferrières-Saint-Hilaire

This remains of the forge and the forge master's manor still stand.

Saint-Quentin-des-Isles

Below the 19C château, there is a textile plant. A dovecote stands on an island.

Brionne

Medieval Brionne was a Risle Valley stronghold. When William of Normandy besieged it 1047–1050, he met the monks of Bec-Helloüin abbey, an event that would profoundly affect English religious life.

SIGHTS

Donjon

Park at place du Chevalier-Herluin or by church. Take r. des Canadiens, then right on "sente du Vieux-Château".

Steep path to ruins of one of Normandy's best examples of a square keep (11C). Lovely view of town and Risle valley. The **Église St-Martin** has a 15C nave; 14C vaulting. The **Musée de la Poupée** (*38 r. de Calleville; contact for details;* ✆ *02 32 45 76 24*) exhibits antique dolls. Riverside garden in **Jardin de Shaftesbury** (*other side of Risle*). The tourist office is in an 18C **press**.

Visit **La Champignonnière** (*r. de la Briqueterie;* ✆ *02 32 57 87 99; by appointment*). Mushrooms grown in a cave.

🚗 DRIVING TOUR

🚗 LIEUVEN

55km/34mi. Allow about 2h30.

The Lieuven is a region of pastures and cereal crops, between Caux and Auge.

▷ Leave Brionne N by the D 46. N of Authou turn onto the D 137.

Saint-Grégoire-du-Vièvre

16C figures and rebuses on stone church's southern side.

▷ Contine W on the D 137.

Saint-Georges-du-Vièvre

👣 A waymarked Resistance itinerary starts here (*38km/23mi. Brochure from tourist office, 1 route de Montfort;* ✆ *02 32 56 34 29*).

▷ Leave St-Georges NW on the D 29; left on D 98 for Saint-Étienne-l'Allier.

▷ **Population:** 4 325.
🚲 **Michelin Map:** 304: E-6.
ℹ **Info:** 1 rue du Générale-de-Gaulle. ✆02 32 45 70 51.
▷ **Location:** Brionne is 40km/25mi NW of Évreux via D 613 and D 130, and nearly the same distance E of Lisieux.
👁 **Don't Miss:** The square Norman keep and the banks of the Risle.
🕐 **Timing:** After 1–2hr in the village, visit Le Bec-Helloüin and the châteaux of Harcourt and Champ de Bataille nearby.

Saint-Étienne-l'Allier

11C church with interesing 14C recumbant figure. The **monument des Maquisards** (*at the D 98 and D 29 crossing*), recalls that the village was one of Normandy's most active Resistance units.

▷ Leave Saint-Étienne to continue N to Saint-Martin-Saint-Firmin.

Saint-Martin-Saint-Fermin

The chapel of St Firmin was a major pilgrimage site; there are beautiful wood carvings inside.

🥾 **"Chemin de la Fontaine Fiacre"** – *Leaves from church – 7km/4mi. Brochure from Lieuvin tourist offices (www.lieuvin-paysdauge-tourisme-normandie.fr). This pretty walk follows the Véronne.*

▷ At St-Siméon turn left, S, on D 810 to Lieurey.

Lieurey

🥾 **"Les chemins de l'eau"** – 250km/155mi of waymarked foot, cycling and horseriding Lieurey-Pont-Audemer paths. *Brochure from Lieuvin tourist offices (www.lieuvinpaysdauge-tourisme-normandie.fr).*

▷ Continue W on D 810 to Cormeilles.

Cormeilles

Distillerie Busnel – *R. de Lisieux.*
℘02 32 57 38 80. www.distillerie-busnel.
fr. Cider distillery.

"Le sentier de la biodiversité" –
*From tourist office, first right; "Les Monts
du Bourg". After avenue, left, park at
water tower; second left.* This route offers
a 6km/3mi stroll.

▷ Return by D 810 to Lieurey; D 137
to St-Georges-du-Vièvre, then D 38 SE.

Château de Launay

Note the chateau's **dovecote★**.

▷ Continue on the D 38.

Saint-Benoît-des-Ombres

Beyond the small mairie, there is a
chapel hidden in greenery. Its 15C
wooden porch bears a wooden St
Benedict.

▷ Head S and SW for St-Victor-
d'Epine and the D 31; gardens on right
after about 2km/1mi.

Jardins du clos Saint-François

St-Victor-d'Épine.
🕙*May–Aug Fri–Mon 10am–noon,
2–6pm.* ∞€5. *℘02 32 45 98 90.*
English-style garden around thatched
cottage. Rose collection.

**From the St-Victor-d'Epine mairie,
there is the **Circuit de la Grande Boissière**, a 6–9km/3–5mi trekking path.

▷ D 31 towards Berthouville, but
turn left on D 26. At Brétigny, take
D 48 N, then left on D 38.

Livet-sur-Authou

Quaint village with half-timbered
houses, a castle and a church.

Abbaye du Bec-Hellouin★★

Le Bec-Hellouin abbey, a medieval
religious and cultural centre,
produced two great Archbishops of
Canterbury for England.

A BIT OF HISTORY

In 1034, the knight **Herluin** found God
and founded the Bec Abbey; its pious
reputation attracted an Italian scholar,
Lanfranc, who later became young
Duke William's trusted adviser.
Pope Alexander II, a former student
of Lanfranc at Bec, appointed him
Archbishop of Canterbury, which made
him virtual Regent of England whenever
William returned to Normandy.
On Lanfranc's death in 1093, **Anselm**,
the theologian who was now Abbot
of Bec, was transferred to Canterbury.
In the 17C, Bec rose to new eminence
under **Guillaume de la Tremblaye**
(1644–1715), one of the greatest
sculptors and architects of his period.

▶ **Population:** 404.
Michelin Map: 304: E-6.
▷ **Location:** The abbey is
35km/22mi SW of Rouen
and within 40km/25mi of
Honfleur (NW), Lisieux (W)
and Évreux (SE). Rouen is
52km/32mi NE, Harcourt
10km/6mi SE.
Don't Miss: The abbey
of Le Bec-Hellouin, the
château and gardens at
Champ-de-Bataille, and the
Harcourt fortress with its
arboretum.
🕙 **Timing:** Spend your
morning at the abbey, then
go to Champ-de-Bataille or
Harcourt in the afternoon.

The monks were driven out during the
Revolution and the church, one of the
largest in Christendom, was demolished
under the empire. In 1948 the site was
restored to the Benedictine Order.

VISIT

Abbaye de Bec-Hellouin★★

🕐 *Unaccompanied visits daily 8am–9pm.* 🚶*Guided tours Jun–Sept 10.30am, 3pm, 4pm, 5pm; Oct–May 10.30am, 3pm, 4pm.* 📞*02 32 43 72 60. www.abbayedubec.com.*

New Abbey Church

The new abbey stands in the former Maurist refectory. At the entrance is a 14C statue of the Virgin; the Fathers of the Church are 15C. The altar was presented in 1959 by Aosta, birthplace of Bishop Anselm. Before the high altar lies the 11C sarcophagus of Herluin, founder of Bec. Turn left on leaving to reach the other sights.

Old Abbey Church

Only the column, foundations and fragments of the south transept of the old abbey church remain.

Cloisters

A monumental 18C grand staircase leads to the cloisters. Built between 1640 and 1660, the cloisters were modelled on those of Monte Cassino (Italy). Northeast of the cloisters is a beautiful, 14C Gothic doorway.

Tour St-Nicolas

🔒*Closed to the public.*
The 15C tower is the most important remainder of the old abbey church. A plaque recalls the abbey's ties with England in the 11C and 12C.

🚗 DRIVING TOURS

The Neubourg plain south of the Seine, and the Roumois plateau north are both ideal for the flourishing cereal crops, spreading here amid charming country churches and noble châteaux.

🚗 LE ROUMOIS

50km/31mi. Allow 2h30.

▷ Leave Le Bec by Pont-Authou and take the D 38 to Boissy-le-Châtel.

Château de Tilly

🔒*Closed to the public.*
Lozenge-patterned stone and glazed-brick façade, perimeter wall quartered by pointed turrets.
The winding **staircase★** in brickwork in the courtyard recalls the Rihour Palace in Lille.

▷ Come back on the D 124; 4km/2mi further, take D 576 on right.

Écaquelon

The church contains beautiful 16C wood carvings.

▷ Take D 582 through Les Epinais and N to Illeville-sur-Montfort. Then D 94 to Rougemontier, right on D 144.

Routot

Romanesque church; the **Maison du Lin** on mairie ground floor tells the story of linen (🕐*Mar and Oct–Nov Sun 2–6pm; Apr–Jun and Sept Wed–Sun 2–6pm, and Wed 10am–noon; Jul–Aug daily except Mon 2.30–6.30pm.* ⊜ *€3.* 📞*02 32 56 21 76; www.lamaisondulin-en-normandie. fr).*

▷ D 144 Bouquetot.

Bouquetot

There is an 11C–12C **church** with statues and 18C paintings. Note the 700-year-old hawthorn.

▷ D 675 to Bourg-Achard.

Bourg-Achard

The **church** has 16C stained glass, and remarkable 15C–16C carved wood. 15C stone Virgin with Bird.

▷ D 313 to Bourgtheroulde.

Bourgtheroude

Church with interesting Renaissance windows. Entrance pavilion and dovecote remains of 16C château.

▷ D 574 to Infreville, 1km/0.6mi to the N

Abbaye du Bec-Hellouin

Infreville

There is a large 18C rocaille altarpiece in the **church**.

▶ D 438 SW to Le Bec-Hellouin.

🚗 LE NEUBOURG
50km/31mi. Allow 2h30.

▶ Leave Le Bec by the D 39 heading SE for Le Neubourg.

Château du Champ-de-Bataille★

Gardens: 🕐*Mar–mid-Apr and Sept–mid-Nov daily 2–6pm; mid-Apr–Jun Mon–Fri 2–6pm, Sat–Sun 10am–6pm; Jul–Aug daily 10am–6pm.* ✎€15.
Chateau and gardens: 🕐*Mid-Apr–Jun and Sept–mid-Nov Sat–Sun and public holidays 2.30–5pm; Jul–Aug daily 2.30–5pm.* ✎€30. 📞*02 32 34 84 34. www.chateauduchampdebataille.com.*
The name, which means "Castle of the Battlefield", may recall a battle in 935 between forces of the Count of Cotentin and of William Longsword, ancestor of the Conqueror. The 17C château was built by Alexandre de Créqui and occupied by the Harcourt family before it was looted in 1795. In the 20C it was used as a hospice, a camp for war prisoners and a jail for women. The Duke of Harcourt bought it in 1947 and began restoration, continued by the present owner, Jacques Garcia.

Interior – *Entrance through the main courtyard on the left.* Grand ceremonial rooms presented with the owner's rich collection of furniture and art objects.
Park★★ – A French-style garden of vast proportions has been recreated, offering spectacular perspectives and subtle plantings reflecting 18C philosophical notions of the orders of nature: animal, vegetable, mineral, etc.

👣**Parcours de découverte du massif du Champ-de-Bataille**.
Contact Le Neubourg tourist office for info: 110 Place du Maréchal Leclerc . 📞*02 32 35 40 57.* To take this nature walk (1.5km/1mi), leave your car at the château; from the entrance head round the estate on right to the GR 26 path (about 2km/1mi) that takes you there; by car, take the D 39 for Le Neubourg; before La Mare Auzanne, right (indicated).

▶ Continue on the D 39 to Le Neubourg.

Le Neubourg
50km/31mi. Allow 2h30.
The capital of the plain of the same name. The church has a 17C **main altar** decorated with pretty statues.

Musée de l'Ecorché d'anatomie
♿🕐*Daily (except Mon and Tue) 2–6pm.*
🕐*Mid-Dec–Jan, 1 May.* ✎€4.50.
📞*02 32 35 93 95.*
www.musee-anatomie.fr.

Château d'Harcourt

© C. Michaud/Eure Tourisme

In the early 19C Dr Auzoux, who comes from the region, invented an anatomy model for his medical students that could be taken apart to see muscles, membranes and nerves. This museum shows how he conceived it, along with a room devoted to local fauna.

⚲⚲ From Le Neubourg there are five cycling itineraries. Contact the tourist office for information (in converted former train station).

🚲 The green route through Le Neubourg also offers beautiful cycling excursions.

▶ Head S on the D 840.

Le Tremblay-Omonville
The château has a curious fore part (18C); terraces and imposing service quarters.

▶ Come back to Le Neubourg and take the D 137 for Brionne.

Harcourt★
This small town near Le Neubourg is at the intersection of roads leading to the banks of the River Risle and River Charentonne and Beaumont Forest. Not far from the 13C **church** the old wooden marketplace stands intact.

🚶🚶 Two waymarked treks (6km/3mi and 20.5km/12mi) leave from the church.

Château d'Harcourt★
🕐 Mar–mid-Jun and mid-Sept–mid-Nov Wed–Mon 2–6pm; mid-Jun–mid-Sept daily 10.30am–6.30pm. ⚬€5.
📞 02 32 46 29 70.

www.harcourt-normandie.fr.
Late 12C castle built by Robert II of Harcourt, companion to Richard the Lionheart, modernised in the 14C and made a comfortable residence in the 17C. The imposing mass of the castle stands sheltered by its curtain wall, 20m wide moat, and ramparts flanked by dilapidated towers. Restored medieval entrance and bridge.

Arboretum★
Adjoining the main courtyard, a 10ha/25acre arboretum presents over 400 tree species coming from the five continents.

ADDRESSES

The Perche is a region subdivided into two: the Norman Perche and the southern sector, the Perche-Gouët or Lower Perche. The Perche countryside is thick with forests, hedgerows, gentle hills and green dales, while Perche buildings offer interesting architecture. Pays d'Auge manors look like country homes; in the Norman Perche, they resemble small stone fortresses. Although most of these late 15C and early 16C lordly homes are now farmhouses, they still have their towers, elegant turrets and delicately carved façades.

Percheron Horse

The large, powerful Percheron horse is known for gentleness and manoeuvrability. Its capacity to pull heavy loads at a trot long made it ideal for draft work, and especially for coaches from the 17C on. By the 19C it was one of the most common horses in the UK and the United States. However, with the development of motorised vehicles its numbers dropped. In 2009, only 20 000 horses were known of worldwide, and the Perche horse is today considered dangerously close to extinction. French breeders are now attempting to cross it with American stallions to make it a lighter horse for racing.

Cider Country

Cider was originally a peasant's drink. As early as the 16C Rabelais called himself "an apple-gatherer in the Perche countryside", and the Perche countryside has indeed long been one of orchards and cider-making. The 1950s brought modernised farming and the decline of the industry. The drink itself had become

Highlights

1 Climb 155 16C steps to the fortress in **Nogent** (p240)

2 Learn about medieval abbey life in **Thiron-Gardais** (p241)

3 Admire the chapels in **La Ferté-Bernard**'s church (p242)

4 Taste real Norman farm cider in **Le Theil-sur-Huisne** (p245)

5 Visit ancient oaks in **Perche** and **Trappe forests** (p249)

unfashionable, and the orchards were abandoned. Fortunately, the 1990s brought with them a desire to save this important part of the Perche identity. More than 150 unique Perche apple and pear varieties were rediscovered and logged.

Today orchards are being replanted, local apple varieties are being grafted, and the region has the new ambition of obtaining the coveted AOC label for its unique Perche cider.

Percheron Horse

© Dominique VERNIER/Fotolia.com

237

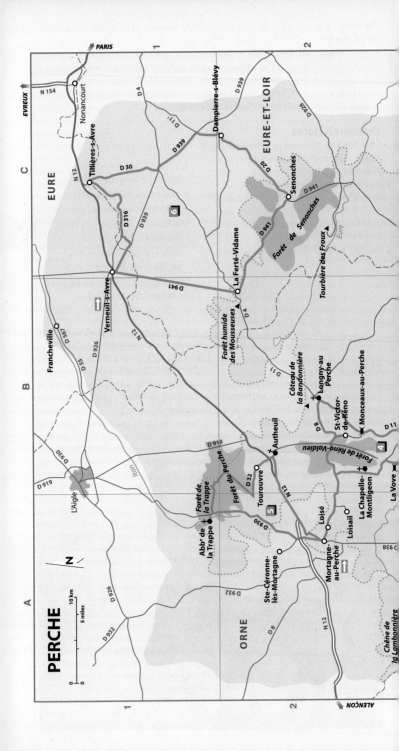

PERCHE

N

0   10 km
0   5 miles

A

B

C

1

2

EVREUX
PARIS
ALENÇON

N 154
Nonancourt
N 12
Tillières-s-Avre
D 30
Dampierre-s-Blévy
D 4
D 939
D 11
D 938
EURE-ET-LOIR
D 939
EURE
6
D 316
D 941
Senonches
D 941
D 20
Forêt de Senonches
La Ferté-Vidame
Tourbière des Froux
Eure
D 4
Verneuil-s-Avre
D 567
D 926
D 55
Francheville
N 12
Forêt humide
des Mousseuses
D 11
Coteau de
la Bandonnière
Longny-au-
Perche
St-Victor-
de-Réno
Monceaux-au-Perche
D 11
Autheuil
D 918
Forêt de Réno-Valdieu
4
D 32
Forêt du Perche
Tourouvre
L'Aigle
D 930
D 919
Iton
Abⁿ de
la Trappe
Forêt de
la Trappe
N 12
5
D 930
Loisé
La Chapelle-
Montligeon
Loisail
La Vove
D 938
Mortagne-
au-Perche
Ste-Céronne-
les-Mortagne
D 932
D 926
D 932
D 8
N 12
ORNE
Chêne de
la Lambonnière

238

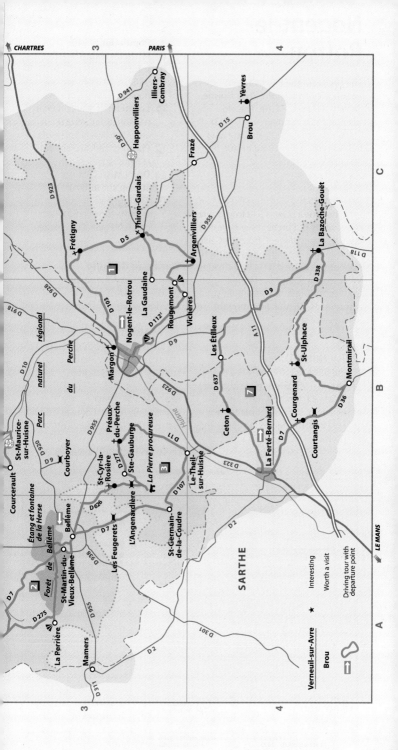

CHARTRES

PARIS

LE MANS

Illiers-Combray

Yèvres

Happonvilliers

Brou

Frazé

D 941

D 15

D 50²

D 923

Frétigny

Thiron-Gardais

Argenvilliers

La Bazoche-Gouët

D 5

La Gaudaine

D 955

D 118

D 928

Nogent-le-Rotrou

Rougemont

Vichères

D 112²

D 9

Les Étilleux

D 338

St-Ulphace

D 918

Parc

naturel

régional

du

Perche

Margon

D 9

A 11

Courgenard

Montmirail

D 10

D 923

Huisne

Ceton

D 637

Courtangis

D 36

St-Maurice-sur-Huisne

D 955

Préaux-du-Perche

La Pierre procureuse

D 11

La Ferté-Bernard

D 7

Courcerault

Courboyer

St-Cyr-la-Rosière

Ste-Gauburge

Le-Theil-sur-Huisne

D 323

D 9

D 277

D 107

SARTHE

Étang et fontaine de la Herse

Bellême

L'Angenardière

St-Germain-de-la-Coudre

D 626

D 2

Forêt de Bellême

St-Martin-du-Vieux-Bellême

Les Feugerets

D 938

D 7

D 955

D 2

La Perrière

Mamers

D 7

D 275

D 301

D 311

1 **2** **3** **7**

Verneuil-sur-Avre ★ Interesting

Brou ● Worth a visit

Driving tour with departure point

A B C

3 4

3 4

239

Nogent-le-Rotrou

The capital of the Perche region lies on the banks of the River Huisne, dominated by its castle. The old town borders the main road (N 23) at the foot of St John's Hill; the new town covers the flat land beside the River Huisne.

A BIT OF HISTORY

Between 925 and 1226 the Gallo-Roman town became a powerful Rotrou family fief; counts of Perche, they gave the town its name (Nogent, from the Gallic *novio-mago*, meaning new market). Nogent was burned in 1449 at Charles VII's command, to prevent the English from capturing it. It was rebuilt soon afterwards, in the Flamboyant or Renaissance style.

SIGHTS

Église Notre-Dame

The building was formerly the chapel of the Hôtel-Dieu (workhouse) and dates from the 13C and 14C. At the end of the north aisle there is a 16C–17C crib; the figures are of painted terracotta.

▶ **Population:** 9 940.
  Michelin Map: 311-A-6.
  Info: 9 rue Villette-Gate. ℘02 37 29 68 86. www. nogentlerotrou-tourisme.fr.
▶ **Location:** Nogent-le-Rotrou is 91km/56.5mi SW of Dreux and 77km/47.8mi S of L'Aigle.
🅿 **Parking:** Park in place de la République.
  Don't Miss: Château St-Jean; the tomb of Sully.
  Timing: Take time to tour the surrounding Parc naturel régional du Perche.

Tombeau de Sully

Access is through rue de Sully.
Daily 9am–4.30pm.
The doorway pediment to the Hôtel-Dieu (17C) displays Sully's coat of arms and emblems. As Sully was Protestant, his tomb is nearby but not part of the church. Barthélemy Boudin of Chartres sculpted his empty tomb.

Marches St-Jean

Initially only rue du Château led to the fortress; the "Demoiselles d'Armagnac", the duc de Nemours' daughters, had these 155 steps built in the 16C.

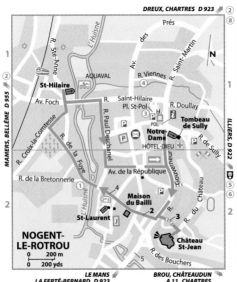

Château St-Jean

By the Marches-St-Jean, or by car along rue de Sully, then rue du Château-St-Jean. ◷*Daily except Tue: May–Oct 10am–noon, 2–6pm; Nov–Apr 10am–noon, 2–5pm.* ◷*1 Jan, 1 May, 1 Nov, 25 Dec.* ◉€3.50. ℘02 37 29 12 04.

This impressive castle is on a rocky spur. The Rotrous, counts of Perche, lived in the huge rectangular keep (35m high), which is supported by unusual buttresses. The enclosing wall with its semicircular towers was built from the 12C–13C. The remarkable gatehouse has two round towers with arrow slits and machicolations. View from courtyard.

◉ At foot of r. des Marches-St-Jean, cross r. Gouverneur; take r. Bourg-le-Compte which extends r. St-Laurent.

Rue Bourg-le-Comte

Several of the houses are of interest: a 13C turreted house (No. 2), which is better seen from rue des Poupardières; a 16C house (No. 4); a Renaissance house with mullioned windows (No. 3).

Maison du Bailli

47 rue St-Laurent.
Two turrets flank the entrance to the 16C mansion built by Pierre Durant, Bailiff of St Denis' Abbey, and his wife, Blanche Dévrier.

Église St-Laurent

The building is in the Flamboyant style, surmounted by a tower with a Renaissance top.

Église St-Hilaire

The church (13C–16C) stands beside the River Huisne. Its square tower dates from the 16C. The unusual polygonal chancel (13C) was modelled on the Holy Sepulchre in Jerusalem.

🚗 DRIVING TOUR

🚗 1 NEAR THE PERCHE CAPITAL

50km/31mi. 5h (including château).

Head northeast from Nogent on the D 103. At La Hurie, turn right on D 5 to go to **Frétigny**. **St Andrew's church** has 12C–13C frescoes.

Now take the D 5 S for **Thiron-Gardais**, to **Thiron Abbey** (◷*Mon–Fri 9am–5.30pm; May–Oct 3.30–6pm; ℘02 37 49 49 49*). Founded in 1114, the Benedictine Order of Thiron was influential 12C–13C. The vast church has 14C stalls. Visitors can learn about medieval abbey life in the gardens.

Drive south on the D 5 to **Argenvilliers**, to the 18C **Château d'Ourisères** (*park open 10am–5pm, no charge; ℘02 37 29 43 68*).

From there, take the D 371 to **Ferme de Rougemont** where there is an immense view of the region. From here, head for Vichères, take the D 112.1, NW. Just before Nogent, turn at the chapel on your left for a beautiful view of the countryside around the Perche capital.

ADDRESSES

🛏 STAY

🍽🛏 **Auberge de l'Abbaye** – *15 r. du Commerce, 28480 Thiron-Gardais (14 km/8mi E of Nogent). ℘02 37 37 04 04. www.aubergedelabbaye.fr. 7 rooms. Restaurant* 🍽. Good for exploring around Thiron-Gardais. Simple, comfy rooms.

⊜⊜ **Chambre d'hôte Au Clair de l'Huisne** – *3 r. Bretonnerie.* ☎*06 11 43 46 72. 3 rooms.* Attractive 18C riverside farm with comfortable rooms. Bicycle loan, kayak hire; pool.

⊜⊜ **Hôtel Au Lion d'Or** – *28 pl. St-Pol .* ☎*02 37 52 01 60. www.hotel-chartres-le-mans.com.* **P**. *18 rooms.* Former relay station with nice clean rooms.

⊜⊜ **Hôtel Sully** – *51 r. des Viennes.* ☎*02 37 52 15 14. www.hotelsullynogent.fr.* **P**. *42 rooms.* In quiet neighbourhood; good functional rooms.

⊜⊜⊜ **Domaine du Bois Landry** – *La Graiserie, 28240 Champrond-en-Gâtine.* ☎*02 37 49 80 01. www.boislandry.com. Seven treehouses for 2 or 4.* Unusual – good beds but no water or electricity.

⊖/**EAT**

⊜⊜ **L'Alambic** – *20 av. de Paris, 28400 Margon (exit N of Nogent).* ☎*02 37 52 19 03. www.lalambic-margon.fr. Open Tue–Sun lunch.* Former lorry-driver eatery has become a restaurant offering traditional cuisine.

⊜⊜ **La Forge** – *1 rue Alfred-Chasseriaud 28480 Thiron-Gardais.* ☎*02 37 49 42 30. www.a-la-forge.com.* Artist-chef; his paintings decorate this 16C abbey forge.

La Ferté-Bernard★

In Ferté-Bernard, canals wend their way among Renaissance houses, the fountain, market and superb Flamboyant-Renaissance church.

▸ **Population:** 8 848.
◔ **Michelin Map:** B4
  Info: 15, place de la Lice ☎02 43 71 21 21; www. tourisme-lafertebernard.fr.
▸ **Location:** 40km/24mi E of Mans, 90km/55mi SW of Chartres
⊘ **Don't Miss:** Discovering the town via its canals – and in a canoe!
◔ **Timing:** 1hr for the historic centre.

SIGHTS

Begin by the 15C **Porte St-Julien** (*pl. St-Julien*), which once had a drawbridge. It takes you to a few Renaissance **old**

Place Sadi Carnot

© Nicolas Thibaut/Photononstop

houses in rue de l'Huisne: (*No. 15, caryatid*). There are more in rue Carnot: a 15C inn and house with lively painted caryatids.

The **Église Notre-Dame-des-Marais★★**, built over two centuries, is both Flamboyant and Renaissance. Don't miss the three **absidal chapels★**: 16C windows and one has a stunning coffered ceiling; also look out for the sacristy's 15C painted alabaster panels. The 15C–16C **fountain** (*pl. Carnot*), 16C **market** (*between pl. de la Lice and r. Carnot*) and 12C **St Liphardus' chapel** (*imp du Château, near market*) deserve a visit.

Église Notre-Dame-des-Marais

© CSP_clodio/age fotostock

🚗 DRIVING TOUR

🚗 ⑦ LE PERCHE-GOUËT
87km/54mi. About a half day.

Meadows and orchards flourish here.

▶ D 153, via Cherrau; D 136 to Ceton.

Ceton
St Peter's church has a Romanesque belltower with Gothic choir and nave.

▶ Take D 637 for Coudray-au-Perche.

Les Étilleux
South of the village on D 13, near a tiny farm, take the path up for a view.

▶ On D 124 to Coudray-au-Perche, then Authon-du-Perche (D 9) and continue on D 9 to La Bazoche-Gouët.

La Bazoche-Gouët
12C–13C **church**, extended 16C *(access by covered passageway)*.

▶ Now head SW on D 927.

Montmirail
Viewed from the terrace, Montmirail **Château**'s classical west façade contrasts with the eastern medieval front; the château enjoys a panoramic view of Perche-Gouët (🕐*Jul–Aug daily except Sat 11.30am–12.30pm, 2–4.30pm; early Apr–Jun and early-mid Sept Sun and public holidays 2.30–6.30pm.* 👓€5. 📞*02 43 93 72 71*). Montmirail also has a 12C–16C **church**.

▶ Take Ferté-Bernard road by the D 36.

Château de Courtangis
This is a gracious 16C manor.

▶ Leave on D 36 for Courgenard.

Courgenard
Courgenard's church has 16C murals.

▶ Take D 7 to La Ferté-Bernard.

ADDRESSES

🛏 STAY
🍽🍽 **Chambre d'hôte La Veronnière** – *61260 Le Theil (8km/5mi NW of La Ferté-Bernard by D 323).* 📞*02 37 49 76 01. 2 rooms.* Environmentally conscious establishment in a stone barn; absolutely fresh ingredients.

🍴 EAT
♿🍽🍽 **Le Dauphin** – *3 rue d'Huisne.* 📞*02 43 93 00 39. www.restaurant-du-dauphin.com. Closed Sun–Mon.* 16C house with cachet of yesteryear but warm and peaceful decoration. Up-to-date cuisine.

Bellême

Bellême, a typical village of the region, overlooks the forest and the beautiful Perche countryside. The town had a particularly turbulent history in the Middle Ages, when Blanche of Castile and the future St Louis (Louis IX, 1214–70) took the fortress by storm in 1229.

SIGHTS

Ville-Close

The **gate**, flanked by two reconstructed towers, together with towers now incorporated into domestic buildings, are the only remains of the 15C ramparts, which once enclosed the town and were built upon 11C fortress foundations.
Rue Ville-Close, on the site of the former citadel, is lined with fine 17C and 18C houses. Outstanding are No. **24**, the Governor's house, and especially No. **26**, the **Hôtel Bansard des Bois**.

Église St-Sauveur

pl. de la République.
The late 17C St Saviour's church has a richly decorated interior. Note in particular the imposing high altar and canopy (1712) made of stone and marble, the chancel woodwork from the old abbey of Valdieu, and the windows, each composed of six scenes from the life of Christ. The font, decorated with garlands, stands against a three-panelled altarpiece.

🚗 DRIVING TOURS

🚗 ② FORÊT DE BELLÊME

Forêt de Bellême★
35km/21mi. About 3h.

This forest (2 400ha) is one of the most beautiful in the Perche.

▶ From Bellême take D 938 NW. There is a very pretty view from road.

▶ **Population:** 1 515.
🚗 **Michelin Map:** 310: M-4
ℹ **Info:** Bd Bansart-des-Bois. 𝒫02 33 73 09 69.www. perchenormand.fr/ tourisme.
▶ **Location:** Bellême is 22km/ 13.5mi NW of Nogent-le-Rotrou and 17km/10.5mi S of Mortagne-au-Perche.
👁 **Don't Miss:** The old houses of the Ville-Close, and the forest walks.
🕐 **Timing:** Give yourself 1hr to see the town and 3hr to visit the Écomusée at Ste-Gauburge.

Étang et Fontaine de la Herse
A path circles the pool – 15min on foot. A lovely cool spot. Opposite the forester's lodge is a Roman fountain and two stone blocks with Latin inscriptions.

▶ Backtrack to Colbert crossroads; turn right, W.

The forest road (surfaced) affords lovely views.

▶ At the Montimer crossroads turn left and head down for 400m/0.2mi.

Chêne de l'École
This 300-year-old oak is 40m tall; its circumference is 22m.

▶ Return to the Montimer crossroads and continue to La Perrière.

La Perrière
The name comes from the Latin *petraria* (stone quarry). Many houses are in dark-red ferruginous sandstone *(grison)*.
To look at the town's old streets and 15C–17C homes, take the **"sentier découverte"** (ℹ *Rue de la Juiverie, La Perrière; 𝒫02 33 73 09 69*). From the cemetery path near the church there is a **panoramic view★** of the Perche countryside with Perseigne and Écouves Forests.

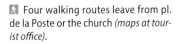

Forêt de Bellême near La Perrière

© Hervé Lenain/hemis.fr

▶ Four walking routes leave from pl. de la Poste or the church *(maps at tourist office).*

◉ Take the D 210 NE for Bellavilliers, then D 7 (passing by the D 931 and D 27) to reach Pervenchères. Continue NW on the D 27. After Vauvineux, turn left into marked road for the Chêne de la Lambonnière.

Chêne de la Lambonnière
This oak, over 500 years old, has a trunk 7.32m in circumference.

◉ Return to Pervenchères and continue on D 27/D 931 to La Gravelle; take the D 7 (right) to Bellavilliers, then D 310 to St-Martin-du-Vieux-Bellême.

St-Martin-du-Vieux-Bellême
The village clusters around the 14C–15C church. ▶Three walking routes from the church to Bellême forest.

◉ Take D 955 on left for Bellême.

⇌ ③ BELLÊME COUNTRYSIDE
34km/21mi. Allow about 3h.

◉ From Bellême take D 7 south.

Château des Feugerets
⊶*Closed to public.* A harmonious, well-balanced château design.

◉ Take the D 7 to St-Germain-de-la-Coudre.

St-Germain-de-la-Coudre
The church has an 11C crypt. The **Manoir de La Fresnaye** (◐*Late Jun–mid-Sept Sun–Thu 1–7pm; ⇆€4. ☏07 83 81 02 06 www.fresnaye-perche. fr*) has a pretty view from the keep of its 14C–16C manor.

◉ D 107 for Le Theil-sur-Huisne.

Le Theil-sur-Huisne
The **Cidrerie traditionnelle du Perche** (*at "Tronas" on the D 107. ◐Apr–Oct*

Mon–Sat 10am–noon, 3–8pm, Sun and public holidays 10am–noon; Nov–Mar Mon–Sat 10am–noon, 3–7pm; ◐Sun in Nov–Mar; ⇆no charge. ☏02 37 49 67 30; www.cidrerie-traditionnelle-du-perche. fr) offers guided tours of cider-making facilities.

◉ Leave on the D 11 to Saint-Agnan-sur-Eure, then left on D 634 for Préaux-du-Perche.

Préaux-du-Perche
The very pretty **church** of St-Germain has architecture ranging 12C–18C.
▶ Three walking routes depart from the war memorial; a fourth leaves from the nature park's car park.

◉ Take the D 277 W.

Prieuré de Sainte-Gauburge
At St-Cyr-la-Rosière.
The church is now the **Écomusée du Perche** (◐*Apr–Sept daily 10.30am–6.30pm, Oct–Mar Mon–Fri 10.30am–5.30pm, Sat–Sun and public holidays 2–5.30pm.* ◐*Christmas to late Jan,. ⇆€6. ☏02 33 73 48 06. http://ecomuseeduperche.com*) where past crafts live again.
▶Three walking routes leave from here to the manors and La Pierre Procureuse.

▶ Head towards Le Theil, but follow signs to "La Pierre Procureuse".

La Pierre Procureuse
This stone roof on a late Neolithic (2500 BCE) dolmen, brings luck if you touch it.

▶ Head N to Clémancé.

Manoir de l'Angenardière
☞ *Closed to public.* This manor house, built 15C and 16C, has a rampart.

▶ Continue to St-Cyr-la-Rosière.

St-Cyr-la-Rosière
The church has a Romanesque portal and 17C terracotta **Entombment★**.

ADDRESSES

🏠 STAY
☞ **Relais Saint-Louis** – *1 bd Bansard-des-Bois. ℘02 33 73 12 21. https://relais-saint-louis.com. 9 rooms. Restaurant ☞ ☞.* Delightful, classically decorated rooms; dining room fireplace, earthy cuisine.

Mortagne-au-Perche

This pretty village retains a medieval design with the houses clustered together, presenting a jumble of brown-tile roofs contrasting with the lighter-coloured façades.
The village was once a stronghold of the Perche region.

- ▶ **Population:** 3 873.
- ◔ **Michelin Map:** 310: M-3.
- ⓘ **Info:** 36 place du Général de Gaulle. ℘02 33 83 34 37. www.ot-mortagne auperche.fr.
- ▶ **Location:** Mortagne is 35km/21.7mi S of L'Aigle; 74km/46mi SW of Dreux.
- ◈ **Don't Miss:** Approaching from the N you will enjoy an excellent view of the town.
- ◔ **Timing:** After 1–2hr in town, take one of the described driving tours.

VISIT
Jardin Public
These gardens *à la française* offer good views of the Perche countryside. An outstanding equestrian statue by E Frémiet (1824–1910) depicts Neptune as a horse, setting out to conquer Ceres.

Hôpital
Delightful 16C cloisters with panelled vaulting and an 18C chapel are all that remain of the former convent of St Clare.

Porte St-Denis
Musée Percheron
rue du Portail-St-Denis.
◔ *Mid-Jun–mid-Sept Tue–Sun 3–6pm.*
☞ *No charge. ℘02 33 25 25 87.*
The St-Denis Gate is the sole remnant of the town's fortifications. In the 16C two storeys were added to the original 13C Gothic arch and they now house the Musée Percheron.

Maison des Comtes du Perche
This 17C house stands on the site of a former manor house. The ground floor houses the public library, and the first floor contains the Musée Alain.

Église Notre-Dame
The church, built between 1495 and 1535, combines both Flamboyant Gothic and Early Renaissance styles on the exterior decoration. There is an 18C **altarpiece★** in the apse. The stained-glass window in the third chapel recalls the role of local people in the colonisation of Canada in the 17C.

MORTAGNE-AU-PERCHE

0 ———— 200 m
0 ———— 200 yds

D 930, L'AIGLE, PARIS, N 12

ALENÇON · D 912

Maison du doyen de Toussaint

R. du Fg St-Éloi

R. Ferdinand de Boyère

R. de Rouen

R. du Mail

R. de Paris

Cloître

Hôpital

R. de Longny

Crypte St-André

Notre-Dame

R. du Gén. Leclerc

Musée Alain

Musée percheron

Pl. du Palais

R. des Quinze-Fusillés

D 8, LONGNY

R. Aristide Briand

R. de la Croix de Son

R. du Fg St-Langis

Cinéma

R. Ste-Croix

Jardin public

Montcacune

R. des Déportés

Rte de Mamers

D 9

MAMERS · D 931

LE MANS, BELLÊME, D 938

RÉMALARD

N

WHERE TO STAY	
Miottière (Chambre d'hôte la)	①
Tribunal (Hôtel du)	②

WHERE TO EAT	
Notre-Dame (R.)	2
Colonel-Guérin (R.)	4

Musée Alain

8 rue du Portail St-Denis.
Late May–mid-Sept Thu–Sat 2.30–6pm. No charge. 02 33 25 35 75. www.alainmortagne.fr.
French philosopher **Alain** (1868–1951), whose real name was **Émile Chartier**, was born in Mortagne. The museum displays personal belongings.

DRIVING TOURS

4 MORTAGNE-AU-PERCHE TO LONGNY

50km/31mi. Allow about 1h30.

Leave Mortagne by the D 8, going E.

Loisé

16C church with monumental tower.

Continue on the D 8; you pass the Château de la Goyère (left).

Forêt de Réno-Valdieu★

Forest of very old trees; the most beautiful in the **Série artistique★** (*Degraine crossroads; indicated*). Nature walk.

Cross forest; take D 29, right.

Saint-Victor-de-Reno

The church has a Renaissance statue of St Gilles.
From the church there are walks to Commeauche and Réno-Valdieu.

Return to D 8 to Longny-au-Perche.

Longny-au-Perche

Pleasant spot on Jambée; good view of 16C **Chapelle de Notre-Dame-de-Pitié** (*r. Gaston-Gibory, right of Mairie*). The **Église St-Martin** is 15C–16C.

D 111, SW to Monceaux-au-Perche.

Monceaux-au-Perche

The **Manoir du Pontgirard** has fine terraced **gardens** (*mid-Jun–Sept daily 10am–6pm; no charge; 02 33 73 61 49*).
There are three marked walks from the Mairie.

Take D 111, S to Boissy-Maugis. Cross the Huisne; then 1km/6mi NW to St-Maurice-sur-Huisne.

Saint-Maurice-sur-Huisne

At **Jardins des Perrignes** (*mid-Apr–mid-Jul daily 2–6pm; no charge; 02 33 73 77 33*), **English gardens** are set around an old manor house

Head for Courcerault.

Courcerault

The **Ferme-Musée de la Tonnelière** (*Jul–Sept by appointment. 02 33 83 91 32*) displays old farm and craft tools.

D 629 N; after 1.5km/1mi turn left.

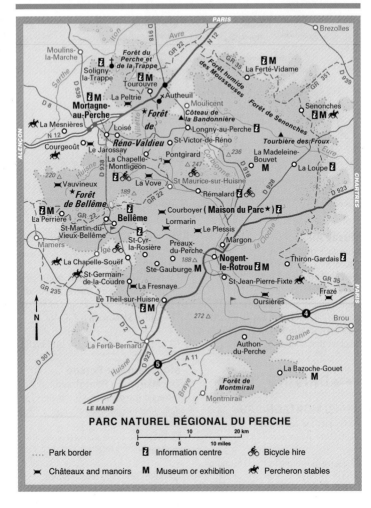

.... Park border	🛈 Information centre	🚲 Bicycle hire
✈ Châteaux and manoirs	M Museum or exhibition	🐎 Percheron stables

Parc Naturel Régional du Perche★

This regional park was created in 1998 to protect and showcase 1 820sq km/702.7sq mi of gentle hills, deep forests, hidden ponds, hedgerows, green valleys and interesting architecture; it also takes numerous initiatives on behalf of sustainable development. The Maison du Parc (*Courboyer, 61340, Nocé. ✆02 33 25 70 10. www.parc-naturel-perche.fr*) has been in the estate of **Courboyer** since 2000. This former manor house's surrounding buildings now house not only the administrative services, but also a shop, a dining space for tasting Perche gourmet specialities and a tourist information centre. Courboyer is a natural emblem for all there is to discover in the Perche, reflecting the rich architectural heritage to be found here in
addition to its typical country estate.

Owing to its rich meadows the Perche is devoted to stock raising, particularly the breeding of the draught horses known as **Percherons**.

Manoir de Courboyer, Parc Naturel Régional du Perche

Manoir de La Vove
Exterior can be visited all year, Mon and Sat 2–6pm. Park outside. No charge. This is one of the oldest manors in the Perche. Its keep dates back to the 14C.

▶ Backtrack to D 10 and turn left; D 5 for La Chapelle-Montligeon, right.

La Chapelle-Montligeon
A vast neo-Gothic **basilica** (1896) with a view.

▶ D 5 again N for pretty drive to D 8; turn left to return to Mortagne

🚗 5 THE PERCHE AND TRAPPE FORESTS
54km/33mi. About 2h.

These forests are in the **Parc naturel Régional du Perche**★ *(see box opposite).*

▶ From Mortagne take D 912 and then N 12 northeast; after 11km/6mi , right on D 290.

Autheuil
The Romanesque church has a fine chancel arch at the transept, and handsome capitals.

▶ Take D 290 NW to Tourouvre.

Tourouvre
Here you can discover the origins of modern Quebec, at the **Musée de l'Émigration française au Canada**★, which tells how Tourouve inhabitants left for "New France" in the 17C.

▶ Beyond the church turn right.

After a steep climb the road enters the **Perche forest** and reaches the beautiful Étoile du Perche crossroads. Continue straight ahead and on reaching the Avre valley turn left to admire the various pools. West of Bresolettes the road enters **Trappe forest**.

▶ At junction with D 930, turn right and later left on D 251.

Abbaye de la Trappe
The 12C abbey was named after an area where hunters caught game using a *trappe.* 🚶 Forest walk.

ADDRESSES

🛏 STAY

🍽🛏 **Chambre d'hôte La Miottière** – *61400 Le Pin-La-Garenne (12km/7.5mi S).* ☎02 33 83 84 01. *2 rooms.* 🅿 🚭. Set in the countryside in an area of 53ha. Spacious rooms, copious breakfasts.

🍽🛏 **Hôtel Le Tribunal** – *4 pl. du Palais.* ☎02 33 25 04 77. www.hotel-tribunal.fr. *18 rooms.* Family-run, in a house built 13C–18C in old Mortagne.

Verneuil-sur-Avre ★

Verneuil comprises three districts, the main streets of which are rue de la Madeleine, rue Gambetta and rue Notre-Dame. In the past each district was like a mini-town protected by a fortified wall and a moat, just as the whole town was surrounded by an outer wall and moat. Some fine half-timbered houses and old mansions have been preserved in the town.

A BIT OF HISTORY

Verneuil was formerly a fortified city created in the 12C by Henry Beauclerk, Duke of Normandy, third son of William the Conqueror. Together with Tillières and Nonancourt it formed the Avre defence line on the Franco-Norman frontier.

In 1204, the town became French under Philippe Auguste, who built the Grise Tower and its defence system.

After many battles with the English, the French victory of 1449 was achieved through the guile of miller Jean Bertin.

▸ **Population:** 8 164.
⌖ **Michelin Map:** 304: F-9.
▯ **Info:** 129 place de la Madeleine. ℘02 32 32 17 17.
◖ **Location:** 36km/22.4mi W of Dreux on N 12.
◔ **Timing:** Count on 1 1/2 hr to visit the town.
▲▲ **Kids:** Don't miss the the the birds at the Bois des Aigles in Bâlines.

SIGHTS

Tour Grise

The sentry walk at the top of this 13C tower is built of red agglomerate, from which it takes its name.

To the south, cross the small bridge over the Iton River to view the tower together with a charming little house at its base. The pleasant and relaxing **Fougère Park** lies near the bridge.

The partly ruined **Église St-Jean** has retained its 15C tower and its Gothic doorway.

The term Promenades refers to boulevard Casati and its prolongation. Remains of several of the old outer fortifications are visible. From avenue du Maréchal-Joffre and avenue du

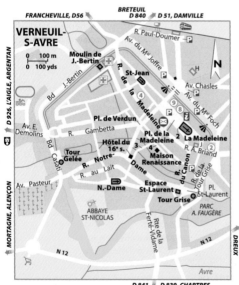

WHERE TO STAY

Saumon (Hôtel du).....................⑧

WHERE TO EAT

Collectionneur Gourmand (Le).........................②
Madeleine (Le)..............................④
Patate Gourmande (La)...........⑨

Maréchal-Foch are interesting views of the town.

The many old houses are extremely well restored and add to Verneuil's charm. Note for instance the 15C residence at the corner of rue de la Madeleine and rue du Canon, with its chequered walls and turret, which now houses the public library. Between rue Canon and rue Thiers, on rue de la Madeleine, stand a number of attractive stone or timbered houses. The 18C Hôtel Bournonville has wrought-iron balconies. Note also the houses at Nos. 532 (behind a courtyard), 466 and 401.

A Renaissance house stands at No. 136 rue des Tanneries, with a carved wooden door surmounted by wooden statues. At the corner of rue Notre-Dame and rue du Pont-aux-Chèvres stands a 16C town house with decorated turret. On place de Verdun, place de la Madeleine, rue de la Poissonerie there are more picturesque old wooden houses.

Église de la Madeleine★

The **tower★** abutting the church dates from the late 15C–early 16C. The third of the four tiers is surmounted by a richly decorated belfry.

The Renaissance-style porch is flanked by mutilated but beautiful 16C statues of the Virgin and of St Anne. The interior is lit by 15C and 16C stained-glass windows and has several 15C and 16C artworks. The nave ceiling is vaulted in wood.

Église Notre-Dame

pl. Notre-Dame.

The church, built of the red stone known as *grison* in the 12C, has been remodelled and possesses a number of 16C **statues★** carved by local sculptors. The illustration (below) shows: **1)** St Denis (14C). **2)** St James the Great. **3)** St Christopher. **4)** St Christine. **5)** St Fiacre. **6)** St Susanna. **7)** St Barbara. **8)** St Francis of Assisi.

9) St Benedict. **10)** Joan of Arc, as a Lorraine country girl. **11)** Renaissance *Pietà*. **12)** St Lawrence. **13)** St Augustine. **14)** St Denis with open skull. **15)** St Louis (17C). **16)** Two Prophets (Renaissance

15C and 16C stained-glass windows depicting the Passion of Christ, Église de la Madeleine

© DEA/G DAGLI ORTI/age fotostock

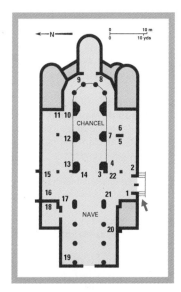

woodwork). **17)** St Sebastian (17C woodwork). **18)** 15C chest and altar base. **19)** 11C font. **20)** 14C Trinity (early Norman Renaissance). **21)** Virgin at Calvary (13C). **22)** St John.

EXCURSION
Francheville

9km/5.6mi NW on D 56.

Village on River Iton with pretty church. Ironwork museum, the **Musée de la**

Ferronnerie (*place Modeste Leroy.* ⏱*Contact tourist office for access*).

🚗 DRIVING TOUR

🚗 ⑥ VALLÉE DE L'AVRE TO FORÊT DE SENONCHES

64km/39mi. Allow 2h.

▷ From Verneuil, drive along the D 839, then D 316 (left) becomes D 102: Montigny-sur-Avre and Bérou-la-Mulotière for Tillières.

Tillières-sur-Avre

Tillières was the first Norman fortified town built (1013) to guard the Avre defence line. The church, with its Romanesque nave and panelled vault, was rebuilt in the 16C. From the garden called the Grand Parterre, there is a fine view of the Avre valley.

▷ Head S by D 30 to Brezolles; continue on D 939. At Chennevières, right for Dampierre-sur-Blévy.

Dampierre-sur-Blévy

The **Maison de Maître des Forges** (⏱*mid-Jul–late Aug daily 1–7pm;* ✺*No charge*) has a an old 17C forge furnace still in very good condition.

▷ Continue on D 20 to reach Senoches.

Senoches

This flower-decked little town has the remains of a 12C **castle** (château), under restoration.
The real treasure is the surrounding 4 300ha of **forest.** 🚶 There are about a dozen waymarked walks in the forest (*ask for the map at the tourist office: 1 Rue du Château.* 📞*02 37 37 80 11*).
To the southwest, near Manou on the D 140, the site of the **tourbière des Froux** has been protected and turned into a place to learn about the fragile eco-system of the peat bog.

▷ From Senoches, the D 941 crosses the forest NW to take you to La Ferté-Vidame.

La Ferté-Vidame

This is a lovely, immense ruined château, set in a vast 18C French-style **park** and forest. Louis de Rouvy, duc de St-Simon – a celebrated memorialist at Louis XIV's court – owned a château here once, but the remains are that of the château of the Marquis Jean Joseph de Laborde, which was subsequently built here in 1770.

The **pavillon Saint-Dominique** (*left at park entrance*) contains two exhibition rooms recounting the lives of the writer and the Marquis de Laborde in La Ferté-Vidame (⏱*May–Jul and Sept 2.30–6pm; Sun 2–6.30pm; Aug Wed–Sun 2.30–6.30pm;* 📞*02 37 37 64 09*).

▷ Return to Verneuil on the D 941.

ADDRESSES

🛏 STAY

🍽 **Hôtel du Saumon** – *89 pl. de la Madeleine, Verneuil.* 📞*02 32 32 02 36. www.hoteldusaumon.fr. 29 rooms. Restaurant*🍽. Rooms in the main building decorated with antique furniture.

🍴 EAT

🍽 **La Patate Gourmande**– *15 pl. de la Madeleine.* 📞 *02 32 38 58 53. Closed Sun. and Wed evening.* Small, charming dining room; big servings made with farm-fresh products.

🍽 **Le Collectionneur Gourmand** – *Ruelle de l'Abreuvoir, 63 r. Gustave Roger.* 📞*02 32 60 11 11. www.lecollectionneur gourmand.com.Closed Mon, Sun evening and Tue noon. Reservations advised.* Bric-a-brac decorates a gourmet restaurant. Look at fascinating old objects while waiting for your food. Tea room in the afternoon.

🍽 **Le Madeleine** – *206 r. de la Madeleine.* 📞*02 32 37 91 81. www. lemadeleine.fr.* Nice little traditional restaurant that makes the most of local produce.

The future of the city of Caen was bound to that of England when Duke William conquered that powerful country facing Normandy across the Channel. During the Hundred Years' War, the English occupied and developed the ducal city. Centuries later, on 6 June 1944, Caen found itself at the epicentre of a global power struggle with the Normandy Landings, the decisive battle to liberate France and Europe. Today, Caen's message of peace won it honourable mention in 1999 at the UNESCO Cities for Peace Prize.

City of William the Conqueror

The first mention of the name "Caen" was in 1025. Founded in the Roman period, the growing town had been ceded to the Vikings a century before. The Normans were great warriors, and it was one of their greatest, William the Bastard, who in 1066 invaded England, to become William I, the Conqueror.

From the Conquest onwards, ties between Caen and England were close, and it was the English who developed the ducal city, especially under Henry VI, who built what is now one of France's oldest universities.

Caen bloomed in the Renaissance, developing an intense intellectual life. Up to the Age of Enlightenment Caen's citizens lived in peace and prosperity, shaping their city. During the 19th century industrial age, rail linked Caen to Paris. With the canal running from the city to the sea, its trading port developed internationally.

Normandy Landings

On 6 June 1944, Caen was the theatre of the decisive battle of World War II.

Highlights

1 Contemplating **St-Pierre**'s church (p256)

2 Admiring paintings at Caen's **Musée de Beaux-Arts** (p263)

3 D-Day memories at **American Military Cemetery** (p283)

4 Reliving history with the. **Bayeux Tapestry** (p288)

5 Visiting an 18C **Garden of Surprises** (p297)

Three million soldiers engaged in the titanic conflict, with Allies landing at five Normandy beaches – code-named Sword, Utah, Gold, Omaha and Juno – and parachuting behind enemy lines. A year later the war was over, but the Allied bombings meant Caen had to rebuild itself almost entirely. In so doing it created the Memorial Museum, a commitment to peace, solidarity and defence of human rights. It is this message that Caen seeks to convey to the world today as a City of Peace.

Le Mémorial, Caen

© Loïc Durand/Calvados Attractivité

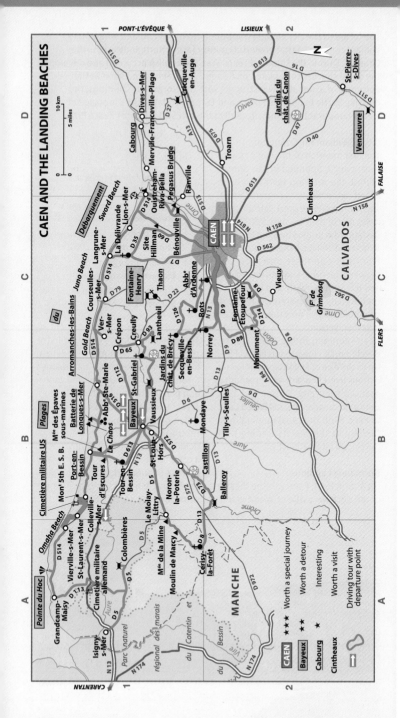

CAEN AND THE LANDING BEACHES

Caen★★★

Caen is the capital of Calvados and the cultural heart of the Basse-Normandie, a lively city with a distinctive identity. The bombs that fell here in 1944 could have left Caen lifeless, but the city proved resilient and drew on the strength of its history to rebuild and recreate. Today Caen is a charming place to visit. It has a modern spirit and a well-regarded university, founded in the 15C and now with almost 25 000 students.

A BIT OF HISTORY

William and Matilda

The city achieved importance in the 11C when it became Duke William's favourite place of residence.

After establishing himself as Duke of Normandy, William asked for the hand of Matilda of Flanders, a distant cousin. She replied that she would rather take the veil than be given in marriage to the bastard son of the beautiful Arlette.

One fine day, mad with love and anger, the duke rode headlong to Lille and burst into the palace of the Count of Flanders. According to the Chronicler of Tours, he seized Matilda by her plaits and dragged her round the room, kicking her as he did so. Then he left her gasping for breath and galloped off. Matilda admitted defeat and consented to the marriage. The Pope, however, objected to the cousins' distant kinship. In 1059, through the efforts of **Lanfranc**, the Pope relented.

As an act of penitence the duke and his wife founded two abbeys – the Abbey for Men (Abbaye-aux-Hommes) and the Abbey for Women (Abbaye-aux-Dames). Bayeux remained the episcopal See. When William departed to conquer England, faithful Matilda became regent of the duchy; in 1068 she was crowned queen of England. She was buried in the Abbey for Women in 1083.

William died in 1087 and was buried in the church of the Abbey for Men.

▶ **Population:** 105 403.
〇 **Michelin Map:** 303: J-4.
▢ **Info:** 12 place St-Pierre. ℘02 31 27 14 14. www.caenlamer-tourisme.fr.
◖ **Location:** At the junction of the rivers Orne and Odon, Caen can be reached by the A 13, some 2.5h, or 235km/146mi from Paris.
◉ **Don't Miss:** The Mémorial, the Abbaye-aux-Hommes and the Fine Arts Museum (Musée des Beaux-Arts) housed in the château.
◔ **Timing:** You need at least 2h to visit the Mémorial.
▲▲ **Kids:** There is an amusement park called Festyland nearby. ◖See p271.

WALKING TOUR

Hôtel d'Escoville★

pl. Saint-Pierre.

This mansion, which now houses the tourist office and the Artothèque, was built between 1533 and 1538 by Nicolas Le Valois d'Escoville, a wealthy merchant. The bomb damage incurred in 1944 has been repaired. Behind the plain street façade there is a **courtyard** flanked by two wings at right angles; the harmonious proportions, the arrangement of the various elements and the majestic sculptures make an elegant composition.

The main block facing the entrance is surmounted by an unusual ornament: a large two-storey dormer window supported by flying buttresses projecting from a steep pavilion roof. Climb up to the loggia for a view of the whole courtyard.

◖ Opposite the Hôtel d'Escoville stands the impressive Église St-Pierre.

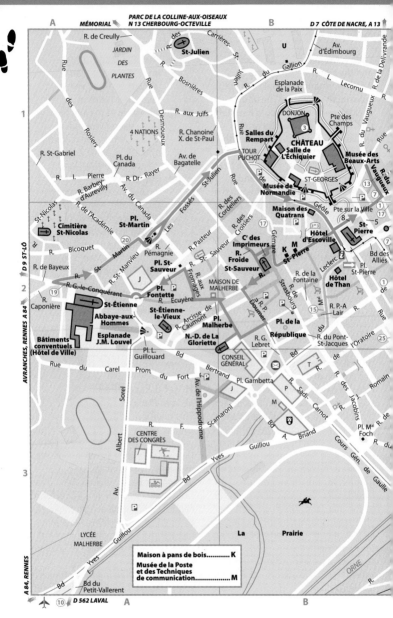

Église St-Pierre★

Although only a parish church, St Peter's is richly decorated. Construction started in the 13C, was continued during the 14C and 15C and completed in the 16C in the Renaissance style. The impressive tower (78m), which dated from 1308, was destroyed during the Battle of Caen in 1944. "The king of Norman belfries" has, however, been rebuilt, as well as the nave into which it fell (all the vaulting has been redone). The west front has been restored to its 14C appearance; the Flamboyant porch is surmounted by a rose window.

The **east end★★**, built between 1518 and 1545, is remarkable for the richness of its Renaissance décor, in which the

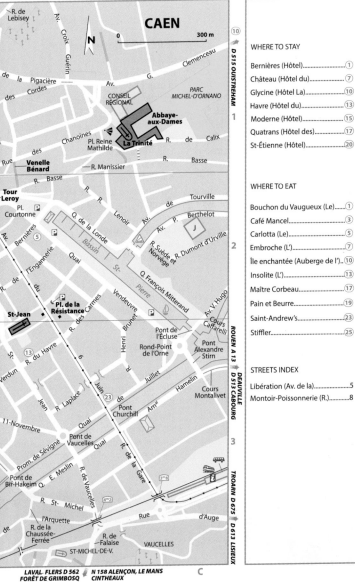

CAEN

0   300 m

shapely and graceful furnishings (ornate pinnacles, urns, richly scrolled balustrades, carved pilasters), have replaced the Gothic motifs.

Some of the **capitals**★ are interesting for their carvings, which are taken from the bestiaries of the period and chivalrous exploits.

The third pillar shows Aristotle on horseback threatened with a whip by Campaspe, Alexander the Great's mistress; the Phoenix rising from the flames (Resurrection); Samson breaking the lion's jaw (Redemption); the Pelican in her Piety (Divine Love); Lancelot crossing the Sword Bridge to rescue his Queen; Virgil suspended in his basket by the daughter of the Roman emperor; the Unicorn (Incarnation), pursued by hunters; Gawain on his deathbed with an arrow wound *(image is damaged)*.

The Renaissance vaulting in the second part of the nave, near the chancel, contrasts with the vaulting in the first part: each arch is embellished with a hanging keystone, finely carved. The most remarkable keystone, in the fifth arch over the high altar, is 3m high and weighs 3t; it is a larger than life-size figure of St Peter.

The chancel is enclosed by four arches (late 15C–early 16C) surmounted by a **frieze★★** in the Flamboyant Gothic style with a delicate decoration of flowers and foliage.

The Gothic style prevails up to 2.75m from the ground but above that level the Renaissance influence increases to predominate in the **vaulting★★** by Hector Sohier. The vaulting in each chapel is highly ornate; the pendants look like stalactites.

▶ At the church entrance, turn left onto rue St-Pierre.

Rue St-Pierre

This is a lively shopping street. Nos. **52** (Postal Museum) and **54**, beautiful **half-timbered houses★** with steep gables, are early 16C; very few have survived in Caen. The profusion of carved decoration and the numerous small statues of saints are in the Gothic style, but there are some Renaissance elements.

Cour des Imprimeurs

Place Pierre-Bouchard.

These early 16C houses used to be home to major printing presses that were in operation here until the early 20C. Take a look at the Flamboyant Gothic windows; their decoration combines vine leaves with curly cabbage leaves.

Rue Froide

In the shadow of St-Saviour's church, this very discreet little street still has interesting houses from the 15C to 19C.

Église St-Sauveur

Also known by its old name of Notre-Dame-de-Froide-Rue, St Saviour's church has twin chevets facing rue St-Pierre: Gothic (15C) on the left and Renaissance (1546) on the right. Rue Froide contains interesting old houses, dating from the 15C to the 19C.

▶ Turn left on rue Paul-Doumer.

Place de la République

The pedestrian precinct, between place St-Pierre and place de la République, is lively both day and night. Place de la République, which is laid out as a public garden, is bordered by beautiful Louis XIII houses (Hôtel Daumesnil at Nos.

Gargoyles, Église St-Pierre

© Loïc Durand/Calvados Attractivité

Caen, June–July 1944

© R. Delassalle/Collection A. de Valroger/Michelin

Battle of Caen

Two Agonising Months – The battle lasted for over two months. On 6 June 1944 there was a heavy bombing raid; fire raged for 11 days and the central area was burnt out. On 9 July the Canadians, who had taken Carpiquet Airfield, entered Caen from the west, but the Germans, who had fallen back to the east bank of the Orne in Vaucelles, began to shell the town. The liberation ceremony took place in Vaucelles on 20 July, but German shelling lasted another month.

Under the Conqueror's Protection – On 6 June many people sought shelter in St-Étienne Church. During the battle, more than 1 500 refugees camped out in the abbey church. An operating theatre was contrived in the refectory of the Lycée Malherbe, which was housed in the monastery buildings of the Abbey for Men. The dead were buried in the courtyard. Some 4 000 people found accommodation on the Hospice of the Good Saviour (Bon Sauveur) nearby. The Allies were warned of this by the Préfet and the Resistance and these buildings were spared. The quarries at Fleury, 2km/1mi south of Caen, provided the largest refuge. Despite the cold and the damp, whole families lived there until the end of July.

23–25) and the modern offices of the Préfecture.

▷ Turn into rue Jean-Eudes, and continue to rue St-Laurent.

Notre-Dame-de-la-Gloriette, a former Jesuit church standing on rue St-Laurent, was built between 1684 and 1689.

▷ Take rue St-Laurent, and head up to place Malherbe.

Place Malherbe

This square is named after a beautiful restored house where the poet Malherbe is said to have been born in 1555. Heading up toward St-Etienne, la rue Écuyère (*at No. 9, pretty Renaissance façade*) then, to the right, little rue aux Fromages (*pedestrian*), with half-timbered houses on either side, leads to place St-Sauveur.

Place St-Sauveur

A fine collection of 18C houses borders the square, where the pillory stood until the 19C. At the centre is a statue of Louis XIV as a Roman emperor. The northeast side of the square is the site of the old St Saviour's, which was destroyed in 1944.

▷ Turn left and continue to a traffic circle. Follow rue Guillaume-le-Conquérant, which takes you to the

Abbaye-aux-Hommes and the Église St-Étienne (*described below*).
To continue the walk, turn right on rue Jean-Marot.

On your way, note the row of attractive houses in rue Jean-Marot; they date from the early 20C.

▶ Turn left on rue St-Martin.

Place St-Martin

Note the statue of Constable Bertrand du Guesclin. There is an interesting view of the two towers of St-Étienne.

▶ Continue NE along the Fossés St-Julien and turn right onto rue de Géôle.

The 15C half-timbered house (No. 31) is called **Maison des Quatrans**.

Rue du Vaugueux

Rue Montoir-Poissonnerie leads to this lovely pedestrian street, which has kept its quaint charm: cobblestones, stone and timber houses, old-fashioned street lights.

▶ Return to place St-Pierre.

ABBAYE-AUX-HOMMES★★

100 Rue de l'Ancienne Mairie.
🕐*Apr–Jun and and Sept Mon–Thu 8am–6pm, Fri 8am–5pm, Sat–Sun and public holidays 9.30am–1pm, 2–6pm; Jul–Aug Mon–Fri 8am–6.30pm, Sat–Sun and public holidays 9.30am–6.30pm; Oct–Mar Mon–Thu 8am–6pm, Fri 8am–5pm, Sat 9am–1pm, 2–5.30pm, Sun during holidays 9.30am–1pm, 2–6pm.* 🕐*1 Jan, 1 May and 25 Dec.* 👓€3. 📞*02 31 30 42 81.*
Despite their different styles, St-Étienne church and the monastery buildings of the Abbey for Men constitute an historical and architectural unit.

Église St-Étienne★★

This is the church of the abbey founded by William the Conqueror; Lanfranc was the first abbot, before being appointed Archbishop of Canterbury and it was probably he who drew up the plans. The church was started in 1066 in the Romanesque style, and was completed in the 13C in Gothic style (east end, choir, spires). The building was damaged during the Wars of Religion in the 16C and painstakingly restored in the early 17C by Dom Jehan de Baillehache, the Prior. Following the Maurist reforms of the Benedictine order (1663) the abbey enjoyed a period of prosperity until the French Revolution: the church was richly furnished and the monastery was rebuilt. In the 19C St-Étienne became a parish church and the monastery was converted for use as a school. Fortunately, the buildings survived the Battle of Caen unscathed.

Romanesque art has produced few more striking compositions than this plain **west front**; there are no ornate porches, no rose windows, only a gable end resting on four sturdy buttresses and pierced by two rows of round-headed windows and three Romanesque doors. Lanfranc seems to have exercised the artistic severity of Ravenna and Lombardy in his native country. The austerity of the west front is, however, tempered by the magnificent soaring towers (11C). The first storey is decorated with fluting, the second with single pierced bays and the third with paired bays. The octagonal spires with their turrets and lancets in the Norman Gothic style were added to the two towers in the 13C; the north tower is finer and more delicate in style.

The vast nave is almost bare of ornament except for the great round-headed arches. The construction of the sexpartite vaulting in the 12C altered the arrangement of the clerestory, which is decorated with fretwork typical of the Norman style. At the west end of the church is the organ (1747) flanked by two telamones, i.e. supports sculpted in the form of a man.

The lantern tower above the transept crossing was constructed in the 11C but rebuilt early in the 17C. The gallery in the north transept houses a large 18C clock in a carved wooden surround. In the 13C the Romanesque chancel was replaced by a Gothic construction, including an ambulatory and radiating chapel; it was the first of the Norman Gothic chancels and subsequently served as a model. With the Gothic style, new decorative motifs were introduced: chevrons on the archivolts, rose windows in the spandrels of the lateral arches, trefoils piercing the tympana of the bays in the galleries, capitals ornamented with crochets and foliage. Note the spacious galleries above the ambulatory and the elegant central arches. The handsome stalls and pulpit are 17C.

In front of the altar is a stone inscribed with an epitaph. The sarcophagus containing the body of William the Conqueror was originally placed beneath the lantern but when the church was sacked by the Huguenots in the 16C, the Conqueror's remains were scattered; all that remains is a femur, which is interred beneath the stone. A monumental 18C paschal candlestick stands on the north side of the altar. The chancel is enclosed by a beautiful 19C wrought-iron screen; the cartouches bear the names and arms of the former abbots, priors and other dignitaries of the abbey.

In the sacristy there hangs an unusual portrait of William the Conqueror, painted in 1708, in which he is made to resemble Henry VIII.

◗ Leave the church by the chancel door and skirt the handsome *east end*★★ of St-Étienne (13C–14C) to reach the gardens in esplanade Louvel, which have been restored to 18C plans.

Monastery Buildings★

These fine buildings were designed early in the 18C by Brother Guillaume de la Tremblaye, the great master builder of the Congregation of St Maur; the **woodwork**★★ is particularly beautiful. The east wing comprises the monks' **warming room**, now a municipal exhibition hall; the **chapter house**, formerly a collegiate chapel and now a registry office, is panelled in light oak and hung with 17C paintings; the chapel **sacristy**, panelled in oak, contains a painting by

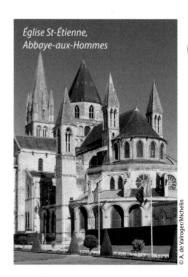

Église St-Étienne, Abbaye-aux-Hommes

© A. de Valroger/Michelin

Charles Lebrun (1619–90) *(Moses Confronting an Egyptian Shepherd)* and a collection of Norman headdresses.

The hall, which features 18C stairs with a wrought-iron banister, leads to the **cloisters** (18C), where the groined vaulting centres on octagonal coffers. From the southeast corner of the cloisters there is a very fine **view**★★ of the towers of St-Étienne and the south side of the church. Fixed to the door into the church is a dark oak timetable of the offices said by the monks (1744).

A doorway leads into the **parlour**, a large oval room with an unusual elliptical vault and beautiful Louis XV wooden doors. The **refectory**, now used for meetings, is sumptuously decorated with late 18C oak panelling and broken barrel vaulting. Some of the paintings above the door and the blind apertures are by Lépicié, Restout and Ruysdael. The wrought-iron banister of the **grand staircase** is decorated with floral motifs. The bold design has no central support. The remarkable Gothic hall in the courtyard, known as the **guard room**★, was built on the remains of a Gallo-Roman structure and is now used for meetings. The panelled ceiling is shaped like an upturned hull. Originally there were two rooms, as the two chimneys suggest.

View of the Abbey★★

Walk through the gardens in esplanade Louvel to reach the east side of place Louis-Guillouard near Old St-Étienne Church (Vieux St-Étienne), an attractive ruin, with the Jesuit church of Notre-Dame-de-la-Gloriette in the background. This is the best view of the 18C monastery buildings flanking the impressive east end of St-Étienne with its bristling bell turrets, flying buttresses, clustering chapels and steep roofs, topped by the lantern tower and the two soaring spires.

ABBAYE-AUX-DAMES★

pl. Reine-Mathilde.
Guided tours daily 2.30pm and 4pm. 1 Jan, 1 May, 25 Dec. No charge. 02 31 06 98 98. http://caen.fr/adresse/abbaye-aux-dames.

Founded in 1062 by **Queen Matilda**, the Abbey for Women is the sister house to the Abbey for Men. It is located on the northeast side of the old city, about 2km/1mi from the Abbaye-aux-Hommes. From place de la Reine-Mathilde, the towers of St-Étienne Church can just be seen at the end of rue des Chanoines.

Église de la Trinité★★

The old abbey church, which dates from the 11C, is a building in the Romanesque style. Its original plan was inspired by that of Benedictine abbeys, characterised by sturdy tiered apsidioles. The spires were replaced early in the 18C by heavy balustrades. The vast nave of nine bays is a fine example of Romanesque art. Broken barrel vaulting marks the transition from the nave into the spacious transept. Adjoining the south transept is an attractive chapel, which is now used as the chapter house. It was built in the 13C, replacing two Romanesque chapels similar to the two in the north transept. The late 11C groined vaulting in the chancel covers a magnificent span. In the centre of the chancel is Queen Matilda's tomb, a simple monument consisting of a single slab of black marble, which has survived unscathed despite the

Wars of Religion and the Revolution. The crypt *(access by steps in the chapel in the south transept)* is well preserved. The groined vaulting rests on 16 columns, standing close together, which define five bays. An attempt at historiated decoration can be seen on one of the capitals, illustrating the Last Judgement, in which St Michael is portrayed gathering up the dead as they rise from their graves.

Conventual Buildings

Daily 2–5.30pm. Guided tours daily 2.30pm and 4pm. 1 Jan, 1 May, 25 Dec. No charge. 02 31 06 98 98.

From the French-style garden in the main **courtyard** one can admire the luminous golden façades. The cloisters (only three sides were completed) are a replica of the one in the Abbey for Men. Leading off them is a small oval room, the washroom *(lavabo)*, decorated with stone pilasters and a carved frieze like those in Greek temples; it is furnished with four black-marble basins set in recesses ornamented with a shell. In the **refectory** *(used as a reception room or as a gallery for temporary exhibitions)*, pilasters with Ionic capitals and two columns which flanked the abbess' chair have survived, whereas the oak panelling which covered the lower walls has been removed.

The **Great Hall**, which is the focal point of the whole abbey and leads into the church, is graced by **two flights** of stairs decorated at first-floor level with a cartouche bearing a plant motif; the walls are adorned with portraits of the two last abbesses, Anne de Montmorency and Marie-Aimée de Pontécoulant.

CHÂTEAU★

Sept–Jun Tue–Sun Mon–Fri 9.30am–12.30pm, 1.30–6pm, Sat–Sun and public holidays 11am–6pm; Jul–Aug daily. No charge. 02 31 30 47 60. www.chateau.caen.fr.

The imposing citadel dominating the mount was begun by William the Conqueror in 1060 and fortified in 1123 by his son, Henry Beauclerk, who added a mighty keep (demolished in

Château Ducal de Caen

© Loïc Durand/Calvados Attractivité

1793). During the 13C, 14C and 15C it was repeatedly enlarged and reinforced. Throughout the 19C it was used as soldiers' barracks and was severely damaged in the bombardment of Caen in 1944. Since then its massive walls have been restored to their early grandeur. The line of the ramparts has changed little since the days of William the Conqueror. In some places the walls date from the 12C, but most of them were built in the 15C. The two main gateways are protected by barbicans.

▶ Enter the castle by the ramp which approaches the south gate opposite Église St-Pierre.

After passing a round tower, a defensive outwork, you enter the citadel by the town gate *(porte sur la ville)*. From the terrace *(east)* and the rampart sentry walk there are fine **views★** of Église St-Pierre and western Caen as far as the Abbey for Men. On the west side of the gate, behind the Normandy Museum, a platform provides an interesting **view★** over the southwest sector of the town and the belfries of the many churches. The **north rampart**, the first to be restored under the current programme, can be visited for a remarkable **view★** of Caen.

The **rampart rooms** offer temporary Musée de Normandie exhibitions. Very contemporary, there is an astonishing view here of the rampart and walkway. The castle precinct encloses the modern **Musée des Beaux-Arts** *(east)* near the **Porte des Champs** (Field Gate), an interesting example of 14C military architecture; the **Chapelle St-Georges**, a 12C chapel which was altered in the 15C; the **Musée de Normandie** *(west)* in a building that was the residence of the bailiff in the 14C and of the governor of Caen in the 17C and 18C; a rectangular building, incorrectly called the **Salle de l'Échiquier** (Exchequer Hall), which is a rare example of Norman civil architecture in the reign of Henry Beauclerk and was the great hall of the adjoining ducal palace (foundations only visible); adjoining it was the Normandy Exchequer (the Ducal Law Court). Further north lie the foundations of the keep, which was built by Henry Beauclerk and altered in the 13C and 14C; it was a huge square structure, a round tower at each corner, surrounded by a moat which was joined to the castle moat. ▶*You can stroll in the castle moat; descend from the porte des Champs.*

Musée des Beaux-Arts★★

Located within the château.
&. ⏱*Tue–Fri 9.30am–12.30pm, 1.30–6pm, Sat–Sun 11am–6pm (Jul–*

Musée des Beaux-Arts de Caen

© L. Sangor/Musée des Beaux-Arts de Caen

Aug daily). 🕐*1 Jan, Easter Sunday, 1 May, Ascension Day, 1 Nov, 25 Dec.* 🎟*€3.50–€5.50 depending on exhibition; no charge 1st Sun of month.* 📞*02 31 30 47 70. http://mba.caen.fr.* 🍴*The Café Mancel offers a pleasant break inside the museum, where you can enjoy a meal or a drink.*

Situated within the precinct of William the Conqueror's castle, the Fine Arts Museum displays its collections from a chronological, thematic and geographical point of view. Large religious paintings and imposing historical and allegorical scenes hang in vast halls, bathed in light, whereas works of religious fervour and smaller paintings are displayed in the small cabinets. The large galleries display landscapes, battle scenes and portraits.

The first three rooms on the ground floor are devoted to 15C, 16C and 17C Italian paintings: the *Marriage of the Virgin* by Perugino, with a remarkable new frame, a triptych representing the *Virgin and Child Between St George and St James* by Cima da Conegliano; in a room entirely devoted to Veronese, two paintings are of particular interest: the *Temptation of St Anthony* and *Judith and Holofernes*; also worth noting are *Coriolanus Implored by His Mother* by Il Guercino and *Glaucus and Scylla* by Rosa Salvatore.

The next room deals with 17C French paintings with outstanding works by Philippe de Champaigne *(Louis XIII's Vow)* and religious and mythological paintings by Vouet, Vignon, La Hyre and Le Brun.

Three intimate rooms are devoted to Dutch and Flemish 17C paintings with works such as *A Seascape* by Solomon van Ruysdael, *Virgin and Child* by Roger van der Weyden and *Abraham and Melchizedek* by Rubens.

In the gallery devoted to the 18C are displayed works by French and Italian portrait and landscape painters: Hyacinthe Rigaud *(Portrait of Marie Cadenne)*, François Boucher *(Young Shepherd in a Landscape)*, Locatelli, Lalemand, Tournières. On the lower level, the various aspects and the evolution of painting during the 19C and the early 20C are depicted through works by Romantic painters (Géricault, Delacroix, Isabey), Realists (Courbet: *The Lady with the Jewels*; Ribot), landscape painters (Corot, Dupré), Impressionists (Vuillard: *Portrait of Suzanne Desprez*; Bonnard, Dufy, Van Dongen: *Portrait of Madame T Raulet*), and Cubist painters (Gleizes, Villon, Meitzinger). Local artists are also represented: Cals, Fouace, Gernez, Lemaître, Lépine, Lebourg, Rame. Innovations by contemporary painters such as Tobey *(Appearances)*, Mitchell *(Fields, 1990)*, Soulages, Dubuffet

(*Migration*), Vieira da Silva, Szenez, Asse and Deschamps illustrate the different post-war trends: Conceptual art, Abstract landscape, Abstract art, Environmental art. From one end to the other, the museum thus presents an impressive chronology of the history of painting.

Musée de Normandie★

Located within the château.
⊙*Jul–Aug Mon–Fri 9.30am–12.30pm, 1.30–6pm, Sat–Sun 11am–6pm; rest of year Tue–Sun.* ⊛*€3.50, no charge ist weekend of month.* ⊙*1 Jan, Easter Sunday, 1 May, Ascension Day, 1 Nov and 25 Dec.* ℘*02 31 30 47 60.*
http://musee-de-normandie.caen.fr.

The history and traditions of Normandy are illustrated by the presentation of the many archaeological and ethnographical exhibits.

The first section is devoted to the prehistoric period up to the arrival of the Vikings in 911 and concentrates on the culture and technology of the era: excavated artefacts, miniature replica of the burial mound at Fontenay-le-Marmion, statue of a mother goddess found at St-Aubin-sur-Mer, weapons and jewellery found in medieval cemeteries (tomb of a metalworker).

The second section follows the evolution of agriculture: land use (models comparing different types of cultivation and farms), agricultural techniques (display of ploughs, scythes and millstones). The third section is devoted to crafts and industrial activities: stock breeding, ceramics (jugs, funerary ornaments and decorative ridge tiles), wood (beautifully carved marriage chests), metallurgy (iron and copper work: craftsmen's tools, copperware from Villedieu-les-Poêles), textiles (costumes, headdresses and bridal-ware in silk lace). The last room concentrates on the work of the candlemaker (interesting collection of candles for Easter, funerals and as votive offerings) as well as ceremonial articles belonging to the different brotherhoods (gold thread embroidery and tintenelles, the tiny hand bells used in processions by the Brothers of Charity).

ADDITIONAL SIGHTS

St-Nicolas Cemetery★

Rue Saint-Nicolas.
⊙*Daily Mar–Oct 8am–6pm; Nov–Feb 8am–5pm.*

St Nicholas' church (deconsecrated) was built late in the 11C by the monks of the Abbey for Men and has not been altered since. The west door is protected by a beautiful triple-arched Romanesque porch, an exceptional feature in Normandy.

The church is surrounded by an old graveyard (entrance left of the west front); one may stroll among the mossy tombstones under the shade of the trees and admire the magnificent apse at the east end beneath a steep stone roof.

Église St-Jean

Place St-Ouen.
The fine Flamboyant Gothic building was begun in the 14C, and repaired in the 15C. The belltower, of which the base and first storey are 14C, was inspired by the tower of St Peter but, owing to the instability of the marshy ground, the spire and the belfry were never built, nor was the central tower; the lower courses of its second storey were capped with a dome.

The vast nave has a remarkable Flamboyant triforium and a highly ornate cylindrical **lantern tower★** over the transept crossing. The highly venerated statue of Our Lady of Protection dates from the 17C. In the south transept there is an old retable (17C) from the Carmes Convent depicting the Annunciation and bearing statues of St Joseph and St Teresa of Ávila. In 1964 a statue of Joan of Arc was transferred from Oran to a site near the east end of the church in place de la Résistance.

Église St-Julien

1 r. Malfilâtre.
The old church, which was destroyed in 1944, was replaced in 1958 by this modern building. The sanctuary wall, elliptical in shape, forms a huge piece of latticework like that of a stained-glass window.

Port of Caen

Although the River Orne has always enabled Caen to serve as a port, no major development took place until the middle of the 19C, when Baron Cachin dug a canal parallel to the river. The canal (12km/7.4mi long) was regulated by several locks and served by an outer basin at Ouistreham. Since then the increased output of the Caen steelworks has required the deepening and widening of the canal and the creation of five more docks: St-Pierre for pleasure boats, the New Dock, the Calix Dock, the Hérouville Dock and the Blainville Dock, which came into use in 1974. Today the transportation of cereals is the chief function of Caen harbour, the largest one in Basse-Normandie, which can receive ships of up to 19 000t fully laden and up to 30 000t partially laden. Because of its broad range of activities, this port is ranked 11th in France. The opening of a cross-Channel car ferry service on 6 June 1986 has established daily links between Caen-Ouistreham and Portsmouth, catering to an estimated one million passengers every year.

Le Mémorial★★

espl. Général-Eisenhower.
♿ ✗ ⏰*Apr–Sept daily 9am–7pm; Feb–Mar 9am–6pm; Oct–Dec 9.30am–6pm; Jan check website for details* ⏰*25 Dec.* 👁*€19.80.* ✆*02 31 06 06 44. www.memorial-caen.fr.*

The memorial erected by the city, which in 1944 was at the centre of the Battle of Normandy, takes the form of a Museum for Peace; it is primarily a place of commemoration and of permanent meditation on the links between human rights and the maintenance of peace. As such it is one of the mosts important contemporary history sights in Europe.

The façade of the sober building of Caen stone, facing esplanade Dwight-Eisenhower, is marked by a fissure that evokes the destruction of the city and the breakthrough of the Allies in the Liberation of France and Europe from the Nazi yoke. It stands on the site of the bunker of W Richter, the German general, who on 6 June faced the British-Canadian forces.

The main events of World War II, the causes and the issues at stake, are presented in the light of the latest historical analysis. A particularly imaginative display on such themes as the inter-war years and the advance of Fascism centres on a spiral ramp. This, together with the use of extensive archive material, including a gripping panoramic projection of D-Day, seen simultaneously from the Allied and the German stand-

points, as well as moving testimonies by witnesses of and participants in the drama, confers on this presentation of the recent past the authenticity of living experience.

The **Jardins du Souvenir** are dedicated to the memory those resistance fighters and allied forced killed in Normandy.

Parc floral de la Colline-aux-Oiseaux

Avenue Amiral Mountbatten.
⏰*Daily from 10am: closing time depends on the season: Apr–Aug 8pm, Mar and Sept–Oct 6.30pm; Nov–Feb 5.30pm.* 👁*No charge.* ✆*02 31 30 48 38.*
Lying northwest of Caen, not far from the Memorial, this park (17ha) created in 1994 for the 50th anniversary of the Landings, is actually on a former rubbish tip – hence the name, "Bird Hill". There are themed gardens and a beautiful rose garden.

Jardin des plantes

Place Blot.
⏰*Mon–Fri open at 8am, Sat–Sun and public holidays 10am. Close Apr–Aug at 8pm, Mar and Sept–Oct 6.30pm, Nov–Feb at 5.30pm.* ⏰*1 Jan, 25 Dec.* ✆*02 31 30 48 38.*
A botanical garden and a garden for botanical research, both in the same place, bring together specialised plant collections. The botanical garden for research goes back to the 17C; in particular it includes a tropical hothouse

with South American giant waterlily flowers.

OUISTREHAM-RIVA-BELLA★★

15km/9mi – 15min. Leave Caen NE by the D 515, then the D 514.

Located at the mouth of the Orne and astride the canal from Caen, the combined facilities of the town of Ouistreham and the beach of Riva-Bella make an excellent seaside resort. As the seaport for Caen, the harbour bustles with trawlers, pleasure craft and the cross-Channel ferries plying between Ouistreham and Portsmouth.

Église St-Samson★

Place Lemarignier.

This ancient 12C fortress church was built on the site of a 9C wooden church destroyed by Norsemen. The gabled west front with its three superimposed tiers of blind arcades above the recessed doorway is particularly remarkable. Step back to get a good view of the late 12C belfry supported by buttresses.

In the nave, note the round piers with gadrooned capitals and the lovely clerestory windows.

Port de Plaisance

A large basin on the opposite bank of the canal (Canal de Caen à la Mer) provides berths for many yachts. In season it is a lively and colourful spot.

Plage de Riva-Bella

The beach closest to Caen, this magnificent extent of fine sand invites families from Caen to enjoy the sea as soon as the sun rises.

The resort, which has the French *station nautique* label of certification, authorises all sailing and board sports, on water or sand.There is also a karting track, a horseriding club, a kite-flying club and a miniature golf course.

Lighthouse

Quai Georges-Thierry.

From the top of the lighthouse (30m high, 171 steps) there is a good view of the harbour and marina.

Ouistreham-Riva-Bella

A busy port since medieval times, Ouistreham derives its name from Saxon words meaning "western" *(ouistre)* and "farm" *(ham)*.

The name "Riva Bella", or "beautiful coast" in Italian, derives from the name of the first of many residences constructed in the 19C, when the splendid 5km/3mi beach attracted fashionable visitors.

Musée du Mur de l'Atlantique – Grand Bunker

Av. du 6-Juin, near the tourist office. Apr–Sept daily 9am–7pm; Oct–early Jan 10am–6pm; early Feb–Mar. 1 Jan, 25 Dec. €7.50. 02 31 97 28 69. http://museegrandbunker.com.

This museum, located in a former German range-finding station, overlooks the mouth of the River Orne from a height of 17m; it sent firing instructions to the artillery units in Ouistreham. Rooms are arranged as they were in 1944. In the range-finding room, you can study the horizon with the range-finder over a 180° angle and a distance of 45km/28mi.

Musée du Débarquement "No 4 Commando" - Riva-Bella

Pl. Alfred-Thomas. Apr–early Nov daily 10.30am–1pm, 1.30–6pm. €5. 02 31 96 63 10. www.musee-4commando.fr.

The 4th Anglo-French Commando under Commander Philippe Kieffer reduced the enemy strong points on the morning of 6 June. The museum contains original artefacts from the operation.

SOUTH AND EAST OF CAEN

Cintheaux

15km/9mi. From Caen take N 158 S.

The village, renowned for its late 12C church, stands on the southern edge of the Caen countryside, in an old mining area marked by solitary slag heaps.

The road from Caen to Falaise passes through country laboriously recaptured during the Battle of Normandy between 8 and 17 August 1944 by the Canadian 1st Army (Gaumesnil cemetery) and its Polish units (Langannerie cemetery).

Troarn

14km/8.5mi. Leave Caen going E and then take D 675. In Troarn take rue de l'Abbaye (second turn on the right after the church).

This little town, which was founded in 1048 by Roger de Montgomery, contains the remains of a 13C abbey.

Vieux

18km/11mi – 19min. Leave Caen by the SW on the D 405; take the D 8, then the D 147A on the left and the D 212 on the right.

Today it is difficult to imagine that the peaceful village of Vieux was Aregenua, the former capital of the Viducasses, during the Roman period. The archaeological digs over the past decades have brought to light rich findings, presented in a clear and modern way in the **museum** (&⏰*Mar–Dec Mon–Tue, Thu–Fri 9am–5pm, Sat–Sun 10am–6pm;* ⏰*1 May, 1 and 11 Nov, 24–25 and 31 Dec;* ✆*€5 (under 18, no charge);* 📞*02 31 71 10 20; www.vieuxlaromaine.fr).* The visit continues on the site itself. While difficult to recreate, it nevertheless has some interesting vestiges, including the sumptuous Villa au Grand Péristyle *(follow the signposting on the site).*

Forêt de Grimbosq

19km/11mi. Leave Caen S by the D 562a, then the D 257. 📞*02 31 75 49 50.*

Crisscrossed with little streams, the superb 475ha Grimbosq Forest has belonged to the City of Caen since 1973. Its walking routes, picnic area, animal park (with deer and boar) and arboretum make this the destination for numerous Caen families, as is the charming St Anne's chapel at the edge of the River Orne.

For sports-lovers, there are well-signposted treks (1½ hrs to 3hrs) and a fitness circuit leaving from the St-Laurent-de-Condel car park *(on leaving the village, follow the blue "Parking" sign to right).*

🚗 DRIVING TOURS

🚗 1 NORTH OF CAEN
Round-trip of 31km/19.2mi. Allow 1h.

▶ From Caen take D 7 and at the top of the hill, turn right on D 401, then D 60 to the left.

The road bends to the right and there is a panoramic view of Caen.

Bléville-sur-Orne

The blind arcades and oculi which decorate the west front of the church recall the architecture of Tuscany.

▶ Continue to Périers-sur-le-Dan on D 60, then D 222 to Cresserons, and D 35.

La Délivrande
👆*see p 274.*

▶ Head back down to Caen by the D 7.

Epron

This small locality, which was razed in 1944, has been called the Village of the Radio since 1948.

The origin of the nickname was a radio programme that sought to determine which of France's *départements* had been most severely damaged. Calvados was named, and a lottery draw among ten communes fell to Epron. The village was rebuilt thanks to a collection of small change taken up on its behalf.

🚗 2 CHURCHES AND ABBEYS
35km/21mi. Allow 2h.

▶ From Caen take D 9 west towards Bayeux on rue de Bayeux and then rue du Général-Moulin. Halfway up a hill on the outskirts of the town turn right onto the road to the abbey.

Abbaye d'Ardenne★
&⏰*Tue–Fri 9am–6pm.* 🚶*Guided tour Jul–Sept Mon and Wed 2.30pm and 4pm.* ✆*No charge.* 🅿*Leave the car at*

the main gate (12C). 📞 *02 31 29 37 37.*
www.imec-archives.com.
The abbey, which was founded in the
12C by the Premonstratensians, fell into
ruin during the 19C, but has recently
benefited from a major restoration
project. An exhibit describing its
history can be seen at its sister abbey
of Mondaye. In the first courtyard stands
a huge 13C tithe barn (*back left*) with
aisles covered by a single asymmetrical
wooden roof (🕐*during temporary
exhibitions*). The 13C **abbey church★**
has been damaged on the outside but
the nave is a very pure example of the
Norman Gothic style.
Since 1998, the abbey has housed a
major archive of French publications.
The abbey church is now a research
library.

▷ Drive west to Rots via Authie.

Rots
The **church** here has an attractive
Romanesque west front; the nave dates
from the same period; the chancel is 15C.

▷ Take D 170 north; in Rosel turn left
onto D 126.

Secqueville-en-Bessin
The 11C **church** has a fine three-
storey tower and a 13C spire. The nave
and transept are decorated with blind
arcading.

▷ Take D 93 and D 83 south.

Norrey
The little Gothic **church** has a great
square lantern tower but no spire; the
interior is richly carved; the chancel
was built in the 13C.

▷ Return to Caen by D 9.

�car 3 THE BATTLE OF ODON
37km/23mi. Allow 2h.

The name of this river recalls the
hard-fought battles which took place
between 26 June and 4 August 1944
southwest of Caen.

▷ Leave Caen by the rue de Bayeux,
then take D 9.

The road skirts the airfield which the
12th SS Panzers held for three days,
from 4 to 7 July, against the Canadian
3rd Division.

▷ After another 3km/2mi bear left
on D 170. in Cheux turn left behind
the church onto D 89; after crossing
D 175, at the top of a slight rise, follow
D 89 round to the right and straight
through Tourville.

This is the line of the British advance,
which began on 26 June in pouring rain
at Tilly-sur-Seulles; the objective was the
River Orne to the southeast. A memorial
has been erected to pay tribute to the
men of the 15th Scottish Division who
fell here.
Just when it seems that the road has
reached the floor of the Odon valley
it drops into a rocky ravine, hitherto
hidden by thickets; the river has created
a second valley within the main one. It
is easy to see what a valuable line of
defence this would have been and to
appreciate the difficulties of the British
troops exposed to heavy fire from the
Germans on the far side of the valley. In
fact the British lost more men crossing
the Odon than crossing the Rhine.
The road climbs the opposite slope to a
crossroads. The road on the left (D 214)
passes straight through Baron-sur-Odon
and continues to a T-junction marked
by a stone monument surmounted by
an iron cross *(right)*.
The raised roadway to the right, an old
Roman road also known as Duke William's Way, leads to another T-junction
where a stele has been set up to commemorate the battles fought by the 43rd
Wessex Division. To the south stands **Hill
112** later known as Cornwall Hill.

▷ Take D 8 to the left towards Caen.

A monument at the junction with D 36
recalls the operations that took place
in July and were marked by fierce duels
between armoured vehicles. A night

attack on 15 June took place by the light of an artificial moon created by the reflection of searchlights on low cloud.

▶ Turn left onto D 147A.

Near a farm on the right the Château de Fontaine-Étoupefour comes into view.

Château de Fontaine-Etoupefour

Access by a track on the right beyond the farm.

🔑 *Guided tours Jul–Sept Sun–Wed 2–6pm. ℰ02 31 26 73 20.*

Nicolas d'Escoville, who built the Hôtel d'Escoville in Caen, owned this castle. It is surrounded by a moat spanned by a drawbridge, which leads to an elegant 15C gatehouse bristling with turrets and pinnacles. The dining room is hung with three interesting paintings of hunting scenes. On the far side of the paved courtyard stand the ruins of one of the two main blocks (late 16C), currently undergoing restoration.

The refectory houses an exhibit about the battle of Hill 112 in 1944, of which the château was the centre.

▶ Return to D 8 to reach Caen.

ADDRESSES

🏨 STAY

CAEN

⊖ **Hôtel Bernières** – *50 rue de Bernières. ℰ02 31 86 01 26. www.hotelbernieres. com. 17 rooms.* Friendly hotel, charming breakfast room, lounge.

⊖ **Hôtel du Havre** – *11 rue du Havre. ℰ02 31 86 19 80. www.hotelduhavre.com. 18 rooms.* Near La Prairie and racecourse; post-war hotel with modern, quiet rooms.

⊖ **Hôtel St-Étienne** – *2 rue de l'Académie. ℰ02 31 86 35 82. www. hotelsaintetiennecaen.com. 10 rooms.* Dating from 1789, this house is near Abbaye-aux-Hommes. Some rooms with fireplaces.

⊖⊖ **Hôtel des Quatrans** – *17 rue Gémare. ℰ02 31 86 25 57. www.hotel-des-quatrans.com. 47 rooms.* Central family hotel with colourful, functional rooms. Rear rooms quieter.

⊖⊖ **Hôtel du Château** – *5 av. du 6-Juin. ℰ02 31 86 15 37. www.hotel-chateau-caen.com. 24 rooms.* In the town centre, between marina and château. Rooms small but pleasant.

⊖⊖ **Hôtel-Restaurant la Glycine** – *11 pl. du Commando No. 4, 14970 Bénouville. ℰ02 31 44 61 94. www.la-glycine.com.* 🅿 *35 rooms. Restaurant⊖⊖.* Near Pegasus Bridge; pleasant lodgings.

⊖⊖⊖ **Best Western Hôtel Le Moderne** – *116 bld Mar.-Leclerc. ℰ02 31 86 04 23. www.bestwestern-moderne-caen.com. 40 rooms.* Discreet post-war building. View from breakfast room.

OUISTREHAM-RIVA-BELLA

⊖⊖ **Hôtel de la Plage** – *39–41 avenue Pasteur, 14150 Riva-Bella. ℰ02 31 96 85 16. www.hotel-ouistreham.com. 16 rooms.* 🅿. Early 20C quiet Anglo-Norman villa near the beach.

⊖⊖⊖ **Best Western La Mare Ô Poissons** – *68 Rue Emile Herbline, 14150 Ouistreham. www.lamareopoissons.fr. ℰ02 31 37 53 05. 30 rooms.* 🅿. Just 1.2 miles from the ferry terminal and 4.3 miles from Normandy's famous landing beaches. There is also a **restaurant** (⊖⊖) offering refined regional cuisine.

🍴 EAT

CAEN

⊖ **La Patisserie Stiffler** – *72 r. St-Jean. ℰ02 31 86 08 94. www.stifflertraiteur.fr. Open Tue–Sat 9am–7pm, Sun 9am–1pm.* Magnificent pastry shop with celebrated *charlotte aux fruits de saison.* Also good for inexpensive lunch dishes.

⊖⊖ **Le Bouchon du Vaugueux** – *12 r. Graindorge. ℰ02 31 44 26 26. www. bouchonduvaugueux.com. Closed Sun and Mon. Reservations required.* Popular tavern near château and old Caen.

⊖⊖ **Café Mancel** – *At the Château. ℰ02 31 86 63 64. www.cafemancel.com. Closed Sun evening and all day Mon.* This café and shop has high-quality local produce and also goods from Italy, Flanders, Holland and the UK.

⊖⊖ **Le Carlotta** – *16 quai Vendeuvre. ℰ02 31 86 68 99. http://lecarlotta.fr. Closed Sun.* Art Deco-inspired brasserie; meats, wide range of seafood.

😑🍽 **L'Embroche** – *17 r. Porte-au-Berger.* 𝒫*02 31 93 71 31. Closed Sat lunch, Mon lunch and Sun. Reservations advised.* Regional specialities include camembert with Calvados, steak with a caramelised balsamic sauce, and tripes Père Michel.

😑🍽 **L'Insolite** – *16 r. du Vaugueux at foot of château.* 𝒫*02 31 43 83 87. www.restaurantlinsolite.com. Closed Sun–Mon except May–Sept. Reservations advised.* Half-timbered 16C house with unconventional interior, rustic and retro.

😑🍽 **Saint-Andrew's** – *9 quai de Juillet.* 𝒫*02 31 86 26 80. http://restaurant. st.andrew.free.fr. Closed all day Sun, Sat munch and Wed dinner.* Good place to eat after a stroll along the Orne. Recalls an English pub, traditional menu.

😑🍽–😑🍽 **Restaurant les petites bouches** – *46 r. Guillaume-le-Conquérant.* 𝒫*09 83 30 45 30.* Near the Mairie and the Abbaye-aux-Hommes. Fine cuisine: authentic and exotic.

😑🍽–😑🍽 **Auberge de l'Île Enchantée** – *1 rue St-André, 14123 Fleury-sur-Orne.* 𝒫*02 31 52 15 52. www. ileenchantee.fr. Closed Mon–Tue and Sun dinner.* Riverside; warm welcome, gourmet French cuisine.

OUISTREHAM-RIVA-BELLA

😑🍽 **Le Normandie** – *71 av. Michel-Cabieu.* 𝒫*02 31 97 19 57. www.lenormandie.com. Also has 22* **rooms** 😑🍽. Old Norman house on the port; brightly coloured, well-lit dining room, and an elegant veranda.

😑🍽 **Villa Andry** – *51 avenue Andry.* 𝒫*02 31 97 18 79. Closed Sun eve, Mon noon. Also has 18 rooms* 😑🍽. Seafood specialities. Two dining rooms: modern, with large picture windows with panoramic coastal view; traditional with wood ceiling, fireplace.

NIGHTLIFE

Caen is a highly convivial and lively town. In the evening, tour the small pubs and restaurants in the Vaugueux district.

Centre dramatique national de Normandie (Comédie de Caen) – *32 rue des Cordes.* 𝒫*02 31 93 83 78.* Classical, contemporary theatre; two halls: 300 and 700 seats.

Théâtre de Caen – *135, boulevard Maréchal Leclerc.* 𝒫*02 31 30 48 00. www.theatre.caen.fr.* Opera, ballet and

Market, Caen

© Arnaud Guérin/Calvados Attractivité

contemporary dance; theatre, classical concerts, jazz sessions and traditional music.

SHOPPING

Librairie générale du Calvados – *98 rue St-Pierre, Caen.* 𝒫*02 31 85 43 13. www. librairie-guillaume.fr. Open Mon–Sat 9.30am–7pm.* 1902 carved-wood façade. Books on the region and first-rate antique books upstairs.

Charcuterie Poupinet – *8 rue St-Jean, Caen. Open Mon–Sat 9am–noon, 2–6pm.* To taste authentic *tripes à la mode de Caen*, you must visit Poupinet. Regional specialities: pâtés, terrines, country-style blood puddings, pork ears in jelly, etc.

Markets – Marché St-Pierre *(Sun am)*, rue de Bayeux *(Tue am)*, boulevard Leroy *(Wed am, Sat am)*, boulevard de la Guérinière *(Thu am)*, Marché St-Sauveur *(Fri am)*, Christmas Market *(Dec)*.

LEISURE

Caen Racecourse – *Boulevard Yves Guil-lou.* 𝒫*02 31 27 50 80. www.hippodrome-caen.com. Closed Jul–Aug.* Racecourse nearly 2km/1mi long, in central Caen. Panoramic view from restaurant (2nd floor). Tours on race mornings (30 times a year). Don't miss it.

👪 **Festyland** – *rte de Caumont.* 𝒫*02 31 75 04 04. www.festyland.com. Open Jul–Aug 10am–6.30pm, but check website for other months.* €*21 (child undere 12, €18).* Typical fairground rides, including attractions: *Le Grand Tournoi, Le 1066, Le Carrousel de Jules, Le Valhala, Le Pont de Cordes*, etc. Great for kids.

Plages du Débarquement★★

Normandy Landing Beaches

The choice of Normandy as the landing point for the invasion of Europe was not evident. Defended by the Atlantic Wall, the coast had choppy water and tricky tides. Italy seemed a more likely option, but the invasion, begun in July 1943, proved slow and costly. At the Teheran Conference in late 1943, Churchill, Roosevelt and Stalin agreed on a French front. Men and arms were massed in Britain and intense bombing raids over Germany and France were intended to soften defences. The tour described in this section includes that part of the Calvados coast between the mouths of the Orne and the Vire, also known as the Côte de Nacre, where the D-Day landings took place on 6 June 1944. The marked itineraries, known as Overlord – L'Assaut (Overlord – The Onslaught) and D-Day – Le Choc (D-Day – The Impact), are two of several such itineraries in the Historical Area of the Battle of Normandy.

- **Michelin Map:** F3-K4.
- **Info:** Port-en-Bessin: ℘02 31 22 45 80. Longues-sur-Mer: ℘02 31 21 46 87.
- **Location:** This section covers the Calvados coast between the mouths of the Orne and the Vire, also known as the Côte de Nacre (Mother-of-Pearl coast) where the Normandy landings took place on D-Day, 6 June 1944.
- **Timing:** Each of the circuits described below takes half a day.

A BIT OF HISTORY
Operation Overlord

The Normandy Landings, or D-Day, for which the code name during preparations for this massive Allied invasion was Operation Overlord, were commanded by US General Dwight D Eisenhower, with British General (later Field Marshal) Bernard Montgomery

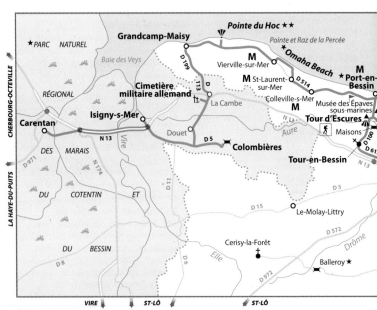

in charge of land forces. Transport involved an armada of 7 000 ships and landing craft, and 12 500 aircraft. Some 156 000 troops landed, supported by 195 000 sailors. Preparations were epic: finally, all depended on the tides, to bring landing craft to shore.

See The D-Day Landings on p275 for a more detailed history of events.

D-Day Landings: A Turning Point

Field Marshal Erwin Rommel, inspecting the Atlantic Wall, pointed out that if the Allies succeeded in breaching it, the Third Reich would fall. Germany fell on 8 May 1945, after a long stuggle, but the end had begun 11 months earlier.

65th Anniversary: 2009

Leaders of France, Great Britain, the USA and Canada met on the beaches of Normandy to mark the June 1944 landings, probably the last commemoration where significant numbers of veterans would be able to take part.

🚗 DRIVING TOURS

🚗 ① SWORD BEACH–JUNO BEACH–GOLD BEACH

71km/44mi. Allow 1h15.

▶ From Caen take D 515 northeast.

The road to Riva-Bella runs down the lower Orne valley west of the ship canal.

Bénouville

The town hall, which stands alone in a fork in the road near Pegasus Bridge, was occupied by the British 5th Parachute Brigade at 11.45pm on 5 June.

The **château**★ (*not open to the public*), one of the major works by the Parisian architect **Claude-Nicolas Ledoux** (1736–1806), is a fine example of French neo-Classical architecture at the end of the 18C.

The interior contains a suite of five rooms and a magnificent **staircase**★★ rising through three landings to the first floor. The château was virtually undamaged in the war.

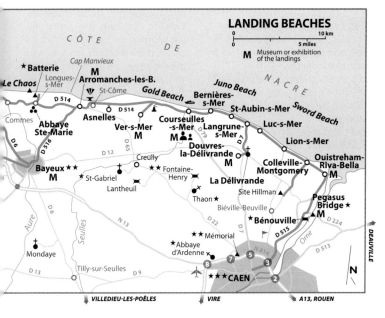

Pegasus Bridge★

The two Ranville-Bénouville bridges were captured soon after midnight during the night of 5–6 June 1944 by the British 5th Parachute Brigade: **Pegasus** was their emblem.

Major Howard had won the Battle of Pegasus – a field where the Horsa and Hamilcar gliders could land, a mobile bridge made of steel, a house at the water's edge... and the Gondrée family, who waited until **Lord Lovat** (1911–95) and his Green Berets arrived, to the strains of Bill Millin's bagpipes (*see panel, p276*).

Mémorial Pegasus★

Av. du Major-Howard, Ranville.
Daily: Apr–Sept 9.30am–6.30pm; Feb–Mar and Oct–Nov 10am–5pm.
€8. 02 31 78 19 44.
https://musee.memorial-pegasus.com.
Near the commemorative stelae stands a museum devoted to life during the Occupation and the Normandy landings.

Ouistreham-Riva-Bella⚓⚓

See CAEN, p255.

From Riva-Bella to Asnelles, the D 514 follows the Mother-of-Pearl coast.

Colleville-Montgomery

At dawn on 6 June, the 4th Anglo-French commandos landed here under the command of Captain Kieffer.

In gratitude, the commune of Colleville-sur-Orne added to its name that of General (later Field Marshal) Bernard Montgomery, the victor of El Alamein and commander of the British forces.

South of the town, going towards Biéville-Beauville, a former coastal defence has been transformed into a **memorial** for the Suffolk Regiment (*Jun–Aug Mon 10am–noon, 2–3.30pm, Tue–Sat 10am–noon. 2.30–6.30pm.* *Guided tours (2h: Jun–Sept) Tue at 3pm; no charge; 02 31 97 12 61; www.amis-du-suffolk-rgt.com*).

Lion-sur-Mer

This seaside resort has a 16C–17C **château**. The **church** has a 11C Romanesque tower and handsome capitals.

Luc-sur-Mer

Luc is a seaside resort known for its bracing air. The spa offers hydro-sodium iodate cures. The beautiful **municipal park★** (*35 r. de la Mer*), is an oasis of greenery.

Langrune-sur-Mer

The name of this resort on the Mother-of-Pearl coast is Scandinavian in origin and means green land, probably due to the abundant seaweed, which fills the air with the smell of iodine. The 13C **church** has a handsome belltower similar to the tower of St-Pierre in Caen.

Take D 7 inland.

La Délivrande

The tall spires of the basilica in La Délivrande, the oldest Marian sanctuary in Normandy, are visible for miles across the Caen countryside and far out to sea. The present **basilica**, Notre-Dame de la Délivrande, is a neo-Gothic 19C building housing a highly venerated statue of the Virgin (late 16C).

At the convent of **Notre-Dame-de-Fidélité** (Our Lady of Fidelity), the last house on the Cresserons road, the chapel chancel is lit by three stained-glass windows (1931), made of crystal and chrome, by **René Lalique**, who was also responsible for the door of the tabernacle.

Continue on D 7 for 3km/2mi until you reach D 404. Follow signs for the Musée-Radar up to D 83 on the right.

Douvres-la-Délivrande
Musée-Radar

rte de Basly.
Daily late May–Aug Tue–Sun 10am–6pm. *Guided tours mid-Jul–mid-Aug 11am, 3pm (in English). €5.50.*
02 31 96 45 66. www.musee-radar.fr.
The **Musée-Radar** retraces the history of radar equipment. Blockhouses,

D-Day Invasion, 6th June 1944

© Underwood Archives/age fotostock

The D-Day Landings

Dawn of D-Day – The formidable armada, which consisted of 4 266 barges and landing craft, together with hundreds of warships and naval escorts, set sail from the south coast of England on the night of 5 June 1944 (for further details, see the Battle of Normandy in the Introduction); it was preceded by flotillas of minesweepers to clear a passage through the mine fields in the English Channel.

As the crossing proceeded, airborne troops were flown out and landed in two detachments at either end of the invasion front. The British 6th Division quickly took possession of the Bénouville-Ranville bridge, since named Pegasus Bridge after the airborne insignia, and harried the enemy positions between the River Orne and the River Dives to prevent reinforcements arriving. West of the River Vire the American 101st and 82nd Divisions mounted an attack on key positions such as Ste-Mère-Église or opened up the exits from Utah Beach.

British Sector – Although preliminary bombing and shelling had not destroyed Hitler's Atlantic Wall, they succeeded in disorganising German defences. Land forces were able to reach their objectives, divided into three beachheads.

A German counter-attack was crushed under naval bombardment.

Sword Beach – The Franco-British commandos landed at Colleville-Plage, Lion-sur-Mer and St-Aubin. They captured Riva-Bella and the strongpoints at Lion and Langrune and then linked up with the airborne troops at Pegasus Bridge. The main strength of the British 3rd Division then landed. This area, exposed to the Germans' long-range guns in Le Havre, became the crucial point in the battle.

Juno Beach – The Canadian 3rd Division landed at Bernières and Courseulles, reaching Creully by 5pm. They were the first troops to enter Caen on 9 July 1944.

Gold Beach – The British 50th Division landed at Ver-sur-Mer and Asnelles; by the afternoon they held the area and the artificial Mulberry harbour could be brought into position. The 47th Commandos advanced and captured Port-en-Bessin during the night of 7 June. On 9 June, the British sector joined up with the Americans from Omaha Beach. On 12 June, after the capture of Carentan had enabled the troops from Omaha and Utah beaches to join forces, a single beachhead was established.

American Sector – The events involved in the landing of American troops at **Omaha Beach** and **Utah Beach** are described under *Omaha Beach* and *Presqu'île du Cotentin*.

Bill Millin and his Bagpipes

Down the road came Lord Lovat's commandos, cocky in their green berets. Bill Millin marched at the head of the column, his pipes blaring out *Blue Bonnets over the Border*. On both sides the firing suddenly ceased, as soldiers gazed at the spectacle. But the shock didn't last long. As the commandos headed across the bridges the Germans began firing again. Bill Millin remembers "just trusting to luck that I did not get hit, as I could not hear very much for the drone of the pipes". The most famous literary work about the Battle of Normandy is undoubtedly *The Longest Day*, written by the late Irish author **Cornelius Ryan** (published by Simon & Schuster in New York).

situated on the site of the German radar station at Douvres, have been renovated and provide insight into the daily life of German soldiers stationed along the Atlantic Wall. The role of aerial and maritime search equipment in World War II and their evolution since 1945 is explained with the help of realistic scenery.

St-Aubin-sur-Mer⌂

Bracing seaside resort with an offshore reef for shrimping and crab catching.

Bernières-sur-Mer

The French-Canadian Chaudière Regiment landed on this beach. Press and radio reporters came ashore here and sent the first reports of the landings. The church has a justly famous 13C **belltower★**; the three storeys and the stone spire together measure 67m.

Courseulles-sur-Mer⌂

It was on this beach west of the locality – a Juno Beach sector – that Winston Churchill set foot on 12 June 1944; on 14 June General De Gaulle went to Bayeux and on 16 June King George VI came to spend a few hours with his troops. A major pleasure port, Courseulles is also a seaside resort.

Centre Juno Beach

Voie des Français-Libres.
&⌚*Daily Apr–Sept 9.30am–7pm; Mar and Oct 10am–6pm; Feb and Nov–Dec 10am–5pm.* ⊘*25 Dec.* ⊜€7.
&02 31 37 32 17. www.junobeach.org.
At Centre Juno Beach, a short film introduces you to the role of Canadian

soldiers and sailors, as well as the heroic performance of Canadian industry in the war effort. Multimedia guideposts and interactive exhibits enliven the displays.

Val-sur-Meregasus

On 6 June 1944, this tiny resort was the main British bridgehead in the Gold Beach sector. A monument commemorating the landing stands where D 514 meets avenue du Colonel-Harper. The **tower★** of St Martin's church is the original robust 11C Romanesque structure of four storeys.

The **lighthouse** works in conjunction with the lights of Portland and St Catherine's Point in England and at Antifer, Le Havre and Gatteville in France to guide channel shipping. There is an extensive view from the lantern.

America-Gold Beach Museum

2 place Amiral-Byrd.
⌚*Jun–Aug daily 10.30am–1pm, 2–6pm; Apr–May and Sept daily except Mon 11am–1pm, 2–5pm.* ⊜€4.50. &02 31 22 58 58. www.goldbeachmusee.fr.
The first exhibit describes pioneering transatlantic flights, notably that of the triple-engine Fokker *America* which landed at Ver in 1927. Homage is also paid to the British troops who landed at Gold Beach on 6 June 1944 to liberate Bayeux. West of Ver-sur-Mer, the cliffs of come into view.

Asnelles

This little resort with its sandy beach lies at the eastern end of the artificial harbour established at Arromanches. From the sea wall there is a good view

Beach of Asnelles

© Jean Michel Gatey/Calvados Attractivité

of the cliffs and the roads (traces of the Mulberry harbour still exist). On the beach stands a monument raised to the memory of the British 231st Infantry Brigade.

West of Asnelles the road climbs to the eastern edge of the Bessin plateau; the Romanesque church in St-Côme comes into view. West of St-Côme, on the right-hand side of the road, a belvedere *(viewing table and parking area)* offers a beautiful **view★** down over the harbour and the last remaining elements of the Mulberry harbour.

Arromanches-les-Bains

♿*See ARROMANCHES-LES-BAINS, p281.* The road passes through the fields of Bessin. Further on you can see the belltowers of Bayeux.

⬤ 2 LA CÔTE DU BESSIN

From Bayeux to Port-en-Bessin – 34km/21mi. Allow 1h45.

▷ Leave Bayeux NE on D 516.

Arromanches-les-Bains

♿*See ARROMANCHES-LES-BAINS, p281.*

▷ After visiting , return to the road you came in on and, about 1km/0.6mi outside of town, turn right on the road to Port-en-Bessin. At Longues-sur-Mer, turn right on D 104 towards the sea.

Batterie allemande de Longues-sur-Mer★

Half a mile down this road, a surfaced road *(left)* leads to the site of the powerful German battery. In spite of the

---

Crabs and AVREs and DD Tanks
Ingenious Fighting Machines to Breach the Atlantic Wall

These bizarre fighting machines, known as Hobart's Funnies, formed the 79th Armoured Division, commanded by their foremost inventor Major-General Sir Percy Hobart. The tanks were designed to swim ashore (Duplex Drive: Sherman amphibious tank); to clear a path through the minefields (Crab: Sherman flail tank); to double as flame-throwers (Crocodile: Churchill VII tank); to lay matting on soft sand (Bobbin); and to double as bridges to carry other tanks over obstacles (Ark: Churchill tank). The tanks were a complete surprise to the enemy and after the Normandy landings the 79th Armoured Division pursued its advance, crossing the Rhine and entering Germany.

Eisenhower paid a vibrant tribute to Hobart's Funnies, pointing out that many lives had been saved thanks to the "successful utilisation of our mechanical inventions". A Duplex Drive can still be seen on Canada Beach (Plage du Canada) at Courseulles-sur-Mer.

The Norman Ancestors of Walt Disney?

As is well known, in 1066, Duke William of Normandy sailed across the channel and conquered England. After these historic events, two Norman soldiers who had accompanied his troops, **Hugues d'Isigny** and his son **Robert**, chose to settle on British soil. They were born in Isigny-sur-Mer, a small village near the mouth of the River Vire. Over the years, their surname d'Isigny underwent a series of changes, becoming Disgny, then Disney, which sounded decidedly more Anglo-Saxon. In the 17C, a branch of the Disney family emigrated to Ireland. In 1834, Arundel Elias Disney and his brother Robert, along with their families, embarked on a voyage to North America. Leaving from Liverpool, they arrived on Ellis Island off New York on 3 October, after travelling for a month. That was the start of their American adventures. On 5 December 1901, Elias Disney's fourth child was born in Chicago: he was to become the famous illustrator **Walt Disney**, whose legendary animated cartoon characters like Mickey Mouse and Donald Duck have delighted many a generation of children. He died on 15 December 1966.

release by 124 RAF planes of 600t of bombs during the night preceding 6 June, the four German guns began firing at 5.37am on 6 June. The French cruiser *Georges-Leygues* returned fire, followed by the *Montcalm* and the American battleship *Arkansas*.

The Germans were silent for a while but resumed firing in the afternoon; the battery was finally silenced at 7pm by two direct hits from the *Georges-Leygues*. Built on a picturesque cliff, it was composed of four 150mm guns with a range of 20km/12.5mi, which enabled it to control Omaha and Gold beaches. The observation post and control room, on the cliff-edge, appeared in a famous scene from the film *The Longest Day* (1962).

Le Chaos

The track descends steeply and is liable to rockfalls; there is a view of the coast from Cap Manvieux in the east to the Pointe de la Percée in the west.
This part of the Bessin coast has eroded into a chaotic jumble.

▷ Take D 104 south towards Bayeux.

Abbaye Ste-Marie de Longues

◷*May–Jul Tue–Sat 2–6pm.* ✆€5.
✆*02 31 21 78 41.*
Only the main door and some of the coir and transept remain of the 12C abbey

church. Tombstones of the lords of Argouges in the refectory.

▷ Return north to D 514; continue west to Port-en-Bessin.

Port-en-Bessin★

From the jetties there is a view of the Bessin coast, Cap Manvieux to Pointe de la Percée. A 17C tower dominates the eastern outer harbour. Good harbour **view** from the clifftop blockhouse; outside Bayeux on the D 6, good **view** of **Château de Maisons** (15C–18C).

3 OMAHA BEACH★

From Bayeux to Carentan 75km/46.6mi. Allow 2h45.

▷ Leave Bayeux by the N 13 going northwest.

Tour-en-Bessin

The church has a 12C doorway; the transept spire is 13C, while the Romanesque nave has been renovated. On the arcade columns to the right are scenes of the 12 months of the year.

Tour d'Escures

🚶*Park beside D 100; take the private path (left) uphill (15min on foot there and back).* Steps on the outside of the wall lead to the top of the round tower (**view**).

Pointe du Hoc

Port-en-Bessin★
See p278.
From Port-en-Bessin, as far as Grandcamp-Maisy, the road continues through the Bessin region, which is crisscrossed by hedgerows.

Omaha Beach
See OMAHA BEACH, p282.

Pointe du Hoc★★
From D 514 coming from Bayeux, just after a manor house, turn right to the ▣ *car park. 1h on foot.*
The Pointe du Hoc was heavily defended by the Germans; their observation post covered the whole area where the American invasion fleet appeared on the morning of 6 June 1944. As the troops landing on **Omaha Beach** would have been particularly vulnerable to attack from this battery, the **Texas** fired 600 salvoes of 35.5cm shells.
The 2nd Battalion of Rangers captured the position by assault at dawn on 6 June, scaling the cliffs with ropes and extendible ladders but with heavy losses – 135 Rangers out of 225. Commandos of the 116th Regiment of the US infantry, assisted by tanks, subdued the German defence. The gaping craters and battered blockhouses give some idea of the intensity of the fighting. Fine **views★** of the sea and the coast.

▷ Continue west on D 514.

Grandcamp-Maisy
A little fishing port and marina.

▷ Take D 199 and D 113 inland.

Cimetière militaire allemand de la Cambe
This impressive German cemetery with its rectangular lawn (2ha) is the last resting place of 21 500 German soldiers who fell in the fighting in 1944.

Château de Colombières
Guided tours only (45min): Jul–Aug Mon–Thu 2–7pm; Sept Sat–Sun 2–7pm. €6. *02 31 22 51 65. www.chateau-colombieres.fr.*
This feudal military **château** was HQ for the American press after the Normandy landings.
Today, a guided tour of this exceptional building, owned by the Maupeou d'Ableiges family, gives an insight into a fascinating period of history from William the Conqueror to the Allied Forces Landing on 6 June, 1944.

Isigny-sur-Mer
The town has been famous for the production of milk and butter since the 17C.

Carentan
See PRESQU'ÎLE DU COTENTIN, p384.

ADDRESSES

🛏 STAY

🍴 Chambre d'hôte La Ferme d'Escures
– *Escures village, 14520 Commes.* ☎*02 31 21 79 56.* 🅿🍴. 17C farm near Bayeux, ideal base for touring area. Simple, pleasant rooms; self-catering cottage used to be a boulangerie and has its own garden.

🍴🍴 Chambre d'hôte Le Logis – *Escures village, 14520 Commes.* ☎*02 31 21 79 56. http://le.logis.monsite-orange.fr.* 🅿🍴. *4 rooms.* Old houses inhabited by hospitable family. Breakfast in the former stable; comfortable rooms.

🍴🍴 Chambre d'hôte Ferme du Mouchel – *At "Le Mouchel", 14710 Formigny.* ☎*02 31 22 53 79. www.ferme-du-mouchel.com.* 🅿🍴. *4 rooms.* On a little country road, a pleasant dairy farm, probably dating from the 16C.

🍴🍴 Chambre d'hôte La Faisanderie
Av. du Col.-Courson, 14450 Grandchamp-Maisy. ☎*02 31 22 70 06.* 🅿. *3 rooms.* Vine-covered house at horse farm. Pretty, individual rooms; fireplace in dining room.

🍴🍴🍴 Hotel-Restaurant Domaine de L'Hostréière – *rue du Cimetière-Américain, 14170 Colleville-sur-Mer.* ☎*02 31 51 64 64. www.domainehostreiere.com.* ♿🅿. *22 rooms, 5 apartments.* Modern rooms, each with terrace, in old farm near US cemetery of St-Laurent-sur-Mer. Gym, spa and sauna.

🍴🍴🍴 Chambre d'hôte Château de Vouilly – *14230 Vouilly-Église.* ☎*02 31 22 08 59. www.chateau-vouilly.com.* 🅿. *4 rooms.* A moat abounding with fish, handsome gardens, an orangery, imposing drawing rooms and dual-coloured paving in an 18C residence.

🍴🍴🍴 Chambre d'hôte Manoir de l'Hermerel – *14230 Géfosse-Fontenay (7km/4.3mi N of Isigny via D 514 then D 199).* ☎*02 31 22 64 12. www.manoir-hermerel.com.* 🅿 *4 rooms.* Fortified 17C farm; visit the 15C Gothic chapel.

🍴 EAT

🍴 Café Gondrée – *Pegasus Bridge – 12 Avenue du Commandant Kieffer, 14970 Bénouville (9km/5.6mi N of Caen via D 514).* ☎*02 31 44 62 25. www.pegasus-bridge-cafe-gondree.com.* 🅿🍴. Small, authentic pre-war café, the first house on French soil to be liberated in 1944. Arlette Gondrée, who was four at the time, makes traditional omelettes with salad.

🍴🍴 Hotel-Restaurant Les Alizes – *4 quai Ouest, 14470 Courseulles-sur-Mer.* ☎*02 31 36 14 14. www.restaurant-hotel-courseulles.fr.* Loyal regulars for food; oysters and mussels at any hour; 3 guest **rooms** (🍴).

🍴🍴 Le Bistrot d'à Côté – *12 r. Michel-Lefournier, 14520 Port-en-Bessin.* ☎*02 31 51 79 12. www.barque-bleue.fr.* Seafood a speciality; the day's catch on a blackboard menu.

🍴🍴 La Trinquette – *7 rte du Joncal, 14450 Grandcamp-Maisy.* ☎*02 31 22 64 90. Closed Mon and Tue from end Aug–Easter.* ♿🅿. Try the local fishermen's dish, *la marmite grandcopaise.*

🍴🍴 Le Vauban – *6 rue du Nord, 14520 Port-en-Bessin.* ☎*02 31 21 74 83. http://restaurant-levauban.fr. Closed for lunch Tue–Wed and Fri.* One of the locals' favourite eating places.

🍴🍴🍴 Hotel Mercure Omaha Beach – *On the golf course, 14520 Port-en-Bessin.* ☎*02 31 22 44 44. www.accorhotels.com.* Hotel restaurant, open to public; superb view over Omaha Beach Golf Club. Generous Sunday brunch. Brasserie-restaurant at club house.

🍴🍴🍴 Hotel-Restaurant La Pêcherie – *7 place du 6-Juin, 14470 Courseulles-sur-Mer.* ☎*02 31 37 45 84. www.la-pecherie.fr.* Storm lanterns, oars and port-holes. A few guest **rooms** (🍴🍴).

🍴🍴🍴 Restaurant l'As de Trèfle – *420 rue Léopold-Hettier, 14990 Bernières-sur-Mer.* ☎*02 31 97 22 60. www.restaurantasdetrefle.com. Closed all day Mon and Tue evening.* 🅿. Unattractive post-war building, but delicious seafood, well worth the trip.

Remains of a Mulberry harbour, Arromanches-les-Bains

Arromanches-les-Bains★

A modest seaside resort that owes its fame to the gigantic landing operation of June 1944. In the little port are the remains of a Mulberry harbour, the most extraordinary maritime achievement of the war.

▶ **Population:** 503.

♣ **Michelin Map:** 303: I-3.

Info: 2 Rue Maréchal Joffre, 14117 Arromanche. ₮02 31 22 36 45. www.bayeux-bessin-tourisme.com.

▶ **Location:** On the coast, 10km/6.2mi NE of Bayeux via D 516, 38km/23.6mi NE of Caen via D 516 and N 13.

Don't Miss: The remains of the allied artificial "Mulberry" port.

Timing: 3h for the beach, museum and film.

VISIT

Artificial Port★

"As we have no harbour at our disposal, we shall bring ours," said Lord Mountbatten to Churchill.

Arromanches was chosen for "Mulberry B", the floating artificial harbour for British troops; "Mulberry A" was for the Americans (♣ *see Omaha Beach, p282*). There were 230 Phoenix caissons (500 000t of concrete; the largest were 70m long, 20m high and 15m wide), 33 pierheads and 18km/11mi of floating roads that crossed the Channel at 6km/3mi an hour. The floating port at Arromanches allowed 9 000t of equipment to be landed daily, the same tonnage handled by Le Havre's port prior to the war.

Reinforced after the terrible storm of 19 June 1944 that destroyed the Omaha artificial port, Arromanches still has imposing sections left, including about 20 Phoenix caissons, part of the 8km/4mi jetty closing in the harbour.

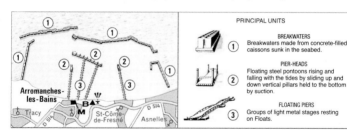

Arromanches-les-Bains

Tracy · St-Côme-de-Fresné · D 514 · Asnelles

PRINCIPAL UNITS

BREAKWATERS
① Breakwaters made from concrete-filled caissons sunk in the seabed.

PIER-HEADS
② Floating steel pontoons rising and falling with the tides by sliding up and down vertical pillars held to the bottom by suction.

FLOATING PIERS
③ Groups of light metal stages resting on Floats.

Concrete floating docks and part of the platform lie on the beach. The best view (preferably at low tide) is from the belvedere situated on the D 514 heading for Asnelles.

Musée du Débarquement
&🕐May–Aug 9am–7pm; Sept 9am–6pm; Feb and Nov–Dec 10am–12.30pm, 1.30–5pm; Mar and Oct 9.30am–12.30pm, 1.30–5.30pm; Apr 9am–12.30pm, 1.30–6pm. 🎫€8.20. ✆02 31 22 34 31. www.musee-arromanches.fr.
The D-Day Landing Museum contains a collection of models, photographs, arms and equipment. A large model of the Mulberry port shows how it functioned regardless of the tides. Graphic films of the landing are shown using nine large screens.

Arromanches 360°
&🕐Feb–Mar and Oct–Dec 10am–5pm; Apr and Sept 10am–6pm; May–Aug 9.30am–6pm. 🎫€6.50. ✆02 31 06 06 44. www.arromanches360.com.
Normandy's 100 days mixes archive footage with scenes re-enacted on the landing sites, on a 360-degree screen.

Omaha Beach★

Omaha Beach, which until 6 June 1944 existed only as an operational code name, has continued to designate the beaches of St-Laurent-sur-Mer, Colleville-sur-Mer and Vierville-sur-Mer, in memory of the American soldiers of the 1st (5th Corps of the 1st Army) Division, who suffered heavy casualties in the most costly of the D-Day battles.

A BIT OF HISTORY
Normandy Landings – When the American forces landed at Omaha Beach on 6 June 1944, they met an extremely well-organised German defence, aided by a strong coastal current that swept landing craft off course, and beach shingle that proved at first insurmountable to heavy armour. Companies at first baulked, later rallied and by evening the 116th Regiment had taken the Port-en-Bessin-Grandcamp road, enabling the motorised units to gain the plateau. The austere and desolate appearance, especially of the eastern part, a narrow beach backing on barren cliffs, makes the invasion scene easy to imagine.

- &b **Michelin Map:** 303: G-3.
- ▷ **Location:** Omaha Beach is some 20km/12mi northwest of Bayeux.
- ⊛ **Don't Miss:** The American Cemetery at Colleville-sur-Mer holds some 9 400 crosses and Stars of David, perfectly aligned. Note the extreme youth of many of the fallen soldiers.
- 🕐 **Timing:** You will need 3h to see the sights.

🚗 DRIVING TOUR

🚗 COLLEVILLE-SUR-MER TO VIERVILLE
9km/5.6mi. Allow 1h.

Colleville-sur-Mer
The last Germans did not leave the area around Colleville's village church until 10am on 7 June 1944.

▷ Just before the church, turn right towards the coast.

Monument to the 5th Engineer Special Brigade
The monument, built on the remains of a blockhouse, commemorates those who died protecting movements between

Monument Signal, Omaha Beach

© A. de Valroger/Michelin

the landing craft and the beach. This is the best belvedere on Omaha Beach.

American Military Cemetery

The 9 385 Carrara marble crosses and Stars of David stand aligned in an impressive site. A memorial stands in the central alley and is surrounded by trees. The commemorative list includes 1 557 names.

A **viewing platform** overlooks the sea. The path down to the beach (*30min there and back*) passes a second viewing table. A monument to the US 1st Infantry Division stands just outside the cemetery.

▶ Continue west on D 514 to St-Laurent-sur-Mer.

St-Laurent-sur-Mer
Musée Omaha 6 juin 1944
Av. de la Libération.
♿🕐*Daily: early–end Feb 10am–5pm; Mar 10am–6pm; Apr–May and Sept 9.30am–6.30pm; Jun 9.30am–7pm; Jul–Aug 9.30am–7.30pm; Oct–mid-Nov 9.30am–6pm.*
📞€7. ☎02 31 21 97 44.
www.musee-memorial-omaha.com.
This village was not liberated until 7 June after heavy combat. The **museum** describes life under occupation.

▶ Take D 517 down to the beach: the road runs through a valley.

Les Moulins

This site is marked by the **Monument to the D-Day Landing**. Turn right onto the road that runs along the beach and follow it to the end; there, at the foot of the American cemetery, you can look out onto the Ruquet valley and the road opened by the Engineers unit after the blockhouse was destroyed around 11.30am. Heavy equipment, motorised units and the infantry were able to reach the plateau and then advance to the town of St-Laurent.

▶ Return to the Monument to the D-Day Landing.

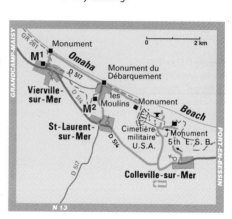

American Military Cemetery, Colleville-sur-le-Mer

© Vincent Rustuel/Calvados Attractivité

The first units found shelter here at dawn on 6 June 1944. From a platform erected for the Omaha Beach Monument there is a view of the cliffs the infantry had to scale to reach the plateau.

Vierville-sur-Mer

Taking boulevard Maritime westwards, a few hundred metres away is a stele marking the temporary burial place of the remains of soldiers fallen in the battles on the beaches. The village was besieged from the morning of 6 June 1944, and the church seriously damaged after its belltower fell. The road leaves the coast by another "beach exit", only open later in the day. A monument to the United States National Guard forces who fought in the two world wars is at one of the blockhouses the assailants dreaded most.

Musée D Day-Omaha

Rte de Grancamp (D 514).
  Apr–May and Sept 10.30am–6pm; Jun–Aug 10am–7pm. €6 (child 8+ years, €3.50). 02 31 21 71 80. www.dday-omaha.fr.
This former aircraft hangar displays objects from World War II, including an Enigma machine, aeroplane motors and paratrooper motorcycles.

ADDRESSES

STAY

Chambre d'hôte Ferme du Clos Tassin – *498 route d'Omaha Beach, 14710 Colleville-sur-Mer. 06 88 48 82 27. www.clostassin.fr. Closed Jan. 5 rooms.* Farm owners make cider, calvados and pommeau. Taste it in the shop, where meals are taken. Cosy rooms.

Hôtel du Casino – *Rue de la Percée, 14710 Vierville-sur-Mer. 02 31 22 41 02. 13 rooms. Restaurant.* Seaside hotel from the 1950s. Ask for a room with a view; enjoy seafood in the dining room.

EAT

L'Omaha – *Rue Du 116e Régiment USA, 14710 St-Laurent-sur-Mer. 02 31 22 41 46. Open daily from 11am.* Restaurant facing the sea, a stone's throw from Omaha Beach. Plain interior and two summer terraces. Fresh, grilled meat; seafood.

LEISURE

Eolia Normandie – *Le Cavey, Omaha Beach sea base, 14710 Colleville-sur-Mer. 02 31 22 26 21. www.eolia-normandie. com.* Guided outings on sand-yachts, wakeboards, catamarans and kayaks.

Château de Fontaine-Henry★★

This beautiful building is a fine example of Renaissance architecture. A member of the Harcourt family built it in the 15C and 16C over the dungeons, cellars and foundations of the original 11C–12C fortress.

VISIT

Late Apr–May and mid-end Sept Sat–Sun and public holidays 2.30–6.30pm (Guided tours at 3.15pm and 4.45pm); Jun–mid-Sept Wed–Mon 2–6.30pm (Guided tours at 3.15pm, 4.15pm, 5.15pm). €8.50.
02 31 26 93 67.
www.chateau-de-fontaine-henry.com.
An immense, steeply sloping **slate roof**, taller than the building itself, covers the 16C pavilion on the left. The **main building** is a wonder of delicately worked stonework. Inside is similar stonework, including the **François I staircase**.
Furnished throughout, the château has some fine paintings, as well as a rare collection of engravings by **Van der Meulen**. The nave of the 12C chapel was altered in the 16C; don't miss the sculptures inside, as well as the stone-work staircase.

Michelin Map: 303: J-4.
Location: Fontaine-Henry is in the Mue Valley, near the Côte de Nacre and the D-Day beaches, 18km/11mi N of Caen and 25mi/15.5mi E of Bayeux.
Don't Miss: The stone stalls in the château chapel.
Timing: 1h30 to see the château.

EXCURSION

Allow 15min on foot there and back. The lane branches off D 170 on a corner, about 500m from Thaon parish church. This downhill path will take you to the bottom of the valley.

Ancienne église de Thaon★

http://vieilleeglisedethaon.free.fr.
This small 12C Romanesque church is enhanced by its attractive setting in an isolated valley. The belfry, one of the most original in Normandy, is capped by a pyramid roof and deeply recessed twin bays.

Château de Fontaine-Henry
© P. Enticknap/age fotostock

Bayeux★★

Today the Bayeux Tapestry still presents a unique record of the events of 1066 and the Battle of Hastings. Its home, the former capital of the Bessin, was the first French town to be liberated (7 June 1944) in World War II. The town escaped damage during the war, leaving a cathedral and old houses – many tastefully restored – as well as a pedestrian precinct, for explorers in the 21C.

▶ **Population:** 13 525.
🚗 **Michelin Map:** 303: H-4.
🛈 **Info:** Rue St-Jean. ✆02 31 51 28 28. www.bayeux-bessin-tourism.com.
▶ **Location:** A short distance away from the D-Day beaches of Omaha, Bayeux is midway between Caen (30km/18.6mi SW) and Carentan (47km/29.2mi NW).
👁 **Don't Miss:** The Bayeux Tapestry; Notre-Dame Cathedral; Battle of Normandy Museum; gardens of the château of Brécy; Priory of St-Gabriel.
🕐 **Timing:** At least 1h to view the Bayeux Tapestry.
👫 **Kids:** The children's audioguide will make the tapestry more interesting for them.

A BIT OF HISTORY

Cradle of the Dukes of Normandy – Bayeux, a Gaulish town, became a Roman centre, then was successively captured by the Bretons, the Saxons and the Vikings.

Rollo, the famous Viking, married Popa, the daughter of Count Béranger, governor of the town. In 905, their son, the future William Longsword, ancestor of William the Conqueror, was born here.

Oath of Bayeux – In the 11C Edward the Confessor ruled over England. He had previously found refuge in Normandy for many years, and Norman accounts claim that he thus chose his cousin, William of Normandy, as his successor. He allegedly sent **Harold**, a powerful favourite of the Saxon nobles, to officially inform the duke.

Harold was shipwrecked on the coast of Picardy and captured by Count Guy of Ponthieu. Freed by **William**, he was received at the Norman court where the duke's daughter, Edwige, was presented as his wife to be.

Harold swore on saintly relics to recognise the duke's right to the English throne. However, when Edward died on 5 January 1066, Harold accepted the English crown.

The Conquest of England – Harold's accession provoked William to set sail with the Norman fleet on 27 September 1066 from Dives-sur-Mer, to fight for his claim to the throne. On 28 September the Normans set foot on English soil

at Pevensey in Sussex and occupied Hastings. Harold dug in on a hill. On 14 October William advanced and emerged victorious by that evening. The Bayeux Tapestry, a propaganda created after the invasion, claims that Harold fell in the fighting with an arrow in his eye.

👣 WALKING TOUR

45min to visit historic centre.
Start from the tourist office.

Rue St-Jean

East of rue St-Martin, partly an attractively restored pedestrian precinct. At No. 53 is the Hôtel du Croissant (15C–16C).

▶ Turn back and head for rue des Teinturiers.

Quai de l'Aure

Fine view of the river, the water mill in the former tanning district, the arched bridge, the old fish market and the cathedral's towers in the background.

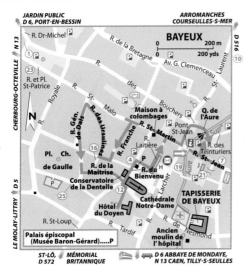

WHERE TO STAY

Argouges (Hôtel d')..............(23)
Churchill (Hôtel).....................(21)
Les Remparts
(Chambre d'Hôte)...........(25)
Petit Matin
(Chambres d'hôte Le).........(16)
Reine Mathilde
(Hôtel)...............................(19)

WHERE TO EAT

Bristot de Paris (Le)....................(1)
L'Assiette normande.............(12)
Pommier (Le)..............................(4)
Rapière (La)...............................(7)
Saint-Martin (Hostellerie).....(10)

◗ Take rue Maréchal-Foch; turn right.

Rue St-Martin

No. 6 is the 17C Maison du Cadran, so called for the sundial on the façade. There is a beautiful **half-timbered house**★ with two overhanging upper storeys and slate roof on the corner of r. des Cuisiniers. Just after the rue Franche, right, is the 15C **Hôtel d'Argouges** (wood sculptures).

◗ Turn into rue Franche.

Rue Franche

Several townhouses: No. 5, **Hôtel de Rubercy**, is a 15C–16C turreted manor house; No. 7, Hôtel de la Crespellière, after a courtyard, is early 18C.

◗ Turn right into rue de la Juridiction to get to rue des Ursulines.

Rue des Ursulines

A charming Louis XV hotel opens onto a street dotted with beautiful houses, often hiding behind tall enclosing walls. At No. 11, the **Hôtel de Marguerie** (17C) has an imposing stone portal. At the end of the street, at the crossroads and to the right, notice the beautiful hotel with delicately worked window frames.

Rue du Général-de-Dais

No. 10, Hôtel de Castilly (18C), in the Louis XV style. No. 14, Hôtel de la Tour du Pin (18C), has a majestic Louis XVI façade.

Place Charles-de-Gaulle

On this immense esplanade, a column commemorates General de Gaulle's 14 June 1944 speech: "In our Normandy, glorious and mutilated, Bayeux and its surrounding area witnessed one of the greatest clashes in History…" He had a triumphant return here on 8 July 1960.

◗ From place Charles-de-Gaulle (public garden) head back down to the cathedral by rue de la Maîtrise.

Cathédrale Notre-Dame★★

The cathedral is the seat of the former bishopric of Bayeux, created by St Exupery in the 4C; it became the diocese of Bayeux-Lisieux in 1855, bearing the French title of *"insigne cathédrale"* ("cathedral of note"). The **east end** of this beautiful Romanesque and Norman-Gothic edifice is a graceful composition. Flying buttresses sustain the choir, flanked with two bell turrets. The central tower dates from the 15C, but its crown, "the bonnet", was redone in the 19C. The portal represents the history of St Thomas Becket, the Archbishop

© Image Asset Management/age fotostock

Details of the Bayeux Tapestry showing Harold's Oath

Bayeux Tapestry★★★

The ♿👤**Bayeux Tapestry** *(Tapisserie dite de la Reine Mathilde)* is displayed in the **Centre Guillaume le Conquérant**; the work is the most accurate and lively document to survive from the Middle Ages, providing details on the period's clothes, ships, arms and general lifestyle.

Presentation of the famous tapestry has been organised in two spaces. The masterpiece itself is in a glass case in the dimmed Harold Room.

Wrongly attributed in the 18C to Queen Matilda, the tapestry (in fact an embroidery) was probably commissioned in England soon after the conquest from Saxon embroiderers by Odo of Conteville, Count of Kent and Bishop of Bayeux. In coloured wool on linen, it is 50cm high by 70m.

The outstanding sections are Harold's embarkation and crossing (4–6), his audience with William (14), crossing the River Couesnon and Mont-St-Michel (17), Harold's Oath (23), the death and burial of Edward the Confessor (26–28), the appearance of Halley's comet, an ill omen for Harold (32), the building of the fleet (36), the Channel crossing and the march to Hastings (38–40), cooking and eating of meals (41–43), the battle and Harold's death (51–58).

The English are distinguished by their moustaches and long hair, the Normans by their short hairstyles, the clergy by their tonsures and the women (three in all) by their flowing garments and veiled heads.

On the first floor, an exhibition makes it possible to understand the origin and history of the tapestry, and to place it in its context. Informative panels and display cases explain the reign of William the Conqueror, as well as the secrets behind the embroidery of the tapestry and the difficulties in preserving it. The visit is organised by themes, easy for young children to understand. At the end of the circuit, the film illustrates the history of the tapestry and the conquest of England. Scholars agree, however, that the final scenes of the tapestry, showing the coronation of William the Conqueror, were missing. During 2015, the 'Finale' Bayeux Tapestry, created by the inhabitants of the tiny Channel Island of Alderney was displayed in the museum alongside its historic original.

Centre Guillaume-le-Conquérant, r. de Nesmond. ♿🕐*Nov–Feb 9.30am–12.30pm, 2–6pm; Mar–Oct 9.30am–6.30pm (7pm May–Aug).* 🕐*Jan, 24–25 Dec.* 👁️*€9.50.* 📞*02 31 51 25 50. www.bayeuxmuseum.com.*

Watermill over the Aure, towers of the Cathédrale Notre-Dame in the background

© Danita Delimont/Getty Images

of Canterbury, on the tympanum; his murder in the cathedral was ordered by King Henry II.

The **façade** has two Romanesque towers. The upper windows in the vaulting are 13C, but the wide arches are in the best 12C style. Their justly famous decoration is typical of Norman Romanesque sculpture. In the right transept arm notice, down and to the right, two interesting paintings: *The Life of St Nicholas* and the 15C *Crucifixion*. The tympanum of the left portal represents the Passion; that of the right represents the Last Judgement.

The three-storey choir is a magnificent example of Norman Gothic architecture. The stalls are 16C. The high altar is a majestic 18C piece; the six candelabras in chased bronze, the tabernacle and the cross are by Caffieri the Elder. Notice the paintings on the choir vaulting, depicting the first bishops of Bayeux.

The third and fourth chapels on the south side contain 15C frescoes.

The 11C **crypt** beneath the choir is divided into three small naves each containing six bays. Above the remarkably delicate foliage of the capitals are 15C frescoes of angel musicians. A recess contains the 15C recumbent figure of a canon, his tomb set into the wall.

The chapter house is a beautiful late-12C Gothic construction. The vaulting, which was renewed in the 14C, is supported

by consoles decorated with monsters or grotesque figures. Paintings and a crucifix thought to have belonged to the Princesse de Lamballe are presented here. The floor of 15C glazed bricks has a labyrinth in its centre. The tiles on the risers at the back of the room depict hunting scenes.

▷ On leaving the cathedral, take rue Lambert-Léonard-Leforestier, left.

Musée d'Art at d'Histoire Baron Gérard

37 rue du Bienvenu.
🕐*Feb–Apr and Oct–Dec 10am–12.30pm, 2–6pm; May–Sept 9.30am–6.30pm.* 🕐*Jan, 24–25 and 31 Dec.*
🎟€7.50. ✆*02 31 92 14 21.*
www.bayeuxmuseum.com /mahb.html.
A huge 17C porch leads into the 18C mansion, which houses the collection of the **Baron-Gèrard Museum**. Themed tours as well as workshops for children are still offered *(call the number above for information).*

▷ Backtrack and take rue Bienvenu, before the cathedral.

Conservatoire de la Dentelle de Bayeux

6 rue du Bienvenu. 🕐*Mon–Sat 9.30am–12.30pm, 2.30–6pm (Mon and Thu, 5pm).* ✆*02 31 92 73 80.*

http://dentelledebayeux.free.fr.
This edifice, called the "Maison d'Adam et Eve" owing to the wood sculptures depicting religious or legendary subjects on its façade, is a shop and workshop where lace-makers continue the generations-old tradition of *point de Bayeux*, the Bayeux pattern. Several beautiful pieces are displayed.

▷ Take rue de la Chaine, which turns into rue Laitière, to get to rue St-Martin; then take rue St-Jean.

ADDITIONAL SIGHTS

Musée-Mémorial de la Bataille de Normandie★

Bld Fabian-Ware.
&⊙*Feb–Apr and Oct–Dec 10am–12.30pm, 2–6pm; May–Sept 9.30am–6.30pm.* ⊙*Jan, 24 pm–25 and 31 pm Dec.* ⊛€7.50. ℘02 31 51 46 90. *www.bayeuxmuseum.com.*
Situated on the line that separated the British and American sectors in 1944, the Memorial Museum recalls the dramatic events of summer 1944. A clear and explicit layout retraces the Battle of Normandy from 7 June to 29 August 1944, alternating chronology and themed spaces (the French Resistance, war correspondents, destroyed towns and cities, civil engineering, etc.). Equipment and uniforms illustrate each phase. A film in the last room *(25min)* is projected at regular intervals, and gives a good summary.

Jardin Botanique

By rue du Dr.-Michel, then the D 6.
⊙*Apr–Sept 9am–8pm; Oct–Mar 9am–5pm.* ℘02 31 51 60 60. *www.bayeux.fr.*
The garden was created under the second Empire by the famous architect and landscaper, Eugène Buhler. Among the little hills and dales, notice the surprising dimensions of the **weeping beech**: its 40m diameter has caused it to be classified as a "natural monument" and an "important tree of France". Pond with flowers, glass houses.

▲▲ A botanical itinerary for children is available at the tourist office.

EXCURSIONS

Abbaye de Mondaye

11km/6.8mi – allow 45min. From Bayeux take D 6 S. After 8km/5mi turn right onto D 33; follow the signs.
&☞*Guided tours Jul–Aug daily at 2.30pm; rest of the year Sun 3.30pm.* ⊛€5. ℘02 31 92 58 11. *www.mondaye.com.*
Also called St Martin's abbey, it was founded in 1215 but rebuilt in the 18C and 19C. The abbey church, which also serves the parish, is in the classical style (early 18C). Its uniformity of design is due to its architect and decorator, **Eustache Restout**, a canon in the Premonstratensian Order. The interior contains some fine pieces: high altar, woodwork in the chancel including a beautiful Crucifixion, the Assumption (a terracotta group in the Lady Chapel) and the Parizot organ (restored).
The 18C conventual buildings – refectory, sacristy (18C woodwork) and library – are open to the public.

Tilly-sur-Seulles

12km/7mi SW of Bayeux, by the D 6.
Completely destroyed in June 1944, Tilly saw bloody combat between British troops and the Panzer Lehr in June 1944. A visit to the cemetery gives a good idea of scale (986 British, 232 German graves) as does the **Musée de la Bataille de Tilly-sur-Seulle** in a former chapel (&⊙*May–Sept Sat–Sun and public holidays 10am–noon, 2–6pm.* ⊛€4. ℘02 31 80 92 10; *www.tilly1944. com/musée).*

🚗 DRIVING TOUR

🚗 ① SOUTHWEST OF BAYEUX

Round-trip of 50km/30mi. 3h30.

▷ From Bayeux take D 572 towards St-Lô.

St-Loup-Hors

The 12C–13C church has retained its Romanesque tower and old tombs.

Noron-la-Poterie

This is a well-known centre producing salt glaze ware; some of the workshops are open to the public.

▷ In La Tuilerie turn left onto D 73, which leads to Balleroy via Castillon.

Château de Balleroy★

🕐*10.45am–6pm: Apr–Jun and Sept Wed–Sun; Jul–Aug daily.* ⊜*€7 (chateau and museum €9; museum only €4.50; Park only €3).* 📞*02 31 21 06 76. www.chateau-balleroy.fr.*

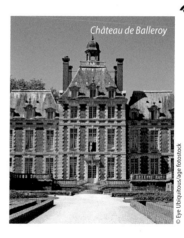

Château de Balleroy

© Eye Ubiquitous/age fotostock

The Château of Balleroy was built between 1626 and 1636 and designed by François Mansart (1598–1666) for the chancellor of Gaston d'Orléons, Jean de Choisy. His descendants, the successive marquises de Balleroy, have occupied it for three centuries. It is today the property of the family of publisher, balloonist and millionaire Malcolm Forbes, who bought it in 1970 and created the Musée des Ballons here. Built in local materials, grey stone and red schiste, the château expresses the style dear to the architect, although it was one of the first of Mansart's private works: the staging of buildings in a perspective of successive courtyards, pyramidal composition of pavilions, etc. The former stables, laid out here and there with interlacing flower beds; and the terrace, flanked by two pavilions, create a setting worthy of the building. The foliage of the romanticised park (135ha) and the French-style gardens, complete the theatrical staging.

Interior★ – On the ground floor are the paintings of Albert de Balleroy, a 19C painter of animals: in the Louis XIII salon are hunting scenes and in the smoking-room, portraits. Two of them represent the count: one (on the easel) is by Paul Baudry and the other is signed by Manet (Albert de Balleroy shared an art studio with him in Paris for seven years). In the dining room, the wood paneling is decorated on the theme of the fables of La Fontaine. Of revolutionary design, the staircase suspended on the vaulting leads to the first floor where three bedrooms pay homage to some well-known figures: Queen Victoria, Louis-Philippe, and finally Napoleon and Wellington in a shorthand version of the facts, under the imperturbable eye of Blucher.

The **Salon d'honneur** has superb décor, embellished with a collection of royal portraits by Juste d'Egmont; from floor to ceiling it is painted in the French style (the four seasons and the signs of the zodiac).

Musée des Ballons – Hot air and gas balloons, gondolas, trophies, photographs, models, medals and fantasy objects in this museum bring the period of ballooning and dirigibles to life.

Église paroissiale

The church stands before the château entrance. Built in 1651 in the local brown schiste, it is attributed to Mansart. Its octagonal belltower sets it apart. Inside, there is an Annunciation of the 18th century Italian school, over the altar.

▷ On leaving, turn left onto D 13. At the crossroads take D 13 and D 8 west through Cerisy forest.

Ancienne Abbaye de Cerisy-la-Forêt★

At the exit from the forest of Cerisy near D 572. Allow 2h.
🕐*Apr daily except Mon 11am–6pm; May–Aug daily 10am–6pm; Sept daily 11am–6pm; Oct Sat–Sun noon–6pm.* ⊜*€6. (*👥*Guided tours Wed at 3pm,*

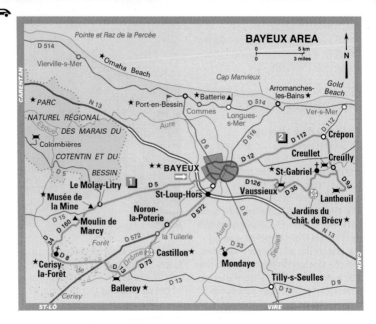

BAYEUX AREA

€8). ☏ 02 33 57 34 63.
www.abbaye-cerisy.fr.

The abbey at Cerisy is a remarkable
example of Norman Romanesque
architecture. The first monastery dates
from around 510. In 1032 Robert I of
Normandy, the father of William the
Conqueror, founded a new monastery
here dedicated to Vigor, former bishop
of Bayeux.

Église Abbatiale★ – The nave is
remarkable for its height. The choir and
especially the **apse★** are striking examples of Romanesque architecture, characterised by delicacy and abundance
of light, when most 11C buildings were
massive and sombre.

Walk round the church to the east end
to admire the **chevet★** with its tiered
effect formed by the apse, the choir and
the belfry.

Bâtiments conventuels – Following
the Revolution, these 13C buildings were
used as a stone quarry.

Musée lapidaire – A low chamber with
pointed vaulting houses the Archaeological Museum. At the far end of the
chamber, on the left, is a dungeon with
15C and 16C graffiti.

Chapelle de l'Abbé – The Abbot's
Chapel, built in the 13C with a gift from

St Louis, is a good example of Norman
Gothic architecture.

Salle de justice – This contains the
monks' furniture, as well as documents
and manuscripts.

▶ Leave Cerisy by the D 34, to the
north, heading for Molay-Littry.
The Moulin de Marcy is near the
intersection of the D 160 and D 189.

**Musée de la Meunerie – Moulin de
Marcy**
Le Molay-Littry.
🕐2–6pm: May–Jun and 1-mid Sept
Wed–Sun; Jul–Aug daily except Tue.
€5 (child 6+, €2). Ticket combined
with the Musée de la Mine €8 (childr 6+,
€3) . ☏02 31 21 42 13.

In this green setting, watered by the
Siette, the water mill can be seen;
the last miller lived here until 1975.
Remarkably well preserved, it offers
you a chance to discover a complete,
functioning water mill.

▶ Continue on the D 160.

Le Molay-Littry
The village was once a busy coal mining
centre. The mine was opened in 1743

Ancien Prieuré de St-Gabriel

and flourished until the late 19C. During World War II it was reopened and produced coal until 1950.

The **Musée de la Mine**★ ♣♣ (⟨♿⟩*same hours and charges as the Moulin de Marcy. ℘02 31 22 89 10; www.ville-molay-littry. fr*) presents the history of mining and the life of the miners through an audiovisual presentation, a reconstruction of a mining gallery, a scale **model**★ of a pithead, and a range of tools.

A tall chimney and significant archaeological vestiges mark the former Frandemiche pit; with informational panels, it is the material link to the presentation at the museum.

▷ Take D 5 east to return to Bayeux.

🚗 2 EAST OF BAYEUX
Round-trip of 34km/21mi. Allow 2h.

▷ From Bayeux take the D 12 (east) and D 65/D 112 towards Ver-sur-Mer.

Crépon
Admire the Romanesque church with its 15C tower and the prosperous farms.

▷ Turn south on D 65.

Creully
The **château** is built on the foundations of an 11C castle. The main 12C building is flanked by a 16C round tower adjoining a square keep. During World War II, the BBC used it to relay news of the Battle of Normandy.

From the terrace there is a view of **Château de Creullet** standing in a loop of the road. On 12 June 1944 King George VI and Winston Churchill met here with General Montgomery.

Grange aux Dîmes
On the Bayeux road, level with No. 82.
The tithe barn is a powerfully buttressed building where wheat was stored and taxes were collected.

▷ Take D 93 southeast to Lantheuil.

Château de Lantheuil
This imposing castle, built in the reign of Louis XIII, has remained in the same family ever since. The rooms have retained their original décor: woodwork, furniture, sculptures and paintings including a remarkable collection of family portraits.

▷ Return to Creully; turn left onto D 35. Enter St-Gabriel-Brécy; turn right.

Ancien Prieuré de St-Gabriel★
The old priory of St-Gabriel was founded in the 11C as a daughter house of Fécamp abbey. The attractive buildings surround a courtyard with a monumental entrance gate. A spiral staircase leads to the **priory room**.

The **church** is reduced to the magnificently designed and decorated east end and chancel (11C–12C).

Beyond the church is a **garden**, planted with fruit trees and banks of flowers. The 15C **Justice Tower** contained a prison on the lower floor and a lookout at the top.

▶ Return to D 35; continue west towards Bayeux; then follow signs south.

Jardins du Chateau de Brécy★

St-Gabriel-Brécy. ⏱*Easter–early Nov Tue, Thu, Sun and public holidays 2.30–6.30pm (Jun Sat 2.30–6.30pm).* ℘*02 31 80 11 48. https://jardins-de-brecy.business.site.*

The castle is approached through a magnificent great **gateway★** (17C). The terraced **gardens★** offer a beautiful perspective, which terminates in a high wrought-iron grill ornately decorated.

▶ Take D 158c; just before the church turn right onto a narrow road; after 2km/1mi turn left onto D 35; after 2km/1mi turn right towards Esquay-sur-Seulles.

Château de Vaussieux

Vaux-sur-Seulles. ☛*Closed to the public.* In 1778 the American owner of this 18C mansion gave it to Marshal Broglie to hold manoeuvres designed to intimidate England. The château is an elegant building set in its own park; the outbuildings are half-timbered or of stone.

▶ Continue onto Esquay-sur-Seulles; take D 126 to return to Bayeux.

ADDRESSES

🏠 STAY

🛏 **Chambre d'hôte La Ferme des Châtaigniers** – *14400 Vienne-en-Bessin (7.5km/4.6mi E of Bayeux via D 126).* ℘*02 31 92 54 70. https://fermechataigniers. wixsite.com. 4 rooms.* 🍴. Set apart from farmhouse, this converted stable has simple yet pleasant, comfortable rooms.

🛏🛏🛏 **Chambre d'hôte Le Manoir de Crépon** – *1 Rue du Calvaire, 14480 Crépon.* ℘*02 31 22 21 27. 5 rooms.* House built 17C–18C. Vast, tastefully furnished rooms.

🛏🛏🛏 **Chambre d'hôte Le Moulin de Hard** – *At "Le Moulin de Hard", 14400 Subles (6km/3.7mi SW of Bayeux).* ℘*02 31 21 37 17. www.moulin-de-hard.com. 4 rooms.* 🍴. Restored 18C watermill near a small river with a beautiful garden.

🛏🛏🛏 **Chambre d'hôte Le Petit Matin** – *2 bis. r. Quincangrogne.* ℘*02 31 10 09 27.* 🍴. *3 rooms.* Small hotel near cathedral.

🛏🛏🛏 **Hôtel-Restaurant Reine Mathilde** – *23 rue Larcher.* ℘*02 31 92 08 13. www.hotel-bayeux-reinemathilde.fr. 16 rooms.* Family hotel near cathedral.

🛏🛏🛏 **Hôtel Ferme de la Rançonnière** – *rte d'Arromanches-les-Bains, 14480 Crépon.* ℘*02 31 22 21 73. www. ranconniere.fr.* 🅿. *35 rooms. Restaurant* 🛏🛏🛏. Rustic, cosy 15C–18C rooms; breakfast in bed!

🍴 EAT

🛏🛏 **Le Pommier** – *40 r. des Cuisiniers.* ℘*02 31 21 52 10. www.restaurantle pommier.com. Open daily for lunch and dinner.* Restaurant near cathedral; Norman specialities.

🛏🛏 **Le Bistrot de Paris** – *place St-Patrice.* ℘*02 31 92 85 05.* The daily menu of this bistro-style restaurant is based on the day's market produce. Reasonable prices.

🛏🛏🛏 **Hostellerie St-Martin** – *place Edmond-Paillaud, 14480 Creully.* ℘*02 31 80 10 11. www.hostelleriesaintmartin.com.* 16C building, formerly village market. Curious décor. Classic cuisine. A dozen bedrooms 🛏.

🛏🛏🛏 **Rapière** – *53 r. St-Jean.* ℘*02 31 21 05 45. www.larapiere.net. Open for dinner Tue–Sat.* A 15C house in quaint old Bayeux street. Tasty food, Norman produce.

SHOPPING

Markets – *rue St-Jean. Wed 7.30am–2.30pm; place St-Patrice. Sat 6.30am–2.30pm.* St-Jean has 25 greengrocers, butchers, fishmongers, etc; St-Patrice has 120 sellers, about half of them with foodstuffs.

Naphtaline – *14–16 parvis de la Cathédrale.* ℘*02 31 21 50 03.* Two shops in an 18C building: antique and modern lace, Bayeux porcelain, reproduction tapestries. Next door a third shop specialises in medieval items.

Jardins du Château de Canon★

An invitation to time-travel, the gardens of the Château de Canon submerge the visitor in the world of the Age of Enlightenment, in a realm between reason and imagination: Romantic ruins, chinoiseries, grottoes, walled gardens protecting fruit trees, and trees three centuries old and still intact. This is, as Élie de Beaumont, enlightened member of parliament and friend to philosophers, would have wished it.

- **Michelin Map:** 303 L5.
- **Info:** ℘02 50 93 65 17.
- **Location:** Mézidon-Canon is 29km/18mi SW of Caen by the D 613 and D47, and 28km/17mi NE of Falaise by the D 511 via St-Pierre-sur-Dives.
- **Don't Miss:** the château's *chartreuses* (walled gardens)
- **Timing:** Allow 1½ hours, to take your time.

CHÂTEAU DE CANON
Mézidon-Canon.
⟐⟲*Apr–Sept daily except Tue 2–7pm (Jul–Aug daily 10.30am–7pm); Oct Sat–Sun 2–6pm.* ⟐€7 (chld 6–18, €3). ℘*02 50 93 65 17.*
www.chateaudecanon.com.

The Château de Canon comes into view at the end of a long avenue bordered with trees and strips of lawn. J.-B. Élie de Beaumont, a brilliant lawyer at the Paris Parliament, stewarded the finances of the Comte d'Artois and was a great friend of Voltaire; he created the estate in 1768. The elegant 18C construction is surrounded by service buildings in an L-shape.

Park and gardens★ – The château is embellished with 15ha of gardens, decorated with statues and follies, which juxtapose the French and English styles. Among the main points of interest are the Temple de la Pleureuse, in memory of Mme Élie de Beaumont, who died in 1783. Also of interest is the Miroir d'eau, a body of water surrounded by antique busts; a rare Chinese pavilion; and above all the **chartreuses★**, a series of 12 fruit gardens enclosed by high walls, sheltering a profusion of flowers. Finished in 1780, they are the perfect illustration of the 18C sense of order. In each "room", or enclosed space, fruit trees are trained to

Gardens, Château de Canon

© A. de Valroger/Michelin

grow *en espalier* along the walls, which preserve the sun's heat to ripen the fruit. The park itself still has a few superb trees, especially 300-year-old Middle Eastern plantains. Some have huts that can be rented for the night (*www.coupdecanon.fr*).

In the surrounding buildings, which include an 18C cider press, you can buy cider produced on the estate.

Each year in August the park is lively with the evening performances of the **Féeries de Canon**, followed by fireworks over the Miroir d'eau.

👥 To perpetuate the idea of organic, integrated agriculture, such as Élie de Beaumont would have wished it, the château has an organic farm and a wide range of domestic animals, that will delight children.

St-Pierre-sur-Dives★

St-Pierre-sur-Dives developed around an 11C Benedictine abbey founded by William the Conqueror's aunt; the old abbey church still remains.

SIGHTS

Église Abbatiale★

Tour St-Michel, was originally a dove-cote, doubling as a keep. The **convent buildings** are 17C; the **cloister** is 18C.

Salle capitulaire

23 r. St-Benoist.
13C Gothic chapter house.

♜♟ Jardin conservatoire des fleurs et des légumes du pays d'Auge★

R. St-Benoist across from the tourist office.
♿⏱*Daily May–Sept Mon–Fri 10am–12.30pm, 2–6pm, Sat 10am–noon, 2–5pm. ✆02 31 20 97 90.*
450 varieties of regional plants, flowers and vegetables are curated here; some of them are on the brink of extinction.

▶ **Population:** 3 635.
⚲ **Michelin Map:** 303: L-5.
ℹ **Info:** Rue St-Benoist. ✆02 31 48 18 10. www.lisieux-tourisme.com.
▶ **Location:** St-Pierre-sur-Dives is 43km/21mi SW of Caen.
🕐 **Timing:** The Monday morning market is one of the largest in Normandy.

Halles★

The 11C–12C market, which was burned down in 1944, has been faithfully rebuilt, even to the use of 290 000 chestnut pegs in its **timber-work**.

16C village market place; on Monday morning some 150 merchants sell cheese, charcuterie, fruit, vegetables and a variety of crafts.

On 1st Sun of the month, 8am–6pm, there are antique dealers.

Église Abbatiale, St-Pierre-sur-Dives

© A. de Valroger/Michelin

Château du Vendeuvre★★

In 1750 Alexandre le Forestier d'Osseville, Count of Vendeuvre, commissioned the architect Jacques-François Blondel to build him a summer residence on the banks of the Dives. The château and its beautiful gardens, with their delightful surprise fountains, continue to delight visitors.

VISIT

The château offers five sights: the **Musée du mobilier miniature** (Miniature Furniture Museum), the château interior, the collection of shelters for pets, the garden and the 18C kitchens. Ticket prices depend on how many venues you want to visit (*Daily: Apr and Sept 2–6pm; May–Jun 2–6pm; Jul–Aug 12.30–6pm; Oct Sun and public holidays 2–6pm. €11.90 (children €9.50). 02 31 40 93 83. www.vendeuvre.com*).

Musée du mobilier miniature★★

The lovely vaulted rooms of the orangery are the setting for an exceptional collection of miniature furniture, models and masterpieces of skilled craftsmen. About 100 pieces dating from the 16C to the present, are exhibited.

Château★

Same hours as museum.

The rooms are attractively furnished. In the dining room, with a great view of the sunset, the table is laid with a linen cloth woven with the family arms and the rear façade of the château. The reception room has lovely carved panelling.

Two popular 18C games are on display: loto and tric-trac on a special table. Note the chair designed for a woman wearing panniers, and in the main bedroom the toiletry set, the pastels in the salon, the study (collection of goose feathers), the smoking room (paraphernalia of an 18C smoker) and the kitchens. Behind the château there is a water garden.

- **Michelin Map:** 303: L-6.
- **Info:** 02 31 40 93 83. www.vendeuvre.com.
- **Location:** The château is 5km/3mi SW of St-Pierre-sur-Dives.
- **Don't Miss:** The Musée du mobilier miniature, a collection of tiny masterpieces; the park has remarkable water features, including surprise fountains.
- **Timing:** You will need 3hr to see the miniature museum and enjoy the garden.
- **Kids:** There is an amusing collection of shelters for pets.

Château du Vendeuvre

© Philippe Blanchot/hemis.fr

Garden of surprises★

Among the fanciful delights of the garden, the spray of fountains may catch you by surprise. True to the playful spirit that motivated 18C landscape artists, the many wonders include a not-to-be-missed grotto made of 200 000 seashells. Vendeuvre celebrates the **tulip festival** in April, with the wonderful blossoming of tens of thousands of bulbs; the **iris festival** is in May.

Due south of the city of Caen and the Invasion Beaches, this part of Basse Normandie is quiet and mostly agricultural, with no major towns, no "Incontournables" – "must-see" – visitor attractions. Anyone who has been to Devon in southwest England will be familiar with the countryside of Le Bocage, where sunken country lanes wind between banks, surmounted by tall thick hedgerows which border woodland pasture and fields. It gained notoriety during the Battle of Normandy in 1944, severely hampering the Allies' tank advances. Covering the Orne and parts of Calvados (famous for its apple brandy) it makes for leisurely picturesque drives.

Highlights

1 Visiting the **castle** where the Conqueror was born (p300)

2 Walking the **Circuit des Belvédères** for its views (p304)

3 Driving along the beautiful **Vallée de l'Orne** (p306)

4 Taking in the stunning views from the **Roche d'Oëtre** (p307)

5 Watching the equestrian shows at the **Haras du Pin** (p318)

Falaise

William the Conqueror was born here and would be proud that one of his many mighty castles commemorates his legacy. However, even he is over-shadowed by the terrible events of 1944 that took place near the town in what is known as the Falaise Gap (or Pocket). Here the retreating German forces were surrounded and fought to the death with tens of thousands of casualties. Today's peaceful bucolic surroundings belie the bloody past.

La Suisse Normande

Don't expect mountains or skiing here, but there are plenty of spectacular cliffs and crags, many fine walking trails and some wonderful hilltop lookout points in Normany's "Little Switzerland". The picturesque River Orne, carving sweeping meanders and gorges in the process, flows through the heart of the area. La Suisse Normande is a highly popular destination whether you simply enjoy it from the comfort of your car, or are more daring and take to the water.

Le Pays d'Argentan

The northernmost part of the département of Orne, this area is also watered by the river that forms a major attraction. The area's most popular visitor attraction is also here, the Haras Stud Farm, which has plenty of interest whether or not you are a lover of equestrian pursuits.

Take time out to visit the Memorial Montormel Museum, which is the best place to understand the heroism and horrors of the Battle of Normandy.

Sport and Leisure

With so many rivers, the Suisse-Normande is a natural playground for water sports enthusiasts and many sites offer equipment rentals. At **Clécy**, look for Au fil de l'eau, le Beau Rivage and Lionel Terray; at **Thury-Harcourt**, La Roc qui Beu and the Kayak Club; at **Pont-d'Ouilly**, the Base de Plein Air. Clubs in Pont-d'Ouilly, Clécy and Thury-Harcourt offer opportunities to canoe and kayak along the Orne. On the reservoir at **Rabodanges**, you can also windsurf and waterski.

The area is full of woodland trails and there are also dozens of accessible craggy promontories that provide tre-mendous views for walkers: the most renowned is the **Roche d'Oëtre**, near Pont-d'Ouilly, which achieves almost Alpine grandeur; others are the Pain de Sucre at Clécy and Mont Pinçon at Thury-Harcourt. None of these requires any climbing ability. However, if you do have that ability, Rochers des Parcs is ideal.

At Pont-d'Ouilly and Notre Dame du Rocher horseriding is available. And at La Route des Crêtes, near Clécy, you can take to the skies strapped to a paraglider.

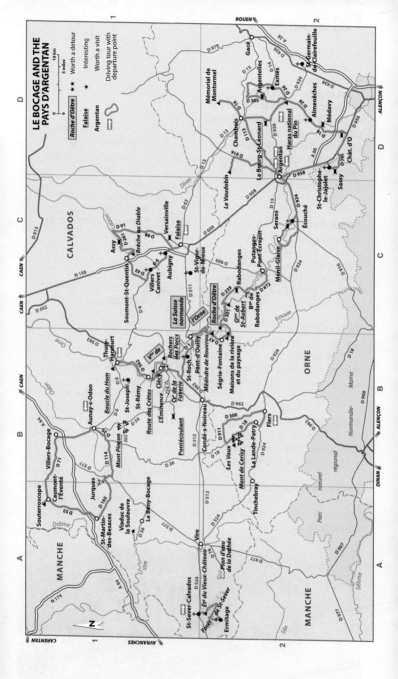

LE BOCAGE AND THE PAYS D'ARGENTAN

Roche d'Oëtre

★★ Worth a detour
★ Interesting
★ Worth a visit

Driving tour with departure point

Falaise
Argentan

0   5 miles
0   5   10 km

CALVADOS

ORNE

MANCHE

Normandie-Maine
Parc naturel régional

ROUEN
CAEN
CARENTAN
AVRANCHES
DINAN
ALENÇON

Gacé
St-Germain-de-Clairefeuille
Exmes
Argentelles
Mémorial de Montormel
Almenêches
Médavy
Chambois
Haras national du Pin
Le Bourg-St-Léonard
Argentan
Chât. d'O
St-Christophe-le-Jajolet
Sassy
Écouché
Serans
Putanges-Pont-Écrepin
Méhil-Glaise
Rabodanges
Gros de St-Aubert
Bois de Rabodanges
Le Vaudobin
St-Vigor-de-Mieux
Versainville
Falaise
Assy
Brèche au Diable
Soumont-St-Quentin
Villers Canivet
Aubigny
La Suisse normande
Roche d'Oëtre
l'Orne
Pont-d'Ouilly
St-Roch
Méandre de Rouvrou
Ségrie-Fontaine
Maisons de la rivière et du paysage
Thury-Harcourt
Vee de
Rochers des Parcs
Clécy
Cr de la Faverie
L'Éminence
Route des Crêtes
St-Joseph
St-Rémy
Boucle du Hom
Aunay-sur-Odon
Mont Pinçon
365
Pontécoulant
Condé-sur-Noireau
Les Vaux
Mont de Cerisy
La Lande-Patry
Flers
Villers-Bocage
Caumont-l'Éventé
Souterroscope
Jurques
St-Martin-des-Besaces
Viaduc de la Souleuvre
Le Bény-Bocage
Tinchebray
Vire
Plan d'eau de la Dathée
St-Sever-Calvados
Ermitage
Forêt de St-Sever
Ee du Vieux-Château

Odon
Orne
Dives
Rouvre
Maine
Vire
Drôme
Séline
Sée

N 158
N 174
A 84
A 88
A 28
D 979
D 13
D 14
D 926
D 438
D 958
D 924
D 916
D 872
D 239
D 301
D 562
D 6
D 36
D 511
D 658
D 606a
D 916a
D 63
D 91
D 6
D 562
D 562a
D 34
D 54
D 114
D 71
D 577
D 26
D 512
D 962
D 911
D 300
D 18
D 924
D 524
D 53
D 165
D 577
D 907
D 977
D 88a

299

Falaise★

The town's setting in the Ante valley is dominated by the enormous fortress, one of Normandy's first stone castles, where William the Conqueror was born about 1027. In August 1944, Falaise suffered cruelly during the fighting in the Falaise-Chambois pocket (also known as the Falaise Gap). Today the town is a centre for excursions into the Suisse Normande.

TOWN
Église de la Trinité★
The west front of the church features a triangular Gothic porch. On the south side, note the gargoyles and small carved figures. At the east end the Renaissance flying buttresses are highly ornate.

Église St-Gervais
The church dates from the 11C to the 16C; the lantern tower is 12C. Inside, the contrast between the Romanesque south side and the Gothic north is striking.

Porte des Cordeliers
This lovely stone gateway, part of the town wall, is flanked by a round tower and has a 14C–15C porch.

Fontaine d'Arlette
The fountain of the Val d'Ante (Fontaine d'Arlette) provides an impressive view of the castle towering above.

▶ **Population:** 8 214.

Michelin Map: 303: K-6.

Info: 5, Place Guillaume le Conquérant. ℘02 31 90 17 26. www.falaise-tourisme.com.

Location: Falaise is to the east of the N 158 between Caen, 41km/25.5mi to the north and Argentan, 22km/14mi to the southeast.

Don't Miss: The château of William the Conqueror.

Timing: Visit the château in the morning, lunch in Falaise and finish the day by touring the valley of the River Laizon.

Kids: Children will enjoy the Automates Avenue exhibit.

Château Guillaume-le-Conquérant★
Daily 10am–6pm (Guided tours Sat–Sun 3.30pm). 1 Jan, 25 Dec. €8.50. ℘02 31 41 61 44. www.chateau-guillaume-leconquerant.fr.
This medieval ensemble (12C–13C), characteristic of defensive Anglo-Norman architecture, has been heavily restored. William the Bastard, Duke of Normandy, was born here in 1027, to a local girl, the beautiful Arlette.

Château Guillaume-le-Conquérant

© A. de Valroger/Michelin

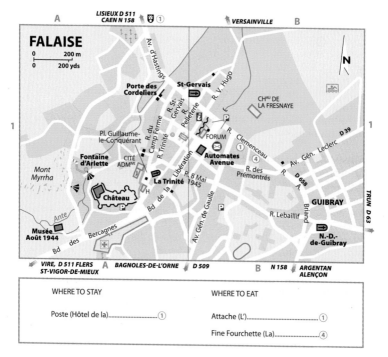

FALAISE

0 — 200 m
0 — 200 yds

LISIEUX D 511
CAEN N 158

VERSAINVILLE

Av. d'Hastings

Porte des Cordeliers

St-Gervais

R. St-Gervais

R. du Camp Ferme

R. Trinité

R. Peleterie

R. V. Hugo

CH^{AU} DE LA FRESNAYE

Pl. Guillaume-le-Conquérant

FORUM

Automates Avenue

R. Clemenceau

D 39

Av. Gén. Leclerc

R. D 658 A

Fontaine d'Arlette

CITÉ ADM^{VE}

La Trinité

R. 8 Mai 1945

R. Libération

R. des Prémontrés

Mont Myrrha

Château

Bd de la

Av. Gén. de Gaulle

GUIBRAY

R. Lebaillif

R. Briand

TRUN D 63

Musée Août 1944

Ante

Bd des Bercagnes

N.-D.-de-Guibray

N

VIRE, D 511 FLERS
ST-VIGOR-DE-MIEUX

BAGNOLES-DE-L'ORNE

D 509

N 158

ARGENTAN
ALENÇON

WHERE TO STAY	WHERE TO EAT
Poste (Hôtel de la)............................①	Attache (L')............................①
	Fine Fourchette (La)....................④

Inner courtyard

Visitors walking through the Porte St-Nicolas enter a large area of about 1ha, defined by 15 towers.

Main keep

This rectangular 12C structure is surprisingly large; great impregnable-looking flat buttresses mark the line of the walls. Restoration of the huge *aula,* or main reception room, involved sophisticated techniques: the flooring is made of alternating squares of glass and lead, and the ceiling consists of Teflon stretched over an iron frame. Note the Chapelle St-Prix, a small oratory.

Small keep

This luminous, well-balanced construction commissioned by Henri I Plantagenet in the late 12C was designed to guard the main keep from attack from the rock platform.

Tour Talbot

This impressive round tower, 35m tall with walls 4m thick, recalls John Talbot, governor of the castle in 1449.

An incredibly deep well (65m) provides water to the entire castle.

The rock platform commands a lovely **view** of the surrounding countryside.

The Battle of the Falaise Gap

Between 12 and 21 August 1944, the last bloody battle of the Normandy campaign was fought near Falaise, the name Falaise Gap referring to the corridor that the Germans sought to maintain to allow their escape. They were unsuccessful and with withdrawal forbidden by Hitler, terrible carnage ensued. In the aftermath of the battle General Eisenhower recorded: *"Falaise was unquestionably one of the greatest 'killing fields' of any of the war areas. Forty-eight hours after the closing of the gap I was conducted through it on foot… It was literally possible to walk for hundreds of yards at a time, stepping on nothing but dead and decaying flesh…"*

🏛👤 Automates Avenue

Boulevard de la libération.
⏱10am–12.30pm, 1.30–6pm: Apr–Sept and Dec daily; Oct–Nov and

Jan–Mar Sat–Sun, public and school holidays. ⏱24–25 and 31 Dec, 1 Jan, 2nd week of Jan–1st week of Feb. ◉€8 (child 4–12, €6). ℘02 31 90 02 43. www.automates-avenue.fr.

Until the 1950s, the Decamps company decorated the windows of Parisian department stores with animated scenes, of which some 300 are displayed.

Musée André-Lemaître

bld de la Libération.

♿⏱10am–12.30pm, 1.30–6pm: Apr–Aug, Sept and Dec daily; Oct–Nov and Jan–Mar Sat–Sun, public and school holidays. ⏱1 Jan, last 2 weeks of Jan–1st week of Feb, 25 Dec. ◉€5 (children under 12, no charge). ℘02 31 90 02 43. www.musee-andre-lemaitre.fr.

Local artist **André Lemaître** (1909–95) is renowned for his paintings of the area around Falaise and Honfleur.

EXCURSIONS

Faubourg de Guilbray

The **Église Notre-Dame-de-Guibray** dates from the days of William the Conqueror. The apse and the apsidal chapels are still pure Romanesque. The organ is by Parizot (1746).

Versainville

2.5km/1.6mi. Leave Falaise, heading north on rue Victor-Hugo. Turn right after le pont sur l'Ante onto the Versainville road.

The 18C château (⛔closed to the public) features a central wing with a peristyle, linked by a gallery to a huge pavilion forming the left wing.

Chapelle St-Vigor-de-Mieux

3km/1.8mi west of Falaise.

Ruined and abandoned, this 15C chapel has been totally transformed by Japanese artist, Kyoji Takubo, into a work of art, featuring a roof of coloured glass and a floor mural on sheets of lead. The building is called "chapelle des Pommiers" (Chapel of Apples), after the trees represented on the walls, and is now a French-Japanese cultural exchange centre; exhibitions are held in summer.

🚗 DRIVING TOUR

37km/23mi. Allow 3h.

▷ Leave Falaise, north on the D 658.

Aubigny

At the entrance to the village, on the left, stands a late 16C château. The parish **church** contains statues of six consecutive lords of Aubigny. Notice the 13C belfry of **Soulangy** to the left.

▷ Join the D 6 west, in the direction of Thury-Harcourt. Before Villers-Canivet, the abbey is signposted on the left.

Abbaye de Villers-Canivet

🚶Guided tours only 2–6pm: May–Jun and Sept Wed–Sun; Jul–Aug daily except Tue. ◉€4. ℘02 31 90 81 80. www.villers-canivet.com.

Founded in 1127 by the nuns of Savigny, and rebuilt in the 18C, the abbey is now mere ruins, though excavations reveal its historical importance. The abbey farm has retained its beautiful fortified gatehouse and a large tithe barn.

▷ Continue towards Ussy, then right towards Potigny and Soumont-St-Quentin and follow the signposts.

Brèche au Diable (The Devil's Gap)

This picturesque **gorge★** at the foot of Mont-Joly has been occupied since 3500 BCE) according to flints found here. There are numerous hiking trails.

▷ Head back northeast towards Ouilly-le-Tesson and take a right towards d'Assy.

Assy

A magnificent avenue (left) leads to the **Château d'Assy**, a handsome 18C mansion with an elegant Corinthian portico; the chapel dates from the 15C.

▷ Return to Falaise via Rouvres, Olendon and Épaney.

ADDRESSES

🛌 STAY

🍽🍽 **Hôtel de la Poste** – *38 r. G. Clemenceau.* ☎*02 31 90 13 14.* The 17 bedrooms in this 1960s building are well kept; those at the rear are quieter. The restaurant (🍽🍽) serves traditional dishes.

🍽 EAT

🍽🍽 **L'Attache** – *rte de Caen (1.5km/ 0.9mi N).* ☎*02 31 90 05 38.* A former coaching inn with a charming façade and attractive interior. The focus is on local cuisine with the occasional heirloom variety of herbs and vegetables.

🍽🍽🍽 **La Fine Fourchette** – *52 r. Clemenceau.* ☎*02 31 90 08 59. www. finefourchette-falaise.fr. Closed Tue evening Oct–May.* Modern cuisine on five set menus is served in two bright and cheery semi-formal dining rooms.

Clécy★

Tourist centre of the Suisse Normande, the town of Clécy is close to some of the most beautiful spots in the Orne valley and is the starting point for many walks.

SIGHT

👥 Musée du Chemin de Fer Miniature

Rue d'Ermington, Clécy.
♿🕐*Early Apr–Oct, but check website for times, which vary.* 🎫*€9 (child 3–12, €6.50).* ☎*02 31 69 07 13. www.chemin-fer-miniature-clecy.com.* The model railway that is the centrepiece of this museum covers 300sq m, with backdrops ranging from Switzerland to Flanders. The lights are dimmed to create a magical dusk of illuminated, houses, factories, castles and, of course, trains. The museum is set on a former quarry and a miniature train takes visitors around. In a huge vaulted former lime kiln cellar, cider is now made. A terrace café serves cider and crêpes.

🚶 WALKS

None of these walks is strenuous though Le Pain de Sucre and the Circuit des Belvédère do involve ascents.

Bords de l'Orne

From Le Pont du Vey, just outside town, the banks of the Orne, with their *guinguettes*, make for a pretty scene. A footpath along the river heads south to

▸ **Population:** 1 259.
🧭 **Michelin Map:** 303: J-6 – Local map, 📖*see LA SUISSE NORMANDE, p305.*
ℹ **Info:** Place du Tripot. ☎*02 31 69 79 95. www.suisse-normande-tourisme.com.*
◑ **Location:** Clécy is between Caen (40km/24.8mi N) and Flers (23km/14.3mi S) via D 562.
😎 **Don't Miss:** The many scenic walks, with panoramic views.
🕐 **Timing:** Spend the day enjoying the scenery on foot.
👥 **Kids:** The Model Railway Museum is a sure bet.

the Lande viaduct (1km/0.6mi), beside which the Rochers des Parcs attract climbers.

Rochers des Parcs★

🚶 *Allow 1h round-trip. Leave the village of Bo, 5km/3mi southeast of Clécy, on the D 168. At the church a path joins the GR 36 (red and white markings).*
The trail climbs the ridge, revealing stunning views of the Orne, the viaduct and the typical Suisse Normande countryside. At the viaduct, the trail descends towards Vey and Clécy.

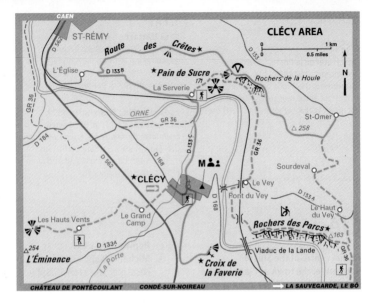

CLÉCY AREA

CAEN

ST-RÉMY

Route des Crêtes★

L'Église

D 133 B

★Pain de Sucre
171

La Serverie

Rochers de la Houle

St-Omer
△ 258

ORNE

GR 36

Sourdeval

M

★CLÉCY

Le Vey

Pont du Vey

D 133 A

Le Haut
du Vey

Les Hauts Vents

Le Grand
Camp

D 133 A

Rochers des Parcs★
△ 163

△ 254

L'Éminence

La Porte

Viaduc de la Lande

★Croix de
la Faverie

CHÂTEAU DE PONTÉCOULANT   CONDÉ-SUR-NOIREAU   ⟶ LA SAUVEGARDE, LE BÔ

Le Pain de Sucre★

Allow 3h round-trip. From Clécy take the route de La Serverie. Cross the bridge over the Orne and the level crossing; after 100m turn right. A sign (left) shows the start of the path to the Pain de Sucre (Sugar Loaf).

The path *(marked red and white)* climbs up a valley on the right bank of a stream. Cross the stream. Entering the copse, keep to the right of a trail that rises obliquely to the right and leads to the foot of a hillock and a vast **panorama** of the Orne. Going down, on reaching the foot of the hillock, along the slope opposite the one you came by, follow a winding path (well marked) which, passing below the Rochers de la Houle, comes out at the rustic church of Vey.

Circuit des Belvédères★★

Allow half a day.

This circuit allows you to make a neat loop, joining the two walks above. Start from La Sauvegarde, or from the church at Bô, and take the GR 36 to Les Rochers des Parcs. The trail leads to Vey, where, near the church, you will find the start of the path to Le Pain de Sucre. Take a well deserved break at the lookout, retrace your steps a short way down, and follow the path marked

yellow (the middle one), that ascends to La Route des Crêtes (the Road of the Peaks). Turn right and follow the road, passing two open areas, one of which may be in use by paragliders. Ignore the first path, down to Vey; instead take the second right, leading down to Sourdeval, a small hamlet where you turn left towards Haut-du-Vey. Follow the yellow signs to La Bruyère and Les Rochers des Parcs, where you will find the GR 36 and your starting point.

L'Éminence

2h round-trip. Leave Clécy on the D 168. Around 300m from the village, up the hill, turn left, past the police station, cross the D 562 towards Grand-Camp, go right into the village and turn left towards Hauts-Vents; the path rises north to l'Éminence, peaking at 254m. You don't need to climb right up, however, to enjoy a beautiful view of the Normandy countryside and the valley of the Orne.

EXCURSIONS

Route des Crêtes★

8km/5mi – allow 45min. From Clécy church take the D 133c north towards La Serverie. After the bridge, turn left to

The Orne and Clécy viewed from Route des Crêtes

St-Rémy; after 1.5km/0.9mi turn sharp right and follow the "Route des Crêtes". The road looks down onto the valley, with beautiful views of the meandering River Orne and surrounding areas, particularly the Pain de Sucre and Les Rochers de la Houle.
Follow the wooded slopes and bear left *(beware, sharp bend)*; continue on to St-Omer.

Croix de la Faverie★

45min round-trip. Leave from the car park between the post office and the church, and head towards Croix de La Faverie. At the stop sign turn right; then turn left and continue to climb. Follow the signposts to the Croix.

Opposite the cross, a path leads to a grove of pine trees *(picnic site)* with a beautiful **view**: the Rochers des Parcs overlooks the Lande viaduct.

ADDRESSES

🛏️STAY AND 🍴EAT

Hotel-Restaurant au Site Normand – *2 rue des Châtelets, Clécy.* ℘*02 31 69 71 05. www.hotel-clecy.com. 18 rooms. Restaurant closed Sun–Mon.* Set on the heart of La Suisse Normande, the 18C building is also home to a spa and wellness centre.

La Suisse Normande★★

This odd name denotes the area that straddles the **Orne** and **Calvados** regions. It has neither mountains nor lakes in the Swiss sense, and does not even include Normandy's highest points, but nevertheless draws tourists to its attractive landscape. The River Orne winds its way through the ancient rocks of the Armorican massif, bordered by steep banks surmounted by rocky escarpments.

A BIT OF GEOGRAPHY

Located in the midst of Calvados *bocage* country, some 30km/18.5mi south of Caen, and extending into the Orne

- **Michelin Map:** 303: J-6 to K-7.
- **Info: Clécy:** Place du Tripot. ℘02 31 69 79 95. **Thury-Harcourt:** 2 Place St-Sauveur. ℘02 31 79 70 45. www.suisse-normande-tourisme.com.
- **Don't Miss:** The remarkable view of the gorge of the River Rouvre from the belvedere of the Roche d'Oëtre.
- **Timing:** Tour the area in your car before deciding on which of the many walks to try.

département, the Suisse Normande lies between the towns of Condé-sur-Noireau, Thury-Harcourt and **Putanges**; some definitions extend the range eastwards to Falaise and the rugged Ante valley. Besides the Orne valley, the area takes in several small tributaries, including the Noireau, the Vère, the Rouvre and the Baize. Deeply eroded valleys and escarpments appear in stark contrast with the flat plain around Caen.

The curious name, Suisse Normande, was coined by tourism promoters in the 19C, as first the train, then the car, brought city-dwellers into the area. Switzerland, then (as now), evoked images of inspiring scenery, clean air, vigorous sports and healthy living. Tourism aside, the Suisse Normande is resolutely rural, with pastures for horses and cattle, fields of rapeseed, winding roads between ancient hedgerows, swathes of forest and picturesque little villages.

🚗 DRIVING TOURS

🚗 VALLÉE DE L'ORNE★★
99km/61.5mi. Allow 3h.

ⓐ *Nearly all sights require a short walk. Be sure to wear suitable shoes.*

Thury-Harcourt
The town stands on the banks of the Orne and is now a tourist centre for the Suisse Normande to the south. In 1700, Thury became the Harcourt family ancestral seat and was famous for its **château** (o—▪ *closed to the public*), burned down by the Germans in 1944.

▷ From Thury-Harcourt take the D 562 south.

The road drops down into the valley. Ahead, perched on a hillock, is the small Chapelle de la Bonne-Nouvelle, followed immediately by Caumont with its abandoned sandstone quarry (left) and finally St-Rémy.

St-Rémy
The St-Rémy iron mines, once the most productive in Normandy, were worked from 1875 to 1967, though surface mining had also taken place since medieval times.

About 700m off the D562 an 11C Romanesque **church,** renovated in the 19C, stands under an enormous yew tree on a promontory; there is a pretty **view** over the Orne valley from the cemetery. The Château de la Maroisière (o—▪ *closed to the public*) dates from the 18C.

Clécy★
ⓒ*See CLÉCY, p303.*

▷ Leave Clécy along the D 562 south. In Le Fresne turn left onto the D 1.

The road follows the crest of the ridge separating the valleys of the Orne and Noireau and then joins up with the Béron crest. East of the Rendezvous des Chasseurs (500m) there is a view north of the Orne valley, and of the Rochers des Parcs.

The downhill stretch offers a view (right) of the Roche d'Oëtre, before reaching **Chapelle St-Roch,** a 16C pilgrimage chapel where a *pardon* is held on the Sunday after 15 August.

Continue on to **Pont-d'Ouilly**, a busy tourist centre at the confluence of the River Orne and River Noireau.

▷ Take the D 167, south.

Leaving Pont-d'Ouilly, the road passes the foot of a rock whose top is shaped like a lion's head. The road runs along the Orne to Pont-des-Vers.

Take the D 43 to the right. The road climbs, offering glimpses of the beautiful meandering river Rouvre. At Rouvrou, take the sign for « Site de St-Jean ».

Méandre de Rouvrou
🚶 *15mn round-trip.*
Follow the road to the war memorial and leave your car there. The monument has been built in the neck of the winding

Roche d'Oëtre

river meander, surrounded by a copse of shady pines.

▶ Head in the direction of Ségrie-Fontaine, then towards Bréel.

Ségrie-Fontaine
Maison de la rivière et du paysage
Mon–Fri 9.30am–5pm (5.30pm in Jul–Aug, and 1.30–6.30pm on Sat); Apr–Sept Sun and public holidays. ℘02 33 62 34 65.
The Ségrie-Fontaine Nature Centre gives details of four walks along the river and gorge.

▶ At Bréel, take the D 229, then the D 329 left.

Roche d'Oëtre★★
The Roche d'Oëtre enjoys a superb **setting**, dominating the Gorge de la Rouvre with its steep escarpment. This is the highest point in La Suisse Normande and the view of this mighty cliff from the viewpoint indicator is breathtaking. To the right of the indicator, note, beneath the main lookout point, a rocky ridge in the shape of a human profile.
Relax and learn more about the site in the well equipped modern **Visitor Information Centre**, which includes films on various aspects of the area, including its flora and fauna, plus impressive multimedia terminals and an interactive map.

If you want to stretch your legs, a signposted circular walk *(1h, steep in parts, walking shoes recommended)* goes down to the river and offers superb views. There are three other marked trails (from 600m to 8.5km/5mi) departing from the centre.

▶ East of the Roche d'Oëtre the road runs along the valley; the final viewpoint is at the bridge in La Forêt-Auvray.
At this point on its course, north of the Argentan region, the Orne flows through, the **Gorges de St-Aubert★**, a succession of narrow gorges which are accessible only on foot (*see below*).

Rabodanges
A 17C moated castle (*closed to the public*) is set in a park overlooking the Orne valley. Further on, at the Barrage de Rabodanges, the road follows the shoreline of the 95ha artificial lake. There are fine views of the lake from the road and also from the bridge in Ste-Croix.

▶ Take the D 121 to the dam. From the car park, a steep path leads to the trail head, off to the right. At Ste-Croix, turn left on D 872, to join D 15 (turn left).

Putanges-Pont-Écrepin
This little town on the Orne is the departure point for walking the **Gorges de St-Aubert**.

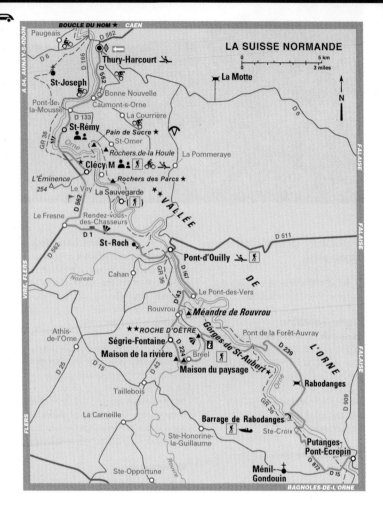

BOUCLE DU HOM★ CAEN

LA SUISSE NORMANDE

0   5 km
0   3 miles

N

Paugeais
Thury-Harcourt
St-Joseph
La Motte
Pont-de-la-Mousse
Caumont-s-Orne
La Courrière
St-Rémy
Pain de Sucre ★
St-Omer
Rochers de la Houle
La Pommeraye
Clécy M
Rochers des Parcs ★
L'Éminence 254
Le Vey
La Sauvegarde
Le Fresne
Rendez-vous-des-Chasseurs
St-Roch
Pont-d'Ouilly ★
Cahan
Noireau
Le Pont-des-Vers
Rouvrou
Méandre de Rouvrou
Athis-de-l'Orne
★★ROCHE D'OËTRE
Ségrie-Fontaine
Pont de la Forêt-Auvray
Maison de la rivière
Bréel
Maison du paysage
Rabodanges
Taillebois
La Carneille
Barrage de Rabodanges
Ste-Croix
Ste-Honorine-la-Guillaume
Putanges-Pont-Ecrepin
Ste-Opportune
Ménil-Gondouin
BAGNOLES-DE-L'ORNE

VALLÉE DE L'ORNE
Gorges de St-Aubert

🚗 BOUCLE DU HOM★

5km/3mi.

◗ Leave Thury-Harcourt west on the D 6. After around 1.5km/1mi, take the D 212 right.

The road follows the west bank of the Orne with fine views overlooking the Orne and its verdant riverbanks.
Turn right at Le Hom where the road leaves the river, to enter a deep cutting through the rock.

◗ Return towards Thury-Harcourt on the D 6.

🚗 MONT PINÇON★

◗ 14km/9mi. Leave Thury-Harcourt west on the D 6. At the Vallée de Hamars, turn left onto the D 36, then right on the D 108. At Plessis-Grimault, turn sharp right onto the D 54, towards Aunay-sur-Odon.

The **Pré-Bocage** is a picturesque rural area which borders the Caen plain, the Bessin, and the *bocage*.

◗ The road climbs to an altitude of 365m. At the top, near the television transmitter, turn left and continue for another 600m.

Leave the car and cross the heathland on foot (⊘*Beware in winter, the rough stony path can be difficult*); your reward is an extensive **panorama** of the *bocage*.

⌁ CHAPELLE ST-JOSEPH

🔵 17km/10.5mi. Leave Thury on the D 6 towards Bayeux; after rossing the river bridge, turn south onto the D 166. The road climbs up through the valley of the Orne. Turn right at Mesnil-Roger (D 134) to St-Martin-de-Sallen, and turn right onto a narrow road leading uphill, from which a single-track road leads off to the right to the Chapelle St-Joseph.

From behind the chapel, there is a beautiful **panorama★** of the Orne valley and the heights of the Suisse Normande.

🔵 Return to St-Martin-de-Sallen and take the next road on the right to rejoin the D 6 back to Thury.

Aunay-sur-Odon

This small modern town, rebuilt entirely in 1947–50 as a result of the Allied bombardments of 1944, is an ideal base for several excursions, notably in the Suisse Normande.

⌁ DRIVING TOUR

⌁ LE BOCAGE

Villers-Bocage
7km/4mi north of Aunay-sur-Odon on the D 6.

Like Aunay-sur-Odon, the town of Villers-Bocage was completely rebuilt after the war, but its style is much more daring, radical even, with an interesting mix of modern buildings, not least the Église St-Martin, built of stone and concrete.

ADDRESSES

🛏 STAY

⊖ **Chambre d'hôte La Ferme du Vey** – *Le Vey. ℘02 31 69 71 02. www.fermeduvey.fr. 3 rooms.* This working cattle farm offers comfortable rooms in an outbuilding.

🍴 EAT

⊖⊖ **Auberge Saint-Christophe** – *5 Saint-Christophe, Pont-d'Ouilly (12km/7.5miSE of Clécy). ℘02 31 69 85 54.* This old house, covered in Virginia creeper, sits on a quiet country road very close to the River Orne. Rustic dining room, regional cuisine. Bright cheerful modern rooms (⊖⊖).

⊖⊖ **Relais de la Poste** – *7, rue de Caen, Thury-Harcourt. ℘02 31 79 72 12. www.hotel-relaisdelaposte.com.* This Caen-stone house has an elegant dining room serving traditional cuisine with an extensive wine list. Comfortable characterful rooms (⊖⊖); lovely garden.

ℹ **Info:** 8 Rue d'Harcourt, 14260 Aunay-sur-Odon. ℘02 31 77 60 32. www.bocage-normand.com.

👁 **Don't Miss:** Going underground at Caumont-l'Évente; the bird shows at the zoo.

🔵 Take the D 71 west.

Caumont-l'Évente
The exposed hilltop situation of this small town explains its unusual name, as well as a lot of storm damage. Abandoned in the late 19C the old slate quarries of **Souterroscope des ardoisières** (⌁*guided tours only: Jul–Aug daily 10am–6pm; early Feb–Jun and Sept–late Nov daily except Mon 11am–5pm; ⊛€10; ℘09 74 56 76 97; www.souterroscope-ardoisieres.fr*) were dug by hand. Today they provide a window into a subterranean world.

Only a small part of the quarries are accessible, but these include vast chambers, a lake and a sound-and-light show with fountains. Information boards and a small museum relate to the underworld of fauna, geology and caving and includes an interesting collection of minerals. Wear warm clothes and sturdy shoes, the constant temperature underground is 12° C.

▷ Leave town south on the D 53.

**St-Martin-des-Besaces,
Musée La Percée du Bocage**

Apr–Sept Sat–Sun and public holidays 10am–6pm. €6. *02 31 67 52 78. www.laperceedubocage.fr.*
This gripping museum (its name means Bocage Breakout) tells the story of how the British army liberated the area in July 1944. It includes a graphic diorama, a large collection of contemporary photos, documents and relics from the battle, a superb audio-visual display, and moving accounts from combatants.

▷ Leave St-Martin-des-Besaces south east on the D 165, then follow the signs in the direction of la Cabosse.

Zoo de Jurques

Mid-Feb–mid-Mar 11am–5pm; Apr–mid-Jul and Sept and last 2 weeks of Oct 10am–6pm; Jul–Aug 10am–7pm. €18.50 (child 3–11, €12.50). *02 31 77 80 58. www.zoodejurques.fr.*
Set in a wooded 15ha park, the zoo is home to dozens of species of animals in near-wild conditions. It specialises in endangered creatures, including snow leopards, Siberian tigers and three very rare white lions. Other highlights include its birds of prey, feeding times for the wolves and penguins, and its parrot **shows★**. Look out too for the reptiles and mini-farm.

▷ Return to Aunay on the D 114/ D 26, which passes through the Bois de Buron.

Vire

Vire stands on a small hill overlooking the rolling Normandy *bocage*. The town grew up around its castle in the 8C. In the 12C Henry Beauclerc (King Henry I of England, fourth son of William the Conqueror), strengthened the castle's fortifications and built the keep. In the 13C the population increased and trade flourished, but the Wars of Religion (1561–98) led to decline and in 1630 Cardinal Richelieu dismantled the castle. The 17C and 18C brought another period of prosperity. Vire is an important road junction and as such it was almost annihilated in 1944.

SIGHTS
Église Notre-Dame
pl. Notre-Dame.
This 13C–15C Gothic church was erected on the site of a 13C Romanesque chapel

▶ **Population:** 17 425.
Michelin Map: 303: G-6.
Info: Square de la Résistance, 14500 Vire. *02 31 66 28 50. www.bocage-normand.com.*
▷ **Location:** On the route between Caen and Fougères.

built by Henry Beauclerc. The 13C porch is flanked by a slate-roofed tower. The belltower is surmounted by a balustrade; its spire succumbed to lightning in the 15C. In the south transept is a gilded Baroque altarpiece and a 19C *pietà* by a sculptor from Lisieux. The church suffered heavily during wars and the French Revolution, but has been well restored.

Les Vaux de Vire
Access via rue du Valhérel.
The Vaux de Vire refers to where the steep-sided Vire and Virenne valleys

meet. It is a popular place for walking and intriguingly gave its name to a local collection of 15C satirical drinking songs. The clipped form *"vau de vire"* was in common use by around 1500. This was subsequently conflated to *"voix de ville"* and eventually became part of the English language as vaudeville.

Tour de l'Horloge

pl. du 6 Juin. ⊙*Jul–mid-Sept Tue–Thu 2–6pm, Fri–Sat 10am–12.30pm, 2–6pm* ⊛*No charge.*

The old main gate (13C) to the fortified town is flanked by twin towers and surmounted by a 15C belfry, built to include both a clock *(horloge)* and a bell. A niche holds a wooden statue of the Virgin dating from the 16C.

© Arnaud Guérin/Calvados Attractivité

Tour de l'Horloge

EXCURSIONS

Plan d'Eau de la Dathée

S on D 577, then turn right onto D 76.
There are good views and a walk (7km/4.3mi) round the shore, as well as a water sports centre, a bird reserve and picnic area.

Le Bény-Bocage

15km/9mi north on the D 577 (the Caen road).
The streets of this pleasant village, which boasts a beautiful market hall, are often decked with flowers. Nearby is the Vallée de la Souleuvre, which is very popular for horseriding

Viaduc de la Souleuvre

6 km/3.8mi west of Bény-Bocage on the D 56, signposted to La Ferrière-Harang.
Built in 1869 to plans by Gustave Eiffel for the Vire–Caen railway, the viaduct was all but destroyed in World War II and abandoned. Partially rebuilt,It is now a famous bungee jumping point.

Saint-Sever-Calvados

13km/8mi west of Vire, on the D 524, on the edge of the Forêt de St-Sever.
The church takes its name from Sever, a slave who in the 6C, having converted his pagan master, was offered land, where he established a religious com-munity. Eventually appointed Bishop of Avranches, he returned to the abbey built in his name to die, and his tomb became a place of pilgrimage. In the 11C, the establishment became a Benedictine abbey.

The abbey church we see today was built in the 13C and 14C though it suffered a partial destruction of the nave in 1821. The separate belltower dates from the 17C. The transept crossing is dominated by a graceful lantern; the choir is lit by large lancet windows, two of which retain their 13C stained glass. Note, on the south side, the 15C window.

🚗 DRIVING TOUR

17km/11mi. Allow 1h15.

🚗 FORÊT DE ST-SEVER

Comprising 618ha of oak, beech, pine, fir and larch, the forest lies south of Vire.

▶ Leave St-Sever-Calvados on the D 81 southbound. At the end of the village, take the forest road left.

The road goes deep into the forest and at a crossroads is the small chapel, **La Vierge à la Vilaine**. A little further on,

© S. Sauvignier/Michelin

Vire Chitterlings

This well-known local speciality *(andouille de Vire)* is prepared to a traditional recipe.

The stomach and the smaller intestines of the pig are cleaned, chopped, salted and marinated and then stuffed into the larger intestine, which is smoked over a beechwood fire for several weeks.

The black colour produced by the process is proof of authenticity. The sausage-like chitterlings are then cooked in water and tied off.

anglers can fish in the pond of Vieux-Château. Continue on and you will find a series of slightly raised ponds. After the ponds, the road rises a little (*a footpath branches off right, leading to the ruins of the old castle*), then passes through open countryside before arriving at a crossroads.

Turn right onto the D 299. This road rejoins the D 81 where you turn left.

Ermitage/ Monastere du Carmel

During the early 16C reign of Louis XIII, a small colony of hermits established itself in this retreat, living according to the rules of the Camaldolese, a religious order founded in the village of Camaldoli in Tuscany in 1010. The monks lived here until the French Revolution. Of the original settlement, only the monastery gate (1776), and the Chapel of Our Lady of the Angels, almost entirely paved with granite tombstones, remain.

The buildings have been occupied since 1984 by a group of Carmelite nuns from Avranches, hence its current name. The public are welcome to attend services.

Flers

Situated in the heart of a *bocage* – a region of traditional hedgerows – Flers' traditonal way of life was producing textiles, based on local linen and hemp. This has given way to new industries, notably mechanical engineering and electrical appliances.

Musée du Château

av. du Château.

Mid-May–Nov Tue–Sun 2–6pm.

13 Jul, 11 Nov. €3. 02 33 64 66 49. *www.flers-agglo.fr*

The present castle, with a moat on three sides, has a 16C main building by the alchemist **Nicolas Grosparmy**, lord of Flers from 1527 to 1541, with

▸ **Population:** 14 766.

Michelin Map: 310: F-2.

Info: 2 pl. du Dr-Vayssières. 02 33 65 06 75.

Location: Flers is at the crossroads of the Paris–Granville and Caen–Laval routes: 92km/57.5mi S of Caen via D 562; 58km/36mi N of Mayenne via D 962 and D 23; 30km/18.6mi SE of Vire; 44km/27mi W of Argentan via D 924.

Don't Miss: The view from the château at Mont de Cerisy.

Timing: You need half a day to see Flers and its surroundings.

an 18C classical main façade. The first-floor rooms contain the painting and decorative art sections. In the gallery devoted to the regional schools of the 19C there are works from the Barbizon School by Corot and Daubigny, pre-Impressionists such as Boudin and Lépine, and Impressionists including Caillebotte.

EXCURSION
Prison royale, Tinchebray
Guided tours Jul–Aug Tue, Wed, Fri, Sun 2.30. €4. *02 33 96 19 49.*
The old *prison royale* now houses a local ethnography museum. The revolutionary tribunal was set up on the first floor. Two cells have fireplaces; prisoners were allowed coal, if they paid for it. The thick walls and wooden doors with impressive locks bear graffiti – some dates from 1793.

🚗 DRIVING TOUR

🚗 AROUND MONT DE CERISY
Round-trip of 24km/15mi. Allow 3h.

Argentan

The small town of Argentan looks down from its hillside site onto the confluence of the River Orne and the River Ure. The itinerary known as L'Encerclement (The Encircling Movement) – one of eight trails in the Historical Area of the Battle of Normandy – goes through the town. France's most renowned stud farm, the Haras du Pin, lies nearby.

A BIT OF HISTORY
Kingly Disputes and Lacemaking – It was in Argentan in the 12C that the papal legates assembled to settle the disagreement between the English king, Henry II Plantagenet, and his chancellor,

▷ Take the D 924 west.

La Lande-Patry
Two giant yews dating back over 1 000 years grow in this old cemetery

▷ Continue northeast on D 18 to Cerisy-Belle-Étoile.

Mont de Cerisy★
A road bordered by rhododendrons, climbs up the slope to the ruined castle, which commands extensive **views**★ over the countryside, as far as the foothills of the Suisse Normande. The plateau is the venue for the local **Rhododendron Festival** (*la Fête des Rhodos*).

▷ Turn around, go back to the D 18 and turn left, and shortly left again on a minor road.

Les Vaux
After passing between Mont de Cerisy and Rocher de St-Pierre, the road ends in the old hamlet of St-Pierre where a small Roman bridge spans the river.

▷ Return to Flers via St-Pierre-d'Entremont on the D 18.

- ▶ **Population:** 13 866.
- **Michelin Map:** 310: I-2.
- **Info:** Chapelle St-Nicholas, 6 place du Marché, 61200 Argentan. *02 33 67 12 48.* www.tourisme-argentan-intercom.fr.
- **Location:** Argentan lies on the River Orne, surrounded by forests, between Flers and Alençon, each 45km/28mi away.
- **Don't Miss:** The Château de Bourg-St-Léonard.
- **Timing:** Allow 1 day.

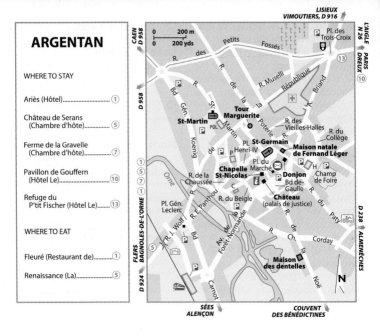

ARGENTAN

WHERE TO STAY

Ariès (Hôtel)........................... ①

Château de Serans
(Chambre d'hôte)............... ⑤

Ferme de la Gravelle
(Chambre d'hôte)............... ⑦

Pavillon de Gouffern
(Hôtel Le)........................... ⑩

Refuge du
P'tit Fischer (Hôtel Le)........ ⑬

WHERE TO EAT

Fleuré (Restaurant de)............ ①

Renaissance (La)..................... ⑤

Thomas Becket, Archbishop of Canterbury. Ironically Becket's assassins also set out from here.

Although Colbert, Louis XIV's minister, chose nearby Alençon to set up the Royal French Lace Workshop, he did not entirely neglect the lacemakers of Argentan. The rediscovery of 18C lace patterns for the Point d'Argentan in 1874 enabled the characteristic Argentan pattern to regain its popularity.

TOWN
Église St-Martin
The church, which was damaged in 1944, is dominated by an octagonal tower surmounted by a decapitated spire. The overall style is Flamboyant Gothic but includes several Renaissance innovations.

Église St-Germain★
pl. du Marché.
The church, badly damaged by shelling in 1944, was built in the Flamboyant style from the 15C to the 17C.
Walk round the church clockwise to view the unusual pentagonal east end (16C) and the unusual circular chapels at the ends of the transepts. At the base of the

belfry a fine Flamboyant **porch** opens on to rue St-Germain.

Château
⚭ *Closed to the public.*
The castle now serves as the Law Courts. This imposing rectangular building, flanked by two square towers, was built in 1370 by Pierre II, Count of Alençon.

Ancienne chapelle St-Nicolas
pl. du Marché.
Built in 1773, this chapel belonged to the castle. The Tourist Information Centre occupies the ground floor, and the first floor *(open on request)* houses a beautiful carved 17C altarpiece.

Maison des dentelles
34 r. de la Noë.
&⚭Mar–Jun and Sept–Nov Tue–Sun 1.30–6pm; Jul–Aug Tue–Sat 10am–12.30pm, 1.30–6pm, Sun 1.30–6pm. ⚭€3.50. ✆02 33 67 50 78.
The town's lace museum presents a charming introduction to the history of local lacemaking right up to the present day. A number of dresses and other outfits are on show, many the work of famous designers.

Abbaye des Bénédictines

2 r. de l'Abbé.
♾🕐*Mon–Sat 2.30–4pm.* ✈*€2.*
☎*02 33 67 12 01.*
www.abbaye-argentan.fr.
This enclosed order of nuns has exclusive rights to the Argentan stitch, a needlepoint lace style comprising a variety of motifs on a honeycomb-like background. There are no workshops, but you can ask to see specimens illustrating stages in the development of Argentan lace and samples of old and modern needlepoint lace.

DRIVING TOURS

PAYS D'ARGENTAN

Around Argentan is a plain circled by woods: Écouves to the south, Gouffern to the north. The Orne valley, separating this region from the Pays d'Auge, entered into military history in August 1944.

BANKS OF THE RIVER ORNE

32km/20mi. 1h round-trip from Argentan.

▷ Leave Argentan southwest on the D 924.

Écouché

At the crossroads marking the start of the town, stands a tank, acting as a war memorial.
The imposing 15C–16C **church** was never completed and the ruined 13C nave never rebuilt. The Renaissance triforium in the transepts and the chancel are worthy of note.

▷ Leave Écouché heading northwest on la Grande-Rue, in the direction of Falaise. Where the town ends, follow the road left, which leads to the Château de Serans.

Château de Serans

🕐*May–Sept daily; Oct–Apr Sat–Sun and public holidays only 2–7pm.*
☎*02 33 36 69 42. www.atelierbalias.com.*
Built in the early 19C, in the style of the villas of the Veneto, since 1991 this castle has been the property of the Greek painter, Balias (b.1943). This versatile artist has applied his talent to the castle interiors and exteriors, with unusual bas-reliefs and contemporary frescoes that take inspiration from neoclassical and ancient designs. The castle grounds are home to a sculpture park.

▷ Return on the D 771, then head in the direction of Ménil-Glaise.

Ménil-Glaise★

The **view**★ from the bridge takes in the rock escarpment crowned by a castle on the south bank of the Orne; there is another good view from a terrace.

▷ Turn round; continue straight ahead passing (left) the path from the bridge and (right) the Batilly road; at Écouché turn left onto the D 424 to return to Argentan.

LE VAUDOBIN

🚶 *12km/7.4mi – plus 15min walk (round- trip);* ⚀ *Beware slippery paths.*

▷ From Argentan take the D 916 northeast; after 7km/4.3mi (beyond Gouffern forest) turn left and cross La Londe. Park near the quarry; take the path left of the quarry entrance.

🚶 The path crosses the Meillon stream, bears left round a large rock and climbs uphill past a rock bearing fossil imprints. From the top of the grassy mound there is a view of the Meillon gorge and the Dives valley.

FOREST AND CHÂTEAUX

68km/42.5mi. Allow one day.

▷ Leave Argentan to the east on the D 916. Then turn left onto D 113.

As you leave Argentan, the road crosses Gouffern forest, then winds back down into the Dives valley.

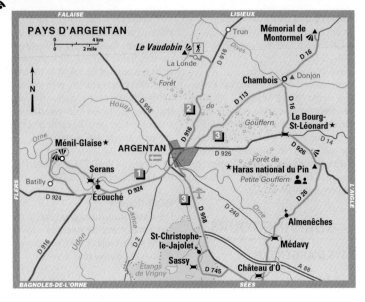

Chambois

A stele near a central crossroads recalls the joining up of the Polish 1st Armoured Division (attached to the 1st Canadian Army) and American 3rd Army troops on 19 August 1944 to cut off the retreat of the German 7th Army.

The huge rectangular **keep** *(donjon)* buttressed by four towers is a good example of 12C military architecture. The church has an 11C stone spire and a fine Descent from the Cross.

▶ Take D 16 northeast up hill to Montormel.

Mémorial de Montormel

Apr and Sept–Oct daily 10am–5pm; May–Aug daily 9.30am–6pm; Nov–Mar Wed, Sat–Sun 10am–5pm. €5.50. *02 33 67 38 61.*
www.memorial-montormel.org.

This museum and memorial commemorates the Battle of Normandy, and in particular, the **Battle of the Falaise Gap** (*see p301*) which raged from 12 to 21 August 1944, resulting in 10 000 to 12 000 deaths (some estimates put the figures much higher). Field Marshall Montgomery declared that it marked the "beginning of the end of the war". From here there is a superb

panoramic **view★** over the plain. Two galleries are of particular interest: in one, a large relief map describes the battle; the other is devoted to the soldiers of the Polish 1st Armoured Division. Its eye-witness accounts are harrowing.

Le Bourg-St-Léonard★

11km/7mi E by N 26.
Château. *Guided visit (45min): May–Jun Sat–Sun and public holidays 2.30–4.30pm; Jul–Aug daily 2.30–5.30pm; Sept daily 2.30–4.30pm.* €5. *02 33 36 68 68.*

This elegant 18C château was built by the chief of the Treasury under Louis XV. The interior is embellished with panelling, tapestries and 18C furniture. Take a walk to enjoy the views from the paths in the huge English-style park.

Haras National du Pin★

From France's most famous stud farm, (*see p318*) you can see the outline of the Écouves forest (*www.haras-national-du-pin.com*).

Almenêches

The Renaissance church here was once part of a Benedictine **abbey**. The altars are decorated with sculptures representing historical events, including the canonisation of St-Opportune, a local abbess.

Château de Médavy

Guided visits only: Jun–Sept Sat–Sun 1–7pm (daily from mid-Jun–mid-Sept. €6. ℘02 33 35 05 09. *www.chateau-medavy.com.*
Surrounded by a moat fed by the Orne, and by formal gardens, this 18C château was rebuilt for a French Marshal on the ruins of an ancient fortress. All that remains of the latter are two 15C towers, one of which houses a chapel with a beautiful marble altar. An extensive restoration project is currently under way, and will last several years. At the same time the owners are refurnishing the château. Don't miss the Russian winter sled, the Atlas Hall, the great staircase, and the remarkable parquet floor in the grand salon.

Château d'Ô

This late 15C château combines the Flamboyant Gothic and Renaissance styles. For generations the château belonged to the Ô (pronounced the same as *eau*) family, who were royal courtiers. The name is appropriate, as the sloping roofs, slim turrets, delicate ornamentation and brick-and-stone façade reflect beautifully in the water of the moat.

◯ Take the D 958 in the direction of Argentan. After 3.5km/2mi, turn left onto the D 222/D 745, then right onto the D 752.

Château de Sassy

Guided tours only (45min): Easter–Sept Sat–Sun 3–6pm (mid-Jun–mid-Sept 10.30am–12.30pm, 2–6pm). €7. ℘02 33 35 32 66. *www.chateaudesassy.fr.*
Building began in 1760, was interrupted by the Revolution and continued in 1817. The main salon holds several 17C tapestries. The **chapel**, partly hidden by trees, contains a 15C Flemish oak altarpiece carved with scenes from the Passion. The **terraces** and **gardens** of the château are delightful.

◯ Continue on the D 752.

St-Christophe-le-Jajolet

The village church is a place of pilgrimage to St Christopher, the patron saint of travellers. On the day of pilgrimage *(last Sun in Jul and first Sun of Oct)* a procession of cars files past.

ADDRESSES

⌂ STAY

⊖ **Le Refuge du P'tit Fischer** – *1 pl. des Trois-Croix.* ℘02 33 67 05 43. *17 rooms.* At the entrance to Argentan, on a busy street, this hotel offers modern, fuctional rooms on three storeys, well soundproofed. Brasserie-style restaurant.

⊖⊖ **Arlès** – *La Beurrerie Route d'Écouché (1km/0.6mi via 4 on map).* ℘02 33 39 13 13. *www.aries-hotel.com. 43 rooms.* Simple and functional accommodation, on a busy road (but well insulated against noise), with bistro-style dining (⊖⊖).

⊖⊖ **Chambre d'hôte Ferme de la Gravelle** – *41 r. de la Gravelle, Sarceaux (2.5km/1.5mi W).* ℘02 33 67 04 47. *3 rooms.* Set in a small rural village. There is a peaceful atmosphere in this country house. Rooms are pretty and a gîte is also available. Restaurant (⊖⊖).

⊖⊖ **Pavillon de Gouffern** – *Silly-en-Gouffern (11km/7mi E).* ℘02 33 36 64 26. *www.pavillondegouffern.com. 20 rooms.* The exterior of this former 19C hunting lodge, is rustic, with typical Norman half-timbering, the renovated interior is chic and contemporary. Restaurant (⊖⊖⊖).

⊖⊖⊖ **Chambre d'hôte Château de Serans** – *Écouché (10km/6mi SW).* ℘02 33 36 69 42. *www.atelierbalias.com. 2 rooms.* This fascinating château, graced with contemporary art by the owner, offers two bedrooms with views of the estate.

⫚ EAT

⊖⊖ **Clérembaux Denis** – *22-39 Le Bourg-Est, 61200 Fleuré (6.5km/4mi SW).* ℘02 33 36 10 85. Tradtional cuisine of the region.

⊖⊖⊖ **Hostellerie La Renaissance** – *20 av. de la 2e Division-Blindée.* ℘02 33 36 14 20. *www.arnaudviel.com. Open Tue lunch to Sat dinner.* Hotel restaurant with a quiet, friendly atmosphere and a choice of fine dining menus.

Haras National du Pin★

Le Pin Stud Farm, "the equestrian Versailles", dating from 1665, enjoys a magnificent setting amid woods and meadows; its grounds were designed by the king's landscape architect, André Le Nôtre. Nearby Gacé was home to the heroine of La Dame aux Camélias, who inspired Verdi's opera *La Traviata*.

- Michelin Map: 310: J-2.
- Info: Association Haras du Pin Tourisme. ℘02 33 36 68 68. www.haras-national-du-pin.com.
- Location: The Haras is some 15km/9mi E of Argentan via D 926.
- Don't Miss: The Cour d'Honneur on Thursdays, with stallions and carriage teams.

VISIT

Apr–Sept daily 10am–6pm; last two weekends of Mar and Oct 2–5pm. ∞€8. ℘02 33 36 68 68. www.haras-national-du-pin.com.
Three magnificent woodland rides converge on the horseshoe-shaped *cour* (courtyard), surrounded by splendid buildings. It is named the Cour Colbert, after Jean-Baptiste Colbert, chief minister of Louis XIV, who founded the stables in 1665.

The **château** (*only open certain days off-season, see website*) holds offices and reception rooms. Guided tours take visitors through the stables to see the 40 or so horses, the 19C carriage collection and to explore the equestrian world, past and present, through its modern interactive visitor centre. The harness room, paddocks and forge are also open on certain days in the summer (*see website*).

EXCURSIONS

St-Germain-de-Clairefeuille

10km/6mi SE (via Nonant-le-Pin).
The church is distinguished by its magnificent woodwork including 13 **painted panels★** of the Life of Our Lord by the early 16C Flemish School.

Gacé

13km/8mi N. Head towards Exmes on the D 26, then turn right onto the D 14.
Severely damaged during the battles of 1944 Gacé was fortunate to retain its imposing brick **château** built between the 15C and 18C.

The town is famous for being the home of Marie Duplessis. immortalised as "the Lady of the Camelias" in the novel *La Dame aux Camélias*, by Alexander Dumas *fils* (the younger) and is the basis for Verdi's *La Traviata*. She is celebrated in a special museum as part of the castle tour.

🚗 DRIVING TOUR

🚗 VUE SUR LA DIVES

23km/14mi. Allow 1h30.

This short tour takes in beautiful countryside, calling at **Exmes**, the historic capital of the Argentan, and the nearby 15C **Manoir d'Argentelles**.

▶ From Argentan take the D 926 east and, at the Tête-au-Loup, turn left onto the D 26 on the edge of the woods.

After visiting Exmes and its Romanesque parish church, go west on D 14, then north on D 305 to Villebadin.

The views around here are particularly fine. At the end of the village, turn right to the **Manoir d'Argentelles** (Easter–Sept Sat–Sun 3–6pm).

Return to the D 14 and turn righ (west) on the D 926 to return to Argentan.

ALENÇON *and the Parc Regional Normandie-Maine*

Created in 1975 and spread over the two regions of Basse-Normandie and the Pays de Loire, the **Parc naturel régional Normandie-Maine** covers 2 350sq km/907sq mi and includes 150 communes from the Orne, Manche, Mayenne and Sarthe *départements*. Lying on the boundaries of both Normandy and Maine, the park can be divided into an upper stretch *(haut pays)*, featuring crests and wooded escarpments in the Alpes Mancelles, and a lower stretch *(bas pays)*, characterised by a *bocage* landscape, the rolling hills of Saosnois and open fields around Sées and Alençon.

Alençon

Just outside the park boundary, the main town of this region, Alençon became famous in the 17C for its lace, once in high demand throughout Europe. Lace-making as a serious commercial enterprise has long gone and the town now has a thriving plastics industry in its place. Unlike many towns in the region, however, Alençon retains much of its historic fabric, escaping the Battle of Normandy with only minor damage.

Alpes Mancelles

Just south of Alençon, this picturesque region of small villages, hills and river valleys clad in woodland, heather and broom, spans the Normandy and Pays de Loire border. It follows the twists and turns of the Sarthe river valley as far as Fresnay-sur-Sarthe. The villages of St-

Céneri-le-Gérei and St-Léonard des Bois are particularly attractive and the latter has plenty to offer outdoor enthusiasts.

Highlights

1. Admire **Alençon** lace at the town museum (p323)
2. Take a trip along the **Alpes Mancelles** (p326)
3. Marvel at the medieval crafts-manship of **Sées** cathedral (p327)
4. March up the grand staircase of the Château de **Carrouges** (p330)
5. Stroll through the historic town centre of **Domfront** (p332)

Domfront

© Musat/iStockphoto.com

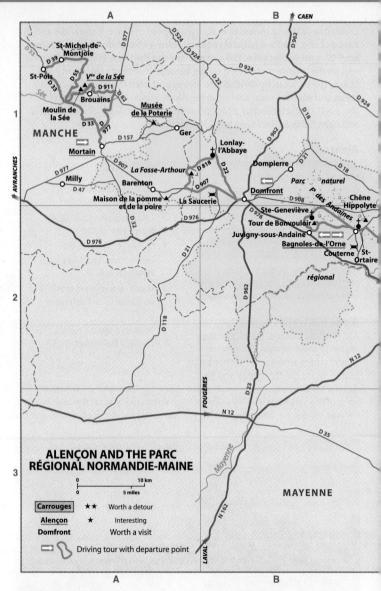

ALENÇON AND THE PARC RÉGIONAL NORMANDIE-MAINE

0   10 km
0   5 miles

Carrouges	★★	Worth a detour
Alençon	★	Interesting
Domfront		Worth a visit

Driving tour with departure point

Around Carrouges

This is the centre of the national park with the Château de Carrouges being the region's single biggest visitor attraction in every sense. The little hilltop town makes a good base. Nearby, don't miss the fascinating Champ de la Pierre gardens.

Around Domfront

The charming historic town of Domfront with its half-timbered houses is the best stopover for exploring the west of the Parc. From here you can make an excursion to the attractive town of Mortain, to the west, with its lovely waterfalls.

Sport & Leisure

If you like messing about in boats, you can navigate a good stretch of the River Sarthe through the Alpes Mancelles by canoe or kayak. Try Alpes Mancelles Aventures in St-Léonard-des-Bois.

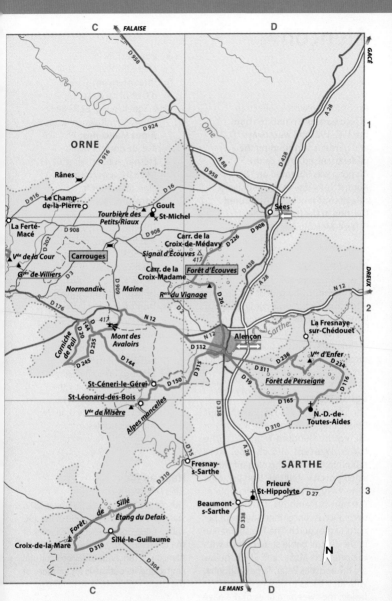

If you prefer wheels to water, hire mountain bikes from Espace VTT FFC, also in St-Léonard-des-Bois. Also near here is the Parc aventure du Gasseau, offering an excellent Acrobranche course navigating the treetops while suspended on wires. Horseriding is popular in many areas, particularly the Écouves forest. Pamper yourself by taking one of the many hydrotherapy treatments available at Bagnoles-de-l'Orne. Untypical of

the region, this posh spa town attracts wealthy clients from all over France and is not the sort of place you want to visit on a tight budget. Even if you have an aversion to spas, however, it's worth a quick visit to admire the town's early 20C Belle Époque architecture.

Alençon★

A royal lace-making town under Louis XIV, Alençon has a rich architectural heritage, a Fine Arts Museum with a collection of lacework and paintings from the 15C–19C; and waterways and gardens surrounding the pedestrianised town centre. Alençon was liberated on 12 August 1944 due to the decisive role of the French 2nd Armoured Division in the Battle of the Falaise-Mortain Pocket.

- ▶ **Population:** 26 129.
- **Michelin Map:** 310: J-4.
- **Info: Alençon:** Maison d'Ozé, place de la Magdeleine. ℘02 33 80 66 33. www.visitalencon.com. **Alpes Mancelles:** 19 ave. de docteur Riant, Fresnay-sur-Sarthe. ℘02 43 33 28 04. www.tourisme-alpesmancelles.fr.
- ▶ **Location:** From Alençon, roads lead to Paris (195km/122mi E via N 12), and to Brittany, Belgium and Spain. The A 28 leads to Le Mans (58km/36mi to the S) and to Rouen (160km/100mi to the N).
- **Don't Miss:** The little villages of the Alpes Mancelles, especially St-Léonard-des-Bois and St-Céneri-le-Gérei.
- **Timing:** Take a half-day in the town, then enjoy the lovely countryside in the forest of Perseigne or in the Alpes Mancelles.

SIGHTS
Maison d'Ozé
pl. de la Magdeleine.
Now home to the tourist office, this attractive 15C house, according to local lore, sheltered the future king, Henri IV, in 1576. It is named after the first prefect of Orne (who held the post 1800–1815), though it belonged to the Le Coustelier family.

Église Notre-Dame★
The beautiful 14C–15C Flamboyant Gothic Church of Our Lady was begun during the Hundred Years' War. The tower, transept and chancel were rebuilt in the 18C. The elegant three-sided **porch★**, built by Jean Lemoine from 1490 to 1506, is an example of the purest Flamboyant style. All the decoration is concentrated on the upper parts of the church. The Transfiguration in the central gable shows Christ with the prophets Moses and Elijah; below are the apostles Peter, James and John, with their backs to the street.
Inside, the sweeping lines of the nave rise to the highly decorated rib **vaulting**. The lines of the triforium merge with those of the clerestory to form a unified whole. Note the **stained glass★** by the master-glaziers of Alençon and the Maine region. The glass in the clerestory windows dates from 1530.
The first chapel off the north aisle is where Marie-Françoise-Thérèse Martin (1873–97), better known as St Theresa of Lisieux, was baptised.

Halle au Blés
r. des Filles Notre-Dame.
The old circular grain market, built 1812, was covered towards the end of the 19C with a glass dome, which the ladies of the town nicknamed "the hoopskirt of Alençon". It functions today as a cultural centre and its outline is an emblem of the city.

Musée des Beaux-Arts et de la Dentelle★
Cour carré de la Dentelle.
&⊙*Jul–Aug daily 10am–noon, 2–6pm; Sept–Jun Tue–Sun 10am–noon, 2–6pm.* ⊙*1 Jan, 1 May, 25 Dec.* ⊚€4.10 *(free for under 26, and 1st Sun of month).* ℘02 33 32 40 07. *http://museedentelle.cu-alencon.fr.*
Located in the old 17C Jesuit college, the Museum of Fine Arts and Lace houses

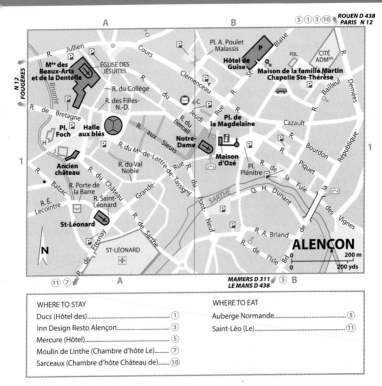

ROUEN D 438
PARIS N 12

ALENÇON

WHERE TO STAY		WHERE TO EAT	
Ducs (Hôtel des)	①	Auberge Normande	⑤
Inn Design Resto Alençon	③	Saint-Léo (Le)	⑪
Mercure (Hôtel)	⑤		
Moulin de Linthe (Chambre d'hôte Le)	⑦		
Sarceaux (Chambre d'hôte Château de)	⑩		

From Venice Lace to Alençon Lace

Lace-making began in Alençon during the 16C, but took off in the mid-17C after it perfected the art of imitating the finest Venetian techniques – then regarded as the best in Europe. Louis XIV's minister, Colbert, established a Royal Workshop and an industry developed, employing around 8 000 people. So there would

Point d'Alençon lace

© Orne Tourisme

be no competition from Venice, or indeed anywhere else, Colbert banned all imported lace. The Alençon lace-makers subsequently developed their own style, Point d'Alençon lace, an even more delicate stitch than that of the Venetians. The industry survived the Revolution and reached new heights under Napoléon I. From 1880 onwards, however, mechanical lace making and changes in fashion meant the decline of Alençon hand-made lace. Today, the last vestiges of the craft are kept alive by the Atelier National du Point d'Alençon (⚊ *closed to the public*), created by the State in 1976, to uphold lace needlepoint traditions, and who still supply needlework to the highest government establishments.

L'Encerclement

The itinerary known as L'Encerclement (The Encircling Movement), one of several in the Historical Area of the Battle of Normandy, runs from Alençon to L'Aigle, tracing the progress of the 2nd Armoured Division under General Leclerc.
Find out about this and other routes at http://en.normandie-tourisme.fr by entering "Battle of Normandy" in the search box.

paintings from the 15C to the 19C as well as collections of lace. The French and Nordic Schools of the 17C are well represented, with canvases by Philippe de Champaigne, Jean Jouvenet, Allegrain, Voet, Ryckaert and Wyck. There is also a fine selection of 19C French painting with works by Boudin, Courbet, Fantin-Latour, Lacombe, Laurens, Legros and Veyrassat.

The presentation of the **lace collection★** offers a broad review of the principal lace-making centres in Italy and France. Its display of Alençon lace, which uses a needlepoint technique unique in France, includes the elegant creations of the Alençon lace-makers from the 17C to the present day.

There is also a collection of Cambodian objects brought back by **Adhémar Leclère** (1853–1917), a native of Alençon and 19C governor of Cambodia.

Ancien Château

49 r. du Château.
From place Foch, you can see the 14C and 15C towers of the old castle, built by Jean II le Beau, first Duke of Alençon and an ally of Joan of Arc.
The central tower, known as the crowned tower, has an unexpected outline: the main tower with machicolations is itself crowned by a slimmer, round tower. The other two towers, which defend the main gate, can be seen from rue du Château.

Église St-Léonard

pl. Marguerite-de-Lorraine.
The rebuilding of the present church was begun in 1489 by René, second Duke of Alençon, and was completed in 1505 by his widow, Marguerite de Lorraine.
Nearby (*No. 10 rue Porte-de-la-Barre*) is a 15C house (*Maison à l'Étal*) with a slate-hung façade.

Hôtel de Guise

The local Prefecture and Départment offices now occupy this beautiful 17C building, which, despite its name, was formerly a military headquarters.

Maison de la famille Martin - Chapelle Ste-Thérèse

r. St-Blaise.
🕐*Contact tourist office for information.*
This is the birthplace and childhood home of Thérèse Martin (1873–1897) who became St Theresa of Lisieux in 2008. A double staircase leads to the chapel, which adjoins the house.

EXCURSIONS

Fresnay-sur-Sarthe

21km/13mi S of Alençon.
Fresnay occupies a picturesque site, perched high above the River Sarthe. The town centre is a preserved network of narrow streets bordered by beautiful medieval houses. It is also a centre for excursions into the Alpes Mancelles or Sillé Forest.

La Belle Échappée

8 rue de la Forêt de Perseigne, La Fresnaye-sur-Chédouet.
♿🕐*Apr–Sept Wed–Sun 10am–1pm, 2–6pm.* 🕐*25 Dec–2 Jan.* ⊚€5.
☎*02 43 34 39 11.*
www.lemuseeduvelo.fr.
The name means "the beautiful journey" and the exhibits and exhibitions in this museum of cycling celebrate the history of this popular national sport and of its many great French champions.

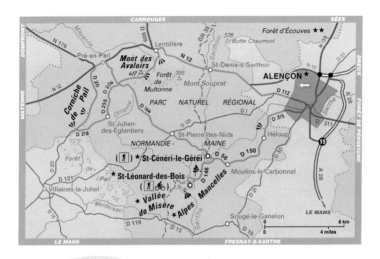

🚗 DRIVING TOURS

🚗 FORÊT DE PERSEIGNE★
Round-trip 53km/33mi. About 3h.

▷ Leave Alençon heading southeast on the D 311 in the direction of Mamers.

Bordered by the former provinces of Perche and Champagne Le Mans, the Perseigne forest, comprising mainly oak, beech and fir, covers more than 5 000ha and is marked by deep valleys. The route initially bypasses the forest to the north before penetrating its depths via the D 236.

▷ On leaving the hamlet of Buisson, turn left on the D 236; 4 km/2.5mi further on, turn right at a sharp bend towards Aillières-Beauvoir, then go right again for Ancinnes, on the forest road leading to Croix-Pergeline. At the last intersection (note the boundary marker stone), take the road left, the Route Forestière du Gros-Houx.

▷ The road leads downhill into a valley where you can walk through a beautiful series of oak, beech and fir copses. At the Trois-Ponts junction, follow the road up the hill; to the left is the picturesque Route Forestière de vallée d'Enfer (Hell's Valley), at the bottom of which is a meandering stream. Climb the belvedere tower (30m high) to enjoy the views from the highest point (349m) in the Sarthe district.

🚶 *There are 8km/5mi of waymarked paths round the belvedere and in Hell's Valley.*

▷ Join the D 234 and go southeast to the twin villages of Aillières-Beauvoir then the D 116 south via Villaines-la-Carelle. At the crossroads with the D 311 continue southwest on the D 310.

Chapelle Notre-Dame-de-Toutes-Aides
The doorway of this graceful pilgrimage chapel is surmounted by a Virgin and Child. Above the 17C altarpiece is an Assumption; below is a painting of the Annunciation.

▷ In St-Rémy-du-Val turn right in front of the church onto the road to Neufchâtel-en-Saosnois (D 117). Turn left onto the D 311, and left again onto the D 165 to reach the D 19.

▷ From Ancinnes take the D 19 back to Alençon.

Old bridge over the Sarthe, St-Céneri-le-Gérei

© Hervé Lenain/hemis.fr

THE ALPES MANCELLES★

See map p325. 82km/51mi – approx 3hr round-trip from Alençon (excluding the Misère valley).

The Alpes Mancelles is a particularly picturesque part of the Normandie-Maine Regional Park on the border with the Pays de Loire.

▶ On leaving Alençon take the N 12 west via St-Denis-sur-Sarthon. Continue to Lentillère and there turn left towards Champfrémont; then bear right to Mont des Avaloirs.

Mont des Avaloirs

A belvedere marks the summit (417m); this is one of the highest points in western France.

▶ At the second crossroads turn left onto the D 204 and then fork right onto the D 255. In St-Julien-des-Églantiers turn right onto the D 245, right again onto the D 218 and right again onto the D 20.

Corniche de Pail

The road, which climbs slowly, provides a view over the Mayenne basin.

▶ In Pré-en-Pail take the N 12 east and the D 144 south via St-Pierre-des-Nids.

St-Céneri-le-Gérei★

This picturesque village, often listed as one of the most beautiful in France, has a charming setting with a hilltop Romanesque church, a bridge spanning the Sarthe and ancient stone houses. For many years it has been a centre and source of inspiration for artists, painters and sculptors and there is an artists' exhibition centre here.

▶ From St-Céneri-le-Gérei take the D 56 south; then turn right onto the D 146.

St-Léonard-des-Bois★

This attractive village is an ideal excursion centre for the Alpes Mancelles and is home to several outdoor pursuits operators (*see Introduction*).

Vallée de Misère★

🚶 *1h30 round-trip.*

From the church square take the path at the corner by the Hôtel Bon Laboureur. At the crossroads marked by a stone cross take a path uphill. Beyond Le Champ-des-Pasfore turn left. At the next crossroads turn left onto a path marked in red and white. From a bench there is a fine **view**★ of the wild Misère valley, St-Léonard and the Manoir de Linthe further downstream.

From St-Léonard-des-Bois return on the D 146 north. Turn right onto the D 56; in Moulins-le-Carbonnel turn left onto the D 150, which becomes the D 315, and will take you back to Alençon.

ADDRESSES

🏠 STAY

⊜ **Inn Design-Resto Novo Alençon** – *rue de Gatel, 61250 Valframbert (1km/0.6mi N of Alençon).* ℘*02 33 27 42 64. www. hotel-inn-alencon.fr. 45 rooms.* The rooms in this traditional family hotel offer contemporary furnishings and modern plumbing.

⊜⊜ **Chambre d'hôte Le Moulin de Linthe** – *route de Sougé-le-Ganelon, 72130 St-Léonard-des-Bois.* ℘*02 43 33 79 22. http://chambres-hotes.alpesmancelles.com. 5 rooms.* The bedrooms have character in this picturesque old mill, still with paddle wheel.

⊜⊜⊜ **Château de Sarceaux** – *61250 Valframbert.* ℘*02 33 28 85 11. www. chateau-de-sarceaux.com. 4 rooms.* A large park with a pond surrounds this 17C–19C château. South-facing rooms are elegantly decorated with antique furniture and family portraits.

⊜⊜⊜ **Mercure** – *187 av. Gén-Leclerc, 2.6km/1.6mi SW.* ℘*02 33 28 64 64. 53 rooms.* Fairly recent building in a small commercial park. Rooms are practical and well soundproofed.

🍴 EAT

⊜ **Auberge Normande** – *Le Pont-du-Londeau, 61250 Valframbert.* ℘*02 33 29 43 29. Closed Sun dinner and Mon dinner.* Often fully booked for lunch, as the locals appreciate the updated regional cuisine and reasonable prices. 9 **rooms**.

⊜ **Le Saint Leo Creperie - Saladerie** – *pl. de l'Église, 72130 St-Léonard-des-Bois.* ℘*02 43 33 29 09.* A simple, convivial stop in this picturesque village. The dining offers salads, galettes and crêpes.

Sées★

The quiet old cathedral town of Sées, with its several religious communities, has been the seat of an episcopal See since St Latuin converted the district to Christianity in the year 400. Its historic centre has been sensitively restored.

▶ **Population:** 4 182.
🎯 **Michelin Map:** 310: K-3.
📋 **Info:** place du Général de Gaulle. ℘02 33 28 74 79. www.tourisme-sourcesdelorne.fr.
▶ **Location:** 22km/13.5mi SE of Argentan, or 19km/11.8mi N of Alençon, near the Forêt d'Écouves.
🔔 **Don't Miss:** The chancel of the cathedral; Forêt d'Écouves.
🕐 **Timing:** Take a day to see the town and enjoy the forest.

SIGHTS

Cathedral★★

♿🕐*Daily 9am–6.30pm.* ℘*02 33 27 81 76.*

The cathedral is one of the finest examples of 13C and 14C Norman Gothic in the country.

Exterior – The porch on the west front is disfigured by heavy buttresses, added in the 16C when the cathedral began to lean alarmingly.

Interior – In the **chancel★★** and the **transepts★★** the triforium is a fascinating example of Gothic art, lit by magnificent 13C **stained glass★★** and rose windows in the transept. In the south transept is the "Beau Dieu" Carrara marble bust by Bernini (1678), one of the last works of the Italian Baroque master. Note, too, the beautiful marble altar from the Louis XVI period, executed by Brousseau, the architect

Cathédrale Notre-Dame de Sées

© Hervé Lenain/hemis.fr

of the diocese. One side of the gilded bronze represents the Entombment, the other scene carved into the marble relates to the discovery of the relics of the two saints, Gervais and Protais.

Musée départemental d'Art religieux

pl. du Gén. de Gaulle.
🕓*Early Jul–Sept Wed–Mon noon–6pm.*
💶*€2.* 📞*02 33 28 59 73.*
The museum, in the former canons' residence, presents a varied collection (12C–19C) of religious art and objects.

Ancien évêché (Palais d'Argentré)

The Old Bishops' Palace was built for Bishop Argentré in 1778.
The beautiful wrought-iron gate has an escutcheon and foliated scrolls.

Ancienne abbaye St-Martin

⊶*Closed to the public.*
The old abbey is now a children's home. However, through the great main gate the gracious 18C abbot's lodging can be glimpsed.

Église Notre-Dame-de-la-Place

The organ loft is Renaissance, and twelve bas-relief sculptures, which illustrate scenes from the New Testament, date from the 16C.

Anciennes halles

This unusual covered market, a rotunda with a peristyle, dates from the 19C.

Basilique de l'Immaculée-Conception

Built in 1872 in Gothic-Revival style, and featuring murals enriched with gold-leaf, the Basilica has a calm meditative atmosphere.
Opposite stands la tour d'Argentan, a remnant of the city's 12C fortifications.

🚗 DRIVING TOUR

🚗 ÉCOUVES FOREST★

29km/18mi. About 2h15.

This itinerary explores a diversity of forests (oak, beech, fir, pine, spruce).

▷ Past Sées, the D 908 leads into the forest via Choux.

✍ Guided tours on foot or on horseback through the forest massifs (Écouves, Andaines, Bellême and Perche-Trappe, Réno-Valdieu, Moulins-Bonsmoulins) are available on request one month in advance from the Office National des Forêts. 📞*02 33 82 55 00. www.onf.fr.*
As you reach the top of the hill, turn left onto the D 226 for views over the Argentan countryside.

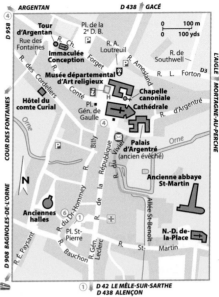

SÉES

WHERE TO STAY

Ferme équestre des Tertres
(Chambre d'hôte)............... ①

Île de Sées (Hôtel).................. ④

Roses et les Pivoines
(Chambre d'hôte Les)............. ⑥

WHERE TO EAT

Cheval Blanc (Le)........................ ①

Normandy (Au)........................... ④

🐾 The various visitor facliities include a Fitness Trail at Chêne-au-Verdier and a Discovery Trail at the Rendez-Vous crossroads. The forest is home to kites and deer.

Carrefour de la Croix-de-Médavy

The Sherman tank (*Valois*) at this crossroads belonged to the 2nd French Armoured Division (*2e division blindée, 2eDB*) under the command of General Leclerc. At the other side of the crossroads, a board recalls the battles fought by the 2eDB during the Battle of Normandy.

The **Signal d'Écouves** is, with the Mont des Avaloirs, the highest point (417m) in western France.

Carrefour de la Croix-Madame

Turn left onto the path to Sapaie-Pichon and keep following the trees marked with yellow stripes. 🐾 *1hr 30min approx round-trip.*
Fine vistas can be enjoyed on this trail.

▶ Return to your car and follow the D 204.

The road descends quickly, with fine views. After the Chêne-au-Verdier crossroads there are beautiful woodlands.

▶ At the Rochers-du-Vignage crossroads, turn right onto the D 26 then immediately right onto a forest track.

Rochers du Vignage★

🚶 *1h45 round-trip.*

The path *(marked with yellow stripes)* leaves the forest road to follow a low rock crest from which there are outstanding views over the forest. The path reaches the Chêne-au-Verdier, runs parallel with the Aubert forest road for around 300m, forks right, then returns downhill to the forest road and back to your car.

▶ Follow the D 26 towards Alençon.

At the exit to the forest, at the junction with a forest trail is a monument and cemetery, some 200m south, both commemorating the 2eDB.

ADDRESSES

☜ STAY

☞ Chambre d'hôte Ferme Équestre des Tertres – *61500 La Chapelle-près-Sées (4km/2.5mi S of Sées). ℘02 33 27 74 67. www.fedestertres.com. 5 rooms.* This farm is the starting point for horse rides through the Écouves Forest. Walkers can follow waymarked trails; other guests could try a barouche ride. Stylish bedrooms with robust furniture.

☞☞☞ Hôtel-Restaurant Île de Sées – *61500 Macé (5.5km/3.5mi NW of Sées). ℘02 33 27 98 65. www.ile-sees.fr. 16 rooms.*

This former dairy is set in a park amid peaceful countryside. Dark woodwork adds warmth to the interior decoration. Restaurant (☞☞).

☟ EAT

☞☞ Au Normandy – *20 pl. du Gén.-de-Gaulle. ℘02 33 27 80 67. www.au-normandy.com.* Behind a 17C façade lies a dining room with blackened beams and a welcoming atmosphere. The menus have regional accents, but the pizza and crêpes also provide good quality comfort food.

Carrouges

Located in the centre of the Parc naturel régional Normandie-Maine, this immense château and park (10ha), belonged to a famous Norman family, Le Veneur de Tillières, for almost five centuries. in 1936 it was bought by the nation. The town is a good base for exploring the region, and its Maison du Parc visitor centre is an indispensable source of information.

▶ **Population:** 671.
◔ **Michelin Map:** 310: I-3.
▤ **Info:** 1 place Charles de Gaulle. ℘02 33 27 20 38.
◐ **Location:** Set on a high point NW of the Écouves forest, Carrouges is 26km/16mi E of Bagnoles-de-l'Orne and 30km/18.5mi NE of Alençon.
🅐 **Don't Miss:** The majestic grand staircase at the château.
◷ **Timing:** Allow at least 90min to see the château.

Château de Carrouges★★

◔*Daily: Jan–Apr and Sept–Dec 10am–12.30pm, 2–5pm; May–Aug 10am–12.45pm, 2–6pm.* ◔*1 Jan, 1 May, 1 and 11 Nov, 25 Dec.* ☜€6. ℘*02 33 27 20 32. http://carrouges. monuments-nationaux.fr.*

From the park with its fine trees and elegant flower beds there are good views of the château.

The **Conservatoire botanique des pommiers de Bretagne et de Normandie** includes 152 varieties of apple trees. The 16C **gatehouse★** is an elegant brick building with decorative geometric patterns. Surrounded by a moat, the château is austere but imposing; its buildings are arranged around an inner courtyard. The stables and domestic quarters occupy the ground floor; the apartments and state rooms occupy the first floor.

The **kitchen** presents an imposing array of copper pans. The **Louis XI Bedroom** was named after the king's visit on 11 August 1473.

The panelling is adorned with delicate panels of foliage highlighted in a different colour.

In the principal **antechamber** the chimney breast is decorated with a hunting scene. The remarkable fireplace in the **dining room** is flanked by two polished granite piers with Corinthian capitals. The sideboards are Louis XIV; note the Restoration chairs.

The **portrait gallery** with its Louis XIII chairs assembles past lords and owners. The **drawing room** occupies part of one of the corner towers. The straw-coloured panelling dates from the late 17C or early 18C.

Château de Carrouges

© Orne Tourisme

The visit ends with the monumental great **staircase★** and its brickwork vaulting and round-headed arches as they wind up and round the square stairwell.

Parc naturel régional Normandie-Maine: Maison du Parc

🕐 *Apr–mid-Oct daily 10am–1pm, 2–6pm (Jul–Aug 6.30pm).* 🕐 *1 May.* 📞 *02 33 81 75 75.* *www.parc-naturel-normandie-maine.fr.* This is the principal visitor centre for the park, with interesting exhibitions and interpretations of the park, and provides a comprehensive information service whatever your interests. The park can be explored by car, on foot (2 499km/ 1 553mi of signposted paths) or by bike (via four themed itineraries). Details and maps are available here.

The centre occupies the restored buildings of a 15C chapter of canons, and is an outbuilding of the château. Next door is the **Conservatoire botanique des pommiers de Bretagne et de Normandie**, a collection of the 152 apple varieties to be found in the two regions.

EXCURSIONS

Goult

13km/8mi E of Carrouges via D908, then left on D 204.
A road lying between two farms leads to the **Chapelle St-Michel**, all that remains of the La-Lande-de-Goult Priory, once a stop on the medieval pilgrimage route to Mont St-Michel.

The 12C Romanesque porch has remarkable capitals carved with complex designs of birds and mythical beasts, as well as hunting scenes. From the cross, there is a fine view of the Écouves forest. Nearby earthworks indicate remains of a Roman military camp.

Tourbière (peat bogs) des Petits-Riaux – follow the signposts. Guided walks are organised by the park rangers – enquire at the Maison du Parc.

A discovery trail *(1.4 km/0.9mi)*, partly on a boardwalk, allows visitors to safely explore this fragile ecological treasure, which includes a spongy carpet of sphagnum moss, ferns and all sorts of amazing carnivorous plants such as round-leaved sundew (Drosera).

Le Champ de la Pierre

8km/5mi northwest via the D 908 and the D 909.
🕐 *Mid-Jul–Sept 10am–noon, 2.30–6.30pm.* 👥€3.50. 📞*02 33 27 21 70. http://lechampdelapierre.com.* Created in the late 18C, this delightful romantic 4ha/10 acre "Jardin remarquable" is full of pretty features and surprises. Take the bridle path lined by lime and beech trees to the lakeside where you will find an 18C blast furnace and forges *(visit possible by arrangement;* 👥€3. *call* 📞*02 33 28 83 93).* This metal-working industry was the mainstay of the local community for nearly

three centuries until being abandoned around the mid-19C. It made fixings, locks and general hardware; one of its notable commissions being the superb main gates for the Château Carrouges. The iron ore came from the bois de Ranes and the charcoal from the forêt d'Ecouves.

ADDRESSES

🛏 STAY

🛏🛏 **Gite de Mary** – *St. Martin des Landes (3km de Carrouges). ☎02 33 28 84 21. http:// gite.de.mary.pagesperso-orange.fr.* This well-equipped cottage, sleeping 8, is in an idyllic country location.

🍴 EAT

🍴 **La Gourmandie** – *19 av. du Maréchal-Leclerc. ☎02 33 29 10 37. Closed Sun and weekday evenings in winter.* Choose from their delicious galettes and crêpes or the *plat du jour.*

Domfront★

Domfront en Poiraie lies spread along a rocky ridge over a gorge carved by the River Varenne, affording a panorama of the Passais *bocage* country. In addition to its **strategic site★** on the old route between Mont St-Michel and Paris, the town features historic ruins and a well-restored town centre.

A BIT OF HISTORY

Under English Rule

In 1092, the townspeople of Domfront rose up against their overlord Roger de Montgomery and rallied to **Henry Beauclerc**, the son of William the Conqueror.

In 1100, Henry became king of England and Domfront an English possession. In the 12C, Henry II Plantagenet and his queen, Eleanor of Aquitaine, often visited with their brilliant court.

Papal legates met here in August 1170 to attempt to reconcile Henry and his estranged Archbishop of Canterbury, Thomas Becket. Domfront passed from English to French hands, and back again, during the Hundred Years' War. It became French for good in 1450.

Matignon's Siege – In 1574 Gabriel, Comte de Montgomery (1530–74), who had mortally wounded the French king Henri II in a tournament, defended Domfront against the royal forces under the Comte de Matignon. Montgomery

- ▶ **Population:** 4 276.
- ⌚ **Michelin Map:** 310: F-3.
- ℹ **Info:** 12 place de la Roirie. ☎02 33 38 53 97. www.ot-domfront.com.
- ▶ **Location:** Domfront lies between Mayenne (36km/22.4mi S) and Flers (22km/13.5mi N).
- ◉ **Don't Miss:** The Old Town and its half-timbered houses; Notre-Dame-sur-l'Eau.
- ◕ **Timing:** Several bike tours have been mapped by the tourist office.

surrendered, believing that his life would be spared, but was executed on the orders of Henri's widow, Catherine de' Medici.

OLD TOWN CENTRE★

Allow 30min.

The old town is enclosed by a wall and 13 of the original 24 towers. The best preserved are those on the south side; one is still crowned with machicolations. For a good view walk along rue des Fossés-Plisson. Several 16C stone houses, formerly inhabited by noble or well-to-do families, have been restored.

Grande-Rue

This sloping street, now a pedestrian zone, has kept its original paving.

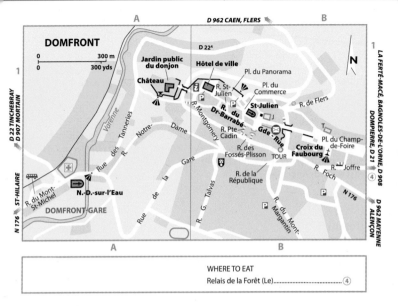

WHERE TO EAT
Relais de la Forêt (Le)............................④

Rue du Docteur-Barrabé
There are some lovely timber-framed houses, notably No. 40 and at the corner of ruelle Porte-Cadin.

Église St-Julien
This modern church (1924) in neo-Byzantine style is dominated by a tall cement belfry. Inside, an immense mosaic depicts Christ in Majesty. The area around the church, in particular rue St-Julien and place du Commerce, is a pleasant area for a stroll.

Hôtel de Ville - Musée
 ⌖◷Mon–Fri 9am–noon, 1.30–4.45pm. ℘02 33 30 60 60.
www.ville-domfront.fr.
In the town hall, the **Salle Charles-Léandre** houses paintings and drawings by local artist Charles Léandre (1862–1941).

Terre-plein nord des remparts (City Walls north)
From la place du Panorama is a beautiful (partial) view into the deep Varenne valley, better known by the townfolk as the "val des Rochers".

ADDITIONAL SIGHTS
Jardin public du Donjon★
Cross the bridge over the old moat to the public gardens, laid out on the site of the fortress destroyed in 1608.
Of Henry Beauclerc's 1092 fortress there remain two imposing sections of the keep's walls and two towers from the flattened curtain wall.
Inside the curtain walls stand the ruins of the late 11C Chapelle St-Symphorien. Eleanor of Aquitaine's daughter was born in Domfront and christened in this very chapel. Skirt the ruins of the keep to reach the terrace which affords a **panorama★** of the Passais countryside. A view indicator points out the three rivers; Mayenne, Varenne and Égrenne.

Église Notre-Dame-sur-l'Eau★
Under the château on the Varenne river.
This charming Romanesque church of Our Lady on the Water (late 11C) was badly damaged in the 19C when five of its seven nave bays were destroyed to make way for a road. Following war damage in 1944 the church was restored. According to legend, at Christmas 1166, Thomas Becket, Archbishop of Canterbury, celebrated Mass in this church while in exile in France.

Several 12C frescoes have been uncovered in the south transept representing the Doctors of the Church (theologians who expounded the Christian doctrine). A Gothic canopy covers a recumbent figure with a lion at its feet.

Croix du Faubourg

From the foot of the Calvary, there is a **panorama★** similar to the one from the public gardens, but it extends further east towards Andaines Forest.

EXCURSION

Dompierre

9 km/5.6mi northeast on the D 21.
The wealth of this village was based on iron working and its **Museum of Iron** (⊙*May–Sept Mon–Fri 10am–noon 2.30–6pm; Sun 2.30–6pm;* ⊸ *no charge;* ℘*02 33 38 03 25; http://lesavoiretlefer.fr*) has displays not only on iron but on other traditional local trades such as cotton spinning, shoemaking, lace-making and farming.

🚶 To see traces of the industrial past still in situ, pick up the leaflet from the museum, which details a 10km/6mi walk around Dompierre's old mineworks. It is marked in yellow and takes around 3h.

🚗 DRIVING TOUR

🚗 NORTHWEST OF DOMFRONT

Round-trip of 35km/22mi. About 2h.

▷ Leave Domfront heading north on the D 22.

Lonlay-l'Abbaye

The church, once part of an 11C abbey, enjoys a pleasant country setting. It was damaged in 1944. The 15C porch opens directly into the transept; the south arm is typical of Romanesque construction and decoration. The Gothic chancel and its granite pillars have been restored.

▷ 5km/3mi west of the village turn left onto the D 134.

La Fosse-Arthour

From the high rocks to the left is a view down into the 70m deep gorge of La Fosse-Arthour. The River Sonce runs swiftly between the gorge before opening out into a swirling pool then continuing on its way in a series of small cascades.

The gorge is the subject of many local legends, the most popular being that it is named after the mythical King Arthur, said to have ended his days here. Fishing and canoeing are popular along this stretch of water.

▷ Take the D 134 south towards St-Georges-de-Rouelley; at the first junction turn left onto the Rouellé road. In Rouellé turn left onto the D 907 to Domfront. After 1.5km/0.9mi turn right onto a narrow unsurfaced road, towards the end, which leads to the Manor ruins.

Manoir de la Saucerie

⊙*Mid-Jul–early Sept 10.30am–1pm, 2.30–7pm.* ⊸€3. ℘*02 33 38 99 08.*
The name comes from Robert le Saucier who was a favourite servant of Eleanor of Aquitaine; at the end of the 12C she gave him the land on which the current manor stands.

The Manoir is a most unusual and attractive building with a fortified appearance, though it has never seen battle. In fact it is a small Châtelet (gatehouse) flanked by two round towers with loopholes and is all that remains of the original 16C manor house. Its unusual picturesque stone, brick and timber upper storey and roof construction is said to be unique in France.

▷ Return to the D 907 for Domfront.

ADDRESSES

🏠 STAY

⊸ 🍴 **Le Presbytère** – *2 rue de la Poste, 61700 St-Bômer-les-Forges (10km/6mi N). ℘02 33 38 83 20. www.stbomer.com. 4 rooms.* A 19C house set in 3ha of grounds. A charming retreat. Open all year.

♀/EAT

🍽 **Bistrot St Julien** – *2 pl. St-Julien.* *☎02 33 37 14 60. Closed Sun and Wed.* This Bordeaux-style bistro with a sunny terrace is as good for a sandwich or salad for lunch, as it is for a nice plate of roast lamb with rosemary for dinner.

🍽 **L'Échauguette** – *12 Grande rue.* *☎02 31 37 71 71. www.lechauguette-domfront.com. Closed Mon.* The salads, pizzas, galettes and crêpes taste even better here when taken on the shady terrace.

🍽🍽 **Le Relais de la Forêt** – *Le Bourg, Dompierre (9km/5.6mi NE). ☎02 33 30 44 21. Closed all day Tue and Sun, and Mon evening.* Slightly old-fashioned décor; expect local seasonal produce, accompanied by local cider.

🍽🍽🍽 **Auberge du Grand Gousier** – *1 pl.de a Liberté. ☎02 33 38 37 25. www. restaurant-grandgousier.com.* Enjoy fine local cuisine such as monkfish in red wine, or veal sweetbreads with shallots and basil, in this charming cosy half-timbered house.

Bagnoles-de-l'Orne★

In addition to its healing waters, the spa town of Bagnoles-de-l'Orne has a lovely serene lakeside setting★. The lake is formed by the Vée, a tributary of the Mayenne, before it enters a deep gorge cut through the massif of the Andaines forest. It is best appreciated by taking a stroll from Tessé-la-Madeleine to the Roc au Chien.

- ▶ **Population:** 2 674.
- ⏱ **Michelin Map:** 310: G-3.
- 🛈 **Info:** Place du Marché. ☎02 33 37 85 66. www. bagnolesdelorne.com.
- ▶ **Location:** Bagnoles is 2km/1mi N of the D 176, which links Alençon (47km/29mi SW) to Mont St-Michel (90km/56mi W). The town comprises two distinct parts: to the W Bagnoles-Château and E, Bagnoles-Lac.
- 🅿 **Parking:** Near the château, the museum, the casino and the place du Marché.
- 🚫 **Don't Miss:** Roc au Chien.
- 🕐 **Timing:** Half a day for the spa waters.
- 👪 **Kids:** Forêt des Andaines.

BAGNOLS-LAC
Parc de l'établissement thermal★

The park surrounding the spa building is planted with pines, oaks and chestnut trees. The Allée du Dante on the east bank of the Vée, which is often crowded with bathers, leads from the lake to the spa building. Other alleys in the park wind towards Capuchin's Leap and to the pictureque site known as the Abri Janolin. Shops along rue des Casions line the lake front.

BAGNOLS-CHÂTEAU
Le Roc au Chien★

🚶 *45min round-trip.* Start from the church and walk up the avenue du Château; the main gateway opens on to the avenue and the public park of Tessé that holds an arboretum containing 150 different tree species, a bird-watching trail, a children's playground and other amusements. The château, built in the

19C in neo-medieval style, now houses the town hall.

Take the avenue on the right, which overlooks the Bagnoles gorge and leads to the rocky promontory, the Roc au Chien, where there is a lovely **view★** of Bagnoles beside the lake and the spa building and its park.

EXCURSIONS
Château de Couterne

1.5km/0.9mi south of Bagnoles on the D 335. Park the car by the bridge. ⊶*The interior is closed to the public.*

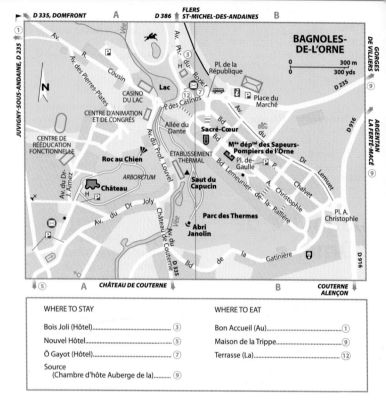

WHERE TO STAY		WHERE TO EAT	
Bois Joli (Hôtel)	③	Bon Accueil (Au)	①
Nouvel Hôtel	⑤	Maison de la Trippe	⑨
Ô Gayot (Hôtel)	⑦	Terrasse (La)	⑫
Source (Chambre d'hôte Auberge de la)	⑨		

The massive brick and granite château (16C and 18C) is reflected in the waters of the Vée.

La Ferté-Macé

6km/4mi north via the D 916.

This small town has retained a number of 18C and 19C buildings and houses that recall its past role in the textile industry. It is also famous for *tripes en brochettes*, tripe skewered on hazel wood sticks.

There is a large tourist complex, including a leisure park (pedalos, windsurfing, fishing, climbing, swimming, golf, etc.) and a dozen holiday houses. A lively market is held on Thursday mornings. An 11C Romanesque tower is all that remains of the old parish church, demolished in 1861.

The **hôtel de ville** (town hall) houses works by the local artist **Charles Léandre**, as well as fascinating 19C paintings celebrating the postal service and local manufacturing.

👥 Musée du Jouet

32 r. de la Victoire.

🕙*Easter–early Nov Wed and Sat 2–5pm.* 🎫€3.30. 📞*02 33 37 10 97.*

This museum of 19C and 20C games and toys has been set up in the former municipal baths.

Rânes

13km/8mi northeast from La Ferté-Macé via D 916.

Rebuilt in the 18C, the castle, which now houses the local *gendarmerie*, has retained its 15C two-storeyed keep, complete with crenellations and machicolations. Enjoy the panoramic view from the top.

🚶 WALKS

The Andaines forest (🧭*see Driving Tour*) is ideal for walking. We offer two suggestions below (for more ideas visit the tourist office).

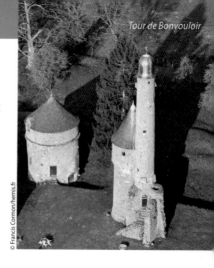
Tour de Bonvouloir

© Francis Cormon/hemis.fr

Circuit de St-Ortaire et du chêne Hippolyte

4.5km/2.8mi – allow 1h45.

Start near the Market Square. Walk beside the train tracks. The first place you come to is the Priory of St Ortaire, an ancient establishment founded by Jean de Valois, dedicated to the saints Radegund and Ortaire. A little further on, in the heart of the forest, is a giant 300-year-old oak (known as the Hippolyte) with a girth of around 5.25m and a height of 30m.

Gorges de Villiers★

12km/7.5mi southeast, near St-Ouen-le-Brisoult.

There are several well marked walking trails in this beautiful gorge, which has been created by the River Gourbe. The Chapelle St-Antoine trail takes around an hour. It initially leads to the river, passing over an impressive scree slope; look out for the small cave of the fairy, Gisele, who, according to local lore, protects travellers. Near the bridge, across the Gourbe, is a hot spring, which in Roman times attracted a cult following. The trail crosses the river and climbs up to a wide path. Go right on here and this takes you back into the forest. Set in a beautiful glade, the chapelle St-Antoine (built 1875) appears in a beautiful glade. Walk back along the river to the starting point of your walk.

DRIVING TOUR

VALLÉE DE LA COUR

11km/6mi northeast.

Take the D 916, turn right onto the D 387 and then right again, after 600m onto the D 20, then follow the signs.

A road leads to a lake where there is good fishing.

Forêt des Andaines

Part of the Normandie-Maine Regional Nature Park the forest offers pleasant walks and, if you're lucky (and quiet), a glimpse of deer, stag or roe deer.

*Popular places include the slender **Tour de Bonvouloir** observation tower; the **Chapelle Ste-Geneviève**, a picnic site; and, best of all, the heavy-horse shows at **Ferme du Cheval de Trait** (Juvigny-sous-Andaine; Apr–Oct check the website for details; €13.50 (child 5–12, €5); 02 33 38 27 78. www.lamichaudiere.fr).* Book for lunch on the farm.

ADDRESSES

STAY

Auberge de la Source– La Peras, 61600 La Ferté-Macé (5km/3mi NW). 02 33 37 28 23. http://auberge.lasource.pagesperso-orange.fr. 5 rooms. This building is in old Norman-style with bricks and half-timbering. Rooms have excellent beds and parquet floors. The restaurant serves regional fare and has an open fire.

Ô Gayot – 2 av. de la Ferté-Macé. 02 33 38 44 01. www.ogayot.com. 16 rooms. This town centre hotel offers minimalist rooms, bar, tea room, gourmet shop, and modern bistro serving contemporary cuisine. Terrace.

Nouvel Hôtel – 8 Avenue Pierre Noal, 61140 Tessé-la-Madeleine (0.5km/0.3mi S). 02 33 30 75 00. http://www.lenouvelhotel.fr. 30 rooms. This lovely, thoroughly renovated villa dating from 1900 lies close to the thermal spa. Modern rooms are decorated in warm colours. Covered terrace.

♥/EAT

🍽 **Maison de la Trippe** – 20 pl. du Gén.-Leclerc, La Ferté-Macé. ☎02 33 37 11 85. http://lamaisondelatripe.unblog.fr. Open Tue–Sat 7am–7.30pm, Sun 8am–1pm. Offal is the house speciality at this small daytime restaurant and shop.

🍽🍽 **La Terrasse** – r. des Casinos. ☎02 33 37 81 44. Closed Sun and Wed evenings, and all day Mon. Excellent regional cuisine with fish specialities are served in an inviting rustic interior with a sheltered terrace.

🍽🍽 – 🍽🍽🍽🍽 **Le Bois Joli** – 12 av. Philippe-du-Rozier. ☎02 33 37 92 77. www.hotelboisjoli.com. Overlooking the lake, this beautiful Anglo-Norman villa offers three prix-fixe gourmet menus.

🍽🍽🍽 **Au Bon Accueil** – 23 pl. St-Michel, Juvigny-sous-Andaine. ☎02 33 38 10 04. www.aubonaccueil-normand.com. Closed Sun eve, Mon. This elegant establishment serves fine, light regional cuisine using the freshest local produce.

Mortain★

This small, well-kept town is built halfway up a hillside in an attractive setting★ where the River Cance, cutting through the last of Basse-Normandie's southern hills, emerges on to the vast wooded Sélune basin, leaving in its wake a rock-strewn countryside. The name of the town is derived from the word Maurus and could refer to the Moors who served in the Roman army. During the Middle Ages Mortain was the capital of the county held by Robert, the stepbrother of William the Conqueror. The town has been rebuilt over the ruins left by the Battle of Normandy.

- ▸ **Population:** 2 955.
- ◔ **Michelin Map:** 303: G-8.
- ▯ **Info:** Rue du Bourg Lopin. ☎02 33 59 19 74.
- ◖ **Location:** Mortain is 25km/15.5mi S of Vire via D 577 and D 977. Avranches is 42km/26mi W via D 5.
- ◉ **Don't Miss:** The picturesque Grande and Petite Cascades and the "Chrismal" treasury at St-Évroult Church.
- ◕ **Timing:** You will need at least a half day to tour the Cascades, which involve a fair amount of walking; and the Abbaye Blanche.

SIGHTS

Grande Cascade★

🅿 Use the car park at avenue de l'Abbaye-Blanche (at a bend in the road) and take the path downhill, or park in rue du Bassin (signposted) and take the path that follows the river bank.
The waterfall (25m) is created by the River Cance flowing through a wooded gorge; the foaming waters are reminiscent of the mountain streams of the Pyrenees or the Alps.

Petite Cascade★

🚶 45min round-trip. From place du Château take the downhill path south (left) along the wall of the Caisse d'Épargne (signpost).

The path crosses the River Cance and follows the bank upstream past the Needle Rock. It then crosses the Cançon stream on stepping stones before reaching the waterfall (35m) in a rock amphitheatre.

Petite Chapelle★

From Mortain take the road south towards Rancoudray; in front of the Gendarmerie turn left. Park in the car park at the top of the hill; walk up the avenue of fir trees.
To the left and beyond the chapel there is a belvedere providing a **view**★ of the

wooded heights of Mortain and Lande-Pourrie, with an indicator to identify the various points of interest.

On a clear day Mont St-Michel and the Breton coast are visible on the horizon (right).

Abbaye Blanche
At edge of town.

This 12C former monastery, now a nunnery, sits amid a landscape of rocky outcrops. It was founded in the 12C by Adeline and her brother Vital, chaplain to Count Robert, stepbrother of William the Conqueror.

The chapter house is composed of two bays with pointed vaulting. The cloister gallery, unlike other Romanesque cloisters in the region, which have twinned columns or clusters as at Mont St-Michel, consists of a simple row of single columns. The vaulting is of timberwork.

The church displays the usual features of the Cistercian plan: flat east end with an oculus and transept chapels. The diagonal ribs are a precursor of the Gothic style. The groined vaulting of the Lay Sisters' Refectory is supported by two central columns.

Collégiale St-Évroult
Town centre.

This old collegiate church, reconstructed in the 13C, is built of sandstone in a severe Gothic style. The 13C belfry is plain and simple. The door in the second bay shows all the fine decorative elements known to Norman Romanesque. The single arch relies neither on columns nor capitals. The chancel stalls have carved misericords representing satyr-like figures.

The **treasury** contains the **Chrismal**, an exceptional 7C casket (portable reliquary) of Anglo-Irish origin, made of beechwood, lined with copper and engraved with runic inscriptions and images of sacred personages.

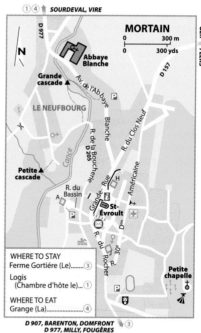

EXCURSIONS

Barenton
9 km/5.6mi southeast. Leave Mortain on the road to Domfront.

Near Barenton in the Normandie-Maine Regional Park is **La Musée du Poiré** cider and perry farm (◷Apr–Oct 10am–1pm, 2–6pm (6.30pm in summer); ◷1 May. ℘02 33 59 56 22. www.parc-naturel-normandie-maine.fr). Here you can learn all about the making of cider,

Petite Cascade

© FLPA/David Burton/age fotostock

perry and calvados and its wider economic importance to the region, take a tour of the orchards and, of course, enjoy a tasting at the end of your visit. Children can join in the fun too with a special interpretive trail of their own

Ger

The town is famous for its distinctive brown pottery which reached its zenith in the 19C, employing 700 workers. Production concentrated on stoneware pots, fired at very high temperature (1 260°C), which were sold through western France. The industry has now all but gone, though you can explore its history at the nearby regional Museum of Pottery, located on the road to Flers some 15km/9.5mi from Mortain.

▷ From Mortain take D 157, then D 60 on the left, heading towards Le Placître.

Musée régional de la Poterie★

3 rue du Musée.
Jul–Aug 10am–6pm; Apr–Jun and Sept Wed, Sun and public holidays 2–6pm. 1 May. €5 (child 7–18, €2.50). 02 33 79 35 36.
The museum comprises 12 buildings: a potter's house, three long tunnel-kilns from the 17C and 18C, a drying device for pots, various workshops, a bakery, etc. There is an interesting **demonstration★** of manufacturing techniques. Pottery is still made on the premises and is available for sale.

🚗DRIVING TOUR

🚗 VALLÉE DE LA SÉE
Round-trip of 58km/36mi. Allow 3h.

▷ From Mortain take D 977 north towards Vire.

North of La Tournerie, where the road winds downhill, there is a view of the vast Sourdeval basin, through which runs the River Sée.

▷ In Sourdeval turn left onto the D 911.

The road follows the curves of the narrow **Sée valley★**, offering a new view at each bend.

Moulin de la Sée

Brouains. Apr–Jun Sun and public holidays 10.30am–6pm; Jun and Sept Wed–Sun and public holidays; Jul–Aug Tue–Sun and public holidays 10.30am–6pm. Oct–Mar. €3. 02 33 59 20 50. https://moulindelasee.wixsite.com/ecomusee.
This mill is also known as the **Écomusée de la Vallée de Brouains**, a museum devoted to rivers and related activities, including fish breeding (the River Sée is one of France's finest salmon runs), the development of hydraulic energy, and the development of water-powered industries, from pewter ware to stainless steel cutlery.

▷ After passing the church in Chérencé-le-Roussel, turn right onto the D 33.

St-Pois

From here there are fine views south of the Sée valley.

▷ In St-Pois turn right, then right again onto the D 39 which climbs uphill.

St-Michel-de-Montjoie

At the southwest entrance to the village, a terrace affords a fine view which, on a clear day, extends to Mont St-Michel. The village is known for its granite quarry *(northwest off the D 282 towards Gast)* and for its mineral water, Eau de Montjoie.
The **Parc-musée du Granit** (*Apr–May Sun and public holidays 10am–6pm; Jun Wed–Sun 10.30am–6pm; Jul–Aug Tue–Sun 10.30am–6pm; Sept 10.30am–6pm; no charge. 02 33 59 02 22*) explains the local history of quarrying and displays objects fashioned from the quarry – capitals, pediments, sarcophagi, balusters, millstones – in a wooded park.

▷ Return to Chérencé-le-Roussel. Turn left onto the D 33 to return to Mortain.

ADDRESSES

🛌 STAY

🛏 **Le Ferme Gortière**– *28 route de St-Hilaire, 50640 Le Teilleul (13km/8mi south). ℰ02 33 59 43 29. www.chambres-hotes-gortiere.com. 2 rooms.* On a working farm operated by the Rousseau family who will pleased to tell you all about it. Walk in the orchard and meet the goat!

🛏🛏 **Hôtel de la Poste** – *place des Arcades. ℰ02 33 59 00 05. www.hoteldelaposte-mortain.fr. 25 rooms.*

Opposite the Collegiate Church. Choose a room with a view of the valley. Seasonal menus in the restaurant (🍴🍴).

🍴 EAT

🍴🍴 **La Grange** – *Bellefontaine (7km/4.3mi North). ℰ06 69 41 83 07. www.village-enchante.fr.* Situated at the entrance to the village, this charming barn conversion is a delight if rather touristy. The menu features snacks, salads, simple grills and fixed-price meals.

Sillé-le-Guillaume

Occupying a strategically important site, which protected northern Maine from Norman invasion, the small town of Sillé-le-Guillaume had a rich and eventful past.

Château

🕐*Jul–Aug 10.30am–12.30pm, 1.30–6.30pm; Apr–Jun and Sept Wed–Sun 2–6pm. ≈€3.*
At the end of the Hundred Years' War, the English sacked the 11C fortress. The 15C castle was built on the ruins.

Église Notre-Dame

The church stands upon the site of a former Romanesque church of which the **crypt** and the south transept gable remain.

🚗 DRIVING TOUR

🚗 LA FORÊT DE SILLÉ
30km/19mi. Allow 1h.

▷ Leave Sillé-le-Guillaume northeast on the D 310.

This short tour takes you into the forest, which is popular with walkers.

▶ **Population:** 2 312.
◔ **Michelin Map:** 310: I-5.
🛈 **Info:** Place de la Résistance ℰ02 43 20 10 32. www.tourisme.sille-le-guillaume.fr.
▷ **Location:** Sillé-le-Guillaume is 35km/22mi NW of Le Mans and 17km/10.5mi SW of Fresnay-sur-Sarthe.

▷ Take the D 105 towards Sillé-Plage then left on the D 203.

Sillé-Plage is a popular lake with a beach. The information office (*see above*) is a useful resource. On the Coco-Plage part of the beach are the remains of an ancient medieval castle.

▷ Continue around the lake, in the direction of Sillé-le-Guillaume and take the forest road right towards Grand-Ligne which leads via a crossroads to **Croix-de-la-Mare**. A 45min round-trip walk leads to the highest point in the forest, marked by a cross (erected by a penitent after the French Revolution) and a chapel dating from 1862.

▷ At the Croix de Mare crossroads take the D 103 towards bis-Rouessé Vasse, then the D 310 back to Sillé-le-Guillaume.

The northern portion of the Mayenne *département* that extends into Normandy is also known as the lower Maine or the black Maine, remnants of a former province. Through it flows the River Mayenne, on which sit the ancient fortress cities of Laval and Mayenne. The navigable river system once formed a vital transport artery, defended by picturesque forts and castles; today, marinas line the river banks. The landscape, part of the Amoricain massif, is rocky and forested, crisscrossed with hedgerows planted to contain the marshy soil, and dotted with gardens, orchards and pastures where horses graze.

Highlights

1 The imposing château at **Lassay-les-Chateâux** (p346)
2 The extensive remains of the Roman past at **Jublains** (p347)
3 The Chapelle St-Créspin of La Basilique **Évron** (p348)
4 **Laval** Old Town, for its history, art, architecture (p353)
5 Milking a visit to the Lactopôle at **Laval** for all it's worth (p356)

Ste-Suzanne
© Philippe CAHAREL/Mayenne Tourisme

Around the Mayenne

Laval is both a thriving modern city and one that enjoys the title "City of Art and History". Its delightful old town, made up of medieval and Renaissance buildings, clusters under the castle on the bank of the Mayenne River. The terraced **Perrine gardens**, noted for their magnificent trees and water features, offer views of the town and river. Tucked away among the surrounding countryside are abbeys, castles and Roman ruins, ideal for driving tours.

Mayenne is the main city of this region, with an old Carolingian core and the eponymous river flowing through the heart of town. It is a good base from which to explore the many picturesque

Lassay-les-Châteaux
© Dominique VERNIER/Mayenne Tourisme

villages and surrounding countryside. Chief among these are the ancient market town of **Lassay-les Châteaux**, with its splendid little-visited castle, and the well-preserved town of **Évron**, set among forests and lakes at the foot of the Coëvrons hills.

At the little village of **Pontmain**, a magnificent basilica marks the site of an apparition of the Virgin and the beautiful **La Pellerine gardens** bloom all summer long. The 11C keep at **Ste-Suzanne**, set on a commanding promontory above the River Erve, offers splendid views of this village, voted one of the most beautiful in France. For the archaeologically inclined the most impressive sight in the Mayenne is probably the remains of the ancient Roman garrison town at **Jublains**, with its fortress, temple, amphitheatre and public baths.

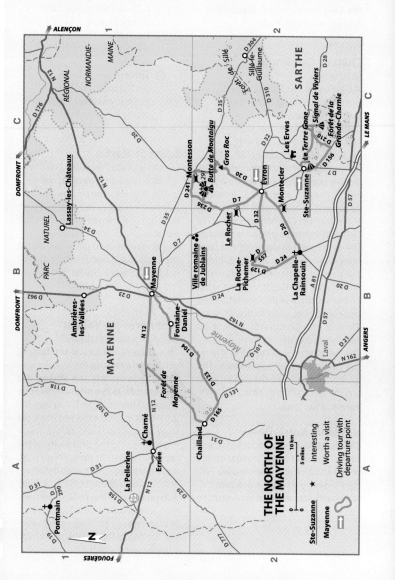

Mayenne

Historically Mayenne was a fortified "bridgehead" town, defending the river, which has been navigable to Laval since the 17C. Its strategic importance was reinforced in June 1944, when the town had been nearly levelled, but thanks to the heroism of American Sergeant Mack Racken, the bridge remained intact. It was the only bridge still spanning the River Mayenne and allowed the Allies to march on Paris.

▶ **Population:** 12 893.
⏲ **Michelin Map:** 310: E-5.
ℹ **Info:** quai Waiblingen. ℘02 43 04 19 37. www.hautemayenne-tourisme.com.
▶ **Location:** Mayenne is on the route from Le Mans (104km/64.5mi SE) to Mont St-Michel. It is also between Caen (120km/74mi N) and Laval (32km/20mi S).
👁 **Don't Miss:** The pretty villages in the forest of Mayenne.
🕐 **Timing:** Take a day to see the town, and to enjoy the many nautical activities on the Mayenne river.

SIGHTS
Château Carolingien
pl. Juhel.
&⏲*Mar–Jun and Sept–Oct daily except Mon 10am–12.30pm, 2–6pm; Jul–Aug daily 10am–76m; Nov–Dec and Feb daily except Mon 10am–12.30pm, 2–5pm.* ⏲*Jan, 1 May, 25 Dec.* ◉€4. ℘02 43 00 17 17. www.museeduchateaudemayenne.fr.

During construction work on a new cultural centre in 1993, workers discovered an old fortress dating from the time of the Carolingian kings (751–987), and archaeologists were called in. The new museum presents artefacts from 15 years of digs, in lively displays. The present castle, reinforced several times in the 11C–15C, stands on the hill on the west bank of the river. It suffered frequent sieges, most famously when William the Conqueror took it by cunning, rather than by force.

The perimeter wall remains, giving the castle a feudal appearance. The promenade between the curtain walls and the town gardens commands a fine **view**★ of the town.

Basilique Notre-Dame
This church has been remodelled several times. The west front, along with the pillars and arches in the nave, are 12C; the transept walls and windows are 16C. The church was rebuilt at the end of the 19C in the Gothic style.

Église St-Martin
Located opposite the château, on the hillside on the other side of the river.
In the 11C the church belonged to Marmoutiers abbey in Tours, and both the apse and transept date from this period.

The modern stained glass, like that in the Basilique Notre-Dame, is by the master glazier Maurice Rocher.

EXCURSIONS
Ambrières-les-Vallées
12km/7.5mi north on the D 23.
This ancient medieval settlement perches on a rocky peak.

Near the town hall, the **Musée des Tisserands mayennais (**Mayenne Weavers Museum. ⏲*Jul–Aug Tue–Sun 2.30–6.30pm.* ℘02 43 04 96 19) tells the story of how cloth and canvas weaving was vital to the prosperity of the region. Housed in three former 18C weavers'cottages, it traces all the production stages of sheets, clothing, ships' sails and more. The cellar-workshop, with period tools, a large loom and furnishings, gives a good idea of the workers' lot during this time. Audio-visuals complement the visit.

Mayenne by the river with Château Carolingien

© Joel Damase/Mayenne Tourisme

Ernée

24km/15mi west via the N 12.

At the town entrance, on the edge of the road, sheltered by trees, stands the chapel of Charné. It is all that remains of the ancient village of Charné, which was abandoned centuries ago, when the people moved to the new town of Ernée. It features a Gothic choir and transept, and Romanesque tower. Balzac set part of his novel *Les Chouans* in and around Ernée.

🚗 DRIVING TOUR

🚗 FORÊT DE MAYENNE

50km/30mi.

▷ Leave Mayenne to the southwest on the D 104.

Fontaine-Daniel

A beautiful lake overlooked by a lovely chapel, flower-decked houses and a former Cistercian abbey all contribute to the charm of Fontaine-Daniel.

The village was created around a fabric manufacturer's known as the **Toiles de Mayenne**. Founded in 1806, it was installed in the grounds of the old Cistercian abbey (which had lost its property during the Revolution), and has produced nationally acclaimed upholstery fabrics here ever since. An exhibition centre and shop (◯*Mon–Sat 9am–12.30pm, 1.30–6pm.* ✆*02 43 00 34 80.*

River Mayenne

Cruises depart daily in summer; the standard cruise lasts 2hr, there is also a 1hr mini-cruise, or you could make a night of it by going on a dinner cruise. Alternatively you can explore the river independently by hiring a pedalo or electric motorboat from the Base Nautique Halte Fluviale at Quai Waiblingen. Visit www.paysdemayenne-tourisme.fr for more details on both cruising and hiring boats. For canoe and kayak rentals, visit www.kayakmayenne.fr.

www.toilesdemayenne.com) displays its high-quality fabrics.

▷ The D 104 and D 123 lead to St-Germain-le-Guillaume, then Chailland on the D 165.

Chailland

This small town is dominated by a rocky outcrop, on top of which stands an over-size statue of the Virgin.

▷ Turn right before the church.

The road bypasses the rocky outcrop and passes between the Château de la Touche and a pond, before entering the oak-and-elm coppiced Mayenne forest, which is privately owned. Gradually the forest subsides to thickets.

ADDRESSES

🛏 STAY

🍴🍴 **Best Hotel Mayenne** – *2 Route de Saint-Baudelle.* ☎*02 43 00 71 71. www. besthotel.fr/Mayenne. 39 rooms.* Cheap and cheerful good-value no-frills chain hotel with spotless rooms, in the city centre.

🍴🍴🛏 **Hôtel la Tour des Anglais** – *13 bis, place Juhel.* ☎*02 43 04 34 56. http://latourdesanglais.com. 20 rooms.* This centrally located hotel compensates for its basic rooms with a breathtaking view of the river and town from its historic tower, parts of which date back over 1 000 years; once a fortress and a prison, it is now a lounge bar. Guests can also relax in the terraced gardens.

🍴🍴🛏 **Hôtel Beau Rivage** – *route de Ste Baudelle, Moulay (1.6km/1mi south).* ☎*02 43 00 49 13. www.restaurantbeaurivage.com. 8 rooms.* The hotel occupies a former riverside dance hall in a lovely grassy spot, with a terrace shaded by a large horse chestnut tree. A veranda seating 80, with sliding windows, looks onto the river (🍴*see EAT*).

🍴 EAT

🍴🍴 **Beau Rivage** – *route de St-Baudelle, Moulay (1.6km/1mi south).* ☎*02 43 00 49 13. www.restaurantbeaurivage.com. Closed Sun evening and all day Mon.* The River Mayenne flows just below the shaded terrace of this beautifully sited hotel restaurant. In cool weather you can relax in the spacious dining room with exposed timber work and watch meat and fish being grilled in the brick-built fireplace.

🍴🍴🛏 **Hotel-Restaurant La Marjolaine** – *Le Bas-Mont, Moulay (1.6km/1mi south).* ☎*02 43 00 48 42. www.lamarjolaine.fr. Closed early Jan, Feb school holidays, Mon lunch and Sun eve.* This splendid old stone house stands in its own grassy grounds with a swimming pool. In the evening, dine on refined modern cuisine, either inside the cosy dining room, or out on the terrace. 35 **rooms** (🍴🍴🛏).

🍴🍴🛏 **La Forge** – *Fontaine-Daniel (5km/3 mi southwest).* ☎*02 43 00 34 85. www.restaurantlaforge.fr. Closed Sun evening and all day Mon.* The old forge in the centre of this charming village has been transformed into a contemporary restaurant, serving dishes focusing on textures, herbs and aromatic plants.

Lassay-les-Châteaux★

On the edge of this ancient market town stands an imposing fortress. Some of its buildings have recently been restored, revealing some splendid red-granite façades such as that of the Maison du Bailly.

THE CHÂTEAU★

🔍 *Guided tours: May Sat–Sun and public holidays 2.30–6.30pm; Jun–mid-Jul and Sept daily except Mon 2.30–6.30pm; mid-Jul–Aug daily 1.30–7.30pm.* ≋€7. ☎*02 43 04 05 47. http://chateaudelassay.fr.*
The castle, which dominates the village, features eight pepper-pot towers linked by a strong curtain wall. It was built in 1458 in place of an older building, dismantled in 1417 during the Hundred Years' War. A prime example of military architecture under the reign of Charles VII, the castle

▸ **Population:** 2 293.
🜨 **Michelin Map:** 310: G-4.
▤ **Info:** 8 rue du Château. ☎*02 43 04 74 33. www.hautemayenne-tourisme.com.*
◉ **Location:** On the D 34 between Bagnoles-de-l'Orne (17km/10.6mi NE) and Mayenne (19km/12mi SW).
◈ **Don't Miss:** For a good overall view of the castle take the path under the stone bridge at the foot of the towers.
🕐 **Timing:** Allow time to take a walk in the surrounding countryside among the hedgerows *(bocage)*.

has links with King Henri IV, the writer and poet Victor Hugo and the chemist A L de Lavoisier, who was a prisoner here during the Revolution. During World War II the castle was used as a German command post.

The working drawbridge, which spans the moat, leads to the barbican, a fortified structure defending the entrance. The two towers guarding the drawbridge are linked by living quarters, in which 16C and 17C weapons and furniture are displayed. The casemates can be seen at the foot of the barbican.

ADDRESSES

🛏 STAY

🍽🍽 **La Ferme de la Prémoudière** – *St-Denis-de-Villenette (11.5km/7mi north). ℰ02 33 37 23 27. www.lapremoudiere.com. 5 rooms.* These attractively converted farm buildings provide the best of both worlds, combining B&B and self-catering. There is a kitchenette for guests' use, pre-prepared farm-fresh meals to buy, and a communal breakfast area.

Ville Romaine de Jublains★

This archaeological site, comprising baths, the ruins of a fort, a temple and theatre are the best Gallo-Roman period remains in the region and offers a valuable insight into local life under the Romans.

A BIT OF HISTORY

Following the conquest of Gaul by Julius Caesar (50 BCE), the Romans divided the country into districts and built towns; the town of Noviodunum (Jublains) was built at an ancient crossroads as an important link in the road network of the Roman Empire. Its main role, as a sanctuary, is shown by the alignment of the public buildings along the axis of the temple.

SIGHTS

Musée archéologique départemental

Situated at the entry to the fortress, 13 r. de la Libération.
🚸🕐*May–Jun and Sept daily 9am–12.30pm, 1.30–6pm; Jul–Aug 9am–6pm; Oct–Apr Thu–Tue 9.30am–12.30pm, 1.30–5.30pm.* 🕐*Mid-Dec–Jan.* 🎫*€4. ℰ02 43 58 13 20. www.museedejublains.fr.*
This modern museum not only interprets the adjacent Roman site, but also other archaeological themes of the Mayenne region, in particular the palaeolithic site

- ▶ **Population:** 727.
- 🚲 **Michelin Map:** 310: G-5
- 🗎 **Info:** Mairie: 6 imp Romaine. ℰ02 43 04 30 33. www.jublains.fr.
- ▶ **Location:** The remains of the Roman city are 10km/6mi SE of Mayenne; 14km/8.5mi NW of Évron.
- 👁 **Don't Miss:** The remarkably preserved theatre.
- 🕐 **Timing:** If you are near Jublains in late July or early August, try to attend a musical performance organised by Les Nuits de la Mayenne (*www.nuitsde lamayenne.com*).

at Saulges with its decorated cave, the Gaulish and Gallo-Roman sanctuaries and the development of the Roman town, then called Noviodunum. A large-scale model gives a good idea of what the town looked like in ancient times.

Fortresse gallo-romaine

This consists of three concentric parts. The central building – the oldest part of the fortress, dating from the early 3C – is a massive rectangular storehouse with four angle towers. During the late 3C crisis (invasions, military anarchy and peasant rebellions), which shook

Fortresse gallo-romaine

the Roman Empire, the storehouse was surrounded by a rampart of raised earth and a moat. This moat was later filled in, and fortified walls were erected in around 290, just before the whole site was abandoned.

Les Thermes (Public Baths)
Below the church.
&♿⏲*Same times as museum.*
The building, which dates from the late 1C, was altered in the 3C and transformed into a Christian church at the end of the Gallo-Roman period. The layout of the baths and main rooms is shown on a plan: the cold bath (*frigidarium*) paved in blue schist;

the warm room (*tepidarium*); and the sweating room (*laconicum*). The hot bath (*cella soliaris*) is situated beyond the excavated part.

Theatre
The theatre was offered to the town by a rich Gaul, Orgetorix (c. 81–83).

Temple
The temple can be visited freely; brochures are available at the museum.
The temple is situated at the other end of the Roman town, 800m from the theatre. Its proportions were vast (each side 80m long). It was built of limestone brought in from the Loire region.

Évron★

This small town at the foot of the Coëvrons possesses one of the finest churches in the Mayenne, visible from up to 10km/6mi away. In the 19C the town's linen mills prospered; today it is classified as a "station verte de vacances" – recognised for the beauty of its surroundings.

BASILIQUE NOTRE-DAME★
pl. de la Basilique.
⏲*Daily 9am–6.30pm.* ✆€5.
☎*02 43 66 85 04.*
www.evron.fr/La-Basilique.html.
A massive square 11C tower, embellished with corner buttresses and turrets, links the Romanesque part of the nave to the 18C abbey buildings. The nave's four

▶ **Population:** 7 200.
🕐 **Michelin Map:** 310: G-6.
🛈 **Info:** Mairie: 4 rue de Hertford. ☎02 43 01 78 03. www.evron.fr.
◐ **Location:** Évron, surrounded by forests and lakes, is 26km/16mi SE of Mayenne via D 7, and 33km/20.5mi ENE of Laval via D 32.
✦ **Don't Miss:** The St-Crespin chapel in the Notre-Dame Basilica.
🕐 **Timing:** After an hour or so of seeing the town, make an excursion into the surrounding countryside.

original bays are Romanesque, while the remainder of the basilica was rebuilt in the 14C in the Flamboyant Gothic style. Note the fine 16C organ case and in the trefoil the fragments of a fresco depicting the Nursing Virgin.

The bare Romanesque nave enhances the sense of space, soaring height and luminosity and contrasts with the Gothic decoration elsewhere (restored 1979).

Chancel

Slender columns, pure lines and subtle decoration give the chancel considerable elegance. The overall effect is embellished by five windows with 14C stained glass, restored in 1901. During repair work to the chancel paving, a crypt and several sarcophagi were discovered, one dating to the 10C.

Chapelle St-Créspin★★

This 12C chapel opens off the north side of the ambulatory. Christ is shown in a mandorla surrounded by the symbols of the Evangelists. Four lovely Aubusson tapestries represent Abraham's Sacrifice of Isaac, Hagar and Ishmael in the desert; Lot and his daughters leaving Sodom; and Jacob's Dream.

At the altar is a large 13C statue of Our Lady of the Thorn (the full name of the basilique is Notre-Dame-de-l'Épine) in wood plated with silver. Beneath a remarkable 13C crucifix, a cabinet contains two outstanding pieces of metalwork: a delightful 15C silver Virgin and a 16C reliquary.

Frescoes in Chapelle St-Créspin

© S. Sauvignier/Michelin

Le Gros Roc

From this rocky escarpment, surrounded by vegetation, there is an extensive view over the *bocage* countryside.

▷ Turn left onto the D 241 just before a bridge at Bais.

The road passes the **Château de Montesson**, encircled by a moat; its lodge is crowned by an unusual roof and the adjoining round tower also has a highly original onion-domed roof.

▷ In Hambers, opposite the church, turn left onto the D 236. After 2.5km/1.5mi turn left again onto the narrow road leading to the Butte de Montaigu.

Butte de Montaigu★

Allow 15min on foot there and back from the car park.

The butte (mound or hillock), crowned by an old **chapel**, is only 290m high but, because of its isolation, makes an excellent viewpoint from which to see the hills of the Coëvrons rising to the southeast: Évron, Ste-Suzanne on its rocky spike, to the south; Mayenne and its forest to the northwest; the forests of Andaines and Pail to the north and northeast.

▷ Return to the D 236 and continue south through Chellé. At the

🚗 DRIVING TOURS

🚗 LE BOIS DE MIREBEAU

35km/22mi. Allow 1h45.

▷ From Évron take the D 20 north.

As the road climbs there are views to the west over woods and lakes.

▷ Beyond Ste-Gemmes-le-Robert turn right onto the Mont Rochard road, which is sometimes in poor repair.

T-junction turn left onto the D 7 at the entrance to the village of Mézangers; turn right to the Château du Rocher (where you must park and walk).

Château du Rocher★

Allow 30min on foot there and back.
Grounds only: mid-Jun–mid-Oct daily 10am–noon, 2–6pm.
A gallery of five low rounded arches runs the length of the Renaissance façade. Delicate sculptures adorn the buildings. The more austere 15C façade faces the lake in the park.

Return to the D 7 and continue south to return to Évron.

LES BOIS DES VALLONS

36km/22.5mi. Allow about 1h.

From Évron take the D 32 west. On the west side of Brée, turn right onto the D 557. On approaching St-Ouen-des-Vallons, turn right to the Château de la Roche-Pichemer.

Château de la Roche-Pichemer

Grounds only: Jul–mid-Aug 2–6pm.
No charge. Park near the moat, outside the gate.
The château consists of two main Renaissance wings built at right angles and covered with tall slate roofs. Massive square pavilions project from each corner, considerably enhancing the building, which is fronted by formal gardens.

From St-Ouen-des-Vallons take the D 129 and D 24 south via Montsûrs to La Chapelle-Rainsouin.

La Chapelle-Rainsouin

A room off the church chancel contains a beautiful 16C polychrome stone **entombment★**.

Take the D 20 northeast. In Châtres-la-Forêt turn right onto the D 562. Continue on, and turn right again to the Château de Monteclerc.

Château de Monteclerc

Closed to the public. Leave the car at the beginning of the avenue.
This plain but elegant building, dating from the beginning of the 17C, stands at the far end of a vast courtyard. The drawbridge lodge has a rounded roof crowned by a lantern turret.

Return to Châtres-la-Forêt; turn right onto the D 20 to return to Évron.

Ste-Suzanne★

In the 11C the viscounts of Beaumont built this peaceful village, nicknamed "pearl of the Maine", in a **picturesque setting★** on a rocky promontory commanding the north bank of the Erve. It is one of the most important strongholds in the region and was the only one to successfully resist William the Conqueror.

SIGHTS

Tour d'orientation

Via rue du Grenier à Sel.
From the top of the tower you can see the old town nestled around its 11C keep,

▸ **Population:** 1 314.
Michelin Map: 310: G-6.
Info: 1 rue de Bueil. 02 43 01 43 60. www.coevrons-tourisme. com.
Location: Ste-Suzanne is 50km/31mi W of Le Mans, 32km/20mi E of Laval.
Don't Miss: The view from the castle keep.
Timing: Half a day.
Kids: The Théatrales Pitchoun runs a summer programme for children.

the new town beyond the ramparts, and the surrounding countryside.

Promenade de la Poterne

This 3km/2mi walk along the ramparts starts at the Tour du Guet (watchtower), and passes the castle and the Porte de Fer (Iron Gate). The second half of the walk, ending at the Porte du Guichet (Wicket Gate), provides distant views *(northeast)* of the Coëvrons hills and *(north)* of Mont Rochard and the Butte de Montaigu, topped by St Michael's Chapel. Before you set off, pick up a leaflet from the tourist office for points of interest en route.

Parish church

Go inside to see the graceful 16C polychrome wood statue of Ste-Suzanne, and a 14C stone Virgin and Child statue.

▲≗ Musée de l'Auditoire

7 Grande-Rue. ⏱*Mid-May–Sept daily 2.30–6pm.* ⚏€5. ✆*02 43 01 42 65. http://museeauditoire.jimdo.com.* Housed partly in a courthouse dating from the 17C and also in an ancient mill house, this exhibition looks back on the medieval town of Ste-Suzanne.

Château de Ste-Suzanne

⏱*Feb–mid-Dec 10am–12.30pm, 1.30–5.30pm (Jul–Aug 10am–7pm; Weekends in May–Jun and Sept 10am–1pm, 2–7pm).* ⏱*Mid-Dec–early Jan.* ⚏€6. ✆*02 43 58 13 00. http://chateau-de-sainte-suzanne.fr.* The second floor of this handsome early 17C château is devoted to an architectural and regional heritage centre, and features a remarkable **timberwork roof** in the shape of an upturned ship's keel. There is a great **view★** from the castle keep.

EXCURSIONS

La Ferté-Clairbois – Domaine du Chevalier

2km/1.25mi south of Ste-Suzanne, towards Sablé.
⏱*Jul–Aug daily. Call for details of shows.* ✆*02 43 01 42 15.*

This medieval recreation of a small castle is brought to life by costumed actors who re-enact chivalrous days of old, including medieval banquets, tournaments and horseriding spectacles.

Dolmen des Erves

3km/2mi on the D 143, Assé-le-Béranger road.
This megalithic monument, now restored, dates from the 4th millennium BCE.

🚗 DRIVING TOUR

🚗 LA FORÊT DE LA GRANDE-CHARNIE

26km/16mi. Allow 1h30.

▶ Leave Ste-Suzanne east on the D 9. After 1km/1/2mi, turn right onto a minor road 700m further on. Leave your car beside the houses.

Point de vue du Tertre Gane

Cross a picnic area in the woods to get to a viewing platform strewn with boulders. From here there is a panorama of Ste-Suzanne and the surrounding plain.

▶ Return to your car, go as far as "La Foussillère" retirement home and then turn right. After crossing the D 210, turn right taking the road up the hill.

Signal de Viviers

The road ends at the edge of a steep wooded area with La Grande-Charnie forest ahead. The path to the left, takes you to you can reach a rock surmounted by a statue of Sacré-Cœur; through the gaps in the trees you can see the Coëvrons hills.

▶ A long descent leads north towards Torcé-Viviers en Charnie. Turn left at the end of the hill, go through the village and turn south on to the D 210. After 5.5 km/3.5mi, take a right turn onto the D 156 and D 7 to return to Ste-Suzanne.

ADDRESSES

Pontmain

Legend has it that here, on the border with Brittany, on 17 January 1871, during the Franco–Prussian War, the Virgin appeared to several of the village children, including Eugène and Joseph Barbedette, offering a message of hope. An armistice was declared 11 days later.

▶ **Population:** 848.

⏱ **Michelin Map:** 310: C–4.

🅘 **Info:** 5 rue de la Grange. 📞02 43 11 26 55.

▷ **Location:** Pontmain is 16km/10mi NE of Fougères, 45km/28mi NW of Mayenne, 6km/4mi SW of Landivy and 35km/22mi SW of Mortain.

👁 **Don't Miss:** The excursion to the lovely garden of la Pellerine.

SIGHTS

Grange Barbedette

It was from this thatched barn that some of the village children, and then the other villagers, allegedly saw the Virgin in the sky above the house of Augustin Guidecoq on the far side of the square.

Basilique

The vast neo-Gothic basilica was built at the end of the 19C. The ten stained-glass windows in the chancel depict the Virgin's Apparition at Pontmain, at Lourdes, and at La Salette, as well as scenes from the life of Christ.

Chapelle & Musée des Missionaires Oblats

Behind the basilica is the Mission of the Oblate Fathers of Mary Immaculate. The interior of the chapel (built in 1953) is surprisingly attractive, illuminated by a golden light diffused by stained-glass windows.

EXCURSION

Jardin de la Pellerine★

La Larderie, La Pellerine (21km/13mi S of Pontmain, on the N 12 between Fougères to the W and Ernée to the E). 🕐*May–Oct Thu–Fri 10am–6.30pm, Sat–Sun and public holidays 2–6.30pm.* 👓*€8.* 📞*02 43 05 93 31. http://lejardin-delapellerine.simplesite.com.* Lovely gardens surround a 17C house: roses, shrubs, arbours and ponds with aquatic plants, including water lilies, on a 2ha site.

Jardin de la Pellerine

© Mayenne Tourisme

Laval★

The first thing that strikes any visitor to Laval is the River Mayenne, which flows gently through the centre of town, under the river bridges and creating fords, as it has since the city was founded in the year 1000. Laval has a picturesque château, many venerable half-timbered houses, and has produced many distinguished citizens (🔗 *see box, p355*).

OLD TOWN★
Place de la Trémoille
The square is named after the last of the local lords, guillotined during the Revolution. On the east side stands the Renaissance façade of the 16C **Nouveau Château** built for the Count of Laval; it was enlarged in the 19C and now houses the law courts.

Vieux Château★
Pl. de La Trémoille.
🕐 *Tue–Sat 9am–noon, 1.30–6pm, Sun 2–6pm.* 👁️*Guided visits: Jul–Aug Tue–Fri 11am, 2pm, 3.30pm, 5pm, Sat–Sun 2.30pm, 3.30pm, 4.30pm; Sept–Jun Sat–Sun 3pm, 4.30pm.* 🎫€3.
📞 *02 53 74 12 30. www.laval.fr.*
To the right of the railings in front of the law courts stands a handsome 17C porch, next to an early 16C half-timbered house. Through the porch is the courtyard of the Old Castle, enclosed by ramparts; from here there is a picturesque **view★** of the old town. In its present state the bulk of the castle dates from the 13C and 15C; the windows and dormers in white tufa, carved with scrolls in the Italian style, were added in the 16C. The crypt and the keep (12C–13C) are the oldest parts.

Donjon
Originally separated from the courtyard by a moat, the keep was later incorporated between the two wings of the castle. Within the keep, the most interesting feature is the extraordinary **timber roof★★**, which was built c.1100 to an ingenious circular design. Great beams, radiating from the centre like the spokes of a wheel, project beyond the walls (which are over 2m thick) to support the wooden defensive gallery that projects out to defend the gate and the base of the walls.

Musée d'Art naïf★
Within the Vieux Chateau.
🕐 *Same hours as for the Vieux Château.*
The Museum of Naïve Painting, which can be visited separately from the castle and the keep, displays a number of canvases by painters from France and around the world. A reconstruction of the studio of **Henri Rousseau**, born locally (🔗*see p355*) contains mementoes of the artist.

Rue des Orfèvres
The narrow street that runs south into Grande-Rue is lined with beautiful 16C overhanging houses and 18C mansions. At the T-junction stands the Renaissance house (1550) of the Master of the Royal Hunt (Grand Veneur).

Grande-Rue
This was the main street of the medieval city; it descends to the River Mayenne between rows of old houses, some half-timbered with projecting upper storeys, others in stone with Renaissance decoration.

▶ **Population:** 49 492.
🗺️ **Michelin Map:** 310: E-6.
ℹ️ **Info:** 84 avenue Robert Buron. 📞02 43 49 46 46. www.laval-tourisme.com.
▶ **Location:** Laval is 32km/ 20mi S of Mayenne by D 162. Le Mans is 86km/ 53.4mi to the E on N 157.
🕐 **Timing:** Allow about an hour to see the Old Town, not including visits to the château, museums and churches.
👁️ **Don't Miss:** A walk along the docks to see the old *bateau-lavoir* St-Julien.

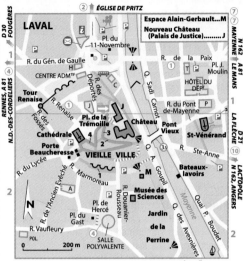

▶ Turn right onto rue de Chapelle.

The street climbs between medieval and Renaissance houses to a charming statue of St René in a niche (*right*) at the top.

▶ Go straight ahead onto rue des Serruriers.

South of the Beucheresse Gate are two slightly askew half-timbered houses.

Porte Beucheresse

In former days this 14C gate, then called Porte des Bûcherons, opened directly into the forest; its two round towers, topped with machicolations, were once part of the town walls. Henri Rousseau was born in the south tower, where his father worked as a tinsmith.

Cathédrale

The building has been altered many times but the nave and the transept crossing are covered with Angevin vaulting, characterised by curved rib vaulting in which the keystones are at different heights.

The walls are hung with Aubusson tapestries (early 17C) depicting the story of Judith and Holofernes in six panels. On the left pillar near the chancel is a beautiful triptych painted by the Antwerp Mannerist School in the 16C; when closed it presents the Martyrdom of St John the Apostle, and when open, three scenes from the life of John the Baptist. In the north transept there is an imposing revolving door, which was carved in the 18C.

On leaving the cathedral, walk round the east end to admire the northeast door (facing the law courts), which is decorated with 17C terracotta statues.

Rue de la Trinité

Look out for the 16C house along here, adorned with statues of the Virgin and the Saints.

Old town

© Dominique VERNIER/Mayenne Tourisme

Famous Citizens

Laval is the birthplace of many exceptional men. **Ambroise Paré** (1517–90) was the first to practise the ligature of arteries during amputations and is deserving of his reputation as the father of surgery: yet he was modest about his success, "I dress their wounds, God cures them."

Henri Rousseau (1844–1910), whose nickname was Le Douanier (the Customs Officer), was originally a tax collector in Paris. He was the archetype of the modern naïve artist and was known for the meticulous approach which he brought to his paintings of lush jungles, wild beasts and exotic figures.

Alfred Jarry (1873–1907) was the inventor of pataphysics, the science of imaginary solutions, and the forerunner of the Surrealists. He created the grotesque satirical character of *Père Ubu, King of Poland*, when he was still in his teens. Jarry died destitute and largely unappreciated. Today, however, he is honoured as one of the creators of the Theatre of the Absurd.

Alain Gerbault (1893–1941) was a renowned tennis player, as well as a sailor. In 1923 he made the transatlantic crossing single-handed; he died in the Polynesian islands. His second boat, the *Fire-Crest II*, is exhibited in the Jardin de la Perrine.

Jean Cottereau (1757–1794), called Jean Chouan, led Royalist troops during the French Revolution. In 1793 the Royalists occupied Laval and beneath its walls defeated the Republican army of General Lechelle. The name **Chouan** was adopted from their rallying cry, the hoot of the tawny owl *(chat-huant)*.

Quays★

The quays on the east bank provide the best overall **views★** of Laval across the River Mayenne. From the **Pont Vieux**, a 13C humpback bridge, there is a more detailed view of the old town. Intriguing relics of the past, **bateaux-lavoirs** (floating public wash houses), are moored along quai Paul Boudet. One of these, the **St-Julien** (◔*Jul–Aug Tue–Sun 2–6pm*), has been restored.

Jardin de la Perrine★

These public gardens are home to many kinds of tall trees, ponds, waterfalls, lawns, a rose garden and flower beds. The views from the terraces are excellent.

Musée des Sciences

21 rue Douanier-Rousseau.
◔*Tue–Fri 10am–noon, 1.30–6pm, Sat 10am–noon, 2–5.30pm, Sun 2–6pm.*
◉€2 (free on 1st Sun of month).
℘02 43 49 47 81. www.ccsti-laval.org.
This Science and Culture Museum is housed in an imposing building. In addition to scientific subjects it also includes archaeological exhibits from local exca-

vations. Don't miss the 19C astronomical clock in its own carved wooden case.

OTHER SIGHTS

Notre-Dame-d'Avesnières Basilica

1.5km/1mi S, via the quai d'Avesnières.
This ancient sanctuary dedicated to the Virgin Mary was made into a basilica in 1898. The Romanesque **east end★** is best seen from the Pont d'Avesnières. The attractive Gothic-Renaissance spire is an identical copy, made in 1871, of the original, which was erected in 1538. The fine Romanesque chancel consists of three storeys of arches and bays. The modern stained glass is by Max Ingrand.

Église St-Vénérand

The nave of the church is flanked by double aisles. The north front, facing the street, has a Flamboyant **door★** decorated with an attractive 17C terracotta figure of the Virgin.

Tour Renaise

This 15C round machicolated tower was part of the old city walls.

Église Notre-Dame-des-Cordeliers★

Built between 1397 and 1407, this former Franciscan monastery chapel contains a remarkable set of seven 17C **altar pieces★★**. Six of them can be seen in the north aisle; they were carved out of tufa and marble by the local architect **Pierre Corbineau** (1600–78).

👥 Lactopôle André-Besnier★★

10 rue Adolphe-Beck.

♿🚶*Guided tours only: school holidays, Mon–Fri at 3pm (daily at Easter); Jul–Aug daily, 3pm.* ⊚ *€10 (child 12–18, €6.50).* ☎*02 43 59 51 90. www.lactopole.com.*

Everything you ever wanted know about milk, cheese and other dairy products is answered in this exhibition, which claims to be the biggest of its kind in the world. Looking nostalgically at the past – it counts Marie Antoinette's milk churn among its 2 500 or so exhibits – it also deals with present-day issues and looks at future trends in this industry, which is of such importance to Normandy

Ancienne Église de Pritz

2km/1mi N. Leave Laval by allée de la Résistance, rue du Vieux-St-Louis and D 104. ⌖*Closed to the public.*

This simple ancient church stands on the right-hand side of the road in a garden in the hamlet of Pritz. It dates from about the year 1000 and was altered and enlarged in the Romanesque period.

EXCURSIONS

Abbaye de Clermont

16km/10mi west on the D57; turn right at the Chapelle-du-Chêne, then take the D115.

♿🕐*All year, daily 9am–nightfall. Unaccompanied visit* ⊚*€6.*

🚶*Guided visits Jul–Aug Sun 6pm.* ⊚*€4.* ☎*02 43 02 11 96. www.abbaye-de-clairmont.com.*

The ruins of this once great house stand in open country watered by many streams. The abbey was founded in 1152, on lands gifted by the Count of Laval. It housed a thriving monastic community until the Revolution.

The square east end of the **church** comes into view before the dilapidated west front and the austere Romanesque porch with its three round-headed openings. South of the church is the **cloister garth**. The wooden cloister galleries have not survived, but the **lay brothers' range** (west) contains the cellar and the refectory.

Entrammes Gallo-Roman Baths

13km/8mi south of Laval via the N 162.

♿🚶*Guided tours: May–early Jul and 2nd week in Sept Sun and public holidays 2.30–6.30pm; early Jul–Aug daily 2–6.30pm.* ⊚*€4.* ☎*02 39 90 20 72. www.laval-tourisme.com.*

During restoration work inside the church in 1987, remains of the former town's **Gallo-Roman baths** were discovered in a remarkable state of preservation. These included Roman walls, up to 8.5m high, four bathrooms in a row, arcades and various religious finds including a sarcophagus. An audiovisual presentation also interprets the site.

The town's claim to more recent historical fame is that, until 1959, the famous Port-Salut cheese was made here by Trappist monks, in the **Abbaye du Port-du-Salut** (1.6km/1mi west). The cheese is still sold today, under the label "Entrammes", available locally. Two **chapels** of the abbey are open to the public.

Parné-sur-Roc

14km/8.5mi south of Laval via the N 162, then the D 21. E of Entrammes.

The 11C parish church contains some interesting **mural paintings** (late 15C to early 16C). On the left mural is the silhouette of the resurrected Christ against a background of red stars and a Madonna Dolorosa; the right mural depicts the saints Cosmas and Damian, popular in the Middle Ages. These Greek twins were physicians, thought to have been martyred in the year 287.

ADDRESSES

🛏 STAY

🛏 **Camping Village Vacances Pêche** – *Villiers-Charlemagne (20km/12.5mi S of Laval via N 162).* ℘*02 43 07 71 68. www. vacancesetpeche.fr. Open Apr–Oct. 20 sites each 100sq m. Reservations advised.* Campers have their own bathroom and you can rent small chalets with individual terraces. Keen anglers will enjoy themselves here; the lake abounds in pike, pike-perch and carp.

🛏🛏 **Marin'Hotel** – *102 av. Robert-Buron.* ℘*02 43 53 09 68. www.marin-hotel.fr. 26 rooms.* This no-frills hotel is opposite the train station in a thoroughly modernised old building. Rooms are functional and well soundproofed from the street noise.

🛏🛏🛏 **Best Western Hôtel de Paris** – *22 r. de la Paix.* ℘*02 43 53 76 20. www.hotel-laval.fr. 50 rooms.* Situated right in the town centre, close to the shopping area this hotel offers simple soundproofed rooms with white roughcast walls and coloured wood furniture.

🛏🛏🛏🛏 **Chambre d'hôte Chateau Le Bas du Gast** – *6 rue de la Halle-aux-Toiles, across from the Salle Polyvalente.* ℘*02 43 49 22 79. www.chateaulebasdugast.fr. 4 rooms.* In the centre of Laval's old quarter, this 17C–18C château is surrounded by a beautiful garden featuring trimmed box hedges. The oak parquet flooring and period furniture in the vestibule set the scene and atmosphere as soon as you enter. The spacious guest rooms have been thoughtfully decorated.

🍴 EAT

🍴🍴 **L'Antiquaire** – *64, rue de Vaufleury.* ℘*02 43 53 66 76. www.restaurant-lantiquaire.fr. Open Tue–Fri for lunch and dinner, Sat evening and Sun lunch.* This restaurant occupies the ground floor of an old Laval house in the old town. It has a cosy dining room, with turn-of-the-20C British décor in tones of red. Generous portions of traditional cuisine, showing flashes of modern creativity.

🍴🍴 **Bistro de Paris** – *67 r. du Val de Mayenne.* ℘*02 43 56 98 29. www.lebistro-de-paris.com. Closed Sat lunch, Sun eve, all day Mon.* In the heart of the historic centre, the locally renowned Bistro de Paris has

a classic façade and elegant atmospheric Art Nouveau brasserie decor. Refined brasserie food is on the menu.

🍴🍴 **L'Édelweiss** – *99 av. R-Buron.* ℘*02 43 53 11 00. Closed Sun eve, Mon and holidays.* Next to the train station, this is a contemporary dining room in pastel tones, where you can enjoy traditional and modern cuisine using regional produce to offer a wide range of menus in a friendly setting, without fuss.

🍴🍴 **Le Johannesburg** – *5 r. de la Trinité. Old Laval, near the Cathedral.* ℘*02 43 53 21 21.* Behind a 17C façade, formerly housing a Cistercian abbey, this building has been converted into a beautifully decorated pub tucked away in a deep cellar. One of the most pleasant spots in Laval for a beer, it specialises in stone-grilled steaks. Live music.

🍴🍴 **À La Bonne Auberge** – *170 r. de Bretagne.* ℘*02 43 69 07 81. www. alabonneauberge.com. Open Mon–Fri lunch and dinner, Sat evening.* The pastel-coloured decoration of the dining room gives this inn an intimate, muted atmosphere. The veranda adds light and an impression of space. Well-prepared cuisine at reasonable prices. 17 **rooms** (🛏🛏–🛏🛏🛏).

🍴🍴🍴 **La Bastide d'Elva** – *9 Place Christian d'Elva, Changé (4km/2.5mi N of Laval via the D 104).* ℘*02 43 53 43 33. www. bastidedelva.com. Closed Sun evening, all day Mon, Tue evening and public holidays.* Opposite the château. Gastronomical restaurant in a delightful setting serving refined, traditional cuisine.

SHOPPING

Abbaye de la Coudre – *rue St-Benoît.* ℘*02 43 02 85 85. www.abbaye-coudre. com. Closed Easter, 25 Dec.* Beneath exposed rafters illuminated by lightwells in the roof, the abbey shop offers all kinds of food and drink products made by monastic communities from near and far: jams and conserves, beer and wine, coffee from Cameroon, biscuits, Bonneval chocolate, honey, nougat and caramels. The speciality of the house is Trappist cheese aged in the abbey cellars.

EVENTS

Mayenne Nights – *mid-Jul–mid-Aug.* Shows and performances of music and theatre at several sites including Ste-Suzanne, Jublains and Laval. ℘*02 43 67 60 90. www.nuitsdelamayenne.com.*

GRANVILLE *and the Bay of Mont-St-Michel*

Tucked into the bottom of the Cotentin peninsula on its western side, lies the fabulous Bay of Mont St-Michel which, along with the world-famous abbey dedicated to the Archangel Michael, was added to the list of UNESCO World Heritage Sites in 1979. Situated at the junction of the regions of Normandy and Brittany, there is a great diversity of landscape on offer, both maritime and urban, with headlands and plentiful viewpoints from which to enjoy the extensive vistas.

Highlights

The Tides

The bay experiences the highest tides in Europe, which are the source of many local legends. The author Victor Hugo compared the speed of the tide with that of a galloping horse.

There is approximately 14m between high and low tide, and due to the aforementioned rapidity with which it covers the sand flats, it is no wonder that the pilgrims, known as "miquelots", crossing them named the Abbey "St Michael in Peril of the Sea". Even today it is very dangerous to try to reach the abbey from the nearby coast and it is essential to approach it by the designated route only.

However, there are beneficial effects of the tides. The creation of polders led to the establishing of salt-marsh meadows, locally known as "herbus", which are well suited to grazing the 7 000 sheep of the area. The result is salt-flavoured meat or "agneau de pre-salé" which is a speciality of the region and can be found in local restaurants whose trade is derived in large part from visitors to Mont St-Michel and the bay.

History

Much of the history of the bay is bound up with the abbey, which dates from the early medieval period, and the pilgrimages that have taken place over the years. Once located on a small rocky island, the area between the mainland and the island became silted up and engineering works have been carried out to reverse this process. A new hydraulic dam will use the waters of the River Couesnon to flush away the silt and

Falaises de Champeau, Carolles, Mont St-Michel bay

© Francis Leroy/hemis.fr

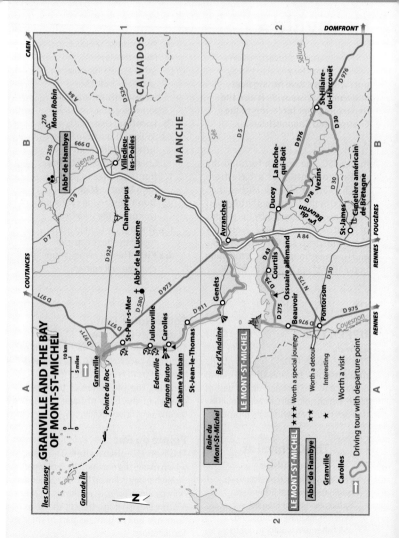

GRANVILLE AND THE BAY OF MONT-ST-MICHEL

LE MONT-ST-MICHEL ★★★ ★★ ★

★★★ Worth a special journey
★★ Worth a detour
★ Interesting

LE MONT-ST-MICHEL
Abb⁰ de Hambye
Granville
Carolles

Worth a visit

Driving tour with departure point

restore island status to Mont St-Michel. Instead of visitors crossing the causeway, which helped to create the silt build up, they now cross an elevated bridge by shuttle, thus allowing the water to flow naturally beneath.

The main towns of the area, Avranches at the head of the bay and Granville in the east, both have interesting histories. Avranches was where Henry II made his public penance for the murder of Thomas Becket, and it was from here that General Patton launched the attack that was to cripple the German Army and allow the Americans to advance.

Today

The area is primarily agricultural, with sheep farming, cereal production, fishing and shellfish farming being the main industries. The bay acts as a nursery for flat fish such as plaice and sole and is one of the largest producers of shellfish in France, with about 10 000 tonnes of mussels and 3 000 tonnes of oysters produced here every year. Of course, tourism has become vitally important to the region and the abbey attracts more than 3 million visitors per year.

Granville★

This lively seaside resort, set on a rocky promontory, is also a busy port with an active fishing fleet and a marina. Granville is also the departure point for ferries to the Chausey and Channel Islands.

A BIT OF HISTORY

In the 15C, the English fortified the rocky promontory as a base from which to attack Mont St-Michel, then occupied by the Normans. The town was recaptured permanently by the knights of Mont St-Michel in 1442. Prosperity came with deep-sea fishing in the 18C, and Granville flourished with the rising popularity of sea bathing in the 19C.

▶ **Population:** 12 900.

Michelin Map: 303: C-6.

Info: 4 cours Jonville.
℘02 33 91 30 03.
www.tourisme-granville-terre-mer.com.

▶ **Location:** Granville is 350km/218mi from Paris; 105km/65.8mi from Cherbourg; 108km/67.7mi from Caen; 48km/30mi from Mont St-Michel.

Don't Miss: A look at haute couture in the Villa Dior.

🕐 **Timing:** Try to fit in a day trip to the Îles Chausey.

Kids: There is an aquarium children will enjoy.

👣 WALKING TOURS

UPPER TOWN

Allow 2h.
The Main Gate (Grand Porte) with its drawbridge remains the principal entrance to the fortified upper part of town, which holds all Granville's military and religious past within its ramparts.

The Carnival at Granville

This long-standing tradition was originated by local fishermen. Before leaving for long fishing expeditions in Newfoundland, cod fishermen would go out to spend their money in the streets of the city, dressing up in various costumes for the occasion. Today the Carnival takes place during Shrove Tuesday celebrations (the day before the beginning of Lent); it lasts for four days and includes a funfair with a procession of floats, an orchestra and majorettes.

On the last day the residents, dressed up and masked, pay a visit to their friends; a Carnival effigy is burned on the beach, marking the end of festivities.

Église Notre-Dame

pl. du Parvis, Upper Town.
The oldest parts of this austere granite church go back to the 15C. The nave and the west front were erected in the 17C and 18C. The 14C statue, in the north chapel, of Our Lady of Cape Lihou is greatly venerated locally.

Pointe du Roc

This is an exceptional **site★**. The point which marks the northern limit of Mont St-Michel bay is linked to the mainland only by a narrow rocky isthmus. In the 15C the English dug a trench, known as Tranchée aux Anglais, as part of their fortifications.

🚶 *The walk (the path starts from the harbour) to the lighthouse offers a fine view of the sea and the rocks.*

👣 Roc des Harmonies – Aquarium

Enter from 1 bld Vaufleury.
🕐*Apr–Sept daily 10am–7pm; Oct–Mar 10am–12.30pm, 2–6.30pm. ⊛€9.*
℘*02 33 50 19 83.*
www.aquarium-du-roc.com.
The **tanks** contain fish from local waters – note the sea perch with its powerful jaws – as well as exotic and freshwater species.

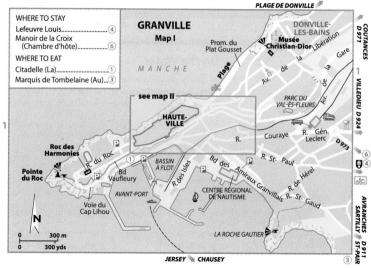

GRANVILLE
Map I

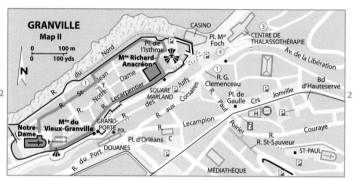

GRANVILLE
Map II

RAMPART WALK★

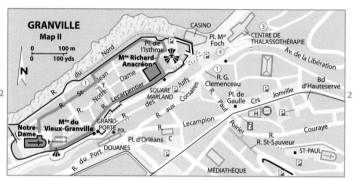 *Park on the parvis of Notre-Dame church.*

▶ Go through the Grand'Porte and over the drawbridge. Turn right onto rue Lecarpentier to follow the south rampart to place de l'Isthme.

The **view★** from the square extends, on a clear day, to the coast of Brittany.

▶ Continue along the inside of the ramparts by rue du Nord. The view is spectacular in stormy weather. The Chausey Islands lie to the northwest.

Turn left onto rue des Plâtriers to reach rue St-Jean, then turn right.

Note, at No. 7 rue St-Jean, an old house with a ground-floor shop and then, at No. 3, a house dating from 1612.

Musée du Vieux Granville

2 rue Lecarpentier.
🕐 *Closed for renovation; check website for updates.* 📞 *02 33 50 44 10. www.ville-granville.fr.*
On the first floor is a collection of Norman costumes and headdresses as well as household furnishings, notably the **toiles de Hambaye**, pieces of

On the Water

Granville is famous for its traditional fishing vessels, such as *la bisquine*, a sailing ship that challenged those of Cancale during fierce regattas as early as the 1850s. Today, cruises are offered aboard some of these, superbly restored by enthusiastic craftsmen.

Traditional fishing vessel "la Granvillaise"

© Hervé Lenain/hemis.fr

canvas or gunny sacks painted in stylised decoration, and used as bed curtains. On the second floor are exhibitions about the sea.

Musée d'art moderne Richard-Anacréon

pl. de l'Isthme.

🕐*Early Feb–May and Oct–Nov, outside school holidays Fri–Sun 2–6pm; during school holidays Tue–Sun 2–6pm; Jun–Sept Tue–Sun 11am–6pm.* ⇔€5.
📞*02 33 51 02 94.*

This museum of modern art presents a permanent collection of works by major 20C artists including Derain, Utrillo, Signac and Van Dongen, as well as temporary exhibits.

LOWER TOWN
La Plage

The narrow beach at the foot of shale cliffs is overlooked by the Plat-Gousset breakwater promenade.

Musée and Jardin public Christian-Dior

🕐**Museum:** *end Apr–Sept daily 10am–6.30pm; Oct–mid-Nov 10am–12.30pm, 2–6pm: during school holidays daily; outside school holidays Tue–Sun.* ⇔€9.
Gardens: *Apr–May and Sept 9am– 8pm; Jul–Aug 9am–9pm; Nov–Feb 9am–5pm; Mar and Oct 9am–6pm.* 📞*02 33 61 48 21.*

http://musee-dior-granville.com.

This public garden and museum are located in the childhood home of the famous couturier. From the upper terrace you look down on the Granville promontory, north towards Regnéville and out to the Chausey islands. The cliff path passes the cemetery to reach the great expanse of Donville Beach. Low tide reveals numerous stakes used for growing mussels.

EXCURSION

Îles Chausey

🕐*See ÎLES CHAUSEY, p364.*

👥⛱ St-Pair-sur-Mer⛱

St-Pair has a breakwater promenade protecting a beach of golden sand, which is perfect for children. The **church** is said to have been founded in the 6C by two local Evangelists, St-Pair and St-Scubilien. The building consists of the Romanesque belfry and the bay beneath, the 14C chancel and a 19C neo-Gothic nave and transepts.

Jullouville

8.5km/5mi. Leave Granville by the D 911. This resort, which is really an extension of St-Pair-sur-Mer, is famous for its fine sandy guarded beach, which is much appreciated by families. In summer it is possible to catamaran, kayak or windsurf, while in low season there is sand yachting. Two clubs for children complete this range of activities. There is a pleasant walk along the sea front which is lined with 19C villas, palms and mimosas. When you reach the Pignon Butor the view extends north as far as the Pointe du Roc at Granville.

There is also a small beach to the south at Edenville that extends towards Carolles.

Abbaye de La Lucerne

12km/7.5 mi SE of Granville via D 973 until just before St-Pierre-Langers. Turn left (east) on D 580.

The sizeable restored ruins of Lucerne abbey stand in a fine parkland setting in the Thar valley. Founded in 1143, construction started in 1164.

Abbey church

🚻♿*Apr–Sept Mon–Sat 10am–noon, 2–6.30pm, Sun 2–6.30pm; Oct and Christmas period Mon–Sat 10am–noon, 2–5pm, Sun 2–5pm.* ⏱*During religious holidays.* ⊜€7. ☎*02 33 48 83 56. www.abbaye-lucerne.fr.*

The doorway in the 12C façade is Romanesque. The transept crossing (restored) supports a late-12C Gothic square **belltower★**. The south transept houses a fine 18C **organ★** with 33 stops.

Cloisters and Conventual Buildings The arcades of the northwest corner and the entrance to the chapter house still stand. In the southwest corner, is a 12C *lavatorium,* with four Romanesque arcades. Note the old tithe barn and the dovecote.

ADDRESSES

🛏 STAY

⊜ **Chambre d'hôte Lefeuvre Louis –** *3 impasse du Puits, 50740 Carolles (11km/7mi S of Granville).* ☎*02 33 58 05 40. 3 rooms.* A modern house with cliffs on two sides giving a splendid view over the Bay of St Michel. Spacious, comfortable rooms, including one family room, on the first floor. For walkers, the GR223 is close by.

⊜⊜ **Chambre d'hôte Manoir de la Croix –** *La Croix du Gros Chêne, 50530 Montviron (8km/5mi south of l'abbaye de la Lucerne by the D 335 to the southeast of Sartilly, then the D 61).* ☎*02 33 60 68 30. www.manoirdelacroix.com. 2 rooms and 2 suites.* This 19C residence has a tree-planted garden. There are very large suites furnished with collections of period furniture, and two other cosy rooms.

⊜⊜🍽 **Hôtel des Bains –** *19 rue Clemenceau.* ☎*02 33 50 17 31. www. hoteldesbains-granville.com. 54 rooms.* Right on the coast in the bay of Mont St-Michel; ask for a room with a view, or one equipped with a relaxing jacuzzi. Restaurant (⊜⊜).

⊜⊜⊜🍽 **Hôtel Mercure Granville Le Grand Large –** *5 rue de la Falaise.* ☎*02 33 91 19 19. www.accorhotels.com.* ♿ 🅿 *(paying). 66 rooms.* Looking down from the beach from the clifftop, this hotel offers duplex or studio accommodation, mostly with sea views.

🍴 EAT

⊜⊜ **Au Marquis de Tombelaine –** *25 route des Falaises, 50530 Champeaux (3km/2mi southeast of Carolles by the D 911).* ☎*02 33 61 85 94.* The two parts of the hotel are separated by the coast road. On one side is the restaurant, with meals served in a rustic setting and on the other are 6 **rooms** enjoying a view of the bay.

⊜⊜ **Crêperie l'Échauguette –** *24 rue St-Jean.* ☎*02 33 50 51 87.* Nestling in one of the narrow streets of old Granville, you can enjoy buckwheat galettes and pancakes.

⊜⊜⊜ **La Citadelle –** *34 rue du Port.* ☎*02 33 50 34 10. www.restaurant-la-citadelle.fr. Closed Wed.* Before setting off for the islands, stop and have a meal here in the dining room with its blue-wood panelling or sit on the small raised terrace. Specialities are seafood, including lobster.

⊜⊜ **Le Terra Nova –** *Place du Mar.-Foch.* ☎*02 33 50 00 79. www.restaurant-terranova. com.* ♿. This restaurant occupies part of the Casino. There is a view of the sea from the dining room and in good weather you can see the Channel Islands.

Îles Chausey★

According to legend, the Chausey Islands were part of the ancient Scissy forest submerged by the sea in 709. The islands are a popular day excursion *(1h by boat)* and are uninhabited except for Grande Île, which has a population of up to 400 in summer, and only a dozen in winter.

- **Michelin Map:** 303: B-6.
- **Location:** The islands are 17km/10.5mi from Granville.
- **Don't Miss:** The remarkable spectacle of the high tide.
- **Timing:** The excursion takes a day; you can spend the night.

VISIT

La Grande Île★

The Island (2km/1mi long by 700m at its widest point) is the largest, and the only one accessible to visitors. Spring flowers are especially lovely. The **lighthouse** stands 37m above the sea.

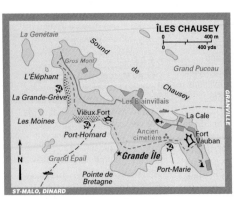

Fort

The fort was built between 1860 and 1866 against a British attack that never came. It now serves as a shelter for local fishermen.

▷ Go round the fort. The path goes past an old cemetery with four tombs.

Vieux Fort

The Old Fort was rebuilt in 1923. Below it, on the beach at Plage de Port Homard, the enormous tidal range is 14m.

The Moines and the Éléphant

These granite rocks, which can be reached at low tide, are thought to resemble monks and an elephant. More than 200 rocks, known locally as *grunes*, are revealed when the tide is out. Sailors should get some advice and double-check charts before setting out on an adventure.

Port-Marie, La Grande Île

© Christophe Boisvieux/age fotostock

ADDRESSES

🛏 STAY

🍽🍽 **Hôtel Fort et des Îles** – *50400 Îles Chausey.* ✆*02 33 50 25 02. www.hotel-chausey.com. 8 rooms. Reservations for half or full-board only essential.* The sounds of wind and waves will lull you in this white house set in a flower garden. Its the only hotel on the island, with a few simple rooms. Local seafood can be enjoyed in the **restaurant**.

Mont St-Michel ★★★

Why is the world fascinated by Mont St-Michel? No doubt it is not just the beauty of the architecture and the length of the mount's history. Perhaps it is the sense of mystery in the movement of the tides that separate this rocky outcrop from the mainland, or the play of twilight on the water and walls, or the cry of gulls gliding above the salty grass marsh. It is impossible to take the measure of Mont St-Michel without including its unique natural setting: the rock and the bay of this UNESCO World Heritage Site are truly one.

A BIT OF HISTORY

An amazing achievement – The abbey dates back to the early 8C when the Archangel Michael appeared to Aubert, Bishop of Avranches. He founded an oratory on the island, then known as Mount Tombe. In the Carolingian era (8C–10C), the oratory was replaced by an abbey. From then until the 16C a series of increasingly splendid buildings, in the Romanesque and then the Gothic style, succeeded one another on this mount dedicated to the Archangel Michael. The abbey was remarkably well fortified and never fell to the enemy.

The construction is an amazing achievement. The blocks of granite were transported from the Chausey Islands and Brittany, then hoisted up to the foot of the building. The crest of the hill was very narrow, so the foundations had to be built up from the lower slopes.

Pilgrimages – Pilgrims flocked to the mount, even during periods of attrition like the Hundred Years' War. The English, who had possession of the area, granted safe conduct to the faithful in return for payment. People of all sorts made the journey: nobles, rich citizens and beggars who lived on alms and were granted free accommodation by the monks. Hotels and souvenir shops flourished. The pilgrims bought medals

▶ **Population:** 30.
♿ **Michelin Map:** 303: C-8.
ℹ **Info:** Grande Rue. ℰ02 33 60 14 30. www.ot-montsaintmichel.com.
▶ **Location:** Mont St-Michel is at the northern limit of D 776, which connects with N 175 at Pontorson, 10km/6mi S, which in turn leads to Avranches (25km/15½mi NE) via N 175 and major national arteries.
🅿 **Parking:** Pay at Centre or by credit card at exit barrier (€14 *high season, €9 low season, includes shuttle*). The visitor centre is on the mainland 2.5km/1.5mi from the Mont. Access the Mont from here by frequent shuttle service ("le Passeur"; 12min: departs from "place de navettes").
👁 **Don't Miss:** Walk out, bus back – for an improving view of the island as you walk. If you have the time, try to catch the miraculous spectacle of sunset over the bay from the ramparts.
🕐 **Timing:** Allow 1–2 hours just for the climb up through the streets of the Mont, which are invariably thronged with slow-moving visitors.
👪 **Kids:** The Maison de la Baie offers guided tours of the bay (ℰ*02 99 48 84 38. www.maison-baie.com*). The nature centre at Relais de Vains-St-Léonard explains the fauna and flora of the bay (&*see Relais des Genêts p373*). Alligator Bay (&*see p374*) displays alligators, crocodiles, turtles, etc.

© José Antonio Moreno/age fotostock

bearing the effigy of St Michael and lead amulets which they filled with sand from the beach. In periods of widespread disaster the pilgrimage incited such excesses of fervour that the church authorities were obliged to intervene. Of the many thousands of people crossing the bay, some drowned, others perished in the quicksands. The deaths led to the lengthening of the prayer to St Michael in Peril of the Sea.

Decline – The abbey came to be held *in commendam* (by lay abbots who received the revenue without exercising the duties) and discipline among the monks grew lax. In the 17C, the Maurists (monks from St Maur) were made responsible for reforming the monastery, but they only made some disappointing architectural changes and tinkered with the stonework. Further dilapidation ensued when the abbey became a prison.

From being the local Bastille before the Revolution, it was converted afterwards into a national prison for political prisoners, who included Barbès, Blanqui and Raspail. In 1874 the abbey and the ramparts passed into the care of the Historic Monuments Department (Service des Monuments Historiques). Since 1966 a few monks have again been in residence conducting the services in the abbey church.

THE ABBEY★★★

Daily: Jan–Apr and Sept–Dec 9.30am–6pm; May–Aug 9am–7pm. 1 Jan, 1 May, 25 Dec. €10 (under 18 years, no charge: audioguide +€3). 02 33 89 80 00. *www.abbaye-mont-saint-michel.fr.*
The tour, which is given in French and English plus other languages during the high season, passes through a maze of corridors and stairs floor by floor, not from building to building or period by period.

Outer Defences of the Abbey

A flight of steps, the Grand Degré, once cut off by a swing door, leads up to the abbey. At the top on the right is the entrance to the gardens; more steps lead up to the ramparts.

Through the arch of an old door is a fortified courtyard overlooked by the fort, which consists of two tall towers linked by machicolations. Even this military structure shows the builder's artistic sense: the wall is attractively constructed of alternate courses of pink and grey granite. Beneath a flattened barrel vault a steep and ill-lit staircase,

---

✄ DOGS ✄

Dogs are not allowed in the shuttles, except those transported in a closed bag or basket, and guide or assistance dogs. Nor are they allowed in the abbey precincts. There are kennels (*Le Chenil*) at the Visitor Centre where pets can be left for short periods. €8.50 per dog per day. (*www. bienvenueaumontsaintmichel.com*).

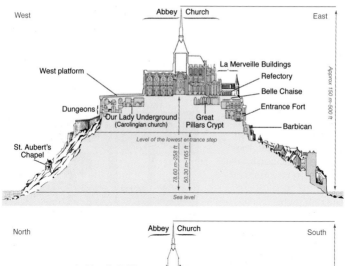

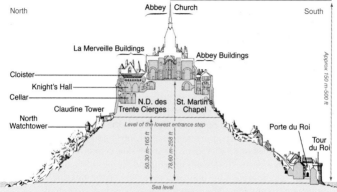

the Escalier du Gouffre (Abyss Steps), leads down to the beautiful door that opens into the guard room, also called the Porterie.

Salle des Gardes or Porterie

This gatehouse was the focal point of the abbey. Poor pilgrims passed through it on their way from the Merveille Court to the Almonry.

Abbey Steps

An impressive flight of 90 steps rises between the abbatial buildings *(left)* and the abbey church *(right)*; it is spanned by a fortified bridge (15C).

The stairs stop outside the south door of the church on a terrace called the Saut Gautier **(Gautier Leap)**, after a prisoner who is supposed to have hurled himself over the edge. The tour starts here.

West Platform

This spacious terrace, which was created by the demolition of the last three bays of the church, provides an extensive **view★** of the bay of Mont St-Michel.

Church★★

The exterior of the church, particularly the east end, with its buttresses, flying buttresses, bell turrets and balustrades, is a masterpiece of light and graceful architecture. The interior reveals the marked contrast between the severe, sombre Romanesque nave and the elegant, luminous Gothic chancel.

La Merveille★★★

The name, which means the Marvel, applies to the superb Gothic buildings on the north face of the mount. The eastern block, the first to be built between 1211 and 1218, comprises, from

Stages of Construction

Cloisters

© M. Gaspar/Michelin

Romanesque abbey

11C–12C: Between 1017 and 1144 a church was built on the top of the mount. The previous Carolingian building was incorporated as a crypt – Notre-Dame-sous-Terre (Our Lady Underground) – to support the platform on which the last three bays of the Romanesque nave were built. Other crypts were constructed to support the transepts and the chancel, which projected beyond the natural rock. The convent buildings were constructed on the west face and on either side of the nave. The entrance to the abbey faced west.

Gothic abbey

13C–16C: This period saw the construction of:

◆ The magnificent Merveille buildings (1211–28) on the north side, used by the monks and pilgrims and for receiving important guests.

◆ The abbatial buildings (13C–15C) on the south side, comprising the administrative offices, the abbot's lodging and the garrison's quarters.

◆ The main gatehouse and the outer defences (14C) on the east side, protecting the entrance, which was moved to this side of the mount.

◆ The chancel of the Romanesque church had collapsed and was rebuilt in the Flamboyant Gothic style (1446–1521) above a new crypt.

Alterations

18C–19C: In 1780 the last three bays of the nave and the Romanesque façade were demolished. The present belltower (1897) is surmounted by a beautiful spire that rises to 157m and terminates in a statue of St Michael (1879) by Emmanuel Frémiet. The 4.5m tall archangel, in position for over 100 years, was recently restored after lightning struck off St Michael's sword.

Returning Mont St-Michel to the Sea

Every year, the sea deposits tonnes of sediment in the bay. In part, this can be blamed on man, since between the mid-19C and 1969 a number of regional building initiatives were taken that accelerated the formation of polders (canalisation of the River Couesnon, building of a dyke, then a dam). A 1995 project was commissioned by the State and local authorities, intended to return the Mount to the sea by allowing cross-currents to flow between the mainland and island, while restoring the scouring action of coastal rivers and streams. A new dam was built in 2011 and a parking and visitor centre followed, from which visitors can access the mount either on foot, by shuttle bus, or the 'Maringote' horse-drawn carriage (✍ *www.bienvenueaumontsaintmichel.com*).

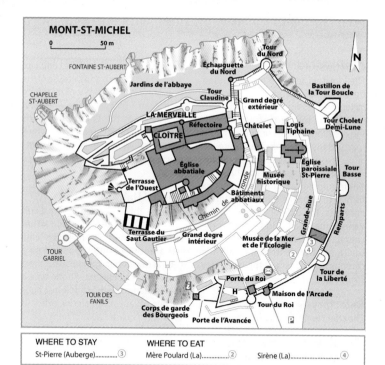

MONT-ST-MICHEL

0   50 m

N

FONTAINE ST-AUBERT

Tour du Nord

Échauguette du Nord

CHAPELLE ST-AUBERT

Jardins de l'abbaye

Tour Claudine

Grand degré extérieur

Bastillon de la Tour Boucle

LA-MERVEILLE

Réfectoire

CLOÎTRE

Châtelet

Logis Tiphaine

Tour Cholet/ Demi-Lune

Église abbatiale

Terrasse de l'Ouest

Chemin de Ronde

Musée historique

Église paroissiale St-Pierre

Tour Basse

Bâtiments abbatiaux

Grande-Rue

Remparts

Terrasse du Saut Gautier

Grand degré intérieur

Musée de la Mer et de l'Écologie

③

② ④

TOUR GABRIEL

Tour de la Liberté

TOUR DES FANILS

Porte du Roi

Maison de l'Arcade

H

Tour du Roi

Corps de garde des Bourgeois

Porte de l'Avancée

WHERE TO STAY	WHERE TO EAT	
St-Pierre (Auberge)............③	Mère Poulard (La)............②	Sirène (La)............④

top to bottom, the refectory, the Guests' Hall and the Almonry; the western block, built between 1218 and 1228, consists of the cloisters, the Knights' Hall and the cellar.

From the outside the buildings look like a fortress, although their religious connections are indicated by the simple nobility of the design. The interior is a perfect example of the evolution of the Gothic style, from an almost Romanesque simplicity in the lower halls, through the elegance of the Guests' Hall, the majesty of the Knights' Hall and the mysterious luminosity of the Refectory, to the cloisters, which are a masterpiece of delicacy and line.

Salle des Chevaliers, La Merveille.

© René Mattes/hemis.fr

Cloisters★★★

The cloisters seem to be suspended between the sea and the sky. The gallery arcades display heavily undercut sculpture of foliage ornamented with the occasional animal or human figure (particularly human heads); there are also a few religious symbols. The double row of arches rests on delightfully slim single columns arranged in quincunx format to enhance the impression of lightness. The different colours of the various materials add to the overall charm. The *lavatorium* (washroom) on the right of the entrance recalls the ceremonial washing of the feet every Thursday.

Refectory★★

The effect is mysterious; the chamber is full of light, although it appears to have only two windows in the end wall.

To admit so much light without weakening the solid side walls that support the wooden roof and are lined with a row of slim niches, the architect introduced a very narrow aperture high up in each recess. The vaulted ceiling is panelled with wood and the acoustics are excellent.

Old Romanesque abbey

The rib vaulting marks the transition from Romanesque to Gothic. The tour includes the Monks' Walk and part of the dormitory.

Great Wheel

The wheel belongs to the period when the abbey was used as a prison. It was used to haul provisions and was operated by five or six men turning the wheel from within as if on a treadmill.

Crypts

The transepts and chancel of the church are supported by three undercrofts or crypts; the most moving is **Notre-Dame-sous-Terre** (*accessible only during guided tours*): the Carolingian structure that stands where St Aubert officiated, is a simple rectangle (8x9m), divided into two small naves by a couple of arches resting on a central pillar. The place is awe-inspiring because of the complete silence that prevails and because of the memory of events which took place here more than 1 000 years ago. The most impressive is the **Crypte des Gros Piliers★** (Great Pillared Crypt), which has ten pillars (5m in circumference) made of granite from the Chausey Islands.

Guests' Hall★

Here the abbot received royalty (Louis IX, Louis XI, François I) and other important visitors. The hall (35m long) has a Gothic ceiling supported on a central row of slim columns; the effect is graceful and elegant. At one time it was divided down the middle by a huge curtain of tapestries; on one side was the kitchen quarters (two chimneys) and on the other the great dining hall (one chimney).

Knights' Hall★

The name of this hall may refer to the military order of St Michael, which was founded in 1469 by Louis XI with the abbey as its seat. The hall is vast and majestic (26x18m) and divided into four sections by three rows of stout columns. It was the monks' workroom or *scriptorium* where they illuminated manuscripts, and read and studied religious or secular texts, and for this reason it was heated by two great fireplaces. The almonry and cellar occupy the rooms on the lower floor.

Cellar

This was the storeroom; it was divided into three by two rows of square pillars supporting the groined vaulting.

Almonry

This is a Gothic room with a Romanesque vault supported on a row of columns.

Abbey gardens★

🕐*Closed in winter and in bad weather.*
A pleasant place for a stroll with a view of the west side of the mount and St Aubert's chapel.

THE VILLAGE

The cobbled streets are uneven and steep here, and the abbey is a labyrinth of corridors and cloisters. Wear comfortable shoes.

Outer Defences

The outer gate opens into the first fortified courtyard. On the left stands the Citizens' Guard room (16C) occupied by the tourist office; on the right are the Michelettes, English mortars captured in a sortie during the Hundred Years' War.

A second gate leads into a second courtyard. The third gate (15C), complete with machicolations and portcullis, is called the King's Gate because it was the lodging of the token contingent maintained by the king to assert his rights; this gate opens onto the Grande-Rue where the abbot's soldiers lodged in the fine arcaded house *(right)*.

Grande-Rue★

This picturesque narrow street climbs steeply between old (15C–16C) houses and ends in a flight of steps. In summer it is crowded with stalls of souvenir merchants just as in the Middle Ages.

Ramparts★★

These are 13C–15C. The sentry walk offers fine views of the bay; from the North Tower the Tombelaine Rock, which Philippe Auguste had fortified, is clearly visible.

👤👤 Musée de la Mer et de l'Écologie

9am–6pm. €9 (children under 18, €4.50), €18 (€9) gives entry to the four museums. 02 33 60 85 12.
Films and an audio-guided tour explain the environment of the mount, including the tides, the dangers in the bay and the silting-up process. There are also 150 models of old boats.

👤👤 Musée historique

Same hours and conditions as the Musée de la Mer. 02 33 60 07 01.
This historical museum retraces the history of the Mount back 1 000 years,

using a sound and light show and with glass cases of old objects and weapons. The tour ends in the dungeons.

Église paroissiale St-Pierre

The 11C parish church has been much altered. The apse spans a narrow street. The church contains a crucifix and other furnishings from the abbey; the chapel in the south aisle houses a statue of St Michael covered in silver; in the chapel to the right of the altar there is a 15C statue of the Virgin and Child and another of St Anne and the Virgin as a child.

Logis Tiphaine

Same hours and conditions as the Musée de la Mer. 02 33 60 23 34.
When the 14C warrior Bertrand du Guesclin was captain of the Mount, he had this house built (1365) for his wife Tiphaine Raguenel, an attractive and educated woman from Dinan, while he went off to the wars in Spain. The house was heavily restored in the 19C.

🚗 DRIVING TOURS

🚗 MONT ST-MICHEL BAY★★
About 100km/62mi of coastline border the bay.

The islands, cliffs, beaches and dunes form a series of ecosystems that are home to many species of flora and fauna. Travelling along the coast, you will be rewarded by stunning views of Mont St-Michel, and you can enjoy walks along pleasant paths rambling between the polders and grassy fields.

Tall Tales and Natural Phenomena
Pilgrims liked to tell frightening tales of the perils of Mont St-Michel, but the natural phenomena of the site are now well understood. What used to be called quicksand is really the effect of swathes of firm sand sitting on top of pockets of more liquid sand.
The fearsome fog that occasionally envelops the whole bay with such speed can now be predicted by weather fore-

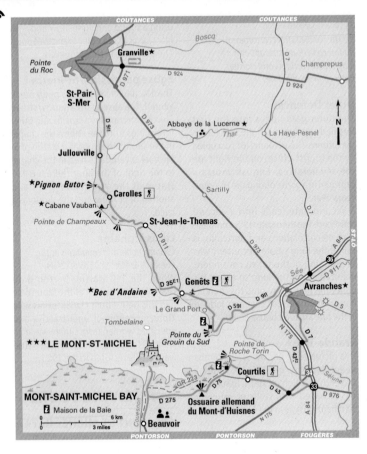

casters, and there is no longer a need to ring the church bell to warn of its imminence. And as for the tide racing in faster than a galloping horse? Well, although there are specific points where the action of the spring tide combines with geological features to create a movement of water at a speed of up to 25–30kph/15.5–18.6mph, the average rate of speed of the incoming tide is 3.7kph/2.3mph – about the speed of a person walking.

🚗 GRANVILLE TO MONT ST-MICHEL
40km/25mi. Allow 2h30.

Between Granville and Carolles, there is a wide open view of the bay.

St-Pair-sur-Mer
🔖 See GRANVILLE, p360.

Jullouville
The town is renowned for its fine sand beach. A pleasant walk leads along the seafront, passing 19C houses scattered among pine trees. The view extends from Pignon Butor to the Point du Roc.

Carolles
The village is set on the last headland before the sandy expanse of Mont St-Michel bay. As you drive between Carolles and St-Jean-le-Thomas, there is a splendid **view ★★** of the bay. Don't hesitate to stop the car to enjoy it.
🔲 In the vicinity there are also several attractive walks with fine views.
The **Vallée des Peintres** (Artists' Valley) is an attractive spot, green and rock-

strewn (⊞*Car park at Carolles-Plage, N of Carolles*).

The **view**★ from **Le Pignon Butor** on the clifftop extends north to Granville Rock and west to the Pointe du Grouin and Cancale in Brittany (*1km/0.6mi – 1hr on foot there and back, NW of the village*).

🚶 The path through the **Vallée du Lude** crosses an area of gorse and broom to reach the lonely cove, Port du Lude, on the coast. ⊞*Follow the signs to the car park, 1h on foot there and back.*

▷ South of Carolles on D 911 beyond the small bridge turn right; park at the end of the road; take the downhill path (left) which then climbs (right) towards the cliff.

The **view**★ from the Vauban Hut, a stone building standing on a rocky mound, includes Mont St-Michel.

St-Jean-le-Thomas

This seaside resort is very busy in the summer months.

▷ On entering Genêts turn right.

Bec d'Andaine★

There is a good **view** of Mont St-Michel from this beach backed by dunes.

Genêts

The solid granite 12C–14C **church** is preceded by an attractive porch with a wooden roof. Inside, the transept crossing leaves an impression of considerable strength, as it rises from four square granite piers with animal- and foliage-decorated capitals. The high altar is crowned by a canopy resting on gently swelling columns. Note the 13C stained-glass window at the east end.

Relais des Genêts

Guides offer visitors an opportunity to join walking tours through the bay area, some with special themes, and all centred around enjoying the natural beauty, learning about the flora and fauna (*4 pl. des Halles, 50530 Genêts;* ◷*Apr–Sept daily 9am–6pm; Oct–Mar Mon–Fri 9am–1pm, 2–5.30pm.* 𝄢*02 33 89 64 00*).

Reservations are required, and you are asked to wear boots and warm clothing in winter and carry a windproof jacket, a snack and water at all times.

▷ On leaving Genêts turn right before the calvary.

The coastal road goes through Le Grand Port and offers good views, at very close quarters, of Mont St-Michel, especially from the **Pointe du Grouin du Sud** (Grouin du Sud Point). The famous salt-marshes can also be seen.

♟ Maison de la Baie-Relais de Vains-St-Léonard (Bay Centre)

Relais de Vains Saint-Léonard, route du Grouin du Sud, 50300 Vains. ♿◷*Jul–Sept 10am–6pm; Apr–Jun and school holidays 2–6pm.* ◷*1 May.* ⊚€*5 (child 7–18, €2.50).* 𝄢*02 33 89 06 06. http://manche.fr/patrimoine.*
Before undertaking a walking tour of the bay, lead your children through this exhibition to introduce them to the flora and fauna they will encounter.

▷ Take D 591 and D 911 to Avranches.

Avranches★

⌘*See AVRANCHES, p376.*

▷ From Avranches take the N 175 south, leaving it after Pontabault for the D 43 to Courtils.

▷ At Bas-Courtils, turn left onto D 75; after 2km/1mi turn right onto D 107.

Ossuaire Allemand du Mont-d'Huisnes

This circular construction with 68 compartments, built in 1963, contains the remains of 11 887 German soldiers who fell in France. From the belvedere there is a good view of Mont St-Michel.

▷ Continue along D 275.

The coastal road skirts the salt-marshes where flocks of sheep are put out to graze on the special grass.

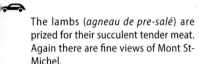

The lambs (*agneau de pre-salé*) are prized for their succulent tender meat. Again there are fine views of Mont St-Michel.

👥 Alligator Bay

Located at the entrance to Beauvoir, on the edge of D 976. 62 rte Mont St-Michel. ♿⏱*Apr–Sept daily 10am–7pm; Feb–Mar and Oct–Nov daily 2–6pm; Dec–Jan Sat–Sun 2–6pm, and school holidays 10am–6pm.* ⏱*1 Jan, 25 Dec.* ✎€14 (child 3–12, €9.50; 13–18, €11.50). ✆02 33 68 11 18. www.alligator-bay.com.

Thrills are guaranteed at this reptile breeding centre where you can see a wide variety of tortoises, snakes and crocodiles.

ADDRESSES

🛏STAY

🍽🍽 **Maison d'hôtes Les Epinettes** – *8 bis route du Mont St-Michel, 50170 Beavoir (4km/2.5mi S of Mont-St-Michel).* ✆02 33 68 02 65. www.les-epinettes-normandie.fr. *6 rooms and suites.* The owners have converted their grandparents farm buildings into pleasant spacious rooms. Picnic lunches can be provided. Several restaurants can be found close by.

🍽🍽🍽 **Chambre d'hôte Les Vieilles Digues** – *68, route du Mont St-Michel, 50170 Beauvoir (3 km/2mi south of Mont St-Michel in direction of Pontorso).* ✆02 33 58 55 30. www.lesvieillesdigues.com. 🅿. *7 rooms.* This pretty stone house has large bright rooms, well furnished, view of Mont St-Michel on request. Pleasant half-timbered breakfast room and landscaped garden.

🍽🍽 **Hôtel de la Digue** – *La Digue.* ✆02 33 60 14 02. https://lemontsaintmichel. info. 🅿. *36 rooms.* This coastal hotel has been a relais since 1877. Functional rooms. Dining room with a view of Mont St-Michel. **Restaurant** (🍽🍽)Traditional cooking using seafood.

🍽🍽🍽 **Âuberge St-Pierre** – *Grande-Rue.* ✆02 33 60 14 03. www.auberge-saint-pierre.fr. *23 rooms. Restaurant*🍽🍽. This half-timbered inn has a restaurant and small, well-kept bedrooms. Choose between a brasserie on the road side, a dining room upstairs, or the terrace.

🍴EAT

🍽 **La Gourmandise** – *21 route du Mont St-Michel, 50170 Beauvoir (4km/2.5mi S of Mont St-Michel).* ✆02 33 58 42 83. www.lagourmandisebeauvoir.fr. This Breton house transformed into a crêperie enlivens the village. Simple décor, lit by large bay windows. The extensive menu offers a choice of crêpes, etc.

🍽🍽 **Auberge de la Baie** – *44 route de la Rive, 50170 Ardevon (3km/2mi SE of Mont-St-Michel, direction Avranches).* ✆02 33 68 26 70. www.aubergedelabaie.fr. This restaurant on a main road is a welcome break from the bustling tourism of Mont St-Michel, at least for an hour or two. On the menu: traditional and regional dishes, plus a short list of galettes.

🍽🍽 **La Promenade** – *pl. du Casino, 50610 Jullouville.* ✆02 33 90 80 20. Closed Mon. Reservations advised. It would be difficult to find a better view of Mont St-Michel Bay than at this elegant restaurant-tearoom on the ground floor of the former casino hotel (1881). Handsome antique furniture.

🍽🍽 **La Sirène Lochet** – *16 Grande-Rue.* ✆02 33 60 08 60. Take the spiral staircase to enter the crêperie in this 14C house that was an inn for many years. The frosted-glass windows confirm the genuine flavour of the place.

🍽🍽 **Restaurant Le Pré Salé** – *route de Mont St-Michel 50170 (2 km/1.25mi south of Mont-St-Michel).* ✆02 33 60 24 17. https:// restaurants.le-mont-saint-michel.com/le-pre-sale. On the banks of the River Couesnon, the Mercure Hotel invites you into a well-lit, renovated dining room. Taste the famous meat from sheep that graze on the local salty pastures.

🍽🍽🍽🍽 **La Mère Poulard** – *Grande-Rue, 50170, Mont St-Michel.* ✆02 33 89 68 68. www.merepoulard.com. This hotel-restaurant is famous for Mother Poulard's omelette, which rubs shoulders with appetising regional recipes.

Stained-glass windows, Église Notre-Dame

Pontorson

Pontorson is a favourite stopping place for visitors on their way to Mont St-Michel. The town is named after a local baron, Orson, who in 1031 built a bridge (*pont* in French) over the Couesnon.

VISIT
Église Notre-Dame
The 11C church is said to have been founded by **William the Conqueror** to thank the Virgin for saving his army from the Couesnon quicksands. The episode is portrayed in a stained-glass window and also in scene 17 in the Bayeux Tapestry. The church was given pointed vaulting at a later date and has been remodelled several times. The massive rough granite west front has kept its Romanesque appearance, with a great arch, only slightly pointed.

Note the tympanum on the south doorway, carved with a man and a bird. A Gothic arch opens into the chapel of St Saviour, where there is a fine 15C altarpiece: the Broken Saints. Despite being mutilated during the Wars of Religion and the Revolution, it is a work of great richness.

EXCURSION
St-James
15km/9mi ESE by D 30.
This is one of western Normandy's oldest cities, founded by William the Conqueror in 1067. Several old streets and 15C ramparts recall the historic past. The **Cimetière américain et Mémorial**

- ▶ **Population:** 4 350.
- ◔ **Michelin Map:** 303: C-8.
- ▤ **Info:** Place de l'Hôtel-de-Ville. ℘02 33 60 20 65. www.mont-saint-michel-baie.com.
- ◖ **Location:** Pontorson is 9km/5.6mi S of Mont St-Michel on D 776.
- ◈ **Don't Miss:** The chapel of the St-James American Military Cemetery.

de Bretagne is on the outskirts of St-James (◖ *Take D 230 in the direction of Louvigné*). This cemetery holds the graves of more than 4 400 Americans. In the chapel are regimental colours, stained-glass windows, coats of arms and maps that commemorate the events of 1944.

ADDRESSES

⌂ STAY

⌐ **Hôtel La Tour Brette** – *8 r. Couesnon, 50170 Pontorson (9km/5.6mi S of Mont St-Michel).* ℘02 33 60 10 69. http://fraysse.phpnet.org. *10 rooms. Restaurant⌐.* This well-situated little hotel owes its name to an old tower that protected Normandy from the dukes of Brittany.

⑂/EAT

⌐⌐ **Restaurant Eugénie** – *59 rue Couesnon, 50170 Pontorson (8km/5mi S of Mont St-Michel).* ℘02 33 59 45 89. This regional-style house has lovely 18C wood panels, a grey-marble fireplace.

Avranches★

The pretty and lively city of Avranches is one of the oldest towns in Normandy; its origins date to early antiquity. St Aubert, Bishop of Avranches in the 8C, instigated the foundation of Mont St-Michel and the two centres are therefore closely linked, not only geographically but historically. The surrounding area is known for the Avranchin breed of sheep.

SIGHTS

The museum, the Plate-forme and the town hall (Mont St-Michel manuscripts) are located around the site of the former episcopal palace, while the botanical gardens are slightly down the hill. The Basilica of saints Gervais and Protais is a short walk from the town hall.
Entry to the Basilica Treasury is included in the museum and manuscript ticket. The Patton Monument is a 20-minute walk down rue de la Constitution.

Jardin des Plantes

pl. Carnot.
🕐*8.30am–dusk.*
The botanical gardens were once the property of a Capuchin monastery that was destroyed during the Revolution. From the terrace at the far end of the garden is a **panorama**★ of the bay.

La Plate-forme

From place Daniel-Huet, walk along the garden of the Sous-Préfecture to reach the site of the old cathedral. This little square contains the paving stone on

▸ **Population:** 7 719.
⚙ **Michelin Map:** 303: D-7.
🅘 **Info:** 2 rue Général de Gaule. ☎02 33 58 00 22. www.avranches.fr.
◖ **Location:** The town, on a granite spur, has a commanding view of Mont St-Michel, 25km/15.5mi to the SW. It can be reached by A 84, linking Villedieu-les-Poêles (23km/14.3mi) to the NE and Rennes, 82km/51mi to the SSW.
🅿 **Parking:** In the town centre, near the museum, Plate-forme and gardens.
☺ **Don't Miss:** The superb view of Mont St-Michel from the Jardin des Plantes.
🕐 **Timing:** Half-day is adequate; longer is better.
👫 **Kids:** At the Scriptorial, children are welcomed with a special tour led by the elf Titivillus.

which Henry II made public penance in 1172. From the terrace there is a wide **view**★ embracing Mont St-Michel.

Monument Patton

This memorial commemorates the deployment of General Patton's troops towards Brittany and the Basse-Normandie (in July 1944 with the American 3rd Army). The square on which it stands is now American territory.

Henry II Repents (12C)

Relations between the King of England, **Henry Plantagenet**, who was also Duke of Normandy, and his Archbishop of Canterbury, **Thomas Becket**, became very bitter. It is said that one day the king cried, "Will no one rid me of this turbulent priest?" Four knights took the words as a command and, on 29 December 1170, Thomas Becket was murdered in Canterbury cathedral.
The Pope excommunicated Henry II, who begged absolution. Robert of Torigni, Abbot of Mont St-Michel, held a council attended by the king at Avranches, and so it was that at the door of the cathedral (collapsed in 1794) Henry II, barefoot and dressed only in a shirt, made public penance on his knees on 22 May 1172.

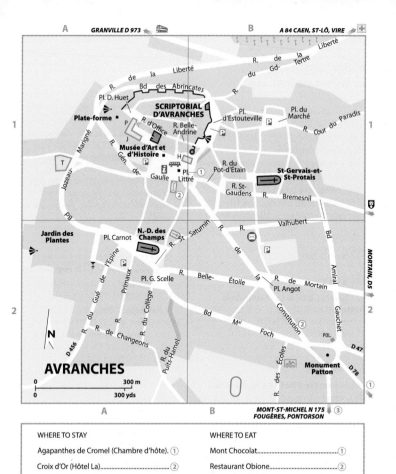

AVRANCHES

0   300 m
0   300 yds

SCRIPTORIAL D'AVRANCHES
Plate-forme
Musée d'Art et d'Histoire
St-Gervais-et-St-Protais
Jardin des Plantes
N.-D. des Champs
Monument Patton

MONT-ST-MICHEL N 175
FOUGÈRES, PONTORSON

WHERE TO STAY		WHERE TO EAT	
Agapanthes de Cromel (Chambre d'hôte).	①	Mont Chocolat..	①
Croix d'Or (Hôtel La)...............................	②	Restaurant Obione..	②
Moulin de la Butte (Chambre d'hôte Le)......	③		

Musée d'Art et d'Histoire

pl. Jean de St-Avit.
🕐*Jun–Sept Wed–Sun 10am–12.30pm, 2–6pm.* 📞*02 33 58 25 15. www.avranches.fr.*
The museum contains varied collections illustrating the history of the town.

Scriptorial – Musée Manuscrits du Mont St-Michel★★

pl. d'Éstouteville.
♿🕐*Jul–Aug daily except Mon 10am–1pm, 2–7pm; Apr–Jun and Sept, Tue–Sun 10am–1pm, 2–6pm; Oct–Dec and Feb–Mar Tue–Sat 2–6pm.* 🕐*Jan, 1 May, 1 Nov, 25 Dec.* 💶€8.
📞*02 33 79 57 00. www.scriptorial.fr.*
The Scriptorial houses a collection of precious 8C–15C **manuscripts★★**.

13C manuscript showing the sacrifice of Abraham

© Hervé Gyssels/Photononstop

Basilique St-Gervais-et-St-Protais Treasury

pl. St-Gervais.

🕐 *Jul–Sept daily 10am–noon, 2–6pm; Jun Mon–Sat 10am–noon, 2–6pm, Sun 2–6pm.* 🚫*No charge.* 📞*02 33 58 00 22. www.ville-avranches.fr.*

This vast late 19C basilica contains several gold objects, including a gold and silver **reliquary** containing the skull of St Aubert, the 8C bishop, which legend says was pierced by St Michael's finger.

ADDRESSES

🛏 STAY

🛏 **Chambre d'hôte Le Moulin de la Butte** – *11 rue du Moulin-de-la-Butte, 50170 Huisnes-sur-Mer (18km/11mi SW).* 📞*02 33 58 52 62. 5 rooms.* At the entrance to the village, opposite Mont St-Michel, this large, modern house has light, spacious rooms.

🛏🛏 **Chambre d'hôte les Agapanthes de Cromel** – *5, route de Quintine, 50220 St Quentin (6.5km/4 mi S of Avranches).* 📞*02 33 58 04 56. www.cromel.com. 3 rooms.* This

authentically renovated stone house is ideally located close to Avranches and a short drive from Mont St-Michel. Tastefully decorated rooms and a pleasant garden with a pool.

🛏🛏🛏 **Hôtel La Croix d'Or** – *83 rue de la Constitution.* 📞*02 33 58 04 88. www.hotel-restaurant-avranches-croix-dor.com. 27 rooms.* 🅿. This low, half-timbered house extends into an attractive garden full of flowers in season. Some guest rooms overlook the garden. Restaurant (🛏🛏🛏).

🍴 EAT

🛏 **Mont Chocolat** – *9 place Littré.* 📞*02 33 58 05 74. www.montchocolat.fr.* This pleasant patisserie is great for a quick lunch: sandwiches, *crêpes* and more.

🛏🛏 **Restaurant Obione** – *8 rue du Docteur Gilbert.* 📞*02 33 58 01 66. www.lelittre.fr. Closed all day Sun, and Mon dinner.* The regulars occupy low chairs in the bar, but you can sit comfortably at a table in one of the two dining rooms.

Saint-Hilaire-du-Harcouët★

St-Hilaire-du-Harcouët knows how to gain the maximum profit from its charms: the little Normandy town has adopted green tourism, and upholds its traditions. Sited on the strategic frontier between Brittany, Normandy and the Loire, the town was built and fortified by Harcouët, comrade-in-arms of William the Conqueror. Destroyed during World War II, the town had to be rebuilt at the end of the hostilities.

THE TOWN

The town is dominated by a neo-Gothic church (1855). Just below the priory, a stretch of water, graced with two lakes, has been created in the Airon valley. Areas for picnics or sports line the banks.

▶ **Population:** 6 120.
🕐 **Michelin Map:** 303: F-8
ℹ **Info:** 25 Avenue du Mal Leclerc, 50 600 Saint Hilaire du Harcouët. 📞02 33 79 38 88. www.st-hilaire.fr.
▶ **Location:** 28km/17.5m SE of Avranches.
🅿 **Parking:** On the street or by the lake.
👁 **Don't Miss:** The Musée de la Verrière.
🕐 **Timing:** About 2 hours to see the town and museum.
👪 **Kids:** Picnics and sports areas by the lake.

Musée de la Verrière★

37 bld Gambetta. 🕐*Closed for renovation until 2020; check for details at tourist office.* 📞*02 33 49 13 43.*

The nuns of the order of St Francis D'Assisi and St Claire had to abandon the building some time ago as the convent was not suitable for such a small number. Nowadays it houses an exhibition about the principle Norman Cistercian abbeys, as well as an important collection of sacred art.

The centre also presents an excellent view of the cloistered life of the nuns: the visit is brought to life by video evidence, pictures and waxwork models based on the faces of the nuns themselves.

🚗 DRIVING TOUR

🚗 LA ROUTE DES BARRAGES
50km/31mi. Allow 1h30.

▶ Leave St-Hilaire by the D 976, direction Avranches.

Ducey-les-Chéris
The 17C Montgomery castle is now being restored.

🕙 *For information about guided visits contact the tourist office.*

▶ Follow the D 78.

Barrage de la Roche-qui-Boit
Unfortunately it is not possible to visit this small dam, dating from 1919.

▶ At the junction with the D 582, turn left onto the road marked "le Rocher, accès au lac". After 2km/1.25m, the route passes a holiday village, leading to the lake, which is very pleasant and well shaded.

▶ Return to the D 582 and turn left.

The road leads you back to a view of the valley. After the bridge over the river, take a small road on the right, which climbs rapidly to the Auberge du Lac, on the ridge of the Vézins dam.

Barrage de Vézins
This curved structure (1931) with multiple buttresses has created a long artificial lake.

Villedieu-les-Poêles★

The town occupies a bend in the River Sienne and is an important road junction. It takes part of its name (*poêle* means pot or frying pan) from the making of pots and pans – a local activity here since the 12C. By 1740, there were 139 workshops in the town.

From making the great round-bellied copper milk churns (*cannes*), the local factories now make copper and aluminium boilers for domestic and industrial use. The town has retained its medieval appearance with many attractive inner courtyards, stepped streets, alleys and old houses.

▶ **Population:** 3 893.
🕙 **Michelin Map:** 303: E-6.
🛈 **Info:** 8 Rue des Costils. 📞02 33 61 05 69. www.tourisme-villedieu.com.
▶ **Location:** From Granville, Villedieu is 29km/18mi E.
👥 **Kids:** The zoo in Champrepus.

SIGHTS
Église Notre-Dame
This 15C church in the Flamboyant Gothic style was built on the site of a 12C church. The square transept tower over the crossing is emblazoned with various heraldic emblems. The chancel contains an 18C gilt wooden tabernacle.

Atelier du Cuivre

54 rue Général Huard.

♿⏱*Mon–Fri 9am–noon, 1.30–5.30pm, Sat 9am–noon, 2–5pm. ✏Tours Mon–Sat 10–11am, 2–3.30pm (Jul–Aug 4.45pm); ☞€8.20. ⏱Public holidays. ☞€5.50. ✆02 33 51 31 85. www.atelierducuivre.fr.* The story of copper working in Villedieu is explained: the copper deposits, techniques of copper working and a tour.

Musée de la Poeslerie and Maison de la Dentellière

25 r. Général Huard, cour du Foyer.

⏱*Apr–Oct: Mon–Sat 10am–12.30pm,*

2–5.30pm (Jul–Aug also open public holidays 2–6pm). ☞€5. ✆02 33 69 33 44. www.museesvilledieu.sitew.com. A reconstruction of an old workshop shows the copperware-making process. The lace-maker's house displays Villedieu lace, popular in the 18C.

Fonderie de Cloches★

rue du Pont-Chicnon.

♿⏱*Early Feb–mid-Nov (Tue–Sat 10am–12.30pm, 2–5.30pm (mid-Jul– Aug daily 9.30am–6.30pm). ☞€8.50 (child 6–11, €7.50). ✆02 33 61 00 56. www.cornille-havard.com.* The foundry still produces bells for belfries, ships and other public buildings, exported worldwide.

Musée du Meuble normand

9 rue du Reculé.

⏱*By arrangement during 2019; call for opening hours for 2020.*

✆02 33 61 11 78. The collection of Norman furniture dates from 1680 to 1930.

EXCURSIONS

Abbaye de Hambye★★

12km/7.5mi N of Villedieu by D 9 and D 51.

⏱*Apr–Sept daily except Tue 10am–noon, 2–6pm (Jul–Aug daily 10am–6pm).*

Fonderie de Cloches Cornille Havard

© Hervé Hughes/hemis.fr

Abbaye de Hambye

© Olivier Rault/Fotolia.com

🕐 *1 May.* ♿ *€5.50.* 📞 *02 33 61 76 92.*
Beside the River Sienne are the majestic ruins of Hambye abbey, which was founded around 1145. The **church★** is imposing, although it lacks a roof, a west front and the first bay of the nave. The narrow 13C nave was extended in the 14C by three bays.
The exceptionally large Gothic chancel has pointed arches, an ambulatory and radiating chapels. The tombstones are those of Jeanne Paynel, last descendant of the founders of Hambye, and her husband, Louis d'Estouteville.
The lay brothers' refectory (now used as a conference room) is furnished with 17C Rouen tapestries and a collection of old furniture.

Mont Robin

13km/8mi N by D 999. About 2km/1mi beyond Percy turn right towards Tessy-sur-Vire and right again almost immediately to Mount Robin.
From this point (276m) there is an expansive **view** east in the direction of the Suisse Normande.

👥 Parc zoologique de Champrepus

8km/5mi W by D 924 toward Granville. Picnic area and adventure playground.
♿🕐 *Apr–early Sept daily 10am–7pm; rest of year see website.* ♿ *€18 (child 3–12, €12) – online discounts.* 📞 *02 33 61 30 74. www.zoo-champrepus.com.*

Over 80 species are presented in a pleasantly shaded setting of parkland covering 6ha. There is also an amusement park and snack shops.

ADDRESSES

🛏 STAY

🍴 **Auberge de l'Abbaye** –
50450 Hambye. 📞 *02 33 61 42 19. www.aubergedelabbayehambye.com. 7 rooms.*
You cannot fail to notice this large hotel near the abbey. The dining room is bright with floral decoration and coloured net curtains. Restaurant (🍴🍴) serving classic cuisine open Tue lunch–Sun lunch.

🍴🍴🍴 **Le Fruitier** – *Place des Costils.*
📞 *02 33 90 51 00. www.le-fruitier.com.*
Functional and well-presented rooms and apartments in this family hotel near the tourist office. Restaurant bistronomique.

🍽 EAT

🍴 **Manoir de l'Acherie** – *37 rue Michel de l'Epinay, 50800 Ste-Cécile (4km/2.5mi E).*
📞 *02 33 51 13 87. www.manoir-acherie.fr. Closed Mon.* Enjoy a meal (or a night) in this beautiful 17C manor house. The restaurant fare is plentiful; wood fire in dining room.

🍴🍴 **Restaurant La Ferme de Malte** –
11 rue Jules Tétrel. 📞 *02 33 91 35 91. www. lafermedemalte.fr.* A touch of luxury at this comfortable, highly rated restaurant in the town.

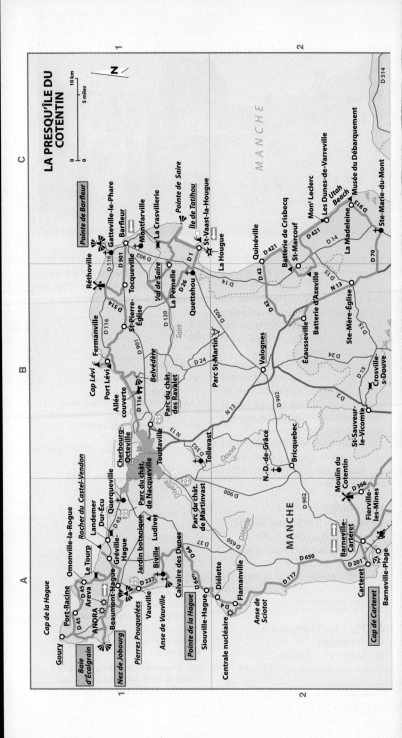

LA PRESQU'ÎLE DU COTENTIN

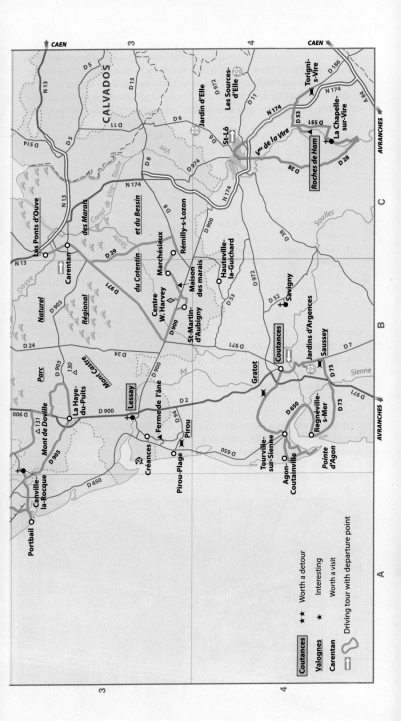

CAEN

CALVADOS

D 5
D 15
D 11
D 5
D 514
N 13

Les Ponts d'Ouve
Carentan
N 13
D 903

Naturel

Régional

du Cotentin
et du Bessin
des Marais

Canal de Vire-Taute
Taute

D 29
D 971
D 8

Marchésieux
Centre
W. Harvey
St-Martin-d'Aubigny
Maison
des marais
Remilly-s-Lozon

D 900
D 900
D 900

Hauteville-
la-Guichard

Jardin d'Elle
Les Sources-
d'Elle
D 972
D 11

CAEN

Torigni-
s-Vire
N 174
D 186

N 174
D 53
SSS a
La Chapelle-
sur-Vire

V^ce de la Vire
St-Lô
D 974
Vire

N 174
D 38
D 38

Roches de Ham
D 28

AVRANCHES
A 84

C

Savigny
D 52
D 53
D 972

B

Mont Castre
△ 130

D 24
D 24

La Haye-
du-Puits
D 900

D 006 900
D 903
△ 131
Mont de Doville

Parc

Douve

D 24

Lessay
+
D 900
Fermede l'âne
D 94
Pirou
Pirou-Plage

Créances

D 2
Ay

D 650

Gratot
Coutances
Jardins d'Argences
Saussey
D 73

D 971
D 971
Sienne
D 7

Regnéville-
s-Mer
D 73
D 650

Tourville-
sur-Sienne
D 650

Agon-
Coutainville
*Pointe
d'Agon*

AVRANCHES

Canville-
la-Rocque
+
D 903
D 650

Portbail

3
4

A

Coutances   ★★ Worth a detour

Valognes   ★   Interesting

Carentan   ⬆   Worth a visit

                    ◯   Driving tour with departure point

3
4

383

LA PRESQU'ILE DU COTENTIN

The pronounced thrust of the Cotentin peninsula, or La Presqu'Île du Cotentin, into the Atlantic corresponds with an equally uncharacteristic landscape: the austere surroundings of La Hague are more like Brittany than Normandy. Geographically speaking, the area can be divided into three parts: the Cotentin Pass is the lower plain, the Val de Saire includes the river valley and the whole northeast part of the peninsula, the Cap de la Hague is the granite spine jutting out into the sea. The wooded hinterland was the cradle of Norman adventurers who once controlled the central Mediterranean area.

Highlights

Geography

Surrounded on three sides by the sea, and separated from the mainland by swamps, the peninsula extends from south of Granville in the west to Carentan in the east, passing through Cherbourg in the north, from which it gets the name by which it is most commonly known in English: the Cherbourg peninsula. The whole peninsula lies within the Manche *département* of the Basse-Normandie Region. Off the west coast lie the Channel Islands known to the French as Les Îles Anglo-Normand and, of course, in the east are the westernmost of the beaches used for the Allied Landings in 1944.

Today

The peninsula is very rural and agriculture is one of the most important economic activities, with dairy farming and vegetable growing being the most prominent. Cider and Calvados are also produced here from locally grown apples. Being a coastal region, fishing is also much in evidence and the oysters from St- Vaast-la-Hougue are renowned throughout France.

There are two important nuclear facilities in the area, one at Flamanville, but better known is the plant at La Hague where there is a nuclear waste reprocessing and storage site.

Like many rural regions tourism is becoming increasingly important, especially to the D-Day beaches, the nearby town of St-Mère-Église and, of course, the various war cemeteries.

Musée Airborne, Ste-Mère-Église

© Walter Bibikow/hemis.fr

St-Lô

In 1944 St-Lô acquired the sad title of Capital of Ruins. On 19 July, the day the town was liberated, only the battered towers of the collegiate church and a few houses in the suburbs remained standing. Since then St-Lô has been rebuilt and it is now the site of one of the largest stud farms in France.

A BIT OF HISTORY

Key Town – St-Lô, a vital communications centre, was destined to play a strategic role in the Battle of Normandy. Owing to its position at a crossroads, the town underwent heavy bombing from 6 June, aimed at dispersing enemy forces. The battle for St-Lô began early in July in the middle of the War of the Hedgerows to capture the Lessay-St-Lô road, the base for Operation Cobra.

The town, which was the centre of German resistance, fell on 19 July. A monument, erected in memory of Major Howie of the American army, recalls a moving episode in the town's liberation. Howie had wanted to be one of the first to enter St-Lô, but he was

- ▶ **Population:** 18 961.
- ⚅ **Michelin Map:** 303: L-5.
- 🛈 **Info:** 60 rue de la Poterne - Plage Verte. ℘02 14 29 00 17. www.ot-saintloagglo.fr.
- ▶ **Location:** St-Lô lies between Coutances (29km/18mi W) and Bayeux (35km/22mi NE).
- 👁 **Don't Miss:** The outdoor pulpit at the Église Notre-Dame.
- 🕑 **Timing:** In late summer, attend the Thursday exhibition at the stud farm.
- 👥 **Kids:** Haras national stud farm.

killed on 18 July. To fulfil his wish, the first Allied troops to enter St-Lô carried his coffin in with them, setting it down in the ruins of the belfry of Holy Cross Church.

A week later, after an unprecedented aerial bombardment – when 5 000 tonnes of bombs fell on an area of 11sq km/4sq mi – the German front

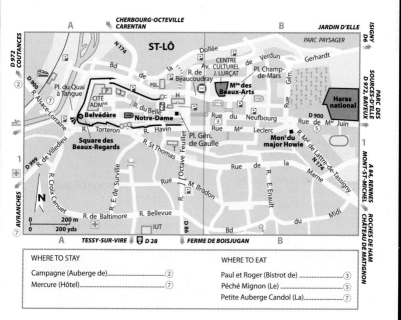

broke in the west and the Avranches breakthrough was launched.

Reconstruction – A new town has arisen from the ruins, planned so that you can now clearly see the outline of the rocky spur, ringed by ramparts and towers, which have become the landmark. The oldest district, the Enclos, in the upper part of the town includes the Préfecture and administrative buildings, which make an interesting post-war architectural group. The extremely modern tower in place Général de Gaulle is an amazing contrast to the former prison porch nearby, now a memorial to Resistance fighters and the victims of Nazism.

SIGHTS

Église Notre-Dame
rue de la Chancellerie

The west front of the church (13C–17C) and the two towers have been shored up, but otherwise left as they were in 1944 as a witness to the ferocity of the bombardment.

In St Thomas Becket's chapel, note the large window by Max Ingrand. There is an outside pulpit against the north wall, level with the chancel.

St-Lô and the Unicorn

Strolling through the streets of St-Lô, the attentive visitor will glimpse many versions of the unicorn, a handsome white horse with a goat's beard, cloven hooves and a narwhal's spiralled horn growing from his forehead. Considered as shy, wary creatures embodying purity, chastity and loyalty, unicorns in the Middle Ages came to symbolise the Virgin Mary. The devotion of the inhabitants of St-Lô for the Virgin may account for the presence of a unicorn on the city's coat of arms, in rue de la Porte-au-Lait, and even leaping from a stone fountain on the corner of rue Leturc and rue du Neufbourg.

Belvédère

From the tower overlooking the spur on which the town stands there is a view of the Vire valley and the *bocage*.

Hôpital-Mémorial France-États-Unis
By rue de Villedieu to the SW.

The hospital was built jointly by the two nations and has a Fernand Léger mosaic on one of its façades.

Musée des Beaux-Arts
In the Centre Culturel Jean-Lurçat, pl. Champ-de-Mars.

&♿ ◷Jul–Aug Tue–Sun 1.30–6.30pm; Sept–Jun Tue–Sun 2–6pm. ◷1 Jan, 1 May, 1 Nov, 25 Dec. ⊜€4.50. ℘02 33 72 52 55.

The museum has a good collection of tapestries as well as 19C French painting: Boudin, Miller and Corot.

♟♟ Haras national / Pôle Hippique de Saint-Lô ★
437 r. du Maréchal-Juin, dir. Bayeux

&♿ ◷Jul–Aug self-guided tours daily 2–6pm; ⟷⟶Guided tours Jul–Aug at 11am, 2pm, 3pm, 4pm and 5pm; rest of year daily except Sun at 2.30pm, 3.30pm and 4.30pm. ◷Nov–Feb. ⊜€6 (under 12, €4). ℘02 14 29 00 17.

The St-Lô stud, initially created by Napoleon, and now the biggest of the national studs, specialises in breeds such as Norman cobs, trotters and French saddle-horses. There are eight stable blocks around the central courtyard, housing around 40 stallions. Possibility of pony trekking by arrangement (℘02 33 57 27 06). Or you can become a show jumper using virtual reality helmets.

Hôpital-mémorial France-États-Unis
route de Villedieu, west of the town.

This edifice exists thanks to a Franco-American initiative. In the entrance, a huge mosaic by Fernand Léger celebrates the friendship between the Allies.

Musée du Bocage normand

bld de la Commune, 50000 St-Lô, on the road south to Vire.

♿⏰*Apr–Oct daily except Mon 2–6pm (Jul–Aug 1.30–6.30pm).* ⏰*1 May.*
✎*€5.50 (12–30 years, €2.75, under 12 no charge).* ✆*02 33 72 52 55.*

Situated around a huge square courtyard, the restored buildings of this large farm (dating from the 17C–19C) showcase a modern and interactive interpretation of rural life. Emblematic rooms featuring country life have been recreated – the butter-making facility, the stables and valet's room, the cow byre and workshop.

The creation of these collections allows visitors to follow the evolution of methodology in agricultural life and raising animals. One floor is dedicated to equine and cattle breeding, a tradition in Normandy.

EXCURSIONS

Parc des Sources-d'Elle

At Rouxeville, 14 km/8.75m east of St-Lô by the D 11, on the the left near the road to Caumont-l'Éventé.

⏰*Feb and Oct Tue–Sun 8am–6pm; Mar–Jun and Sept Tue–Sun 7.30am–6.45pm; Jul–Aug daily 7.30am–6.45pm; Nov Mon–Fri 8am–6pm.* ⏰*Dec–Jan.*
✎*€3.* 🅿*€2.* ✆*07 62 89 55 39.*
www.sourcesdelle.com.

With no lack of fish, fishermen are happy in this huge 37ha park, boasting eight lakes and splendid rhododendron shrubberies.

Jardin d'Elle

At Villiers-Fossard, 6km/3.75m north east of St-Lô by the D 6.

⏰*Mar–Nov Tue–Sat 9am–noon, 2–6pm, Sun–Mon and public holidays 2–6pm.* ⏰*Dec–Feb.* ✎*€6 (child 8–14, €3).* ✆*02 33 05 88 64.*
www.dellenormandie.com.

More than 2 500 varieties of plants, trees and bushes are spread among a multitude of small themed gardens. You can lose yourself in this labyrinth of greenery, abundant with flowers, some scented, in which all the plants are indentified, which is a good way of encouraging you to stop in the garden centre located at the entrance and exit of the garden.

🚗 DRIVING TOUR

🚗 VALLÉE DE LA VIRE
20km/12.5mi.

▶ Leave St-Lô SE on the D 974.

Torigni-sur-Vire

Since the 19C the **Château des Matignon** (⏰*During journées du patrimoine only; groups by reservation during rest of year.* ✆*02 33 56 71 44*) has consisted of only the west wing (restored). The main staircase (17C) leads to the reception rooms, which contain a very fine collection of tapestries, Louis XIII, Louis XV and Louis XVI furniture and works by the wildlife artist Arthur Le Duc. The park includes three ponds encircled by shaded paths.

▶ From Torini take D 974 north. Cross the N 174 on the D 53 to Condé-sur-Vire. Then turn south on D 86, D 151 and minor roads.

Roches de Ham★★

Alt 80m.

From the magnificent escarpment (above the river) there is a **view** of a beautiful bend in the River Vire.

▶ Return downhill; turn right onto D 551 and right again onto D 396. Pass through Troisgots and descend southeast on D 159 to La Chapelle-sur-Vire.

La Chapelle-sur-Vire

This small village has been a centre of pilgrimage since the 12C. In the church stand a statue of Our Lady of Vire (15C) and a low relief of St Anne, the Virgin and Child.

▶ Continue south along D 159.

Roches de Ham and the Vire

© Bertrand Rieger/hemis.fr

The shaded road crosses the River Vire, then follows its course.
Along the way there is a view of the **Château de l'Angotière** (⌣ *closed to the public*).

▶ Continue to Tessy-sur-Vire, and turn right to return to St-Lô on D 28.

ADDRESSES

🏨 STAY

⊜⊜⊜ **Auberge de Campagne** – *Château de la Roque, 50180 Hébécrevon (7.5km/4.7mi W of St-Lô towards Coutances, then towards Périers). ℘02 33 57 33 20. www.chateau-de-la-roque.fr. 15 rooms.* This beautiful 16C–17C residence appears at the end of a poplar-lined approach. Tastefully decorated rooms, lovely park for strolls, spa, sauna and plenty of activities on offer. By reservation only, the *restaurant*⊜⊜ offers fine local cuisine in its dining room, which displays exposed beams.

⊜⊜⊜ **Hotel Mercure Saint Lo Centre** – *1 avenue de Briovère. ℘02 33 05 10 84. www.accorhotels.com. 67 rooms.* Opposite the ramparts two hotels have united to

become a contemporary establishment. The rooms are comfortable. The restaurant (⊜⊜*Le Tocqueville*) has traditional cooking with a regional accent.

🍴 EAT

⊜ **Bistrot de Paul et Roger** – *40 rue du Neufbourg. ℘02 33 57 19 00 . Closed Sun and Sat evening.* In the middle of this crazy bric-à-brac of glazed tiles, Louis XVI chairs, old posters and black-and-white photographs, don't miss the priceless collection of old radio sets.

⊜⊜ **La Petite Auberge** – *Candol, St-Lô (1216 rte de Candol, exit towards Canisy). ℘02 33 05 34 11. www.aubergedecandol.fr. Closed Mon and Tue all day, and Sun evening.* After long years of travel, the chef has settled here to create delicious seafood dishes served on the terrace or close to the fireplace.

⊜⊜ **Le Péché Mignon** – *84 rue du Maréchal-Juin. ℘02 33 72 23 77. www. lepechemignon.restaurant. Closed Sun eve and all day Mon.* Near the Haras national, the owner/chef prepares regional dishes adapted to today's tastes. Two dining rooms, including a more modern one with brightly coloured tablecloths.

Coutances★★

Coutances is perched on a hillock crowned by a magnificent cathedral, miraculously saved from the bombardments that destroyed two-thirds of the town in June 1944. The name of this religious and judicial centre of the Cotentin peninsula recalls the Roman Emperor Constantins-Chlorus (293–306). In the 14C Coutances acquired an aqueduct (*ancien aqueduc*) of which only three arches remain standing to the northwest of the town on the Coutainville road.

▶ **Population:** 8 624.
Michelin Map: 303: D-5.
Info: 6 Rue Milon. ℘02 33 19 08 10. www.tourisme-coutances.fr.
Location: Coutances is at a crossroads: D 972 links it to St-Lô (29km/18mi E), D 2/D 900 heads towards Cherbourg (77km/48mi N) and D 971 leads to Granville (29km/18mi S). The coast is 10min to the W.
Don't Miss: The Gothic cathedral, and the display of old Nativity crèches at the manor of Saussey.
Timing: Take 2h to see the town and cathedral, before embarking on one of the excursions in the area.

👤👤 CATHÉDRALE★★★

🕐*Daily 9am–7pm. ℘02 33 19 08 10. http://cathedralecoutances.free.fr.*
One of the best views of the cathedral is when arriving at Coutances from the south; the elegance of the proportions and the purity of the lines are starkly outlined against the sky.

Geoffroy de Montbray, one of those great prelate knights Duke William gathered round him, completed the first nave in 1056. Then, thanks to the generosity of the sons of Tancrède de Hauteville, whose amazing Mediterranean adventure had just begun, he built the chancel, transept, central tower and the façade with its twin octagonal towers reminiscent of those at Jumièges.

In 1218, after the town had been burned down, a new Gothic cathedral was mounted on the remains of the 11C church, involving prodigious adaptations of style, as can be seen from the way the Romanesque towers of the old façade were incorporated into a new rectangular front and surmounted by spires.

Exterior

Above the great window a beautiful gallery crowns the façade, whereas on either side rise the towers, quartered at their highest, octagonal level, by graceful elongated pierced turrets. The profusion of ascending lines, so remarkable in their detail, culminates in the flight of the spires, which rise to 78m. The bold turreted lantern tower at the transept crossing is noteworthy for its slender ribbing and fine, narrow windows.

Interior

Pause at the beginning of the nave for a remarkable general view of this singular building with its upswept lines: to right and left wide arcades are lined above by galleries where the lower windows, surmounted by blind rose windows, have been blocked up; above again, along the bottom of the clerestory windows, a second balustrade of a different design lines the walls.

Dominating the transept crossing is the octagonal **lantern tower★★★**. It is 41m high at its apex and the best example of its type in Normandy. At the base of the south transept pillar stands the beautiful and deeply venerated 14C statue of Our Lady of Coutances, which miraculously survived the 1944 bombing of St Nicholas' church. The north transept contains the oldest, 13C stained-glass windows; the south,

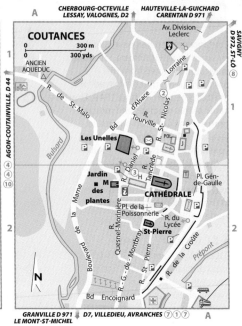

WHERE TO STAY

Cositel (Hôtel)............................ ④

Quesnot
(Chambre d'hôte Le)............. ⑦

Refuge
(Chambre d'hôte Le)............. ⑧

Roses (Les).............................. ⑩

WHERE TO EAT

Fleur de Sarrasin (La)............... ②

Jules Gommes (Le).................... ①

Taverne du Parvis...................... ③

Tourne-Bride (Le)...................... ④

Verte Campagne (La).............. ⑦

Musée Quesnel-Morinière.... M

a 14C window, in sombre tones, of the Last Judgement. The chancel, with the same architectural simplicity as the nave, is later in date and wider. As you walk round the two ambulatories, note the false triforium formed from two arches, each covering twin bays. The radiating chapels are shallow and the ribs of their vaulting combine with the corresponding ambulatory bay rib to form a single arch. The central apsidal chapel, known as the Circata, was enlarged during a late 14C rebuilding by Sylvestre de la Cervelle. Above the slender painted columns small figures and animals peer out from the foliage of the capitals.

Upper Storeys★★

⏳*Guided tour (1h30), reserve beforehand (children under 10 years not permitted). Jul–Aug Mon–Fri.* ⊜€8. ℘02 72 88 14 25.
The walk, which explores the Romanesque parts of the original building, starts at a west front tower, continues through the attic of the aisle then on to the third-floor galleries to finish at the top of the lantern tower.

The **panorama** extends from Granville, over the Chausey Islands to Jersey and on a clear day even Mount Pinçon is visible.

ADDITIONAL SIGHTS

Jardin des Plantes (Botanical Garden)★

rue Quesnel-Morinière.
⏳🕐*Daily: Feb–Mar and Oct 9am–6pm; Apr–Jun and Sept 9am–8pm; Jul–Aug 9am–11pm; Nov–Jan 9am–5pm.* ⊜*No charge.* ℘02 33 19 08 10.
The garden's entrance is flanked by an old cider press on one side and the Quesnel-Morinière Museum on the other. The terraced promenade traverses the sloping gardens with their many flower beds and pine trees.

Musée Quesnel-Morinière

2 rue Quesnel-Morinière.
🕐*Daily except Tue: Jul–Aug 10am–noon, 2–6pm; Sun 2–5pm; Sept–Jun 10am–noon, 2–5pm, Sun 2–5pm.*
🚫*Public holidays.* ⊜€2.50 *(no charge for temporary exhibitions, under 18s and Sun afternoon).* ℘02 33 07 07 88.

Ambulatory, Cathédrale de Coutances

The museum is in the former Hôtel Poupinel, which was bought in 1675 by the king's counsellor of the same name. The collections are mainly local: regional pottery and paintings by local artists. Outstanding, however, are Rubens' *Lions and Dogs Fighting* and the *Last Supper* by Simon Vouet. The popular arts and traditions section includes 18C–20C costumes from the Coutances area, 18C–19C regional pottery, headdresses, furniture and kitchen utensils.

Les Unelles

A new steel frame and glass-walled building adjoins the former seminary buildings which have been transformed to house an arts centre, the tourist office and the local authority offices. The name is derived from the Unelli whose capital was Cosedia, present day Coutances.

Église St-Pierre

This fine 15C–16C church, built by Bishop Geoffroy Herbert, was given a lantern tower over the transept crossing. In accordance with Renaissance custom, it was decorated ever more richly as the height increased.

EXCURSIONS

Savigny

11 km/7m east by the D 972, then right on D 52 towards Savigny.
Savigny's Romanesque church (12C) is renowned for its 14C frescoes. On the left hand wall of the nave, one depiction of the Last Supper is particularly well preserved. In the chancel, four scenes illustrate the martyrdom of St Barbe; the last one on the left dates from the 19C. Visit the sacristy behind the altar, where you can see a large sculpted relief of Christ, from the 11C.

Hauteville-la-Guichard

15km/9mi NE. Leave Coutances to the N on D 971 heading for St-Sauveur-Landelin, then turn right onto D 53. Just after Moncuit, turn left towards Hauteville (D 435).
The **Musée Tancrède de Hauteville** (✖️ ⏱Jul–Aug Tue–Sun 2–6.30pm, rest of year, last Sun of each month 2–6pm. ⏱public holidays and Dec–Jan; ✆02 33 47 88 86) plunges you into the heart of the Norman conquest of Sicily and southern Italy at the beginning of the 11C. Tancrède and his 12 children (the most famous were Robert Guiscard and Roger I of Sicily) were the true founders of Norman power in the Mediterranean. Incredibly well organised and extremely cunning, they created a powerful state remarkable for its military achievements as well as its cultural influence.

🚗 DRIVING TOUR

🚗 COUTANCES TO THE COAST

Round-trip of 47km/29mi. Allow 1h30.

Château de Gratot

© A. de Valroger/MICHELIN

▶ Leave Coutances west on the D 44 and then turn right onto D 244.

On the way out of Coutances the road passes the overgrown remains of the aqueduct.

Château de Gratot★

🕐 *Daily 10am–7pm.* ⊕€4 *(child 10–18, €1.50).* 📞 *06 64 01 05 82.*
www.chateaugratot.com.
For five centuries the château belonged to the Argouges family. Long abandoned, it has been restored and converted into an arts centre.
A small three-arched bridge over the moat leads to the entrance gatehouse and then the inner courtyard. Within the courtyard from left to right are the 18C pavilion and the 17C main building, flanked by the Round Tower, and the Fairy's Tower with the North Tower to the rear.

Maison seigneuriale

Two flights of steps lead to the entrance of the now roofless former living quarters. The ground floor was lit by tall windows, the upper floor by dormers.

Tour ronde

This early 15C round tower is quite medieval in appearance. The narrowing of the staircase as it moved upwards was devised to hinder an attack as only one person could pass at a time.

The entrance to the basement is at the foot of this tower.

Caves

The groined vaulting of these fine cellars is supported by stout piers. The masonry is composed of stones placed edgewise. The late 15C tower, now called the Fairy's Tower, is reinforced by a powerful buttress. It is octagonal at the base but becomes square at the top and is crowned by a saddleback roof.

Tour d'angle

This corner tower, the only part of the medieval castle that remains, probably dates from the late 13C or the early 14C; the door has been walled up.

Communs

One of the rooms in these 16C outbuildings hosts an exhibition on the château, its construction and restoration.

▶ In St-Malo-de-la-Lande take D 68 south towards Tourville-sur-Sienne then turn right onto D 272 and D 72 to Agon-Coutainville.

Agon-Coutainville

Coutainville is one of the more popular resorts on the west coast of the Cotentin peninsula, bounded by the Channel to the west and the Sienne estuary to the east. At low tide these great wet sandy stretches are popular with those looking for shrimps, cockles and clams.

▷ Take the road leading to the Pointe d'Agon.

Pointe d'Agon

The line of stones on the right-hand side of the road is a memorial to the author **Fernand Lechanteur** (1910–71), who wrote in the Norman dialect.

From the headland there is a good view of this part of the Channel coast and especially of the port of Regnéville on the other side of the estuary.

▷ Return to Agon-Coutainville, then follow the D 72 to the hamlet, la rue d'Agon.

Thereafter, the road overlooks the silted up port of Regnéville. Turn right on D 44.

Tourville-sur-Sienne

The roadside statue is of Admiral de Tourville, who lost the Battle of La Hougue (1692). From the terraced cemetery (*road from the statue*) there is a good view of Regnéville harbour, closed off by the sandy headland, Montmarin belfry, the Rocher de Granville, and in clear weather, the Chausey Islands.

▷ Drive to Pont-de-la-Roque along D 650, then via the D 20 to Regnéville-sur-Mer along D 49.

Regnéville-sur-Mer

From the 13C **church**, follow signposts to the **Musée du Littoral et de la Chaux** (*14 rte des Fours-à-Chaux*. ⏰*daily 9am–7pm;* ⊕*€2.50;* ✆*02 33 46 82 18*), set up in the former Rey lime kilns. This splendidly restored example of mid-19C industrial architecture presents traditional activities connected with the Channel coast.

▷ Leave Regnéville on D 49 towards Montmartin-sur-Mer, then Hyenville (D 73). Continue on D 73 until you cross D 7 and drive towards Coutances via Saussey.

Manoir de Saussey★

⏰*Easter–Sept daily 2–6.30pm.* ✆*02 33 45 19 65.*

The 17C buildings are enhanced by a pretty rose garden, an orchard, a vegetable patch and a series of delightful flower beds. Note the collection of **Nativity scenes** and a lovely exhibition of **glassware**.

▷ Go back to D 7 and follow signs to the Manoir d'Argences.

Jardins d'Argences

⏰*Mid-May–mid-Oct daily 2–6pm.* ✆*02 33 07 92 04.*

The grounds surrounding this manor house (15C–18C) are enchanting and laid out along a series of pretty itineraries.

▷ Drive back to Coutances.

ADDRESSES

🛏 STAY

⊖ **Maison d'hôtes Les Roses** – *11 rue du Vieux-Lavoir, 50560 Blainville-sur-Mer (2km/1mi N of Agon-Coutainville).* ✆*02 33 47 20 31. 5 rooms.* This village used to be exclusively fishermen's homes. In this house, bedrooms with wood panelling make for a fine halt right by the sea.

⊖⊜ **Chambre d'hôte Le Quesnot** – *3 r. du Mont-César, 50660 Montchaton (6.5km/4mi SW of Coutances via D 20 then D 72).* ✆*02 33 45 05 88. https:// chambreslequesnot.wixsite.com. 3 rooms.* Guests have the use of a small 18C stone-built house with its own terrace and tiny garden and a view of a little church perched on a promontory. Modern bedrooms above the large country-style dining room.

⊖⊜⊜ **Hôtel Cositel** – *rue de Saint Malo.* ✆*02 33 19 15 00. www.cositel.fr. 55 rooms.* Modern construction in the town. Rooms are functional; the bistro offers light fare.

🍴 EAT

⊖ **Le Jules Gommes** – *34 r. du Vaudredoux, 50590 Regneville-sur-Mer (10km/6mi SW of Coutances via D 20, rte de Montmartin-sur-Mer and then D 49).* ✆*02 33 45 32 04. www.le-jules-gommes.com.*

Open Wed lunch to Sun dinner. Reservation required at weekends. This establishment, which shares its name with a late 19C three-masted schooner, positively exudes charm. Handsome rustic interior featuring exposed stone, a fireplace and watercolours. Both seafood and inland cuisine, crêpes, and a pub featuring a healthy choice of ales and whiskies.

La Verte Campagne – *Le Hameau Chevalier, 50660 Trelly (13km/8mi S of Coutances via D 7, D 49, then D 539 and a minor road).* 02 33 47 65 33. *www.laverte campagne.com.* This 18C farm, covered with Virginia creeper in summer, has retained its authentic charm: wide ceiling beams, stone walls and old fireplaces. This renowned restaurant serves dishes prepared with care. **5 rooms** () available.

Le Tourne-Bride – *85 r. d'Argouges, 50200 Gratot.* 02 33 45 11 00. *www. letournebridegratot.com. Closed Sun eve and Mon.* The proprietors of this former post-coach relay, Martine and Denis Poisson, offer a warm and attentive welcome. In the two rustic-style dining rooms, the menu focuses on traditional Norman cuisine, with produce straight from the sea and the local fields.

SHOPPING

Market – *pl. du Gén. de Gaulle, 50560 Blainville-sur-Mer.* An extremely animated and colourful market. Country produce of every kind can be found here, including, *naturellement*, the local cheese: le Coutances.

L'epicerie Gosselin – *27 rue de Verrüe.* 02 33 54 40 06. *www.maison-gosselin.fr. Closed Sun pm–Mon.* This well known traditional family grocery store established in 1889 offers traditional quality and service. Run by the founder's great-grandaughter Françoise there is locally roasted coffee, rare spices and forgotten liqueurs amongst the cheeses, charcuterie and vegetables.

LEISURE

Several beaches are found on this part of the west coast, within 12–15km/7.5–9mi of Coutances. From north to south:
Anneville-sur-Mer, a little beach with fine sand, set in the dunes;
Gouville-sur-Mer, a beach 6km/4mi long with several acres of oyster beds (*for a guided tour of the oyster beds,* 02 33 47 84 33);
Blainville-sur-Mer, another beach with a reputation for oysters, also offers fishing and a wide sand beach much appreciated by families;
Agon-Coutainville is the furthest south, and you will find here a golf course, a casino and all sorts of sports and nautical activities.

Lessay★

Lessay grew up round a Benedictine abbey founded in 1056 by a Norman lord. The first monks came from Le Bec-Hellouin. The town is particularly lively in September during the Holy Cross Fair, which originated in the 13C. Attended by about 400 000 people, it is one of the oldest and most important in France.

ABBEY CHURCH★★
Av. Paul Jeanson.
Daily 9am–6pm, except during services. No charge. Guided tours Jul–Aug Wed 3pm (check exact details at tourist office).

▶ **Population:** 2 246.
Michelin Map: 303: C-4.
Info: 11 place Saint-Cloud. 02 33 45 14 34. www.tourisme-cocm.fr.
Location: Lessay lies between Coutances, 21km/13mi to the S on D 2, and Valognes, 36km/ 22.4mi N on D 900.
Don't Miss: The impressive view of the abbey nave.
Timing: Allow an hour or so to explore the abbey.
Kids: There are several nature trails; ask at the tourist office.

The magnificent Romanesque abbey church, damaged during the war, was reconstructed between 1945 and 1957, using original building materials wherever possible; the result is one of the most perfect examples of Romanesque architecture in Normandy.

Building of the original church began in 1098 with construction of the apse, chancel transept and two bays of the nave, with their vaulting; the remaining bays of the nave were completed several years later.

Exterior

The full beauty of the lines of the apse, abutting on a flat gable, can best be seen from the War Memorial Square. The rather squat square belfry with its Hague schist slates is also worth noting.

Interior

The seven broad bays of the nave and the transepts are roofed with pointed vaulting; there is rib-vaulting in the aisles. The gallery in front of the clerestory windows passes round the entire building in the thickness of the walls.

The chancel terminates in an oven-vaulted apse lit by two rose windows. A 15C chapel with a cobbled floor (right of the chancel) contains the baptistry and the font. The new windows are inspired by Irish manuscripts.

EXCURSIONS

Créances

3 km/2mi southwest.

This commune owes its fame to its marshland and notably to its famous carrots grown in sand (Red Label). The

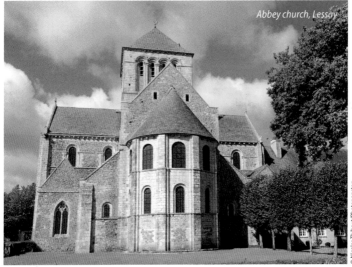
Abbey church, Lessay

© Nicolas Thibaut/Photononstop

The Legendary Geese of Pirou

When the Norse invaders failed to take the Pirou fortress they decided to lay siege to it. After several days of waiting they realised that there was no longer any sign of activity within the castle but, being suspicious, they decided to delay a little longer before making the final assault. Imagine their surprise when they found that the only remaining occupant was a bedridden old man, who informed them that the lord, his wife and other occupants of the castle had transformed themselves into geese, to escape from the hands of their attackers. Indeed, the Norsemen recollected having seen a skein of wild geese flying over the castle walls the previous evening.

According to Norse traditions, the human form could only be reassumed once certain magic words had been recited backwards. The geese came back to look for their book of magic spells but, alas, the Norsemen had set fire to the castle. Legend has it that the geese return every year in the hope of finding their book of spells, which explains why there are so many skeins of geese in the vicinity of the castle.

mielles, sandy areas close to the sea, provide perfect conditions for growing this sweet fleshed carrot, which has such a tender skin that it does not need to be peeled. The sand provides excellent drainage, with nearby seaweed acting as fertiliser. The beach, a huge stretch of sand, bordered with gorse lined dunes, is much loved by kite fliers, sand buggy enthusiasts, windsurfers and shore fishermen.

Château fort de Pirou★

8km/5mi SW of Lessay.
🕐*Daily: Apr–Sept 10am–noon, 2–6.30pm; mid-end Oct 10am–noon, 2–5pm; Christmas and New Year holidays 10am–noon, 2–5pm.* 🎫€7 (child 7–17, €4). 🕿02 33 46 34 71. www.chateau-pirou.org.

The 12C fortress, which once stood on the coast beside an anchorage, since silted up, is one of the oldest Norman castles and served as an outpost for the defence of Coutances under the lords of Pirou who owned it from the 11C to the 14C. These lords were related to the House of Hauteville, of which several members contributed to the formation of the Norman kingdom of Sicily.

The castle passed to other noble families until the late 18C, when it was used as a hideout for smugglers dealing in tobacco from Jersey, before finally becoming a farm in the 19thC.

Three fortified gatehouses – there were originally five – lead to the old sheepfold, the outer bailey and then to the castle itself, a massive structure encircled by a moat, whose towers are constructed directly on the top of the ramparts, with no overhang.

The courtyard is bordered to the left with outhouses. As you progress you will see firstly the bakers (with a monumental chimney, and a huge oven), the press room, the chapel and the Plés room, where justice was dispensed. Here a **tapestry** is displayed, similar in style to the Bayeux Tapestry, recounting the conquest of southern Italy and Sicily by the Cotentin Normans. The original tapestry can be seen only in July and August; otherwise a copy is on display. After the last room a staircase leads to the ramparts.

There is a lovely view of the surrounding countryside from the top of the castle's square tower, which dominates the entrance.

Pirou-Plage

2km/1.25mi SW of Pirou by the D 650.
This small resort has a 6km/3.75mi expanse of fine sand (swimming supervised in summer) running alongside the promenade and a seawater swimming pool. Fishing, windsurfing and water sports are all available here.

Barneville-Carteret★

This popular seaside resort, the closest port to the Channel Islands, is lively, the dunes windswept, and the long beach is of fine sand.

SIGHTS

The resort was created in 1965 by the coming together of the communes of Barneville and Carteret. It is now based around three relatively distant centres: Barneville-Bourg, Barneville-Plage and Carteret. It is best to have some means of transport to move from one to another.

Carteret★

This is the oldest area, along with Barneville-Bourg. Even in the 1820s, the 19C writer Jules Barbey d'Aurevilly spent family holidays here. Chateaubriand visited in 1842. At the end of the 19C, the fashion for sea bathing dramatically changed this fishing village into a spa resort. Carteret still has a sense of quiet charm, thanks, in the main, to the villas that were built there around the beginning of the 20C. Most of them are built above the port.

Finally, the magnificent **rocky headland ★★** which, to the north, shelters the Gerfleur estuary, and its beach (beware of strong currents offshore), and is hidden in a ravine, makes Carteret one of the most agreeable coastal resorts of the Cotentin peninsula.

Ports – Carteret port remains very active. Today there are twenty or so fishing vessels, which trawl for sole and ray, set pots for lobster and crab, and drag net for whelks and scallops. When they return, the port comes to life and visitors can enjoy this authentic snapshot

- **Population:** 2 227.
- **Michelin Map:** 303: B-3 – Local map, *see PRESQU'ÎLE DU COTENTIN, p384.*
- **Info:** 15 Rue Guillaume le Conquérant. ℘02 33 04 90 58. www.barneville-carteret.fr.
- **Location:** Valognes is 29km/18mi NE, Cherbourg 37km/23mi NNE via D 650 and Caen 120km/74.5mi to the E.
- **Don't Miss:** You may want to tour Carteret on the tourist train, before trying some of the walks giving views over the sea.
- **Timing:** The Saturday morning market is worth your time.
- **Kids:** The tourist train.

of life that adds to the charm of the resort. In addition, Carteret possesses a yacht harbour with 300 moorings and an embarkation point for the Channel Islands.

Beaches – Above and beyond Barneville beach (*p398*), which is family orientated and has a life guard, the resort has two

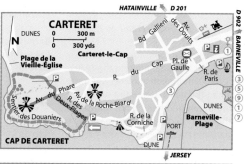

Cap de Carteret

© C. Brett/Michelin

other beaches which are quite different in style. Carteret, facing south, has cabins set in the shade of the cliffs, forming a continuation of the port, and is also guarded. This is not the case for the Vieille-Église beach, which is situated at the foot of the dunes, from the north of the Carteret headland to the Rozel point. Wild, and made rather dangerous by violent currents, this is the favoured spot for windsurfers and speed sailors.

≛≛ Le train touristique du Cotentin: Carteret-Porbail – *28 Avenue de la République, 50270 Barneville-Carteret.* ⏱*Early Jul–Aug, Sun; mid-Jul–mid-Aug Wed. Trains depart Carterets at 3pm, and Barneville at 3.10pm, Saint-Georges 3.15pm, arriving Portbail at 3.35pm.* ⊜*€10 (child 5–12, €5).* ⊟. ℘*02 33 04 70 08. www.train-touristique-du-cotentin. com.* This train, dating from the 1930s, runs 10km/6mi on a former rail track along the beaches and the surrounding dunes and heathland. Known as the coast train during the weekend, it becomes the market train twice a week.

Barneville-Bourg

Just behind the dunes and beaches lie shops and banks. The town's Saturday morning market attracts the surrounding population, who come to buy their provisions from local suppliers. The market is held next to the church, surrounded by granite mansions which are 16C – the oldest in the area.

Église St-Germain

The 11C church of St-Germain of Auxerre, standing high on the town's central hill, was given a fortified tower in the 15C. A late 19C restoration disfigured the chancel, which lost its ceiling, but the arches and capitals of the Romanesque nave have delightful **decoration★**.

On one of these capitals, note the figure portraying the Prophet Daniel confronting a fierce lion. The monument on the way out of Barneville commemorates the cutting-off of the Cotentin Peninsula on 18 June 1944 during the Battle of Normandy.

Barneville-Plage

The seafront boulevard bordered by villas leads to the popular beach.

☇ WALKING TOUR

Cap de Carteret★★

Allow a total of 2h for these two walks.

🚶 Follow the signs La Corniche and le Phare; park near the roundabout by Carteret beach. Take sentier des Douaniers *(left)*, which is very narrow and requires care. The view changes constantly on the way to Carteret's second beach, the extensive Plage de la Vieille-Église.

🚶 Take the road leading down to this beach to return inland. At the crossroads either turn right up to the **lighthouse** (*phare*) for an overall view or turn left (*avenue de la Roche-Biard*) to a viewing table: **views★** of the coast, the Channel Islands and inland.

▷ Alternatively, continue straight ahead at the crossroads to return to your car.

🚗 DRIVING TOUR

52km/32.5mi.

▷ Leave Barneville-Carteret by the road for Coutances. At La Picauderie, turn right onto the D 50 which goes to the harbour at Portbail.

Portbail
The former port was improved to provide a yachting basin and in 2012 was further upgraded to provide 240 moorings. This, plus two beaches of fine sand 2km/1mi away, and a sailing school, have made the area the place of choice among the resorts of the Cotentin. Sea fishing competitions, sand yachting, golf and horseriding complete the range of activities on offer.

Église Notre-Dame – Now disused, the church is a building from the start of the Romanesque era, dominated by a 15C tower. The columns and the chapels decorated with interlacing patterns and animals form one of the main attractions of the interior. To the left of the altar, there is a 16C statue of St Jacques made from multicoloured stone. The church also hosts temporary exhibitions.
As you leave, note the 13 arch bridge to your right which links the town to the port and the beaches. It separates the southern harbour, which is still functioning, from the northern one, which is now polder.
Baptistry – Excavations have revealed the remains of the ancient baptistry. From the original hexagonal structure only the lower parts of the exterior walls remain, with fragments of blue schist, the font, and water drainage systems.

▷ Follow the signs to St-Sauveur-le-Vicomte passing St-Lô-d'Ourville. At the crossroads of the D 15 and the D 903, turn right and then left on the D 147 to Canville-la-Rocque.

Canville-la-Rocque
Église St-Malo – the north chapel of the church has frescoes from the 16C. This is well conserved, illustrating the history of the Pendu-dépendu. This legend relates the tale of a young man who was falsely accused of a crime and hung by the roadside in St-Jacques-de-Compostelle. On their return from pilgrimage, his parents found him still hanging there, but still alive. Justice was served and he was taken down, to be replaced by the guilty party. Note also the 17C fonts, the door panels and the stalls.

▷ Return to the D 903 and turn left.

La Haye-du-Puits
Still dominated by its redoubtable dungeon from the 11C (*no visits allowed*), the town was heavily damaged during the liberation of Normandy in 1944. The town is at the heart of an area that has been long renowned for witchcraft.

▷ Cross the town and continue on the D 903 east towards Carentan. Shortly before Lithaire, turn right (sign "Lac du Mont-Castre") and follow the signage.

Mont Castre★
Dubbed "Hill 122" during the Battle for Normandy, Mont Castre cost the 90th division of the US infantry dear, with a loss of more than 2 000 men.
Aside from these memories, follow the road after the houses, which leads to an area for relaxation and discovery on Mont Castre. A huge lake has been created in a former quarry.
🚶 There are several possibilities for circular tours, one of which is a panoramic walk, which includes a Gallic covered alley, dating from 1500 BCE, the ruins of

a Roman lookout post and the remains of a former 11C church in Lithaire.

▶ Returning on the D 903, go to Lithaire where you take several left-hand turns in the direction of Neufmesnil (D 67).

🚶 A circuit of 11km/6.9mi, marked in yellow. Use the car park of the church at Doville.

Mont de Doville
This mount, which is 129m high, deserves its name, if you believe in its Scandinavian origin – "Bald Escarp-ment". Also known as "Mont Colquin", it is one of the principal hills of the area along with Mont Castre and Mont Eten-clin. From the orientation table there is a panoramic view of the countryside around La Haye-du-Puits and the marsh-land of La Sangsurière (a nature reserve).

▶ Rejoin the D 137, then the D 127 to the north. After Besneville, follow the signs to Fierville-les-Mines.

Fierville-les-Mines
Moulin à vent du Cotentin – This 18C windmill, restored in 1997 with a mecha-nism imported from the Vendée, is the only working example in the Cotentin and continues to produce wheat, buck-wheat and spelt wheat flour.

▶ Return to Barneville-Carteret following the D 50, and the D 650.

ADDRESSES

🛏 STAY

⊜⊜ **Chambre d'hôte La Roque de Gouey** – 16 rue Gilles-Poërier, 50580 Portbail (8km/5mi SE of Barneville). ✆02 33 04 80 27. 🍽🚭. 4 rooms. Simply decorated rooms; pleasant garden area.

⊜⊜ **Chambre d'hôte La Tourelle** – 5 rue du Pic-Maillet. ✆02 33 04 90 22. 🚭. 3 rooms. This 16C house faces the village church: an old-fashioned place offering good breakfasts. Garden, BBQ, garage for bicycles or motorbikes.

⊜⊜⊜ **Chambre d'hôte Le Logis de la Mare** – 14, route de la Mare du Parc, 50270 Surtainville (11 km/6.9mi north of Carteret by the D 650, then the D 66 to the left). ✆02 33 04 35 50. www.logisdelamare duparc.com. 5 rooms. In this extensive lovely 18C house are five very large well-equipped comfortable en-suite rooms. Four on the first floor for 2 or 3 people and one on the ground floor accessible for people of reduced mobility, with an adapted bathroom.

⊜⊜⊜ **Hôtel-Restaurant Les Ormes** – Promenade Barbey-d'Aurevilly. ✆02 33 52 23 50. www.hotel-restaurant-les-ormes.fr. 12 rooms. Restaurant (⊜⊜) open Tue–Sat for lunch and dinner. Opposite the marina. 19C building and beautiful landscaped garden, with a relaxing interior in pastel shades. Rooms are small and cosy.

🍴 EAT

⊜ **Le Berlingot** – route de Bricquebec, (D 902), Hameau Costard, 50270 Sortosville-en-Beaumont (7km/4.3mi NE of Barneville). ✆02 33 53 87 16. Closed Tue and Wed out of season. This restaurant, specialising in crêpes, is popular with locals.

⊜ **Bar Restaurant La Cale Marine** – Port de Carteret --2 prom. Abbé-Lebouteiller. ✆ 02 33 53 82 50. Closed Wed. Called "la Cala Kiki" by the locals, this café-brasserie is appreciated for its terrace ideally situated opposite the fishing quay with its floats and lobster pots, and also for its moules marinière. Nothing sophisticated, but a pleasant stop to have a meal and enjoy the sun in the company of seagulls awaiting the return of the fish from the high seas.

⊜⊜ **Restaurant Pom'Cannelle** – 10 rue du Gén.-Leclerc, 50250 La Haye-du-Puits. ✆02 33 46 45 57. www. restaurantpomcannelle.fr. Closed Mon and Wed eve mid-Sept–mid-Jun). Crêpes and country cooking, fish and seafood, home-made duck foie-gras, duck cutlet with camembert cream, etc., all served in a pleasant environment with matching colour scheme. Revealed beams and wooden panelling complete the attractive décor.

SHOPPING

L'Hermitage – 4 Prom. Abbé Lebouteiller, 50270 Carteret. ✆07 66 03 34 29. Home good store selling the work of 12 artisan craftspeople.

Pointe de la Hague★★

Some of the highest cliffs in Europe, interspersed with small sandy beaches and charming ports, all linked by the Customs Path, which is well known to walkers. This "end of the world" place with its dramatic cliffs is renowned for its spectacular scenery as well as the beauty of its gardens, which have a tropical feel. Although often associated with the nuclear power industry the name of La Hague is particularly associated with the generosity of nature.

- **Michelin Map:** 303: AB1/2.
- **Info:** 1 Place de la Madeleine, 50440 Beaumont-Hague. ✆02 33 52 74 94. www.lahague-tourisme.com/.
- **Location:** La pointe de La Hague is at the extreme north west of the Cotentin peninsula: 20km/12.5mi W of Cherbourg, and 39km/24mi N of Barneville-Carteret.
- **Don't Miss:** the dunes between Carteret and Hatainville.
- **Timing:** Allow a day to do both tours.

🚗 DRIVING TOURS

🚗 WEST COAST★★
45km/28mi. Allow 1h30.

▶ Leave Carteret and drive north on the D 201.

Between Carteret and Hatainville, the road wanders along the highest dunes on the Normandy coast. The dunes separate grassy hollows known as *"mielles"*, where rare and brightly coloured plants grow, such as the blue of sea lime-grass to the bright pink of the pyramidal orchid.

▶ Continue towards Surtainville and Le Rozel.

Between Le Rozel and Flamanville, the road runs above Sciotot cove. You can see the Flamanville headland to the North. Cliffs replace the dunes.

Flamanville
Centre nucléaire de production d'électricité de Flamanville
⊶*For security reasons, the nuclear power station no longer receives visitors.* This nuclear power station, occupying 120ha, stands in part on the granite bedrock, and in part on an artificial platform that juts into the ocean. Two production units have

an installed capacity of 1 300 million kWh each. Each unit produces 9 000 million kWh.
Between Flamanville and Le Rozel the road overlooks a small bay, the **Anse de Sciotot**. Cap de Flamanville and, to the south, the Pointe du Rozel, are visible. The cliffs become lower, giving way to dunes. Between Hatainville and Carteret the road runs along the dunes, the highest on the Norman coast. The grass covered hollows between the dunes are known locally as *mielles*.

▶ Continue along the coast, passing Flamanville.

Diélette
The small port of Diélette, at the foot of the dark cliffs, is the only refuge between Goury and Carteret. As the tide goes out, a beach of fine sand appears between its two breakwaters.

Siouville-Hague
Siouville's long gently sloping beach is the spot for surfing on this coast. The waves are ideal for learning to surf, windsurf, and kite surf safely, as well as for experienced surfers. Competitions for water sports, such as the French championships for skimboard, the Siouville Surf Open, etc. take place here. If

offers walkers the chance to enjoy the sight of acrobatic men and women enjoying their various water sports.

Biville★

The village is set on a plateau overlooking the desolate shoreline of Vauville bay. The Blessed **Thomas Hélye** (1187–1257), a native of Biville, lies in the 13C chancel. On the north side is a 19C bronze group showing Thomas Hélye with some of his followers.

The arrival of the Allies and the liberation of the region is commemorated in a stained-glass window by Barillet (1944) *(first on the right in the nave).*

▷ Walk along the street beside the church; by a fence, make some sharp turns and take the path that passes in front of a chapel dedicated to the Virgin, and continue to the calvary.

Calvaire des Dunes★
45min on foot there and back.

▷ At the end of the street next to the church, go through the gate and take the path which passes by a little chapel and leads up to the cross.

From the foot of the cross there is a panoramic view: in the foreground the desolate landscape of Vauville Bay stretches from the Nez de Jobourg to the cliffs at Flamanville.

▷ Continue towards Vauville.

Beyond the village of Petit Thot the road affords a good **view★** of the moorland around the bay of Vauville.

Vauville

The **Botanical Garden★** (& ⏲*Apr–Sept daily 2–6pm (7pm in Jul–Aug); Oct Sat–Sun 2–5pm;* ⊜€9; ℘*02 33 10 00 00; http://jardin-vauville.fr)* in the grounds of the manor specialises in evergreen plants.

The 12C church and the 17C manor make an attractive picture.

👥 **Réserve naturelle de la mare de Vauville** – *Entry at the side of the Munici-pal Camping de Vauville –footpath with information boards or guided visit organised by le Groupe ornithologique Normand.* ℘*02 33 08 44 56. www.reserves-naturelles.org/mare-de-vauville. Binoculars advised.*

Created in 1976 and managed since 1983 by the Normandy Ornithology Group, this nature reserve, possessing a huge 62ha natural water lake, cut off from the sea by a cordon of dunes and ringed with reeds, allows visitors to discover an exceptionally rich flora and fauna; numerous species of birds (snipe, mallard, reed warbler, etc.), invertebrates and amphibians.

Pierres Pouquelées★
45min round-trip on foot from D 318.

🚶 Leave the car 200m before the first houses of Vauville and walk inland up a path on the right. When it reaches the plateau turn left to reach the Pierres Pouquelées gallery grave. Continue right to a small rise from which there is a **panorama★** of the coast from the Nez de Jobourg to the Flamanville cliffs.

🚗 LA CÔTE NORD ET LA BAIE D'ÉCALGRAIN
55km/35mi. Allow 2h45.

The road rejoins the north coast, near-Gruchy, then follows the road west along the Bay d'Écalgrain before returning to Beaumont-Hague.

Beaumont-Hague

This was the home town of the 17C smuggling family, the Jallot de Beaumont.

▷ Leave Beaumont-Hague going east on the D 245/D 901e, then take the D 237 left and the D 45 until Gréville-Hague (4.5 km/2.8mi).

Gréville-Hague

The small church was a model for the painter **Jean-François Millet** (1814–75) in his works of Norman landscapes. The artist's bust sits on a rock at the crossroads. He was born in the nearby village of Gruchy.

◐ From Gréville-Hague, take the D 237 to the right for Gruchy.

Rocher du Castel-Vendon★
Allow 1h round-trip on foot.
Leave the car at the entrance to the village and continue on foot to the public wash-house by a sunken road that then becomes a footpath:
 Parts of this itinerary are difficult.
 The path follows the right-hand side of the valley. From a rocky promontory, there is a **view** of the coast from Cap Lévy to Pointe Jardeheu. In the foreground stands the granite rock spine called the Rocher du Castel-Vendon.

◐ Leaving Gruchy by car, leave the D 45 for a moment to make a detour via **Quervière bay**. Take the road towards **Éculleville**, then take a left, just before a sign marked "Baie de Quervière". At the end of the road, enjoy the **panorama**.

◐ Return to the D 45.

Omonville-la-Rogue
Manoir du Tourpa
 Early Feb–early Apr and Sept–early Jan daily 2–6pm; early Apr–Jun Mon–Sat 2–6pm, Sun and holidays 10.30am–6pm; Jul–Aug daily 10am–7pm. 1 Jan, 8 Jan–early Feb, 1 May, 25 Dec. No charge.
 02 33 01 85 89. http://letourp.com.
This magnificent manor house (15C and 16C), was bought back by the coastal Conservatoire and has been completely restored to create a major tourist and cultural centre for the north of the Cotentin. The Tourp exhibitions remind visitors of the beauty of its rich and varying landscape, the variety of its fauna and flora, and the history of a region with strong traditions. The huge outhouses of the manor are grouped around a large enclosed courtyard.

Omonville-la-Petite
A pretty little country graveyard surrounds the church: the poet Jacques Prévert (1900–77) lies here beside his ancestors. (to the left of the entrance).

Baie d'Écalgrain, Cap de la Hague

© Christophe Boisvieux/hemis.fr

Maison de Jacques Prévert
 Daily Jul–Aug 11am–7pm; Jun and Sept 11am–6pm; Apr–May and school holidays 2–6pm. €5.
 02 33 52 72 38.
Parking on the square in front of the church (*300m on foot*). Bought in 1971 by Prévert, this house was his last refuge before his death in 1977. Annual temporary exhibitions recreate his, and his painter and writer friends', work. A film portrays the life of the poet.

 Towards l'anse St-Martin – leave from Prévert's house and after 5km/3mi, follows yellow signs (*1h30 on foot, there and back*).
Straight after Prévert's house, take the the road sloping uphill to the left. At the next intersection, turn at the panel marked "Hameau Henry" then take a left straight away after leaving the village, before the wash house. The walk passes by the Mont-Clin cross, which offers a 360° view over St-Martin bay and the surrounding area.
At the hamlet of Guillemins-de-Bas, note the head of a policeman sculpted on the roof of the last house, placed there to scoff at the customs men who were on the hunt for smugglers. Bas-Monterie farm, his hide-out, can be seen just before the hamlet of Fours.
The path opens out onto the gorgeous beach of St-Martin cove where several boats usually lie at anchor. Return on the tarmac road to the left and turn right 300m further on to get back to Omonville-la-Petite church.

Port-Racine★

The climb towards St-Germain-des-Vaux reveals this liliputian harbour, considered to be the smallest active port in France. The name of Port-Racine comes from a ship's captain who had established his base here, under Napoleon I.

From the lower parking place, a road (600m) leads to a pleasant shaded garden.

Jardin en hommage à Jacques Prévert

Easter–Sept daily 2–7pm (Jul–Aug 11am–7pm). €5. 02 33 52 11 00.
Prévert loved this calm and verdant valley, fed by a river. Since 1981, one of his close friends, Gérard Fusberti, has brought these charming places to life with little scarlet bridges and benches, andexamples of his poetry placed here and there.

Leaving for Goury, you pass through heathland, which is littered with numerous rocks. Upon entering Auderville on the right, the descent to Goury offers a good view of La Hague.

Goury★

The small harbour is an important coastguard and lifeboat station.

♁♁ Ludiver – Observatoire – Planétarium de La Hague

1700 r. de la Libération.
Feb–early Jul and Sept–Dec daily except Sat 2–6pm (Planetarium, 3pm); Jul–Aug daily 11am–6.30pm (Planetarium 11.30am, 3pm, 4.30pm). Jan, 1 May, 1 and 11 Nov, 24–25, 31 Dec. €8.50 (child 7–18, €6.50). 02 33 78 13 80. www.ludiver.com. See also Cherbourg-Octeville entry on p408).
Set on the Tonneville and Flottemanville-Hague plateau (180m), this new centre comprises a museum on astronomy and the universe, a planetarium with a seating capacity of 80 and an interior amphitheatre where the images of a 600mm/23.6in telescope are projected live to the public.

Return to Goury and take the D 401.

Baie d'Écalgrain★★

This desolate beach, backed by heathland, is one of the area's wild beauty spots. To the left of Alderney are Guernsey and Sark.

From Dannery, take D 202, right to the Nez de Jobourg.

Nez de Jobourg★★

Off D 901 in Beaumont-Hague.
The long, rocky and barren promontory is now a bird sanctuary. Walk along the **Nez de Voidries**.
From the Auberge des Grottes there is a view north of Écalgrain bay, the lighthouse off Cap de la Hague and the Channel Islands: Alderney, the nearest, Sark, Guernsey and Jersey. Farther south the Nez de Jobourg itself comes into view, separated from the Nez de Voidries by Senneval bay.

Return to Dannery, then rejoin the D 901 and turn right.

ANDRA – Centre de stockage de la Manche

For security reasons visits are suspended.
This storehouse for radioactive waste, opened in 1969, received 527 000m^3 of so-called "parcels", up to 1994. From 1991 to 1997 works were carried out to make the site water tight, to ensure that the waste was contained and the environment protected.

Usine Areva

For security reasons visits are suspended.
This factory by the D 901 processes nuclear fuel. Facing the factory, take the D 403, which descends steeply. Between Herqueville and Beaumont the road is rather rough. There is a great view from the place known as "13 Winds", which looks down on Vauville harbour and the cliffs of Flamanville.

Cherbourg-Octeville★

Cherbourg is a seafaring town with the largest artificial harbour in the world. Here, on the northern shore of the Cotentin peninsula, this city has beautiful monuments and is known for its remarkable breakwater.

A BIT OF HISTORY

Titanic Undertakings – The great military architect **Vauban** (1633–1707) saw the possibilities of Cherbourg as an Atlantic port. An attempt in 1776 to create an offshore barrier by submerging 90 huge timber cones filled with rubble failed when the sea washed it all away. However, over time all of the material that had accumulated on the sea bed began to form an artificial island. A fortified breakwater was eventually completed in 1853.

Today the breakwater remains essential for maintaining a safe haven against often violent storms.

Frogmen at Work – The capture of Cherbourg on 26 and 27 June 1944 marked a decisive stage in the Battle of Normandy, allowing for the landing of heavy equipment on a large scale. When the American 7th Corps took Cherbourg they found the harbour completely devastated and mined. Mines were cleared by Royal Navy frogmen, so

- ▶ **Population:** 80 076.
- **Michelin Map:** 303: C-2.
- **Info:** 14 quai Alexandre III, 50100 Cherbourg-Octeville. ℘02 33 93 52 02. www.cherbourgtourisme.com.
- **Location:** The N 13 ends in Cherbourg, after passing through Caen (123km/77mi SE) and Bayeux (93km/58mi).
- **Don't Miss:** The Cité de la Mer and a boat tour of the port area.
- **Timing:** Count on 3hr to see the Cité de la Mer.
- **Kids:** See the aquarium and the submarine at Cité de la Mer.

that Cherbourg could supply the Allied armies. The undersea pipeline **PLUTO** (**P**ipe **L**ine **U**nder **T**he **O**cean) from the Isle of Wight emerged at Cherbourg, bringing gasoline to the Allies from 12 August 1944.

SIGHTS

Six historic trails wind through the city, with explanatory markers in French and English. They start across from the SNCF train station, across from St-Trinité and from the former Transatlantique station.

Fishing boats, Cherbourg Harbour, Fort de l'Est in the background

© Jean-Daniel Sudres/hemis.fr

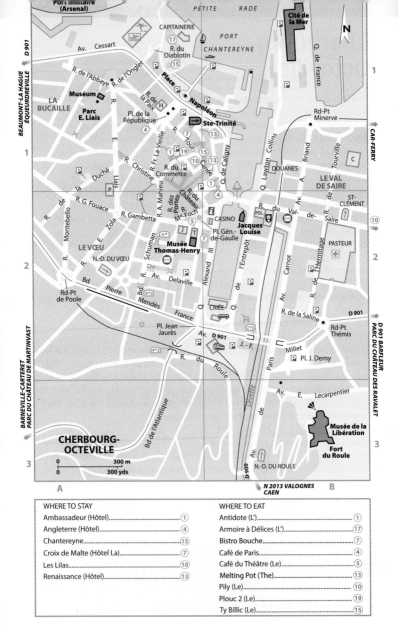

WHERE TO STAY	
Ambassadeur (Hôtel)	①
Angleterre (Hôtel)	④
Chantereyne	⑮
Croix de Malte (Hôtel La)	⑦
Les Lilas	⑩
Renaissance (Hôtel)	⑬

WHERE TO EAT	
Antidote (L')	①
Armoire à Délices (L')	⑰
Bistro Bouche	⑦
Café de Paris	④
Café du Théâtre (Le)	⑤
Melting Pot (The)	⑬
Pily (Le)	⑩
Plouc 2 (Le)	⑲
Ty Billic (Le)	⑮

Muséum Emmanuel-Liais

19 ter, rue Bonhomme.

🕐*Feb–mid-Oct Tue–Fri 10am–
12.30pm, 2–6pm, Sat–Sun 1–6pm;
mid-Oct–Jan Tue–Fri 10am–12.30pm,
2–5pm, Sat–Sun 1–5pm.* ⃝*Public
holidays.* ⃞*€2.* 📞*02 33 53 51 61.*
On the ground floor are exhibits of
shells, mammals and birds. Upstairs
Egypt, Asia, Africa, Oceania and the
Americas are represented.

Place Napoléon

A bronze statue of the emperor
dominates the square. Nearby is the
Église de la Trinité, a Flamboyant
Gothic church.

Cité de la Mer

© B. Almodovar/La Cité de la Mer

Musée d'Art Thomas-Henry

🕐 *Tue–Fri 10am–12.30pm, 2–6pm, Sat–Sun 1–6pm.* ☞€5. 📞*02 33 23 39 33.*

The first gallery is devoted to paintings with Cherbourg and the sea as themes. The 15C–19C paintings are on display in the other galleries, including Fra Angelico's altarpiece panel, *The Conversion of St Augustine* and Filippo Lippi's *Entombment*. The local artist **Jean-François Millet** (1814–75) is well represented.

Cité de la Mer★★

♿🕐*Apr–Jun and Sept 9.30am–6pm; ul–Aug 9.30am–7pm; check website for other dates and times, which are variable.* 🕐*1 Jan, 7 Jan–8 Feb, 11 and 18 Mar, 4 and 18 Nov, and Sun in Dec, 25 Dec.* ☞€19 *(child 5–17,* €14. 📞*02 33 20 26 69. www.citedelamer.com.*

The Art Deco former hall of the transatlantic passenger station has information kiosks, but the core of the museum lies in adjacent wings with basins and tanks that present marine fauna and flora. *Le Redoutable,* the first French nuclear submarine, is here.

Quai de France

Behind the Cité de la Mer the port also regularly handles cruise ships such as the *Queen Mary II* at the Gare Maritime Transatlantique on the Quai de France. Information about the arrivals and departures of these ships can be obtained from the tourist office.

Fort du Roule

A road winds up to the fort on Roule Hill (112m). In June 1944, the Germans entrenched here offered fierce resistance before surrendering. The ramparts offer a good **panorama★**.

Musée de la Libération

av. Étienne-Lecarpentier, Fort du Roule. ♿🕐*Early May–early Dec Tue–Fri 10am–12.30pm, 2–6pm, Sat–Sun 1–6pm.* 🕐*Public holidays.* ☞€4. 📞*02 33 20 14 12.*

The museum in a 19C fortress retraces the dark years of French history from 1940 to 1944 as well as hopeful events such as the D-Day landing, the liberation of Cherbourg and the rebuilding of the port.

EXCURSIONS

Tourlaville

5km/3mi E. From Cherbourg take avenue de l'Amiral-Lemonnier SE. In Tourlaville, at the crossroads before the Hôtel Terminus, turn right onto rue des Alliés. 800m farther on at the junction with D 63 turn right again onto D 32. Park the car and continue on foot.

Château des Ravalet – park★

♿🕐*Daily from 8am (8.30am in winter) until 8pm in summer and 5pm in winter.*

The park of this lovely Renaissance château includes tropical plants, lovely stretches of water and fine beech trees.

Martinvast
10 km/6.25mi south of Cherbourg by the D 900.

Château de Martinvast – park
🕐 *Daily 10am–noon, 1.30–6pm.*
📞 *02 33 87 20 80.*
Although the château is not open to the public, its attractive **park** offers seven signposted trails.

Tollevast
10km/6.25mi south of Cherbourg by the D 900, then left towards Hardinvast.
Église –You need to take your time, and if possible binoculars, to discover this small Romanesque church (12C). At first sight, there is nothing exceptional about it, apart from the harmony that its sober architecture exudes. Its main interest lies in the abundant sculpted décor that is found on the masonry on the exterior, the tops of the columns of the western porch, and the diagonally ribbed chalice forms of the chancel.

👤👤 Ludiver – Observatoire – Planétarium de La Hague
Leave Cherbourg going west on the D 901, in the direction of Équeurdreville-Hainneville. At the roundabout, take the Cap de La Hague direction for 4km/2.5mi. At the intersection, go towards Tonneville and follow the signs.
🕐 *See p404 for details.*
Set on Flottemanville-Hague and Tonneville plateau (180m), the aim of this centre is the discovery of the sky, stars and planets. The site incorporates a museography area dedicated to the universe, a planetarium with 80 places, an inside amphitheatre (images from a 600mm telescope are projected live to the public). The observation site is blessed with ideal conditions, because atmospheric and light pollution is minimal here.

▶ Return towards the coast.

Querqueville
7.5km/4.5mi northeast of Cherbourg via D 901.
Beside the parish church stands the 10C **Chapelle St-Germain**, the oldest religious building in the Cotentin area. From behind the church (*path between the chapel and the church*) there is a view over the Cherbourg roadstead stretching from Cap Lévy to Pointe Jardeheu.

Château de Nacqueville
9.5km/6mi northwest of Cherbourg by the D 901, the D 45, then left to La Rivière.
🕐 *Park only: May–Sept Thu–Fri, Sun and public holidays noon–5pm.* 👝€7.
📞 *02 33 03 21 12.*
http://nacqueville.com.
This beautiful 16C edifice, built as a fortified manor, covered with ivy, makes a romantic sight, standing by a pool in a **park★** of oak trees and flowering shrubs. The park was created by an English landscape designer in 1830 and is resplendent with rhododendrons, azaleas and hydrangeas.
Only the great hall with a beautiful Renaissance fireplace is open to the public.

Landemer
10km/6mi to the northwest of Cherbourg by the D 901 and the D 45.
Le manoir is situated at the entrance to Landemer, next to the road, on the left.
Manoir de Dur-Écu – 🕐 *Jul–Sept Tue–Thu 11am–1pm, 3–7pm.* 👝€5 *(free for 2 children under 18, then €5 for 2 further children).* 📞 *06 10 58 68 41.*
https://durecuf.wordpress.com.
A 16C manor house with bizarre groups of towers, built on 9C foundations. Only the courtyards and the *pigeonnier* can be visited, but there is also a maze in the cornfield next to the manor.
After Landemer, the road goes into the ravin du Hubiland and soon, on the right, you will have a beautiful view of the lighthouse at Cap Levi at the Pointe Jardeheu.

ADDRESSES

🏨 STAY

🛏️🛏️ **Hôtel Angleterre** – *8 Rue Paul Talluau.* 📞*02 33 53 70 06. www. hotelangleterre-fr.com. 23 rooms.* Situated in a quiet part of the town centre, a simple hotel with a white façade. Rooms are a bit small, but perked up with pastel colours. Reasonable prices.

🛏️🛏️ **Hôtel De La Croix De Malte** – *5 rue des Halles.* 📞*02 33 43 19 16. www. hotelcroixmalte.com. 24 rooms.* A stone's throw from the theatre and the casino. The rooms are well soundproofed.

🛏️🛏️ **Chambre d'hôte Les Lilas** – *163 rue du Val de Serre, 50100 Cherbourg-Octeville.* 📞*02 33 43 06 93. www.chambres-hotes-cherbourg.com. 3 rooms.* Located in the centre of Cherbourg, this 19C mansion was used by the German and American armies during WWII, with the remains of a bunker in the lovely garden to prove it! All rooms are on the first floor, two with views over the garden. If you look carefully you will find souvenirs of the owner's extensive travels in Asia.

🛏️🛏️ **Hôtel Ambassadeur** – *22 quai de Caligny, 50100 Cherbourg.* 📞*02 33 43 10 00. www.ambassadeurhotel.com. 40 rooms.* This hotel overlooks the port, providing a view of constant activity. But the rooms are well soundproofed. Reasonable prices.

🛏️🛏️🛏️ **Hôtel Renaissance** – *4 rue de l'Église.* 📞*02 33 43 23 90. www.hotel-renaissance-cherbourg.com. 12 rooms.* This hotel has bright, soundproofed rooms and modern bathrooms.

🍽️ EAT

🍴🍴 **L'Antidote** – *41 rue au Blé.* 📞*02 33 78 01 28. www.restaurant-cherbourg.fr. Reservations advised.* A pleasant terrace and a wood-panelled dining room. The specialities include duck, lobster and salmon.

🍴🍴 **Café de Paris** – *40 quai Caligny.* 📞*02 33 43 12 36. www.restaurant cafedeparis.com. Closed Mon lunch and Sun.* This bistro-style restaurant is bright and warm. Enjoy a selection of seafood while admiring the view of the harbour in one of the two dining rooms.

🍴🍴 **The Meltin Pot** – *17 rue du Port.* 📞*02 33 01 24 09. https:// lemeltingpotcherbourg.wordpress.com. Closed Sun.* Very much an idiosyncratic mix of dishes from slow-cooked stews, to goulash, cassoulet and wok-fried dishes.

🍴🍴🍴 **Bistro Bouche** – *25 rue Tour-Carrée.* 📞*02 33 04 25 04. www. bistro-bouche.fr.* An attractive retro façade in pale blue, and a handsome wood-panelled décor, like that of a ship, inside. Traditional cuisine and Norman specialities. Everything made to order, and totally Fait Maison.

🍴🍴🍴 **Le Pily** – *39 Grande Rue.* 📞*02 33 10 19 29. www.restaurant-le-pily.com. Closed late June–Aug all day Sun and Mon lunch; rest of year Sun–Mon.* Warm welcome in a soothingly decorated dining room, with a cosy lounge area. Delicious contemporary cuisine.

LEISURE

Station Voile Nautisme et Tourisme de Cherbourg Hague – *rue du Diablotin, quartier Chantereyne.* 📞*02 33 78 19 29.* This club offers many activities: canoeing, kayaking, sailing, diving, beach sports, mountain biking, paragliding, hang-gliding, etc. Lessons and equipment rentals are available.

ON THE TOWN

Cherbourg is a sailors' town and under its peaceful daytime atmosphere runs a fun-loving, wild streak that surfaces after midnight.

Café du Théâtre– *8 place du Gén.-de-Gaulle.* 📞*02 33 42 15 45. Closed Sun.* A great place to meet after a movie or show, or just to hang out. A glass-enclosed terrace lets you enjoy the view over the public square in all weathers. A lounge with red plush seats recalls the days when this was a theatre.

Casino de Cherbourg– *18 quai Alexandre III.* 📞*02 33 43 00 56. www.casinocherbourg. com.* Built in 1827, this casino is the oldest in France. Gamblers can try their luck, but others might prefer the leather armchairs of the elegant bar, or the 1950s style pub "Fifty's Diner". The disco plays golden oldies.

Barfleur★

This charming fishing port, with its granite houses and quays, is one of the most beautiful villages of France. Tradition has it that the boat that carried William, Duke of Normandy, to England was built here. A bronze plaque placed in 1966 at the foot of the jetty marks his departure in 1066.

SIGHTS

Église St-Nicholas

Set in a cemetery on a rocky promontory, this squat 17C church has the appearance of a fort. In the south transept is a remarkable 16C *Pietà* while in the north transept above the font is a stained-glass window depicting Ste-Marie-Madeleine Postel (1756–1846).

Maison de Julie Postel

Julie Postel was born in Barfleur in 1756. As Sister Marie-Madeleine she founded the Sisters of the Christian Schools of Mercy (La Congrégation des Sœurs de la Miséricorde), now called Sisters of Ste-Marie-Madeleine Postel.

🚗 DRIVING TOURS

🚗 POINTE DE BARFLEUR
4km/2.5mi N by D 116 and D 10.

Reach the Pointe by the GR 223 Coastal Footpath or by the D 116 to Gatteville and right onto the D 10.

Gatteville-le-Phare
The church, rebuilt in the 18C, still has its original 12C belfry. The Mariners' Chapel (Chapelle des Marins), in the square, is built over a Merovingian necropolis.

Phare
🕐*May–Aug 10am–noon, 2–7pm; Apr and Sept 10am–noon, 2–6pm; Mar and Oct 10am–noon, 2–5pm; Feb and Nov–Dec 10am–noon, 2–4pm.* 🕐*Jan, 1 May, 25 Dec, and if winds are too high.* 🎫€3. 📞*02 33 23 17 97. www.phare-de-gatteville.fr.*

- ▶ **Population:** 577.
- 🚗 **Michelin Map:** 303: E-1.
- ℹ **Info:** 2 rond-point Guillaume-le-Conquerant. 📞02 33 54 02 48. www.encotentin.fr.
- ◐ **Location:** Barfleur is reached from Cherbourg (28km/18mi to the W) via D 901.
- ☝ **Don't Miss:** The view from the top of the Gatteville lighthouse, and the arrival of the day's catch from fishing boats in the port.
- 🕐 **Timing:** The area requires at least a half day of your time.

The lighthouse, on the northeastern extremity of the Cotentin Peninsula, is one of the tallest in France (71m). The light, with a range of 56km/35mi, and the radio beacon, installed in a small 18C tower, guide ships into Le Havre.

From the top (*365 steps*) there is a **panorama**★★ stretching over the east coast of the Cotentin peninsula, St-Marcouf islands, Veys bay and, in clear weather, the cliffs at Grandcamp. The shallow waters and swift currents have caused many shipwrecks, including the *White Ship* in 1120, with Henry's heir, William Atheling, and 300 members of the Anglo-Norman nobility on board.

Montfarville
2km/1mi S of Barfleur by D 155.
This 18C granite church has a chapel and belfry dating from the 13C and a highly colourful **interior**★. The paintings on the vaulting are by a local artist, Guillaume Fouace.

🚗 THE NORTH COAST – BARFLEUR TO CHERBOURG★★
38km/23.6mi. Allow 1h30.

◐ Leave Barfleur by the D 901.

Phare de Gatteville

© José Antonio Moreno/age fotostock

Tocqueville
This was the family seat of **Alexis de Tocqueville** (1805–59) the author of *Democracy in the United States* and *The Ancien Régime and the Revolution*.

▷ Turn right (north) on D 226.

Réthoville
Moulin de Marie Ravenel – 🚫🕐*Apr–Sept Wed, Sat–Sun 2–5.30pm (Jul–Aug daily 2–6.30pm).* 🔦*Guided tours at 2.30pm, 3.30pm, 4.30 (and 5.30pm in Jul–Aug).* 🕐*Oct–Mar, 1 May.* 🎟€4 *(child 7–17, €1.50).* 📞*02 33 54 56 18. http://moulinmarieravenel.fr.* This 18C mill was the residence of the miller/poetess Marie Ravenel in the 19C

▷ Take the D 514 to rejoin the D 901 west in the direction of St-Pierre-Église.

St-Pierre-Église
The fortified 17C church has a 12C Romanesque doorway. The 18C **château** was the family home of the Abbé de St-Pierre (1658–1743), the author of a plan for peace entitled *Projet de Paix Perpétuelle*.

▷ Leave St-Pierre-Église by the D 210 in the direction of Fermanville.

Fermanville
A flower bedecked village, with granite houses which are typical of the region. **Vallée des Moulins** – 🔦Leave from the tourist office car park; 8km/5mi – waymarked in yellow.

▷ Leave Fermanville by the small road signposted "Phare du cap Lévi". 600m after leaving the hamlet of La Bourdette, a surfaced path on the right leads to the Cap Lévi Semaphore.

Cap Lévi
Encircling a harbour near to Fermanville, Cap Lévi has three buildings which are dedicated to coastal watch, unique in Europe.

Sémaphore du cap Lévi – Destined to give assistance to ships in distress, by bringing them help, this semaphore was demilitarised in 1999.

▷ Rejoin the road to the Lighthouse.

Phare – reconstructed in granite in 1946, it has a height of 28m.

▷ Return to Fermanville then take a turn to the right which is the fort road that runs along the small port.

Port-Lévi – Small anchorage port.

▷ Drive in the direction of Fermanville and follow the signs for "Port-Lévi".

Fort du cap Lévi – Constructed in the 19C to defend this coastline, which faces England, the fort today houses a chambre d'hôte.

▷ Just after the harbour in Brick, turn left, in front of the Maison

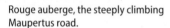

Rouge auberge, the steeply climbing Maupertus road.

Belvédère★
There is a magnificent view of the coast and Cherbourg in the distance.

▶ Return to the D 116; continue southwest along the coast; in Bretteville take the D 320 left towards Le Theil, crossing the D 901 en route.

Allée Couverte (Gallery Grave)
This collective burial chamber consists of a double row of upright stones supporting flat slabs laid horizontally.

▶ Return to Bretteville; take D 116 west.

On approaching Cherbourg you can see the roadstead (offshore anchorage area) and Pelée Island, which serves as an anchor for the mole. With the great breakwater, this divides the harbour from the sea. To the left is Roule Fort.

St-Vaast-la-Hougue

Among the good reasons to visit this popular seaside resort with a marina and a mild climate are the delicious *huîtres* **(oysters).**

SIGHTS
Phare
The lighthouse is situated at the end of the large granite jetty. The Chapelle des Marins was a landmark for sailors.

Fort
Follow the direction of La Hougue. The road along the Grande Plage is bordered by tamarisks and at the end of the beach the keep of the fort stands proud.

EXCURSION
Île de Tatihou★
Crossing (10min) from Saint-Vaast every 30min (high tide) and every hour (low tide). An amphibious vehicle takes visitors over to Tatihou. Book in advance at the Quayside Office, Quai Vauban.
€8 return fare (€10.50 ticket includes museum and Tour Vauban).
02 33 54 33 33.
http://manche.fr/tatihou.
The **Musée maritime départemental** has sections on naval architecture and objects from the site of the Battle of La Hougue (1692).

▶ **Population:** 1 779.
◉ **Michelin Map:** 303: E-2.
🈯 **Info:** 1 Place du Général de Gaulle, 50550 Saint-Vaast-la-Hougue. *02 33 71 99 71. www.encotentin.fr.*
◐ **Location:** St-Vaast is 12km/7.5mi S of Barfleur; 18km/11mi NE of Valognes.
◉ **Don't Miss:** Vauban's Tower.

🚗 DRIVING TOUR

🚗 LE VAL DE SAIRE
40km/25mi. Allow 2h30.
The circuit offers beautiful views of the Cotentin coast and countryside.

▶ Leave St-Vaast heading west on the D1.

Quettehou
The 13C granite **church** is flanked by a tall 15C belfry. From the cemetery there is a view of Morsalines bay, the Hougue Fort and the Pointe de Saire.

▶ Leave Quettehou by the D 902 north and turn left onto the D 26. Turn right on the D 25 to Valcanville. There take the D 125, southeast. At the crossroads with the D 238, turn left to

La Pernelle, then at 300m follow the signs "Église, panorama".

La Pernelle

Beyond the rebuilt church of **La Pernelle** is a former German blockhouse, once an observatory, which commands a **panorama★★** extending from the Gatteville lighthouse (north) to the Grandcamp cliffs (south) by way of the Pointe de Saire, Tatihou island, Hougue Fort and the St-Marcouf islands.

⊙ Cross the D 902 then take the D 328 as far as Jonville.

Pointe de Saire

Beyond Jonville, by the sea, is an old blockhouse that offers a good **view★** of the attractive rock-strewn beaches of Pointe de Saire and of Tatihou Island with St-Vaast in the background.

⊙ Return to Réville and continue north on D 1.

Beyond Réville the road passes **La Crasvillerie**, a delightful 16C manor house. As you approach Barfleur, the countryside gradually changes, becoming more like the neighbouring region of Brittany, with houses made of granite hewn from local rocks, rocky bays and gnarled trees bent by the wind. Gatteville lighthouse stands to the north.

ADDRESSES

🛏 STAY

⊜ Chambre d'hôte Marie Marie – *10 route du Martinet, 50760 Réville (3.5km/2.2mi N of St-Vaast). ℘02 33 54 48 42. 3 rooms.* 🍽. A poplar-lined alley leads to this fortified 15C farm. The guest rooms are nice and bright.

⊜⊜ Hôtel les Fuchsias – *20 Rue Maréchal Foch. ℘02 33 54 40 41. www.hotel-fuchsias.com. 35 rooms. Restaurant⊜⊜*. When the fuchsias are in bloom they cover the walls of this 100-year-old hotel set back from the harbour. Some rooms overlook the garden. Meals in the dining room, on the veranda or the terrace.

🍽 EAT

⊜⊜ Le Chasse Marée – *8 place du Gén. de Gaulle. ℘02 33 23 14 08. www. chassemaree.net. Closed Tue–Wed except in Jul–Aug.* The dishes are mostly locally caught seafood. On the walls, the pennants of prestigious yacht clubs and old photos form an appropriate setting for the refined cuisine.

Valognes★

Valognes is an important road junction at the heart of the Cotentin peninsula and is the market town for the surrounding agricultural area. The aristocratic town described by Barbey d'Aurevilly was partially destroyed in June 1944; it has been rebuilt in the modern style and expanded. Several traces of the past have survived including Gallo-Roman ruins, 11C–18C churches, and private mansions built in the 18C when local high society made Valognes the Versailles of Normandy.

▸ **Population:** 6 779.
◔ **Michelin Map:** 303: D-2.
🛈 **Info:** 25 Rue de l'Église. ℘02 33 40 11 55. www.ot-cotentin-bocage-valognais.fr.
⊙ **Location:** Valonges is at a major crossroads: Cherbourg is 20km/12.5mi NW, Barnville-Carteret 29km/18mi SW, St-Sauveur-le-Vicomte is 16km/10mi SW.
◔ **Timing:** Allow a good half day, and maybe visit the cider museum.

SIGHTS

Hôtel de Beaumont★

9 rue Barbey-d'Aurevilly.

⏤⏤Guided tours (1hr). ◷*Jul–mid-Sept Mon–Sat 10.30am–noon, 2.30–6.30pm, Sun 2.30–6.30pm.* ⊜*€8 (child 7–12, €4); gardens only €4.* ✆*02 33 40 12 30. www.hoteldebeaumont.fr.*

This noble 18C residence, miraculously spared by the bombings, has a splendid front in dressed stone. Inside, the sweeping flight of steps with a double winding stairwell gives access to the upper floor by a stone arch ending in mid-air. The terraces are laid out as formal gardens.

Hôtel de Grandval-Caligny

32 rue des Religieuses.

◷*Not open to the public.*

The 19C novelist **Jules Barbey d'Aurevilly** once lived in this handsome 17C–18C mansion. Note the staircase with its wrought-iron banister, the Empire-style ceramic stove in the dining room, and the alcoved bedrooms.

Musée Régional du Cidre

rue du petit-Versailles.

◷*Apr–Jun and Sept Wed–Sun 2–6.15pm; Jul–Aug Mon–Sat 11am–6.15pm, Sun 2–6.15pm.* ⊜*€4.50.* ✆*02 33 40 22 73.*

The Cider Museum is in the **Maison du Grand Quartier**, one of a group that housed a 15C–18C linen factory.

Musée de l'Eau-de-Vie et des Vieux Métiers

◷*Closed for restoration work.* ✆*02 33 40 26 25.*

Housed in the **Hôtel de Thieuville** (16C–19C), this museum displays equipment for distillation, stonemasonry, iron and copper work from the 11C to the 20C.

EXCURSIONS

Bricquebec

From Valognes, go west on the D 902 about 13km/8mi.

The town is known for its old **castle** and its Trappist monastery. The inner courtyard of the castle is still enclosed by a fortified wall. The 14C **keep** is a handsome polygonal tower (22m high). The sentry walk between the keep and the clock tower offers a view of the town. The **Tour de l'Horloge** (Clock Tower) houses a small regional museum where there is a collection of old furniture, some medals and mineral samples. There is also a restored 13C crypt.

▶ From Bricquebec take D 121 north; just before the calvary turn left onto a path.

Abbaye Notre-Dame-de-Grâce

☺*The abbey is not open for tours, but it is possible to attend services.*

The Trappist monastery, which is occupied by a community of Cistercian monks, was founded in 1824 by Abbot Dom Augustin Onfroy, a local priest.

♣♟ Parc animalier St-Martin

Montaigu-la-Brisette, at 12km/7.5mi to the NE of Valognes by the D 902.

◷*Daily Apr–Oct 9am–6pm; Nov–Mar 10am–4pm.* ◷*When it snows and 25 Dec. May close early in winter due to bad weather.* ⊜*€16 (child 3–9, €12).* ✆*02 33 40 40 98.*

www.espace-zoologique.com.

The exhibits in this park, which is located in the heart of the forest, come from all five continents: from Bactrian camels (Asia), to the amusing maras, a type of hare from Patagonia; watusi cattle from Africa, to llamas, not forgetting the baboon colony which delouse themselves all day, nor the multicoloured macaws and arrogant ostriches.

ADDRESSES

🛏 STAY

🛏 **Chambre d'hôte Le Haut Pitois** – *50700 Lieusaint (2km/1mi S of Valognes via D 2, small road to left on leaving the village).* ✆*02 33 40 19 92. 4 rooms.* ⊐. A superb woodland road leads to this former farm in a peaceful setting. The rooms, located upstairs in an outbuilding (2 can sleep 4 or 5 people) are sparse but functional with complete bathrooms.

⊜⊜ **Grand Hôtel du Louvre** – 28 r. des Réligieuses. ☎02 33 40 00 07. www. grandhoteldulouvre.com. 20 rooms. ▣ Restaurant⊜⊜. Near the centre of town, this hotel has character: Barbey d'Aurevilly, a 19C Gothic novelist, stayed in room No. 4. Rooms, reached by a spiral staircase, have been renovated but retain their 19C character, as does the dining room.

ⴲ/EAT

⊜⊜ **L'Agriculture** – 18 rue Léopold-Delisle. ☎02 33 95 02 02. www.hotel-agriculture.com. Closed Sun evening. In the centre of Valognes, this vine-covered building sits on a quiet little square. The interior is charming and rustic. Delicious house specialities using the best Normandy produce selected according to season. The 30 guest **rooms** (⊜⊜) are modern and comfortable.

St-Sauveur-le-Vicomte

St-Sauveur-le-Vicomte, standing on the banks of the Douve in the heart of Cotentin, is closely associated with the 19C writer **Jules Barbey d'Aurevilly** and Ste-Marie-Madeleine Postel, who founded the Sisters of the Christian Schools of Mercy in the 19C.

SIGHTS
Château

⊸•Guided tour (1hr) Jul–Aug Sat at 5pm. Gardens open all year. ⊜€4. ☎02 33 21 50 44.
The bust at the entrance is that of Jules Barbey d'Aurevilly, by Rodin. This 12C castle was the ancestral home of two Norman families, the Néels and the Harcourts.

▶ **Population:** 1 762
ⴵ **Michelin Map:** 303: C-3.
ⴲ **Info:** Le Vieux Château. ☎02 33 21 50 44. www.ville-saint-sauveur-le-vicomte.fr.
⏵ **Location:** St-Sauveur-le-Vicomte is 15km/9.6mi S of Valognes on D 2 and 19km/12mi E of Barneville-Carteret via D 650 and D 15.
ⴲ **Don't Miss:** The keep of the Vieux Château.
🕑 **Timing:** You will need 3hr to see the château and the abbey.

The castle has suffered many a siege, notably by the English in 1356 and the French in 1375. Louis XIV had the castle converted into a hospice in 1691.

Château de St-Sauveur-le-Vicomte

© Franck Guiziou/hemis.fr

Église

Only the transept dates from the 13C. The rest of the church was rebuilt in the 15C. At the entrance to the chancel are a 16C Ecce Homo (left) and a 15C statue of St James of Compostela (right).

Musée Barbey-d'Aurevilly

64 rue Bottin-Desylles.

⏱ *Apr–May and Oct Tue–Thu and Sun 2–6pm; Jun–Sept Tue–Thu and Sun 12.30–7pm.* ⏱ *1 Jan, 1 Nov, 24–25 and 31 Dec.* ✆ €5. ✆ 02 33 41 65 18.

The museum contains mementoes of Jules Barbey d'Aurevilly (1809–89), a critic and writer of popular fantastical novels who was born in the town and is buried in the castle cemetery.

Abbaye

♿⏱ *Daily 10am–noon, 2–6pm (9.30am in Jul–Aug).* ✆ *No charge.* ✆ 02 33 21 50 44.

The abbey was founded in the 10C by Néel de Néhon, Vicomte de St-Sauveur. The Hundred Years' War ruined the abbey and forced the monks into exile. At the Revolution the building was further dismantled. In 1832 it was bought by Mother Marie-Madeleine Postel to serve as the mother house for the order, which she had founded in Cherbourg in 1807. Although damaged in World War II, the abbey was repaired between 1945–50.

Abbatiale – The plain round-headed windows in the south aisle of the abbey church date from the Romanesque period. The tomb of Ste-Marie-Madeleine Postel lies in the north transept.

Park – The well-tended park with its fine trees and colourful flower beds is a pleasant place for a stroll.

EXCURSION

Château de Crosville-sur-Douve

Proceed towards Valognes for 5km/3mi and in Rauville-la-Place take D 15 towards Pont-l'Abbé, then follow the signposts.

⏱ *Easter–mid-Nov daily 2–6pm.* ✆ €6 *(includes the garden).* ✆ 02 33 41 67 25. *www.chateaucrosville.org.*

The oldest part of this imposing 17C château is the round, machicolated tower with its staircase turret.

Ste-Mère-Église

This town entered modern history brutally on the night of 5–6 June 1944 when troops from the American 82nd Airborne Division landed to assist the 101st Division in clearing the exits from Utah Beach. Ste-Mère-Église was liberated on 6 June, but fighting continued until tanks advanced into the town from Utah Beach the following day.

SIGHTS

Église

The solid 11C–13C church was damaged particularly during the dislodging of German snipers from the belfry. A dummy at the end of a parachute hangs from the steeple as a reminder

- ▶ **Population:** 2 531.
- **Michelin Map:** 303:E-3.
- **Info:** 6 rue Eisenhower. ✆ 02 33 21 00 33. www. ot-baieducotentin.fr.
- **Location:** The N 13 between Bayeux (56km/ 35mi E) and Valognes (17km/10mi NW) passes by Ste-Mère-Église.
- **Don't Miss:** Look up to the church steeple at the paratrooper dangling there.
- **Timing:** Take 2h to see the village and the Airborne Museum.
- **Kids:** The Cotentin Farm Museum.

of Private John Steele's ordeal: dropped over the area during the night of 6 June 1944, he was caught dangling from the steeple by his parachute. He played dead for two hours, a few feet from a bell that never stopped ringing. The Germans eventually unhooked him.

Borne O de la Voie de la Liberté
In front of the town hall.
This is the first of the 12 000 symbolic milestones *(bornes)* along the Road of Liberty followed by General Patton's 20th Corps of the American Third Army to Metz and Bastogne.

Musée Airborne★
14 rue Eisenhower.
&.⚡︎©*Daily: Apr and Sept 9.30am–6.30pm; May–Aug 9am–7pm; Oct–Mar 10am–6pm.* ⊛€9.90 *(child 6–16, €6).* ©*Dec–Jan except during Christmas holidays.* ☎02 33 41 41 35. www.musee-airborne.com.
A parachute-shaped building in a large park at the entrance to the town houses the Airborne Museum, which contains mementos of the fighting on D-Day.

Ferme-Musée du Cotentin
1 rue de Beauvais.
&.©*Daily Jul–Aug 11am–7pm; Apr–Jun, Sept Sun–Fri 2–6pm.* ©*1 May.* ⊛€5. ☎02 33 95 40 20.
Housed in the Beauvais farm (16C), this Cotentin farm museum recreates rural life of the early years of the 20C.

🚗 DRIVING TOUR

🚗 IN THE FOOTSTEPS OF THE AMERICAN LANDINGS
43km/27mi. Allow 2h15.

▷ From Ste-Marie take D 974.

Écausseville
👥 **Hangar à dirigeables** – *Cross the town and follow the red signs "Hangar"* &.©*Mar Sat–Sun 2–6pm; Apr–May and Sept–Oct daily except Fri 2–6pm; Jun daily 2–6pm; Jul–Aug daily 10am–6pm (also open for longer hours during*

school holidays). ⊛€6 *(child 8–14, €2).* ☎02 33 54 01 02. www.aerobase.fr.
This huge hangar in the middle of nowhere offers rare evidence of infrastructures used for air combat during the 1914–18 war. Built in the last year of the war, it formed part of the air station of Montebourg-Écausseville, whose mission was to spot German submarines and mines in order to provide safe passage for maritime convoys. Its 150m length and 30m width houses airships. After the abandonment by the Navy of these dirigibles in 1936, it served as a storage centre for tanks and cannons, and spare parts for ships and planes, etc.

▷ Continue north to Montebourg, then follow the D42 to Quinéville.

Quinéville
This is a family seaside resort. Good view of St-Vaast roadstead from the square near the church.

World War II Museum (Mémorial de la Liberté retrouvée)
18 avenue des Plages, Quinéville.
&.©*Apr–Sept daily 10am–7pm.* ⊛€7. ☎02 33 95 95 95.
https://worldwar2-museum.com.
This museum recreates daily life during the dark days of the Occupation. There is a village street, a blockhouse, and miscellaneous documentary material from the period.

▷ Follow the coastal route south D 421 to Gougins.

Gaps in the cordons of dunes provide views that change, along the coast, from the cliffs of Grandcamp to the fort of La Hougue and Saire point. Single storey granite houses with slate roofs, are a forerunner of the Sairea valley.

▷ At Gougins, turn right onto the D 69 towards Crisbecq.

St-Marcouf
Batterie de Crisbecq – ©*Daily Apr–Nov 10am–6pm (Jul–Aug 10am–7pm).* ⊛€10 *(child 6–14, €6).* ☎06 68 41 09 04.

www.batterie-marcouf.com. The St-Marcouf Battery had vital strategic interest, because its 210mm guns could sweep the Utah beaches. It was therefore the target of terrible attacks aimed at neutralising and removing the position. Crisbecq was struck by hundreds of tonnes of bombs, which reduced the major arms to silence, but did not destroy the pillboxes. On 8 June 1944, during a fierce attack by American troops, Lieutenant Ohmsen requested that the Azeville battery fire above him to ease the vice he was caught in. The garrison held until the morning of 12 June. Resistance was strong and only 78 out of more than 350 men survived the battle, before reaching Cherbourg. The shattered pillbox on the left is impressive, but it was the Americans who shelled it, after the surrender.

▷ Continue 1.6 km1mi on the D 69, then turn left into the D 269. At 1km/0.6mi, follow the directions for Azeville.

Azeville

Batterie – ⏰*Daily Jun–Aug 10am–7pm; Apr–May 10am–6pm; Sept–early Nov 1–6pm.* ⏰*1 May.* ✏€5 *(children under 18, €2).* 📞*02 33 40 63 05.*
Away from the coast, and less exposed than the Crisbecq, this battery has been built near to the village to allow the camouflage of certain pillboxes which were installed in houses. Equipped with 105mm cannons, the battery had no view of the sea, and its garrison lived the good life for a long time with a "casino" – a hut with a bar, stage and dancing girls and even a water reservoir which served as a swimming pool. Exceptionally well preserved, it has notably maintained the core of its underground galleries.

▷ Return and follow the D 420 until Ravenoville, where you turn right onto the D 14 for 300m. Turn left on the D 15, until Ravenoville-Plage. Follow the dunes on the D 421, southeast.

Les Dunes-de-Varreville

In an opening in the dunes, 100m from the route des Alliés, a rose granite **monument** in the form of a ship's prow and bearing the cross of Lorraine commemorates the landing of the 2nd French Armoured Division under General Leclerc on 1 August 1944.

▷ Continue on the D 421.

Utah Beach

Despite murderous fire from the German coastal batteries, the troops of the American 4th Division (7th Corps) disembarked on 6 June near La Madeleine and Les Dunes-de-Varreville and managed to make contact with the airborne troops of the 82nd and 101st Divisions, who had landed in the region of Ste-Mère-Église. Three weeks later the whole of the Cotentin peninsula had been liberated.

At **La Madeleine** there is a milestone – the first on the Road to Liberty – erected in 1947 to honour soldiers killed during the landings and a memorial to the 4th Division. A German blockhouse is now a monument to the dead of the 1st Engineer Special Brigade; a stele and a crypt commemorate the American 90th Division. On an area of dunes, presented by the commune of Ste-Marie-du-Mont as official American territory, there stands a huge stele erected on the 40th anniversary of the landings by the Americans, in homage to those who died at Utah Beach.

Musée du Débarquement

Ste-Marie-du-Mont.
♿⏰*Daily Jun–Sept 9.30am–7pm; Oct–May 10am–6pm.* ⏰*1–25 Dec.* ✏€8. 📞*02 33 71 53 35.* *www.utah-beach.com.*
Utah Beach D-Day Museum displays its magnificent collection in an impressive exhibition space. This includes a hangar to house a full-scale replica of the B-26 *Dinah Might*, whose crew from the 533rd Squadron parachuted safely during the Landings, but were later captured.

Take the D 913 until Ste-Marie-du-Mont (5.5km/3.4mi).

Ste-Marie-du-Mont

The **church** is identified by its square 14C tower, of which the top storey is a Renaissance addition. A roadside monument honours 800 Danish sailors who took part in the **D-Day landings**.

ADDRESSES

⌂ STAY

⊜⊜⊜ **Château de Quinéville** – 18 rue de l'Église, 50310 Quinéville. ☎06 52 45 09 55. www.chateau-de-quineville.com. 30 rooms. 🅿. Restaurant⊜⊜⊜ (closed out of season). Rooms in the former stables are more modern than those in the 18C château. The garden has Roman ruins, a 14C tower and a pond.

Carentan

Carentan is an important cattle market town and one of the largest centres of the regional dairy industry. Known as the gateway to the Cotentin peninsula it is surrounded by the magnificent wet pastureland of the Marais, much appreciated by the cattle and horses of the region.

SIGHTS

The octagonal spire of the belfry of the **Église Notre-Dame** (12C–15C) dominates the whole region. The fine stone house at the corner of rue de l'Église and place Guillaume-de-Cerisay was described by Balzac under the name Hôtel de Dey in his work Le Réquisitionnaire.

The arcades of the old covered market in **place de la République** date from the late 14C. The **hôtel de ville** (town hall) occupies a 17C–19C convent.

The port, situated to the northeast of town, was inaugurated in 1982 at the end of the canal that links with the sea in the Baie des Veys.

⍩/EAT

⊜⊜ **L'Estaminet** – 44 pl. de l'Église, 50480 Ste-Marie-du-Mont. ☎02 33 71 57 01. https://restaurant-lestaminet-saintemariedumont.fr. Stop on the tiny, charming square next to the church, which on 6 June 1944 was stormed by thousands of Allied vehicles on their way from Utah Beach. This lovely Norman inn is the right place to recover from an emotional visit to the beaches. Seafood on the menu.

⊜⊜ **Auberge John Steele** – 4 rue du Cap-de-Laine, 50480 Ste-Mère-Église. ☎02 33 41 41 16. www.auberge-john-steele. com. Closed Sun eve and all Mon. Situated near the famous church, this inn (1730) pays homage to the soldier John Steele. Typically Norman dining room with exposed beams and stone walls. Regional cuisine. A few simple rooms.

▸ **Population:** 7 880.
⌖ **Michelin Map:** 303:E-4.
▯ **Info:** 24 Place de la République, 50500 Carentan. ☎02 33 71 23 50. www.ot-baieducotentin.fr.
▸ **Location:** Carentan marks the entry to the Cotentin peninsula. Bayeux is 44km/27.5mi E and Cherbourg 51km/32mi NW.
⍟ **Don't Miss:** the spire of Église Nôtre-Dame.
◷ **Timing:** Allow at least half a day to see the town and do the driving tour.

🚗 DRIVING TOUR

🚗 PARC NATUREL RÉGIONAL DES MARAIS DU COTENTIN ET DU BESSIN
40km/25mi. Allow 2h30.

▷ Leave Carentan by the D 974 in the direction of St-Côme-du-Mont.

Cycling along the canal de Vire et Taute, Carentan

Les Ponts d'Ouve★ – Maison du Parc
3 village Ponts d'Ouve, 50500 St-Côme-du-Mont. 🕐*Open daily all year .* ✆*02 33 71 65 30. www.parc-cotentin-bessin.fr.* Near Carentan is a visitor centre for the Marais du Cotentin et du Bessin Park. In addition to the exhibits indoors on flora and fauna, there is a **discovery trail** through the park with informative panels. There are observation areas set up for bird-watchers.

The nature park, formerly known as the Marais de Carentan, was inaugurated in June 1991. With a total area of 145 000ha these wetlands stretch from the Bay of Veys on the east coast of the Cotentin peninsula to Lessay haven on the west coast. This area of marshland *bocage* with its many canals is rich in plant and animal life.

▷ Return to Carentin, leave the town by the D 971 southwest, then turn left on the D 29. Keep going for 13km/8mi, then right on the D 8.

Rémilly-sur-Lozon
The village is renowned for its reed work, which developed considerably in the 19C.
Château de Montfort – L'art du bois.
♿ 🕐*Daily Jul–Aug 2.30–6.30pm; Apr–Jun and Sept–Oct Sat–Sun 2.30–6pm.* ✆*02 33 55 30 11.* Visitors first fall for the charm of this former castle, dating from 15C, then enjoy exploring a restored outbuilding that houses an astonishing exhibition of sculptures in balsa wood. A passionate wood worker, Gilbert Hous-

set has amused himself by creating life-size models of his motorbike, a tractor, aircraft engines, clothes, etc.

▷ Take the D 94 in the direction of Marchésieux (2.5km/1.6mi).

Marchésieux
In this southern section of the Parc, this commune, with several interesting features, has a church decorated with remarkable 14C frescoes.
Maison des marais – *Signed on the D 900 at the entry to St-Lô and Périers.* ✆*07 81 69 69 73. www.adame-des-marais.fr.* Remarkably restored, this large house illustrates perfectly what traditional accommodation was like in the marshlands, that is to say, built on a foundation of stone by adding layers or levees of earth, without any wooden structure. The region has preserved several thousand, most of which date from the 19C.

▷ Leave Marchésieux to the SW and follow the D 433 until Le Bourg-d'Aubigny. Turn right on the D 142.

St-Martin-d'Aubigny
Maison de la brique de Basse-Normandie – 🕐*Jul–Aug daily 2.30–6.30pm; mid–end Jun and Sept Sun 2.30–6.30pm.* ♿€3. ✆*02 33 07 61 95.* With a chimney, a vast flame oven, drying rooms…the brickworks has kept the core of its installations and offers the opportunity to discover an activity about which not much is known.

The nine Channel Islands are divided into two territories known as **Bailiwicks.** The **Bailiwick of Jersey** includes Jersey plus the two uninhabited rocky islets of the Minquiers and the Ecréhous; the **Bailiwick of Guernsey** includes Guernsey, Alderney, Sark and Herm, plus the tiny privately owned isles of Brecqhou and Jethou. All the principal islands encourage tourism, maintaining marinas to attract sailors, ensuring clean beaches for surfers and swimmers, and conserving the countryside, to the delight of bird-watchers, walkers and cyclists.

Governance

The Channel Islands have been associated with the English crown since the Norman conquest, despite the fact that they lie much nearer to the French coast – Jersey is a mere 22km/14mi from the Cotentin Peninsula, but 160km/100mi south of Britain – and were largely French-speaking until the 20C. However, English is now the universal language of the islands; the native tongue is a dialect of Norman French, the language of William the Conqueror, and is rarely heard. However, beneath the apparent English atmosphere lie 1 000 years of Norman tradition and sturdy independence. The original Norman laws and systems have been renewed and modified by subsequent monarchs, though in matters of defence and international relations, the islands are subject to decisions made by the Home Office. The most significant constitutional change in recent years was in 2008, when Sark discarded its feudal system and introduced a (largely) democratic constitution.

Highlights

1. **St Peter Port**, Guernsey (p428), particularly **Hauteville House**.
2. Go wild in Jersey's near-natural **Jersey Zoo** (p441)
3. Imagine Nazi occupation in the **Jersey War Tunnels** (p442)
4. Explore the fine fort of **Mont-Orgueil Castle** (p448)
5. Get away from it all on beautiful natural, car-free **Sark** (p451)

The islands yesterday and today

The islands are rich in prehistoric tombs and monuments indicating human habitation from 7500 BCE–2500 BCE. They were annexed by the Normans in 933 and later attached to the English crown by William the Conqueror. Some customs and traditions and the Norman-French dialect heard on these islands, which have only been universally English-speaking since the early 20C, date back to this period. In 1204, King John was forced to cede Normandy to the French, but the Channel Islanders chose to remain loyal to the English Crown in return for certain privileges, one of which was an independent parliament. Despite this, the French tried repeatedly to capture the island. Threats of invasion by Napoleon account for the many Martello defence towers built along the coasts. The islands were occupied by the Germans from 1940–45, the only British territory to fall to the enemy during World War II, and the islanders suffered considerable hardship during this period.

By contrast today the Channel Islands are known for their high standard of living compared to the rest of the UK, benefitting from a VAT-exempt economy and lower rates of income tax. This has encouraged the islands to become a tax haven for wealthy British citizens, and a buoyant industry in financial services has developed. Farming, however, still plays an important part in the local economy and maintains a supply to mainland Britain of early vegetables (potatoes, tomatoes, grapes), cut flowers and rich Channel Island milk.

THE CHANNEL ISLANDS

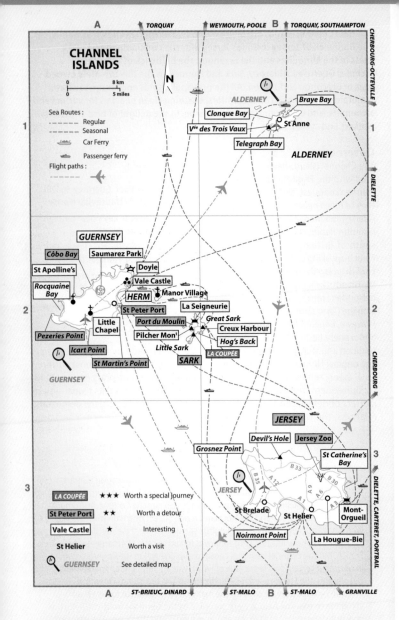

CHANNEL ISLANDS

0 — 8 km
0 — 5 miles

Sea Routes:
— — — Regular
— — — Seasonal
🛳 Car Ferry
⛴ Passenger ferry
Flight paths:
— — — ✈

TORQUAY
WEYMOUTH, POOLE
TORQUAY, SOUTHAMPTON
CHERBOURG-OCTEVILLE
DIÉLETTE
CHERBOURG
DIÉLETTE, CARTERET, PORTBAIL

ALDERNEY
Braye Bay
Clonque Bay
Vic des Trois Vaux
St Anne
Telegraph Bay
ALDERNEY

GUERNSEY
Côbo Bay
Saumarez Park
St Apolline's
Doyle
Vale Castle
Rocquaine Bay
HERM
Manor Village
St Peter Port
La Seigneurie
Little Chapel
Port du Moulin
Great Sark
Creux Harbour
Pezeries Point
Pilcher Monᵗ
Hog's Back
Icart Point
Little Sark
LA COUPÉE
St Martin's Point
SARK
GUERNSEY

JERSEY
Devil's Hole
Jersey Zoo
Grosnez Point
St Catherine's Bay
JERSEY
B 33
A 12
B 35
A 9
A 6
B 30
St Brelade
St Helier
Mont-Orgueil
Noirmont Point
La Hougue-Bie

LA COUPÉE ★★★ Worth a special journey
St Peter Port ★★ Worth a detour
Vale Castle ★ Interesting
St Helier Worth a visit
🔍 GUERNSEY See detailed map

ST-BRIEUC, DINARD
ST-MALO
ST-MALO
GRANVILLE

Geography

Owing to their situation and the Gulf Stream, the islands enjoy a mild climate that nurtures spring flowers and semi-tropical plants. Long sandy beaches contrast with rugged cliffs, and quiet country lanes meander between traditional granite houses. Tidal currents in the islands are among the strongest in the world; at low tide, when the sea may retreat as much as 12m, huge areas of rocky reefs are exposed, greatly increasing the land mass and making it possible to walk further out (up to 3km/2mi).

The islands are served by ferries from France and England, and by flights to Jersey, Guernsey and Alderney. Scheduled ferries also connect the islands.

Alderney

Measuring a mere 5.6km/3.5mi long by 2.4km/1.5mi wide, Alderney slopes gently from a plateau in the southwest, to a tongue of low-lying land in the northeast. There is one main settlement, St Anne, also known as The Town. Alderney is a haven for nature lovers: flora includes wild broom, thrift, sea campion, ox-eye daisies, wild orchids and the bastard toadflax *(Thesium humifusum)*; among the fauna are black rabbits and, even rarer, blonde hedgehogs. Bird-watchers can spy hoopoes and golden orioles, birds of prey and the occasional white stork or purple heron. Seabirds include fulmars, guillemots and kittiwakes, as well as colonies of gannets and puffins.

▶ **Population:** 2 020.
🕭 **Michelin Map:** 503.
🔲 **Info:** 51 Victoria Street, St Anne. ☏01481 822 333. www.visitalderney.com.
◑ **Location:** Alderney is the most northerly of the Channel Islands and lies 12km/7.5mi W of the Cherbourg peninsula, separated from the Cap de la Hague headland by the treacherous tidal current known as the Alderney Race.
☺ **Don't Miss:** The best beaches are in the bays of Braye, Clonque and Telegraph. Also try the cliff walk from Haize to Giffoine.

A BIT OF HISTORY

Owing to its key position, nearest to England, France and the Channel shipping lanes, Alderney has frequently been fortified. The Romans seem to have used it as a naval base; there are traces of a late-Roman fort at the Convent. The first English fortifications were initiated by Henry VIII on the hill south of Longis Bay. In the Napoleonic period, the British strengthened existing defences and sent a garrison of 300.

Between 1847 and 1858, alarmed by the development of a French naval base at Cherbourg, the British Government created a safe harbour at Braye by constructing a huge breakwater and built a chain of ten forts along the north coast.

In June 1940 almost all the population left the island and the livestock was evacuated to Guernsey. During their five-year occupation, the Germans re-fortified most of the Victorian forts and built masses of ugly concrete fortifications. They also built three labour camps and a concentration camp, which mainly held Russian prisoners. When the islanders returned late in 1945 they found their possessions gone and their houses derelict or destroyed. It took ten years and substantial government aid to make good the damage.

Constitution

Alderney is part of the Bailiwick of Guernsey. Since the introduction of the new constitution on 1 January 1949, the budget and other financial matters have to be approved by the States of Guernsey. Otherwise, all island business is decided by the Committees of the States of Alderney, which consists of ten elected members and an elected president, who serve for four years. The court consists of six Jurats under a chairman, all of whom are appointed by the Home Office.

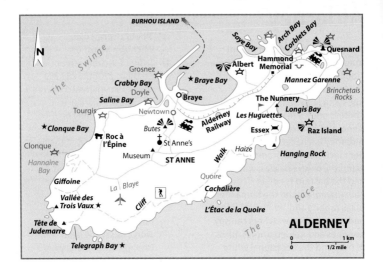

ST ANNE

St Anne, with its cobbled streets and smart whitewashed granite houses, lies about half a mile from the north coast on the edge of the best agricultural land, known as La Blaye.

The original medieval settlement was centred on **Marais Square**. As in ancient times, narrow lanes or *venelles* lead out to the un-enclosed fields divided into *riages*, each consisting of a number of strips: Alderney is one of the few places in Britain still to use this archaic system of managing open agricultural land.

Another settlement grew up at **Le Huret**, where the people assembled to decide when to gather the seaweed (*vraic*) used to fertilise the land. In the 15C, more houses were built to the east of the square and the Blaye was extended to support a population of 700. In the 18C the huge profits made from privateering led to a building boom; thatch was replaced by tiles, the first Court House was built and the governor improved the communal buildings as well as his own residence. The northern part of the town – **Queen Elizabeth II Street**, **Victoria Street**, **Ollivier Street** – developed in the early Victorian era.

Workmen's cottages were built at Newtown and elsewhere. Many attractive houses and gardens line the green lanes, such as La Vallée, which run from St Anne down to the north coast.

St Anne's Church

Consecrated in 1850, this church was designed by Sir Gilbert Scott in the transitional style from Norman to Early English cruciform and is known as the "Cathedral of the Channel Islands". English was then replacing Norman French as the local language; the lectern holds two Bibles, and the texts in the apse and near the door appear in both languages.

During the war the church was used as a store and the bells were removed; two were recovered on the island and the other four were found in Cherbourg. The churchyard gates in Victoria Street, erected as a memorial to Prince Albert, were removed by the Germans but replaced by a local resident.

Alderney Museum

&. ⏱*Apr–Oct Mon–Fri 10am–noon, 2.30–4.30pm, Sat–Sun 10am–noon.* ⬭£3. ☎01481 823 222.

The Alderney Society's museum, installed in a former school founded in 1790 by former island governor Jean Le Mesurier; geology, flora, fauna, archaeology – particularly finds from the Iron Age settlement at Les Huguettes – domestic and military history, including the Victorian fortifications and the German occupation.

The **Clock Tower** (1767) standing nearby is all that remains of the old church, which was pulled down when the present one was built.

The elegant Royal Connaught Square, renamed in 1905 after a visit by the Duke of Connaught, third son of Queen Victoria, was the town centre in the 18C. **Island Hall** (*north side*), a handsome granite building which is now a community centre and library, was enlarged in 1763 by Governor John Le Mesurier to become Government House. Mouriaux House was completed in 1779 by the governor as his private residence.

Alderney Courthouse

The present building in Queen Elizabeth II Street dates from 1850. Both the court and the States of Alderney hold their sessions in the first-floor courtroom.

The name of Victoria Street, the main shopping street, was changed from rue du Grosnez to celebrate Queen Victoria's visit in 1854.

The Butes recreation ground provides fine views of Braye bay (*northeast*), across Crabby bay and The Swinge to the Casquets (*northwest*) and the English Channel.

🚗 DRIVING TOURS

🚗 TOUR OF THE ISLAND

14km/8.5mi. Allow one day.

🚶 It is possible to walk round the whole island following the clifftop footpath (you can also drive around).

Braye

The harbour is protected by Fort Grosnez (1853), which was built at the same time as the massive **breakwater** (914m long plus another 548.5m submerged).

The first quay, the Old Jetty, was built in 1736 by the governor to provide a safe landing-stage for the privateers and smugglers he protected. The modern concrete jetty dates from the turn of the 20C.

Burhou Island

🐾*Take water.* ⛵*Boat trips on Sula of Braye (Wed and Sat 2pm; ☎01481 822935), Lady Maris (Tue and Fri 2.30pm; www.alderneygiftbox.com) and Avante (Wed–Sun; ☎07781 115132 or 823307) depart from Alderney on advertised days during the summer months taking visitors on a round island trip to visit the puffins on Burhou, as well as touring the rest of the Ramsar site, including the gannet colonies on Les Etacs and Ortac and the Atlantic seal colony near Burhou Reef.*

🕐*15 Mar–1 Aug (breeding season).*

The island, which lies northwest across The Swinge (about 2km/1mi), is riddled with rabbit warrens and supports large colonies of puffin, razorbill, gannet and storm petrel as well as other seabirds.

Alderney Railway (Petit chemin de fer)

🕐*Operates bank holidays and weekends Easter–Sept 2.30pm, 3.30pm.* 🎫*£6 return.* ☎*01481 823 580. www.alderneyrailway.com.*

Opened in 1847, the railway was built to transport the blocks of granite from the quarry to the port for breakwaters and forts. Today, it is the only train in the Channel Islands and runs from Braye Road Station to Mannez station at the eastern end of the island. Two 1959 Metro-Cammell London Underground carriages serve as coaches.

Braye Bay★

The largest bay on the island offers a sandy beach with good bathing and a fine view of the harbour. Skirting the beach is a strip of grass, Le Banquage, where the seaweed (*vraic,* gathered for manure and fuel*)* was left to dry.

Fort Albert

Mount Touraille, at the east end of Braye Bay, is crowned by Fort Albert (1853). There is a fine view inland to St Anne, westwards across Braye bay to Fort Grosnez and the breakwater with Fort Tourgis in the background, and eastwards over the northern end of the island.

Beach, Braye Bay

© Catherine Philip/iStockphoto.com

Hammond Memorial

At the fork in the road E of Fort Albert.
Slave labourers from France, Spain, Ukraine, Russia and North Africa, who worked and died during the Nazi occupation under the auspices of the infamous Organisation Todt – are recalled by plaques inscribed in their languages. There were four camps on Alderney which each held 1 500 men, including the only concentration camp on British soil, Lager Sylt, near the old telegraph tower at La Foulère. Many Jews and Russians lost their lives here but little is known about the camp's precise activities.

Controversially, the States (Alderney's governing body) do not commemorate the sites of the four camps, possibly to dissociate themselves from accusations of collaboration.

North Coast

Three excellent sandy bathing bays cluster round the most northerly headland beneath the walls of Fort Château à l'Étoc (1854), now converted into private flats: **Saye Bay**, nearly symmetrical in shape; **Arch Bay**, named after the tunnel through which the carts collecting seaweed reached the shore; **Corblets Bay**, overlooked by Fort Corblets (1855), now a private house with a splendid view.

Mannez Garenne

The low-lying northern end of the island, known as Mannez Garenne (Warren), is dominated by the remains of a German observation tower.

Mannez Lighthouse

🕐*For opening times telephone the Alderney visitor centre* 📞*01481 822 333.* 🚶*Guided tours every Sun, May–Sept, at 3pm.* 💷*£4 (children under 16, £3). Steep steps; children under 1.1m tall may not ascend.* 📞*01481 823 077 or 01481 823 737.*

Built in 1912, the lighthouse stands 37m high and casts its beam nearly 27.5km/17mi. From the lantern platform there is a magnificent **view★** of the coast and the Race and, on a clear day, of the nuclear power station on the French coast. Many ships have come to grief on this coast.

Three mid-19C forts command the coastline: Les Homeaux Florains, now in ruins; Fort Quesnard, on the east side of Cats Bay, and Fort Houmet Herbe.

Raz Island

A causeway, covered at high tide, runs out to Raz Island in Longis bay. Its fort (1853) has been partially restored and there is a fine **view** southwest of Essex Castle and Hanging Rock.

Longis Bay

The retreating tide reveals a broad stretch of sand, backed by a German tank trap which provides excellent shelter for sunbathing. The shallow bay was the island's natural harbour from prehistoric times until it silted up early in the 18C. Traces of an Iron Age settlement were discovered at **Les Huguettes** in 1968; the finds are displayed in the Alderney Museum. Various relics indicate the existence of a Roman naval base protected by a fort.

The Nunnery

Parts of this building, thought to be the oldest on the island, date back to the 4C. It became a garrison and British soldiers based here in the 18C gave it its present name. It is now private dwellings owned by the States of Alderney.

Essex Castle

The present structure, which takes its name from a previous castle on the site, was built in 1840 to be used first as a barracks and then as a military hospital; it is now private property.

Hanging Rock

The tilt of this 15m rocky column projecting from the cliff face at a 45-degree angle is jokingly said by locals to have been caused by the people of Guernsey trying to tow Alderney away.

⚡ CLIFF WALK

From Haize around to Giffoine there is a magnificent walk served by several footpaths running inland back to St Anne. The view of the steep cliffs plunging into the rock-strewn sea is spectacular.

Cachalière

A path leads down past the old quarry to an abandoned pier. From here the rocks of **L'Étac de la Quoire** can be reached at low tide.

Telegraph Bay★

Access to the tower is by a path and steps, which are not recommended as they are steep and difficult. Beware being cut off from the steps by the tide.
The Telegraph Tower (1811), which provided communication with Jersey and Guernsey, has given its name to the bay below. Except at high tide, there is excellent bathing, sheltered from all but a south wind. There is also a good view of La Nache and Fourquie rocks.

Tête de Judemarre

The headland provides a fine **view** of the rock-bound coast and of the islands of Guernsey, Herm and Sark.

Vallée des Trois Vaux★

This deep cleft is in fact three valleys meeting on a shingle beach.

Giffoine

From the cliff it is possible to see the gannets on their nests in the colony on Les Étacs. The remains of a German coastal battery crown the headland above Hannaine bay, where sandy spits between the rocks provide reasonable bathing. There are fine **view** of Burhou, Ortac and the Casquets to the north.

Clonque Bay★

A path descends the gorse-and-heather-clad slope above the attractive bay. A causeway runs out to Fort Clonque (1855), now flats; two futher causeways enabled horse-drawn *vraic* carts to reach the seaweed beds.
Just south of Fort Tourgis (1855), at the northern end of the bay, is the best-preserved burial chamber on the island, **Roc à l'Épine**, a capstone supported by two upright stones. Alderney once had many such megaliths, sadly destroyed when the Victorian fortifications were built.

Saline Bay

The shore, exposed to heavy seas so that bathing can be hazardous, is commanded by Fort Doyle, now a youth centre; beyond lies **Crabby Bay** in the lee of Fort Grosnez.

ADDRESSES

STAY

🪙🪙🪙 **The Victoria Hotel** – *1 Victoria Street.* ℘*01481 822 754. www.victoria hotelalderney.com. 6 rooms.* This small family-run hotel in a Victorian terraced house is set in the conservation area of St Anne's. Cosy and spacious bedrooms.

🪙🪙–🪙🪙🪙 **Farm Court** – *Les Mouriaux.* ℘*01481 822 075. www.farmcourt-alderney. co.uk. 9 rooms, plus self-catering cottage (sleeps 5).* In a quiet location on the edge of St Anne's, this attractive complex of renovated farm buildings is set around a lovely cobbled courtyard garden. Rooms are large with contemporary and antique furnishings.

Guernsey★

Smaller and less sophisticated than Jersey, Guernsey has its own particular charm and a slower tempo. Visitors come for the Regency elegance of St Peter Port, its wild, dramatic southern cliffs, and the bathing, swimming and surfing on the sandy beaches and rocky promontories of the west and north coasts.

- ▶ **Population:** 63 026.
- ◔ **Michelin Map:** 503.
- 🛈 **Info:** North Esplanade, St Peter Port, GY1 3AN Guernsey. ℘01481 723 552. www.visitguernsey.com.
- ▷ **Location:** Guernsey is the second largest of the Channel Islands (63sq km/24sq mi). The south coast, higher, rocky and ragged, contrasts with the sandy bays of the rest of the coast.
- ⊛ **Don't Miss:** A stroll down the streets of St Peter Port, a swim in Côbo bay, and the panoramic view from Icart Point in the south.
- ◕ **Timing:** You'll need a half-day at St Peter Port, plus a day or two to tour the island by car or bicycle, with time for swimming, of course.
- 👥 **Kids:** The Folk Museum; the Aquarium.

ST PETER PORT★★

The island capital is built on the east coast overlooking an anchorage protected from high seas by Herm and Sark. The medieval town by the shore was rebuilt after bombardment during the Civil War (1642–46).

Profits from privateering in the late 18C produced a delightful Regency town. Guernsey's popularity as a tourist destination was assured when Queen Victoria visited in 1846.

As you walk up Market Street, to the right is the covered market comprising Les Halles, with the Assembly Rooms above, completed in 1782. Opposite

is the Doric-style meat market (1822). Les Arcades, 1830 (*on the left*), is very handsome despite the loss of the final bay. The Fish Market was finished in 1877. Finally, the Vegetable Market was constructed in 1879.

The large modern harbour bustles with car and passenger ferries, fishing boats and private yachts. Stroll out to White Rock or visit the castle for a fine **view** of the town, the harbour and the neighbouring islands.

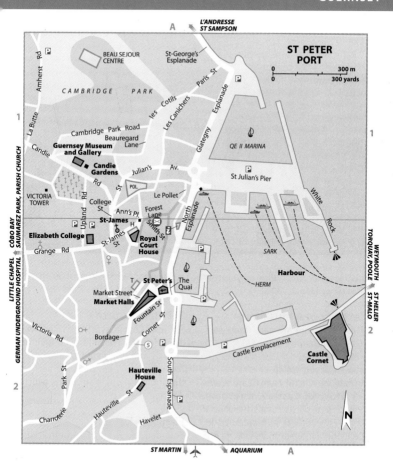

ST PETER PORT

L'ANDRESSE
ST SAMPSON

BEAU SEJOUR
CENTRE

St-George's
Esplanade

CAMBRIDGE PARK

Cambridge Park Road

Beauregard
Lane

Guernsey Museum
and Gallery

Candie
Gardens

Julian's

Le Pollet

VICTORIA
TOWER

College St

Ann's Pl

St-James

Forest
Lane

Elizabeth College

Grange Rd

St-James St

Royal
Court
House

St Peter's

The
Quai

Market Street

Market Halls

Fountain St

Victoria Rd

Bordage

Cornet St

Park St

Hauteville
House

South Esplanade

Hauteville St

Charroterie

Havelet

ST MARTIN

AQUARIUM

QE II MARINA

St Julian's Pier

SARK

Harbour

HERM

Castle Emplacement

Castle
Cornet

White Rock

WEYMOUTH
TORQUAY, POOLE

ST HELIER
ST-MALO

LITTLE CHAPEL
CÔBO BAY
GERMAN UNDERGROUND HOSPITAL
SAUMAREZ PARK, PARISH CHURCH

N

0   300 m
0   300 yards

Hauteville House★★

38 Hauteville.

Guided tours only (1h) early Apr–
Sept daily except Wed 10am–4pm.
£10. 01481 721 911.
www.maisonsvictorhugo.paris.fr.

Victor Hugo was exiled from his native
France for political reasons in 1851. After
time in Brussels and Jersey, he bought
this impressive white house in 1856.
During his 14 years' residence Hugo
redecorated the interior, doing much
of the work himself, sometimes with
eccentric results; note the position of
mirrors, placed so as to enhance the
effect of various features.

Hugo used to work on his poems and
novels standing at a small table in
the **Glass Room,** on the third floor
overlooking the sea. From the **Lookout** where he sometimes slept, he could

Glass Room,
Hauteville House

© Jean-Daniel Sudres/hemis.fr

see the house up the road (*La Fallue,
1 Beauregard Lane*) in which his faithful

St Peter Port

© Arndale/iStockphoto.com

mistress, Juliette Drouot, lived from November 1856 to 1864.

Castle Cornet museums★

🕐 *Late Mar–early Nov daily 10am–5pm (Jul–Aug 9.30am–5pm).* ⬙*£10.50.* 📞*01481 726 518.* *www.museums.gov.gg.*

An exhibition in the Main Guard relates the **Story of Castle Cornet** from prehistoric to present times. The original castle (c.1206) was reinforced under Elizabeth I and again under Victoria. The castle suffered its greatest misfortune in 1672 when a lightning strike ignited the gunpowder store in the old tower keep. On the Saluting Platform in the outer bailey the ceremony of the **noonday gun** takes place daily.

From the citadel there is a fine **view★** of the harbour and town, St Sampson, Vale Castle and Alderney (*35km/21.7mi north*), Herm, Sark and the French coast and Jersey. The **Maritime Museum** relates the island's maritime history from the Gallo-Roman period to the present day. The **201 Squadron Museum** recounts the story of the island's RAF squadron. A **Militia Museum**, housed in the hospital building (1746), contains artefacts of the Royal Guernsey Militia, which was disbanded in 1939. Collections of weapons are housed in the **Armoury**. The **Royal Guernsey Light Infantry Museum** is on the ground floor of the

building and tells the story of Guernseymen who fought in the Great War.

St Peter's Church★

The Town Church, as St Peter's is known, was begun by William the Conqueror in 1048, and completed around 1475. The nave and west door are part of the original Norman structure, which doubled as a fort.

Elizabeth College

Founded in 1563 by Elizabeth I, the Mock Tudor-style building dates from 1826–29.

Guernsey Tapestry★

St James, College Street. 🕐*Apr–Oct Mon–Sat 10am–4.30pm; Nov–Feb Thu only 11am–4pm.* ⬙*£5.* 📞*01481 727 106.* *www.guernseytapestry.org.gg.*

Designed to celebrate the Millennium, this tapestry of ten panels was created in two years by the inhabitants of the ten parishes of the island, and traces the history of Guernsey over the last thousand years.

Royal Court House

🕐*Admission is for small groups only, by prior arrangement.* 📞*01481 725 277.* *www.guernseyroyalcourt.gg.*

The elegant neo-Classical church of **St James**' is now a concert hall. The law courts and the States of Deliberation hold their sittings in the elegant **Royal Court House** (1792); its archives go back 400 years.

Guernsey Museum and Art Gallery

♿🕐*Daily 10am–5pm (4pm during GMT).* 🕐*25 Dec and 1–24 Jan.* ✆*£6.50.* ✆*01481 726 518. www.museums.gov.gg.* A cluster of modern octagonal structures and a former Victorian bandstand, now housing the charming Café Victoria tearoom, is home to the Lukis collection of archaeological artefacts, retrieved from La Varde chambered tomb in 1811, and the Wilfred Carey Collection of paintings, prints and ceramics.

Candie Gardens

Extending below the museum and the Priaulx Library, these splendid Pleasure Gardens were laid out in 1898 and have recently been renovated

EXCURSIONS
Saumarez Park★

In Castel, 3.5km/2.2mi west on the Route de Côbo.
The trees and shrubs of this beautiful park are matched by the formal rose gardens; the pond is alive with wildfowl. The house (**St John's Residential Home**) dates from 1721.

♟♙Guernsey Folk and Costume Museum★

Saumarez Park, Castel.
♿🕐*Daily Apr–Oct 10am–5pm (Sun 11am–3pm).* 🕐*9 May.* ✆*£6 (child 7–18, £2).* ✆*01481 255 384. www.nationaltrust.gg.*
Housed within the farmstead buildings of Saumarez House a series of Victorian interiors are recreated. The collection encompasses a stunning variety of Victorian fashion, including society dresses and a detailed look at Victorian Mourning wear.

Parish Church

3.5km/2.2mi west on Rectory Road.
Early documents list the castle's 12C church of St Mary (**Ste-Marie-du-Castel**

or Our Lady of Deliverance) as belonging to the abbey of Mont St-Michel in 1155; before then, the site may have had a pre-Christian sanctuary and Roman fort. There are fine **views** from here, to the coast and across to Vale Church.

St Andrew
German Underground Hospital and Ammunition Store

La Vassalerie Rd.
🕐*Apr and Oct Fri–Mon 10am–4pm; May–Sept daily 10am–4pm.* ✆*£4 (child under 15, £2).* ✆*01481 235 261. www. germanundergroundhospital.co.uk.* 😷 *Wear warm clothes.*
This huge project took nearly three and a half years to build and consists of a series of tunnels, dug out by hundreds of slave workers, down into the granite bedrock. Today, the miles of hollow corridors and interlocking wards are eerily vacant.

Little Chapel★

Les Vauxbelets, 1km/0.6mi from Underground Hospital.
🕐*Daily: May–Sept 9am–6pm; Oct–Apr 9am–dusk. http://thelittlechapel.gg.*
Possibly the smallest chapel in the world, measuring roughly 3m by 2m, this little jewel was originally built by a Salesian monk, Brother Déodat, in March 1914. It is his miniature version of the famous grotto and basilica at Lourdes, beautifully decorated with seashells, pebbles and colourful pieces of broken china. Now part of Blanchelande Girls College it is open free of charge in daylight hours.

🚗DRIVING TOURS

🚗 CLOS DU VALLE – ST PETER PORT TO VALE CHURCH
8km/5mi. Allow half a day.

Until 1806 the northern part of Guernsey, known as Clos du Valle, was cut off by the Braye du Valle, a tidal channel of mudflats and saltmarsh. The channel was filled in and the reclaimed land (121ha) is now covered with glasshouses.

▶ Leave St Peter Port by the coast road (Glategny Esplanade) north towards St Sampson. Turn left in Belle Grève Bay onto Le Grand Bouet and then take the second right.

Guernsey's second port, St Sampson, lies at the eastern end of the Braye du Valle. Its church, **St Sampson**, is the oldest church in Guernsey, allegedly built where the saint came ashore (c.550), either from Llantwit Major in South Wales or from Dol in Brittany. Its churchyard overlooks the disused Longue Hougue Quarry.

▶ From the bridge take Vale Avenue north and bear left onto the main road (Route du Braye). Oatlands Craft Centre is located opposite a garden centre.

Oatlands Village
Les Gigands.
 🕐*Daily 9.30am–5pm.* 🅿
℘*01481 241 643. www.oatlands.gg.*
Oatlands brick kilns, built in 1892, stand as reminders of a thriving brick-making industry. The site includes several shops, a brasserie, café and children's play area.

Vale Castle★
The medieval castle, now in ruins, was built on the site of an Iron Age hillfort (c.600 BCE) on the only high point in Clos du Valle. There is a fine **view** inland, along the east coast and out to sea to the reef, Alderney, Herm and Sark, and Jersey.
Bordeaux Harbour provides mooring for fishing boats and the only safe swimming in the area.

▶ Follow the main road north; as it curves gently left, turn right onto the minor road; bear left; park by the dilapidated glasshouses (right) opposite the passage tomb.

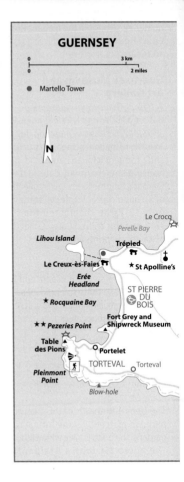

GUERNSEY

| 0 | 3 km |
| 0 | 2 miles |

● Martello Tower

N

Le Croca
Perelle Bay
Lihou Island
Trépied
Le Creux-ès-Faies
★ St Apolline's
Erée Headland
ST PIERRE DU BOIS
★ Rocquaine Bay
Fort Grey and Shipwreck Museum
★★ Pezeries Point
Table des Pions
○ Portelet
TORTEVAL
Torteval
Pleinmont Point
Blow-hole

Dehus Dolmen
🕐*Daily sunrise–sunset. Light switch on the left as you enter.*
www.megalithicguernsey.co.uk/ le_dehus_dolmen
This passage grave has four side chambers covered by seven capstones: crouch down to see Le Gardien du Tombeau, the figure of an archer *(switch for spotlight)*.

▶ Several minor roads meander north to the coast.

The **Beaucette Quarry Marina** was created by a blast in an old quarry, opening a breach to the sea.

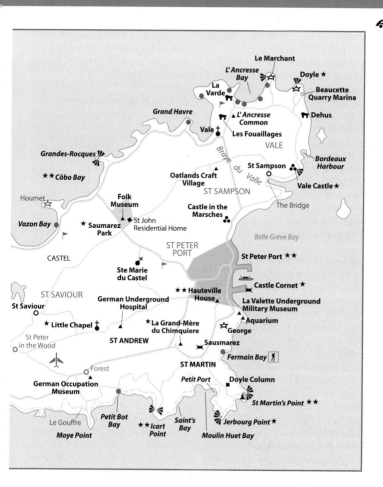

From **Fort Doyle** there is a **view★** of the Casquets reef and Alderney, the French coast, Herm and Sark.

Fort Le Marchant is the most northerly point in Guernsey. It offers a fine view, particularly of **L'Ancresse Common**, the only extensive open space on the island, used for recreation; and of **L'Ancresse Bay**, popular for bathing and surfing.

La Varde Dolmen is the largest passage grave in Guernsey. **Les Fouaillages** burial ground is 7 000 years old.

Vale Church was consecrated in 1117 on the site of an earlier chapel dedicated to St Magloire, who, with St Sampson, brought Christianity to Guernsey in the 6C.

🚗 WEST COAST – LE GRAND HAVRE TO PEZERIES POINT

15km/10mi. Allow half a day.

The **Grand Havre**, a large inlet at the west end of the Braye du Valle, is best admired from the Rousse headland, with its tower and jetty. A more extensive horizon is visible from the German gun battery on the granite headland, the **Grandes Rocques**.

Côbo Bay★★ is a charming combination of sand and rocks, safe for bathing. The huge beach between Fort Houmet and Fort le Crocq at **Vazon Bay** is also excellent for swimming.

In the Grande-Rue at Perelle, **St Apolline's Chapel★** received its charter in 1394. It is decorated with a **fresco** (*light switch*) of *The Last Supper*.

Le Trépied Dolmen burial chamber at Le Cationoc was excavated in 1840 by Frederic Lukis, whose finds are in the Guernsey Museum. In past centuries the site was used for witches' Sabbaths. The tall defensive tower on the L'Erée Headland is called Fort Saumarez.

To the south stands **Le Creux ès Faies Dolmen**, a passage grave dating from 2000 BCE to 1800 BCE.

The grand sweep of **Rocquaine Bay★** is interrupted by the "Cup and Saucer", originally a medieval fort. It is painted white as a navigation mark.

Fort Grey Shipwreck Museum

🕒 *Late Mar–early Nov daily 10am–4.30pm.* ✆£4. 📞 *01481 265 036. www.museums.gov.gg.*

This small museum is dedicated to the many shipwrecks in Guernsey waters, with exhibits from more than 100 wrecks between 1750 and 1978.

The picturesque harbour of Portelet, full of fishing boats, is backed by the houses of the Hanois Lighthouse keepers. Nearby is the **Table des Pions**, a famous local "fairy ring".

Pezeries Point★★ is the most westerly point in all the Channel Islands, a remote and unfrequented place. Its fort was built in the Napoleonic era.

🚗 SOUTHERN CLIFFS – PLEINMONT POINT TO ST PETER PORT

26km/16mi. Allow half a day.

The cliffs along the south coast and round to St Peter Port provide some of the wildest and most dramatic scenery on the island (⚠*beware the cliff face, which can be unstable and dangerous*); a footpath runs to the town.

The headland at **Pleinmont Point** provides an extensive **view**: along the southern cliffs, out to the Hanois Lighthouse and its reefs, across Rocquaine Bay to Lihou Island.

A footpath stretches all along the clifftops, past the watch houses before coming out by the Aquarium in St Peter Port. **La Moye Point**, the smallest of the three promontories on the south coast, is wild and beautiful.

German Occupation Museum

Les Houards Forest, south of the church. 🕒*Daily: Apr–Oct 10am–4.30pm; Nov–Mar 10am–1pm.* ✆£6. ♿ 🅿 📞*01481 238 205. www.german occupationmuseum.co.uk.*

Artefacts from the Nazi occupation: includes weaponry, uniforms, vehicles, personal effects, etc.

Petit Bot Bay, with good bathing and a sandy beach at low tide, lies at the foot of a green valley guarded by a defensive tower (1780).

▷ Return uphill to the main road; turn right down rue de la Villette, which turns inland to rejoin the valley leading down to Moulin Huet bay.

Icart Point★★ is the highest and most southerly headland with very fine **views★** of the coast. On the east side is **Saint's Bay**, a favourite mooring for fishermen. A stream runs down a beautiful valley to **Moulin Huet Bay★**, where it plunges down the cliff face into the sea. The swimming here is good, but even better at neighbouring **Petit Port**. St Martin is of little interest but, near the car park, **St Martin's Point★★** commands is a magnificent view down to the lighthouse on the point, north up the coast to St Peter Port, and seaward to the other islands.

▷ Follow the path along the cliff.

Jerbourg Point★ is Guernsey's southeastern extremity: excavations have revealed Neolithic remains. The Château de Jerbourg protected islanders in the Middle Ages when the French occupied Castle Cornet.

Fermain Bay (*access on foot from the car park or cliff path from Jerbourg; in summer, the bay is accessible by boat from St Peter Port*), with its pebbled cove, backed by densely wooded cliffs and an 18C defensive tower, offers a sandy beach and good bathing at low tide.

▶ Continue east on the main road; on a left-hand curve, turn left beyond the main gate into the shaded car park.

Sausmarez Manor
House: guided tours: 1st week of Apr Mon–Thu 11.30am; 2nd week of Apr–May Mon–Thu 10.30am and 11.30am; Jun–Sept also at 2.30pm. £7.50.
Subtropical Garden and Art Park Sculpture Garden: Daily 10am–5pm. £6.50.
01481 235 571.
www.sausmarezmanor.co.uk.
The elegant Queen Anne house was built in 1714–18 by Sir Edmund Andros, the Seigneur of Sausmarez and former Governor of New York. The interior displays handsome family furniture, portraits and mementoes of the family's 750 years on the island.
The wooded **grounds** are planted with tall bamboo and camellias and include **Subtropical Gardens**, a **Sculpture Park**, a ride-on railway, a pitch-and-putt golf course and a putting green. At the gate into St Martin's churchyard stands a Stone Age menhir, **La Grand'mère du Chimquière★** carved to represent a female figure. The church itself dates from 1225 to 1250; the south porch was added in the 1520s.

▶ Return to the main road; turn right to Jerbourg.

La Valette Underground Military Museum
Mar–mid-Nov daily 10am–5pm. £5.50. 01481 722 300.
www.lavalette.tk
The museum occupies five tunnels that were excavated to hold fuel tanks for refuelling U-boats, Displays relate to the Guernsey Militia, plus German artefacts and mementoes of the occupation.

Guernsey Aquarium
Daily 10am–5pm (Sun 6pm).
1 Jan, 25–26 Dec. £5 (child £3).
01481 723 301.
This is home to local sea fish, European freshwater fish and tropical fish. Also on display are frogs, toads, terrapins, snakes and basilisks.

ADDRESSES

STAY

Sunnydene Country Hotel – rue des Marettes. 01481 236 870. www.sunnydenecountryhotel.co.uk. 20 rooms. Comfortable family lounge, swimming pool, pretty garden and 18-hole putting green. Traditional but unfussy rooms.

Hôtel La Michèle – Les Hubits, St Martins. 01481 238 065. www.la michelehotel.com. 16 rooms. Restaurant (residents only). Near Fermain bay, comfortable, well-equipped rooms. Relaxing lounge, lawned gardens with, terrace and outdoor swimming pool.

Hôtel La Frégate – Les Cotils, St Peter Port. 01481 724 624. www.lafregatehotel.com. 22 rooms. Restaurant . Enjoy a panoramic view over St Peter Port at this welcoming luxury boutique hotel, set in a peaceful location.

EAT

Fleur du Jardin Hotel Bar and Restaurant – Kings Mills, Castel. 01481 257 996. www.fleurdujardin.com. This beautifully converted 15C house serves contemporary cuisine in gastropub surroundings at reasonable prices. The hotel comprises 15 very chic **rooms** ().

L'Escalier – 6 Tower Hill, St Peter Port. 01481 710 088. www.harbourguides.com/lescalier. Closed Mon. This intimate, Anglo-French family-run restaurant is just a short walk from the town centre.

The Pavilion Restaurant – St Peter Port. 01481 728 282 . www.thepavilion.co.gg. Closed Tue. A modern brasserie in the St. Pierre Park Hotel. Menus feature fabulous seafood and regional dishes cooked simply using local produce.

Herm

The broad sandy beaches on Herm's north coast contrast with the steep cliffs at the southern end of the island. Herm has neither roads nor cars, and walkers enjoy a profusion of wild flowers, dunes, trees and cliffs. The deep fringe of rocks offshore is most impressive at low tide. Southwest, across a narrow channel, the islet of Jethou (private property leased from the British Crown) rises like a hillock and is home to thousands of seabirds.

▶ **Population:** 60.
🎗 **Michelin Map:** 503.
🗒 **Info:** North Plantation, St Peter Port, Guernsey. ☎01481 750 000. www.herm.com.
◐ **Location:** Herm is 2.4km/ 1.5mi long, 0.8km/0.5mi wide, and is 5km/3 mi, from Guernsey, a 20-min boat ride away. *A public ferry service to Herm Island is provided by Travel Trident (☎01481 721 379. www.traveltrident.com).*
✎ **Don't Miss:** The view from Grand Monceau.
🕐 **Timing:** Allow one day.

A BIT OF HISTORY

Prehistoric tombs made of granite slabs found in the north of the island are evidence of human settlement in 2000 BCE. In the 6C, Christianity was introduced by St Magloire, who founded monasteries in Sark and Jersey. In the 17C pirates used the island as a base but it remained largely deserted.

In 1947 the Crown sold Herm to Guernsey and in 1949 Major Peter Wood and his wife became tenants. In 1987 the lease was transferred to their family company. The island has been developed for tourism, maintaining its great natural beauty.

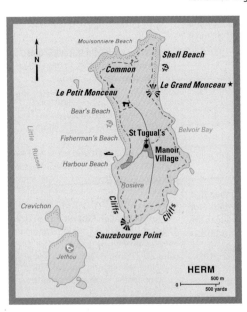

VISIT

Le Manoir Village

A surfaced road climbs up to the tiny hamlet next to the 18C manor house with its square tower. **St Tugual's Chapel** was built in the 11C.

The northern end of the island is composed of sand dunes, known as The Common, covered by prickly vegetation and fringed by sandy beaches, notably Bear's Beach, Mouisonnière Beach and **Shell Beach**, so called because it is composed of millions of shells deposited by the Gulf Stream. From the hillock of **Le Grand Monceau★** there is a splendid panoramic view of the sands, the rocks and the islands. North on the horizon lies Alderney; to the east the French coast. **Le Petit Monceau** beyond is a smaller hillock, overlooking Bear's Beach.

The southern end of the island is composed of steep granite cliffs dropping sheer into the sea. In **Belvoir Bay** nestles a small sheltered bathing beach. The southern headland, Sauzebourge Point, provides a view of Jethou with Guernsey in the background and Sark.

ADDRESSES

STAY

⌂⌂⌂⌂ **The White House Hotel**. ✆01481 750 075. www.herm.com. Open Apr–mid-Oct. 40 rooms. Splendid views of the harbour and beach. Choice of rooms in the main house or in the cottages, and of formal or informal dining (half-board compulsory). Garden with a summer swimming pool.

Jersey★★

Victor Hugo, who spent three years in Jersey (1852–55) was enchanted by the island: "It possesses a unique and exquisite beauty. It is a garden of flowers cradled by the sea. Woods, meadows and gardens seem to mingle with the rocks and reefs in the sea." In addition to the delights of the beaches and the countryside, today's visitors can enjoy a wide range of more sophisticated pleasures with a calendar full of vibrant festivals and events and a lively nightlife.

▶ **Population:** 106 800.
⬤ **Michelin Map:** 503.
▮ **Info:** Liberation Place, St Helier, Jersey JE1 1BB. ✆01534 859 000. www.jersey.com.
◖ **Location:** Measuring 118sq km/45.5sq mi, Jersey lies 19km/12mi W of France's Cotentin peninsula.
◈ **Don't Miss:** Walking the north and east coasts.
⛁ **Kids:** Durrell Wildlife Park; Living Legend amusement park.

A BIT OF HISTORY

The tombs and prehistoric monuments found on the island indicate human habitation between 7500 BCE and 2500 BCE. The Roman presence was brief, and in the 6C St Helier arrived and established Christianity. The dominant influence is that of the Normans who invaded in the 10C and left a rich heritage of customs and traditions.

Famous Sons and Daughters

The most famous name connected with Jersey is **Lillie Langtry** (1853–1929): the Jersey Lily who became an actress and a close friend of Edward VII and captivated British high society with her beauty; she is buried in St Saviour's churchyard.

The fashionable 19C painter, **Sir John Everett Millais** (1829–96), who won acclaim with his painting entitled *Bubbles*, grew up in Jersey and belonged to an old island family. So too did **Elinor Glyn** (1864–1943), who became a novelist and Hollywood scriptwriter. The well-known French firm that makes Martell brandy was started by **Jean Martell** from St Brelade.

After 1204, when King John was forced to cede mainland Normandy to France, the French made repeated attempts to recover the Channel Islands: the last attempt occurred in 1781 when Baron de Rullecourt, a soldier of fortune, landed by night in St Clement's Bay. Under the command of Major Peirson, aged just 24, the militia and British forces defeated the enemy in what came to be known as the **Battle of Jersey**; both leaders were mortally wounded.

Constitution

Jersey is divided into 12 parishes, which together with two groups of islets, the Minquiers to the south and the Ecréhous to the northeast, make up the Bailiwick of Jersey. The parliament, known as the States of Jersey, with 53 elected members, is presided over by the bailiff, who is appointed by the Crown. The three other officers and the Dean of Jersey, an Anglican clergyman, also Crown appointees, may speak in the assembly, but only the 12 senators, 12 constables and 29 deputies, elected to serve for a period of three to six years, may vote.

Economy

Agriculture has long sustained the islanders: wheat and rye, turnips and parsnips, four-horned sheep supplying wool for the famous Jersey stockings and knitwear (dating back to the 17C), apples for cider, table grapes grown under glass and Doyenne de Comice pears. The mild climate continues to favour the cultivation of flowers (daffodils, freesias, carnations and lavender) and vegetables for export, most notable Jersey Royal potatoes. Some crops are grown in the open fields, others under glass. Unique to Jersey is the giant cabbage (*Brassica oleracea longata*), which grows up to 3m tall.

In recent years, the tourism and financial services industries have been driven by competitive young residents who have benefited from an excellent local education.

ST HELIER

St Helier is a lively town, the main commercial centre on Jersey and the seat of government, situated in a sheltered position on the south side of the island.

It is named after St Helier, one of the first Christian missionaries to land in Jersey, murdered by pirates c.555, after living as a hermit there for 15 years. The scant local population was swelled by refugees fleeing the St Bartholomew Day Massacre (1572) and the Revolution (1789) in France.

The shops in the pedestrian precinct formed by **King** and **Queen Streets** are a popular attraction.

Royal Square

The gilded-lead statue of George II, dressed as a Roman emperor, looks down on this charming small square with its spreading chestnut trees; from this point are measured the distances to all the milestones on the island. It was here that the Battle of Jersey erupted. Bordering the south side are the granite buildings of the **Royal Court House**. At the east end of the range of buildings are the **States Chambers** (*entrance at the top of Halkett Place*) where the Jersey

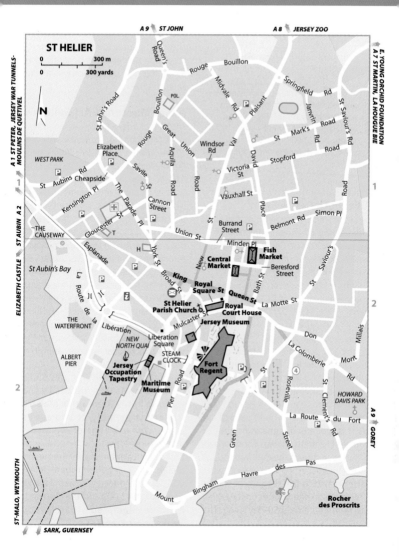

ST HELIER

0 — 300 m
0 — 300 yards

N

Parliament sits in session (🕐*Visitors are welcome to the public gallery of the States Chamber during a States meeting: Tue (and often Wed–Thu) 9.30am–12.45pm, 2.15–5.30pm. https://statesassembly. gov.je*).

Central Market

This Victorian granite building (1882) is furnished with cast-iron grilles at the windows and entrances, and covered with a glass (actually perspex) roof supported by iron columns. Its bustling stalls are arranged around a fountain. The central fish market is around the corner in Beresford Street.

St Helier Parish Church

The foundation of the present pink-granite church with its square tower pre-dates the Conquest. It continues to be the seat of the Dean of Jersey – hence the epithet "Cathedral of Jersey". The altar cross and candlesticks were a gift from Queen Elizabeth, the Queen Mother.

🙂 Jersey Heritage Pass 🙂

Jersey Heritage Pass gives unlimited access to 4 sites for the price of 3 and are valid for 7 days at Elizabeth Castle; Jersey Museum and Art Gallery; Maritime Museum and Occupation Tapestry Gallery, and Hamptonne Country Life Museum. £33.95.
www.jerseyheritage.org.

Elizabeth Castle

Access on foot by a causeway at low tide (30min); otherwise by amphibious vehicle. 🅟*Elizabeth Castle Ferry Kiosk is at Westpark Slip on the Esplanade.*
🍴✕🕐*End Mar–early Nov daily 10am– 5.30pm (or dusk).* 🕐*Jan–Mar, early Nov–Dec.* 🎫*£14.95 (castle and ferry).* 🕾*01534 723 971 (castle) or 01534 634 048 (ferry kiosk).*
www.jerseyheritage.org.
In the 12C William Fitz-Hamon, one of Henry II's courtiers, founded an abbey on St Helier's Isle in St Aubin's bay. The castle buildings were completed shortly before Sir Walter Raleigh was appointed governor (1600), and called Fort Isabella Bellissima in honour of Queen Elizabeth I. It was considerably reinforced during the Civil War (1642–46) while occupied by Royalists who, after resisting the repeated assaults from Parliamentary forces on the island, surrendered after a 50-day siege. The young Prince of Wales stayed here when fleeing from England in 1646, and again three years later when returning to be proclaimed King Charles II. During World War II the Germans added to the fortifications by installing a roving searchlight, bunkers and gun batteries. In 1996 Queen Elizabeth II handed the castle, together with Mont-Orgueil, over to the islanders.
The guard room displays the various stages in the construction of the castle. The **Militia Museum** contains mementoes of the Royal Jersey Regiment. From the keep, known as the Mount, there is a fine **view★** of the castle itself and also of St Aubin's Fort across the bay.

South of the castle a breakwater extends past the chapel on the rock where, according to legend, St Helier lived as a hermit *(procession on or about 16 July, St Helier's Day).*

Jersey Museum & Art Gallery★

The Weighbridge.
🍴🅗✕🕐*Late Mar–early Nov daily 10am–5pm; early Nov–Dec 10am–4pm.* 🕐*24–26 and 31 Dec.* 🎫*£10.25.* 🕾*01534 633 300. www.jerseyheritage.org.*
The island's principal museum and gallery is housed in a former 18C merchant's house and adjoining warehouse. It presents history from 250 000 years ago when the first people arrived in Jersey and continues through the centuries. In particular you can step inside a beautifully restored **Victorian House** and enter the drama of a Victorian family in crisis. Elsewhere there are temporary exhibitions and films about Jersey. By the stairs are displayed a number of silver toiletry articles from the set which accompanied Lillie Langtry on her travels.
The art gallery, which houses much of the Jersey Heritage Trust collection is known as the **Barreau-Le Maistre Gallery** in memory of two Jersey artists, with paintings, drawings and watercolours by local artists or of topographical interest: Sir John Everett Millais (1829–96), Philip John Ouless (1817–85), "the Jersey Turner" John Le Capelain (1812–48) and the illustrator Edmund Blampied (1886–1966). Works by **Sir Francis Cook** (1907–78) bequeathed to the Jersey Heritage Trust are on permanent display in their own gallery, a converted Methodist Chapel, in Augrès *(A 8, Route de Trinité).*

New North Quay

The most prominent landmark is the world's largest **steam clock** (11m high), modelled on a traditional paddle steamer of a type that once shuttled between the islands and Southampton. It was inaugurated in August 1997 as part of the development of the St Helier waterfront.

👥 Maritime Museum

New North Quay.
Late Mar–early Nov daily 10am–5pm; early Nov–Dec 10am–4pm. 1–5 Jan, 24–26 and 31 Dec. £10.25 (child 6–16, £6.65). 01534 811 043. www.jerseyheritage.org.

Installed in converted 19C warehouses, the Jersey **Maritime Museum** has changing displays relating to the fishing, shipbuilding and trading industries, and to piracy.

The **Jersey Occupation Tapestry★** comprises 12 panels (2m x 1m) illustrating the story of the occupation from the outbreak of war to the Liberation: each scene, based on archive photographs and contemporary film footage, has been embroidered by a separate parish.

Fort Regent Leisure Centre

Access by escalators in Pier Road.
Mon–Fri 6.15am–9.pm, Sat–Sun 8.15am–5pm. . Prices depend on activity. 1 Jan, 25–26 Dec. 01534 449 600. www.jersey.com/fort-regent-jersey-leisure-centre.

The massive fortifications of Fort Regent, were built in 1806 to protect Jersey from invasion by Napoleon. Within, topped by a shallow white dome, is a modern leisure centre operated by the government and providing a variety of sports facilities. The rampart walk provides splendid **views★** of the town and St Aubin's Bay *(west).*

EXCURSIONS

👥 Jersey Zoo★★

From St Helier take the A 8 N to Mont de la Trinité; at rue Asplet turn right onto the B 31 towards Trinity Church; this road soon becomes rue des Picots passing in front of the zoo (right).
Daily 9.30am–6pm (5pm in winter). 25 Dec. £16.50 (child 3–16, £12). 01534 860 000. www.durrell.org/wildlife/visit.

This pioneering wildlife park, now known as Jersey Zoo, was founded by the naturalist **Gerald Durrell** (1925–95) in 1963 as a unique centre for research and breeding of rare and endangered species. Today its rolling parkland (10ha) provides suitable environments for around 1 000 animals with exotic species of plants providing both food and natural cover.

Residents include Black lion tamarin from Brazil, Andean bears from the forest uplands of Bolivia and Peru (the only bear indigenous to South America), and an extensive list of birds. Most popular, however, are the primates: a dynasty of lowland gorillas descended from the silverback Jambo (1961–92), orangutans from Sumatra and lemurs from Madagascar, marmosets from Brazil, some of which roam freely in the thick shrubbery.

Tortoises, terrapins, snakes, frogs, toads and lizards, happy to lounge in their warmed enclosures among sprigs of flowering orchids, thrive in the Gaherty Reptile Breeding Centre.

Eric Young Orchid Foundation★

Victoria Village, Trinity.
Wed–Sat 10am–4pm. Mid-Dec–Jan. £6. 01534 861 963. http://ericyoungorchid.org.

A fabulous show of prize orchids is presented here. Displays are regularly reorganised to ensure constant shows of species, the groups arranged to allow close study of their distinctive blooms.

👥 Pallot Steam, Motor and General Museum

Rue du Bechet,Trinity.
Apr–Oct Mon–Sat 10am–5pm. Good Friday. £7 (child £2.50). 01534 865 307. www.pallotmuseum.co.uk.

A fascinating collection of steam engines and organs, farm machinery, motor vehicles, vintage bicycles, locomotives and rolling stock, and lots more besides, that were the passion of the island engineer extraordinaire "Don" Pallot (1910–96). Not only did he refurbish, recondition and assemble this mechanical heritage collection, he also invented several implements to make the life of the Jersey farmer easier.

Jersey War Tunnels★

5km/3mi W. Les Charrières Malorey, Saint Lawrence, Saint Helier, JE3 1FU. Leave St Helier on St Aubin's Road; at Bel Royal, turn right.

♿ ⏰*Mar–Oct daily 10am–6pm; 1–mid-Nov daily 10am–3pm.* ✆*£15 (child 11–15, £9).* ☎*01534 860 808. www.jerseywartunnels.com.*

This large complex of tunnels is kept as a compelling memorial to the forced labourers (Spaniards, Moroccans, Alsatian Jews, Poles, Frenchmen, Russians) who worked on its construction for three and a half years under the severest conditions. Note that some visitors may find the visit rather harrowing, others may suffer from claustrophobia. Hohlgangsanlagen 8 was intended as a secure, bomb-proof artillery barracks. In January 1944, still incomplete, it was converted into a hospital designed to treat the wounded from Hitler's intended invasion of the British mainland. It was equipped with an operating theatre, five 100-bed wards, X-ray room, mortuary, stores, kitchen, staff quarters, etc. Wartime films, archive photographs, newspaper cuttings, letters and memorabilia document the personal suffering and trauma of those caught up in the events.

The **Occupation Walk** opposite the complex leads to an area fortified by anti-aircraft gun positions, crawl trenches, barbed wire entanglements and personnel shelters *(leaflet available from the Visitor Centre).*

Moulin de Quétivel

⏰*Late May–mid-Sept Mon–Tue 10am–4pm.* ✆*£3.* 🅿 ☎*01534 483 193. www.nationaltrust.je.*

The **mill** (pre-1309), on a bend in St Peter's valley, is one of several powered by the rushing water of streams until steam power made them obsolete. During the German occupation the machinery was restored but was largely destroyed by fire in 1969. Since 1979, re-equipped with parts from other disused Jersey mills, Quétivel has ground locally grown grain and produces stone-ground flour for sale.

La Hougue Bie Museum★

From St Helier take either the A 6 (Route Bagatelle) or the A 7 (St Saviour's Hill) NW; at Five Oaks take the A 7 (Princes Tower Road) to the entrance to La Hougue Bie (left).

✂♿⏰*Late Mar–early Nov daily 10am–5pm.* ⏰*Early Nov–Mar.* ✆*£9.55.* 🅿 ☎*01534 853 823. www.jerseyheritage.org.*

A tiny park, encircled by trees, is dominated by a high circular mound. Its strange name may be derived from the old Norse word *haugr* (meaning barrow) and *bie*, a shorthand for Hambye, a Norman lord who, in the Middle Ages, came to rid Jersey of a dragon. Whatever, it is has come to denote one of Europe's finest passage graves.

During the German occupation, the site was heavily fortified, as it provides an excellent **view** over outlying countryside.

Neolithic Tomb★

This cruciform passage burial chamber, excavated in 1924, dates from 3500 BCE. Similar tombs have been discovered in England and Brittany.

The grave was originally built above ground with upright stones and roofed with granite slabs, before being covered by a mound of earth and rubble (12m). A passage (10m long) leads to the funeral chamber (3m x 9m), which is covered with huge capstones (the heaviest weighing 25t). The central granite pillar is a modern addition to support the large capstones, which were found to be cracked.

Archaeology and Geology Museum

The artefacts here are from local excavations – notably from La Cotte de St Brelade, a sea cave in the Ouaisné headland and the Belle Hougue caves on the north coast: remains of mammoths, objects belonging to Neolithic farmers and hunters, Bronze Age metal objects found in St Lawrence, etc. The geology section presents samples of the various rocks and minerals found on the island.

Chapels

The mound is surmounted by two medieval chapels: the **Chapel of Our Lady of the Dawn** (Notre-Dame-de-la-Clarté) dates from the 12C; the altar (late medieval) came from Mont-Orgueil Castle. The abutting **Jerusalem Chapel** was built in 1520 by Dean Richard Mabon after a pilgrimage to Jerusalem. The interior bears traces of frescoes of two archangels.

German Occupation Museum

A German bunker, built in 1942 as a communications centre, houses radio equipment, weapons, medals, original documents (orders and propaganda) and photographs of the period.

🚗 DRIVING TOURS

🚗 THE SOUTH COAST

18km/11mi. Allow about 2h.

▷ From St Helier take the A 1 (Route de St Aubin) west.

Millbrook

The Villa Millbrook was once home to Sir Jesse Boot, first Baron Trent of Nottingham, founder of Boots the Chemists, who is buried at St Brelade. From the outside **St Matthew's Church** is unprepossessing, but in 1934 **René Lalique** (1860–1945), the French glass specialist, was invited by Lord Trent's widow to redecorate the interior with his own style of distinctive **glasswork★** Thereafter, St Matthew's became known as the **Glass Church** (*http://stmatthews.je*).

The entrance doors are made of panels presenting a row of four angels. The flowering lily appears in the windows, screens and in the Lady Chapel. The luminescent, ethereal quality is most apparent at dusk when the lights are switched on.

▷ Follow the main road (Route de La Haule) and then the A 1 (Route de La Neuve).

St Aubin

The little town, which faces east across St Aubin's bay, is particularly picturesque with its long sandy beach, fishermen's cottages and tall granite merchants' houses, lining steep, narrow streets or clinging to the cliffs along the shore. St Aubin was invoked as protector against pirates.

The local church (1892) has a fine stained-glass window made by William Morris & Co. **St Aubin's Fort** on the island *(access at low tide)* was built in the reign of Henry VIII, 1509–47.

The Corbière Walk from St Helier to Corbière follows the line of the old **Jersey Railway**, which opened in 1870.

▷ Turn left off the main road onto the B 57 (Route de Noirmont) for access to the promontory and Portelet bay.

Noirmont Point★

Beyond the pebble beach nestling in **Belcroute** stretches the headland, still scarred by the remains of substantial German fortifications (1941 and 1943–44) including the 12m deep **Command Bunker** (🕐*May–Sept Sun 11am–4.30pm. www.cios.org.je*). Stand on top of the most advanced bastion to get fine views of the rocks immediately below and westwards round to the Île au Guerdain.

▷ Return to the main road, the A 13 (Route des Genets) and then fork left onto the B 66 (Mont Sohier).

St Brelade★

This favourite seaside resort is situated in a sheltered bay; its sandy beaches and usually safe waters (🔾*certain areas can be dangerous*) are ideal for swimming and water-skiing. **Winston Churchill Memorial Park** backs the bay.

At the western end of the beach, behind a screen of trees, lies the parish church and a medieval chapel, surrounded by a graveyard.

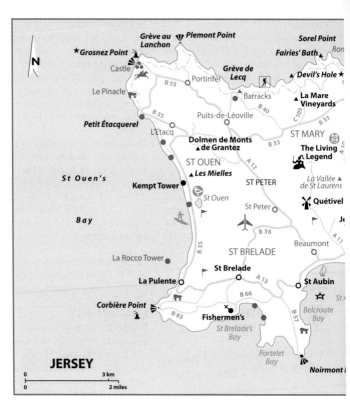

JERSEY

0 ——— 3 km
0 ——— 2 miles

Parish Church

*Light switch inside on the left
of the entrance.*

The cherished church of St Brelade
is built of granite from the cliffs of La
Moye. The chancel, nave and belfry
date from the 11C. In the 12C the church
became cruciform with the addition of
a transept; the aisles were added later.
The altar is a solid slab of stone, marked
with five crosses representing the five
wounds of the Crucifixion. The 15C font
is made of granite from the Chausey
Islands, which lie south of Jersey and
belong to France.

Fishermen's Chapel

*Light switch inside on the left
of the entrance.*

Built of the same granite as the church,
the chapel interior is decorated with
delicate medieval **frescoes★**.

At the east end is an Annunciation
c.1375; the other paintings are from a
second phase of work c.1425: the south
wall (right of the altar) shows *Adam and
Eve* followed by *The Annunciation* and
The Adoration of the Magi; the west wall
bears *The Last Judgement*; on the north
wall fragments have been deciphered
as scenes from *The Passion*.

The paintings probably owe their
survival to the fact that from c.1550
to the mid-19C the chapel was used as
an armoury and as a carpenter's shop,
thus avoiding the attentions of the
Reformation.

Behind the chapel a short flight of
steps leads to a path through the
churchyard to the beach; this is the only
surviving example of a *perquage*: once
commonplace in medieval Europe, these
paths were escape routes from a church,
traditionally a place of sanctuary, to the
shore and away out to sea.

▷ Continue along the road back into
town; turn left onto the A 13 (Route

Orange); bear left down B 83 (Route du Sud) to Corbière.

Point de Corbière★

All that remains of the terminus of the Jersey Railway is the concrete platform. As the road descends, a magnificent view is steadily revealed of the rock-strewn point and the white lighthouse rising from its islet: an excellent place to watch the sun set over the Atlantic. Before the lighthouse (*access on foot at low tide but closed to the public*) was built in 1874, this was a perilous stretch of water where a number of ships foundered; in clear weather the light carries 28km/17.4mi.

🚗 THE WEST COAST

13km/8mi. Allow 1h.

▷ Follow the road round to the junction with the B 35 (rue de Sergente); turn left towards the coast.

St Ouen's Bay

The deep surf which rolls into the bay makes it a favourite spot for experienced surfboarders and windsurfers. The firm sand attracts car and motorcycle racing fans.

In the middle of the bay sits **La Rocco Tower**, the last round tower to be built in Jersey (1800).

Beyond the beach, the landscape is wild and uncultivated, the vegetation sparse. **La Pulente** used to be the main centre for gathering seaweed (*vraic*), which was traditionally used as fertiliser. La Sergenté, also known as the Beehive Hut, is an important Neolithic tomb, near which a large hoard of coins from Brittany was found. The **St Ouen Pond** on the right of the road is a haven for birds and wild flowers, notably the Jersey or lax-flowered orchid. The three upright stones, Les Trois Rocques, are presumed to be part of a dolmen.

Kempt Tower

This defensive tower, built in 1834, has recently been converted into a self-catering apartment. It was previously an interpretation centre for a nature reserve called **Les Mielles** (the Jersey dialect word for sand dunes), set up to monitor and protect indigenous plants, birds and butterflies.

▶ Continue for 500m along the bay.

Channel Islands Military Museum

&🕐 *Mid-Apr–Oct daily 10am–5pm.*
💷£5. ✆01534 732 072.

The rooms and corridors of this former German bunker, which was once part of Hitler's Atlantic Wall defences, are full of artefacts left over from the occupation

▶ Follow the B 35 (Route des Laveurs) onto the B 64 (le Mont Pinel) and turn right into le Vier Mont and le rue de Grantez.

Dolmen de Monts de Grantez

🕐 *Daily.* 💷*No charge* 🅿
✆*01534 483 193. www.nationaltrust.je/ project/grantez-headland.*

The Dolmen de Monts Grantez dates back to between 4000 BCE and 3250 BCE and was used as a burial chamber. Owned and maintained by the Société Jersaise, it was excavated in 1912 and is a fine example of a passage grave constructed of local granite.

There is a roofed passage leading to an oval chamber in which the remains of several humans were found.

The area surrounding the dolmen has six National Trust sites in total and there are wonderful views over St Ouen's bay. Look out for green lizards, kestrels and sparrowhawks, all of which thrive here.

▶ Return to the coastal road; bear right onto the B 35 (Route de l'Étacq).

Petit Étacquerel

A defensive tower guards the point, which marks the northern end of St Ouen's bay. It was here that in 1651 Admiral Blake landed with the Parliamentary forces that defeated the Royalists.

🚗 THE NORTH COAST

38km/24mi. Allow 3h30.

The northern coast of the island is less densely populated. Cliff paths, which stretch from Plémont bay to Sorel Point and beyond, provide spectacular views of the uneven coastline and the open sea to France, Guernsey and Alderney.

▶ Continue north by bearing left onto the B 55 (Route de l'Ouest); bear left again to reach the car park and lookout point at Grosnez.

Grosnez Point★

An area of desolate heathland, covered with gorse and heather and known as Les Landes, extends from Étacquerel to Grosnez Point. Southwest of the racecourse sits **Le Pinacle**, an impressive rock associated with pagan rituals from Neolithic to Roman times. The scant remains of **Grosnez Castle** (c.1373–1540) offer magnificent views out to sea, of Sark and the other islands (northwest).

▶ Return to the B 55; in Portinfer turn left onto the C 105 (Route de Plémont); fork left to Grève au Lançon; eventually the road skirts the holiday village to end in a car park from where a footpath runs along the coast to Grève de Lecq.

Steep cliffs containing caves shelter the attractive small bay of **Grève au Lançon**, which has a sandy beach at low tide. The rocky promontory **Plémont Point** projects into the sea giving a fine view of the cliffs.

▶ Return along the C 105 (Route de Plémont); turn left onto the B 55 (Route de Vinchelez) from Grosnez, which leads to Léoville in the parish of St Mary. Turn left onto the B 65 (Mont de la Grève de Lecq).

Grève de Lecq

The defensive tower on the attractive sandy bay was built in 1780; the conical hill behind is from an Iron Age fortification.

Grève de Lecq barracks were built between 1810 and 1815 to accommodate the 150 British soldiers who manned the gun batteries on the slopes around the bay.

Today they function as a **history and interpretive centre** for Jersey's north coast (⏱*temporarily closed for renovation work: see website for updates: www.nationaltrust.je/project/greve-de-lecq-barracks*). Original features include two prison cells and the ablutions block with outdoor *pissoirs*. In spring and early summer the area is abloom with wild flowers: gorse, daffodils, bluebells and foxgloves.

The water's edge is broken by jagged rocks locally known as **Paternoster Rocks** after the many prayers uttered by passing fishermen, remembering colleagues who perished there. Far out to sea is the French coast.

▶ From Grève de Lecq continue on the B 40 (Mont de Ste-Marie); turn left onto the B 33 (La Verte Rue) and left before the West View Hotel onto the C 103.

La Mare Vineyards

♿⏱*Daily 10am–5pm.* 🗣*Guided tours at 10.45am, 11.45am, 12.45pm, 1.25pm, 2.25pm and 3.30pm.* 💶*£10.50.* ✕🅿 ☎*01534 481 178. www.lamarevineyards.com.*

This is the only vineyard in Jersey, planted on the estate of an 18C farmhouse. Guided tours take visitors around the vineyards, the orchards, the Cognac-style distillery and the chocolate production kitchen. An audio-visual presentation shows behind the scenes, there is a tour of the winery, and, of course, a tasting of the wines, liqueurs and apple brandy.

▶ Continue along the C 103 to the Priory Inn.

Devil's Hole★

🚶 *Park by the inn and take the path down to the cliff.*

This blow hole is an impressive sight, made more dramatic by the amplified thunder of the sea entering the cave below.

▶ Minor roads run east to St John's Parish and north to the coast.

Sorel Point

The section of road, **Route du Nord,** is dedicated to the islanders who suffered during the German occupation. It runs from Sorel Point where a deep pool known as the Fairies' Bath is revealed in the rocks at low tide.

👥 Hamptonne Country Life Museum★

La Rue de la Patente, St Lawrence. ♿⏱*Late Mar–Sept 10am–5pm.* 💶*£9.25 (child 6–16, £5.95).* 🅿 ☎*01534 863 955. www.jerseyheritage.org.*

Six hundred years of Jersey's rural heritage is brought to life in these old farm buildings with the help of lively costumed characters.

▶ Go back the way you came. Just before St John's church, turn right onto the B 52 and then take the C 99.

Bonne Nuit Bay

Once a haunt of smugglers and pirates this is a favourite place for swimming and sailing. The fort, La Crête, at the east end was built in 1835.

▶ From here a footpath follows the coast to Bouley bay; to reach Bouley bay by car, take C 98, B 63, C 97 (rue des Platons).

Bouley Bay

This deep sandy bay protected by a jetty and backed by high granite cliffs, is a safe, popular place for swimming.

▶ Take the C 102, then left on the B 31.

Mont Orgueil Castle

© N. Farrin/AWL Images/Getty Images

ROZEL BAY TO ST HELIER
21km/13mi. Allow 1h30.

Rozel Bay
Part of the bay is taken up by a fishing port where the boats go aground at low tide. Above the bay, at the northern end, traces of a great earth rampart survive from the Castel de Rozel, an Iron Age settlement. At the opposite end sits Le Couperon, a Neolithic passage grave (2500 BCE).

The road turns inland before returning to the coast above Fliquet bay and finally meandering down to the water line. **Fliquet Bay** is a rocky bay between La Coupe and Verclut points: an ideal place for geologists to decipher the volcanic evolution of the island.

Either follow the road to St Martin or make a detour via country roads – B 38 (*Grande Route de Rozel*), B 91 (*rue des Pelles*), B 91 (*Route du Villot*), B 29 (*Mont des Ormes*) to Verclut Point and to Gorey harbour.

St Catherine's Bay★
From the lighthouse there is a magnificent **view★★** of sandy bays and rocky promontories southwards. Out to sea lie the Ecréhou islets, once a favoured

place for smugglers, now a popular spot for a Sunday picnic.

Bear right off the coast road (Route d'Anne Port).

Faldouet Dolmen
This 15m long dolmen dates from 2500 BCE. Digs have revealed vases, stone pendants and polished stone axes.

Gorey
This little port at the northern end of Grouville bay is dominated by Mont Orgueil castle on a rocky spur. Attractive old houses line the quay and yachts add colour in summer.

Mont Orgueil Castle★★
Late Mar–early Nov daily 10am–6pm; early Nov–Dec Fri–Mon 10am–4pm. *1 Jan, 24–26 and 31 Dec.* *£12.95 (child 6–16, £8.35.* *01534 853 292. www.jerseyheritagetrust.org.* Gorey Castle received its present name in the early 15C from Henry V's brother, Thomas, Duke of Clarence, who was so impressed by the castle's position and its defensive strength that he called it Mount Pride (Mont Orgueil in French). Over the centuries the castle has served as a residence for the lords and governors of the island – including **Sir Walter Raleigh**, 1600–03) – a prison for

English political prisoners, and a refuge for a spy network during the French Revolution.

The oldest buildings date back to the early 13C when King John lost control of Normandy and built a castle to defend the island from invasion.

The **view**★★ from the top is extensive: down to Port Gorey, south over Grouville Bay, north to the rocks of Petit Portelet and west to the French coast.

Within the castle's network of staircases, towers and rooms is a series of waxwork tableaux, illustrating significant events in the history of Mont-Orgueil; life-size wooden soldiers guard the castle from attack, "the wounded man" statue shows the fate that could befall those fighting to save the castle from invasion, and in the basement is a witchcraft exhibit.

▶ Take the A 3 along the waterfront.

Royal Bay of Grouville

Grouville is graced with Jersey's finest bay, a magnificent crescent of sand stretching from Gorey Harbour to La Rocque Point. The Seymour and Icho Martello towers (1811) may be reached on foot at low tide. Grouville's **Church** has an unusual 15C granite font.

St Clement

St Clement is Jersey's smallest parish, and it was here that Victor Hugo wrote *Les Châtiments* and *Les Contemplations*, before departing to Guernsey in 1855. The dolmen at Mont Ubé, the 3.4m menhir known as **La Dame Blanche**, and a tall granite outcrop called Rocqueberg suggest that this section of the island was inhabited by Neolithic man.

The oldest extant parts of the present church date from the 12C; the wall paintings date from the 15C (*St Michael Slaying the Dragon*; *The Legend of the Three Living* and *Three Dead Kings*).

St Clement's Bay

This sandy bay stretches from Plat Rocque Point, past Le Hocq Point, (marked by a defensive tower) to Le Nez Point (3km/2mi).

▶ From the A 4 (Grande Route de St Clement) turn onto B 48 (rue du Pontille), which leads onto A 5 (St Clement's Road), to reach Samarès Manor (right).

Samarès Manor

Early Apr–early Nov daily 9.30am–5pm. Gardens and manor £9.75. guided tour of manor house Mon–Sat. +£3.95. 01534 870 551. www.samaresmanor.com.

The name Samarès is probably derived from the Norman *salse marais*, the salt pans that provided the lord of the manor with a significant part of his revenue. Today it is the manor gardens that help earn his keep, created in the 1920s by millionaire shipping magnate and philanthropist, Sir James Knott. The **Herb Garden** is claimed to be the most spectacular in the UK. Also in the grounds is a rare medieval **Colombier** (dovecote), which goes back to at least the 16C, and probably well beyond that. The house is notable for its Norman undercroft and wood-panelled dining room. The **Jersey Rural Life and Carriage Museum** holds a fine collection of carriages, carts and agricultural equipment.

▶ Continue west on the coast road.

Le Rocher des Proscrits

On the east side of the White Horse Inn, a slipway descends to the beach and a group of rocks, Le Rocher des Proscrits (The Rock of the Exiles), where **Victor Hugo** used to meet regularly with fellow exiles.

ADDRESSES

🛏 STAY

🛏🛏 **Chambre d'hôte La Bonne Vie**– Roseville St, St Helier. 01534 735 955. www.labonnevieguesthouse.com. 10 rooms. Close to the beach and the town centre, this flower-decked Victorian house is meticulously looked after.

🛏🛏 **Dolphin Hotel & Restaurant** – Gorey Pier, St Martin. 01534 853 370.

Several of the rooms have panoramic views across the harbour. **Restaurant** (☐☐)open daily for lunch and dinner; adjacent cocktail bar.

☐☐☐ **Old Bank House** – *Main Road, Gorey Village, Grouville.* ☎*01534 854 285. 18 rooms.* Small unpretentious hotel on the coast road. Bedrooms are modern and plain.

☐☐☐ **Prince of Wales** – *Grève de Lecq, St Ouen.* ☎*01534 482 278. www.princeof walesjersey.com. 15 rooms.* This large detached mid–late 20C hotel overlooks one of Jersey's most idyllic sandy bays.

☐☐☐☐ **Harbour View Guesthouse** – *Le Boulevard, St Aubin's Harbour, St Brelade.* ☎*01534 741 585. www.harbourview jersey.com. 14 rooms.* Set right on the quayside overlooking picturesque St Aubins Harbour, this attractive rustic-style guesthouse has a convivial atmosphere and offers large modern bedrooms.

☐☐☐☐ **The Moorings Hotel and Restaurant** – *Gorey Pier.* ☎*01534 853 633. www.themooringshotel.com. 15 rooms.* This small, unpretentious and welcoming hotel enjoys a fine location, facing the harbour just below Mont Orgueil Castle. **Restaurant** (☐☐) open daily for lunch and dinner.

☐☐☐☐ **Somerville Hotel** – *Mt du Blvd, St Aubin.* ☎*01534 741 226. www. somervillejersey.com. 59 rooms.* This grand turn-of-the-20C classic seaside hotel overlooks St Aubin with beautiful views of the bay. **Tides Restaurant** makes the most of local produce.

☐☐☐☐ **Windmills Hotel** – *Mont Gras D'eau, St Brelade.* ☎*01534 744 201. www.windmillshotel.com. 40 rooms.* Discreetly set in luxuriant gardens on the heights above St Brelade's bay, The Windmills has superb sea views and a lovely pool surrounded by gardens.

⚐/ EAT

☐☐ **Old Court House Inn** – *St Aubin's Harbour, St Aubin.* ☎*01534 746 433. www.liberationgroup.com/pubs/the-old- court-house-inn.* This 15–17C inn, full of nooks and crannies, and with ancient blackened beams, has a number of dining areas, There are two main dining

rooms, one a former tribunal, another the reconstructed stern of a galleon looking onto the harbour (as does the terrace). The kitchen specialises in seafood dishes. 10 guest **rooms**.

☐☐–☐☐☐ **The Grill** – *The Royal Yacht Hotel, Weighbridge, St Helier.* ☎*01534 720 511. www.theroyalyacht.com.* This stylish bistro-style space is the place to come for a simple, perfectly cooked steak and an excellent glass of wine, with impeccable service.

☐☐ **Green Island** – *Green Island, St Clement.* ☎*01534 857 787. www.green island.je. Closed Sun eve and Mon.* This attractive informal beachside restaurant is popular with both local people and visitors. A Mediterranean influence is evident throughout – in the décor, the ambience and the style of cooking.

☐☐ **Sumas** – *Gorey Hill.* ☎*01534 853 291. www.sumasrestaurant.com.* This elegant restaurant is a favourite of locals and tourists alike, who come for modern British dishes with Mediterranean flair. Book a table on the glorious terrace to enjoy views of Mont Orgueil castle.

☐☐☐☐ **Bohemia** – *The Club Hotel & Spa, Green Street, St Helier.* ☎*01534 880 588. www.bohemiajersey.com.* One of Jersey's top restaurants, holder of a Michelin star since 2005, produces food that is well-judged and clever, without being gimmicky, and has added a Chef's Table in the heart of the kitchen.

☐☐☐☐ **Tassili Restaurant** – *The Esplanade, Grand Jersey Hotel, St Helier.* ☎*01534 722 301. www.handpickedhotels. co.uk/grandjersey. Closed Sun–Mon.* This restaurant showcases the very best of Jersey's produce in an opulent setting within an intimate ambience. 123 **rooms** and suites.

SHOPPING

Jersey Pottery – ☎*01534 850 850. www. jerseypottery.com.* A paved garden, hung with baskets of flowers and refreshed by fountains, surrounds the workshops where the distinctive pottery is produced. The showroom displays the full range of products for sale.

Sark★★

Offering peace and tranquillity and a traditional way of life without cars, Sark is the smallest independent state in the British Commonwealth and, until 2008, was the last feudal fief in Europe. Its two parts – Great Sark and Little Sark – are linked by La Coupée, a high narrow neck of land that inspired Turner and Swinburne. The island consists of a green plateau bounded by high granite cliffs dropping sheer into the sea or flanking sheltered bays and sandy beaches. Sark is a haven for wildlife – marine creatures in the rock pools and caves; a wide range of bird species; wild flowers in spring and summer.

▶ **Population:** 492.
⊙ **Michelin Map:** 503.
🛈 **Information:** The Avenue 📞01481 832 345. www.sark.co.uk.
◗ **Location:** 12km/7.5mi E of Guernsey, 19km/12mi NW of Jersey. The island is 5.6km/3.5mi long by 2.4km/1.5mi wide.
⊛ **Don't Miss:** The magnificent view from the heights of La Coupée.

A BIT OF HISTORY

Little is known of the island's history before it became part of the Duchy of Normandy, aside from the fact that in the middle of the 6C, St Magloire landed here from Brittany with 62 companions and founded a monastery. In 1042, Sark was given to the abbey of Mont-St-Michel by William the Conqueror. After centuries of intermittent invasions and lawlessness, during which the monks fled, Sark came under English control in the 16C. In 1565, Elizabeth I granted Sark to Helier de Carteret, Lord of the Manor of St Ouen in Jersey, on condition that he establish a colony of 40 settlers prepared to defend the island.

He divided the land into 40 holdings, attributing one to each of the 40 families who had accompanied him from Jersey. Half of the current island population can still trace their descent from these colonists.

The island of Brecqhou (just off the west coast across the Gouliot Passage), a dependent of the fiefdom of Sark since 1565, was acquired in 1993 by the reclusive multi-millionaire British twins Sir David and Sir Frederick Barclay.

Constitution

In 2008, in order to comply with the European Convention on Human Rights, Sark dismantled its 443-year-old feudal system of government. In its place it introduced a 30-member chamber, with 28 members elected in island-wide elections, plus one hereditary member and one member appointed for life. At its head is the hereditary lord *(seigneur)*, while the life member is the *seneschal*, in Sark's case, the local judge.

GREAT SARK

Maseline Harbour

The lighthouse (1912) looks over the harbour from the cliffs on Point Robert.

Creux Harbour★

Opposite the tunnel to Maseline Harbour is a second tunnel to Creux Harbour, dry at low tide.

La Collinette

A short tunnel leads to Harbour Hill (0.8km/0.5mi); at the top is the cross-roads called La Collinette.

Ahead stretches **The Avenue**, the main street lined with shops. The small barrel-

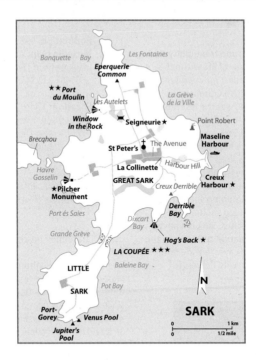

Map of Sark showing: Banquette Bay, Les Fontaines, Eperquerie Common, ★★ Port du Moulin, Les Autelets, La Grève de la Ville, Window in the Rock, Seigneurie ★, Point Robert, Brecqhou, Maseline Harbour, St Peter's, The Avenue, Havre Gosselin, La Collinette, Harbour Hill, GREAT SARK, Creux Derrible, Creux Harbour ★, ★Pilcher Monument, Port ès Saies, Derrible Bay, Dixcart Bay, Grande Grève, Hog's Back ★, LA COUPÉE ★★★, LITTLE SARK, Baleine Bay, Pot Bay, SARK, Port-Gorey, Venus Pool, Jupiter's Pool, N, 0 1 km, 0 1/2 mile

roofed building on the left at the far end is the two-cell island prison built in 1856. Beyond is **Le Manoir**, built by the first seigneur, bearing the De Carteret arms. **St Peter's Church** dates from the 19C.

La Seigneurie★

♿ 🕐 *Easter–Oct Mon–Sat 10am–5pm.*
🎫 *£6.* 👣 *Guided tours Wed 11.30am.*
🎫 *£8 – call to book a place on the guided tours.* 📞 *01481 832 345. www.laseigneuriegardens.com.*

The residence of the seigneur of Sark stands on the site of St Magloire's 6C monastery. Begun in 1565, it was considerably enlarged in 1730. The square tower, built in 1860, provides a splendid view of the island. The house is sheltered from the wind by a screen of trees and high walls. The gardens are luxuriant with flowers and shrubs.

Port du Moulin★★

A road along the north side of the Seigneurie becomes a path along the clifftop. Follow the Window and Bay sign to the **Window in the Rock**, which the Rev William Collings, then lord of Sark, had made in the 1850s to provide an impressive **view** of Port du Moulin.

▶ Return to the fork in the path and take the other branch to Port du Moulin.

Popular with bathers, the bay is flanked by strangely shaped rocks. On the right

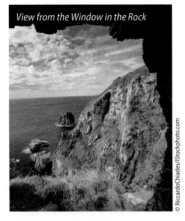

View from the Window in the Rock

© Riccardo Chiades/iStockphoto.com

La Coupée

© chris2766/iStockphoto.com

stand **Les Autelets**, three granite columns, accessible as the sea retreats.

Derrible Bay

At Petit Dixcart turn left onto a stony path, then right onto a path beside a field; a left fork leads down through the trees to Derrible bay, which at low tide has a large sandy beach.

Part way down, a turning to the right leads to the **Creux Derrible**, an enormous hole in the granite cliffs (&*Take care in poor light*).

Return to the first fork and bear left; at the seaward end of the ridge known as the **Hog's Back★** stands an ancient cannon, where a magnificent **view** includes Derrible Bay and Derrible Point, Dixcart Bay with La Coupée and Little Sark in the background.

La Coupée★★★

On either side of the narrow isthmus joining Great Sark and Little Sark steep cliffs drop into the sea. The view is magnificent: Brecqhou, Jethou, Herm and Guernsey to the right; Jersey and the French coast to the left. Grande Grève Bay is a good place for bathing.

Little Sark

On the southern headland lie abandoned 19C silver mines. A footpath to the left of the old mine chimney runs down to **Venus Pool**, visible at low tide, when

visitors (&*check the time of high tide*) can walk from the Venus Pool westward round the headland via Jupiter's Pool, several caves and the rocks in Plat Rue Bay, to **Port Gorey**, which served the silver mines. The clifftop path provides a fine view down into Port Gorey.

ADDRESSES

🛏 STAY

🍴🛏🛏 **Le Vieux Clos Guest House** – *rue de Mouline.* ☎*01481 832 341. www. levieuxclos.co.uk. 6 rooms.* This Georgian-style house is set on one of the highest parts of the island and was home to generations of Sark doctors. Its bedrooms are homely yet elegant, its pride and joy is its beautiful secluded garden.

🍽 EAT

🍴 **Café de la Seigneurie** – *Open Easter to the end of October, 10am–5pm.* ☎*01481 832 345.* Near to the La Seigneurie gardens (&*see p452*). Stop for a spot of tea, a snack or even a light lunch.

🍴🛏–🍴🛏🛏 **La Sablonnerie** – *Little Sark.* ☎*01481 832 061. http://sablonnerie sark.com. Open Easter–mid-Oct.* A country lane leads to this hotel, set in a 16C farm, with an acclaimed restaurant, serving classic unfussy dishes, by candlelight in the evening. An open fireplace contributes to the rural atmosphere. Spacious **bedrooms** (🛏🛏🛏).

INDEX

INDEX

INDEX

INDEX

INDEX

INDEX

INDEX

🛏 STAY

🍴 EAT

MAPS AND PLANS

MAP LEGEND

	Sight	Seaside resort	Winter sports resort	Spa
Worth a special journey	★★★	≜≜≜	✳✳✳	⚕⚕⚕
Worth a detour	★★	≜≜	✳✳	⚕⚕
Interesting	★	≜	✳	⚕

Selected monuments and sights

◉ ⇨	Tour - Departure point
♦ ✝	Catholic church
♦ ✝	Protestant church, other temple
▣ ▣ ▣	Synagogue - Mosque
▩▩	Building
■	Statue, small building
✝	Calvary, wayside cross
◎	Fountain
●━━■━●	Rampart - Tower - Gate
✖	Château, castle, historic house
∴	Ruins
∪	Dam
✿	Factory, power plant
☆	Fort
⌒	Cave
▣	Troglodyte dwelling
⋔	Prehistoric site
▾	Viewing table
॥⁄	Viewpoint
▲	Other place of interest

Abbreviations

A	Agricultural office (Chambre d'agriculture)
C	Chamber of Commerce (Chambre de commerce)
H	Town hall (Hôtel de ville)
J	Law courts (Palais de justice)
M	Museum (Musée)

P	Local authority offices (Préfecture, sous-préfecture)
POL.	Police station (Police)
▯	Police station (Gendarmerie)
T	Theatre (Théâtre)
U	University (Université)

Sports and recreation

⚞	Racecourse
⛸	Skating rink
≈ ▣	Outdoor, indoor swimming pool
★	Multiplex Cinema
⟁	Marina, sailing centre
⌂	Trail refuge hut
□━■━□	Cable cars, gondolas
□+++++□	Funicular, rack railway
🚂	Tourist train
◇	Recreation area, park
⚑	Theme, amusement park
⚞	Wildlife park, zoo
⊛	Gardens, park, arboretum
◉	Bird sanctuary, aviary
🚶	Walking tour, footpath
☺	Of special interest to children

Special symbol

⚲	Beach

Additional symbols

▯	Tourist information
═══ ═══	Motorway or other primary route
❶ ❶	Junction: complete, limited
⊨══⊨ ══	Pedestrian street
ⲉ══ⲉ	Unsuitable for traffic, street subject to restrictions
⁃⁃⁃⁃⁃	Steps – Footpath
🚆 ▣	Train station – Auto-train station
🚌 🚍	Coach (bus) station
─▪─▪─	Tram
⏺	Metro, underground
ℙ	Park-and-Ride
♿	Access for the disabled

✉	Post office
☎	Telephone
⬜	Covered market
⁕⁘⁕	Barracks
△	Drawbridge
∪	Quarry
✗	Mine
Ⓑ Ⓕ	Car ferry (river or lake)
🚢	Ferry service: cars and passengers
⛴	Foot passengers only
③	Access route number common to Michelin maps and town plans
Bert (R.)...	Main shopping street
AZ B	Map co-ordinates

469

COMPANION PUBLICATIONS

travelguide.michelin.com
www.viamichelin.com

MAPS

Regional and Local maps

To make the most of your journey, travel with Michelin maps at a scale of 1:200 000: **Regional map no 513 (Normandy)** and the new local maps, which are illustrated on the map of France below.
And remember to travel with the latest edition of the **map of France no 721** (1:1 000 000), also available in atlas format: spiral bound, hard back, and the new mini-atlas – perfect for your glove compartment.

ROUTE PLANNING

Michelin is pleased to offer a route planning service at **www.viamichelin.com**.

Personalised route plans, comprehensive maps, addresses of hotels and restaurants featured in *The Red Guides* and practical and tourist information.

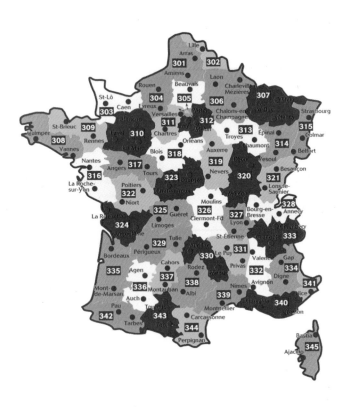

YOUR OPINION IS ESSENTIAL
TO IMPROVING OUR PRODUCTS

Help us by answering the
questionnaire on our website:
satisfaction.michelin.com

Michelin Travel Partner

Société par actions simplifiées au capital de 15 044 940 EUR
27 cours de l'Ile Seguin - 92100 Boulogne Billancourt (France)
R.C.S. Nanterre 433 677 721

No part of this publication may be reproduced in any form
without the prior permission of the publisher.

© Michelin Travel Partner
ISBN 978-2-067243-13-2
Printed: December 2019
Printed and bound in France : Imprimerie CHIRAT, 42540 Saint-Just-la-Pendue - N° 201912.0186

Although the information in this guide was believed by the authors and publisher to be accurate
and current at the time of publication, they cannot accept responsibility for any inconvenience,
loss, or injury sustained by any person relying on information or advice contained in this guide.
Things change over time and travellers should take steps to verify and confirm information,
especially time-sensitive information related to prices, hours of operation, and availability.

The Regions of Normandie Vallée de la Seine

Eastern Normandy - *see the map opposite.*

For western Normandy, known as Normandie Cotentin, see the inside front cover.

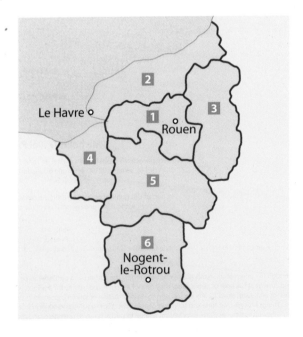